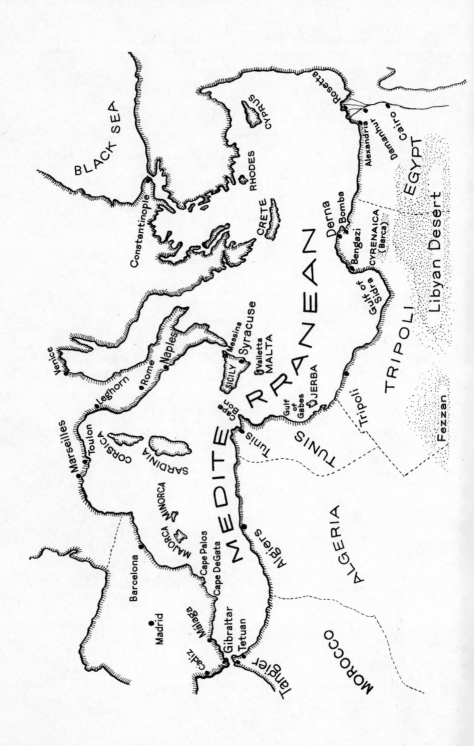

Dawn Like Thunder

Dawn Like Thunder

The Barbary Wars
and the Birth of
the U.S. Navy

GLENN TUCKER

Maps by Dorothy Thomas Tucker

THE **BOBBS-MERRILL** COMPANY, INC.
A SUBSIDIARY OF HOWARD W. SAMS & CO., INC.
Publishers • INDIANAPOLIS • NEW YORK

Library of Congress Catalog Card Number 63-11635

Copyright © 1963 by Glenn Tucker
Printed in the United States of America
First printing, 1963

CONTENTS

Dawn Like Thunder

CHAPTER ONE

New Colors in a Far Port

THE clear, languid dawn of November 9, 1800, crept out of the Bosporus and across the Sea of Marmora and revealed to early watchers along the shore a strange ship riding at anchor inside the Golden Horn.

She had come up under darkness, at 10 o'clock on the night before, and now at daybreak she flew from her mizzenmast a novel flag of red and white stripes and white stars on a field of blue, colors unknown in these waters.

The American frigate *George Washington*, of 24 guns, Captain William Bainbridge commanding, out of Philadelphia, was calling on official business at the Sublime Porte.

Across the city seated on its rolling hills sounded the long, singsong wails of the Moslem priests, calling plaintively from the rooftops, towers, and mosques, notifying the faithful that Allah had bequeathed a new day.

Scarcely were these morning supplications ended and faces turned from Mecca to matters close at hand, when a harbor patrol boat put out from the waterfront castle. Coming alongside the American ship, the captain of the harbor hailed the impertinent newcomer who had penetrated unannounced to the very heart of the Ottoman power, and now held beneath her guns the sacred mosque of Mohammed the Conquerer, Standard Bearer of the Prophet, and the art and treasures of the Moslem world. Captain Bainbridge replied politely that the colors he flew were those of the United States of America. The inquiring officer wasted no time in conversation but turned his boat back toward the shore.

Bainbridge had displayed considerable daring in venturing unheralded into the harbor of Constantinople and might expect to face any consequence, considering that the world was being torn apart by Napoleon's wars, which had fallen with early fury on the Near East. Anywhere in the Levant, unfamiliar elements might be looked on with suspicion. He had effected his passage of the Dardanelles, where it was the imperious rule of the Porte that all vessels must be inspected and those cleared be given the required passport before entering the Sea of Marmora, by a ruse characteristic of the resourcefulness of early American seamanship.

Never before, as long as memory, record, or tradition extended back into Constantinople history, to the year 1453 when the Ottomans overran the ancient seat of Greek and Roman power, had an armed foreign vessel entered the harbor of the Golden Horn without having first been granted leave at the Dardanelles way station, two powerful fortresses overlooking both sides of the narrows near the entrance to the historic strait. What a visitor required was a firman, the distinctive passport of royal decree, issued by the Grand Seignior himself, the Sultan of the Turks.

But Bainbridge was concerned neither with inviolable precept nor Oriental form. He was on a mission which from the beginning had irked his sensibilities and galled his ardent patriotism and he wanted to be done with it with the least possible delay. He was justifiably apprehensive. He had learned back in Algiers that he would probably be compelled to remain in the strait until word of his approach could be carried to Constantinople and the willingness of the government to receive him ascertained. He was taking no chances that his ship might not be cleared and that his long, tedious voyage thus would be rendered fruitless.

As he approached the towering citadel which guarded his side of the passage of the Dardanelles, he directed his crew to scurry across the decks and give evidence that they were taking in sail, indicating that the *George Washington* would heave to and inquire the pleasure of the Turkish commander. Then he began firing a salute—of eight guns, according to the ship's log.

Quickly the fort returned the salute. Bainbridge counted six guns, but they were enough that both ship and fort were soon enveloped in heavy billowing smoke. Under this screen, undetected by the shore batteries, unsuspected by the Turkish captain, the American commander had his seamen hurriedly load on canvas and speed the frigate forward.

Thus, behind the smoke clouds, the *George Washington* moved fleetingly and gracefully out of range. She had already doubled a protecting promontory before the perplexed Turkish commander understood the wily American's stratagem. Bainbridge had a notation entered in his log that the castles "have the Outward appearance of Being very Strong," with eight tiers of guns, the lowest tier being on the water's edge. They were reputed at the time to throw the largest shot in the world, even to cannon balls with a diameter of three feet!

Midshipman Benjamin Page, of Providence, Rhode Island, who kept the log, either was a student of the classics—though his syntax and spelling would not suggest familiarity with his home-town college of Brown or nearby Harvard or Yale—or else he had a translation of Homer on board, for he was entranced with landmarks of the great conflict of Greek against Trojan as he went through the Aegean and Dardanelles. He took note during the voyage of Tenedos, "opposite which stood famous Troy"; of Mount Ida "where the Gods Assembled to view the Battle"; and of the island of Lemnos "where they fed there [sic] horses of Nectar and Ambrosia—the Island where Vulcan Lit when he fell from Heaven and Established his forge."

Now that the *George Washington* was securely in the harbor, how the Turkish government would receive her was any sailor's guess. Soon the dispatch boat returned with the startling message for Captain Bainbridge that neither his flag nor the nation of the United States of which he spoke *had ever been heard of by the Turkish government before.* He was directed to be more specific in explaining whence he came. All that the captain could do was append to his earlier communication a short lesson in history and geography. He said he and his vessel were from the New World which Christopher Columbus long since had discovered far across the seas.

Several hours passed. All aboard the *George Washington* waited patiently in the lower harbor. Finally the dispatch boat put out again and this time the harbor captain, serving as emissary for the Sublime Porte, deigned to set foot on freshly scrubbed New World timber, while behind him came porters bearing to the frigate's deck the symbolic gifts of a lamb and a bouquet of flowers, the first offered as a token of peace, the second an expression of welcome. Obviously someone had been found in Constantinople, and perhaps it was the Sultan himself, a ruler enlightened above most Oriental despots of his day, who had heard something about George Washington, Christopher Columbus, and the United States of America.

By order of the Sultan, the captain of the harbor was to conduct the frigate to the upper bay, and this he did at considerable leisure several days later. Bainbridge, in evidence of his appreciation, fired the recognized international salute of twenty-one guns as he sailed past the royal palace, an act for which the Sultan later made known his gratification. The ship moved about a mile up the harbor and was moored at 3:00 P.M., on November 15.

Thus for the first time in history, by chance rather than orders, without diplomatic exchanges or prearrangement, without the assent of either of the governments involved, an American warship visited the capital

city of the Ottoman Empire, and gave visible notice to the Mohammedan world of the birth of the Western republic.

The *George Washington*—and what name could have been more appropriate for such a pioneering event?—stood at the meeting place of
East and West, the crossroads of the ages, inside the great harbor of the
Golden Horn, five miles wide, big enough to accommodate all the
frigates of both the Old World and the New. She was peacefully at
anchor in front of this vast city of Mussulmans, Greeks, Armenians, and
Jews: the ancient Byzantium of the Greeks; a city reared to world splendor by the Vision of the Flaming Cross; mother of law and of the concept
of society founded on a code of equal justice. *Justice!*—a word synonymous with an era of her imperial past. Nursemaid of learning, theology,
and the arts. City of the impregnable citadel, held in turn throughout
the centuries for Zeus, Jupiter, God, and Allah, but fortress indeed for
any god, where a few might hope to stand off a million, guarded by the
moat of the Bosporus in front and the natural bastions of looming hills
behind.

Bainbridge could well note that almost from the beginning all adventurers had come this way. Here Jason passed in the first war galley, the
Argos, created by Athena for the seekers of the Golden Fleece. Here
dwelt the Harpies who harassed blind King Phineus. Here, much more
securely recorded, Xenophon led his ten thousand Greeks. Here and
along the Dardanelles—the Hellespont of the Greeks, the crossing place
of Helle, daughter of the cloud goddess—the phantasies of antiquity
gave way to the accepted versions of history; legend merged into reality,
myth yielded to verity, the recited narrative became the written word.
Here Constantine conquered, Theodora lived, Theodosius the Great
ruled the better part of the world. Through Constantinople, Tancred,
Bohemond, Geoffrey, and Saint Giles rode with their iron men of the
First Crusade. Here the splendid warrior Suleiman "the Magnificent"
dreamed with his viziers and admirals of the triumph of Islam and
planned campaigns that carried the armies of the Prophet to the walls
of Vienna and Ratisbon.

Yet probably none of these fancies of long-cherished lore or actual
occurrences of ancient, medieval, and modern times was more far-reaching in significance in the long story of human progress than this chance,
unacclaimed, trifling arrival of a single frigate from a faraway shore, if
it may be considered that the raising of the American flag on the mizzenmast of the *George Washington* gave notice to all ancient realms and
distant peoples of the birth of the new American Republic. The United
States, daughter of time, latest of the eager offspring of the ages, was

announcing its fresh, youthful entry, to bid feebly at first, mightily in the end, for a place among the world powers.

Probably the Sultan's decision to accept the uninvited Americans and welcome them cordially was based not so much on prescience as on the caprice of the moment. He liked Bainbridge's flag. As he had scanned the ship from his palace when it came up the bay, he had noticed the stars in the blue field and had commented that the flag of the United States, like that of Turkey, was decorated with heavenly bodies, a coincidence which might be a harbinger of cordial relations between the two nations in future times. Most flags had national insignia or royal coats of arms. Not the American or Turkish. He even went so far as to venture that because of the similarity of the ensigns some affinity in laws and customs must exist between the Moslems and Americans!

Selim III was as good a sultan as the circumstances of the age and the caprices of the Janissaries would permit. Admirous of the cultural distinction that had been won by the French court during the passing century, he aspired to establish French modes and introduce literature and the arts into his physically elegant portal city between East and West. With unusual perception and tolerance, he strove to lift the level of common education among the Turks, where illiteracy was almost the universal rule, and was making strenuous efforts to establish schools and procure Western instructors.

Of equal significance as a measure of popular reform, he was struggling to break the ages-old control of the Janissaries. This austere, rigorously trained and sternly disciplined body of troops, composed mostly of Christian Albanians and Bulgars, was supposed to serve the Ottoman Empire as a hard core of defense, but judged that the best manner of serving was by controlling it. Selim would eventually learn that he could not suppress the Janissaries, who had four centuries of power behind them and nearly three decades ahead. For his efforts to reduce them and break them, his eunuchs would find his richly clad figure on the divan of his seraglio one morning, with a silken cord around his throat.

Undoubtedly the most disconcerting aspect to the Porte involved in the sudden appearance of the American frigate was that the Turkish fleet was absent. Spacious as might be the harbor, it gave berth to few Moslem warships of consequence. The great Turkish fleet, of numerous ships of the line and frigates and a swarm of lesser craft, which would remain one of the most powerful in the world until it encountered Sir Edward Codrington twenty-seven years later in Navarino Bay, was cruising, intent on mopping-up exercises among the Ionian Isles. Under the command of the Capudan Pasha Hassan, Grand Admiral and brother-in-law of the Sultan, it was seeking isolated pockets of the French invaders who had been brought to the Near East by Napoleon's dream of conquest, and left behind when the vision of Oriental empire vanished in the smoke at Acre. The fleet was not expected to return for at least twenty days.

The Sublime Porte was involved at the moment in the most peculiar alliance of its history, a league of the Mussulman and the Slav, which disclosed how the genius of the Corsican might induce desperate enemies to lodge in the same barracks room and mess on victuals from the same galley. A rapport had been established between Turkey and Russia the year before, after nearly a century of conflict. The succession of eighteenth-century wars between the sultans and the czars had been touched off when Charles XII of Sweden, fleeing from Peter of Russia after the disastrous defeat of the Swedes at Poltava, gained sanctuary with Ahmed III. Russian soldiers pursued him across the Turkish border, and the conflicts unloosened came to afflict the Mediterranean shores from Venice to Suez and inland Europe from Vienna to the Caspian Sea.

Now that Bonaparte, a more flashing meteor than Charles XII, was streaking across the military heavens, and since he had deluged the Near East with blood, triumphed over the Mamelukes before the Pyramids, invaded Syria, and threatened to found a new empire in the Levant, Turkey and Russia had united their naval forces for common security. Turkey had fought the heavy part of the desperate war against the Corsican, whose flaming triumphs had announced him to the Ottomans as the "Sultan of Fire" and the "Favorite of Victory."

Aided by British artillerists and engineers, and fortified by the great resolution of Admiral Sir Sidney Smith, the alliance had eventually turned Acre into a French shambles when the loss of that city probably would have laid all Turkey at the invader's feet. Now that Napoleon had returned to France for greater glories on European battlefields, and since Britain was preparing an army for Egypt, and Turkey and Russia were acting in concert, French influence was weakening in the Near East.

But Bainbridge was visiting an Old World still desperately engaged in conflict. Already the new century—if the year 1800 may be regarded as the beginning of the new and not the end of the old—had been stained red at Marengo and would get another blood bath before the year's end at Hohenlinden. The capable French General Kléber, left behind in Egypt, had won another resounding victory over the Turks at sanguinary Heliopolis, then had been stabbed by an Arab assassin—an act which presaged the loss of Egypt to France. In the autumn of 1800, when Bainbridge was crossing the Mediterranean and sailing through the Dardanelles, Lord Nelson, having cleansed the eastern Mediterranean of the French fleet, was making his way by easy land journeys from Naples toward England, feted at all stops for his great triumph in the Battle of the Nile.

Still, enough remained to be done to keep the Turkish fleet employed. For eight days the *George Washington* lay in the harbor of Constantinople, awaiting the pleasure of the Sultan, who in turn awaited the return of his Grand Admiral before entering into matters connected with the visit of the American frigate.

Meantime Captain Bainbridge was visited by the dragoman of the Reis Effendi, the principal civil officer of the Turkish government, who put the American at once on the defensive by inquiring if he did not know that such an office existed. Bainbridge, perceiving there was surely no greater affront in his lack of familiarity with the Reis Effendi than there was in the ignorance of Turkish officialdom about the existence of the United States, replied that he did not. Thereupon the dragoman advised him that he had sailed stealthily into Constantinople Harbor without the advance knowledge or assent of the Ottoman power, then had compounded his disrespect with dereliction by failing to report himself to the proper governmental authority, an oversight and indignity which called for reparation. Consequently, the Reis Effendi summoned the American to appear before him at 10 o'clock on the following morning. It looked as if a fine were in contemplation. When Bainbridge asserted that appearing was the very last thing he had in mind to do, the dragoman advised him that the commands of such a notable official as the Reis Effendi were not to be dismissed so lightly.

A lone American commander in a strange distant port, Bainbridge was sufficiently concerned that he determined to solicit advice. In Algiers he had obtained from the American consul, Richard O'Brien, letters of introduction to diplomatic representatives of some of the European powers residing in Constantinople and these he now brought into play. Going ashore, he called on the Danish and British ambassadors, who received him warmly, the first promptly, the second upon reflection.

Great Britain was represented in Constantinople by one of those men of large capacity often found, at times at the outset of their distinguished careers, in the British diplomatic service. He was the Scotchman Thomas Bruce, seventh Earl of Elgin, statesman and connoisseur, whose striking accumulation of Greek sculptures, known as the Elgin Marbles, became one of the basic collections in the British Museum in London. Though he was to serve for half a century in the House of Lords, his term of three years as diplomat in Constantinople, from 1799 to 1802, was notable not only to British interests in the Near East, and to Britain's treasurers of ancient art—loot, some termed it, though he bought and paid for it with his own coin—but also because of the temporary convenience it gave to the first American naval captain ever to sail a warship into the inner waters of the Ottoman power.

Lord Elgin met Bainbridge cordially and listened without comment to his story about the Reis Effendi. That night Bainbridge, writing to Secretary of the Navy Benjamin Stoddert, said the Briton received him politely but made no offer of services, while the Dane, Baron de Huslech, proffered his good offices in the most friendly terms. But on the following morning Bainbridge was compelled to amend his dispatch. Lord Elgin sent word that his office and services would be at the disposal of the American commander. More than that, he gave assurance that the matter of the Reis Effendi could be forgotten. He would take care of it himself. What the Turkish official had in mind was the procurement of a bribe. Lord Elgin would send his own dragoman with a message covering the circumstances, and the American could rest assured there would be no further annoyance on any score of reparations. For the remainder of the American's stay, no attentiveness could have been more solicitous and helpful than that of this pleasant and accomplished British diplomat.

Lord Elgin's attitude is of interest because his was one of the many actions by British representatives in the Mediterranean during the Barbary War years which tend to refute the long accepted notion of American history that Great Britain, jealous of the rapidly expanding American merchant marine, covertly encouraged the forays of the Barbary powers against American shipping—a belief often expressed in the thought that if a Barbary Coast had not existed Great Britain would have had to create one. This impression that depredations in the Mediterranean were nurtured by British self-interest was first reported in 1783 by Benjamin Franklin, who said he had heard it advanced as a maxim of the London merchants that, in effect, Algerian piracy was a cornerstone of British trade. Whatever may have been the situation regarding American shipping during the Revolutionary War years, the encouragement of piracy against the Americans did not exist after the treaty of peace and ratification of American independence in 1783. While there may have been individual lethargy and disinterest among British representatives about the fate of American ships at times, nothing like fostering the corsairs because of their annoyance to the Americans ever attained the weight of either official or covert policy.

Perhaps never was a more singular voyage made than that of Bainbridge and the *George Washington* to Constantinople in 1800, nor was a sea captain ever cast in a less congenial role.

His ship was one of the merchant vessels purchased and hurriedly converted into frigates when war with France threatened in 1798, at a time when the projected new American warships, authorized under President Washington but delayed in their construction by legislative restraint, were still on the ways. She was bought in Providence, Rhode Island, for $69,025, and when she no longer seemed to be needed was sold for $52,000 in Philadelphia in 1803; but during the five years she was in commission she gave the Navy a full measure of extraordinary service for the $17,025 capital outlay she entailed. Had Jason's Argonauts secured the Golden Fleece and carried it back through the Bosporus, that coveted legendary hide could by no stretch of the imagination have been as valuable as the treasure of coin and cargo carried by Bainbridge aboard the *George Washington* as a tribute from the United States to Algiers, and the specie and cargo he then transported to Constantinople as an abject and placating payment by the Dey of Algiers, a principality of the Porte.

His instructions from the Secretary of the Navy, issued June 25, 1800, when he took command, were to take on only a partial crew, limited to 130 officers and seamen, so that there would be ample room for the necessary six months' provisions, the goodly portion being salt meat, and a large cargo of plank, cables, cannon, foodstuffs and "valuable European goods" which were being assembled under the direction of Secretary of State John Marshall. Still, the ship must not be loaded so heavily that she would be in no condition to fight. The undeclared war with the French Directory was still bursting into sporadic sea clashes and every war vessel had to be prepared.

The *George Washington* weighed anchor at midnight August 8, 1800, and made her way down the Delaware River in fair weather under fresh breezes toward the open sea. On the crossing of the Atlantic she was cleared for action at times and both the "Great guns and small arms" were "exercised," a result of sighting unidentified sails. Though bound on a positive and somewhat urgent mission, Bainbridge could not resist giving chase to two strange schooners. One showed the American colors, but both put on all canvas and outdistanced the *George Washington*, which was a dull sailor. They were judged to have the appearance of French cruisers. Anchoring September 7 at Gibraltar, where he assisted two British frigates which were drifting ashore when their cables parted in heavy weather, he was off Algiers at 4:00 P.M. on September 17, after a passage of forty days from Philadelphia. The American consul, Richard O'Brien, came aboard with the captain of the port, and Bainbridge, unwarned and unsuspecting, allowed the Algerian officer to pilot the ship into the harbor to an anchorage beneath the fort and shore batteries. The British consul, John Falcons, paid a courtesy call to Bainbridge in his cabin.

Two days later the American captain began unloading his cargo of coffee, tea, sugar, herring, bales of nankeen, fustic, gunpowder, chinaware and trinkets such as might have been leftovers from the stocks commonly employed by the treaty-makers on the western frontier in their bartering for Indian lands. He took on board supplies of "fine fruit such as Grapes, Green Figs, Oranges, Almonds, pomegranates & Prickly Pears." Midshipman Page, in keeping the log, was sufficiently initiated in North African fare to drop the capital letters when mentioning pomegranates. He understandably applied capitals to other fresh fruits after a voyage of forty days.

At this juncture Bobba Mustapha, Dey of Algiers, despotic and uncivil,—"an animal," the American consul Eaton termed him—who was recipient of annual tribute paid for the protection of shipping by the new American Republic, as had been his predecessor, Hasan Pasha, after the negotiation of the treaty with the United States in 1795, interposed to demand that the *George Washington* enter into his service under the Algerian flag and sail on his behalf, and with his cargo, to Constantinople. The ship would carry also emissaries to the Sultan, to mollify him with American money. The Sultan's feelings were ruffled because Algiers—remote from the Ottoman capital, which ordinarily governed with a light rein as long as revenues were not in arrears from the satrapies—had negotiated a treaty with France at the very moment when the existence of the Ottoman Empire was menaced by Napoleon's invasion of Egypt and Syria. Any of these Moslem states might consider themselves perfectly free to molest, goad, and pillage the maritime powers of Christian Europe or infant America, but they trembled in terror at any evidence of displeasure by the Porte. President John Adams had sent the tribute to Algiers in a war vessel with a thought that her guns might cow the arrogant Dey, but the captain of the harbor had neutralized Bainbridge's power by giving him a mooring under the harbor batteries which could blast his ship's timbers into splinters before he could let loose a broadside. (A map of Algiers Harbor appears on Page 457.)

The day after he began discharging his cargo Captain Bainbridge called on the Dey to pay his respects, in company with Consul O'Brien. The presumptuous ruler over the city of 100,000 Moslems at once announced from his embroidered cushion that he desired the *George Washington* as a favor to him from the United States to transport his ambassador to Constantinople and then return to Algiers. Consul O'Brien, more accustomed to such negotiations, replied that neither his nor the captain's orders would admit of such a trip, nor were there any powers inherent in their offices that would justify them to comply on their own responsibility. The American frigate would be unable to defend the Dey's ambassador or property from Portuguese or Neapolitan vessels, being authorized to fight only "french Corsairs," as O'Brien put it.

Fat, placid Bobba Mustapha was unimpressed, but closed the conference to reflect. Bainbridge went back to his ship and O'Brien stopped to tell the Algerian Secretary of State precisely what he had told the Dey, that the *George Washington* would not go. Eight days later he was summoned again by the Dey, who inquired if he still declined to allow the ship to carry the ambassador and presents to the Grand Seignior. He answered with all his earlier arguments and explained, as he later put it, that "this ship of the U.S. & Crew would. be in a Very singular Predicia-ment. in going to Constantinople on the business. of the Regency we haveing no Ambasador or Consul at these places." Except for his peculiar use of periods and capitals he got his idea across.

The Dey flew into a passion, saying other nations had rendered such favors to Algiers and why not the United States. But he agreed that if British Consul Falcons would promise on his honor a British warship for the journey the American could go home. Falcons was present and said that Admiral Lord George Keith, commander of British naval forces in the Mediterranean, had promised to supply a warship for the very business of transporting the ambassador and presents to the Porte. The ship might be expected daily. The Dey agreed to wait. The ship, a frigate, arrived shortly, but meantime the Dey's ministers began to object to the employment of a British war vessel for the purpose.

When the Dey, after an outing, returned from his country seat on October 9 he informed O'Brien there was now no alternative. The American ship would have to go. O'Brien remonstrated, but the Dey fell into such a tantrum that it was clear he was resolved. He declared he wanted no more excuses and that "his Mind & his Ministry was Soured against the British." What it amounted to was that neither the Dey nor his ministers wanted to trust the British ship with the amount of money they intended to send, considering the friendly relations they were maintaining with Britain's enemy, France. He made it evident that the American had no choice between compliance and open warfare. Then he heaped on the crowning insult. The American warship would have to fly the Algerian flag from her main topgallant masthead.

When Bainbridge was informed of these decisions he demanded an audience, at which he accomplished nothing. He remonstrated again, then visited the office of the Algerian Marine, where he announced his refusal to hoist the flag of Algiers to the mainmast. After a great deal of discussion and examination of precedents under which warships of

Spain, France, and other nations had raised the Algerian flag to the main while on missions for the Dey, Bainbridge finally acknowledged that if he were under compulsion in one matter he might as well yield on the other, but he merely dropped his remonstrances and made no promise on the flag. Writing to the Secretary of the Navy the next day, October 10, 1800, he explained that every effort had been exerted by both O'Brien and himself to avoid the cruise, which would cost from fourteen to sixteen thousand dollars and promote not a bit of good will for the United States. It was not in the nature of the Algerian regency to consider anything a favor that was done by a Christian nation, he explained.

> The light that this Regency looks on the United States [he wrote], is exactly this: you pay me tribute, by that you become my slaves, and them I have a right to order as I please. Did the United States know the easy access of this barbarous coast called Barbary, the weakness of their garrisons, and the effeminacy of their people, I am sure they would not be long tributary to so pitiful a race of infidels.

The American captain was moved to yield to the obdurate Dey by two considerations. The first was the virtual certainty that if he refused to make the trip Algiers would renounce the treaty with the United States and renew the wanton seizure of American merchant vessels. The second was the probability that if he tried to take his ship out of the harbor it would be sunk before he could inflict any considerable damage on the city. The main elements of the Algerian fleet were the American-built frigate *Crescent,* the American-built brig *Bashaw* and the American-built schooner *Skolderbrand,* all having been offerings from the United States as tribute to the Dey. Apart from these good ships Algiers had a mean hodgepodge of xebecs, schooners, small cruisers, and gunboats. The harbor fortifications were historically among the strongest of the North African coast. Still, although Algiers was a minor naval power and not formidable even in its home waters, Bainbridge was in no condition to fight it. Could he have slipped out by night? It does not appear so. After his discussions with the Dey and later the naval authorities—"a very warm dispute," he termed it, "which was very near causing a declaration of war"—and after his insistence that the ship be allowed to wear its own flag, his decks were overrun by a procession of glowering Moslem officers. The Minister of Marine, the Admiral of the Fleet, and a swarm of Algerian captains came on board without paying the slightest attention to protests or arguments. Some of the officers went impudently to the maintop, where they hauled down the American pennant and hoisted the red Algerian flag in its place. Probably in all its history, the United States Navy never sank to such abjection. What a Preble, a Decatur, or a Lawrence would have done in this situation is anyone's conjecture. Bainbridge was in a tight squeeze, but that was the kind of a risk some young naval officers of the time might have relished.

"Had we 10 or 12 frigates and sloops in those seas," Bainbridge wrote to Secretary Stoddert, "I am well convinced in my own mind that we should not experience those mortifying degradations that must be cutting to every American who possesses an independent spirit."

So Bainbridge was compelled to go to Constantinople. He and O'Brien agreed there was no other course. He explained his compliance to his own satisfaction:

> The loss of the frigate, and the fear of slavery for myself and crew, were the least circumstances to be apprehended; but I knew our valued commerce in these seas would fall a sacrifice to the corsairs of this power, as we have here no cruisers to protect it . . . I hope I may never again be sent to Algiers with tribute, unless I am authorized to deliver it from the mouth of our cannon.

The cargo he took on board, the peace offering from the Dey to the Grand Seignior, was a vast conglomeration of ingredients assembled from animal, mineral, and vegetable worlds. The most important item, apart from the American crew numbering 131 officers and men, and the other humans, was $800,000 in specie, a neat sum which the Dey believed would oil up the creaking political mechanisms that connected the Porte with the remote Algerian satrapy, in spite of his treaty with Turkey's deadly enemy, France. There were jewels of indefinite value, but estimated to increase the worth of the cargo to about a million dollars. Surely the gold in the fleece Jason sought would not have commanded that much on the market of Midas, Croesus, or a Greek demigod. Consul O'Brien had to give the Dey a security for the safe delivery of the money. If it went down, the United States, not Algeria, would have to make the replacement.

In addition to money and jewels there were 100 Negro slaves on board, one-half of them women; 4 lions, 4 tigers, and 4 antelope; 12 parrots, 25 horned cattle, 4 horses, 150 sheep, and several head of ostriches, which apparently were never still long enough for anyone to get a good count. But the problem was not with lions, parrots, horned cattle, ostriches, or jewels. It was with the Algerian ambassador and his suite of 99 other Mussulmans, who overran the decks, got in the way of the sailors, and threatened often to lead to a bloody renewal of time-honored clashes between the Crescent and the Cross.

The *George Washington* made sail out of the harbor of Algiers at 6:00 P.M., October 19, 1800. She fired a signal gun for sailing and was answered by eight guns from the fort. As soon as he was out of range, mindful that he had made no promises, Bainbridge ran up the Stars and Stripes to the position of precedence on the topgallant.

Word of the sailing reached the United States with the arrival of the merchant ship *Brutus,* which made Salem, Massachusetts, December 3, after a forty-day voyage from Algiers. Captain William Brown of the *Brutus* witnessed much of the controversy between the Americans and the Dey and for a time was in danger of having his own ship impressed into the Algerian service. The Dey demanded that the *Brutus* unload her own cargo and go to Rhodes to get a cargo of Turks, at no freightage payment or passenger fare. O'Brien argued that the vessel was privately owned and had a perishable cargo. Unexpectedly he won a stay in the potentate's demands.

Captain Brown reported in Salem that the Dey threatened to hold officers and crew of the *George Washington* as slaves if Bainbridge did not make the voyage to the Levant. After the *George Washington* sailed, Captain Brown got the *Brutus* out of the harbor and made for Gibraltar and the United States. He said Algiers held 2,300 Europeans as slaves, "some of them from the first families of Europe." He, too, declared the place looked strong but thought six or seven ships of the line "could batter it to pieces." His report aroused American opinion to a new attitude about the Barbary powers. The Jefferson administration was soon to take office and it would find the impressment of the *George Washington* humiliating and provocative in the extreme.

Soon after the *George Washington* sailed, friction developed on the main deck. There were too many passengers for a warship of 624 tons, which was not half the capacity of the new frigates *Constitution, United States,* and *President.* With 100 slaves, 100 Mussulmans, and 131 crew, 331 persons jammed a vessel that had to devote much of its space to incompatible and separately caged or stabled animals. Noah might have handled the situation smoothly—Captain Bainbridge was just a seaman, chosen by an obese Dey and not by God. The Mussulmans were noisier than the parrots. The weather turned rainy and squally; then, after a pleasant spell, squally again.

The matter of religion became the Captain's main problem. The faithful to Allah had to pray five times a day and engage in various other devotions exasperating to those manning the ship. They chose to hold their religious observances on the main deck where they could look and bow toward the Kaaba of Mecca with certainty they were facing properly. But on such a voyage amid shifting winds and gales, the vessel had to tack frequently—almost, it seemed to the Mohammedans, by the design of the curs of Christendom—and when the bow on these occasions was pointed in a new direction there was much scurrying and refacing among the worshipers to keep Mecca in their front. These incidents vastly amused the American seamen, who thought that Satan might be in tempest and God more likely in the gentle breeze than around some Black Stone in the Great Mosque in the distant desert town of Mecca. The Americans looked on curiously at first, contemptuously and scoffingly a little later. The conception of religious tolerance was not a common possession of the people of the early nineteenth century. Many rough seamen of that era sailed under the flag of any ship that needed hands. The nationality of the ship was immaterial. They identified God mainly when his name occurred in an oath. The muster roll of the *George Washington* shows barbers, cooks, a cooper, a carpenter's mate, and other specialists, but no chaplain was on board. Probably it was to dampen their ardor and prevent friction with the Moslems that Bainbridge cut his crew to half a rum ration.

Annoying to the Moslems as well as to the crew was the frequent tacking. Finally the Dey's ambassador, who looked on himself as the true commander of the voyage, stationed one of his officers in the binnacle so that he might watch the compass during prayertime. This does not seem to have been to prevent tacking, but to give guidance to the faithful about the direction of the ship and reassure them when they were facing in precisely the proper manner. The voyage progressed with bad spirit but no bloodshed, until finally, at dusk on November 9, Constantinople, recorded by Midshipman Page as "Beautifully situated on the sides of seven hills gently ascending from the sea," was sighted ahead.

Back in Algiers, Consul Richard O'Brien was writing Secretary of State John Marshall a letter heavy with explanations: that the yielding was to save the peace of the United States with Algiers, that the alternative was pillage and slavery; that the $40,000 the voyage would cost was inconsiderable compared with the cost of a war. He denied that he had assumed responsibility for the safety of the money and cargo but stated that if the ship were lost the Dey would cover the loss by capturing other American vessels. In one manner or another the voyage seemed to have been insured by the Americans.

Over in Tunis another American consul, William Eaton, hearing the news, was cast into one of his not infrequent emotional spasms:

> Genius of My Country! How art thou prostrate! Hast thou not yet one son whose soul revolts, whose nerves convulse, blood vessels burst, and heart indignant swells at thoughts of such debasement? Shade of Washington! Behold thy orphan'd sword hang on a slave— A voluntary slave, and serve a *pirate*!

Then, again:

This is the price of peace. But if we will have peace at such a price, recall me, and send a *slave,* accustomed to abasement, to represent the nation. And furnish *ships of war,* and *funds* and *slaves* to his support, and Our immortal shame.

It was all a part of Eaton's routine reports to the Secretary of State—reports undoubtedly without parallel for their heated outbursts in all the Department's long history and its trillions of words, perhaps, of diplomatic correspondence.

CHAPTER TWO

A Firman Bridles the Dey

B AINBRIDGE was a moderate. He was no Thomas Truxtun who could strut as well as he could fight, and Truxtun was no mean fighter; nor an Edward Preble, whose name on his commission ought to have been written in gunpowder with a seaman's oath for an exclamation point; but he was personally brave, outwardly composed, always punctual, generally competent.

Most of his decisions lacked flare or sensationalism. Fame, an uncertain goddess on land and faithless indeed on the water, especially to those who sued her most ardently, seldom sailed with the usually sound Bainbridge, but once or twice she did touch her hand gently to his shoulder. His career as frequently stirred doubt, even distrust, not of his character, but of his capacity.

Dr. Thomas Harris, naval surgeon and a close friend of Bainbridge, who saw him "under all circumstances of disease and health, exhilaration and depression," and judged him a shipmaster of extraordinary capacity, thought the Navy was indeed fortunate in all its first officers.

To them he applied the attributes of "manly dignity," "devoted patriotism," "energetic boldness," and "untiring zeal." Of none did he use such terms with greater assurance than with the New Jersey lad who had won his way up the tough and tricky ladder of the merchant service, where it was easier to become schooled in perfidy and downright meanness than in moral rectitude. That applied to the ordinary-run deckhand. Worthy virtues were not missing in the upper echelons of the naval services of the leading powers, in a period of sea history that was dominated by the deeds of Hood, de Grasse, Rodney, and John Paul Jones, and looked toward the coming of Nelson. The sea during the chivalric era of the great sails was a profession in which knight-errantry lingered and gallantry and courage were recognized as freely in enemy as in friend.

Bainbridge was the fourth son of a Princeton, New Jersey, physician.

He was born in the New Jersey college seat May 7, 1774, too late for par-
ticipation in the Revolutionary War, but in time to feel the impact of its
tremendous patriotic upsurge. The naval exploits of American sea captains during the struggle for independence—John Paul Jones, John
Barry, Richard Dale, Stephen Decatur, Sr., and Bold Joshua Barney of
the *Hyder-Ally* privateer being notable among them—fired his vigorous
mind and robust body with a yearning for action and a longing for the
sea. Though he had gone to Monmouth County, New Jersey, to be educated by his maternal grandfather, John Taylor, he broke away from the
books at the age of fifteen, journeyed by Princeton to gain the assent
of his parents, and soon had a seaman's hammock on a merchant vessel
out of Philadelphia.

His naval career was founded on an incident in the merchant trade
with Holland. He had been appointed first mate, at the age of eighteen,
when he had opportunity to display his resourcefulness and courage.
The crew mutinied. He came on deck just as the mutineers were about
to toss the captain overboard. Of powerful physique and with a strict
sense of duty, he dashed into them, followed by a single old-time sailor
who served as second mate. He liberated the captain, felled mutineers
right and left with his big fists until they were finally all downed or
scattered, and then clapped the ringleader into irons. The result was both
a hearty respect for him among the seamen as the story was spread
through the merchant marine service, and a confidence by the shipowners in his ability to handle unruly crews. They appointed him captain. Thus at the age of nineteen, a year younger than that at which the
celebrated Joshua Barney had become captain of the *Hyder-Ally,* and
with it had captured the British *General Monk* off the Delaware capes,
Bainbridge had his own ship. And like Barney, he had opportunity to
fight an action in the next year, at the age of twenty.

Passing from Bordeaux to the Caribbean with his armed merchant vessel, the *Hope,* he was off St. John of the Virgin Islands when he was
hauled up by an armed schooner showing no flag. The schooner fired
without warning and, when Bainbridge replied briskly, showed the
British ensign.

Bainbridge had but four 9-pounders and eleven men on his small
craft, while the Britisher had a crew of thirty and eight carriage guns.
But Bainbridge pounded the schooner's hull, riddled her decks, and
brought down her spars and rigging. Firing with destructive accuracy,
he crippled the attacking ship and killed and wounded a goodly portion
of her gun crews. The British captain was compelled to strike his colors.
Bainbridge resisted the urgency of his own crew to board and take the
schooner as a prize. He held that his armament was for defense only

and that he had no legal authority for offensive measures, his country being at peace with Great Britain. But he hailed the British captain and told him to "go about your business and report to your masters" and inform them that if they wanted the *Hope* they would have to send more power or better seamanship to fetch her.

Back in the Garonne River, before sailing for the Caribbean, he had reaffirmed his ability to cope with mutineers. While anchored opposite Bordeaux he was hailed by a fellow American merchant captain nearby who asked aid against his rebellious crew. Bainbridge boarded the ship and again quelled the disturbers, though it is not clear that the same amount of fistwork was involved. But there was enough of a melee for the ship's routine and fixtures to be overturned and Bainbridge came within a jot of losing his life when some gunpowder was accidentally ignited. From that time, during a long naval career, he was never again plagued with mutinies.

Some other incidents help one to understand this seafaring Jerseyite, in the light of adversities that were later to beset him. In a crossing from Europe his merchantman was intercepted by the powerful British frigate *Indefatigable,* commanded by Captain Edward Pellew, who had fought against Benedict Arnold on Lake Champlain and in later life was to be distinguished as Lord Exmouth and eventually as Vice Admiral of the British Fleet. A search party headed by a Lieutenant Norton took a member of Bainbridge's crew, despite the irate American's warning to the indifferent British commander that he would retaliate promptly by seizing the first British seaman he could lay hands on.

That chance came five days later when the tough little *Hope* encountered a British merchant brig, which Bainbridge brought up with a shot across her bow. Though the brig had eight guns and twenty men, the American had her broadside to bear, her guns loaded, her matches lit. He sent his first mate, who returned from the British vessel with the required seaman (an unmarried man, as Bainbridge had specified), having left in exchange a message to be delivered to Captain Pellow, stating that Bainbridge had, as promised, retaliated for the seaman Lieutenant Norton had taken from the *Hope.*

When the undeclared war with France broke during the John Adams administration, Bainbridge served under the fathers of two of the great captains of American naval history, and if they imparted to him a modicum of what they must have to their resolute sons, his naval training was well rounded. They were Stephen Decatur, father of the better-known Stephen of the War with Tripoli and the War of 1812, and Commodore Christopher R. Perry, father of Oliver Hazard Perry, who snatched victory out of defeat in the Battle of Lake Erie. In Decatur's squadron, Bainbridge commanded the schooner *Retaliation,* the former *le Croyable* of the French navy. Decatur had captured her and she was the first warship ever captured by the government of the United States.

One bit of unusual recognition came to Bainbridge when, under the orders of Commodore Perry, he patrolled the waters off Hispaniola looking for Frenchmen. At Cap François his ship fired a salute in honor of the Negro government of Toussaint L'Ouverture. When the salute was returned by the fort, Bainbridge went ashore and was received "with great urbanity," according to his friend Dr. Harris, by the Negro leader of Haiti. A little later, though Toussaint had declined to visit French, British, and other American ships, he accepted Bainbridge's invitation to inspect his brig. General Henry Christophe and others accompanied the party, which had such pleasure that Toussaint invited the American captain to dinner on shore, conducted, by Dr. Harris' account, "with great decorum." Bainbridge was the only white man present with about forty of Toussaint's Negro officers.

Bainbridge's great misfortune in these days was to be the first United States naval officer ever to strike his colors to an enemy ship, when he was confronted by overwhelming power. That, taken with his adversities during the approaching wars with the Barbary States, tended to associate his name with failure, and both the government and a vocal public liked successes. But he cleared his record admirably in some spectacular sea duels during the War of 1812.

One cannot understand the resolution in this captain's make-up without looking ahead to the 1812 period, when the long-discussed war with England finally was about to break. Bainbridge had returned to the merchant service after the war with the Barbary powers, had traded in the Baltic, and was on a second visit to St. Petersburg in the winter of 1811–1812. When he heard that war was imminent, the port of St. Petersburg was closed. He was unwilling to await the spring thaw. Hiring bobsleds, he set out across the frozen Russian wastes, and traveled through Finland and almost the length of Sweden, on a journey so hazardous that few would contemplate it. Passing through blizzards and subzero cold, he finally got a vessel to the United States, where he arrived in time to command the *Constitution* in its decisive victory over the *Java* late in the year 1812.

But now he was in the harbor of Constantinople with an Algerian ambassador, much money, and a grotesque cargo of animals and goods to deliver to the Sultan. That sensible potentate, irked by Bobba Mustapha's double-dealings with France, declined to have anything whatever to do with the Algerine ambassador, at least not until the return of the Capudan Pasha with the fleet.

At length the great ships came in—fifteen sail of the line, along with a fleet of frigates and numerous attending craft. The *George Washington*, dwarfed by such naval might, fired a salute and was momentarily perplexed when it was not answered, but it was observed and later verified that at the very instant when the flagship of the Capudan Pasha, Admiral Hassan, was about to reply, a squall from off the Thracian coast struck his ship. All hands had to work diligently to prevent her from being cast on the Bosporus shore. Soon Zacbe, the well-educated, polished private secretary of the Turkish admiral, fluent in English and French, came aboard the *George Washington*, explained the emergency that had prevented a return of the salute, and invited the American captain to the palace of the Capudan Pasha. On the next day, with full formality, the Turkish flagship fired a salute in answer to the *George Washington*'s greeting.

Captain Bainbridge was to learn that all of the courtesy and chivalry did not belong to the navies of the Christian world. When he called at the palace of the Capudan Pasha he was met with cordiality and given what would have been termed in modern times the key to the city of the Golden Horn.

The cosmopolitan Admiral Hassan greeted him: "As the Ottoman Government have sufficient liberality to protect strangers, I beg you will place yourself under my protection, and accept me as your representative to the Sultan."

This was more than Bainbridge could remotely expect. The burst of friendship was clarified somewhat when he noticed that the dragoman of the British ambassador was present and learned that Lord Elgin had assured the Capudan Pasha that the American ship was under his protection. But the Admiral would have none of that, and decided that if the American needed protection, he would take on the job himself. Since the Capudan Pasha and the Sultan were kinsmen as well as brothers-in-law, who had been born in the harem together, been educated together, served Turkey together, and apparently were quite fond of each other, while the Reis Effendi, the grand vizier or secretary of state of the Ottoman power, was not of royal blood, Bainbridge now felt thoroughly secure.

Zacbe, it developed, was not only a gifted linguist but one who knew Occidental history and had no uncertainties about the existence of the United States or the meaning of the American Revolution. Since the Porte was closely allied with Great Britain against France, he saw nothing incompatible in friendship with the new republic, especially when it was being sponsored in Constantinople by the British representative. And was it not battling the frigates of France, the deadly enemy of the Ottomans? One of his heroes, and indeed, friends, had been Benjamin Franklin, whose acquaintance he had formed in Paris. He understood the American Constitution and was intrigued with it. Nothing like it had been known to the East. But his inquiries seemed constantly to go back to the benign Philadelphian who was already being claimed and owned by the world: the seer, scientist, and inventor Franklin. And he took delight in Bainbridge. Years after the voyage of the *George Washington* had passed into history, Bainbridge and Zacbe were corresponding and keeping fresh the friendship they formed during their conversations about the philosopher Franklin, American institutions, and, apparently with more casual concern, the immediate affairs in the Near East.

One of the first instructions Bainbridge received from his new protector Admiral Hassan, and it came in the form of a request, was that the Algerian flag be lowered—Bainbridge had continued to fly it beneath the Stars and Stripes—and that it be kept out of sight while he was in Constantinople. The Turks, it developed, were fully aware of all that had been transpiring in the Mediterranean. Bobba Mustapha of Algiers had been preying on Austrian and Neapolitan vessels, waging war on the enemies of France and consequently on the allies of the home government, Turkey. Nor was the Algerine Ambassador allowed to present his credentials to the Porte.

Bainbridge ran a good ship. A glance through the log shows that when nothing else was transpiring the decks were being swabbed. The crew was responsive, as Bainbridge's commonly were, and the officers were disciplined and well groomed. There was not a slovenly man on board. Among the midshipmen was William Henry Allen, seventeen years old, of Providence, Rhode Island, who was destined to conduct one of the greatest exploits in the history of the Navy. He carried the War of 1812 to the British coast and captured so many British vessels in the Channel and North and Irish seas that the Admiralty, Lloyds, and all London were startled and appalled. He learned much under Bainbridge.

This young mild-mannered Allen was a lieutenant in 1807 aboard the *Chesapeake,* when her commander, James Barron, was about to strike his colors ingloriously to the British *Leopard* and allow native-born American seamen to be taken off an American warship. Revolted at the thought, Allen rushed to the gun deck with a live coal and managed to fire one shot at the British, an unauthorized shot, a shot that rang across the country. That was the only response to the *Leopard*'s devastating broadside to which the ship's commander meekly submitted. This young Allen became a master of rapid firing. He handled the guns for Decatur so rapidly that ditties were written about it when the *United States* captured the *Macedonian*. Then he handled the prize crew, made the *Macedonian* seaworthy, and got her into Newport, Rhode Island.

His cruise in the little brig *Argus*, around Great Britain, won him successes until he met the heavier British brig *Pelican*, and in the desperate battle Allen lost not only his ship but his life, at the age of twenty-eight years. Despite all his destruction to their shipping, the British admired him and gave him a notable funeral in London, with the Royal Marines as an escort, the Royal Marine band for music, and eight captains of the Royal Navy for pallbearers.

Such was the discipline and patriotism of the young men trained under Bainbridge. The Capudan Pasha remarked on his several inspections of the *George Washington*—he took a fancy to this unexpected visitor from across the Atlantic—about the clean ship, the deportment of the crew, the discipline of the officers, and the construction of the ship. On one visit he commented that the *George Washington* was the only foreign warship that had ever reached Constantinople without a firman from the Sultan. He did not complain against Bainbridge, who could not be expected to know Turkish regulations, but he did mention that the officer commanding the Dardanelles fortress had been arrested for neglect of duty and would lose his head as quickly as the Capudan Pasha got around to signing the warrant.

Bainbridge was distressed. He told the Admiral that far from being a culprit entitled to no more than decapitation, the captain was blamable no whit whatever. The Admiral smiled, shrugged his shoulders as though Bainbridge were generous and chivalrous but was pleading a poor case, then asked how in the world a strange frigate could get through the Dardanelles without gross misconduct by the officer set there to prevent that very thing from occurring. The American captain explained that he had feared being turned back and therefore had perpetrated a ruse with the sails and the salute, for which the captain could scarcely be held censurable. Rather than see the innocent captain executed, Bainbridge declared he would take the punishment himself.

The American's frankness delighted the Turkish admiral, who grasped his hand, wrung it warmly, and declared that the custodian of the castle would be saved from the executioner. He did not close his eyes to the fact that the man had been outwitted. Ordinarily that would have been enough, whether or not the misdeed involved culpability. Bainbridge's attitude was so open and refreshing that the matter had to be viewed in a different light. The captain would not only go free; he would retain his position as governor of the Dardanelles castle.

But no such cordial reception or amicable relationship as those accorded Bainbridge were in store for the Algerine Ambassador. He was

ordered aboard the Admiral's flagship, where the Capudan Pasha took
the letter from the Dey, spat on it, stamped it underfoot, and then in a
fury told the bearer to advise the pompous autocrat of Algiers exactly
how his ambassador had been received and to add that the same treatment would be in store for him in person should he come within arm's
length of the Admiral. Still, the cargo was unloaded, lions, tigers, and
ostriches, and most certainly the coin and gems. A million dollars carried
no stigma even if it came from a faithless satrap doing business with
Turkey's enemies. Then the Sultan unloosened the full load on the Ambassador by telling him, through the Admiral, that he was to return to
Algiers, instruct the Dey to declare war on France immediately, liberate
at once the Venetian, Maltese, Sicilian, and Austrian prisoners he had
captured bearing British passports, and to send back to Constantinople
by return voyage, so it would arrive within the period of sixty days,
2,400,000 manbois, equal to $3,240,000, a sum large enough to leave the
Dey and most of his subjects poor indeed. This was to be a fine or "pacification money" due the Porte on account of his "daring presumption,"
plus spoilation money to compensate Greeks and Austrians for losses
at the Dey's hands.

Meantime, before making ready to sail, Bainbridge fell into novel
adventures. He chanced to meet in Constantinople the British author,
traveler, and mineralogist Edward Daniel Clarke, a globetrotter at a
time when much of it was done on foot, who had come down from St.
Petersburg, stopping by way of Moscow and Odessa, to Constantinople,
Egypt, and Palestine. He was also an outstanding collector of Greek
and Egyptian art and into his hands a little later fell the treasures of
manuscripts, maps, statues, and other precious gleanings of French
scholars and savants who had accompanied Napoleon to Egypt. These
Clarke obtained when Sir Ralph Abercrombie's British army captured
Alexandria the next year. His collections went to the British Museum
and to Cambridge University, where he became the first professor in
mineralogy and later the university librarian. In his *Travels in Various
Countries of Europe, Asia and Africa* he told of his jaunts and cruises
with Bainbridge, one in the *George Washington's* longboat to the Black
Sea, where the captain wanted to raise the first American flag ever to
appear on those waters, and others to Thrace and into Asia across the
Bosporus.

Clarke's most interesting story was about the banquet Captain Bainbridge served aboard the American frigate, in return for the numerous
dinners the diplomats had given in his honor. It was something along
the line of Alexander's feast of the "Meeting of East and West," but much
more novel, because on the corners of the table Bainbridge had four
pitchers of water, each from a different continent, and around the table

meats, bread, and fruits, and of each food thus offered the guest might
have portions from Europe, Asia, Africa, and North America. It is not
likely that such a meal was ever served before, most certainly never in
the harbor of Constantinople. It appealed to world traveler Clarke. But
the Britisher explained that it had not been an overly difficult feast to
assemble because Europe and Asia were close at hand, while the *George
Washington* had sailed from North America and touched at Algiers in
Africa.

This American sea captain, just twenty-six years old, having neither a
college nor high-school education, but with the rough spots knocked off
by heavy responsibility and much travel, with an aptitude for command
and possessing an urbanity and civility which made him welcome and
at ease in any company—erect, six feet tall, with black hair and black
whiskers when he let them grow (but usually wearing what in a later
decade came to be known as sideburns), acquitted himself so handsomely in Constantinople and made so many friends that it is difficult to
conceive of a better diplomatic representative who might have been sent
by the American government to the Porte. He raised the question there,
as it was being raised also by the consul to Algiers, Richard O'Brien, of
why the United States had not conducted its negotiations and made its
treaties with Turkey, the overlord of Algiers, Tunis, and Tripoli, instead
of with those suzerainties independently. If necessary, it might have
strengthened the Porte, a responsible power. He might have added that
the Porte could have used better the money the United States was pouring down the drain in the form of tribute to deys, bashaws, pirates, and
corsairs. In any event, Bainbridge, unsent and unexpected, introduced
the United States admirably and left Constantinople with the Ottoman
government—a considerable world power—disposed to be friendly
with the United States.

He did talk with the Capudan Pasha, who requested that he call
before his departure, about a treaty of trade and amity between the
Ottoman Empire and the American Republic. The Admiral was anxious
that the United States send a minister to the Porte. Bainbridge told him a
diplomatic representative, William Smith, had been named but had
progressed no farther than Lisbon and probably would be on in the next
six months. Then the Admiral promised to write the Ambassador giving
protection to his person and to American vessels he might recommend
for voyages to the Levant. He entrusted to Bainbridge letters to the
rulers of Tripoli and Tunis, which were left at Malta for delivery but
came to be largely ignored. They caused Bainbridge to comment that "I
think it very probable, that the states of Barbary will shortly receive
chastisement from the Turks."

As a final good-will gesture, the charmed Turk said to the American captain: "As your ship has been under my protection, she shall receive the honors which are exclusively reserved for my flag." Then he went on to say that as the Captain left Constantinople, and passed the fortress of Tapana, it would salute him, and he, of course, would reply. The rule of the Turkish navy was that this particular fort would salute only the grand admiral of the Turkish fleet, the Capudan Pasha himself, and never had the honor of such a salute been delegated to a foreign warship, or a Turkish ship either, unless he was aboard.

The Capudan Pasha gave Bainbridge one other item, the most prized of all. It was a firman from the Sultan, commanding that he be given respect and safe conduct throughout all Islam. This firman, it developed, was a potent document, more frightening to deys, bashaws, and viziers than cold steel, gunpowder, or the exaction of higher taxes by the Porte.

The *George Washington* slipped from her moorings, fired a departing gun and sailed December 30, 1800, bearing down through the Sea of Marmora under light, fresh breezes on a clear, pleasant day. Bainbridge took under convoy a Russian vessel making for the Mediterranean, whose captain, at a lull on entering the Dardanelles, he entertained at the *George Washington*'s mess. When he reached the fortresses guarding the strait he saluted just as he had done before. The castle replied, but this time the captain in command sent out an officer who invited Bainbridge ashore. As Bainbridge landed he was met with the profuse thanks of the commander, now restored to his rank and the promise of continued good health. Bainbridge was fortunate in dealing here with a man who chose to remember the saving of his head instead of the original deception which imperiled it. The compensation he offered was a lavish table and great quantities of fruit sent out to the ship for officers and crew.

On January 3, 1801, the day on which Bainbridge passed the Dardanelles and tarried for the hospitality at the fort, James Leander Cathcart, United States consul at Tripoli, was reiterating in a circular letter sent to all United States consuls and agents in Europe, a warning informing them of the approach of a rupture between Tripoli and the United States. The heart of the message was that the Bashaw of Tripoli had announced publicly and officially that he would declare war against the United States within six months after October 22, 1800. That would mean war in April, 1801. Cathcart cautioned that it was unsafe for American merchant vessels to sail the Mediterranean. Despite the payment of tributes, right and left, and the dispatch of the warship *George Washington,* conditions in the Mediterranean were not improving, but were growing worse.

By January 21, 1801 the *George Washington* was again off Algiers.

This time it was Bainbridge and not Dey Bobba Mustapha who was making the rules. He would not land the Ambassador and his suite until the Dey agreed to comply with the Grand Seignior's orders: first, that he declare war on his old ally France; second, that he liberate forthwith all his captives who had British "recommendations"; and third, that he agree to provision any British vessels coming his way. Since the American was out of range of the shore batteries, the faithless Dey thought he might be lured in with honey. He made solemn promises that the American ship and crew would not be detained. Bainbridge, knowing he was well prepared, decided to venture in. Before sailing for Constantinople he had loaded some old cannon for ballast to replace the cargo of gunpowder and heavy foodstuffs he had carried to Algiers from the United States. It was necessary to unload these guns, which apparently were not worth much, for the harbor defenses.

So Bainbridge brought in the ship. In company with Consul O'Brien he called at the Dey's Divan, composed of his officers of state, only to find that the oily potentate, backed by fifty armed Janissaries, was wearing a "scouling and vindictive expression." Indifferent to his promise of safe conduct, he began to belabor the American captain and threaten him with bodily chastisement. He reverted to all the arrogance with which he had impressed the *George Washington* into his service. But Bainbridge, forewarned, was forearmed. He drew from his breast the Sultan's firman. When Dey Bobba Mustapha saw it his eyes bulged, his face lost its ferocity and, as Dr. Harris had the story from Bainbridge, the "blood thirsting tyrant became a mild, humble and even crouching dependent." Quick to notice the transformation were the Janissaries, who exchanged startled, then knowing, glances. Of these the Dey must have been conscious, for he ordered the Janissaries away. Then, with only Bainbridge and O'Brien present, his words became soothing and pacific.

For nearly two hundred years the deys of Algiers had inclined toward greater independence from the Porte. They were loosely united with the Ottoman Empire.

(Although the terms dey and bey are often used interchangeably, they are distinct, the dey being, after the revolt of 1710, the head officer of Algiers. The two words have different Osmanli stems, the dey coming from the Turkish *dai*, meaning at first a maternal uncle, but applied by the Janissaries to any well-thought-of elder. When the Janissaries deposed the pasha and elected their own commander the head of the province, they gave him the friendly title of dey, which prevailed until the French conquest of 1830.

(The bey, originally *beg*, meant an Ottoman governor or prince, as

begum meant a princess or queen. It was a more common term than dey.
Eventually *beg* came to be pronounced bey and moved over into the
English language in that form, but its application broadened to include
the ruler of a district, an appointive governor, or an individual of rank.
While there were many beys among the Ottoman rulers, there was prop-
erly only one dey, the half-independent ruler of Algiers.)

The cord with the empire was there, and at times it could be binding.
Bainbridge may have informed the Dey that when he left Constan-
tinople the Capudan Pasha was making ready his huge fleet manned by
a Turkish force of 30,000, including the troops, to rendezvous with the
British fleet under Lord Keith at Rhodes. Keith was transporting a
British army of 20,000. The probability that Bainbridge adverted to the
Turkish mobilization is seen by the inclusion of this information in the
report by Consul O'Brien to the Secretary of State, in which he related
the events of Bainbridge's return and their meeting with the Dey.
Turkey had an additional force of 30,000 at Jaffa. The project described
by O'Brien—and this is what did occur—was the descent on the French
force left in Egypt. In any event the Dey understood that the Porte had
ample power either to unseat him or batter his fortress city to the ground,
and he must have understood that after the Battle of the Nile his old
friend France was in no condition to prevent it. Turkey's problem was
always that of getting her hands free in the Levant or Black Sea, where
she usually was at war with Russia, in order that she might keep the
loosely held colonies of North Africa in line. That she was potentially
dangerous they well understood.

So the orders of the Porte were followed to the letter. First, war was
declared against France. The singular method employed by the North
African satraps to declare war was to send out axemen to chop down the
enemy's flagpole in front of the consulate. It might seem a mild and
juvenile gesture except that along the North African coast a flagpole was
about the most difficult of all objects to obtain. There was an act of finality about chopping down the pole. The desert produced no firs or pines,
which shipbuilders ordinarily got for masts from the Norwegian or North
American hills. A consul who needed a flagpole had to get a mast from
a ship and masts were needed and ships were not plentiful.

The difficulty might be seen by the letter of January 3, from Cathcart,
the United States consul at Tripoli, to the Secretary of State. It told how
peace had been restored between Tripoli and Sweden. The flag of
Sweden was again to be flown. Then the Bashaw's aides brought him
word "that a piece of timber was not to be found in the whole regency
large enough to make a flag staff for the Swedes." The only possibility
was to take a spar from a cruiser. The situation caused the son of the

Bashaw to remark warningly to the American consul that "it is a difficult thing . . . to get a flag staff put up when it once comes down." He went on to threaten that "when the American flag staff comes down it will take a great deal of grease to get it up again." The "grease" he had in mind was a tribute of $20,000 annually as a starter.

The Dey of Algiers in some manner raked together the satisfaction money for the Porte. He emptied the prisons of 400 slaves who had held British protection. They were mainly Venetians, Maltese, and Sicilians. One of their first acts after they breathed the clean air was to find Bainbridge and kiss his garments. From a humanitarian standpoint the voyage of the *George Washington* to Constantinople was paying substantial dividends. The next liberation was of 160 "Imperials," or subjects of the existing Holy Roman Empire, and Venetians. The Dey calculated that if he had to lose all these slaves because he had been allied with the side which displeased the Grand Seignior of the Turks, then when he shifted he ought to be allowed compensation from among his old friends. So unexpectedly he pounced on every Frenchman he could find, rounded up fifty-six men, women, and children, shackled them and clapped a ransom on them of $1,000 each. If the Porte wanted him to treat the French as enemies, he was the Porte's man.

Bainbridge at once saw the injustice of suddenly putting into irons those who had a day earlier supposed themselves to be the Dey's bosom friends. When he had left the United States the infant Navy had been talking about "French pirates," but one of Napoleon's first measures after returning from Egypt and becoming First Consul was to end the undeclared war between the United States and France. The treaty was negotiated between Joseph Bonaparte and an American commission headed by Oliver Ellsworth September 30, 1800, but no inkling of this had reached Bainbridge in Constantinople nor was it known when he returned to Algiers. Still, sea captains were policymakers. His intercession on behalf of the fifty-six French prisoners was humanitarian and not political and the matter of his status with France did not count. The effective weapon he employed was the Sultan's firman. His negotiations with the Dey were protracted but he and Consul O'Brien reached an agreement that the sentence against the French nationals should be changed from imprisonment for ransom to expulsion, provided they would clear out of Algiers within forty-eight hours. The French consul M. Dubois de Trainville was raised from despair to elation and deep gratitude to the American when he learned the terms. But the question of transportation remained. It loomed as a hopeless problem until Bainbridge decided he could speed the unloading and preparing of the *George Washington* and sail in time to get the French out under the deadline. His crew, as anxious as he was to free the innocent civilians, many of them women and children, responded with alacrity. On January 30, 1801, before the forty-eight hours had expired, the *George Washington* was moving beautifully down the harbor, the old cannon unloaded and the entire French contingent on board. He fed them out of the ship's stores and landed them at Alicante, Spain. They were so thankful that they at once got word of the incident to First Consul Napoleon. His gratitude was expressed in the official thanks of the French government to Captain Bainbridge. The action, said the French elaborately, would "be always remembered and reciprocated with pleasure whenever an occasion offered."

Not until he reached Alicante, landed the French passengers and took newspapers on board, on February 6, 1801, did he learn that France and the United States were at peace. The *George Washington* sailed from Alicante on the night of February 8 for the United States. The voyage was hard, the gales heavy. She reached Philadelphia April 19, 1801. "Long Tom" Jefferson, never a pacifist where the matter of tribute was concerned, was President and diminutive Jimmy Madison, who could be expected to look at every paper and ponder over every precept, was the newly appointed Secretary of State, preparing to enter on his duties on May 2.

Both were deeply bothered over the affront to American sovereignty involved in the impressment of the *George Washington* by the Dey of Algiers. That was an action which was not to be repeated under any circumstances at any time. Still, Bainbridge was dealt with gently, as though he had followed a reasonable course. Jefferson received him at the President's mansion and referred to his conduct as "judicious." But it was the kind of prudence that would not be tolerated again.

Jefferson had been thoroughly opposed from the beginning to the policy of protecting shipping in the Mediterranean by paying tribute to the pirate Barbary powers. One of Madison's first directives went to Consul O'Brien in Algiers, dated May 20, 1801, stating that the impressment of the *George Washington*—an American ship of war forced to navigate under a foreign flag—"has deeply affected the sensibility, not only of the President, but of the people of the United States." Madison had no intention to let the matter drop. Whatever the immediate advantages might have been, he stated, "the indignity is of so serious a nature, that it is not impossible that it may be deemed necessary, on a fit occasion, to revive the subject." Therefore the Consul was to say or do nothing which would preclude a reopening of the case.

But even before Madison wrote, American affairs in the Mediterranean had reached a new crisis. They were slipping out of the control of the new administration. The restive Bashaw of Tripoli, jealous that his tributes from the United States had not aggregated anything like the lush payments and costly presents being made to the Dey of Algiers, which had included the frigate *Crescent* and the two brigs, had been threatening open hostilities for months, as Consul Cathcart had been warning American shipping interests in Europe. Now, on May 14, 1801, the Bashaw, Yusuf Karamanli, sent a detail of men to the American consulate with axes, ropes, and instructions that if they could not take down or cut down the flagstaff they should tie halyards to the top and have enough men pull on them to break the staff off in the middle. The Bashaw didn't care about method, so long as the pole was down. They attempted futilely for a time to break it off, then brought out axes and chopped it off, leaving a stump standing. The top of the pole crashed across the terrace of the consulate.

Tripoli, the least considerable of the Barbary powers, but still possessing some elements of strength—a city of perhaps 30,000 with a desert vastness of almost unknown extent but sparse population stretching behind—was at war with the United States. Thus was the first formal declaration of war made against the new American government, which had been slow to build a navy but had been trying to protect its expanding commerce in the Mediterranean by sending tributes instead of warships and guns.

CHAPTER THREE

Piracy, Habit of a Hungry Shore

W HY was the United States government paying tribute to the distant Barbary States, sprawled along the North African coast, and why, despite this tribute, was the new Western republic now involved in a war with one of these regencies and experiencing near belligerent relations with the other three?

The answer lies mainly in the circumstance that the Barbary States for centuries had reverted to piracy whenever the volunteer policemen of the Mediterranean, the stronger European powers, were indolent, weakly led, or engrossed in fighting one another. Usually one or more of those conditions existed. Late in the eighteenth century, after the Revolutionary War, the United States had suddenly shot ahead as a leading marine carrier, with busy shipyards and enterprising masters eagerly participating in the Mediterranean as well as the North Atlantic trade. The new nation had no navy to protect its extensive merchant shipping and the parental surveillance which had been exercised by Great Britain in colonial times had been withdrawn with the recognition of the sovereignty of the States. Moreover, the European powers had again lapsed into conflicts as the wars of the French Revolution merged into the Napoleonic wars, comprising a deadly succession of clashes and an age of bloodletting as effusive as any of modern history.

Piracy had come to be regarded along the Barbary Coast as almost an economic necessity. It was an easy, publicly acclaimed means of making a living, ratified enthusiastically by the Moslem faith as long as it was practiced against Christians. At times it meant great wealth by which the cities along the thin African shore, with the harsh desert or forbidding mountain ranges behind them, reared themselves into imposing principalities and eras of showy splendor. Piracy was far more remunerative to beys and pashas than to the masses of city dwellers or the Bedouins of the back country. But it was more exciting to the ordinary-run Moslem than manning the olive presses, quarrying, or labor-

43

ing in the lead and copper mines. While the lean agriculture and primitive industries might distribute a fairer portion of their benefits to producers and distributors, the fruits of piracy were consumed largely at the top level by luxurious living in the palaces and harems, with few of its bounties trickling down to the dejectedly poor tribesmen who existed on meager desert fare. Still, even piracy was preferable to starvation for a people who were better tradesmen than agriculturalists, who were not temperamentally seafaring, but who could become desperate, fanatical fighters when hungry and in quest of plunder or when fired by religious zeal.

The Barbary States obtained their name from the Berbers, the strong, Hamitic-speaking race which had inhabited northern Africa from Libya to the Atlantic Ocean since before the dawn of history. Over the Berbers the succeeding waves of invaders had thrown their thin film of influence and passed on, without destroying the homogeneousness and stubborn vitality of these indigenous tribes, who bent supplely to the will of the conqueror but preserved their own customs and clannish autonomy and survived where their masters perished.

The Berbers were a nomadic white race, ordinarily dark-haired and brown-eyed but sometimes blond. Their name, though at times traced to the ancient Egyptian, was probably the familiar Greek term of barbarian applied to any non-Hellenic people. They were the Numidae of the Romans, who composed the splendid Numidian cavalry Hannibal threw against the huddled Roman legions at Cannae. Across their land moved Greek, Phoenician, Carthaginian, Roman, Vandal, Arabic, and at length Turkish arms and surface cultures. Fleets harried their seacoasts and distant kings and Caesars ruled their cities. But the hardy Berbers, reasonably honest, tenaciously primitive, having the vast desert behind them and knowing and wanting no other land, maintained their own identity and went their own way with their pristine pursuits.

Perhaps the nearest approach to anything like a fusion of peoples occurred with the coming of the Arabs, who, by the time they reached the Libyan sands west of Egypt, were known as Saracens, the "people of the East." Devastating as had been the tramp of the Vandals across North Africa, moving from west to east in the fifth century, more desolating by far to cities and towns, to aqueducts, cisterns, and circuses, and to the splendor of the Roman edifices of a richly ornamented land, was the sweep of the Arabs during the seventh and eighth centuries, which carried the banner of Islam from the Red Sea to the Atlantic Ocean.

Though the Berbers managed to retain their own language during and after the Saracen inundation, they and the fringe races which remained from the earlier invasions of North Africa yielded readily to the fiery religion of Mohammed. Here were fresh, vigorous men of action before whom the old, apathetic social order tumbled. Islam was an intense, surging force unlike the greedy rule of the Eastern Empire. Why should wanderers who lived in skin tents on the caravan routes, or dwelt in the rubble of decaying cities, be concerned over the passing of Roman elegance? The Bedouins of the sand hills and sparsely scattered oases cared little about the loss of temples, circuses, and baths.

The manner in which the Roman-Berber society of Libya at first resisted, then rallied to the support of the invading horde might be seen from the various steps in the conquest of Tripoli, the first of the North African states west of Egypt to fall before the onrush of the new faith. When in 637 Saad, Moslem governor of Egypt, and brother of the Caliph Othman, and the fervid Zobeir, his general, approached Tripoli across the sands of Barca—over a route a little American army would one day traverse—with an army of 40,000 frenzied Moslems eager to conquer, plunder, and destroy in the name of the Prophet, they came up against the formidable Roman walls of the ancient city. Tripoli was defended by the able soldier Gregorius the Prefect. While the siege was in progress he collected the strength of the province and fought the fierce host outside the walls.

Gregorius was accompanied in battle by his fair but Amazonian daughter, who rode a great charger, wore a burnished suit of mail, and appeared at points on the fighting line where her cause seemed imperiled. She has been likened to the goddess Bellona. But the legions of Augustus and Constantine had long since passed and Roman power was in the yellow leaf. Back and forth the battle surged outside the walls until Gregorius, seeing that his faltering men required greater impetus than the presence of his daughter in combat, proclaimed that whoever should kill the invader Saad should receive not only the handsome prize of one hundred thousand gold pieces (the sums of money the ancients dealt in have not been minimized as the stories have come down through the ages) but an award even more dazzling, the hand of his beautiful and spirited daughter. Thus inspired—and one wonders whether the gold or the warlike maiden was the stimulus—the young men of the Libyan shore battled so nobly for the Empire that the Arab commander sought refuge in his tent. That caused the sturdier general Zobeir, who would aspire later to the caliphate, to scorn and denounce him, and to assert to his followers that the maiden's hand would go not to the slayer of the Moslem chief, but to the soldier of Islam who brought in the head of Gregorius the Prefect.

Again the Saracens surged forward. Zobeir himself, the furious general who had lashed the army across the Libyan wastes, met and slew Gregorius before his daughter's eyes. But the prudent Moslem did not want a virago in his harem, or else he had a dim eye for pulchritude. He rejected the reward. His only comment was that he labored "for a recompense far above the charms of beauty or the riches of this transitory life."

The Tripolitans of the Empire remained tough enough to battle the invaders to a standstill and wealthy enough to purchase a peace from them, though it proved nothing more than a truce. The huge indemnity is calculated to have equaled six million dollars in the money of the early American republic, when dollars were as sturdy as the *Constitution*'s timbers. The sum was far above what any dey or pasha ever aspired to ask in tribute from the United States, but the Greek-Libyans managed to raise it.

The purchase of peace at such a price did not gratify, but aroused the Eastern Emperor at Constantinople, who decided that if there were so much money to be passed around he should receive a more goodly portion. He increased taxes, impoverished the people, and drained and enervated the province. The Empire in its lassitude was stifling its own subjects.

After the passing of thirty-one years, during which the vigor of the Moslems was wasted by civil wars over the succession to the caliphate and by an abortive effort to capture Constantinople, where Greek fire proved a more fearful enemy than imperial resolution, they turned again to the North African shore. Resuming their westward pressure under their zealous general Acbad, the freshly unsheathed sword of Caliph Moawyah I, they came again to Libya, where the people rushed out to greet them as friends and deliverers from the heartless, autocratic Empire of the East.

Thus in 668, soon after the seat of the spiritual and temporal successors of Mohammed had been moved from Medina to Damascus, Tripoli fell. The year was that in which the weak and bloody Greek emperor, Constans II, fleeing always from the ghost of the brother he had murdered, who continually handed him a cup of blood saying "Drink, brother, drink!" was slaughtered by a Syracuse mob. The sternness of the new faith thus prevailed over the decadent successors of the great Justinian. The old Persian empire, given a late bloom by Chosroes, was almost simultaneously extinguished and the conquerors pressed to the Oxus and the Indus.

The welcome to the Mohammedans on their second appearance in Libya was not repeated elsewhere as the sons of the Prophet pushed ahead with their bloody swords. Onward went Acbad, beyond ancient

Carthage and into the Berber country of modern Algiers, battling his way at almost every step, defeating Numidians, Berbers, and Moors, plunging by forced marches across Mauritania, the modern Morocco, until he stood with the banner of Islam and looked out into the Atlantic. It is related in Moslem lore that he even rode into the salt waves up to the girth of his saddle, flourished his scimitar and proclaimed to the Prophet his regret that only the vast ocean frustrated him in continuing the march of the faithful.

But there were reverses and delays. Forces gathering in his rear overcame Acbad and his depleted band. Here and there the Empire made stubborn stands, as that of John the Patrician before Utica and Carthage. Another great soldier of the faith, Hossan Ibn Annoman, finally toward the close of the seventh century took up the crescent banner and with his camels, horsemen, and intrepid Arab infantry again worked his way across North Africa. Carthage was destroyed at last, more effectively than had been done at the call of Cato, and never again did a city rise from the heaps of rubble. Hossan fought desperate battles with Berbers from the Mauritanian hills. Another Amazon warrior, the princess and prophetess Dhabba, brought together a desert army of Berbers and adopted a scorched-earth policy. North Africa, under the battering rams of both invaders and defenders, became a desolation. Dhabba was defeated and her head was sent to Damascus. Quickly the inhabitants of North Africa, Berbers and Moors and the descendants of earlier invaders—Phoenicians, Persians, Greeks, Vandals, and many others—accepted as if by one impulse the new faith. They cast aside the religion of the Cross, though some of the great spiritual leaders of patristic times had dwelt and labored among them. The African Saint Augustine, of Numidian as well as Roman blood, one of the greatest of Christian writers and philosophers, had been Bishop of Hippo Regius, and had died there while the Vandals besieged the town in 430.

The armies of Islam were swelled by accretions from among the Berbers and Moors. The religion of the flaming sword gave a cohesion to North Africa that had never been obtained by Carthaginian or Roman conqueror. As was done some centuries later in the instance of Saint Sophia's Cathedral in Constantinople, the masterpiece of Byzantine art and the flowering creation of Justinian the Great, which became the great mosque of Islam, Christian churches left standing after the wars were turned into mosques of the faithful. The Semitic Arabs became peaceful and usually sympathetic neighbors of the Hamitic-speaking Berbers. Never was there a thorough amalgamation of the peoples or languages, but religious solidarity was achieved. The coins devised by Omar, bearing the inscription *Lo illah il Allah*—"There is no god but

Allah"—came into circulation, replacing the bezant of the Empire. Under the Caliphs Abd-al Malik and Walid I, Islam reached not only across North Africa but into Europe to the Pyrenees. Everywhere the armies of the Prophet were triumphant. Islam, the religion of "submission," did not know how to yield.

Neither would the Jews in matters of their ancient faith. During the dispersal after the Emperor Titus captured Jerusalem in 70 A.D., the fugitives settled in moderately heavy numbers along the Barbary Coast. They maintained their racial and religious integrity and sustained the contempt and periodical persecution of their kindred Semites the Arabs, but they provided the capital and outlets for much of the North African trade.

It is necessary thus to skip through the history of North Africa, in order to understand the character and complexion of the Barbary States of 1800–1815, the period of the American wars. One development of far-reaching significance which occurred while the Saracens were making their way across North Africa was the decision of the general Musa Ibn Nosseyr at Tunis to create shipyards and build a fleet. The Moslems already had taken to the sea. In the great "Battle of the Masts," fought by Abu Sofian, the admiral of Caliph Othman, they had virtually destroyed the fleet of the Emperor Constantine III. All of the religious fervor of the desperately earnest causes had gone into this great clash of the galleys. Constantine entered the fray with his crewmen singing psalms and the cross raised above the prow of his ships. The Saracens looked toward Mecca, recited from the Koran, and flew the golden crescent on their banner of scarlet. So utter was Constantine's defeat that he narrowly avoided capture. His galleys were scattered or sunk.

Now, in Tunis, Musa recruited and trained shipwrights, launched vessels, and sent them to the islands and shores of the Mediterranean to plunder Christian vessels and towns. The seventh century was dying as the corsairs of Islam set out on their first piratical exploit. For the next eleven centuries, from this and other Barbary ports, pirates in sporadic outbursts of rapine would plague the Christian nations of Europe and eventually take notice of the infant United States.

Though the Crusades brought the European monarchies into protracted conflict with the Saracens of Asia, only occasionally did they touch Barbary, which through seven centuries following the conquest of Africa maintained mildly hostile but at times amicable relations with the countries across the Mediterranean. Pirates came and went and were often chastised. Occasionally a crusade, unable to come to grips with the Moslem defenders of Palestine, wore out its fury in Spain or Africa against heretics near at hand. The crusades of Saint Louis of France fell on Egypt, where he was captured and ransomed, and on Tunis. There he was defeated, and killed by the plague instead of the scimitar.

Most bitter among the evils of piracy was not the loss of ships and cargoes but the subjection of Christian captives to perhaps the most abject condition of slavery recorded in medieval or modern times. Mainly the captives wore out their lives as galley slaves. Lashed by a boatswain's whip, they manned the oars of the fleet boats which dashed out on surprise forays from the North African harbors, pounced on unwary vessels of the Christian powers, boarded them, overcame any resistance, and took back the ship as a prize and the survivors, the men to be chained to the oars as galley slaves until death relieved them, and the women, if young, for lives in the harems.

Large-scale raids were launched against Christian cities. Which of the medieval expeditions could be classified technically as warfare and which were piracy could be distinguished only with difficulty. But it would be inaccurate to characterize all the Barbary activities on the Mediterranean as piracy and all those of the Christian powers as recognized war. The Christian navies employed slaves in the galleys, usually Moslem captives, and there was an overabundance of brutality on both sides. Though much may depend on the character of the master, slavery is never attractive. The worst features of Mediterranean slavery disappeared with the passing of the galleys. After the transition to sailing vessels in the seventeenth century, the back-breaking, life-wasting toil beneath the boatswain's whip was largely ended. Slaves were rarely entrusted to the sails but were employed on land in construction gangs, in common labor, and where their education or talents suggested, in clerical and governmental positions.

That the practice of assigning slaves to the galleys was of early origin and was deeply deplored throughout Christendom might be seen from the formation in 1199—the year Richard Coeur de Lion died—by priests of the Church of Saint Mathurin in Paris, who became known as Mathurins, or Fathers of the Redemption, of an organization for the ransom or relief of Christian slaves in the Barbary States. Termed formally the "Order of the Holy Trinity and Redemption of Captives," the Mathurins labored for more than six hundred years transmitting ransoms, maintaining hospitals and missions in Barbary, and relieving as much as they could the suffering of the galley slaves. Thomas Jefferson would come to know them and seek their help.

Nevertheless, Mediterranean piracy remained more an irritant to the pride than a wound to the economies of the North Mediterraneans until the sixteenth century dawned on the restored vitality of the Christian powers, by which time the monarchies of Europe had obtained a fair

ascendancy over the dukes and barons. Civil strife ceased as the discovery of the New World offered an outlet for martial vigor. Trade ex-
panded as art, literature, and learning flourished. Nations long land-
locked by internal concerns were building ships and turning to the sea.
Rich cargoes provided fresh incentives to the sea robbers. The new wave
of nationalism proved in another and unexpected manner a stimulus
to Barbary freebooting. Ferdinand and Isabella, consummating their
dream of a new Spain, captured Granada in 1492 and decreed the expulsion of the Moors, who passed in thousands across the Strait of
Gibraltar. Bitter against the Christians who had driven them from the
land on which they had been settled for seven centuries, vigorous,
skilled, and unemployed, they turned to piracy for both vengeance and
what they regarded economic necessity. Piracy had its great resurgence
in this period following the expulsion and gave to the Barbary States
some of the commanding names among their many scourges of Christendom.

Foremost among them were two red-bearded brothers born on the
olive-covered island of Lesbos in the Aegean, whose leading families
were supposed to have been descendants of Agamemnon. Lesbos had
given the world the clear notes of the unparalleled Sappho. The voices
of Arouj and Khair-ed-Din were harsher. They were known in Christendom as the Barbarossa brothers, though there appears to be a question
whether the origin of the surname was from a mispronunciation of Baba
Arouj (the first in prominence but less durable of the two) or from their
flaming whiskers. Arouj was taken prisoner by the Knights of Saint John
in his first sea battle, held captive at Rhodes, then ransomed by the
Turks. After a spell with the Mamelukes in Egypt he appeared in Tunis,
there to become associated with his brother Khair-ed-Din. Together
they recruited followers from among the exiled Granada Moors and set
out on their piratical careers which made them known, from the standpoint of Christian seamen, as the most unmitigatingly vicious element
ever to infest the Mediterranean.

The Moors were from Mauretania, the old Roman province embracing
parts of Algiers but mainly Morocco. They were white, an admixture of
Berbers and Arabs, originally nomads, fanatically Mohammedan, and
desperate fighters for the faith. They probably descended from the
Zenago Berber tribe of southern Morocco and crossed the Sahara and
Atlas Mountains into the coastal region. The name came into more general use as signifying the Mohammedan invaders of Spain, though apparently it was from the Greek *Mauri*, denoting the area of Northwest
Africa. The Spaniards also applied it in the altered form of *Moros* to a
group of Filipinos in Mindanao because they were Moslems and of a
dark complexion. A not uncommon belief that the Moors were a Negro

race probably has resulted from some admixture south of the Senegal River and from the casting of Shakespeare's Othello.

The North African states meantime were substantially independent for half a century. Both Mohammedism and the Greek Empire were subjected to powerful new attacks. The Crusades had weakened the Saracens and sapped their energies as conquerors and colonizers. The Ottoman Turks, beginning as a nomadic band of not more than 4,000, which had been driven southward by Genghis Khan, appeared in Asia Minor and exerted an insistent pressure against Constantinople and the remnants of the Eastern Empire. Isolating Constantinople on the south, they advanced to the Dardanelles.

Their relations with the Empire grew close by trade and intermarriage until in the first half of the fourteenth century they appeared as arbiter or the balance of power in contests between rivals for the Greek throne. For their aid Emperor Catacuzene gave the hand of his daughter to the Sultan Orchan, son of Othman, or Osman, from whom the tribe took its name. Orchan's son, Soleiman, going to the aid of Emperor Catacuzene, crossed the Dardanelles at the head of 10,000 horsemen. He overran Thrace in 1353, a hundred years before the capture of Constantinople, and the Turks have ever since possessed a foothold of varying size in southeastern Europe.

Another of Othman's sons, Amurath I, conquered northward and made Adrianople the capital of the Turkish empire. His armies overcame the Bulgars, Serbs, Albanians, and Bosnians. From among the most physically sound and intellectually strong of the young men of these subdued peoples he organized and trained the Janissaries, who came to be looked on as the best-drilled and most formidable body of troops in the world. By posting a chain of galleys across the Dardanelles at Gallipoli, the Turks maintained free contact between their Asian and European kingdoms. They withered Constantinople like a vine cut at the root. They reduced the once mighty Empire to the lone city and its outer defenses. Under Amurath's son, Bajazet Ilderim, or "Lightning," the Turks terrorized Europe by attacking Hungary and besieging Constantinople.

The seat of the Empire was saved for little more than half a century by the appearance in Asia Minor and Syria of another greater and more heartless conqueror, Tamerlane. He captured and destroyed the heart of Mohammedism at Damascus. He burned and leveled that city and Aleppo. Then at Angora, which the Sultan Bajazet tried to relieve, he delivered to the Turks a ghastly defeat, July 28, 1402, captured Bajazet, and held sway over all southwest Asia. He died three years later, having retarded the onrush of the Turks for half a century and delivered a vital wound to the Saracen power.

Thus Tamerlane completed the virtual liberation of the Barbary States

from the Empire of the East and the Moslem soldiers of the desert. This
was the splendid, carefree era for the Barbarossa brothers. They warred
against the Spaniards and Genoese, and just as readily against the small
African potentates they had come to represent. They murdered their
masters and took control of large sections of the Barbary Coast, but
mainly made their headquarters in the Gulf of Gabès, east of Tripoli,
on Jerba, the legendary island of the Lotus Eaters, whose ambrosial
sweet dates, or yellow beanlike fruit, or redolent tropical flowers, had
lulled the sailors of Ulysses. When Algiers in 1515 called for help against
the Spaniards they defeated the Spaniards but murdered the Algerian
ruler who had summoned them. A similar fate awaited the ruler Tiemcen
who had sought their support. But now the Spaniards were sued by the
Algerians to give relief from Arouj Barbarossa, and at length the pirate,
one arm already gone, was put to flight in 1518 and killed.

Brother Khair-ed-Din remained. He appealed to Sultan Selim I, known
for his forbidding manner as "Selim the Grim." Selim was extending
Turkish domain over Syria and Egypt, defeating the Mamelukes, and
substituting the Ottoman Empire for the faltering rule of the Caliphs.
The Sultan of the Turks, under the unsmiling Selim, became the head of
the faithful and leader of Islam. When he commissioned red-bearded
Khair-ed-Din his admiral, he cast out his net for Turkish control over
North Africa west of Egypt, and began the process of bringing the
Barbary States under the Ottoman Empire.

Khair-ed-Din, his faithful, rarely sheathed sword, conquered in turn
the independent rulers of North Africa. He ejected the Spaniards from
Algiers in 1519 and eventually took the island off Algiers, Penon de Alger
(later joined to the mainland by a causeway), which controlled the harbor and from which the city and province had its name. Long held by
the Spaniards, it had been a thorn in the vitals of the Moslem city. The
Spaniards also held Oran. They captured it in 1509 and retained it for
two centuries and Khair-ed-Din could do nothing about it.

The Turks now entered into their most splendid era. Selim's only son,
Suleiman the Magnificent, became Sultan in 1520, roughly about the
time when three young, ardent nationalists—Francis I of France; Henry
VIII of England; and Charles V of Spain and Austria, the Holy Roman
Emperor—were taking their thrones. Under Suleiman, Khair-ed-Din
completed the consolidation of North Africa by capturing Tunis in 1534.
He became Capudan Pasha of the Turkish fleet and a noted admiral of
Islam. His greatest naval triumph came over the Genoese admiral An-
drea Doria, who commanded the fleets of Venice, the Empire, and the
Papal States, in 1538, off the west coast of Greece.

Charles V organized a great expedition against him, captured Tunis in 1535, at a time when the Admiral was absent, and scattered the Turkish fleet. Suleiman, clearly the greatest statesman among the later Sultans, turned to diplomacy, formed an alliance with Francis I (to the horror of much of Christendom), and in 1543–1544 sent Barbarossa with a new and reassembled fleet on a visit to the coast of southern France. The mission was one of rapport but the insolent pirate, now cloaked with an official Ottoman office, would not allow the churches of Provence to ring their bells while his faithful of Allah were in the French ports. They made winter quarters in bell-stilled Toulon. Returning toward Constantinople, he sacked the exposed Italian towns enroute. Reggio was burned and pillaged, slaves were captured, Rome threatened. Then Khair-ed-Din died in the seat of the Ottoman Empire, where Sultan Mohammed II, "the Conqueror," had offered the first prayers to Allah in the Cathedral of Saint Sophia in 1453. Khair-ed-Din's son, Hassan Barbarossa, became Capudan Pasha of the fleet and governor of North Africa. Suleiman consolidated Tripoli, Tunis, and Algiers into a single satrapy under him.

The most formidable attack of Charles V against North Africa, delivered against Algiers in 1541, was disastrous to the Empire and Charles's military reputation. The city was defended by a Sardinian eunuch, Hassein Aga, who sallied out and fought a fierce battle. Then the storms came to scatter the Spanish fleet and the Emperor, harried at every step by the Moslems, dragged his army overland to safety removed from the city.

The defeat of Charles—probably as much by the elements as by the Turks and Moors—was the more surprising because the great Genoese admiral, Andrea Doria, commanded the fleet. He had an extraordinary lieutenant. A Spanish contingent was led by one of the boldest and most resourceful captains of history, Hernando Cortez. Even here he likely would have given Charles victory had the arrogant monarch heeded his advice of how and where to make a timely counterattack when Hassein Aga was on the offensive. It being ignored, so the story goes, Cortez elbowed his way through the guards at Charles's carriage. When he mounted the step the astonished Emperor did not know him and asked who he was! "I am the man," answered Cortez, "who has given you more provinces than your ancestors."

Charles did not heed Cortez, who knew how to subjugate territories, else the Barbary States might have become Spanish. Then the depredations against Christian shipping would have ended, and the United States would never have become involved in a Tripolitan war.

The era of the Barbarossa brothers was one of cruelty to the galley slaves. Stories of their suffering have become a part of the literature of most Christian nations. Cervantes, though never consigned to the galleys, was captured and held later in the century by the corsair Arnaut Mami, and liberated in 1580 after five years of slavery under the Sultan's viceroy Hassan. Among the notorious corsairs who swept the Mediterranean in those years was Dragut, a name frightful to Christendom, who under the reign of "the Magnificent" scourged the Italian and Spanish coasts. The Knights of Malta, usually strong in the Mediterranean, held Tripoli, which had been captured by Ferdinand of Spain and transferred to the Knights by Charles V in 1510. Dragut recaptured it in 1551 and reduced most of the city except the castle to ruins. Then he rebuilt the fortress walls.

A succession of renowned corsairs followed—Piri Reis, Salih Reis, Seidi Ali Reis, and Murad Reis—the last worthy of especial note because his name was adopted by a corsair of a later day, who was to become a leading factor in the American wars. The first Murad Reis sacked Reykjavik, Iceland, in 1631. The major check but by no means an elimination of the corsairs came when Don Juan of Austria, commanding the fleets of Genoa, Spain, Venice, and the Papal States, caught the naval power of Turkey in Lepanto Bay in 1571 and defeated it so thoroughly as to "undeceive the world" about Turkish invincibility. Rarely has a naval victory been more complete. Both sides had about 300 galleys. After the fighting all of the Turkish vessels except a small detachment from the left of their line had been captured or destroyed. One admiral, Uluch Ali, found safety in flight. Fifteen thousand Christian galley slaves were liberated. The Christian loss was put at 8,000, the Turkish at 25,000.

Great as was the victory, its lasting significance was minimized because the galley was passing as a warship and the splendid era of the sails was coming in. Though the Turks lost their great rowboats they reappeared on the Mediterranean with polaccas, caravels, and galleons. The great Turkish Empire that had been a threat to Christendom under the gifted Suleiman, declined under his indifferent and profligate son Selim II. But piracy, given greater range by the sails, flourished under petty captains from the North African ports. They not only darted about the Mediterranean but harried the coasts as far away as Britain and Ireland.

Though there must have been numerous earlier English voyages to Barbary, those of the sixteenth century were the first recorded. Apparently the initial controversy arose in 1583 when the ship *Jesus*—the name may have infuriated the Moslems—took to Tripoli a cargo of woolens and linen and a quantity of jewelry made of coral, jet, and amber, and prepared to load a cargo of olive oil, which the Bashaw had promised duty free. When the English cargo was unloaded he demanded a duty for the oil. As Dr. John Leyden, who in 1817 reported on his travels in North Africa, observed about this earlier bashaw, "albeit he was a king he caused the said Sonnings [the master] to pay the custom to the utmost pence."

But that was only the beginning of trouble for the *Jesus*. The incident showed the perils which confronted shipmasters and their necks. The Oriental mind proved more devious than the winds and tides through which mariners navigated in the squally Mediterranean. An Italian who owed some money to a Turk arranged to escape from Tripoli on the *Jesus*, but the lender appealed to the Bashaw. Happy to have an excuse, the Bashaw summoned the master to come ashore. When Sonnings refused the summons the harbor guns fired on the vessel, but so ineffectually that the Bashaw offered any slave his liberty and a hundred crowns if he could hit the ship. A Spanish slave manned a cannon and with three shots demonstrated that if the Captain did not come ashore at once his vessel would go down under him. The Spanish marksman was of course tossed back into his old cell and the Bashaw forgot the hundred crowns.

Then a court was convened, where the English master and his French factor were sentenced to be hanged, one on the starboard and the other on the port. The master judged the time was propitious to become a Mohammedan. Amid ceremonies extending over several days, he was first de-Christianized, then inducted into the Moslem religion. It was an ordeal but safety was worth the price. So it was sadly disillusioning to hear the original sentence repeated with the sly Bashaw's congratulations that he would now have the benefit of dying in the true faith. When he was dangling over the bulwark the Bashaw made his ship a prize and his crew slaves.

England had her first naval brush with the Barbary Powers in 1655. When Oliver Cromwell became Protector, the Dutch ruled the waves and their Admiral Van Tromp moved with his fleet up and down the Channel with a broom fastened atop his mainmast, giving notice that he would sweep England from the seas. After he had been defeated by the English Admirals Blake, Dean, and Monk, and the Dutch Admiral De Ruyter likewise had learned that Blake's broadsides swept cleaner than a broom, England became the leading sea power.

Admiral Robert Blake, sickly with dropsy, scurvy, and other ailments on his voyages but awesome in battle, was in 1654 given secret orders by Cromwell to sail to Tuscany and collect reparations for injuries inflicted on British shipping. Cromwell would not mind if Blake picked up some of the Spanish treasure ships returning from the New World while he was cruising around Gibraltar. But one of his leading tasks was to chastise the Barbary powers and put an end to their raids on British and Irish seacoast towns.

Blake has generally been held to be the first admiral who dared to take wooden ships against stone fortresses. What he accomplished in this respect must have been in the mind of Captain Edward Preble of the U.S. Navy 150 years later. The question was whether mobility was superior to great stationary strength and he gave the odds to mobility. Blake claimed forts were effective only for making noises and arousing fears. He sailed into the harbor of Tunis, gave the two fortresses such a pounding that he battered them down, and here and at Algiers and Tripoli he destroyed the pirate fleets and put a stop for a season to all Barbary depredations. Clearly, Christendom could have used more Admiral Blakes along the Barbary Coast. He managed to pick up part of the Spanish plate fleet as he returned to England. But was that not technically war and in no manner piracy? England and Spain were ever at odds on the sea.

De Ruyter, whose sea greatness was by no means ended by Blake, took a Dutch fleet into the Mediterranean in 1661, dictated treaties with Tunis and Algiers, liberated Christian prisoners, and gave piracy another setback. These nations learned what the United States discerned later, that treaties with petty despots were not worth the paper they were written on. They were forgotten as quickly as hostile cannon ceased to roar across their home waters. But the Barbary States after Blake and De Ruyter never again gained stature as naval powers such as they had enjoyed under the Barbarossas and Dragut. They sought the easy prey of merchantmen, not the old-time frenzied combat with hostile warships. Now and again they became irritating enough to warrant the dispatch of a restraining squadron to one or another of their ports.

Such an expedition by Spain in 1775, under a Spanish captain with the strikingly un-Latin name of O'Reilly, had among its seamen an impressed American lad, Joshua Barney, sixteen years old, who was to become one of the most skillful commanders and rugged fighters of the early American navy. But the fleet was not led as Barney a little later would have commanded it, and the expedition was bootless. Barney had been seized in Alicante, where his ship had put in enroute home from Baltimore after a voyage in the Mediterranean. Already, before this year of the outbreak of the American Revolution, the colonies under the British flag had developed an extensive trade with the Mediterranean countries. The ships were not seriously disturbed by corsairs whose ports had been entertained by Admiral Blake.

CHAPTER FOUR

To Repel Force by Force

THOMAS JEFFERSON, Minister to France, wrote from Paris on July 11, 1786, the year before the Federal Constitution was drafted in Philadelphia, to John Adams, Minister to England, in London.

The letter, one of the best Jefferson or any other American statesman ever wrote, set forth concisely and forcibly his views about the Barbary powers and the policy the American States should pursue respecting them, and his opinions about pirates, tributes, war, and international methods in general.

Often the document has been neglected by later administrations, but the theme of it might well be emblazoned in the entrance corridor of the U.S. Department of State and made one of the pillars of American foreign policy.

In this letter Jefferson, who has been roundly condemned in much American history and especially by some military writers as a visionary and a pacifist, and because of his experiment with the Embargo in 1808 as a peace-at-any-price President, declared with reference to the Barbary regencies and in particular Algiers, that "I very early thought it would be the best to effect a peace through the medium of war."

While conceding that his opinions had no bearing on the issue because he was a minister acting under orders from the home government, and was not the policymaker, Jefferson outlined a course which was to guide him in this same situation when he became President fifteen years later. As between war and paying tribute, he regarded war as more just, more honorable, less expensive, and as more likely to win respect, which he called the "safeguard to interest."

Jefferson saw that a strong stand against the piratical states flouting American sovereignty would arm the executive head in America "with the safest of all instruments of coercion." The budding but still tender government would gain strength at home by acquiring the means of commanding respect overseas.

He wanted a fleet of 150 guns, half of which would be kept cruising constantly. He estimated that the cost would be £450,000, or, in terms of the dollar system he had already instituted into the American currency, about $2,180,000. This was the capital outlay involved in building a fleet and in operation expenses for a period he did not specify. He based his calculations on British naval costs. Even if the entire sum were to be charged against Algiers, which when he wrote was the principal offender in the Mediterranean, the amount would not be much more than the tribute that regency demanded. Still, the American States would have to maintain a naval force in any event and the entire cost should not be charged against Algiers.

"If it be admitted, however," Jefferson wrote, "that war, on the fairest prospects, is still exposed to uncertainties, I weigh against this, the greater uncertainty of the duration of a peace bought with money, from such a people . . . and by a nation who, on the hypothesis of buying peace, is to have no power on the sea, to enforce an observance of it."

Jefferson maintained that other powers—Portugal and Naples if not most of Europe—likely would enter into a confederacy to suppress piracy, which would mean a much smaller cost to the American States. The whole tenor of his letter was that peace by tribute was a hollow peace and that commerce could be maintained and the respect of others won only through the new Western nation's ability and willingness to defend its own interests. What better cornerstone for a foreign policy could be found than that?

John Adams in a previous letter, and in a reply he wrote to Jefferson from London on July 31, 1786, held a contrary view. Though conceding that much Jefferson said was true, he doubted the resolution of Congress and the people. Adams wrote of conditions existing under the loose Articles of Confederation and in a period when the states were reluctant to entrust responsibility to a feeble and uncertain central power, but he did seem to misjudge the temper of the American citizenry which had just made incalculable sacrifices in the cause of freedom during the long struggle of the Revolutionary War. He told Jefferson of the Barbary powers:

> The resolution to fight them would raise the spirits and courage of our countrymen immediately, and we might obtain the glory of finally breaking up these nests of banditti. But Congress will never, or at least not for years, take any such resolution, and in the meantime our trade and honor suffers beyond calculation. We ought not to fight them at all, unless we determine to fight them forever.

This thought, I fear, is too rugged for our people to bear. To fight them at the expense of millions, and make peace, after all, by giving more money and larger presents than would now procure perpetual peace, seems not to be economical . . .

Adams said he would go to all lengths with Jefferson in promoting a navy "but I think, at the same time, we should treat." He had an eye also on the large marine insurance savings, which would tend to offset the cost of tribute, but he did not enter into this in his letter to Jefferson. He felt Jefferson had underestimated the size of the naval force that would be required. He was apprehensive that with the Algerines a naval force "will make bad worse."

He was pessimistic that anything would be done by the home government at all, either by the use of force or money:

A disposition seems rather to prevail among our citizens to give up all ideas of navigation and naval power, and lay themselves consequently at the mercy of foreigners, even for the prices of their produce. It is their concern, and we must submit; for your plan of fighting will no more be adopted, than mine of treating . . .

Thus the two positions that were to be debated in the next two decades in the American government were set forth by two future Presidents; the one, Jefferson, advocating the enforcement of American rights by naval power and direct action, the other feeling that the practical course was to treat with the piratical states and pay money—tribute—for the protection of American shipping. Jefferson was no trimmer, or poltroon, and at this period at least was a disciple of force. A little later he was writing, from France, "The tree of liberty must be refreshed from time to time with the blood of tyrants. It is the natural manure."

Jefferson, during his dealings with the Barbary question, became about as good a student of the methods of the Barbary powers as anyone in the American government. Algiers, the strongest and largest, might be regarded as equal to the other three together, not only in the size of tributes demanded and paid by the Europeans, but also in naval strength. Jefferson, who had learned much, was unawed. Their vessels, he reported later to Congress, were "sharp built and swift, but so light as not to stand the broadside of a good frigate." He obtained reports each of the five years from 1785 until 1789 and found that Algiers ordinarily had only about nine xebecs ranging from ten to thirty-six guns, and four galleys. They had a forty-gun frigate on the stocks and expected two cruisers from Constantinople, which apparently never arrived.

(A xebec, sometimes spelled "zebeck" or, by Jefferson, "chebeck," was the Barbary warship most frequently encountered. It was a type of small Mediterranean vessel with a long, protruding bow that gave more space for boarders, and with three ordinarily short masts. It was lateen-rigged, a term which came from the word "Latin," and designated the triangular sails used from the early days in the Mediterranean. The masts were stumps, probably because tall timbers were difficult to obtain on the African coast. The lateen sail was suspended on a long yard, or tapered spar, slung low to the mast. Xebecs could be identified readily and were peculiar to the North African corsairs.)

Nor was Jefferson impressed with Barbary seamanship or ordnance: "Their guns are of different calibres, unskilfully pointed and worked. The vessels illy maneuvered, but crowded with men—one third Turks, the rest Moors, of determined bravery, and resting their sole hopes on boarding." Like the lion, which at this period still occasionally roamed North Africa, they stalked their prey alone—not as the wolf, in packs. According to Jefferson's information, "they were never known to act together in any instance." When they came out of the harbor they separated immediately and each corsair went his own way. Each year they made three cruises, between April and November. When the winter winds set in, they unrigged the vessels and laid them up until the next spring.

Though the issue of North African piracy presented itself forcibly to the States after they won their independence in 1783, American shipping had long been established in the Mediterranean, and Western world shipowners were not unfamiliar with piratical depredations.

Scarcely was the new continent colonized before Americans took to the seas. During the century of the British settlements, the seventeenth, the first American sail appeared in the Mediterranean, and almost as soon the New England colonies learned of piracy and enslavement. The Plymouth fathers lost two ships in 1625, five years after their landing, which were taken to the Moroccan port of Salé. Unusual notice must have been attracted to the mysterious case of Dr. Daniel Mason, a Harvard graduate who sailed out of Charlestown in 1678 never to return. Harvard graduates were not plentiful in those days and were usually accounted for, but after Dr. Mason had been traced to Algiers he was heard of no more.

Late in the century, during the reign of William III, American sailing vessels reached the Far East, where ginseng, a root procured in the woods by the North American Indians and prized by the Chinese who attributed to it medical or aphrodisiac powers, was exchanged for the rich products of the Orient. This trade went mainly by Africa and the

Cape of Good Hope but other vessels, venturing into the proximity of the Barbary powers, enjoyed the sanctioned status of the English home commerce. Some of the early American sea captains were not far removed from pirates themselves but were given the softer name of freebooters.

Charles Oscar Paulin in his study of early American voyages to the Orient found there was nothing novel during the period of King William's War for Colonial American seafarers to become pirates and for "roistering freebooters" to stagger through the streets of Boston, Newport, Providence, Philadelphia, or Charleston. A typical buccaneer would be decked out in a broad crimson sash worn over the left shoulder, and display a heavy gold chain. He wore a lace cap, ornate jacket, and white knickerbockers, and carried three or four handy pistols around his belt. Fortunes were made for a time in the Chinese trade, but after about 1710 it virtually disappeared, and there was little direct commerce with the Orient during the long period when England controlled the import of tea.

Late in the eighteenth century the Barbary States found that captives were more valuable for ransom than slave labor, and it was not uncommon in the colonies and in Europe that public funds would be subscribed to liberate seamen held in North Africa. Goethe, in Palermo, saw one of the princes walk through the streets making a public collection of money for ransom purposes. When the early New York merchant Jacob Leiser and his two sons and eight seamen were captured by Algerine corsairs with his ship *Pincke*, enroute to the colonies in 1678, he was held for heavy ransom. New York churches collected contributions and secured his release.

An interesting point in this case was that there was an overage of subscriptions and the surplus was set aside by the governor for church construction. Trinity Church on lower Broadway, begun in 1696 and formally opened in 1698, was completed with the unused balance of a fund collected to ransom American sailors. In a collection made in New York and nearby communities in 1793, with the Leiser case as a precedent, 4,302 persons contributed, a goodly number for a smaller colony. More women contributed than men. A noteworthy feature of the subscription was the relatively heavy number of contributions by Negro slaves—13 per cent of the total—though they could have had little money. New York slavery of the period was mainly of a household character and not as onerous as field labor. These contributions indicate that slaves, however gentle their treatment, never looked placidly on slavery.

If credence is to be given the figures commonly accepted by history and embodied in many early reports in Europe and the United States, huge amounts, in consideration of the times, were paid in tribute to the Barbary States during the late decades of the eighteenth century. The payment of France to Algiers alone has sometimes been put at $200,000 annually, and that of Great Britain at a higher figure. Spain presumably turned over a vast sum.

Jefferson gave Congress some estimates of the amounts, though he advanced all the figures as suppositions or reports from individuals resident in the different regencies. Peace with these states was supposed to cost Great Britain about $280,000 annually. He did not know the original lump-sum payment made by France, but the additional annual tribute was estimated at $100,000. As to Spain, "the late peace of Spain with Algiers is said to have cost from three to five million dollars." But he emphasized that after Algiers got the money, it seized Spanish vessels "on the most groundless pretexts," and having made a hard peace, broke it with impunity. Similarly when France became involved in domestic affairs—the outbreak of the French Revolution—Algiers captured six French ships in the year and held the seamen, numbering forty-four, in slavery. The Venetians, Danes, Dutch, and Swedes paid less in a lump sum at the time of settlement but continued annual tributes of from $24,000 to $30,000. The Dutch and Danes paid in naval stores and the other two in money.

Jefferson then made clear a pertinent point about tributes: "But it must be noted that these facts cannot be authentically advanced; as, from a principle of self condemnation, the governments keep them from the public eye as much as possible."

One other essential was that the Algerines never liked universal peace. That would leave no ships on which to prey. They wanted a reserve of one or two enemies and with these they would not consider peace at any price.

The European nations, during this period, were usually at war and hard up for cash. France in the 1780s was on the verge of bankruptcy, when Necker was first being dismissed as finance minister then being recalled to check the deficit spending. It could not be throwing money around recklessly to beys and pashas. All of these nations were anxiously protecting their own interests in an age of great political turmoil. They were accustomed to receive value for everything they spent. Any one of them possessed the means of blockading Algiers or sinking its small navy. Whatever they paid was too much, but the sums reported are to be looked on with suspicion. No doubt the amounts ordinarily cited were those advertised by the Barbary rulers when they came to demand tributes from the second- or third-class powers which had extensive Mediterranean trade but no navy adequate to protect it, such as the

Scandinavian countries, Venice, Naples, and the United States. They were the announced scale that gave support to a high asking price and were not to be taken too seriously in arriving at the final bargain. As Jefferson pointed out, no nation publicized the amount of its tribute and the matter remains surrounded with some vagueness.

The stated tribute payments were not the only thing demanded. Never did a new consular representative or minister present his credentials, nor a new ruler succeed to power over one of the regencies; and almost never, it seemed, did the sharp Mediterranean wind shift to become a warm *ghibli* blowing from the desert sands, but that rich presents were in order to a petty potentate from the obsequious Christian powers.

When Jefferson went to London in company with John Adams to meet the ambassador of Tripoli, Abdurrahman, he found that this least powerful of the Barbary regencies wanted an aggregate of $160,000 from the United States. The Ambassador thought Tunis would settle for the same tribute. The cost for all four of the Barbary States probably would be a million dollars, a figure later considerably increased. The ineffectual Congress which operated under the Articles of Confederation had difficulty in raising any kind of money from the states and had no powers of direct taxation. The request for a million dollars was fantastic. Jefferson was in no temper to pay it even if the money came easily. He rejected it forthwith.

What the expected tribute amounted to may be understood better by a comparison with present-day expenditures. The cost of the federal government for the first ten years under the Constitution, from 1789 to 1800, was roughly $5,775,000 a year. That was the average. The proposed tribute of one million dollars would have aggregated more than one-sixth of the entire federal expenditure. It would have been tantamount proportionally to fifteen billion dollars of federal expenditures in 1963, at a time when money is much easier to procure by taxation than it was in 1786. The comparison, by no means exact, serves to show the corresponding amounts in the two eras of American history when the problem occurred of making payments to foreign governments in the interest of promoting good will and maintaining friendships. Tribute was quite different from grants of foreign aid; but at times one-way giving, when authorized under duress or a threat that the money would be obtained elsewhere and an enmity would thereby be created, comes perilously close to tribute.

England, by naval might and whatever gifts and annuities she allowed the Barbary States—and it is not likely they approached $280,000 annually—had preserved fairly stable trade relations in the Mediterranean prior to 1776. Passports were given to American vessels exempting them from molestation, and American trade flourished. In those years 1,200 American seamen and 20,000 tons of shipping were employed between the colonies and Mediterranean ports. From eighty to one hundred ships went out annually in this trade. The Mediterranean became one of the best American markets. According to Jefferson's statement later to Congress, the ports of the Mediterranean bought one-fourth of the American exports of dry and pickled fish and one-sixth of the wheat and flour, plus some rice, one of the leading South Carolina crops. Other exports not mentioned were rum, lumber, beeswax, and onions, the last an antiscorbutic. This trade came to a complete cessation while the colonies devoted their energies to gaining independence, but once that was accomplished the enterprising North American shipmasters went forth again, this time under the new banner of the Stars and Stripes.

Seizures of American vessels began almost at once after the colonies achieved independence. The Barbary regencies still respected England and issued passports for English vessels. These were withheld from American vessels after 1776. The new American nation could not expect to enjoy the blessings without assuming the responsibilities and duties of liberty. The necessity for action arose rather suddenly when letters began arriving from American seamen held for ransom.

Two noteworthy seizures occurred in July, 1785, which attracted wide notice and possessed the Dey of Algiers with two articulate Americans who were to play important roles thereafter in the bellicose relations between the United States and the Barbary powers. The schooner *Maria* out of Boston, Captain Isaac Stevens, bound for Cadiz, was captured July 25 off Cape St. Vincent by a 14-gun Algerine xebec. One of the seamen on the *Maria* was James Leander Cathcart, a young Irishman who as a child had been brought to the United States, where he had served with distinction in the Revolutionary War and had shown enough resource to escape from the notorious British prison ship *Jersey* in New York Harbor. Scantily educated but possessing strong natural talents, he was to rise to positions of leadership as a slave working for the Algerine government, and then to become an influential factor in the Barbary Wars while an American consul in North Africa.

The other seizure, on July 30, was that of the ship *Dauphin* out of Philadelphia. The master, Captain Richard O'Bryen (who later when in the United States consular service changed the spelling to "O'Brien"), was a native of Maine whose family had taken him back to Ireland, where he was reared. He, too, had meager schooling but possessed marked ability which became apparent during his consular work in the Barbary Wars. Cathcart, though he had difficulty in his reports with his sentence structure, was fluent in Spanish, a language commonly spoken in Algiers after the return of the Moors.

American public opinion was deeply shocked by the seizures of the *Maria* and the *Dauphin*, which brought into focus the terrible scourge existing in the Mediterranean. From the pulpits in New England seafaring villages and towns, pleas for help were read each Sunday, coming from an enslaved lad known to the communicants, or from a father whose children had become a public charge. The horrors of the brutal treatment of slaves on the Barbary shore were recounted and the miserable plight of these friends and neighbors was told, and the distress was heightened because the amount of the ransom demanded was far above the resources of these poor little communities, or even the larger towns. Scrimp as they might, they could not meet the harsh demands of pirate overlords.

The brig *Betsey*, a slight variation of a common name for merchant craft, commanded by Captain James Erving, was captured in 1784 off Tangier by a corsair of Morocco, but the incident served mainly to show the gentler relations which would exist between the United States and that country. Sidi Mohamet, Emperor of Morocco, who held himself independent of the Grand Seignior of the Turks, did not enslave the crew nor ransom them when the *Betsey* was taken into Tangier, but vowed friendship to the United States and maintained a record evidencing his sincerity. He detained the Americans as hostages until a treaty with the United States might be negotiated, a proceeding in which the delay was altogether on the American side. After six months, though there was still no treaty, the American crew and ship were released, with the cargo intact. The Spanish representative to Morocco had interceded in favor of the Americans. But the Emperor issued instructions that no more American vessels should be brought in until time had been allowed for the American government to act on a treaty of friendship.

He wrote to the American Congress: "We have . . . given strict command to the captains of our ports, to protect and assist all ships under American colours, and in short, to show them every favour, due to the most friendly powers; being fully determined to do much, when an opportunity offers."

The Emperor requested no tribute, a policy which was followed by his successors. His attitude was in sharp contrast with that of the Algerine Dey. He seemed to take pride in his claim that he had been the first to recognize the independence of the United States, though in saying so he was overlooking only the earlier and more influential recognition by France. After the treaty with Morocco was finally negotiated occasional differences arose, but while they were temporarily menacing, they proved negotiable. Severe trouble was threatened at one time with his son. Either Muley Soliman's protestations were not as genuine as his father's, or else he lacked the firm control of his governors and harbor commanders, who liked to take a ship now and then.

Jefferson and Adams designated Thomas Barclay, U.S. consul at Paris, to deal with Emperor Sidi Mohamet, and he did his work so effectively that within a month after his arrival at Morocco on June 19, 1786, the treaty was concluded. The helpful Spanish government had eased the way for him. An important factor in the negotiations apparently was the advice given the Emperor by his spiritual adviser that the American religion more nearly resembled that of Morocco than did the religions of the other countries with which he had been treating.

When Emperor Sidi Mohamet died in 1791 his sons fought for four years over the succession. At length, in 1795, Muley Soliman took the throne. His attitude about the United States was not known, and James Simpson, U.S. consul at Gibraltar, waited on him. Muley rode out of his palace at Meshooar on horseback and greeted the Consul with these words: "The Americans, I find, are the Christian nation my father, who is in glory, most esteemed. I am the same with them as my father was; and I trust they will be so with me. I have given orders to Sidi Ben Ottman [his Secretary of State] to write my answer to their letter, which will be given to you, and to tell them I am on the same footing with them as my father was."

Another seizure with perhaps the most dramatic consequences was that of the brig *Polly* which sailed from Boston for Cadiz in 1793. John Foss, an observant lad from Newburyport, kept a diary, which was published in 1798 under the title of the *Journal of the Captivity and Sufferings of John Foss Several Years a Prisoner at Algiers*. It gave the American public a graphic account of the horrors of slavery, the cruelty of the overseers, and the heartless punishment of those guilty of impertinences or derelictions. Foss's pen informed the American people that, even though the galleys had passed, the conditions of North African slavery were as loathsome and degrading and the lives of Christians as worthless as they had been in medieval times.

The *Polly* was off Cape St. Vincent when a vessel wearing the English flag was seen to stand directly for two Danish brigs, but she allowed the Danes to go and made for the American ship. As she approached it was noticed that though she was a brig her sails were not of English cut. The officer who hailed the *Polly* wore Christian garb and was the only person visible on deck. A gang of eager boarders suddenly appeared above the gunnel with long beards and Moslem dress. Amid din, hand clapping, and shouting they swarmed over the deck of the unsuspecting American vessel. Waving scimitars, brandishing pistols, some armed with lances, pikes, and knives, they rushed through the ship like "ravenous wolves," plundering stores and cargo and the ship's equipment, and stripping the American seamen of their clothing. In exchange they gave some rags and tatters, their own vermin-infested garments they were glad enough to shed, and in these the American prisoners were paraded a little later through the streets of Algiers to the palace of Dey Hassan Pasha. The march was to the tune of the "huzzas of thousands of malicious barbarians" who, it developed, were thanking Allah for such a triumph over so many Christian dogs. The Dey made a statement to them—a bit of an apology for the seizure, it might seem—saying he had been trying to negotiate a treaty with the United States but his requests had been neglected with disdain. Then, waxing more spirited in his self-justification, he declared, "Now I have got you, you Christian dogs. You shall eat stones."

Eating stones would have been soothing comfort compared with what was in store for the captives, aside from four likely lads he picked to be his body servants. The others went to the fetid dungeons of the prison, or bagnio, to join other Americans and Christians of other nations—hundreds of captives in all—and were consigned to labor fairly similar to that performed by the slaves who built the Egyptian pyramids. First they were fettered with chains, anklets, and waist shackles weighing altogether up to forty pounds. In the mountain quarries they blasted out stone and hauled it on huge drags made of great square timbers. They rejected the stones which weighed less than twenty tons and took those up to forty tons. Six to seven hundred men pulled each sled with ropes about seven inches in circumference. Said Foss: "The drivers are continually beating the slaves with their stocks & goading them with its end in which is a small spear, not unlike an ox-goad among our farmers."

Each sled was dragged a distance of two miles, where the huge stones were put on scows, then transported and dumped in the harbor side of the mole, which was constantly being washed out and flattened by the heavy storms. Young Foss judged from a view of the harbor that the task would never be finished. This was apparently part of the work of building and strengthening the breakwater to join the island Penon de Alger with the mainland. Other slaves carried smaller stone blocks on wooden frames, four men to a frame, for the new palace the Dey was building. Still others worked fitting out the ships.

For the stone gangs the labor was gruelling and the punishment for faults, even that of fatigue, excessive. The penalty was usually from 150 to 500 bastinados, or blows with a stick or flail, for which the prisoner was stretched out prone, one overseer holding down his head and another his feet, while the blows were inflicted by two others across the buttocks. When half the sentence had been thus imposed the victim was lashed by his ankles to a pole. This was lifted so the soles of his feet would be up, and across them the flagellators would inflict the remainder of the blows. With such crippling and sustained punishment it was a wonder that the victim lived. Many did not.

For each meal a prisoner was served a loaf of black bread weighing three and a half ounces, and once a day a bowl of vinegar was divided among eight men. Theft was punished by a severance of the hand, which was hung around the thief's neck. Should a slave speak disrespectfully of the true Moslem faith he was either roasted alive or given the slightly preferable punishment, at least in contemplation, of being impaled. For the murder of a Mohammedan a prisoner was cast over the city wall to be caught on the iron hooks midway down, where sometimes he would hang in agony for several days before expiring.

While it is impossible to know how many Americans became acquainted with Foss's story, which could not have been a factor in the early negotiations because of the date of its publication in 1798, other accounts of the mistreatment of Americans were common property long before the country became aroused over the impressment of the frigate *George Washington* by the headstrong Dey of Algiers. The crass cynicism of the Dey could be seen from his attitude while the shackles were being fastened to some of the American slaves. As he supervised the riveting he talked in adulatory terms of "the immortal Washington," and called on the American Congress to send him a portrait of the General, "that he might always have before his eyes the asserter of independence and liberty."

Such was the setting for the negotiations of treaties with the remaining Barbary powers, Algiers, Tunis, and Tripoli. The efforts of the Americans were tedious and protracted. When the issue first arose after the ratification of independence, Congress in 1784 designated Benjamin Franklin, the head of the American commissioners in Paris, and the two outstanding Americans who were in the next year to be given the top diplomatic posts, Jefferson (to France) and Adams (to England), to begin negotiations with the Barbary States for the release of American captives. David Humphreys, later U.S. minister to Portugal, was appointed secretary.

Already Franklin had endeavored at the direction of Congress to have a clause inserted in the treaty with France whereby the French monarch would supply the same protection against the Barbary pirates that had been given by England before the incidents at Lexington and Concord

Bridge. France would not go that far, but in the treaty of commerce and
amity ratified in 1778 had agreed that the King would employ his good
offices as far as possible in interceding with the Barbary powers in the
interest of the Americans. The wording was broad and near meaningless.
When the matter got down to cases it developed that, as the French foreign minister Vergennes advised the Americans, his nation was unable
to enforce respect for the American flag. France would give aid if the
Americans wished to negotiate treaties.

Similarly, England in the treaty of 1783 understandably declined the
American request to have British protection of American ships continued in the Mediterranean.

At this stage the committee of three—Franklin, Jefferson and Adams
—began work. They had ample power but Congress neglected to provide any money. The agent they sent to Algiers found the Dey demanding $59,496 for the twenty-one Americans captured on the *Maria* and
the *Dauphin*, which was a rate of almost $2,850 a head.

Jefferson turned in Paris to the Mathurins, the Fathers of the Redemption, who for centuries had been treating with the Barbary States for
the relief of prisoners. Though he had no authorization from Congress
he ventured a commitment of $200 a person, a piddling sum compared
with what the pirates were accustomed to ask, but a considerable risk
for Jefferson, who, while he opposed tribute, was not adverse to the
humanitarian act of ransoming good American citizens who were being
subjected to barbarous cruelties. The Mathurins agreed with the greatest liberality to perform every service they could. They suggested that
their work be conducted in secret for best results, since they had never
before represented American citizens. They had just previously been
able to effect the release of 300 French captives at an unspecified sum
which with the expenses incurred exceeded 2,500 livres, or about $460
per man, an amount considerably in excess of the $200 Jefferson had
offered, but low compared with all asking figures.

Jefferson reported to Congress in February, 1787, on his contact with
the Mathurins and received authorization to pursue this method. Meanwhile the head of the order, known as the Mathurin General, had received word from his agent in Algiers that the American captives were
eating well on funds that were being provided by the American government and by private sources through the Spanish consul in Algiers. In
order not to arouse the cupidity of the Dey by any evidence of American opulence, these allowances were discontinued, much to the anguish
of the prisoners and to the distress of the American government which
had to read their petitions and pleas. This was the first instance in which
Americans were to be ransomed and it was suggested that the price

would set a precedent. Finally word came from the agent of the Mathurins that the ransom situation had grown tight; that slaves were scarce in Algiers and that the Spaniards, Russians, and Neapolitans had paid exorbitant prices in making redemptions. He was authorized to offer 3,000 livres, or $550 per man. Then while the matter was pending, the French Revolution struck the Mathurins. Their lands and revenues were commandeered and their means of continuing their work were destroyed. Jefferson had to gather up patiently the tangled threads of the negotiations and make plans for a fresh effort.

But the term of his service as minister to France was growing toward a close. Franklin, benign and tolerant, who had taken little part in the conduct of the work, had long since left France. He departed from Paris, the scene of his memorable services for the struggling American colonies, July 12, 1785. The sensation connected with his departure was the report which reached Jefferson that he had fallen afoul of the pirates personally. The rumor that his ship had been captured by a Barbary corsair and that "he bore his slavery with admiration" was later found to be groundless.

Jefferson returned home in 1789. He arrived in Norfolk November 23 and was handed a letter from President George Washington inviting him to be Secretary of State in the newly organized government under the Constitution. John Adams had returned more than a year earlier, and became Vice President. Negotiations with Algiers were left in the hands of David Humphreys, secretary of the commission.

Since other efforts had been held in abeyance while the Mathurins were at work, the new government had been organized while the ragged situation still existed for a treaty with Algiers. Secretary of State Jefferson submitted a detailed and closely reasoned report to the Senate, which President Washington forwarded December 30, 1790. It gave a comprehensive picture of conditions in the Mediterranean. He analyzed dispassionately three possible courses. The first was to insure the cargoes, ransom the prisoners regularly at a fixed rate, and pursue commerce in the Mediterranean on a come-what-may basis. The ransom rate would no doubt be high and it would be impossible to tell in advance what portion of the cargoes would be captured. Nor did he regard it as certain that seamen would engage to navigate the Mediterranean with no greater security than hesitant reliance on Algerine faith.

The second plan was peace by purchase. "For this," said Jefferson, "we have the example of rich and powerful nations, in this instance counting their interest more than their honor." The cost would be a matter of conjecture but he devoted some time to the reports of what others had paid and to varying opinions about possible costs to the United States.

Jefferson, who had ransacked the lore of the ages, undoubtedly had read in Machiavelli's *The Prince* that "the friendship which is gained by purchase and not through grandeur and nobility of spirit is bought but not secured."

The third expedient he stated was "to repel force by force." He described the naval power of Algiers, then said it would be the duty of another department to determine what force the Americans should possess to oppose it. He told Congress that Portugal alone had for several years patrolled the Straits of Gibraltar and thereby had confined the corsairs to the Mediterranean and kept the Atlantic free. Only two Algerine vessels had been through the straits in the last five years.

Then he touched a vital question: "Should Portugal effect a peace with them, as has been apprehended for some time, the Atlantic will immediately become the principal scene of their piracies." The reason was that Spain having made peace, there was no longer sufficient prey in the Mediterranean to cover the expenses of their ships and equipment. Then Jefferson stated the question:

> Upon the whole, it rests with Congress to decide between war, tribute, and ransom, as the means of reestablishing our Mediterranean commerce. If war, they will consider how far our own resources shall be called forth, and how far they will enable the Executive to engage, in the forms of the constitution, the cooperation of other Powers. If tribute or ransom, it will rest with them to limit and provide the amount; and with the Executive, observing the same constitutional forms, to make arrangements for employing it to the best advantage.

Jefferson's message was referred to the Committee on the Trade of the Mediterranean, which on January 6, 1791, reported an opinion "that the trade of the United States to the Mediterranean, cannot be protected but by a naval force." Then the committee added the despondent note: "and that it will be proper to resort to the same as soon as the state of the public finances will admit."

That meant the matter of a navy would have to be deferred. Sentiment was divided sharply but in general was hostile. Washington in his second annual message had called to the attention of Congress the distressful state of trade in the Mediterranean and had suggested that "you will not think any deliberations misemployed which may lead to its relief and protection." But in the end it was the policy of expediency instead of the Jefferson policy of meeting force with force which prevailed. The apprehension was more against a strong central government which would divest the people of their liberties than against the distant Barbary powers. Ransom of the captives was agreed to and Washington advised the Senate on February 22, 1791, that he would take measures to that end as soon as Congress appropriated the necessary money. Not until May, 1792, did Congress appropriate $50,000 to cover the expenses of sending an envoy to Algiers. The Senate, which was advising, suggested that it would spend $40,000 for peace with Algiers and make annual payments up to $25,000. As there was no navy, money was to be the weapon.

President Washington appointed John Paul Jones to conduct the negotiations with Algiers. Jefferson had already been in touch with Jones asking him to prod Holland into joint action against the Barbary States and suggesting that Jones would have charge of the naval forces—a good choice, for he not only knew how to command a fleet, but according to hearsay had in his youth served abroad a pirate ship and would understand their methods. He was living in retirement in Paris, forty-five years old, his health broken but with a great career behind him, when Jefferson sent his commission, along with careful and detailed instructions, through Thomas Pinckney, newly appointed minister to Great Britain. A salient point of the instructions was that there should be no ransom without an accompanying peace.

Jones died in Paris in 1792 before Pinckney could reach him. Jefferson had taken the precaution to name as alternate Thomas Barclay, who had negotiated with the Emperor of Morocco so successfully, but unhappily Barclay died in Lisbon January 19, 1793, not long after receiving the delayed instructions. All of the transactions consumed much time in an age of slow communication. The task of dealing with Algiers now reverted to David Humphreys, minister to Portugal, with Nathaniel Cutting as his secretary. They journeyed to Gibraltar to collect presents for the Dey and take passage to Algiers.

At this juncture there occurred one of those coincidental but momentously significant events which enter at times to shape the course of history. Charles Logie, British consul at Algiers, without the assent or even the advance knowledge of the Portuguese government, concluded with the Dey a truce between Algiers and Portugal. The immediate result was to unlock the Straits of Gibraltar and allow the hungry Algerine corsairs to crowd through into the Atlantic. Though Edward Church, U.S. consul at Lisbon, hurried out warnings to American shipping, and Humphreys added his cautioning, a great many vessels were in the Atlantic and in a twinkling the corsairs boarded and captured eleven American ships, confiscated their cargoes, and added to their bag of American prisoners, bringing the total to 119. Moreover, insurance rates on American ships and cargoes, which had been ten per cent, skyrocketed and reached the almost prohibitive figure of thirty per cent.

When the news reached America it created a furor. Nearly everyone attributed the disaster to British perfidy and there the blame has un-thinkingly remained in much history. The attitude of Portugal shows she was in no measure at fault. Portugal was not opposed to peace with Algiers but she had not wanted to distress the Americans, in proof of which, as quickly as she could make arrangements, she began the con-voy of American merchant ships in Portuguese waters. The Portu-guese foreign minister, Louiz Pinto de Souza, was as surprised as were the Americans, and likewise as displeased.

Logie had not negotiated a peace, but merely a truce for one year, at a promise that Portugal would pay a third as much as the vast tribute obtained from Spain; whatever that may have been, it was rated at from three to five million dollars. The plucky Portuguese took the attitude that they would not pay tribute of a farthing. The Portuguese warships had their first inkling of the truce not from Lisbon, but from the Alger-ines. When the corsairs came up to the straits and the Portuguese inter-cepted and were about to sink them, they exhibited the papers nego-tiated by Logie.

For a time it was supposed by Humphreys in Lisbon that the truce was an expression of the individual genius of Charles Logie, but it de-veloped that he had been authorized by the British government to try to bring about peace between Algiers and Portugal. Apparently to the surprise of everyone he had taken the bit in his teeth and run the full distance, and consummated the truce without referring it to the govern-ment of either Portugal or Great Britain. He committed Portugal to the payment of a million or so—if the advertised figures have any weight—without Portugal's assent.

Britain's explanation was simple, plausible, and no doubt sincere. There was not the least intention to injure the Americans. She wanted the Portuguese fleet liberated from the Algerine menace in its rear so it might co-operate with her as an ally against a common enemy. England and Portugal traditionally made common cause. The wars of the French Revolution already were raging on the Continent. Valmy had been fought and the high-spirited armies of the French Republic were on the march. Portugal was to stand with England as a resolute and faithful friend in the long conflict just ahead. And in any event, why was it any longer the responsibility of Great Britain to be concerned about the protection of American commerce? The time had not yet arrived in his-tory when peoples who severed old ties and went their own way might expect to be bolstered up in their self-government by the parent nation they had spurned. Perhaps the British home government would not have been as impetuous as Logie was in putting the truce into effect, but, like Portugal, would have favored a warning period. But the deed was done, the corsairs were released, the unarmed American merchant vessels were captured, and the crews were enslaved.

Washington was deeply appreciative of the resistance by the Queen of Portugal to the unexpected peace with the Algerine pirates. Secretary of State Edmund Randolph stressed in his letter of January 20, 1794, to David Humphreys "how highly the President of the United States esteems the magnanimity with which that truce has been resisted by her Majesty," and then: "The arrogance of the British Consul, in forming the truce, if he acted without orders from home, and the indignity to the Portuguese nation, if no previous assent was given to the measure, strike us here very forcibly." But Washington did not want to offend Portugal and instructed that "nothing be omitted, which is conciliatory, and that everything which may irritate, be avoided."

American public opinion was enraged. The clamor was heard by an irresolute Congress which had haggled about moderate sums of money while the national honor was trampled by the petty Barbary tyrants. Now the winds that blew across the states toward Philadelphia carried the spirit of a new nationalism. Congress pondered again but this time more responsibly, and on March 27, 1794, President Washington signed the bill authorizing the construction of six powerful American warships. The U.S. navy was being born, despite the strong opposition, almost ununderstandable opposition, it now seems. The nation undoubtedly would have built a navy at some time—perhaps months later, possibly years later—because of other urgency. But a later navy would have meant a different history and probably a later blooming of America as a power.

The certain fact is that the navy was authorized and begun because Charles Logie, an obscure British consul about whom nothing else was ever heard, negotiated and put into effect what would ordinarily be looked on as a minor truce between two small nations, one of which did not even know he was representing it. Some day a destroyer, or at least a patrol boat, might be named for Charles Logie, who did not like the Americans very much, but did them a great service.

Jefferson would have his opportunity, after further halts and delays, to try to obtain peace by war, "to repel force by force."

CHAPTER FIVE

The Building of the Ships

ONE major defect existed in the naval construction bill. This was a concession to those who opposed a navy of any character, that if the Algerine menace disappeared and a treaty were negotiated, construction work would be discontinued and the country would revert to its naval impotence.

If peace came, either the United States would have no navy or else the whole question of a navy would have to be threshed out in Congress again. That is precisely what happened. Thus the matter of establishing a navy was dragged out over a number of years, from the first authorization in 1794 until the final impetus by legislation and by the creation of the Navy Department in 1798. All the while the pressure for the new navy was insistent, the opposition aggressive and articulate.

In the sequence of events, the navy was begun, then peace was negotiated and the building was suspended. Then because of both the North African menace and hostilities with the French Directory, construction work on the ships was reauthorized and resumed. In this account the story of the creation of the fleet will be dealt with first, before returning to the negotiations which were almost continually in progress with the Barbary States.

The flaw in the naval act which required a suspension of work if peace with Algiers were negotiated was a necessary compromise, without which the bill would have had no chance of passage. The division in the House was nearly equal. In the first test, in January, 1794, a House resolution expressing no more than an opinion that a naval force to protect commerce "ought to be provided" passed scantily by two votes. Even the influential Madison, who had been fathering a set of punitive resolutions mentioning no names but directed against Great Britain, striking at her in the touchy regions of her commerce, opposed the naval bill because an American navy likely would become involved unfortunately with British seapower. He felt the hazard should be avoided, though he

had earlier asserted that "an acquisition of maritime strength is essential
to this country."

But major opposition during this and ensuing debates came from the
blunt, rough leader of the North Carolina delegation, Nathaniel Macon,
owner of vast Shocco and Roanoke River estates, tobacco planter and
dominant personality cast in a smaller pattern of the Andrew Jackson
mold. He deeply sanctioned and espoused Jefferson's notions of agricultural ascendancy. Fully as restive as Daniel Boone, he did not want
to be crowded in, either as a nation or an individual. Macon's isolation-
ism sprang from the pattern of his plantation life, which he expressed
in the remark that "A man should not live near enough his neighbors to
hear his dogs bark." Later he was to be Speaker of the House under
Jefferson, and always he was to be aligned against navies and foreign
involvements. Years afterward, when the matter of preparing ships for
the oncoming second war with Great Britain was before the House, he
was still insisting that a navy and an industry were to be mistrusted
and feared. "Setfasts," he termed them. Peace in Europe would relieve
the country of embarrassments to commerce whereas once the "setfast"
of a navy was on the back of the nation it could never be removed.

One certain "setfast" brought about by the Barbary pirates was to
cause the House of Representatives to appoint a Ways and Means Committee, a revenue-producing body that has continually grown more
robust.

In this initial stand of the agrarian South and West in 1794, against
a navy they held might ensnare the nation in European affairs, Macon
was able to align the North Carolina delegation for a solid negative
vote, though that state in the later days of the republic was to produce
quite a few secretaries of the Navy, two of them outstanding.

Where North Carolina was unanimously opposed, Massachusetts,
Rhode Island, and Connecticut delegations were unanimously in favor
of the bill. The cleavage over the establishment of a navy which existed
between the commercial East and the agrarian South was emphasized
by the remarks of Samuel Sewall of Massachusetts, a Harvard lawyer
practicing in Marblehead. It is of passing interest to note that the whispers of secession were first heard in Congress from Sewall during this
debate. He maintained that the "gentlemen who depend upon agriculture for everything" need not spend money on commerce, which could
protect itself if permitted. "Let those states which depend on commerce
be separated from the confederacy," he declared. He held that those
who lived by commerce did not do so by the mere good will of the union,
but should be cast on their own "before they were reduced to poverty
and wretchedness." He admonished: "Their collected industry and

property are equal to their own protection, and let other parts of the confederacy take care of themselves."

When the question of the second authorization was before the House, Macon was able to put into the bill a provision that the three American frigates authorized to be continued should not under any circumstances leave American coastal waters. That would have so circumscribed the President's prerogatives as commander in chief and as director of foreign negotiations as to be manifestly unconstitutional. The Senate eliminated this absurd restriction.

Washington Irving, pointing to the argument of the opponents that the act would be "laying the foundation of a large permanent navy and a great public debt," said, "It seems hardly creditable at the present day [1859] that such policy could have been urged before an American Congress, without provoking a burst of scorn and indignation; yet it was heard without any emotion of the kind."

Cost was only the beginning of the argument against a navy. The object of a good number of Congressmen was to emulate China and live in utter detachment from world politics. The ships would lead to unwanted problems. There would be no friendly harbors in Europe to receive them and shield them when they required repair, or provision them when their supplies were exhausted. Moreover, Algeria, when it sensed that the United States was preparing a retaliatory force, would redouble its severity against American captives. Why not pay Portugal to serve as the front-line defense of American commerce? Numbers of Congressmen did not recognize the truism of "No Navy, No Nation." It remained for a gifted young South Carolinian, William Lowndes, seventeen years later to elucidate to the agrarian sections that "the protection of commerce is the protection of agriculture," because the main products of American export and the ones that commanded top prices in a war-torn world had come to be foodstuffs and tobacco, and, feebly beginning its rise toward supremacy, cotton.

Even more than industry, agriculture required tonnage. The argument against the bill was a peculiar reversal of cause and effect, it being contended that because of their navies the great powers of the past, Athens, Carthage, Tyre, had sunk into oblivion. The opposition did not acknowledge that those cities had risen and been sustained through their greatness by naval strength and declined when naval ascendancy passed to others.

While the naval preparation was being directed against the Algerian corsairs who had surged out into the Atlantic, and who might venture even to the North American shores, anger at Great Britain, believed to be the culprit, was in the minds of both legislators and citizenry. War was talked, as it had been and would be many times again before the rupture finally occurred in 1812; recklessly talked by the Republicans, the Federalists contended. But British warships were beginning to stop American merchant vessels and seize seamen alleged to be British. Then the British admiralty had brought out and reinstated in 1793 an old doctrine called the "Rule of 1756," which prohibited trade between an enemy nation and her colonies, or, in this instance, trade between France and the French colonies in the Caribbean. American vessels engaged lucratively in delivering West Indian products to the French homeland were taken into British admiralty courts and condemned. The "Orders in Council" reinstating the rule were published in Philadelphia newspapers in March, 1794.

At about this time charges were circulated widely that the British government was instigating the Indians to rise against the settlers in the Northwest—charges no more substantial than those that recurred in advance of the War of 1812—and members of Congress were inflamed. This flurry of excitement mainly on the frontier resulted from an address to an assembly of Indians by Lord Dorchester (the General Guy Carleton of the British army during the American Revolution), Governor General of Canada, forecasting war between Great Britain and the United States. The accuracy of such a prophecy was seriously questioned by Lord Granville, the Foreign Minister, who gently repudiated Dorchester on behalf of the British ministry. It was not a threat, but a guess, but it was disquieting.

Reprisals against Great Britain that would protect American shipping were discussed in the government and some were instituted, the most drastic of which was an embargo for thirty days imposed by President Washington at the behest of Congress against all foreign vessels in American ports—a forerunner of the Jefferson embargo of 1808. It was extended for an additional thirty days and Congress authorized President Washington to continue it as circumstances might require during the recess.

When all the arguments of cost, involvement in foreign affairs, the advantages of the European system of purchasing peace with tribute, and the menace of a navy to domestic liberty had been presented and explored, the bill was passed by the safe House margin of fifty to thirty-nine. The Senate having concurred, Congress then appropriated $688,-888.82 to pay for the new Navy. The six ships provided for in the act might be obtained "by purchase or otherwise." The President was allowed some discretion about the employment of the money and the selection of the types of ships but no ship should carry less than thirty-two guns.

Forehanded President Washington, much ahead of the legislation, had put Secretary of War Henry Knox to work on plans for a navy. Knox was an artillery officer whose only connection with naval affairs appears to have been that his father was an unsuccessful shipmaster. Plutarch's *Lives,* with its enthralling accounts of Themistocles, Nicias, and other commanders of great naval expeditions and land campaigns, had fallen into his hands when as a lad he had got a job as a bookstore clerk. Plutarch led him into other military and naval history, which he read between customers when he established his own bookstore in Boston. This was the basis of his military education. Nothing in the notable career of this huge, stolid hulk of a man, who turned from bookselling to become Washington's chief of artillery and then his Secretary of War, surpassed in service to his country his discerning labors at this moment, when he had the opportunity to initiate the building of the U.S. Navy. His principal contribution was to turn up some great naval architects and shipbuilders, two of whom, Joshua Humphreys and Josiah Fox, might be accounted geniuses.

Knox sought opinions from all quarters—from skippers, shipbuilders, old soldiers, commercial men, congressmen, and others, and talked with nearly everyone along the Philadelphia waterfront to get ideas. It is a peculiar circumstance that the two top naval designers discovered by his quest, those who conceived ships that remain probably the most famous of all American fighting craft after the wars of nearly two centuries, were the two peace-loving Quakers, Humphreys and Fox. Knox knew Humphreys, who was well established in shipbuilding. Quite by coincidence he found Fox, and largely through them the American navy was born.

Henry Knox had a better impression than some of the congressmen about what had happened to Athens, Tyre, and Carthage. As early as 1792 he had begun his discussions about the type of warships the United States should undertake. Already the Merchant Marine Act of July 4, 1789, was proving a powerful stimulant, advancing American commerce and shipbuilding. This act has been aptly called "a second Declaration of Independence." Under it the foreign trade of the new republic was multiplied more than fourfold in the brief span of half a dozen years. The reason was the 10 per cent tariff differential allowed goods in American holds. Where in 1789 the United States was carrying only 17½ per cent of her imports and 30 per cent of her exports in her own vessels, by 1795 she was carrying 92 per cent of her imports and 88 per cent of her exports. The merchant marine had grown from 123,893 tons to 529,471 in these six years.

American shipyards were busy and overworked. Still, these merchant vessels were principally schooners. The problem Knox faced was the expenditure of a limited sum of money in such a manner that the new American navy might make itself felt against the great, powerful vessels of Europe as well as against the heavily manned xebecs of North Africa. Knox entrusted the designing problem to Humphreys, who with justice has been called "the father of the American Navy."

Born in Haverford, Pennsylvania, in 1751, Humphreys was a descendant of the adventurous Welsh pioneers who settled the Philadelphia back country in the seventeenth century and gave to the area some of the great names of later American generations. He was apprenticed as a ship carpenter, but when his master died in 1771, he established himself, at the age of twenty, in his own business. The most famous of the numerous ships he built during the Revolutionary War, most of them privateers, was the *Randolph*, a frigate of 32 guns destined to an unhappy fate. On her the gallant young Captain Nicholas Biddle met his death when her magazines exploded and she sank during a battle in the West Indies with the British *Yarmouth*, a 64-gun ship of the line. Humphreys was twenty-five years old when he built the frigate, and was forty-one when, in 1792, Knox began to confer with him.

While Humphreys was at work, chance threw young Josiah Fox into the arms of Secretary Knox. Fox was touring the United States studying types of lumber best suited for the various parts of ships. A member of a wealthy English merchant family, he had been apprenticed in the Royal Dockyard at Plymouth, then had toured Europe studying shipbuilding, and finally arrived in Philadelphia, intending to spend one year in America. The Secretary of War took him to Humphreys and the association so influential on the first American frigates was formed. They employed a draftsman, William Doughty, who worked under the skillful Fox as Fox did under the imaginative Humphreys, and later became a builder in his own right.

With Fox doing the drafting and Humphreys supplying the ideas, to which Knox and a congressional committee had contributed their parts, the plans were laid for the first powerful frigate. This design eventually became the sister ships *Constitution, United States*, and *President*, each of 1,576 tons and a rated armament of 44 guns. Then Humphreys and Fox designed the *Constellation* and the *Congress*. Every vessel of their conception in this program became a household word throughout the country and two of them, the *Constitution* and the *Constellation*, are still in service after upwards of 160 years as ships of the U.S. Navy. Quite naturally Fox, a true artist, became so engrossed in his work that he never got back to England. His views and Humphreys' were not always in full accord. His liking was for smaller, Humphreys' for larger frigates.

He came to inspect and remained to labor; he came to learn and in the end remained to direct.

Knox emphasized in his report as Secretary of War, dated December 27, 1794, that no second-rate warships were in contemplation; that "vessels should combine such qualities of strength, durability, swiftness of sailing, and force, as to render them equal, if not superior, to any frigate belonging to any of the European Powers." That was a salutary policy for the country to embark on, and it was one which in its essentials has guided American naval construction to the present day.

Humphreys' attitude as he approached his problem is best seen in two letters he wrote in 1793 to Robert Morris, then a senator from Pennsylvania, which he introduced with the remarks that "From the present apearance of affairs I believe it is time this country was possessed of a navy." His object was to build frigates which "in blowing weather would be an overmatch for double-deck ships" and could evade them in light weather, or else to build double-deck ships which in blowing weather would be superior to three-deckers. He went on with precise specifications: the beams and decks should be of the best Carolina pine, the lower futtocks and knees of live oak. The scantlings should be equal to those used in 74s. He calculated they could be built of red cedar and live oak for about twenty-four dollars a ton, including masts, rigging, sails, and even chandlers' bills. The *Constitution* actually cost a little more than nineteen dollars a ton, and the workmanship and materials were the best procurable.

Then he disclosed his foresight by saying frigates built to carry the conventional 12- and 18-pounders would not serve, for in a war with any powers of the Old Continent, especially Great Britain, having numerous ships of that size, the chance in combat would be equal "that we lose our ships, and more particularly from the Algerians, who have ships, and some of much greater force." He favored large frigates. This he emphasized more fully in his second letter. The United States, he asserted, should take the lead in a class of ships not built in Europe. That would be the only means of "making our little navy of any importance." If the United States had ships the same size as the Europeans, want of discipline and experience, which would not come quickly, would throw the balance to the enemy. His type of frigate would by their great length have the advantage in sailing. They would be superior to any European frigate and fleet enough to keep out of the way of the larger and more heavily armed ships of the line.

Humphreys' plan was adopted and adhered to closely.

The six frigates on which work was commenced, the shipbuilders, places of construction, and the superintendents designated to become captains of the vessels were:

WARSHIP	GUNS	BUILDER	WHERE BUILT	SUPERINTENDENT
United States	44	Joshua Humphreys	Philadelphia	John Barry
Constitution	44	George Claghorn	Boston	Samuel Nicholson
President	44	Forman Cheesman	New York	Silas Talbot
Constellation	38	David Stodert	Baltimore	Thomas Truxtun
Chesapeake	38	John Morgan	Norfolk	Richard Dale
Congress	38	James Hackett	Portsmouth, N.H.	James Sever

And so the fleet was begun. The eminent New York shipbuilder Forman Cheesman laid down the *President,* 44 guns, in Christian Bergh's shipyard, in New York. He had grown up in the shipbuilding business, working in his father's shipyard probably before the Revolutionary War. He, more than any other, made New York a shipbuilding center at a time when other seaports, particularly in Maine and Massachusetts, were buzzing with activity and bidding for supremacy. When she was finally launched April 1, 1800, after her construction had been delayed for a time, the *President* was fleeter than her sisters, the *Constitution* and *United States.* That was because Doughty, who had been made the naval constructor, was allowed to introduce alterations in Humphreys' original design and build her lighter and lower, or with less freeboard. Before she got to the Mediterranean she was a natural choice for the flagship. By that time a plain upright had been substituted for the figurehead carving of George Washington on her stem. One of her broadsides was to echo through newspaper harangue, diplomatic dispatch, and history, when under Commodore John Rodgers she riddled and silenced the British sloop-of-war *Little Belt* after that inferior ship needlessly provoked a combat. The engagement fought off the Virginia capes May 16, 1811, almost caused war between the United States and Great Britain thirteen months ahead of the actual declaration.

The *Constellation,* 38 guns, was built at Baltimore by David Stodert, but under the watchful eye of Captain Thomas Truxtun, one of the best seamen and even more obviously one of the toughest fighters of the early Navy. Vain, stumpy, fearless, severe, hated and in turn idolized by his men, Truxtun won those victories over the French *Insurgente* and *Vengeance* in 1799 which were the first around-the-world rumblings announcing the arrival of a new naval power. The *Constellation* was launched September 7, 1797, but did not go down the Patapsco until April 9, 1798, when Truxtun took her against the French cruisers and frigates that had been seizing American vessels in the Caribbean.

The *United States,* built by Humphreys at Philadelphia, was launched July 10, 1797, with Commodore John Barry in command. Her first task, like that of the *Constellation,* was to blast out the picaroons of the West Indies, an admixture of French and Spanish corsairs almost as nettlesome as the pirates of the Barbary Coast, and much more challenging because they were plying boldly close at hand. Another of her early missions of consequence, before she won a great name under Stephen Decatur, was to convey to France the special mission, consisting of Patrick Henry, Chief Justice Oliver Ellsworth, and William Davie, to negotiate with Napoleon to terminate the sporadic, undeclared naval war that had broken out between the United States and the French Directory, in which the *Constellation* was taking such an active part.

Of the first six frigates the least distinguished was the *Congress,* which fought no noteworthy sea actions, spent much time in "ordinary," and finally was broken up in 1836 at Norfolk, near the spot where her more worthy successor, the frigate *Congress,* of 50 guns, unhappily challenged the *Merrimac* and burned in a fearful holocaust in 1862.

The *Chesapeake,* handsome and fast, was the bad-luck ship of the lot. Her remnants are still scattered in bits of souvenirs over England. Her building had not been far advanced when peace with Algiers halted the construction. When naval building was resumed the timber that had been accumulated for her in Portsmouth was moved over to Norfolk and used for the completion of the *Constellation.* Originally the *Chesapeake* was intended to be of the *Constitution* class, with 44 guns, but when Josiah Fox gained control of the design after building was begun again, he expressed his favoritism for smaller frigates and reduced her to the size of the *Constellation,* with 38 guns. Captain James Barron had her at sea, poorly manned and equipped, in 1807 when she was stopped by the British warship *Leopard* and forced to turn over four members of her crew, after she had received several broadsides which killed three and wounded eighteen American sailors.

The *Chesapeake's* greatest hour was when, under the command of the gallant James Lawrence with a motley crew, she fought the British frigate *Shannon*—an engagement in which Lawrence, mortally wounded, uttered the watchcry of the American navy, "Don't give up the ship."

Before one may recognize fully the virtues that went into the American fleet it is necessary to glance briefly at the type of vessels customarily employed at this period of naval warfare.

At the close of the eighteenth century the conventional navies consisted in general of three classes of ships. These were line-of-battle ships, heavy, slow, but powerful; frigates, which were fast sailors, termed by Nelson the "eyes of the fleet"; and sloops-of-war, a classification which covered most small armed vessels, whether they were identified as schooners, brigs, corvettes, or otherwise.

The identifying point about a sloop was that all her guns were on one deck—the upper deck, or what American seamen named the spar deck. Unlike line-of-battle ships and frigates, she did not fire through portholes where the gunners were given some protection. Her guns were in the open, where those who manned them were exposed to musket fire from the enemy decks and rigging. At times she mounted guns on the forecastle or on a raised quarterdeck, the one fore and the other abaft the mainmast.

The line-of-battle ship, such as made the might of the British navy, was as a classification broad and a bit vague, but in general these ships had guns on three decks. Two decks had complete batteries, each consisting of up to about 30 long guns. In addition to the long guns, they had carronades on the forecastle and quarterdeck above the spar deck, thus giving them a rating of a 68, or a 74 (which was a common rating), or, as in the case of the *Tonnant,* captured by Nelson from the French at the Battle of the Nile, an 80. The figures designated the number of guns. Some line-of-battle ships accommodated 100 or more. Nelson's flagship, the *Victory,* launched in 1766, had 100; the *Royal George,* an older ship, 100.

Long guns were the main armament of big ships. They fired solid shot, canister, grape, and bursting shells. Shrapnel, in 1784, had made his invention of a projectile which scattered bullets, and it had come into use in naval warfare before the close of the century. But the main reliance was on the weight of the round shot to crush the sides of the enemy vessel, preferably at the waterline. Better results than with shrapnel were obtained from marksmen in the rigging of the vessel, where their first object was to pick off enemy officers, as happened to Nelson at Trafalgar and Lawrence when the *Chesapeake* fought the *Shannon.*

The long gun was not only long in measurement, being 9 to 9½ feet in length, but possessed a longer range. The barrel was thick in comparison with the caliber and long guns were consequently so heavy that they could be employed only on strong lower decks. If used on a high deck they made the ship topheavy and unseaworthy. Guns were designated not so much by their caliber as by the weight of their ball, as 18-pounders or 24-pounders. The bore of the 18-pounder was about 5⅓ inches while that of the 24-pounder was slightly under 6 inches.

In 1779 a revolution occurred in naval ordnance with the introduction of the carronade, which took its name from the town of Carron, Scotland, where the guns were first cast. Its main feature was lightness. The value was that with the carronade greater fire power could be placed higher up on the ship, on the spar deck or the forecastle or quarterdeck, without sacrificing seaworthiness. Higher guns were a distinct advantage. They could be fired with greater accuracy in rolling weather when it would be difficult to get an aim from the lower gun deck across the choppy waves. The carronade was not only short, but light. It was not as thick as the long gun, especially not at the muzzle, toward which it tapered. Though its effective range was shorter, it was a powerful weapon on forecastle or quarterdeck as the ships closed. A 32-pounder carronade, 4 feet in length, or not half the length of the long gun, had a bore of 6¼ inches.

Another advantage of the carronade was that the charge of powder required for a 32-pounder was 2½ pounds, while the charge for the long gun was about 6 pounds. Both were loaded from the muzzle. Though this was an era of experimentation with percussion caps they had not come into general use. The cartridge of powder was placed in the chamber of the cannon and it and the shot in front of it were rammed firmly into place. Then a wire was poked down through the vent or touchhole to break the covering of the powder cartridge. Additional powder was poured from a powder horn into and over the touchhole. This powder was lighted with a match when the command was given to fire.

Canister and grape were employed not only against the seamen working on the spar deck but also against the spars and rigging. Though the bullets in the charges of canister were of uniform size, the destructive qualities of this ammunition had not improved greatly above the "land-ridge" fired from the early cannon, which consisted of scraps of iron, nails, and flintstone, thrown together in a sack and forced down the cannon's mouth in front of a charge of powder. Chain shot and bar shot were at times used, as were heated shot for incendiary purposes.

Another type of gun mounted on the ships of the 1800 era was the columbiad, about midway in size between the long gun and the carronade, but it was not so important a factor in American naval armament as the others. It came to have more extensive use in the army.

Great timbers had to be used in the construction of line-of-battle ships so that the decks would sustain the broadsides fired by such heavy batteries. The line-of-battle ship thus sacrificed speed for sturdiness. A vessel of this class was called also a ship of the line or a man-of-war. They had so much weight in their broadsides that it was not expected a frigate would give them battle any more than a sloop would fight a frigate, except under extraordinary circumstances.

Frigates had guns on two decks—the main or gun deck, where the fire was through the portholes, and the spar deck, where the guns were fore and abaft, but rarely in the waist of the ship. Ordinarily the armament was about 30 long guns, mostly 18-pounders, plus carronades above the spar deck. But with the new American vessels, such sturdy construction was introduced by Humphreys, and so deft was his designing that the top American frigates not only retained speed and excelled European vessels of the same class but also were able to bear heavier ordnance. The British in the War of 1812 termed the American frigates "disguised 74s," implying that they were misnamed—a contention which led Theodore Roosevelt into detailed study and discussion of their qualities and to a resounding conclusion that "the American 44-gun frigate was a true frigate, in build and armament . . . [They were] in no way whatever line-of-battle ships."

How they were superior to any other frigates on the ocean, apart from matters of gunnery and seamanship, in which the Americans of this period excelled, may be seen from the qualities of the *Constitution*. She was rated a 44-gun frigate, but her carronades gave her an armament of 55 or possibly 56 guns at the time of her battle with the *Guerrière*. Ira N. Hollis, perhaps the best-qualified student and writer about the *Constitution*, in his detailed study of the ship made about 1900 took a view somewhat contrary to Roosevelt's. He felt the ship corresponded to a razeed 74, or was like a three-decker with her top deck cut away, and that therefore the British with some justification looked on her as a line-of-battle ship in disguise. Thus is seen the confusion, or possibly the overlapping, in the classifications.

Her name, "Old Ironsides," is customarily ascribed to her hard, heavy timbers and planking which, according to one version, gained their toughness because they were bent into place without the customary resort to steam, which was believed to soften the wood. Another belief was that the delay in building the vessel occasioned by the peace treaty with Algiers allowed better seasoning and hardened and toughened the live oak timber. But the folk lore and more attractive tradition is that one of her gunners, begrimed by powder smoke, seeing the enemy shot bounce ineffectively off her sides, much as did the shot of the wooden ships from the *Merrimac*, exclaimed, "Her sides must be made of iron."

Great difficulty was experienced in procuring the exact materials desired. Some were remote, and weather conditions impeded the work on this and other ships. Ship carpenters sent from the northern states to islands off the Georgia coast to cut and hew the live oak did not fancy the climate of the low, hot seacoast, and most of them could not be prevailed upon to remain. Three capable of selecting the proper timber and molding it properly were induced to stay, and they supervised crews of Negro laborers in carrying ahead the work. Transporting the timber to the northern shipyards was another difficulty. Some of the ships that undertook the work made one voyage and because of the sickness and other hardships declined to make a second.

Down on St. Simons Island, off the Georgia coast, a huge stump of a live oak tree was exhibited in those days as the "Constitution oak" or better, the "Constitution stump," because from it the first tree was felled for the timber for this noble vessel. Shipwright John T. Morgan had journeyed with crews of workmen from Boston to Charleston and on to Savannah in his quest to select the best pine, cedar, and live oak—the last being used for the frame.

Colonel George Claghorn, a Revolutionary War veteran, built the *Constitution* at Edmund Hartt's shipyard, Boston, while General Henry Jackson served as naval agent and handled all the business transactions. Claghorn used Joshua Humphreys' design. The over-all cost of this most famous of all American warships was $302,718, including the cannon purchased in England. Much as the Japanese artillerists threw at the American soldiers in World War II iron from the Third Avenue elevated railroad of New York, so the *Constitution* fired at the British in the War of 1812 from guns bearing the familiar symbol of the British monarch, "G.R." This initial armament bought in England consisted of twenty-eight 24-pound long guns for the gun deck and ten 12-pounder long guns for the quarterdeck.

Artistry went into her hardware. Paul Revere put aside his silverware to make her bolts, fastenings, and brasswork. Her anchor was brought down from Hanover, Massachusetts, while her sails were cut and sewed by expert hands on Park Street in Boston.

French naval architecture still prevailed, and strongly influenced the design of the *Constitution,* though it had become less of a factor in the latter part of the eighteenth century. The French tended toward larger ships in their particular classes, such as 80s in place of the customary British 74s. Humphreys explained his object in a progress report he submitted to Congress at the close of 1794, in which he said his plans "appear to be similar with those adopted by France, in their great experience in naval architecture; they having cut down several of their seventy-fours to make heavy frigates; making them nearly of the dimensions of those of the United States." He went on to say that the commanders of the American frigates would have it within their power to engage any ship they desired or to avoid the engagement if they thought proper. Such would be their fleetness. But they could fight, and "no ship under sixty-four, now afloat, but what must submit to them."

Work on the *Constitution* was retarded by the treaty with Algiers, but while Congress was meditating and there was much uncertainty as to what should be done, events occurred which had profound bearing on the future of the Navy. The French Directory, more arrogant than neighborly in its advance toward absolutism, covertly demanded tribute from the United States such as was then going to the Barbary powers. Agent Hottenguer of Talleyrand's staff put the word in the ear of Envoy Charles Cotesworth Pinckney that the increasing strain on relations between France and the United States could be eased by a *douceur* of 50,000 pounds sterling for the Directory plus a governmental loan. That was on October 6, 1797, and Pinckney is supposed to have answered with a phrase that has rung through American history, of "Millions for defense, but not one cent for tribute." Whether it was this or, as another version has it, "Not a sixpence, sir," the American government could see clearly that it needed warships. Tribute was like blackmail—more and more would be demanded and there would be more and more comers.

Early in the next year a French privateer impudently entered the harbor of Charleston, South Carolina, sank a British merchantman, then sailed out to capture two American vessels heading for the port. Congress swung into action. The money was appropriated to complete the first three of the ships—the *Constellation*, the *Constitution*, and the *United States*, all of which had already been launched. This act was passed March 27, 1798. Congress took one other action in keeping with the nation's needs. It set up a Navy Department under its own Cabinet officer. President Adams appointed Benjamin Stoddert, a native of Charles County, Maryland, after George Cabot of Massachusetts had declined the post. Stoddert, whose father had lost his life in Braddock's defeat in 1755, had been a hard-riding cavalryman (as was later his more distinguished nephew, Lieutenant General Richard Stoddert Ewell of the Confederate army). Serving as a major, he had been wounded severely at Brandywine. After the war he became a merchant and prospered in the bustling commercial town of Georgetown and built the house overlooking the Potomac River, which remained a show place in old Georgetown.

With a cavalryman behind it, the Navy began to work up lather, and on July 2, 1798, the mighty frigate on which the hope of the country was centered dropped down from the inner Boston Harbor; later in the month she made for the sea. Her commanding officer was Captain Samuel Nicholson, who like Secretary Stoddert was a Marylander of Scotch descent.

The *Constitution* was not the first, but the fourth, ship of the new Navy to get to sea, but she was almost from the beginning the most distinguished. Her launching, delayed more by the rebellious ways, which did not have the proper incline, than by peace with Algiers, was an epochal event in Boston when she was finally induced to slip into the water. The day was celebrated on stage and in song. John Hodgkinson wrote a special musical piece for a rendition called "The Launch," which was put together, rehearsed, and presented in the short space of two days. The Boston *Commercial Gazette* told of the "elegant and superb specimen of American naval architecture," a unity of "wisdom, strength and beauty."

In the instance of such a historic ship, as with the others, it is permissible to look ahead and glimpse her great career. Her triumph under Captain Isaac Hull over the *Guerrière* resounded as clear and far as did the shots at Lexington Common and Concord Bridge. Long did she serve as a training ship at Annapolis. Distinguished naval commanders learned seamanship on her decks. The only instance in history where the Pope could be said to have stood on United States territory was when Pius IV in 1848 was rowed out to her with the King of Naples, in the ship's boat. After the blazing poem by Oliver Wendell Holmes, none would dare tear a plank from her, but at times the pennies of schoolchildren have gone toward her repair.

Just as with the fleet, so the construction of the navy yards—as distinguished from private shipbuilding facilities—resulted from the Barbary menace. Daniel Ludlow, an agent of the Navy Department, transmitted plans for the Navy Grounds on Long Island, which became the Brooklyn Navy Yard, to Secretary of the Navy Robert Smith March 17, 1802. Along with the plan and map he observed that "If the improvements I have detailed should be compleated [*sic*] it will be the first Naval Yard on the Continent." The estimated cost of dock, rope walk, barracks, dwelling house for shipwright, mast house, mold loft, hemp store and dock, blacksmith shop and foundry, filling, board fence enclosure, and expense of preparing the yard was $54,500. And the estimate, he stated, was "rather above than under the cost!" Plans for a dock and development of a Navy yard in Philadelphia were submitted by George Harrison, Navy agent, on the same date.

Outbursts of patriotic ardor in various cities gave the United States other spendid warcraft. Virtually all in Essex County, Massachusetts, joined in the building of the *Essex*, a fleet frigate of 32 guns, the first vessel to make American seapower felt in the Pacific, and the first American warship to double the Cape of Good Hope and Cape Horn. She gained notice when from her mainmast Captain David Porter at the beginning of the War of 1812 flew the banner, "Free Trade and Sailors' Rights," which so provoked the British commander Sir James Yeo of the *Southampton* that he sent Porter a challenge. Porter, on sea duty, never had opportunity to accept. The *Essex*, of 866 tons, was the smallest frigate in the Navy, but was one of the staunchest. She was built in Salem in 1799, and every cent of her cost was subscribed by the people of Essex County. Much of the timber was cut in the county and dragged by volunteers to the Salem shipyard. Enos Briggs built her, and so enthusiastic were the workers that she was completed in less than six months.

Similarly, the citizens of Charleston, South Carolina, built and presented to the federal government in 1799 the beautiful frigate *John Adams*, while Philadelphians subscribed and built the *Philadelphia*, 38 guns. She was designed by Fox and, as with the *Chesapeake*, reduced from original plans calling for a frigate of the *Constitution* class. Not to be outstripped in patriotism, New York raised by subscription the funds for another handsome frigate of 36 guns, the *New York*, first of the warships bearing that name, which was honored by the flagship of Admiral William T. Sampson's fleet in the Spanish-American War.

Thus four trim, fast, powerful frigates, the *Essex*, the *John Adams*, the *Philadelphia*, and the *New York*, were added to the fleet. These mass subscriptions by different communities came, it is true, before the income and other taxes siphoned off revenues and centered such matters in the national capital, but the citizens who gave their time, products, and money in an hour of emergency to make the infant United States a naval power—minor compared with Great Britain to be sure, but still a power—deserve no less credit for their patriotic exertions. The American spirit which had flamed during the early months of the Revolution was never expressed more enthusiastically or to better purpose than in the building of the fleet.

CHAPTER SIX

Two Poets and a Peace

WHILE the shipwrights labored in the yards, diplomats hurried back and forth across the Atlantic and Europe trying to work out an adjustment with Algiers that would satisfy the government and delight the back-country congressmen by making the Navy unnecessary.

The negotiations fell into the hands of two extraordinary men, gifted along any number of lines. They were sensible and capable, but as envoys, neither was formidable nor wily and duplicitous, and those were the qualities called for by the diplomatic practice of the era. They were Joel Barlow and David Humphreys, Yale classmates thrown together in peculiar roles.

Humphreys was no kin to the ship architect Joshua Humphreys but was almost equally scintillating in other spheres. Few enjoyed closer relations with George Washington than Colonel David Humphreys of the Revolutionary army, who had come up under General Israel Putnam, first as a company commander of Connecticut troops and then as Putnam's aide. Washington picked him in 1780 to be his military secretary, where he helped to fill the gap caused by the departure of Alexander Hamilton in quest of line duty and military glory—and because he was momentarily piqued by Washington's abruptness—and the loss of John Laurens, who was being sent on a diplomatic duty to Europe on which his father, Henry Laurens, who preceded him, had been made a British prisoner in the Tower.

When Washington in the Yorktown campaign had opportunity to go by way of Mount Vernon as the army marched south, Humphreys was the lone officer he picked to accompany him on the long ride from Baltimore, on which they pressed ahead so Washington might sleep that night under his own roof for the first time in six years. To Humphreys' keeping was entrusted the British standards captured at Yorktown. Through Washington's recommendation in 1784, he was appointed secretary to the commission in Paris consisting of Franklin, Jefferson, and Adams, when they were trying to negotiate with the Barbary powers. Jefferson looked on him with some doubts because he appeared to be attracted by the court formalities and aristocratic etiquettes encountered in Europe, and might not be innately republican. His curiosity aroused, Jefferson was on watch for revealing tendencies.

When Washington was inaugurated for the first time he selected Humphreys and Tobias Lear, both of whom were to appear later in the Barbary negotiations, as the attendants to accompany him in his carriage to the ceremonies. Then Washington designated Humphreys, who had become one of his favorites, to work out with General Henry Knox the proper method of conducting state functions. If the story picked up by Jefferson is to be given credence—and Jefferson conceded he did not have it at first hand—Washington did not hesitate to reprimand his trusted and confidential aide cuttingly, even profanely, just as he had been sharp when Hamilton had kept him waiting.

At the first of the state levees after the inauguration, those who had come to pay their respects to the new executive were assembled in a front chamber. When the door to the inner parlor was thrown open, Humphreys escorted Washington and walked ahead of him, crying loudly, much after the monarchial fashion, "The President of the United States." Washington, chagrined by the heavy display of form, was clearly provoked and was scarcely at ease the rest of the evening. When the callers had departed, he turned and said to Humphreys abruptly: "Well, you have taken me in once, but by God, you shall never take me in a second time."

A native of Derby, Connecticut, Humphreys was honored by his home section after the war by being sent to the legislature, and given command of the Connecticut regiment sent to suppress Shays' Rebellion. He disclosed his versatility in Hartford by turning to literary pursuits. His satires gave him a ready place in the select clique known as the "Hartford Wits," where he fell in with his fellow Yaleman Barlow. He found time between his satires to write, at the request of his patron Washington, the *Life and Heroic Exploits of Israel Putnam*, which contains some good Revolutionary War source material.

Humphreys, after his service on the Paris commission and four years as minister to Portugal, was disgusted with the weathervane inconsistencies of the Barbary regencies but remained faithful and persevering in his efforts. Secretary of State Edmund Randolph wrote authorizing him to draw on a sum of $800,000 for the purpose of peace with Algiers, but Humphreys thought the approach should now come from the Dey. Still, when he received word of the high death rate among the American captives in Algiers, he spurred himself to new efforts and gained contact with Pierre Eric Skjoldebrand, brother of Mathias Skjoldebrand, Swedish consul general at Algiers, and asked him to inquire if the Dey would receive an American representative. The answer, dated October 10, 1794, was in the affirmative, but Dey Hassan Pasha served notice that the envoy might as well save his time unless he came with bulging money bags. Cathcart, the American captive now acting as the Dey's secretary, tried unsuccessfully to convince the little potentate that the Americans could pay no more than half a million. Richard O'Brien, likewise a slave, transmitted to Humphreys the Dey's demands, which included two frigates costing together $248,000; a replenishment for the Casna, or state treasury, of $1,080,000; a sum for the Dey's personal enjoyment, $540,000; for redeeming the captives, $354,000; and for the first- and second-class officers of the Regency, $213,000. The aggregate of the items was $2,435,000. These were the terms the Dey would present to Humphreys on his arrival in Algiers, but O'Brien cautioned that this was merely the asking price. He added some advice to guide Humphreys after his arrival:

> If the Dey gets into his usual Blustering Convulsions of Passion, and orders the Ambassador. to be gone from his presence and depart Algiers. Obey these orders Instantaniously. but remember that from the fluctuateing and Variable character of the Dey, that the Ambassador should leave some person of Confidence with the Dey. on the Terms you offered or proposed.

O'Brien thought a peace of sixty years could be obtained for 500,000 Mexican dollars, plus "consolary presents" and money to persons of influence.

Instead of going to Algiers, Humphreys went back to the United States, in 1794, indisposed to continue these irksome transactions. But his experience was urgently required and he was prevailed on to return, this time soon to be appointed minister to Spain and to marry the daughter of John Bulkeley, wealthy British merchant and factor in Lisbon—a marriage which allowed him in later life in Connecticut to write more poetry and raise Merino sheep. But after landing at Gibraltar in company with his new assistant, Joseph Donaldson, Jr., consul-designate to Tunis and Tripoli, Humphreys went on to Paris, to enlist the aid of France, if possible, in negotiating with Algiers. He sent Donaldson from Gibraltar to Algiers to set up the negotiations and in Paris looked in on the American minister James Monroe and his old Yale friend Joel Barlow. With Monroe's aid he induced Barlow to take over the field direction of the negotiations, while he would man the base of opera-

tions in Portugal and Spain. Monroe, then in the bloom of his ardent
Republicanism and in full rapport with the French Revolution, was attracted to Barlow by his espousal of that cause.

Barlow, an ex-patriot merely in residence, was an American literator,
poet, statesman, advanced thinker, ornament of Yale, and for most of
two decades a familiar figure in the French capital. He was a sympathetic observer of the events of the Revolution but he was ardently
American. He had fought in the Battle of Long Island and had taken
part in the weary retreat through New Jersey. He had taught school,
written a considerable amount of poetry and hobnobbed with the Hartford literary coterie before departing for Europe, where from time to
time he represented the United States and did chores for different
Presidents.

The *National Intelligencer* in Washington, a little later, rhapsodized
about him: "Mr. Barlow, so well known for his *Vision of Columbus*, an
Epic Poem not surpassed by any native poetical production, possessed
of an ardent heart . . . gifted with a fertile mind, and holding a classical
pen," wrote of the triumphs of liberty over the old monarchial system.

Barlow went to Paris to convey a sympathetic greeting to the National
Convention from a group of New Englanders. He was so cordially received and proved himself of such harmonious ideas that he was made
a French citizen. He became familiar enough with the Revolution and
commercial conditions in Paris to accumulate money at a time when
most Frenchmen were losing theirs, and to live elegantly, write couplets,
and exchange views with the best minds. Though credited at the time
with authorship of the notorious poem, "God save the Guillotine!" a
parody on "God Save the King," he apparently no more than publicized
it and introduced it at a Jacobin festival in Hamburg, Germany. It was
set to the same old French air as "God Save the King."

Known almost better than his poetry, at least to posterity, was his
beautiful Georgian country house on the outskirts of Washington, called
Kalorama, situated on what is now the street of that name in middle
Washington. Nothing of it remains except the ancient boxwoods and
memories, among them being that there Decatur's body was brought
for burial after the Bladensburg duel with Commodore James Barron,
and there the great crowds went to grieve and do him homage. A plaque
on the house before it was burned told that Barlow lies buried in Zaro-
witch, Poland, where he died.

So during the summer and autumn of 1795 two charter members of
the "Hartford Wits"—one inclined toward satire and the other contemplating in Homeric simile—went about Europe and North Africa
in quest of peace between the United States and the Barbary powers.

It was a concession made by Barlow which could have been induced only by his classmate and Monroe's Republicanism, because he heartily disliked the Federalists for their antipathy to the course taken by the French Revolution, and while he had been one of Washington's soldiers he was not one of his political adherents.

Meantime Donaldson reached Algiers, where, by direction of the Secretary of State, Pierre Eric Skjoldebrand was offered the American consulate and brought more directly into the negotiations. The negotiations began to bear fruit. The progress has been attributed to the Dey's secretary, the Irish-American captive Cathcart, who was putting words into the Dey's ear that the time had come to deal with the Americans on reasonable terms. The Swedish-American consul and his brother, the Swedish consul, Mathias Skjoldebrand, were helpful and won the unstinted thanks and admiration of Barlow for easing conditions for the captive Americans. The French Republic at the instigation of Monroe and Humphreys was supposed to use its good offices, though there seemed to be a question about which side the French consul favored.

But the main reason why the Dey decided to come to terms lay across the Atlantic. Stanley Lane-Poole, the British professor of Arabic and writer about the Moors, Saracens, and Barbary States, reached the reasonable conclusion that the sounds the Dey heard were not the words about the expected tribute, but the saws and axes and the hammers clanging on the forges, telling that the Americans were building a fleet. News about the naval bill "echoed so promptly among the white walls of Algiers" that before the frigates were well advanced Hassan Pasha waved the olive branch for a treaty of amity. But (and here Lane-Poole looked ahead) "like all cowardly compromises, this one shaped itself into a two-edged sword; and soon every rover from Mogador to the Gates of Bosphorus was clamoring for backsheesh."

Both the Dey and Donaldson blew hot and cold for a time. The American negotiator had the spunk to serve notice that he had not come to Algiers to be trifled with, and Dey Hassan Pasha told him to pack his papers back to America, but at length an agreement was reached that the United States should pay a lump sum to Algiers of $642,500 and an annual tribute in naval stores equal to $21,600, the amount in the treaty being stated at 12,000 gold Algerine sequins. The treaty, the original copy in Turkish, was signed at Algiers September 5, 1795. Of the lump sum payment, $240,000 was for the Dey personally and that was a gratifying feature to him. There were other requirements—the United States must give presents twice a year on the same scale as Holland, Sweden, and Denmark. Naval stores were specified to consist of "powder, lead, iron, bullets, bombshells, bomb stones, masts, poles, yards, anchor chains, cables, sailcloth, tar, pitch, boards, beams, laths, and other necessities." But the big feature of the treaty apart from the tribute was that the American captives would be released upon the payment of the ransom.

All was festivity when the treaty was signed. The American flag was flown and saluted with twenty-one guns from the harbor fortress. O'Brien was sent at once to Humphreys with a copy of the text along with a note from Cathcart and a small present from the Dey, "who esteems you as his Friend and Respects you as a worthy & patriotic Citizen of the United States." The present was a sword and a sash.

For a considerable period it appeared that the treaty was just another scrap of paper, though Humphreys approved it and transmitted it to the government and the Senate ratified it March 2, 1796. But the hitch was the money, which the Dey expected promptly but did not get. Donaldson was not the man to salve him and hold him off, and finally on April 3, 1796, nearly seven months after the treaty had been signed, the Dey issued an ultimatum that he would declare war in eight days and begin to capture American vessels in thirty-eight days unless somebody brought in the coin.

The situation was saved, if it might be termed such in a case involving tribute, by the arrival of Joel Barlow. Humphreys had sent him to Algiers on September 7, 1795, well before he knew the treaty had taken final form, though Barlow's formal appointment as an agent of the United States did not come until the following February 10. Donaldson, with worsening health, became less of a factor, and Humphreys named Barlow acting consul to Algiers. But the main trouble was with specie and not personnel. In the war-torn condition of Europe it was difficult to lay hands on $642,500 in cash, though Humphreys loaned to O'Brien the government brig *Sophia* and sent him first to London and then to Hamburg. "I am sorry to inform you," wrote O'Brien, "that in London Gold or Silver cannot be procured."

When Barlow sailed from Alicante for Algiers he wrote Humphreys that "the situation of our affair seems critical and alarming" and that he would "keep the treaty in suspense" until he got the money. What Barlow did was to up the ante. The Dey claimed his position was weakening with his own people because the American funds were not forthcoming. Barlow soothed him with gifts from Paris. Even that was not enough. To stave off what he believed would be an actual renewal of hostilities, he promised on behalf of the United States a 36-gun frigate for the Dey, the guns to be English 8-pounders. The gift nominally was for the Dey's daughter and the estimated cost was $45,000. A commission of $18,000 was promised for the Jewish broker Barci who was handling the Dey's financial transactions and advising him to give the Americans ample time. The money was to be distributed by Barci mainly "at his discretion among such great officers of state" as would be helpful to preserve the treaty.

Barlow had found on his arrival that the Americans before him had been doing business with the wrong Jewish banking firm and shifted to Barci, who filled tacitly though not formally the role of treasurer of the regency. Barlow satisfied himself as to the prudence of the promises by calculating that if the treaty were thrown into the discard the United States would still have to ransom the surviving 100 American prisoners, and at a higher figure, estimated by him at $3,000 a head; that the Algerine pirates would capture at once some unsuspecting American cargo carriers, and that perhaps an additional 100 seamen would fall into their hands for ransom. Further, "as the Dey will be highly exasperated at the failure of the negotiations, which he will ascribe to bad faith & treachery on our part, it will be vastly difficult, if not impracticable, to renew them again during his reign."

Perhaps Barlow did not calculate the influence of the naval building in America on the Dey, but it was fortunate at the moment that the Algerians did not have information on all the developments in the United States. While the Dey and the American representatives haggled, President Washington followed ratification of the Algerine treaty by the Senate with a message to Congress announcing that, in compliance with the act to provide a naval armament, it was incumbent on the executive "to suspend all orders respecting the building of the frigates, procuring materials for them, or preparing materials already obtained, which may be done without intrenching upon contracts or agreements made" before the treaty.

But Washington did not dismiss the workmen or dismantle the yards. Since public loss might result from dissipation of the workmen, the sudden stoppage of partly finished tasks, and "the derangement of the whole system," he judged it advisable to resubmit the question so Congress could determine what course should be taken. He wanted the ships badly but would not deliberately flaunt the law. As a compromise he suspended most of the work but retained the organizations. We have seen that Congress reconsidered the naval bill and authorized the continuance of work on three, but not all six, of the frigates.

Slow communication, at times advantageous, kept the situation from becoming most distressing, for had the Dey known of Washington's message his demands no doubt would have stiffened. Naval building was suspended, but still the treaty was not in effect nor had the captives been released, and Washington in his earlier instructions had made their freedom an indispensable condition for peace. The difficulty was in finding European bankers who would accept the six per cent certificates for $800,000 issued by the Bank of the United States to the London banking house of John and Francis Baring. This house was to sell the certificates and under the order of Secretary of State Randolph make the proceeds available to Humphreys. The key point was that in war-broke Europe the certificates did not sell.

Barlow placated the Dey and saved his face with the other Moslems not only with the promise of the frigate but with the undelayed delivery of better-than-ordinary presents, which consisted of diamond rings and other jewelry, brocade robes of state, linen, damask, carpets, cloth, and jeweled snuffboxes. These involved no trifle, for the aggregate cost was $27,561.96. Some of the items Barlow had brought from Paris but the others he purchased in Algiers. The cost was about $11,000 more than that of the customary consular gifts. "We expect to incur blame," he wrote to Humphreys of his transactions, "because it is impossible to give you a complete view of the circumstances, but we are perfectly conscious of having acted right."

Finally Humphreys, Barlow, and Donaldson raised a considerable part of the money—$400,000 in Leghorn and $200,000 in Lisbon, from bankers willing to trust United States certificates and who had available gold. When Barlow knew the money was in hand he borrowed enough against it from the sympathetic Barci. An instance of his difficulties was when O'Brien, returning in triumph from Leghorn with the first $200,-000, was captured by a corsair from Tripoli. It looked for a period as though the hard-to-come-by gold had gone to the wrong pirates. But O'Brien's vessel, which was owned by the banker Barci, had a passport from Dey Hassan Pasha of Algiers, and the Bashaw of Tripoli hesitated to bring down on his head the wrath of that stronger neighbor, so O'Brien and his ship were allowed to proceed along the North African coast.

Meantime Barlow was anxious to get the captives out of plague-ridden Algiers. Using money he obtained from Barci, he paid the Dey $200,000, against which the prisoners were released. The transaction was a bit unusual. A new French consul arrived in June bringing some presents looked upon as "brilliant"—a moderate term, for they included $200,000 for the Dey. The Dey deposited the money with the banking house of Barci. Barlow then borrowed the money from Barci and returned it to the Dey, who undoubtedly redeposited it with Barci, his regular financial agent. Barlow's dispatch did not cover this last detail. Barci did the Americans a service by standing security for the remainder of the American payment, and the Dey demanded some such guarantee before he would release the prisoners. Six of the captives had died a few days earlier of the plague, but the remainder on July 13, 1796, were loaded aboard an Algerine vessel, *Fortune*—a name her fate did not honor— and sent off via Leghorn to Marseille. The number was 122 at the high point, now reduced to 85 by prison rigors. The ransom had to cover the full number, though 37 were in their graves. With the survivors Barlow sent a message to Secretary of State Timothy Pickering, whom Washington had shifted from the Postmaster Generalship.

When we reflect [said Barlow], on the extravagant sums of money that this redemption will cost the United States, it affords at least some consolation to know that it is not expended on worthless & disorderly persons, as is the case with some other nations who are driven, like us, to this humiliation to the Barbary States. Our people have conducted themselves in general with a degree of patience and decorum which would become a better condition than that of Slaves.

He expressed hope that they would be well received and given jobs or means of livelihood.

Several of them [he continued] are probably rendered incapable of gaining their living. One is in a state of total blindness; another is reduced to nearly the same condition; two or three carry the marks of unmerciful treatment, in ruptures produced by hard labour; and others have had their constitutions injured by the plague.

Barlow's reports were carried to the United States by the Dey's old secretary, Cathcart, who was now to take a forward role in relations between the United States and the Barbary powers. O'Brien, who already had a nominal freedom as a messenger, also won liberty and carried the dispatches to Humphreys, who was returning to Lisbon from Paris. All fared well except the Algerine ship *Fortune*, owned by Barci, which as soon as she had disembarked the freed Americans at Marseille, made again for the Mediterranean under the American flag. She was picked up by a British patrol and held as a prize on the strange theory that she had been a prize of the Algerians. The British beyond doubt made, executed, and profited by the maritime law at this period. The owner Barci, in turn, held the United States liable. Barlow felt himself forced to assume this debt of $40,000 also. Thousands of dollars in those days were tantamount roughly to millions in the mid-twentieth century, measured by the public purse and national wealth.

Thus the tribute and indemnity bill mounted. When O'Brien finally came in with specie from Leghorn via Tripoli and money arrived from Humphreys in Lisbon, there was much jollification in Algiers. In an expansive mood the Dey told Barlow to make any request he desired. The poet immediately concluded he wanted help in rounding out the nasty Mediterranean business, so he requested the Dey's good offices in negotiating pacts with Tunis and Tripoli. These lesser states might be expected to follow the lead of Algiers though no end of haggling was likely. But before these negotiations could be considered, some loose ends remained in the settlement with Algiers.

The irksome problem left to the United States was the payment of an annual tribute, not in money, but in "naval stores," which would strengthen the Dey in his campaigns against the shipping of the Christian nations. When it all came to be added up, peace with Algiers cost the United States not the sum agreed to by Donaldson, but about a million dollars. Although the requirement in naval stores—lumber, rope, masts, and all the things needed for ships—was fixed at $21,600 annually, the Dey put in requisitions and the amount far exceeded any such figure, at least in costs to the U.S. government. The goods the Dey wanted were not always available at a normal market price, as Secretary Pickering was soon to learn. Then there was the money owed to Barci for the *Fortune* and the cost of any number of presents which had to be fed to appease the Dey's ravenous appetite for consular gifts, known as usance, a term employed from the Levant to Tangier.

Foremost among the problems was the frigate Barlow had promised for the Dey's daughter. David Humphreys had written the Dey a letter confirming Barlow's agreement and advising that he had sent O'Brien to the United States as proof of the sincerity of the deal. He was becoming almost fawning. After saying "these repeated demonstrations of the faithfulness of the Government & Citizens of the United States . . . will baffle all the falsehoods & malice of their enemies" he added that they would "tend to produce a stronger affection on the side of your Excellency" than if such falsehood and malice had never existed. He thanked the Dey for the sash and sword, and explained that he had awaited the consent of his government, a constitutional requirement, before accepting them. Then he had to scurry about to obtain more lavish presents as a return favor.

President Washington decided to honor Barlow's compact about the frigate and directed the Secretary of War to take the necessary measures. When Joshua Humphreys had gone over the design made by Fox, the estimated cost was found to be $70,000, plus $5,000 for the provisions and wages of officers and men for four months to navigate her to Algiers. Perhaps Humphreys was incapable of cutting corners. The estimate included live oak and cedar for the hull, where the use of white oak would mean a saving of $2,000. But white oak, while it gives the appearance of strength and durability, was untrustworthy and might rot out in three years. Humphreys' estimate was substantially above that of $45,000 made by Barlow, and as it developed, Humphreys was low himself.

Apparently everyone was reluctant to push the building of the frigate, for Washington, who was at Mount Vernon, wrote rather sharply on July 13, 1796, to James McHenry, who had become Secretary of War early in the year, expressing surprise that nothing had been done though six weeks had passed after the decision was made to comply with the agreement. The matter had been fouled up jurisdictionally between the State and War Departments. He went on to say that "disagreeable as this requisition was found in its reception, and more so in the compliance with it," nevertheless the depredations likely to result from a failure left no other alternative than to comply. He had thought that the matter was being cared for when he left Philadelphia. Congress had not been in session and the decision had to be made without submitting Barlow's agreement to the Senate. The question now was whether to buy a ship and save time or proceed with the building, a decision which he could scarcely make at Mount Vernon, but which he left to the proper executive officers. Washington took the occasion of this delay to lay down a principle which is still a sound guide in government:

> Before I conclude, let me, in a friendly way, impress the following Maxims upon the Executive Officers—In all important matters, to deliberate materially, but to execute promptly & vigorously—and not to put things off until the morrow which can be done, and require to be done, to day—Without an adherence to these rules, business never will be *well* done, or done in an easy manner; but will always be in arrears with one thing treading upon the heels of another.

After that there was no further question about pushing the frigate, though Washington later accepted McHenry's explanation of the delay. The events which followed promptly do not form an attractive page of the American story.

The gift frigate to the pirate power was named the *Crescent* after the symbol on the Turkish flag. The *Crescent* was a trim, handsome frigate, built on the Piscataqua River at Portsmouth, New Hampshire, the very river that had first buoyed up John Paul Jones's sloop the *Ranger*, raider of the English coast and victor over the British *Drake*, and the great ship of the line *America*, built under Jones's watchful eye, which the United States had presented to France. These ships, laid down in the name of independence and freedom, were now followed on the Piscataqua by a frigate being built to augment the forces of piracy and slavery, which was to be presented obsequiously to the Dey of Algiers not even as tribute, but as an apology because tribute had not been forthcoming at the proper season!

What less fitting date could have been selected for the launching of the *Crescent* than July 4, 1797? Captain Timothy Newman, who commanded her, and who had, like Richard O'Brien, one of his passengers, been a captive in Algiers, pronounced the ship as "complete a piece of workmanship as he ever saw." Secretary of State Pickering, writing to Joel Barlow May 13, 1797, apologized that she was incapable of carrying the 12-pounders the Dey desired. "You will recollect," Pickering said, "that your original agreement, accepted by the Dey, was for a frigate of 36 guns, *nine-pounders* on the *main* deck. In exact conformity to your orders, I procured one of the ablest naval architects in the United States to give me the draught of such a frigate . . . agreeably to which she has been constructed." In the same letter he made his government's position clear: "Nothing is to be done to hazard the good opinion of the Dey, or to excite the most distant idea of trespassing on his distinguished benevolence toward the United States." The Dey was really becoming a favorite!

The *Crescent* fired a gun at sunrise January 20, 1798, slipped down the river, and, according to the local press account, "cleared the harbor with a fine leading breeze." She was not only a gift herself, but she bore lavish presents for the piratical potentate. It required twenty-six barrels to hold the silver dollars shipped as tribute and indemnity in her hold. The value placed on ship and cargo was $300,000—a neat offering mainly for being in arrears. The vessel itself, the loudest note of the apology, was judged in Portsmouth to be "one of the finest specimens of elegant naval architecture which was ever borne on the Piscataqua's waters."

The cost of constructing and equipping the *Crescent* was $99,727, while the naval stores she carried to the Dey to augment his piracy were valued at $100,000, and consisted largely of powder, lead, timber, rope, and canvas. The barrels of dollars made up the balance of the value.

The fresh, young nation of the big sinews was showing a weak heart!

What must Jefferson, now out of the government and ruminating at Monticello, have thought of this good-will bonus offering to the faithless Dey? All along he had opposed sending naval stores to North Africa. He had warned that peace might be bought more readily with naval stores than with cash, but concluded, "we think it not right to furnish them the means which we know they will employ to do wrong and because there might be no economy in it to ourselves in the end."

But the blame for the *Crescent* is scarcely assessable against Washington, who had been struggling all along to procure a navy. Washington in his annual message of December 7, 1796, made his position clear on this most acute of the nation's needs. "To an active external commerce the protection of a naval force is indispensible," he said. Then, after asserting that a navy was required to vindicate a neutral flag from insult or aggression, he declared it "may even prevent the necessity of going to war." He said that, from the best information he had been able to obtain, "it would seem as if our trade to the Mediterranean without a protecting force will always be insecure. . . ."

What Washington had to decide was whether the United States should honor a compact entered into by two of its envoys, Barlow and Humphreys. The original fault was in the compact. But Barlow was acting according to his best judgment and was moved by humane considerations for the mistreated American captives. The frigate was not the only ship involved. The Dey now purchased two additional vessels, an armed brig and an unarmed schooner. The brig was designed and built at Philadelphia by Joshua Humphreys and named the *Hassan Bashaw* after the Algerine regent. The schooner, built at Philadelphia by Nathaniel Hutton, had a better name. She was called the *Skjoldebrand* after the Swede who had eased the way for Barlow and mitigated the suffering of the American captives when no American consul was at hand.

President Adams recommended the building and sale of the last two ships. In a message to Congress June 23, 1797, he mentioned that the Dey "has manifested a prediliction for American-built vessels." Then the President explained:

A compliance with the Dey's request appears to me to be of serious importance. He will repay the whole expense of building and equipping the two vessels, and as he has advanced the price of our peace with Tripoli, and become pledged for that of Tunis, the United States seems to be under peculiar obligations to provide this accommodation . . .

The obligation was indeed peculiar! It did not extend to still two other vessels which were thrown in as a substitute for naval stores. These were the schooners *Lelah Eisha* and *Hamdullah,* which became the property of the new Dey, Bobba Mustapha, who succeeded on the death of Hassan Pasha in 1798.

As an instance of where the payment of tribute leads to, some extracts of a memorandum requisition by Richard O'Brien from Algiers, dated January 12, 1797, are of interest:

The Dey wants a complete Cruiser Constructor a single Man one of abilities and sobriety—Also wants a Master Sail maker, a very capable man. 25 Chests of tea of 4 different qualities. 6 Quintal of loaf sugar refined, some elegant penknives, some small guilt thimbles, scissors cases &c calculated for the Queen and daughter, a few shawls, with roses curiously wrought in them—a few rosed China Cups &c &c 20 lb of fine Tea for the prime Minister, the Hasnagee. Drafting pencils and sweeps for the Constructor Seddi Ali Mistrillia Pencils for Hadge Usef—Plank for Hadge Omar & Hadge Hamita the Brothers in laws of the Deys.

The memorandum does not show whether these and other goods mentioned were to be purchased or sent as gifts, but very little was being purchased by the Dey and his household. Considering how amenable the United States had become to his demands, it was not surprising that his successor decided a little later to press the *George Washington* into his service for the voyage to Constantinople.

Among the Dey's requirements under the heading of naval stores were, quite naturally, masts. How this payment of tribute in goods instead of money, and the type of goods pirates would require, could upset a government by pushing them in as priorities might be seen from the letter Secretary Pickering wrote Barlow May 13, 1797. He dwelt on the high price of masts, saying the enormous types required by the Dey would cost $500 each, instead of the original estimate of $30, and much more when delivered in Algiers. Only large ships could transport them and then only a few in each cargo. They had to be cut in the back country of Pennsylvania or New York and floated down the Susquehanna at high water. Less sturdy masts would not satisfy the finicky Mussulman. Pickering was most apologetic but promised to provide precisely the proper type masts if allowed "ample indulgence in point of time," though he hinted that the Dey, if approached at a favorable moment, might be prevailed upon to take more puny masts than the $500 variety. He wanted to substitute also thinner oak and pine planks for those six inches thick which the Dey stipulated, and which were costly and difficult to obtain and transport.

All along, the Americans had seemed to detect that although Monroe was supposed to have obtained the assistance of France in negotiating with Algiers, the French on the ground were anything but helpful. Nevertheless, when Barlow, who loved the French, began negotiations with Tunis, he selected a French merchant there, Joseph Stephen Famin, to represent the United States. Famin negotiated an ineffectual truce of six months. Relations were complicated by the seizure at about the same time of the schooner *Eliza* loaded with brandy, the redemption of which Barlow calculated would cost an additional $30,000. But the

Bey Hamouda Pacha of Tunis put the ransom on ship and crew at $10,000. The happy feature of the truce was that it cost the United States no immediate tribute and gave an opportunity to reflect. The bad feature was that Tunis paid little attention to it and when the chance arose seized American craft.

Now that the Dey of Algiers had become the good receiving friend of the United States he made a show of pressure on Tunis. He even ordered out troops against his neighbor—ostensibly to help the United States but primarily to chastise the Tunisians for stripping an Algerian craft shipwrecked on their shores. Bey Hamouda Pacha sent gifts and the Algerine forces went home. Nevertheless, Dey Hassan Pasha did show his good will by advancing the initial sums of cash which the United States required for peace with Tunis and Tripoli.

Barlow sent Richard O'Brien, the go-between in so many of these transactions, who had flitted back and forth to London, Hamburg, Lisbon, Leghorn, and other ports with money and gifts that would ease the situation along the African shore. Barlow had written offering Tunis $50,000 in ransom and tribute, but when O'Brien arrived the demand figures aggregated $140,000. They haggled. O'Brien went up to $101,350 and Hamouda Pacha came down to $107,000. But there, like stubborn horse-traders, each balked. O'Brien went on to Tripoli to test out Bashaw Yusuf Karamanli, who likewise had been making some recent seizures as a means of building up his asking price. But since Algiers had broken the log jam he was surprisingly willing to float with the stream, though he stormed about a bit because he had heard reports of lavish gifts and commodities being presented to Algiers.

O'Brien was armed with a powerful tool. He had the cash with him, on the brig that had brought him from Algiers, and cash looked good to the money-hungry Bashaw. O'Brien was able to get a treaty for around $58,000, which included a ransom of $18,000 for the brig *Sophia*, the last seizure Tripoli had made. From further developments it was evident that the Bashaw came to believe he had been bilked by the payment of such a small tribute. That was why later in a fit of anger he had the flagpole chopped down and went to war.

The Frenchman Famin continued talks with Bey Hamouda Pacha of Tunis and arrived at a settlement, which cost $60,000 in cash but with extras aggregated the $107,000 the Bey had stood out for in his last conference with O'Brien. The treaties with Tunis, dated August 17, 1797, and Tripoli, November 4, 1796, were signed by Barlow and approved by Humphreys. With some alterations they were ratified by the Senate.

Objectionable provisions found in the treaty with Tunis were attributed to Famin's wiliness. An advantage was given to Tunisian goods.

A duty of three per cent was assessed on American goods in American vessels in a port of Tunis, and a duty of ten per cent on American goods in foreign vessels. Foreign goods in American vessels would pay ten per cent. But all goods from Tunis entering the United States, irrespective of the flag of the carrier, would be assessed only three per cent. This item had not been in Barlow's draft and the Senate found it offensive and struck it out. Another provision which came to irritate Americans in Tunis was objected to by the Senate but left a subject of further negotiation by the President. Under it the United States had to give a barrel of gunpowder to Tunis for every gun fired in a salute to an American warship. Salutes to American warships would be frequent thereafter in Tunis.

Before Barlow left Algiers he waxed almost poetic in a "certificate of gratitude" he presented to Pierre Eric Skjoldebrand and his brother Mathias for "the singular acts of humanity which they had exercised toward our prisoners . . . and advancing them pecuniary succours, before the American Government had made any provision for that purpose." After the United States established a stipend for the captives, Pierre was charged with the payment and distribution of it, and though he did this work over a number of years as a duly appointed consular officer, he declined any fee. Even when Barlow tried to give him a present of articles worth about $2,500, which he thought "not inconsistent with the delicacy that accompanies the most generous minds to accept," this was also refused. The only thing Barlow could give him was the certificate.

CHAPTER SEVEN

Bribes, Tributes, Insults, Haggles

W HEN the treaties of peace were ratified by the Senate—that with Tunis with reservations—President John Adams anticipated the establishment of normal diplomatic relations and appointed U.S. consuls.

Of the three selections, dictated by circumstances and Secretary of State Pickering, two fell to former American captives. They were Richard O'Brien, who was returned as consul general to Algiers, where he had long been a prisoner and a slave, and James Leander Cathcart, recent slave and secretary of the Algerine Dey, who was appointed consul to Tripoli. The third choice went to William Eaton, former regular army officer and protégé of Pickering. O'Brien originally had been appointed by Washington, and was sent back by Adams aboard the *Crescent* with a new commission and enlarged responsibility.

Eaton, who will be met on later pages of this book and ultimately will come to dominate the story of the Tripolitan War, was so surcharged with enthusiasm and devotion to his country that he gave it his thought and energy almost every wakeful moment; but he had to fight, kick, and scratch through controversies and misunderstandings every step of the way, and a full half of his trials were of his own creation. In the end he died poor and neglected, though he might readily have accumulated wealth in North Africa, as many others were doing in the diplomatic and consular service of different governments. Eventually he became the central figure of the Barbary negotiations and the medium through whom O'Brien and Cathcart conducted much of their correspondence.

Both O'Brien and Cathcart, as has been seen, were captured by Algerine pirates in August, 1785, the first being master of the *Dauphin* and the second a seaman on the *Maria*. O'Brien, Maine-born but Irish-reared, was one of several children left in poverty when their father died soon after taking them back to Ireland. The boy made his way to Richmond, Virginia, where he became indentured to a sea captain who taught him well in navigation. About all his other education came from reading the Bible and *Aesop's Fables*, but he had strong native intelligence and courage to assume responsibility. By the time he was twenty-three years old, in 1781, he was a lieutenant in command of the brig *Jefferson*, owned by the state of Virginia and named for the Governor. She was lying in the James River at Osborne's, fifteen miles below Richmond.

British forces under Generals Benedict Arnold and William Phillips, who had already made an earlier raid on Richmond, advanced again, captured Petersburg, and marched overland to Manchester. At Osborne's they shelled and burned the *Jefferson*, along with other Virginia-owned craft, the *Tempest* and *Renown*. The event marked his first contact with Jefferson and put the young lieutenant in a position to perform a service for him later on, after the Governor became President.

Jefferson in 1805 came under bitter partisan attack on the old complaint that when the British approached Richmond on this second invasion of that area he had fled ignominiously and deserted the city's defenders even before Arnold and Phillips left Petersburg; the charge was that he had exhibited complete want of courage. According to the press article, he left his station "with an awkward precipitation, indicative of timidity, unwarranted by any immediate movement of the enemy, and forbidden by a regard to those duties, which belong to the station he held."

The charges of Jefferson's misconduct on this occasion—and they did not apply to his altogether explainable rapid departure a little later from Charlottesville when Tarleton approached with his legion—were advanced by Light Horse Harry Lee, who denounced the Governor though conceding that he was "highly respected for his literary accomplishments."

The Republican press procured and published affidavits and letters defending President Jefferson, showing he was in no manner personally disturbed by Arnold and Phillips, but labored with great diligence to defend the Virginia capital. O'Brien, whose vessel was the smallest of the Virginia fleet, retired to Richmond after it had been lost. There he remained until the British evacuated Manchester and retreated to Warwick. He certified that when he reached Richmond he found Jefferson at his post and knew from his own observation that "he continued upon the spot during the whole scene."

No testimony was considered more valid or impressive in 1805 than that of the unshaken man who had spent ten years in Algerine bondage and whom President Washington, "pleased with his integrity and sagacity," had thereafter appointed consul at Algiers.

O'Brien had performed much of the leg service in the Barbary negotiations and seemed both devoted to his country and adapted to hard work in its cause.

Cathcart's manner was much more bellicose. His role throughout his captivity and during the negotiations, while it did not involve as much physical anguish as was the lot of those who labored in the stone quarries, was in some respects the most difficult. For the better part of ten years he had been the secretary and almost the body servant of a gross and ill-tempered Dey whose pettish anger had a low boiling point and whose supply of humor was scant, harsh, and coarse. This was not Cathcart's first prison experience. The lad who had been brought from Mount Murrah, Ireland, as a poor immigrant with meager education had become while still in his teens a midshipman on the *Confederacy*, a Continental frigate under the able Captain Seth Harding. But being captured, he was thrown into the British prison ship *Good Hope* and then into the hold of the more notorious *Jersey*. After three years, with many dying around him, he managed to escape in March, 1782, when the fighting of the Revolutionary War had ended. Then he went into the merchant marine and appeared in the Barbary negotiations after being captured by the Algerine xebec.

Getting ahead as a slave probably called for more ability than did progress under the gentler sway of freedom. Cathcart's rise in bondage was rapid, from his first post as barkeeper in the prison tavern through the successive jobs of clerk of the Bagnio Gallera, or jail for the galley slaves, and clerk of the Department of the Marine and then of the Prime Minister, to what might have seemed the coveted position of secretary to the Dey. He spoke Spanish readily and had picked up enough of the combination Arabic and Hamitic tongues to serve as a dragoman. He kept a journal and his writings and reports after he became a consul were voluminous, and it was to his credit that he did not allow his ignorance of syntax, punctuation, capitalization, or methods of easy expression to interfere with the telling of a story, the essentials of which he conveyed boldly and forcibly.

When liberated in 1795 by the peace with Algiers, Cathcart had laid by enough money from his service to the Dey to purchase a barque, the *Independent*, a name selected understandably by one with two long prison stretches behind him. In it he carried to Philadelphia the dispatches from Barlow and the Dey announcing the treaty with Algiers. Though his appointment to be consul at Tripoli was made July 10, 1797, he tarried in the United States to pick up the necessary consular gifts for the great and influential of the Tripolitan regency, and select also a Philadelphia bride, Jane Bancker Woodside.

Consul General Richard O'Brien, it will be recalled, already had returned to Algiers on the gift ship *Crescent* and had assumed his post there. Cathcart and Eaton sailed from Philadelphia aboard the brig *Sophia*, a 12-gun sloop-of-war commanded by Captain Henry Geddes, who escorted as closely as the weather and sailing conditions would permit the three vessels which had been built in American yards for the Dey of Algiers, the brig *Hassan Bashaw* and the schooners *Skjoldebrand* and *Lelah Eisha*. Geddes was the rugged captain who in the Revolutionary War commanded several Maryland letters of marque.

With them sailed also the ship *Hero* loaded with masts, planks, and other naval stores for the Barbary States, but this vessel sprung a leak and turned back to Jamaica. After unloading for repairs, she again undertook the voyage but again shipped water and this time returned to New York, where she once more was unloaded and repaired. Her delay was to perplex the American consuls and strain relations with Tunis and Tripoli anew.

Of the ships being delivered to the Dey of Algiers, the beautiful new brig came in first. The arrival of the *Hassan Bashaw* was a notable event in Algiers. It was the Turks' "Sunday" when the sail appeared, bringing the crowds to the waterfront. When off the city she fired a salute. The concourse of people was greater than was seen in years witnessing the arrival of a vessel. The brig had made the passage from Philadelphia in thirty-two days. The schooner *Skjoldebrand* took only twenty-nine days from the Delaware River to Algiers, which caused the Dey and his ministers to express elation over her fleetness.

O'Brien reported that the whole maritime personnel of Algiers was captivated by the American-built craft. They noticed particularly that after the ships had "traversed the boisterous oceon" they reached Algiers without having lost a single yarn from one of their ropes. As the three new corsairs maneuvered in the harbor under the control of the dexterous American seamen the Algerines were "amazed" and "convinced that we have the abilities & resources in the United States to be a very active & stubborn enemy." O'Brien put a price of $98,000 on the vessels built for the Dey, which was about $19,000 more than the price to the United States in Philadelphia. He told the Dey the Portuguese ambassador in Philadelphia had offered $120,000 for the three ships delivered in Lisbon. Altogether it added up that the Dey was well advised in what President Adams called his "prediliction for American-built vessels."

Meantime the *Sophia* made a comparatively rapid passage to Algiers, in thirty-three days, with more storms inside the brig than without. A source of sharp dissention in official relations, though apparently not in family circles, was the beautiful young maid the Cathcarts employed before they left Philadelphia. She was an English girl, Betsey Robeson, of cultivated manner and possessed of a disposition as pleasing as her looks. But she took a sudden and violent dislike to the Cathcarts. The transition which occurred in Betsey Robeson's thinking after her employment is not entirely explained, but apparently a delicate English girl little acquainted with raw life had expected that an official of the American diplomatic service would possess the same marks of refinement ordinarily found among the lesser nobility so often engaged by the British government overseas. It was not to be assumed that Cathcart could have swept off by a single penstroke on the commission all the rough traces of his years of servitude in the filthy Algerine bagnio, or the marks of his incarceration in the dungeon hold of the prison ship *Jersey*. There is ample evidence of Cathcart's roughness. He was quarrelsome and suspicious. The Bey of Tunis called him an *embroglione*, which by Eaton's translation meant a "troublesome litigious trifler." Translated further into ordinary seaman's language, it would have meant something like a bad apple or a rotten egg.

Eaton observed him on the passage and thought he was trying to play loosely with the handsome English girl's morals, which would have implied a none too common triangle because the consul's bride of six months was aboard. In any event, when the *Sophia* reached Algiers, Betsey Robeson served notice that she was parting company with the Cathcarts at once and returning to the United States, even by the ship that had brought her, though it was not scheduled for the voyage any time soon. For protection prior to the sailing she threw herself on the good offices of the American consul general at Algiers, O'Brien.

O'Brien administered his protection in a most tender and sentimental fashion. The graces Betsey had found wanting in Cathcart she encountered full measure in O'Brien, though he too had passed ten years in the bagnio in the very city where he now represented the vast Western republic. The *Sophia* had reached Algiers on February 9, 1799, and a little more than six weeks later, on March 25, O'Brien and Betsey Robeson were married. The matter would have been unimportant except that it threw Cathcart into paroxysms of anger. With violent language he denounced both O'Brien and the bride, declared the Consul had seduced the girl, and to her applied the best bagnio epithets, and broke off all relations with his former companion in captivity, who was, in fact, his superior officer. O'Brien had both seniority and direct instructions which placed him in charge of the negotiations with the Barbary States after the departure of Barlow.

Mrs. Cathcart, who seemed either not to have heard of or given concern or credence to the shipboard gossip that the girl was a rival for her

husband's affections, was almost equally bitter. She found herself superceded in rank and protocol. Much tolerance would have been required
for her to accept calmly the precedence her former maid would now
enjoy in diplomatic formalities and state functions, such as there were
on the Barbary Coast. After the wedding Cathcart declined to have
further personal contact or diplomatic intercourse with his chief O'Brien
and most communications between the two had to be exchanged through
Eaton. But his marriage to Jane Bancker Woodside seemed altogether
happy and was blessed with twelve children.

Before this family situation had developed, O'Brien arranged on
February 22 an audience with Bobba Mustapha, the new Dey of Algiers. The story of this meeting was set down by Eaton with his customary vigor and reverence for detail. The Americans who assembled
to pay their respects to the Dey included besides Consuls O'Brien, Eaton,
and Cathcart, Captain Geddes of the *Sophia*, Captain William Penrose
of the *Skjoldebrand*, Captain John Smith of the *Hassan Bashaw*, and
Lieutenant William Malley, commander of the *Lelah Eisha*.

Reaching the courtyard of the palace, they uncovered their heads,
walked through a hall, and ascended what Eaton described as "a winding maze of five flights of stairs." They went through a dark, narrow
passage which led to the Dey's secluded audience room. Before entering this sanctum they were required to remove their shoes. The audience room, a cramped apartment eight feet by twelve, must have been
mean indeed, for Eaton described it as a "cave," having small, iron-
barred apertures for light. There they met the Dey—"a huge, shaggy
beast, sitting on his rump, upon a low bench, covered with a cushion
of embroidered velvet, with his hind legs gathered up like a tailor or
a bear."

As the Americans approached "he reached out his fore paw as if to
receive something to eat." They seemed to hesitate and the attendant
called out sharply, "Kiss the Dey's hand!" Consul General O'Brien bent
in courtly fashion and kissed the hand, upon which the others followed.
"The animal," wrote Eaton, "seemed at that moment to be in a harmless
mode; he grinned several times, but made very little noise."

That was all of the ceremony except that they stood around for several
minutes "in silent agony" and then were given leave to clear out of the
den and recover their shoes. They left "without any other injury than
the humility of being obliged, in this involuntary manner, to violate
the second commandment of God and offend common decency." Then
Eaton asked: "Can any man believe that this elevated brute has seven
kings of Europe, two republics, and a continent tributary to him, when
his whole naval force is not equal to two line-of-battle ships? It is so."

And so it was, indeed. Rarely has history provided a parallel to a situation so grotesque.

These formalities completed, Captain Geddes took the *Sophia* out of Algiers on March 2 with Eaton on board going to his post at Tunis and Cathcart and bride bound for Tripoli. Arriving at Tunis on March 12, Eaton met the Frenchman, Joseph Stephen Famin, American chargé d'affaires appointed by Barlow, against whom the British consul gave confidential warning. Britain and France were at war, but while the Briton's cautioning might be suspect, it was loaded with merit.

On the day following his arrival Eaton was summoned by Bey Hamouda Pacha and the conversation reverted to the clause in the treaty with Tunis—one of the clauses to which the Senate had objected—requiring payment of a barrel of gunpowder for every gun fired in saluting an American war vessel. The remarks as reported by Eaton were:

"Is your vessel a vessel of war?"

"Yes."

"Why was I not duly informed of it, that you might have been saluted, as is customary?"

"We were unacquainted with the customs."

Eaton went on to pass it off as a trifling matter.

"However trifling it may appear to you, to me it is important," the Bey replied. "Fifteen barrels of powder will furnish a cruiser which may capture a prize and net me $100,000."

Eaton then declared the concession was so degrading the United States would not yield to it. He refused to budge from this position. The Bey spoke to his ministers in Turkish: "These people are *Cheribeenas* [Persian merchants]. They are so hard there is no dealing with them."

The Tunisian Bey had earned a reputation for rapaciousness. He now protested vigorously against the delay by the Americans in the fulfillment of their obligations. The naval stores called for by the treaty had not arrived. The truth was they were back on the *Hero*. The leakage in the *Hero*'s hull almost brought on a war, for Eaton had to suffer through many months of waiting before he was able to square accounts with Tunis, and they were irritating months. By nature he revolted against the payment of even a single copper para, of which it took 200 to make a dollar, in tribute. Everything seemed to contribute to the opinion of his impulsive utterance when he had seen slaves in Algiers that "Barbary is Hell!"

The *Hero*'s cargo, as explained by Secretary Pickering January 15, 1800, to Consul General O'Brien, was found in New York to be so badly damaged that it had to be replaced. Much of the lumber was ruined. The large oak planks had been shipped when they were full of sap. The

green wood had heated and fermented in the West Indies. He had his
agents comb New York for substitute lumber meeting as nearly as possible the specifications, and other supplies that would satisfy the government's agreements with Tunis. He expected the *Hero* would be ready
to sail in early February. She did reach Tunis April 12, 1800. Eaton did
not write of her arrival with elation. He saw fit to instruct the Secretary
of State that "all the *beneficence* of the Jehovah of the Jews would never
have rendered him *respectable . . .* if he had not *thundered from Mount
Sinai.*" Then he admonished that when the United States shipped the
residue of the supplies due Tunis, to send them in "*something Mascu-
line.*" He called the newly arrived ship the "*Heroe-ine,*" since she was in
no condition to fight. He wanted a man-of-war.

This kind of importuning was not without influence on the government. Part of the original cargo of the *Hero* had been intended for Algiers. Now that she had been reloaded with a fresh cargo consigned
directly to Tunis, President Adams and Secretary Pickering fell in line
with Eaton's idea of sending the required goods to Algiers in a warship,
which accounted for the voyage of the *George Washington* a little later.
Pickering wrote of it to Humphreys in Madrid, May 7, 1800, saying the
frigate, formerly an East Indiaman, was preparing to take on timber
and the like.

Eaton explained to the Bey that the first Tunisian treaty had reached
Philadelphia at the time of the yellow fever plague, during which many
governmental departments were closed down. Then the winter closed
the harbors with ice. Finally, the quasi-war with France erupted and
that required some little attention. Tunis and Tripoli were now at war
with France—a part of the general Turkish war against Napoleon—and
whatever the United States accomplished against French commerce was
in the general interest of Tunis also. The Bey maintained that Eaton's
government seemed to have no difficulty in fulfilling obligations with
Algiers, having presented a frigate. He put in his requisition for a frigate
for Tunis.

Eaton early settled down to the chore of negotiating amendments to
the Tunisian treaty which would accommodate the Senate's reservations.
In this he had Cathcart's assistance. Eventually the adjustments were
worked out and a compromise was reached on the nettlesome question
of a barrel of gunpowder for every gun fired in a salute to an American
warship. The provision was made applicable to both nations; that is,
either might demand a salute and get a barrel of powder for each gun.
Thus in a normal instance of a salute and a return salute, the account
would balance, gun for gun and barrel for barrel. But a salute would
not be fired unless one nation requested it.

The tariffs were equalized. A "most-favored nation" provision was inserted, putting Tunis on a footing with others in commercial transactions with the United States. Nearly everything was adjusted on a face-saving basis for both countries and the amended treaty was negotiated May 26, 1799. The Senate ratified it January 10, 1800.

Completion of the treaty did not solve all of Eaton's problems. While he was at dinner a body of Turks invaded his garden and entered his courtyard and demanded money as personal tribute, or indemnification. They asserted that "the government having made peace with everybody had reduced them to famine, but they were resolved not to starve." Eaton cited the incident to show that public opinion demanded the corsairs "must be let loose upon some body."

Scarcely could it be expected that one of Eaton's restless, aggressive temperament would find merit in his predecessor's conduct, but none would have forecast such a violent eruption as occurred against the Frenchman Famin. Eaton had learned even prior to his landing that the Bey had not wanted Famin replaced but had intended to give him a special dispensation even after Tunis and France were at war. Famin's purpose, it developed, was to help the Bey milk the United States of every pailful of tribute the docile republic might yield. Eaton at least was satisfied that such was his intent. Not only did he publicly denounce Famin in the presence of the consuls of Great Britain and Sweden, but with simple directness publicly horsewhipped him in the Tunis street. Such rough treatment for his favorite could not be overlooked by the Bey, who had Eaton arrested. In a letter to Secretary Pickering Eaton denounced the Frenchman as "a thorn in my side" and said he had been insinuating that the United States had no intention of living up to its treaty obligations. "I have uniformly treated this *french pirate* with polite attention, taking care to keep the commanding grounds, until I have fully defeated all his projects of mischief."

Surprisingly, Eaton won before the mercurial Tunisian tribunal. By his firmness he was making an impression. He demonstrated to the court that Famin had been deceitful. He presented his case so well that even the Bey squeezed his hand in congratulation. Eaton turned the tables on Famin by producing a paper in which Famin had referred to the Tunisian Prime Minister and his commercial agents as "thieves and robbers." This did not sit well with the Bey, who declared the American consul had had good reason for his heat. "I have always found him a very candid man, and his concern for his fellow citizens is not a crime," the Bey declared. A little later when he knew Eaton better he would be more critical. Famin left town for a spell and Eaton's influence was in the ascendancy.

Bey Hamouda, with all his avarice and fits of passion, was a man of higher character than was commonly found among the regents of the Barbary shore. He was a sane and sensible ruler of his own people, free from brutal instincts, industrious, disinclined toward luxurious living, and governed in the end of prudence and repect for the facts. Through the years Eaton was able to prevail on him that his best interests were served by harmony with the United States, whose ably handled merchant vessels were the most reliable carriers he could find for his substantial trade with the southern European ports.

One of the Bey's demands thoroughly enraged the Consul. When the Tunisian palace and arsenal were destroyed by fire in June, 1801, just after Tripoli had declared war on the United States, Hamouda Pacha insisted that the 50,000 stands of small arms he had lost should be replaced by the Christian powers on a sort of pro rata basis, the assessment against the United States being 10,000 stands. The demand was so preposterous Eaton would not entertain it. He would not even transmit it to the home government. Though he was cajoled and badgered, the arms, of course, were not supplied. Such a requisition would have swamped the infant arms industry in the United States. The federal arsenal had been established at Harpers Ferry, Virginia, during the threatened war with France, but most firearms manufacture was small-scale forge and hand work.

A noteworthy incident shedding light on Eaton's character occurred during this period. When the *Hero* brought the first consignment of naval stores to Tunis tension was eased and the Bey became friendly. But his corsairs who had been awaiting the signal to leap on American commerce, which was now rapidly expanding in the Mediterranean, required other prey. The pirates selected the hapless Danes, who had a strong enough navy, with twenty-three ships of the line and fourteen frigates, but who were tied down by northern European politics and were soon to have their capital bombarded by Lord Nelson. The Tunisian rovers brought in eight Danish merchant ships, altogether ignoring the circumstance that Denmark had been paying tribute regularly to safeguard her commerce. A complaint was made that the Danish merchandise was inferior, which was sufficient explanation to appease any conscience the Tunisians may have had over their sudden and unexpected breach of peaceful relations with the unoffending Danes. In order to make the seizures a shade less piratical and give them the cloak of legitimate warfare, the Bey belatedly had the Danish flagpole chopped down on June 28, 1800.

Ensuing developments were important in disclosing Eaton's integrity. After the Tunisians had pillaged the cargoes they put the empty ships on the block, and Eaton at the urgency of the Danish masters bid six of them in, pledging himself personally to the payment of $10,000. The amount was meager compared to the worth of the ships. Eaton had opportunity to sell them at a handsome profit which would have given him a pretty nest egg toward a fortune. No official malfeasance would have been involved by the standards of that day. But he handed the ships back to the Danes as quickly as the owners could satisfy his promissory note. Instead of a neat profit from a sale, he received from the King of Denmark cordial thanks for his generous act.

Never was Eaton happy with affairs in Tunis. Other tribute in the form of stores arrived in November, 1800, on the *Anna Maria* and the Bey received them with niggling complaint—the planks were too short and the diamonds too dim—but a nervous peace was maintained and Eaton never deviated a hair's width from his principle that force, not tribute, was the medicine that would cure the Mediterranean sore.

As if the literary habits of Joel Barlow and David Humphreys were contagious in the Barbary negotiations, Eaton in his boredom turned to verse. When Washington, his old commander, died in 1799 he put on mourning and produced an ode which attracted attention, perhaps mostly by its title, "General Washington's Reception in the Capital Above: Written on Hearing of His Ascension."

All along, Eaton's main problem was with the inordinate appetite of Tunisian officialdom for usance, which was plain extortion, or bribery. The Sapatapa, keeper of the seals, ranked only by the Prime Minister and Bey, not only was continually solicitous about what was going to be given to the Bey, but what would go to the Sapatapa. He wanted knickknacks like a gold watch chain and a double-barreled gun, while the admiral of the fleet would have a gold-headed walking stick, gold watch and chain, and a dozen pieces of cloth. Never did an event happen, it seemed, but that usance was in order somewhere along the line. The old Prime Minister demonstrated for Eaton that there could be no corner-cutting in this iniquitous practice. When he was given some cloth he examined the pieces, judged they were not sufficiently valuable for one in his station, and returned them. Eaton reported that the United States in its dealings would have to choose between "gold or cannon balls." He thought the government had been soft in the beginning: "Too many concessions have been made to Algiers. There is but one language which can be held to these people, and this is *terror*."

After Captain Geddes had dropped Eaton at Tunis, he continued with the *Sophia* to deposit Cathcart in his new post as consul to Tripoli. They came to anchor in the harbor at 3:00 P.M. on April 5, 1799, flying both the American and Algerine flags. They informed the captain of the port, who approached to inquire about their business, that they had on board the American consul with letters from the President of the United States, the Dey of Algiers, and the Bey of Tunis, all addressed to His Excellency the Bashaw of Tripoli.

Half an hour later a courteous Englishman, Brian McDonough, British consul at Tripoli, who had been looking after the interests of the United States and Sweden in the absence of any official representative of those countries, came aboard. He informed Cathcart and Geddes that it was customary to notify the Bashaw officially upon the arrival of a ship and to obtain his permission for the officers to land. McDonough offered to perform that service. He returned to the ship shortly before 6:00 P.M. with the disconcerting intelligence that the Bashaw had decided not to receive Cathcart because he had brought neither the stores nor the brig which had been promised by Consul Richard O'Brien when the peace treaty was negotiated.

This was the first anyone on the Sophia had heard about the promise of a brig. But the Bashaw insisted that since the Americans had not fulfilled their contract he was not obliged to fulfill his. For two years he had waited for an American consul and now one appeared without the stores or the brig. He would take the letters but the consul could go. And if within forty days the provisions were not forthcoming, he would order out his cruisers to capture American vessels.

Cathcart gave to the official who accompanied McDonough all of the letters except that from the President, saying he could deliver it only in a personal audience, which he requested because, as he explained, he never put any trust in messages. McDonough stated that the Bashaw certainly would insist on the brig because O'Brien had promised it in the presence of Gerardo Joseph de Souza, the Spanish consul, and Leon Farfara, Jewish banker for the Bashaw. McDonough had not heard the promise but said he had heard these two men repeatedly tell about it to Joseph Ingraham, U.S. chargé d'affaires at Tripoli, who had cleared out all his papers before his departure some time prior to Cathcart's arrival.

The question of whether or not a brig had been promised loomed suddenly as a crucial issue between the United States and Tripoli and had to be disposed of if an outbreak of hostilities were to be prevented. Cathcart told McDonough he was prepared to offer cash in lieu of the promised stores; to give a brig would be entirely out of the question.

At 7:00 P.M. another messenger came with notice that the Bashaw would see Cathcart two hours after daylight. The new Consul now reflected on his own prerogatives and sent word he would come ashore as soon as the fortifications gave the customary salute to the American

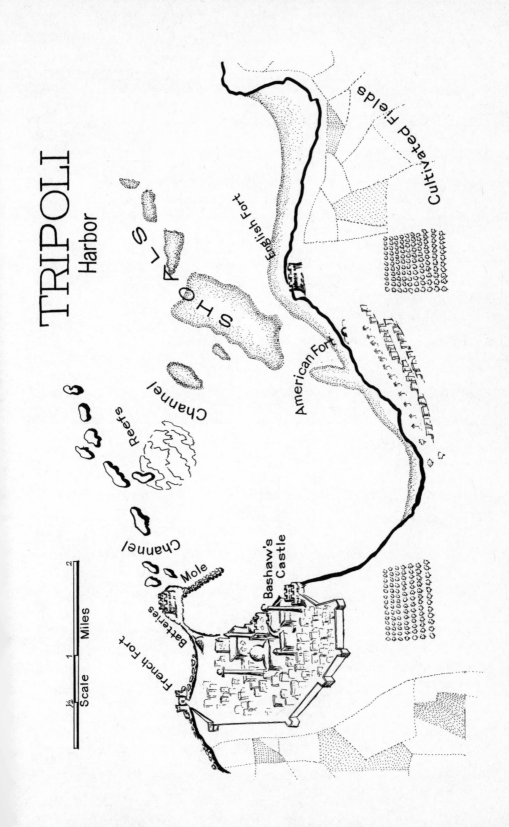

TRIPOLI
Harbor

Cultivated Fields

English Fort

SHOALS

American Fort

Channel

Reefs

Channel

Mole

Bashaw's Castle

Batteries

French Fort

Scale   Miles

½   1   2

ship. The Bashaw's official said the salute would be fired if the American would return it, and to these salutes both agreed. But when at 8:00 P.M. Cathcart and Captain Geddes went ashore the fortifications had not yet fired a salute. Instead, the officers were met at the molehead by a curt officer of the Marine, who served notice impolitely that the Bashaw had ordered they could not land until an English doctor had been on board their ship—apparently a sort of quarantine inspection—that they must return to it; and furthermore, that the Bashaw was asleep and could not be disturbed.

McDonough came on board again next morning with word that Cathcart could not see the Bashaw unless he promised the brig, but that he might see the head of the Marine if he wished. This opportunity Cathcart at once accepted. He wanted to state his position to someone in authority.

The Grand Admiral of the Tripolitan fleet and chief of the Marine Department whom Cathcart was now about to meet was Murad Reis, son-in-law of the Bashaw, and one of the most astonishing figures in all this bizarre history. A few years before he had been a deckhand on the American schooner, the *Betsey*. He was a blond-haired, sandy-bearded Scotchman named Peter Lisle, reared on a Clydebank farm, who had taken to the sea, became an excellent navigator and was to become the principal adversary the United States would encounter in the approaching Tripolitan War.

The *Betsey*, built on the Merrimac River at Amesbury, Massachusetts, and commanded by Captain Chapin Sampson, sailing out of Boston, had been captured by Tripolitan corsairs in 1796, before the treaty was negotiated by O'Brien. When the peace was signed the captain and crew were liberated, but Tripoli kept the *Betsey* and with her remained deckhand Peter Lisle. He became a Mohammedan, which was an elaborate ritualistic procedure for an infidel, married the Bashaw's daughter, and quickly, both because of his seamanship and membership in the ruling family, became High Admiral and a scourge of Christian shipping. The *Betsey*, coppered and converted, became his flagship.

Peter Lisle, who will be given in this account his adoptive name of Murad Reis—which his American adversaries spelled with many variations—was a curious, sometimes sinister, always nebulous character, about whom the available information is scant and usually from an unfriendly source. At some period of his life, apparently in wanderings before he showed up in Massachusetts and took a seaman's berth, he had seen service with the Mamelukes and had become proficient in Arabic. As a seaman he was skillful and resourceful and about the only man in Tripoli, it developed, able to handle a fleet dexterously. He became something of a companion of the British consul McDonough, though it is difficult to believe that friendship existed beyond what McDonough might regard advantageous to his country's interests. Unfortunately Murad Reis will probably remain little more than a name, never an understandable person, in American history. This writer conducted a search in Tripoli, Edinburgh, and in the extensive British Museum and British Records Office in London, including the reading of the British consular reports of the period, without encountering material sufficient to give any very clear, unbiased impression of him. Rarely referred to, he was never described by his companion McDonough or by McDonough's successor, William Wass Langford.

About the only solid characteristic which emerges about Murad Reis was his intense dislike of Americans. Whether it resulted from some incident while he was in the United States or a seaman on the *Betsey*, or was, as is more likely, an attitude whipped up to justify his defection from his crew and his apostasy, is not likely to be determined. He had taken as his Moslem name that of the earlier pirate who had raided Iceland and Ireland in 1631.

When Cathcart went ashore Murad Reis received him "with a great deal of hauteur" and asked where the stores were that had been promised two years before. McDonough was present during the interview. Cathcart told him they were on board the *Hero* which had sailed fifteen days ahead of the *Sophia* and seemed to be lost or captured. He said the Bey of Tunis when the circumstances were explained had agreed to wait nine or ten months longer. Yes, agreed the Grand Admiral, he had agreed to wait because he was paid twenty or thirty thousand dollars. This Cathcart denied, saying the Bey had never hinted that he wanted a dollar and would have been affronted if the Americans had suggested a pecuniary reward.

This remark brought a peal of laughter from the Scotch renegade, who declared the Bey of Tunis was the first Moor he had ever heard of who would be affronted by being offered money. He said he supposed the Dey of Algiers would be similarly affronted. But it happened that he was in Algiers when the *Crescent* came in bulging with guns and ammunition for the Dey, who far from being affronted seemed much gratified. Cathcart said the *Crescent* was delivered in place of the cash required for the redemption of the American captives—a statement which would have applied to the naval stores but not the vessel—and covered the credit established for that purpose when the prisoners were freed. Murad Reis then asked about the consular presents Cathcart had brought on the *Sophia*, and as the American mentioned them McDonough made a list of them and took it to the Bashaw.

Cathcart was confined as a prisoner in the Marine for half an hour until Murad Reis and McDonough returned from the Castle. The list of presents he had brought included three brocaded caftans, one diamond-studded gold watch, eight silver snuffboxes, a brilliant diamond ring solitaire valued at $600 and two smaller diamond rings valued at $300 each, two pieces of holland, and six dozen hankerchiefs, the total value being $2,930. The list clearly made little impression on the Bashaw.

Through the discussions had run a flavor of strong Tripolitan nationalism which Barlow had detected two years earlier. Barlow had reported on August 18, 1797, to Secretary of State Pickering that the Bashaw of Tripoli was becoming powerful and might shake off the influence of the Dey of Algiers, as he "is known to set every principle of honor at defiance more than any prince in Barbary." His navy before the capture of the *Betsey* and the apostasy of Murad Reis consisted of two small cruisers. In a year's time it was almost equal to the navy of Algiers. Beyond this naval strength he seemed to Barlow to be in the good graces of Constantinople. That probably was a conclusion resulting from the remission of the customary payments due from the Tripolitan satrapy, but this was not because of any kindly sentiments of the Porte. The defenses of Tripoli were in miserable condition and the Turkish government wanted the taxes applied to their repair.

Now the Bashaw's jealousy of the other North African regencies was becoming more apparent. In his first message, oral, reported by Cathcart, he had asserted that "the Bashaw of Tripoli is an independent Prince and would be respected as such in spight of the Dey of Algiers Bey of Tunis or even the Grand Signore." When Murad Reis and McDonough returned, the Bashaw had another grievance. The "lying dog O'Brien" had said when Murad Reis was in Algiers that he was consul for Tunis and Tripoli as well as Algiers, and had explained that since the Bashaw of Tripoli and Bey of Tunis were dependent on Algiers, so were the United States consuls dependent on him. Such an arrangement put Tripoli in an inferior status to Algiers and was therefore an affront.

Cathcart vehemently denied that O'Brien could have said any such thing and wished them good morning. Then he stopped and added that the Bashaw seemingly did not want peace but supposed the United States had some rich ships in the Mediterranean which he could pillage. But Cathcart advised that because of the breach between the United States and France, the American vessels were so well armed they could not be captured by anything Tripoli could send out. Nevertheless, he thought it would be unfortunate if the guns intended for their common enemy, France, should be turned against Tripoli. Again Cathcart was advised that the Bashaw "is an Independent Prince & not to be intimidated by Algiers Tunis or even the Grand Signore," and that if the United States wanted to be at peace with him, "we must pay him for it."

The conversation is significant as suggestive of the refractory thinking in Tripoli which a little later brought on the war with the United States. Before Cathcart went back to his ship he sent a messenger to Leon Farfara, the Bashaw's banker, saying he had letters for him from Joseph Coen Barci and Napthali Busnah, Jewish bankers in Algiers. Farfara replied that he desired the letters but "to take care none of the moors should see them, & beg'd for Godsake that I would not mention his name" because it would be detrimental to the affairs of both him and the United States. The contact thus established was important to later negotiations.

Cathcart now wrote a letter to the Bashaw dated April 6, 1799, covering again the denial that he had ever heard of O'Brien's promise of a brig and explaining the delay of the supplies on the *Hero*. He offered to pay the cash equivalent of the stores or to have like supplies delivered in four months. Then he threw discretion overboard in the interests of peace, and wrote that he would give the brig *Sophia* in lieu of the stores, deliverable in nine months, dangers of the sea and enemy excepted, if she would be received as payment in full of all demands from the United States, forever. He promised that on being recognized as consul he would turn over handsome presents to the Bashaw and his chief officers.

On the next day Cathcart finally obtained his audience. The despot of Tripoli, Yusuf Karamanli, was blustering and profane. He used "every invective & term of reproach he could think of and he then swore by God & his Prophet that O'Brien had promised him the brig." Otherwise he would not have made the treaty. What irked him also was that O'Brien had said he, the Bashaw of Tripoli, was dependent on the Algerines. He had already given orders to his cruisers that if they ever caught O'Brien to bring him in and he would be "hung like a dog."

The Bashaw's outburst, which Cathcart called "bravado and huckstering," lasted an hour, after which he offered terms for a continuation of the peace. These were that either the brig should be delivered at once or $18,000 should be paid in cash on the spot; also that $25,000 should be payable in a few weeks in place of the stores lost on the *Hero,* and that consular presents should be given equal to those received from the Danes and Swedes. Cathcart peremptorily rejected the terms and said he would not negotiate again until the Bashaw was in better humor. The Bashaw allowed him twenty-four hours to consider, after which the forty-day period of grace would commence before he ordered an attack on American commerce.

The haggling continued through the next two days while Cathcart awaited a reply to the President's letter, saying he would depart when he received it. He and Captain Geddes circulated a report that the United States had warships in the Mediterranean as a protection of American shipping from the French. Learning that Tripoli had five cruisers at sea, they put out another report that the *Sophia* would sail at once to Malta. This was a hint that they would tell the Portuguese warships operating with Lord Nelson that the Tripolitan corsairs were out of their harbor and could be taken.

Meantime McDonough was continuing the bargaining with the Bashaw. He had been a kind friend to the American captives from the *Betsey* and he wanted peace. Cathcart urged him to get cash substituted for the brig. Giving a brig to Tripoli would mean inevitably that a brig would have to be given to Tunis. Finally, on the morning of April 10, McDonough brought word that he had agreed to a settlement in the name of the American Consul. The United States would pay $10,000 at once for the stores and the delay, and $8,000 in lieu of the brig, as soon as possible. Except for the consular presents worth about $3,000, these sums would satisfy all demands against the United States. Cathcart had to scatter around about $1,500 more in usance to officialdom.

Cathcart immediately accepted. "I assure you," he wrote in his report, "to many encomiums cannot be passed on the conduct of Mr. McDonough during the whole of this negotiation to whom the U S are certainly more indebted as Captn Geddes will inform you more particularly on his arrival in America."

Cathcart could not then know the bitter complaints he would lodge against McDonough after serving alongside him for two years as consul at Tripoli—complaints that never appeared to have much substance.

Late that afternoon he went to the Castle to deliver the consular presents to the Bashaw. There he saw Leon Farfara, the banker, who told the Bashaw he would guarantee such portion of the $18,000 involved in the settlement as the American Consul could not cover. Cathcart had 3,000 mauboobs with him (a mauboob was worth $1.25 in American money), and Farfaro consequently guaranteed $14,250. Even while Cathcart was in the Castle the U.S. flag was saluted by the harbor fortifications with twenty-one guns, which the *Sophia* returned. Flags were hoisted on the Castle and on the consulates of the Christian powers as a compliment to the United States.

Thus again peace was established between the Western republic and the last of the Turkish regencies which maintained fleets of corsairs along the North African shore. The timing was happy for the United States, because during that very spring, eighty American merchant ships entered the Mediterranean and the only American vessel of war in those waters was the small *Sophia*, armed mainly for defense and assigned to diplomatic and not convoy duty.

But the Bashaw of Tripoli was still unhappy with his settlement, in view of the richer tribute paid to Algiers. Tribute, instead of appeasing, only whets the appetite. As soon as Cathcart gave him the consular presents he fingered critically the two pieces of holland, a treated linen fabric, and asked if the United States had sent them merely as samples. Cathcart said no, that they were valuable and not very much could be given at one time. He then asked for two more gold watches. Cathcart fortunately had kept some gifts in reserve, anticipating a second call, and the watches he now presented. That night the Bashaw asked as an especial favor that two of the *Sophia*'s brass guns be traded for two iron guns. As it was the custom on proclaiming peace in Tripoli for the Christian power to present the Bashaw with from three to five barrels of powder, and since no powder could be obtained, Cathcart decided to donate the two brass pieces as a substitute, and to allow the Bashaw to keep his iron guns.

Late on the following afternoon the Bashaw in amiable mood entertained the Americans at coffee. He then wrote new letters to the President and to the rulers of Algiers and Tunis, withdrawing from Cathcart those he had written earlier "in a passion." With that the negotiations ended. As Captain Geddes returned to his ship the Castle saluted with seven guns. The *Sophia* replied, then made sail. She touched at Tunis and picked up Eaton's dispatches, including the amended treaty, and arrived at Lisbon June 18, 1799. Enroute from Algiers she fell in with a British merchant fleet being convoyed by Commander Stephenson of the *Uropa*, who, Geddes reported, "politely took me under his protection." The *Sophia* left Lisbon July 10 for the United States.

That year the United States was fighting its quasi-war with France in the Caribbean. But there was peace, precarious and by anyone's guess fleeting, but still peace, in the Mediterranean.

What brought on the declaration of war by Tripoli two years later was mainly a personality. The Bashaw was moody, suspicious, and a bad loser. Dissatisfied with his own agreements, he sought continually to amend them. He made new requisitions and longed for the brig he thought was due him under O'Brien's promise, but which he did not get. While expressing pleasure over protestations of American friendship, he said he would regard them as more genuine were they accompanied by the gift of a frigate or brig-of-war, such as had been given to the Algerines. Then Tripoli began what amounted to aggressions and at length an overt seizure.

Perhaps the most flagrant incident was the capture by the polacre *Tripolino* of the brig *Catherine*, out of New York bound for Leghorn with a cargo of coffee, sugar, beef, and other goods, valued at $50,000. Master James Carpenter of the craft said the Tripolitan polacre's commander, Raiz Amor Shelli, boarded the vessel on July 25, 1800, robbed the master and seamen, took articles from the cargo, and brought the brig into Tripoli. While the Bashaw held the ship in his harbor he said he would negotiate with the American government for the payment of a regular stated tribute instead of the presents he had been receiving. Cathcart contended it was an improper time to negotiate when the Bashaw had a valuable ship and cargo in his grasp, and that if he ever had a remote idea of an annuity he might as well erase it from his mind.

The Bashaw disavowed the seizure, saying it had been done without his orders. But when Cathcart called on him he again went into a tirade about how well Algiers fared and how poorly he was treated. He said he would hold the brig pending the President's reply to his letter. He changed his mind and she was released after about a month, and after a great deal of arguing by Cathcart. But the Bashaw served notice that he would wait six months for satisfactory answers from the United States and if they were not forthcoming he might declare war. That was approximately the time which did elapse between the release of the brig on October 22, 1800, and the declaration of war against the United States May 14, 1801, a period during which Cathcart was virtually ignored. He passed his time compiling a lengthy protest against the series of irritations, aggressions, and alleged treaty violations, and warning American shipping of approaching hostilities. Meantime, the *George Washington* had been on its enforced voyage to Constantinople. In Washington, the days of the Adams administration were drawing to a close.

CHAPTER EIGHT

The Fleet Goes Out

In the straggling little capital city on the Potomac, the "palace in the woods," with scattered houses far enough apart to win for it the name of the "city of mignificent distances," on March 4, 1801, Thomas Jefferson was sworn in by Chief Justice John Marshall as President.

The unfinished Capitol stood stark and bare as the great crowd estimated at one thousand people packed into the Senate chamber, where the senators retained their chairs but the representatives were required to stand in order to give seats to the ladies.

Jefferson walked. Jefferson was *sans coulettes,* wearing instead of breeches the long pantaloons popularized in Paris, which people pointed to with the comment that they were "an innovation of the French Revolution." Much has been made in history of the walk of the incoming President. He owned at his Monticello estate some of the best-blooded carriage horses in the country. Though not military, he was an equestrian of unsurpassed excellence. But where Washington and Adams had ridden, Jefferson walked. The walk was less than two blocks from Mrs. Conrad's boardinghouse at New Jersey Avenue and C Street, and perhaps without much significance. But there was something fresh and Jeffersonian about the fact that when he returned for dinner he took his customary place at the long dining table, *at the very foot of it,* with thirty seated at the board. He politely declined the seat nearer the head, offered him by Mrs. John Brown, wife of the senator from Kentucky who was Jefferson's fellow veteran of the Continental Congress and also, like Jefferson, a William and Mary graduate.

And there was much of significance in the inaugural address he read in a low voice—he was never a happy speaker—avowing his faith in the purpose of the government and the stability of republican institutions, an inaugural address which remains in the minds of many the greatest ever delivered.

... having banished from our land that religious intolerance under which mankind so long bled and suffered, we have yet gained little if we countenance a political intolerance as despotic ...

If there be any among us who would wish to dissolve this Union or to change its republican form, let them stand undisturbed as monuments of the safety with which error of opinion may be tolerated where reason is left free to combat it ...

... some honest men fear that a republican government can not be strong, that this Government is not strong enough ... I believe this, on the contrary, the strongest Government on earth.

... peace, commerce, and honest friendship with all nations, entangling alliances with none ...

A wise and frugal Government, which shall restrain men from injuring one another, shall leave them otherwise free to regulate their own pursuits of industry and improvement, and shall not take from the mouth of labor the bread it has earned.

... I have learnt to expect that it will rarely fall to the lot of imperfect man to retire from this station with the reputation and the favor which bring him to it ...

He made clear that he harbored no resentments and maintained his customary self-control (another had averred that "no man could put him in a passion") after the harrowing and unexpected contest over the presidency with Aaron Burr in the House of Representatives. "Every difference of opinion is not a difference of principle," he said.

Whatever may have been thought about Jefferson's tolerance to Federalist conservatism at home and to the excesses of French radicalism overseas, nobody doubted that he had principle. "Long Tom's" moral strength was as tough and durable as a post split from a Blue Ridge locust. And if there were one policy against which he had been nursing an aversion through the years, it was the payment of tribute to the little potentates of the Barbary Coast.

Back in 1784, Jefferson, in writing to James Monroe, had stated the opinion which in 1801 still controlled him. Pointing to the difficulty of ascertaining what the other powers paid the Barbary States in tribute, he still thought it would cost the United States "one, two, or perhaps three hundred thousand a year."

Surely our people will not give this [he declared]. Would it not be better to offer them an equal treaty? If they refuse, why not go to war with them? ... we ought to begin a naval power, if we mean to carry on our own commerce. Can we begin it on a more honorable occasion or with a weaker foe? I am of opinion that Paul Jones with half a dozen frigates would totally destroy their commerce; not by attempting bombardments as the Mediterranean States do wherein they act against the whole Barbary force brought to a point, but by constant cruising and cutting them to pieces by piecemeal.

Congress at the end of the Adams' administration, well after the flurry of the quasi-war with France, had again severely curbed the naval strength of the country for economy reasons by authorizing the President to retain 13 frigates of those that had been built or purchased and converted during the crisis with France, but to keep only 6 in active service. The 7 others were to be laid up as a reserve. The list of officers likewise was reduced. It would consist of 9 captains, 36 lieutenants, and 150 midshipmen. Jefferson stated when he took office that he would comply with this law, the economy objects of which he approved, but he did not foresee, of course, the impending hostilities with Tripoli.

By adhering to the law Jefferson did not seriously impair the strength of the Navy, because the ships he retired were the more sluggish, inferior types. Probably the Navy lost no more than twenty per cent of its power. But he did suspend work on six new ships Congress had authorized three years earlier. Among the frigates soon to be retired was the *George Washington*, the converted East Indiaman on which Bainbridge had just made the voyage to Constantinople. After word came of the declaration of war by Tripoli, naval building was soon resumed.

The ingenious Jefferson never had a problem without coming up with some sort of an answer, and this he did with apparently the first suggestion of a "mothball fleet." Since frigates were needed urgently at some times and were judged an unnecessary expense at others, he would lay them by in slack seasons to defray maintenance costs. His object was to preserve a navy so that "at the beginning of the subsequent war, it shall be as sound as at the end of the preceeding [sic] one."

Writing to his architect, Benjamin Henry Latrobe, November 2, 1802, he suggested a drydock covered with a roof so that vessels, shielded from rain and sun, "would last as long as the interior Timbers, doors and floors of a House." He thought a lower basin could be established in the Washington area into which the vessels could be floated at high tide. Then the gates could be closed and water could be introduced from upstream to bring it twenty-four feet higher, which would be the level of an upper basin, built to accommodate twelve frigates. The water could then be drained from the upper basin, leaving the frigates high and dry. A roof could be built over them which need not be wider than 175 feet. He cited a roof of the Halle au blé in Paris as an example of one requiring "no underworks to support it."

He wanted Latrobe to help choose between the streams available for the covered drydock—"the Eastern Branch, Tyber, Rock Creek and the Potomak itself—then to trace the Canal, draw plans of that and the two basons, and calculate the expense of the whole." In the trend of events he never had a chance to carry out the program, because the fleet usually remained busy, but it would have been better than dismantling the vessels or selling them when peace occurred.

Jefferson no longer had Paul Jones, but he had, it developed, some of the best officers who ever walked a ship deck.

James Madison reached Washington from Montpelier on May 1, 1801, to become Secretary of State. As if the deep-seated elements recognized that southern and western Republicanism was supplanting eastern Federalism at the helm of the country's foreign affairs, his arrival was saluted by an earthquake which rocked the New England coast from the Kennebec River to Cape Cod—altogether something of a stir to be set off by the diminutive Jimmy.

He took charge of the State Department only thirteen days before Tripoli declared war on the United States. But well before word of the declaration reached the American capital, the new Jefferson administration was assembling a fleet for Mediterranean service.

Samuel Harrison Smith's *National Intelligencer*, already the mouthpiece for the administration, was saying proudly on May 11 that the United States was at peace with the whole civilized world. Instead, the nation was just about to embark on its first avowed military and naval conflict, already formally declared by one side, and awaiting only the arrival of intelligence before a state of hostilities would be recognized by the other.

By virtue of Truxtun's brilliant successes over the French frigates, and because of his seniority and his standing with fellow officers and the public, he was generally looked on as the officer who would command the Mediterranean fleet. But by the War Department listing of June 5, 1794, Richard Dale ranked him, and Jefferson, who was not partial to Truxtun, appointed Dale. The reasons for the antipathy to Truxtun which kept him out of the Tripolitan War are not entirely clear. Jefferson's first contact with him, so far as his writings disclose, was during his service with Benjamin Franklin and John Adams on the first commission appointed to negotiate with the Barbary powers. Truxtun was the ship captain who carried Benjamin Franklin back to the United States in 1785, on the voyage where it was reported that Franklin had been captured by Algerine corsairs. The report arose from a letter published in England presumed to have been written by Truxtun. Jefferson quickly detected the error in the report and it is not likely that he held Truxtun in any manner responsible. Truxtun was a fighter who could win battles against superior odds. A little later when he was asked to command a fleet the circumstances were such that he did not consider his prerogatives properly respected and his resignation was accepted. His pique against Jefferson was what made Aaron Burr judge—erroneously, it developed—that he would be open to conspiring against the government.

On May 22, 1801, in Hampton Roads, Truxtun turned over the *President* to Dale, saying "she is kind and good humoured in a gale."

He added other complimentary remarks: "In the violent tempest I experienced in September last, when so many ships were dismantled and lost, British Men of War as well as others; I kept the *President* under her main and fore topsails close reefed . . . and never lost a rope yarn or met with the smallest injury, tho' the gale continued an uncommon length of time."

Richard Dale is one of the less vivid figures of the Revolutionary and Tripolitan wars, mainly because he is the only one among the leading naval officers of that period who never had a biographer. James Fenimore Cooper, who talked with him in the days of his retirement in Philadelphia, included a sketch of him in his series dealing with early naval officers, and another brief sketch was published by Nicholas Biddle in the *Portfolio* magazine in 1814. Yet Dale was in the front rank of the intrepid fighters, from the battle of the *Bon Homme Richard* and the *Serapis,* in which, at the age of twenty-three, he was Jones's first lieutenant, until he returned from the Mediterranean after commanding the first United States battle squadron to cross the Atlantic.

In the fight of the *Bon Homme Richard,* when that vessel was sinking and Jones's only recourse was to board the *Serapis,* Dale was the courageous officer who swung by a rope in the moonlight from the faltering American vessel to the *Serapis,* the first man on the deck of the worsted enemy.

Though Dale was Jones's favorite, there was a fading cloud on his early record. None ever more thoroughly effaced a bad start with a strong finish. Jones, in recognition of his staunchness in combat, gave him the handsome, gold-mounted sword, the very one which Jones himself had received from the admirous Louis XVI of France. They had won their brotherhood in stirring combat and it was enduring.

The cloud was that Dale, a mere youth at the outbreak of the Revolutionary War, had embraced first the Colonial, then the British, and again the Colonial cause, as conditions at the moment seemed to suggest. The son of a Portsmouth, Virginia, shipwright, he took to the sea early and by the time the war came had become chief mate at nineteen. Then in 1776 he became a lieutenant on a ship of the rebelling state of Virginia, which had a little navy of its own, and was captured by the British and thrown into a prison ship hold. Friend was fighting friend and one of Dale's schoolmates, Bridger Goodrich, a staunch loyalist, carried on an indoctrination campaign to win young officer Dale back to the King, and finally succeeded.

What went on in Dale's mind at this moment was never fully disclosed. There were a great many arguments to be advanced on each side in 1776, but it was probably craving for action that turned the scales, and action was not to be found in a prison ship. Dale joined Goodrich aboard a tender of a British frigate, the ship that had captured him and taken him into Norfolk, but this time the tender fell in with a little fleet of pilot boats and in a desperate fight in the lower Rappahannock he was severely wounded by a musket ball which hit his head. The tender escaped but Dale was left in a Norfolk hospital, the port being under British control.

Dale's decision that he had made a mistake espousing the British cause is supposed to have taken place while he was reflecting on his hospital bed. He concluded that if he were going to be hit on the head, never again would it be by a bullet from his own countrymen. Opportunity to act on that resolve soon came, when he went with another friend, William Goodrich, to Bermuda. Their boat was picked up by the Yankee captain John Barry, commanding the sloop-of-war *Lexington*.

Meantime the Declaration of Independence had been signed and the war had entered a new phase. Now that Dale had got his affiliations straightened out he became a forthright patriot and served under Barry, one of the leading American naval figures of the Revolution. As a master's mate he was with the *Lexington* on her adventurous cruise to West Indian and European waters. When President Washington established the ranking in 1794 for the new navy—all of the vessels which comprised the Revolutionary War navy having passed out of existence—John Barry was placed first on the list and Richard Dale fourth.

Cooper found him "a man of singular simplicity and moderation," enterprising without bravado, having no sense of exaggeration. Three times during the Revolutionary War he had been a British prisoner and once had dug a tunnel to escape the severe treatment at the Mill Prison at Plymouth, only to be recaptured and returned to the "Black Hole." He did not improve his standing by singing "Rebel Songs." At length he laid hold of a British officer's uniform, donned it, and walked past the saluting sentries, and never in his remaining forty-seven years of life disclosed who gave him the uniform. It was, quite obviously, an inside job.

In order to understand the importance to the government and nation

of the balanced judgment of a squadron commander it is well to reflect
for a moment on the responsibilities of that post. The diplomat's mission
called for even greater discernment then than in the present day when
quick communication makes contact with the home office a matter of
moments and instructions can be transmitted instantly. So also the early
commodore had to possess political insight, emotional balance, an understanding of people, and a strong appreciation of the national interest.
He was, in fact, the United States on the firing line. Perhaps the present
admiral is closer to his earlier counterpart than is the diplomat of today,
because speed has become such an essential in warfare that decisions
must be made instantly and without reference to higher authority. Dale
possessed both the experience and resolute character required of a fleet
commander in the first years of the nineteenth century.

Dale's squadron consisted of the frigates *President,* with 44 guns,
Philadelphia, 38, and *Essex,* 32, and the sloop-of-war *Enterprise,* a trimly
built schooner with 12 guns. Jefferson in a letter to the Bashaw of
Tripoli dated May 21, 1801, called it a "squadron of observation" sent
to the Mediterranean "to superintend the safety of our commerce, and
to exercise our seamen in nautical duties," but his missive contained a
phrase which marked a dramatic change in American policy: ". . . we
mean to rest the safety of our commence on the resources of our own
strength and bravery in every sea." Acting Secretary of the Navy Samuel
Smith wrote several pages of detailed instructions for Dale, the purport
of which was based on the mistaken assumption that the United States
was at peace, and that this squadron might tend to prevent a rupture of
peace by appearing before the harbors of the Barbary powers. Recent
accounts had given cause for fear, he explained, that the corsairs would
attack American commerce if unprotected in the Mediterranean, an apprehension justified particularly by the threats of the Bashaw of Tripoli.
If any regency had declared war their port should be blockaded and
their prizes recaptured.

To show that the United States had no fear of Barbary seamen and
boarders, they were to be liberated: "Any Prisoners you may take, you
will treat with humanity and attention, and land them on some part
of the Barbary shore most convenient to you." A striking part of this first
general order for the conduct of an American squadron at sea, no doubt
the insertion of Jefferson or Madison, but given by Samuel Smith, was:

> In all cases of clashing with the Vessels, Officers or Subjects of other
> Powers, we enjoin on you the most rigorous moderation, conformity
> to right & reason, & supression of all passions, which might lead to the
> commitment of our Peace or our honor. We shall scrupulously & with-

out indulgence, examine that conduct which shall bring us into collision with any other Power—: yet we do not mean that you are to submit to unequivocal insults or wrongs—: and particularly you are not
to suffer your own ships to be entered—or your men examined or taken
out, at sea, by any person or power whatsoever; but to resist such attempt to your uttermost, yielding only to Superior force, & surrendering, if overcome, your Vessel & men, but never your men without your
Vessel.

Searches, such as those of merchant vessels which had been conducted
by the European powers (an area of maritime law which remained
vague and subject to contrary interpretations), were under no circumstances to be permitted by armed warships of the United States.

Commodore Dale sailed aboard the *President*. Captain Samuel Barron commanded the *Philadelphia,* Captain William Bainbridge, returned from Constantinople, the *Essex,* and Lieutenant Andrew Sterrett
the *Enterprise*. Commodore was a courtesy title of that day, and was not
an official rank, the highest in the Navy being captain. But commodore
was invariably employed to designate the officer commanding a squadron.

The contrary wind turned and at 6:00 A.M. on Tuesday, June 2, 1801,
with a smart breeze blowing from westward, the squadron weighed
anchor and made sail out of the Virginia capes.

Jefferson has scarcely received the deserved acclaim or lineage in
American history for dispatching the Dale squadron to the Mediterranean after the sovereignty of the United States had been affronted by the
incident of Bainbridge and the *George Washington*. One of his nine-
teenth-century biographers, the discerning James Parton, who enriched
American history with his gracefully written lives of great Americans,
sensed what had taken place. He found "something really exquisite in
Jefferson's turning the infant navy of the infant government to a use so
legitimate." What in 1785 Jefferson had urged the combined naval
powers to attempt, he was enabled to begin "by the confidence of Congress and the valor of a few heroes." Parton noticed an event "peculiarly
satisfying" in "a peace man making a successful fight" when it had been
clearly thrust on him.

In reviewing Jefferson's qualifications for his office—his service in
subordinate stations, specialized knowledge, insight into the weakness
of particular parts of the system—it was but natural for the biographer
to discern some of Jefferson's qualities which would be regarded as supreme assets whenever possessed by an executive. In an instance like the
Barbary embroilment, the country "derives great benefit if a servant of

State happens to be one of those rarely-gifted men who possess the strength to execute in the presence of mankind what they have meditated in seclusion."

Jefferson's habit during this period was, like Madison's, to pass the warm season in the country. The two lived only thirty miles apart. They exchanged notes and visits and conducted foreign affairs from their plantations almost as readily as they could from the capital city. Jefferson's Monticello plantation near Charlottesville embraced 5,682 acres, operated by 113 slaves, while his Poplar Forest estate near Bedford had 4,164 acres and 85 slaves. That was no small responsibility to add to the tasks of the Presidency.

When autumn and the regular December session of Congress were coming on, they returned to their offices. The *National Intelligencer* scribe, probably Smith, looked the President over after a return at about this time and judged he was in good health. Then he thought the season propitious for all-around felicitations:

> The period of popular delusion and ignorance in this country is past. Tyrants may keep a nation ignorant that has never been enlightened, but they cannot eradicate information when it has once struck its roots and extended its branches.

> Such, at present, is the moral state of the people of the United States. They are the only people on earth that are not governed by a few ambitious men . . . The people of the United States, enlightened to their own interests, have wisely resolved to preserve all power in their own hands, and have patriotically maintained that purpose.

Perhaps no more illuminating thumbnail sketch of Jefferson at this period has been provided than that of Senator William Plummer of New Hampshire—a good historian and founder of that state's historical society—who called at the Executive Mansion with other Congressmen. "In a few moments after our arrival," he said, "a tall, high-boned man came into the room. He was dressed, or rather undressed, in an old brown coat, red waistcoat, old corduroy small-clothes much soiled, woolen hose, and slippers without heels. I thought him a servant, when General [Joseph Bradley] Varnum surprised me by announcing that it was the President."

Dale's passage of the Atlantic was delayed by bad weather. Enroute he gave the fast *Enterprise* authority to sail ahead, with a result that she made Gibraltar several days before the frigates. Off Cadiz, Dale spoke to a British fleet of seven ships of the line commanded by Sir James Saumerez, engaged in blockading that Spanish port. When in sight of

Gibraltar he encountered three French ships of the line bound for Cadiz provided they could get entry through the British squadron. The battle was heard, but two French ships made the entry. Otherwise the voyage was uneventful, though the Napoleonic Wars that were tearing Europe apart were continually spilling over into the ocean.

News of the arrival of American war vessels at Gibraltar reached the *National Intelligencer* in Washington September 7, 1801, in a letter from John Gavino, American consul, dated July 4, 1801. The *Enterprise* under Captain Andrew Sterrett anchored on June 29 in the harbor alongside a Tripolitan schooner commanded by Murad Reis, who was here introduced to the American public as the High Admiral of the Tripolitan navy. To Washington readers he was described as "an English Renegade married to the Bashaw's daughter." On the same date Murad Reis was being denounced in the New York *Commercial Advertiser* in a dispatch from Cathcart, who was quoted: "The admiral is a reputed coward; seldom goes near a vessel that looks warm."

The schooner he commanded was the old converted *Betsey*, rechristened the *Meshuda*. She was crowded with 246 men and armed with 28 guns. She was accompanied by a 14-gun brig, an unusual condition suggesting some extraordinary situation because of the habit of the corsairs to separate on leaving port. The two ships had come into Gibraltar seeking water, after cruising for thirty-five days without making a capture. Murad Reis gave out the false information ashore that Tripoli was not at war with the United States, when in fact the Bashaw had made the declaration before the ships left their home port.

The Tripolitan schooner and the companion brig were making for the Atlantic Ocean, intending to renew the depredations against American shipping such as had occurred after the truce had been negotiated by the British consul Charles Logie between Algiers and Portugal. The schooner had been coppered by the Spaniards. She was now a sloop-of-war, built low at the waist and ornately decorated. Of her twenty-eight guns, eighteen were 9-pounders on the main deck. The other armament was six 4-pounders on her quarterdeck and two chase guns on the bow and two on the stern. She was painted yellow with a white streak across her sides, but with a green stern. The muzzles of her guns were painted red. White flowers were festooned above the stern windows and above them was painted a woman's head in white. These markings made her so easily identifiable that the information that she "looks at a distance like a Spaniard" was scarcely necessary, but it related to her heavy rigging. Still another marking was that in order to mount her two stern guns, the taffrail, or upper part of the ship's stern, had been cut very low, giving her a slinking or down-at-the-hind-end appearance, a very jackal of the sea.

The brig accompanying the flagship was the second strongest vessel of the Tripolitan navy. She was Swedish-built and at the time war was declared was being fitted out at Malta. She carried 120 men and had an armament of fourteen 4-pounders. She also had a white woman's head painted above her cabin windows.

Dale entered Gibraltar Harbor July 2, surprised that not a British war vessel was in the port. The trim *President*, beautiful against the blue waters, sailed majestically ahead of the smaller frigates *Philadelphia* and *Essex*. Anyone of the crowd on the waterfront must have been thrilled as he witnessed the event. For the first time in history a war fleet of the United States was at the entrance of the Mediterranean. A letter from an officer published in the New York *Commercial Advertiser* told that the squadron "received a very handsom reception" from the British authorities of Gibraltar.

Dale brought the *President* close to the *Enterprise* and the two Tripolitan warships. Consul Gavino went on board the flagship and reported the incidents which followed. Dale hailed the Tripolitan admiral and asked if Tripoli was at war or at peace with the United States. Murad Reis replied falsely that the two nations were at peace. Dale then inquired if Consul Cathcart remained in good health at Tripoli. The Tripolitan-Scotchman said Cathcart had gone at his own wish to Tunis, then added that Cathcart "was no friend of the Americans."

On the following morning Gavino had his boat rowed alongside the Tripolitan schooner to speak with Murad Reis, having been informed by the Tripolitan's agent ashore that the Admiral desired words with him. Gavino told Murad Reis that Dale would have no objection to seeing him aboard the *President*, or at the house of the American consul on shore. Both meeting places were rejected by the Tripolitan, who said he would meet the Americans at a tavern and nowhere else. It was his idea of neutral ground. "Indeed, I perceived he was trifling in the business," said the Consul. Commodore Dale agreed.

Dale reported that he took no stock in the Grand Admiral's avowal of peace, since "from every Infermation that I can get here Tripoli is at war with America." How unfortunate it was, he said, that the Tripolitan vessels had not cleared Gibraltar a few days earlier, since he would then likely have encountered them at sea. There he could have handled them, as he could not in the British harbor. Dale looked at the Tripolitan ships closely and concluded that the brig was not a fast sailer but still could catch American merchant ships and could do much damage "if she gits in the Western Ocean."

He detailed the *Philadelphia*, under Captain Barron, to watch Murad Reis—"that Is, to take him when he goes out."

Dale in his blunt sailor language then summed up for the Secretary of the Navy: "This said Admeril is a Scotchman, which makes him the more to be dreded in our Seas—I am very sorry to say our Barbary affairs look very gloomy . . . it is much to be Lemented that the Government has not paid more attention to the information that has been received . . . I am fearful it will cost the United States many Thousand Dollars before things are put at rights; there is ful Employment at present in the Mediterranean, for all Frigates belonging to the United States."

Leaving the *Philadelphia* on guard, he took the rest of the American squadron into the Mediterranean. Before the frigates sailed, one of the officers of the *Philadelphia* took time to write home on July 20: "There are a number of Americans here. One of them challenged the Tripolitan Admiral out to fight him, but the latter would not accept the invitation. He is afraid to leave Gibraltar."

Thus at the very outset the two best vessels of the Tripolitan navy were blockaded in a neutral port and their indispensable Grand Admiral was to all appearances *hors de combat*. But Gibraltar Harbor was not as secure a prison as a Barbary bagnio and Tripoli did possess other warcraft, a close description of which was in the possession of the United States. She had two polaccas (a North African term fairly synonymous with felucca or caravel; comparable to a sloop-of-war). These were described by Cathcart as being "mere shells" but each carried eighteen 4-pounders and a crew of 100 men. One had yellow sides and a red poop, while the other was black. The remainder of the force consisted of two galleys, lateen rigged and identified by their extraordinarily large sails. One carried twenty-eight oars and the other twenty-four, valuable in harbor defense or in a calm, when they might lay under the stern of a becalmed frigate and rake her. Each had a crew ranging from 70 to 100 men. An additional brig, the *Tripoli*, carried 14 guns.

Thus the entire navy of Tripoli at the time of the declaration of war against the United States consisted of seven vessels in active service, carrying 106 guns ranging from 4- to 9-pounders, and a force of around 840 men, and of these, two vessels with 42 guns and 386 men were blockaded. Strength was added subsequently, especially in gunboats.

Reporting on the condition of the enemy fleet, Cathcart, as experienced a judge of maritime matters as anyone could want, rated it badly equipped and as comprising about all the seaworthy personnel the regency could muster: "They have more Vessels But have not People to man them." He described their method of combat and emphasized the importance of Murad Reis to their fleet:

Their mode of attack is first to fire a Broadside, and then to set up a great shout in order to intimidate their enemy, they then board you if you let them, with as many Men as they can, armed with Pistols, large and small Knives and probably a few with Blunderbusses; if you beat them off once they seldom risque a second encounter, and three well directed broadsides will ensure you a complete Victory. The Capture or sinking their Admiral is of such great importance that it will not only ensure us a permanent Peace upon our own terms but will probably effect a revolution in Tripoly favorable to our interests in the whole of the Barbary States.

The Tripolitan craft went through the war largely without names, as far as the American adversaries could discern. Among the exceptions was the flagship of Murad Reis, the *Meshuda*.

Dale now went about the main part of his mission, to demonstrate American strength in front of the Barbary Coast ports. He sent the *Essex* to convoy the *Grand Turk* to Tunis with another quantity of naval stores and articles of tribute, but the more quieting effect was produced on that regency by the splendid appearance of the American squadron. The *Essex*, a frigate smaller than those of the *President* class, excited particular admiration wherever she appeared in the Mediterranean. After this duty the *Essex* went along the southern European shore collecting American vessels and convoying them until they were safely out into the Atlantic. The *Philadelphia* meantime kept watch off Gibraltar to prevent any corsairs from gaining the open ocean.

The *President* and *Enterprise* preceded the *Essex* by a day to Tunis, having dropped in with salutary effect at Algiers. On July 24 Dale arrived off Tripoli with the *President* and *Enterprise* and began a blockade of that port. By July 30 water was running low on both ships. He decided the nearest supply was Malta—though it was never plentiful on that rocky island which frequently experienced long periods of drought—and wrote a letter to the governor of Malta requesting sufficient for his ships.

Lieutenant Andrew Sterrett with the *Enterprise*, 12 guns and 90 men, was making for Malta to obtain the water when, on August 1, 1801, he encountered the Tripolitan ship of war *Tripoli*, 14 guns and 80 men, commanded by Admiral Rais Mahomet Rous. The combat which ensued was one of the strangest ever fought, and unique in some respects in an era that witnessed many unusual ship actions.

Sterrett was a handsome, curly-haired young man who wore what in later years came to be known as sideburns. He possessed a high spirit and such an alertness to defend his rank and prerogatives that it eventually lost him to the naval service, though he was of the precise type who made the best officers and in the end won highest rank. A longer

and more distinguished naval career awaited his second in command,
Lieutenant David Porter, twenty-one years old, who three years earlier,
a recruit from Boston, had entered as a midshipman aboard the *Constellation*. He had won his promotion to lieutenant through gallantry
which everyone aboard could witness—he was in the crow's nest and
rigging—when the frigate, under Truxtun, defeated the French *Insurgente* in 1799. His later cruise of the Pacific Ocean in command of the
Essex, during the War of 1812, formed one of the romantic chapters of
the early Navy.

Sterrett had been one of the reasons why Truxtun, in the quasi-war
with France, had achieved such a splendid record with the *Constellation,*
on which he was one of the lieutenants. The *Constellation* had a mixed
crew—"a tough lot," it has been called. It may not have been impelled
primarily by patriotism for the United States, but the men were devoted
to self-preservation and it was fairly certain in the sanguinary naval actions of the times that it was win or be killed. Sterrett's cold-steel resolution could be seen from his remark after the *Constellation* defeated the
Insurgente: "One fellow I was obliged to run through the body with my
sword, and so put an end to a coward. You must not think this strange,
for we would put a man to death for even looking pale on board this
ship."

These were indeed times when there was nothing to fear more than
fear itself.

If thus on the *Constellation,* so on the *Enterprise.* The little *Enterprise*
was herself a veteran. She had been out eight months during the undeclared war with France and fought seven sea actions and captured nineteen French merchant vessels in that time. Jefferson had included her in
Dale's fleet as something of a tender to the frigates, and that was the
kind of work to which Dale had now assigned her. But even her timbers,
along with her commander, seemed to know she was able to fight.

Commodore Dale instructed Sterrett when the *Enterprise* left the
President off Tripoli to be discreet about the laws and "not suffer your
officers or People to get into any scrapes with the People on shore," but
to liberate any American vessel encountered on the seas which might
have been seized by the enemy. If he fell in with a Tripolitan corsair he
could handle, to "heave all his Guns Over board Cut away his Masts, &
leave him In a situation, that he can Just make out to get into some Port."
Sterrett could use any colors as a deception but was "on no account to
fire under any but our Owne."

Captain Sterrett bore a British flag as he approached the Tripolitan
ship, an expedient frequently practiced in the naval warfare of the day.
He inquired of the Tripolitan the object of her cruise. The commander

replied that he had come out to look for Americans but lamented that he had not yet found a single one. Sterrett promptly lowered the British and hoisted the U.S. colors and ordered a volley of musketry discharged across the Tripolitan's decks. The *Tripoli* replied with a partial broadside.

It was 9:00 A.M. For three hours the ships lay alongside at pistol range and blazed away at each other with broadsides and small arms. Three times they came together and the Moslems tried to board. Each time they were beaten back with severe loss. Fortunately the *Enterprise* had a small Marine Corps detachment, commanded by Lieutenant Enoch S. Lane, whose fire was particularly effective during the boarding efforts.

An equal number of times the Tripolitans seemed to give up the contest and surrender. They struck their colors, but each time as the wary Lieutenant Sterrett drew close for boarding and as the American gun crews relaxed their efforts, came to the spardeck and cheered for their victory, the enemy ship hoisted her flag again, let loose a blast and renewed the battle. After the last deception Sterrett ordered the gunners to sink the craft, whose fire had grown steadily weaker under the unmerciful bombardment from the American guns. The seamen took up the cry of "Sink the villains." Finally the unhappy and treacherous Admiral Rais Mahomet Rous, who like his second in command was wounded, called out for mercy. He bent over the vessel's waist in a supplicating position which appeared to be a genuine surrender.

Sterrett, not to be duped by further trickery, held his fire but told the commander to come aboard the *Enterprise* or send some of his officers. The Admiral replied that the *Tripoli's* boat was so shattered it was unfit for use. Sterrett then inquired what assurance he would have that his men would not be murdered if he sent a detail aboard the Tripoli. The Admiral threw his colors into the sea. After that and other supplications and assurances, the American commander decided to take the risk. When the boarding party headed by Lieutenant Porter reached the enemy deck it found a scene of death and desolation almost unparalleled in such small ship actions. The ship was shot to pieces. Of her eighty men thirty were dead and thirty wounded, leaving but twenty to man the ship. The deck was covered with bodies, splinters, blood, and wreckage. The ship's surgeon had been killed and there was no one on board to care for the wounded. With the two top officers wounded and the third officer dead, the distressed vessel was virtually out of control.

But the strange feature of this battle fought for three hours at close pistol range, with the two ships often lying alongside, was that when Captain Sterrett checked the American gunners, marines, and seamen, *not an American had received a single scratch.* The reason can only be guessed at; partly chance, but mainly because the Barbary powers who were accustomed to boarding defenseless merchant vessels were not fitted by training or temperament for the fierce, desperate, pent-up fury of sea actions in the era of "iron men and wooden ships," in which, for some reason, the Americans of that day seemed to excel.

"When we compare this great slaughter," said the *National Intelligencer and Advertiser* in reporting the event, "with the fact that not a single individual of the crew of the *Enterprise* was in the least degree injured, we are lost in surprise . . .

"All the officers and sailors manifested the truest spirit, and sustained the greatest efforts during the engagement. All, therefore, are entitled to encomium for their valour and good conduct. The marines, especially, owing to the nearness of the vessels, which were within pistol shot of each other, were eminently useful."

Sterrett and his officers and men did what they could to, relieve the suffering of the wounded. Though the enemy admiral could scarcely feel entitled to clemency, he received the American commander's compassion. But Sterrett ordered that the *Tripoli* be dismantled completely, and the American seamen performed the task neatly. Her masts were chopped down, her cannon rolled across the deck and pushed overboard into the Mediterranean. Every cutlass, blunderbuss, and pistol was cast into the sea. The ammunition was dumped. Then they put up a single spar and fastened to it a tattered rag for a sail. Never were orders more exactly obeyed than were Dale's, that an enemy ship should be left in such a shape that she could "Just make out to get into some Port." When the rag was hoisted Sterrett, not being permitted under his general orders to capture prizes, sent her on her way.

She made her home port, where Admiral Rais Mahomet Rous's wounds were no protection from the Bashaw's rage. Some explanation had to be given for such a stinging defeat and the one easiest at hand was the Admiral's incompetence. The charge could not have been altogether unjust, for it is difficult to conceive how any ship commander could have fought a poorer battle. He was broken and publicly disgraced. The second penalty involved the physical shame of being mounted backward on a jackass and ridden through the streets of Tripoli as an object of popular scorn. Then the punishment was capped off with 500 bastinados.

But the punishment did not dispel the wonder or disillusion of the people of Tripoli about such a ghastly defeat, the general circumstances of which soon became common property. According to reports reaching the United States, there was apprehension that the entire fleet of Tripoli would be destroyed by the hard-fighting Americans. Sufficient was this fear, at least, that the seamen Tripoli was employing at the time to fit out fresh vessels to go to sea deserted in a body and went into hiding. Murad Reis was absent and there was none to hold them in line. For a season Tripoli had a fleet but no sailors and no Grand Admiral to navigate it.

Well might the untrained Tripolitans be concerned. Undoubtedly lack of experience with artillery was a factor in the overwhelming defeat of the *Tripoli*. While the Americans were not more experienced in combat, they were more practiced in gunnery. They likewise had a better tradition of teamwork and discipline. Firing the big guns from the deck called for considerable skill. Handspikes had to be used to train the pieces, most of which at this period were without sights. Tackles and breech ropes were employed to hold the guns and check the recoils. Naturally a gun lurched heavily backward when it was fired, causing a great strain on the tackle and the bolts which held it. The strain was especially heavy if the deck at the moment sloped backward. Guns at times broke loose and created havoc. All the while the gunners were under enemy fire, either through the portholes or, as in the case of the smaller craft, on the open deck. Sterrett demonstrated in this first battle that while the Tripolitans might be good boarders, they were not capable or experienced gunners and therefore not good sea fighters.

President Jefferson was a strict constructionist. The reason why he had not allowed Dale's squadron to take prizes was clear from his message to the session of Congress which convened in December, 1801. He told Congress how he had desired to remain at peace and had sent out a squadron of frigates to convey that message and protect American commerce. The action, he said, was "seasonable and salutary" because Tripoli already had declared war and her cruisers were out of their home port. Two were blockaded in Gibraltar. He spoke with pride of Lieutenant Sterrett's sea engagement: "The bravery exhibited by our citizens on that element will, I trust, be a testimony to the world that it is not the want of that virtue which makes us seek their peace, but a conscientious desire to direct the energies of our nation to the multiplication of the human race, and not to its destruction."

Then he explained about the liberation of the *Tripoli*: "Unauthorized by the Constitution, without the sanction of Congress, to go beyond the line of defense, the vessel, being disabled from committing further hostilities, was liberated with its crew." He went on to say that Congress would doubtless consider whether measures of offense should not also be authorized—that is, if a state of war should be acknowledged. On

February 6, 1802, Congress passed what was tantamount to a declaration, authorizing the President to use the Navy as he saw fit to protect American commerce and seamen and to commission privateers.

Perhaps the individual most elated over Sterrett's victory was ex-Consul Cathcart, who after the declaration of war had left Tripoli for Leghorn. Through Commodore Dale, he sent his warmest thanks to Sterrett for having demonstrated to the Tripolines what he had been trying to tell them all along about "the energy of the American character."

Congress passed a resolution commending Sterrett and his men, awarded an extra month's pay to everyone on the ship, and authorized the presentation to the commander of a commemorative sword. The battle, brilliant beyond all expectation, marked Sterrett's only appearance in command of a notable engagement in American history. He continued with the fleet for a time and will be referred to again in these pages. The presentation of the sword was delayed. Congress had voted it but made no appropriation. He returned to Baltimore to supervise the building of the brig *Vixen*. Then when he heard that Lieutenant Stephen Decatur had been jumped to the rank of captain ahead of him, he inquired about it and said if it were true he would have to submit his resignation.

Secretary of the Navy Robert Smith sought to appease him. Perhaps the delay with the sword amid the applause for others was a minor but touchy point. Finally, after nearly four years, the sword was purchased in London. Secretary Smith on July 5, 1805, wrote him an explanation, saying the commodore charged with procuring it had not had opportunity to attend to the matter and therefore Minister James Monroe had been asked to purchase it. Eventually, July 13, 1805, the sword was sent to him with a note from Secretary Smith. But before it arrived he had forwarded his resignation.

The high spirit which makes good officers at times destroys them. He did not recognize that while resignation might appease a fleeting emotion, it sacrificed a lasting opportunity. He quit and passed into obscurity, when he might possibly have commanded the *Constitution* against the *Guerrière*, or the American fleet at Plattsburg or on Lake Erie. Secretary Smith wrote to him with deep regret: "Your high reputation as an Officer & a Seaman and your distinguished energy of character, might and probably would ultimately have raised you to the highest honors in the Navy."

His victory was the first and it was so smashing that it resounded all the way through the Tripolitan War.

Eaton, at Tunis, had been elated when he heard that the Tripolitan High Admiral Murad Reis was blockaded in Gibraltar. He sent word to

Captains Barron and Bainbridge that a Tripolitan vessel had passed Tunis October 31, 1801, going to Gibraltar to get Murad Reis and his crews and carry them back home. He described the ship minutely, a Greek polacre with Ottoman papers, so she would be recognized. Eaton hurried off a small ship with the information in hope it might lead to the capture of the Admiral and his crews.

"This would be an event so fatal to the Bashaw of Tripoli that it would at once put an end to the war," Eaton said. "He can do nothing without the crews of these two corsairs—They are many of them from the first families of Tripoli—this circumstance, if they fall outo our hands, would excite an insurrection in his Kingdom and give us the intire command of terms."

He suggested that the best method would be to let the Greek vessel pass into Gibraltar, take on her passengers, and then seize her when she left port. The crews, he said, about 350 men, in a desperate situation would be apt to try boarding, against which he assumed the American captains were prepared. Then he again emphasized: "I cannot but repeat, if you get possession of the English renegade, Morad Rais, it will decide our contest with Tripoli; But if he escape and return to Tripoli it will prolong the war and be productive of incalculable mischief."

Commodore Dale directed Consul Gavino to keep a sharp lookout in Gibraltar, and in case Murad Reis sailed his vessels from the port, to go to the rock and watch the direction he took. Then he was to dispatch a boat to Captain Barron of the *Philadelphia* so the frigate might give chase. If he went into the Atlantic the *Philadelphia* should follow him and hunt him down.

But the renegade Admiral decided if he could save himself and his men he would let the boats go, prized as they were as the first-line vessels of the Tripolitan navy. Neither the Greek polacre nor his own ships aided Murad Reis. With local connivance he managed to get his crew into small boats on which they could cross the Strait of Gibraltar stealthily at night and land near Tetuan. From there, with great hardships, they made the long, toilsome journey overland through Algiers and Tunis to Tripoli. Murad Reis was permitted by the Gibraltar authorities to take a British ship to Malta, much to the annoyance of the Americans. Then he crossed by another boat to the shore of Tripoli, where he landed at night thirty miles from the city. He walked overland, and thus avoided the American vessels blockading the port.

Meantime off Tripoli, where there was no uncertainty about the war even if Jefferson did not yet have the nod of Congress, Dale was maintaining such an effective blockade that the city began to feel the pinch of hunger. He communicated with the Bashaw through Nicholas C.

Nissen, the Danish consul, whom Cathcart had left in charge of American affairs. The Bashaw asked Nissen to inquire whether the purpose of the American ships was peaceful or warlike, to which Dale replied that his first intentions were friendly but the matter was out of his hands because Tripoli had declared war on the United States. Dale asked the reasons why the regency had gone to war. He wanted to know what he might tell the President as to the principles on which peace could be restored.

Next day the Bashaw sent an agent to Dale to negotiate a peace. He found the Commodore unwilling even to talk on the subject because, first, his letter of inquiry had not been answered, and second, he was not empowered to negotiate a new treaty. If the Bashaw would send out his officers with any serious intent, Dale might treat with them about a truce.

Reporting to the Secretary of the Navy, Dale said:

> ... I have not heard from him since. he wrote me previous to this he had good reasons for Declaring War against the U S but if I would come on shore, he was very certain that we should be able to make a peace,. he said he did not like the 1 & 12 Articles In the Old Treaty,. he did not wish to have any thing to do with the Dey and Algiers that Mr. Cathcart was always telling him of the Dey of Algiers.

Dale told Secretary Smith that if the United States planned to carry on the war against Tripoli it would be necessary to keep that city closely blockaded. Nothing should be allowed to go in or out. This would require two frigates and two sloops, two to be off the harbor and two to cruise. The *Enterprise* after her battle had brought back so little water that Dale had to leave with the *President* after eighteen days, but ordered the Enterprise to take her place. A general rendezvous was established at Gibraltar. The *President* was again off Tripoli on August 15, this time having on board forty-one Tripolitans whom Dale had taken from a Greek ship, among them being a Tripolitan officer and twenty soldiers. When he tried to effect an exchange with the Bashaw, negotiating through Consul Nissen, all he could get for the forty-one Tripolitan subjects was three Americans, *as soon as the Bashaw could capture them.* Not wanting the Moslem prisoners, Dale put them ashore and sailed on September 3 for Gibraltar. When he got there he learned that Murad Reis was gone. The *Philadelphia,* no longer needed at Gibraltar, took up the patrol off Tripoli in September.

Dale's departure did not mean a lifting of the blockade of Tripoli, but it became nominal. Eaton had first proclaimed it—on his own responsibility as consul at Tunis—and now he maintained it at least in theory, and, in his opinion, fairly well in practice. "I kept the enemy three months in a state of blockade when we had not a ship of war within three hundred leagues from his port," he said. His method was to withhold passports in Tunis from all goods consigned to Tripoli. Since it was the custom for most supplies to pass Tunis, Tripoli suffered. The Bashaw longed for the two ships blockaded in Gibraltar so he might have them loaded with grain. The blockade was something new to him in warfare, and something not very palatable. But Consul O'Brien in Algiers declined to sign a passport for the blockaded ships when the Dey of Algiers sought them for the relief of Tripoli. Still, the blockade was not tight and Tripoli did not feel hunger keenly through the winter.

That winter the *Philadelphia* passed in the harbor of Syracuse, which was to become an American headquarters. The *President,* repaired in Toulon after she struck a rock on Minorca, did not get back to the United States until the following spring. She reached Norfolk April 14, 1802. The enlistments of Dale's men were expiring but the United States was preparing to prosecute the Tripolitan War with more ships and, it hoped, with added vigor.

CHAPTER NINE

An Arm's-Length Blockade

OWING mainly to rough weather with strong southerly winds, the blockade of Tripoli during the winter of 1801–1802 was feeble, and, because of the departure of Dale, so haphazard that Eaton complained about it to the State Department. His paper blockade remained more effective than the warships.

On January 12, 1802, Secretary of the Navy Smith issued a series of orders heralding the dispatch of a new squadron. Captain Alexander Murray was given the *Constellation,* the ship which had been most distinguished in the quasi-war with France, but unseen before in the Mediterranean. The *Enterprise,* still under Lieutenant Sterrett, went out first, to be joined by other ships on their arrival, each sailing as she was ready, the *Enterprise* being followed by the *Constellation,* the *Chesapeake,* the *Adams,* the *New York,* and the *John Adams.* The *Essex* and the *Philadelphia* were still in the Mediterranean and a presentable fleet was therefore available to the new commander.

Again the question arose about touchy Commodore Thomas Truxtun. On the previous year, when the command went to Dale, Secretary Smith withheld from Truxtun the carte blanche he wanted in the Mediterranean and thus the post became unacceptable to him. Now, in early 1802, Truxton was offered the command and ordered to take over the *Chesapeake* at Norfolk.

But Truxtun felt a slight was involved in being given the fleet without having an officer of the rank of captain in command of the flagship under him. That would have been the custom in the established navies but one which a less exacting officer might have waived considering the newness of the American naval establishment and the urgency of the situation. Truxtun made a point of it and wrote Secretary Smith March 3, 1802, that unless he had the captain he would resign.

Perhaps he had not expected the Secretary to take him at his word. His letter and Smith's reaction were unfortunate. But Smith answered on March 13 that because of the reduction of the number of officers by Congress in its last session, there was not a captain available in the service who could be required to take a secondary station on a ship. Then he pushed Truxtun aside: "As this must have been known to you—I cannot but consider your notification as absolute." He regretted that Truxtun had not stated the conditions of his service earlier so that he could request a reconsideration, which the situation no longer permitted because the ship was almost ready to sail. He told Truxtun to turn over the *Chesapeake* to Lieutenant William Smith until Captain Richard Valentine Morris could arrive from Boston to take command of both the vessel and the squadron.

The manner of Truxtun's dismissal was a revealment of Jefferson's methods. Truxtun told of it in a letter to Vice President Aaron Burr, March 22, 1802. Suspecting that Jefferson did not want him to command the squadron, he decided to bring things to a point and called at the President's house. Though he had come to Washington to take the command, and was enroute to Norfolk, Jefferson turned to him and asked which way he was traveling, whether northward or southward. "This question was astonishing and the more so—when I assure you he never opened his lips to me on the subject of the Squadron or our Mediterranean Affairs. I think I can with truth say it was never intended that I should proceed on the command in question . . ."

Dale meantime had resigned from the service. He, too, had felt that the reassignment now offered him as commodore with no captain for his ship was a reduction in rank and dignity from his earlier position. His officers of the *President* wrote him an affectionate letter expressing deep regret over his action. He had done well within the limits of his instructions. He had accumulated a competency in the merchant service on which he retired to a quiet life in Philadelphia. There he died in 1832, entitled to the words on his monument, "An honest man, an incorruptible patriot . . ."

Edward Preble, who was considered, was momentarily in ill health. So Morris was the new commodore, but the country would have been better served by the surer hand of vexatious Truxtun or the seasoned judgment of the veteran Dale. The second year of the Tripolitan War may be characterized appropriately by the phrase, *Truxtun was not there.* Morris' name had not appeared on President Washington's original list of six ship commanders appointed when the Navy was formed. Nor was he among the ten captains listed by the Navy Department on

June 11, 1801, as those being retained after the naval reduction imposed by Congress.

One is entitled to wonder about the appointment of Morris. Many have commented on it but as far as has been noted none has criticized Jefferson nor ventured that this may have been an instance where a little political earthliness rubbed off on the great man's slippers.

Morris was the youngest son of Lewis Morris of Morrisania, New York, now a part of New York City. The father had been a member of the Continental Congress and a signer of the Declaration of Independence. He was a brother of one of the noted men of the Revolution, Gouverneur Morris. Jefferson's Republicanism was at the other end of the political pole from Gouverneur Morris' conservative leanings. But Gouverneur's nephew, Lewis Robert Morris, son of the signer and elder brother of the new commodore, had been a Federalist member of the House from Vermont, during the bitter Jefferson-Burr contest over the Presidency. On the thirty-sixth ballot Morris, presumably at the instigation of Alexander Hamilton, withheld his vote and thus allowed the tied Vermont delegation to cast its ballot for Jefferson. That broke the tie in the House. While the appointment of a commodore has never been looked on as payment of a political debt by Jefferson, or as a gesture of gratitude, Richard Valentine Morris, brother of the Vermont congressman, son of Lewis, and nephew of Gouverneur, who had gone to sea early and had been made a captain by the Adams administration in 1798, was given command of the Mediterranean fleet, a post for which he was not suited by achievement or zest. Jefferson could scarcely have been aware of his lack of talent, but it was a risky appointment.

Morris made what many would regard a major error at the start. He obtained from the Secretary of the Navy April 2, 1802, just before sailing, an order authorizing him to take his wife with him. The unusual request had been made by Mrs. Morris. That the Department assented to it during a period of rough naval warfare along the Barbary shore was even more extraordinary. Mrs. Morris was accompanied by her young son. Midshipman Henry Wadsworth, who wielded words almost as dexterously as would his more distinguished nephew and namesake, Longfellow the poet, described her, though she probably would not have arrested his attention had she not been the only woman on the *Chesapeake*. Writing in his journal for the eyes of some other lady, Wadsworth found:

All the Virtues which constitute the chief loveliness of your sex are in her conspicuous. her knowledge of Geo^y History &c are extensive and a passion for reading is predominant; her person is not beautiful, or even handsome, but she looks very well in a veil; a lively passion for domestic happiness adds lustre to her character and her son little Gerard completes the picture.

Then, as indicative that he fully recognized the want of harmony in the scene, he suggested as a subject for a caricature the Commodore seated on a butt, his lady beside him in a chair reading a book, the boy between them holding the hand of each, and on either side a 9-pounder. On the bulwark at their back were battle axes arranged in the form of a half moon, and a row of cannon shot in the shot locker.

That was not precisely the way to go looking for the Barbary pirates. Mrs. Morris seems from the dispatches to have considerable time on board, but was in Leghorn for a period and later was landed on Malta, where her second child was born. Other ladies were given permission to accompany their husbands. The number is not specified but it must have been small.

Captain Murray, who commanded the *Constellation* and whom Eaton called "Old Woman Murray," had mastered a small merchant vessel at the age of eighteen. During the Revolutionary War he had served early with land forces from his native state of Maryland and fought at Long Island and White Plains. Later he had been a privateersman, then joined the Continental Navy, of which he became a lieutenant in 1781. Now, at the age of forty-seven, he was considerably senior to the other captains and lieutenants in subordinate positions in the fleet. Eaton made another uncharitable remark about him, in a letter to Secretary of State Madison, saying the government "might as well send out Quaker meeting houses to float about the sea, as frigates with Murrays in command."

But despite Morris, Mrs. Morris, Murray, and one or two other overly cautious veterans, the fleet of 1802 contained among the junior officers on its roster some of the great names of American naval history. A tall, handsome, muscular midshipman, Oliver Hazard Perry, seventeen years old, was appointed lieutenant when he was in the Mediterranean under Morris. First Lieutenant Isaac Hull, who ten years later would command the *Constitution* against the *Guerrière,* was ten years older than Perry but was having his first experience in a shooting campaign. Stephen Decatur was a first lieutenant on the *Essex.* Another midshipman, Thomas Macdonough, eighteen years old, was the son of an eminent physician who lived at The Trap near Newcastle, Delaware—a name suggestive of the manner in which Thomas would later catch the British squadron at Plattsburg in the War of 1812. James Lawrence, twenty, had been transferred from the *Adams* to be a lieutenant on the *Enterprise*. Lieutenant David Porter, recently of the *Enterprise,* was now assigned to the *Chesapeake.* Others of later fame joined the fleet the following year, but they did not have their best lessons under Morris.

Where Dale had been on an expedition of observation and intimidation, Morris was allowed all the elbow room he required to wage war. His orders authorized him to subdue and make prizes of the vessels of Tripoli, and directed him to blockade the enemy ports, bottle up their raiders, and take other measures necessary to a belligerent power in addition to providing convoys for American merchant vessels. Because the lazarettos (public hospitals) of the Mediterranean coast were justly regarded, according to Secretary Smith, "the graves of all foreigners unfortunate enough to enter them," the Secretary suggested that he set up a hospital at one of the most healthy ports of the Mediterranean, probably Syracuse, if permission could be obtained.

Before Morris left Hampton Roads, Commodore Dale returned with the *President,* but for inexplicable reasons the two did not confer. Dale had written ahead that Emperor Muley Soliman of Morocco had asked permission to send some of his sailors to Gibraltar to get the Tripolitan ships left there by Murad Reis, the *Meshuda* and the brig, disarm them, and take them to Tripoli, along with four other vessels loaded with wheat. He had already sent an agent to Gibraltar to purchase these wheat boats. This was about the same request as was made earlier by the Dey of Algiers and rejected by O'Brien. Dale had vetoed the Moroccan proposition, and he warned Morris that the Moroccan Emperor would stand watching. Morocco had no warships and was in no condition to fight but the Emperor was trying to procure the beginning of a naval force.

Dale on his return reported the Atlantic Ocean free of corsairs, as far as he could determine from his passage and from speaking enroute with a number of other ships. Morris finally weighed anchor April 27. Though he made a late start his fleet was not in top condition, and some of the important ships had to be laid up for repairs in the Mediterranean. About the first incident after the fleet began to arrive was that Lieutenant Sterrett, the flinty commander of the *Enterprise,* was charged with piracy by the Bey of Tunis and considerable time was wasted for the little American schooner which lived up to its name. Sterrett stopped a xebec off Tripoli which proved to be Tunisian. He sent a boarding party which looked over her cargo, then released her for her voyage to Tunis. On her arrival her commander reported that some of his goods—small articles, it developed—were missing, which threw the Bey and his Divan into a frenzy. They lodged with Consul Eaton the charge of piracy against the American commander, whose fierce battle against the *Tripoli* had not endeared him to the Barbary satraps.

Eaton, who had been asking a little while before, "Have we but one Truxtun and one Sterett in the United States?" turned the charge over to Commodore Morris with some loose talk of his own. Before he had investigated he protested the unmilitary conduct of "gentlemen of the fleet" and said the document he forwarded "exhibits a Scene of debasement as dishonorable to our Arms as it is detrimental to our true interests." He thought the incident "below any thing which has hitherto marked our national character." He could not understand how a "gentleman in Commission should accede to a compromise of his reputation." The circumstances admitted no doubt about the veracity of the charges, he stated.

Why Eaton did not throw this document away before he sent it causes one to suspect how much he treasured his own violent rhetoric. But before he could dispatch it he ascertained facts which caused him to write a postscript. In it he rather meekly stated that the violence complained of was the work of three seamen committed when no officer was present. Sterrett had arrived at Tunis with the *Enterprise,* the three seamen were sent away for court martial, and the Bey was placated. Some other seizures the Bey had been complaining about were traceable to Swedish warships which had arrived to protect that nation's commerce. Sterrett brought word that the Swedish flagpole had been chopped down in Tripoli. The United States thus had an ally. Likely it was the sort of letter Eaton wrote against Sterrett—the first part a blistering denunciation and the second a docile retraction—which caused Commodore Murray to judge that the American consul at Tunis was a "man of lively imagination, rash, credulous, and by no means possessed of sound judgment."

Murray countered Eaton from the beginning. When the Captain reached Gibraltar with the *Constellation,* he found awaiting him there a small boat owned by Eaton, the *Gloria,* commanded by Captain Joseph Bounds, who had orders from Eaton to act against the warships or commerce carriers of Tripoli. Possibly Murray looked on the *Gloria* as Eaton's private little navy, though small vessels of this type were precisely what were needed in the Mediterranean. He refused her supplies, enlisted two of her crew on his own ship, and then expelled Bounds from whatever arrangements Eaton may have made with him to serve the government.

"I believe you will find you were unauthorized in employing the *Gloria* on Public account," he wrote to Eaton. He told Bounds to use the vessel as he saw fit, but not for the government: "Duty compels me to check all unwarrantable expense."

Morris reached Gibraltar with the *Chesapeake* on May 31, 1802. Captain Murray had arrived on May 7. Murray's report to Secretary Smith goes a good way to disprove that the British were out of sympathy with the American purpose of cleansing the Mediterranean of the ages-old scourge of the Barbary pirates. Murray was given permission to anchor in Gibraltar and shown great civility and attention by no less a personage than Vice Admiral Lord Keith. Murray and his officers were the guests of Lord Keith at dinner the day after their arrival, and the Vice Admiral gave assurance of his desire to help the American expedition. Murray attended the dinner welcoming the new governor of Gibraltar, the Duke of Kent. With a sure eye for the niceties in naval architecture, the commanders of the vessels in Keith's squadron came to inspect the American frigates—the *Constellation*, the *Philadelphia*, and the *Essex* —and comment about them admirously.

Similar consideration by the British was shown to Commodore Morris when he brought the *Chesapeake* into Gibraltar with her mainmast sprung. The *Essex* was cruising off the harbor, having taken over the blockade of the two Tripolitan corsairs. Morris found Vice Admiral Lord Keith "remarkably friendly," and entirely willing that the *Chesapeake* use the navy yard facilities for the extensive repairs required on her mast. Morris ordered the *Essex* to remain off Gibraltar until either the *Adams,* expected momentarily, arrived, or the repairs of the *Chesapeake* were completed.

Morris declined to entertain the renewed suggestion from Morocco that the *Meshuda,* the blockaded Tripolitan flagship, be released to carry wheat to Tripoli. James Simpson, American consul to Morocco, reached Gibraltar June 25 with intelligence that the Emperor of Morocco had declared war against the United States because Simpson would not issue the required passport for the *Meshuda* to sail. Simpson had referred the matter to Commodore Morris, whom he had met off Tangier, and who held that there would be no consistency in blockading Tripoli on the one hand and authorizing her ships to enter the harbor on the other. Simpson did not seem entirely certain about the translation of the Arabic word which he construed as meaning the declaration of a *state of war*. The situation was momentarily vague. The Emperor still had no ships to fight with. President Jefferson, not wanting an enemy in the rear of the fleet as it fought Tripoli, mollified the Emperor by sending him one hundred gun carriages he had been wanting.

The *Essex* sailed for the United States June 17 and the *Adams* did not arrive until July 21. Captain Murray had gone to the Tripoli coast with the *Constellation*. Morris was alone at Gibraltar with the *Chesapeake* when the emergency flared with Emperor Muley Soliman of Morocco.

But Morocco was not disposed to go to war with the United States,

and whether from the proximity of the *Chesapeake* off Tangier or because of other reflections, Muley Soliman sent word that Simpson might
return to his house for a six months' trial period. There was haggling
about the presents due from the Americans on such an occasion. Simpson, having a good frigate nearby, declined to give any. Peace was preserved but it looked like such a nervous peace that Morris left the *Adams*
under Captain Hugh C. Campbell to patrol the straits and keep an eye
on Tangier.

Already the year was wearing on without much being accomplished.
Sweden conducted a moderate blockade of Tripoli, aided by the one
American frigate, the *Constellation*. Murray was off the city with the
Constellation when, on July 22, 1802, he espied eight Tripolitan gunboats, among them the galley of Murad Reis, about three miles to the
leeward of the city. The galley had one long 24-pounder and two brass
guns, probably those given to the Bashaw by Cathcart in lieu of the
barrels of powder due on the signing of the treaty. The *Constellation*
crowded on sail in an effort to cut off the gunboats but they had both
sail and oars and reached the protection of the harbor forts before the
frigate had them in range. Murray continued after them until half a
mile off the beach. For half an hour the frigate exchanged shots with the
gunboats and inflicted on them, according to Murray, considerable
damage. The most interesting feature of the abortive engagement was
that it brought out the Tripolitan army of about 6,000 men, which paraded on the beach. Murray claimed they were routed by the American
shells. The small action informed the enemy, according to the American
captain, that the Americans had no dread of the formidable Tripolitan
gunboats. "It had a pleasing effect upon our Young Officers, who stood
their fire admirably well," Murray added.

When he had been more than two months in front of Tripoli, Murray
reported to Morris that the blockade was inadequate. The Americans
did not have the required small vessels, brigs, and schooners, which
could lay close to the shore where the frigates could not venture and cut
off the small galleys that were running in and out under cover of darkness. Murray turned back some larger vessels making for Tripoli but
he could not keep out the small Tunisian craft which slipped in despite
his vigilance. All he could undertake was an arm's-length blockade.

The *Boston*, 28, under Captain Daniel McNeill, who had taken Robert
R. Livingston to France to be U.S. minister, had been ordered to join
the Mediterranean squadron and she did put into Gibraltar ahead of
Murray or Morris, then appeared off Tripoli, but never did the Captain
report to the commodore of the fleet or Captain Murray, his senior.
Off Tripoli the *Boston* captured four Tunisian coastal vessels in May,

then encountered a Tripolitan squadron which a Swedish warship, coming up on the windward, drove off with half a dozen shots.

McNeill had appeared in the Mediterranean with the *Boston* before Dale departed for the United States. He commanded loosely. He left some of his officers and men behind at ports and picked up and carried off others, notably three French officers, whom he should have left at Toulon. He was indifferent to quarantine regulations. Dale had to clean up difficulties left in the *Boston*'s wake. "Nothing should tempt a man to deviate from the truth in his report to a Health officer," Dale protested to the Secretary of the Navy. Eventually McNeill was relieved in August at the President's request, but he took the *Boston* home with him that fall. Only Eaton appeared to like him, and that because he would fight.

When the Swedish fleet went off for provisions, the *Constellation* was the sole vessel maintaining the blockade of Tripoli and it was far from effective. In June five row galleys had slipped out of Tripoli and one of them captured the American merchant brig *Franklin,* under Captain Andrew Morris, out of Philadelphia. The capture was made off distant Cape Palos, Spain. The vessel and the cargo, which was being carried from Marseilles to the West Indies, were sold and the master and his crew were taken as captives to Tripoli and paraded through the streets. A little later, through the intercession of Danish Consul Nissen, the master was allowed the freedom of the town. The British Consul McDonough claimed the two sub-officers and one seaman of the *Franklin* as British subjects and procured their release, while two passengers, both French, were liberated. The master, mate, carpenter, steward, and one sailor, all Americans, were held.

The corsair had required a month to take the crew into Tripoli, and the master, Captain Morris, was much disappointed that an American warship did not intercept them somewhere enroute. He admonished the American commanders through Cathcart that they should keep an especial watch off Cape Bon, the northern point of Tunis, which should have been obvious to everyone.

This lapse was minor compared with the nature of the blockade the master observed off Tripoli. When the corsair approached her home port, with loot and the captive Americans in the hold, she began to salute the two frigates on patrol, one Swedish and the other the *Constellation* under Murray; and these ships, according to the master, "never made the least effort to obstruct our progress when it was certainly in their power to Capture or run the Pirate on shore." Morris, the master of the *Franklin,* reported the facts in a letter to Cathcart in Leghorn.

Morris became a sort of official chargé d'affaires for the United States in Tripoli. Eaton, who had no official status in dealing with Tripoli, wrote the Bashaw from Tunis requesting release of the five Americans in compensation for the Tripolitan prisoners Commodore Dale had set free the year before. Finally Consul General O'Brien, who had tried to ransom them when the corsair put in at Algiers enroute from Cape Palos to Tripoli, gave the Bashaw $5,000 for their release, or $1,000 a head. The intercession of O'Brien irritated Cathcart, who was in charge of negotiations with Tripoli though O'Brien was his senior. He thought the Consul at Algiers was not familiar with Dale's release of the Tripolitans as an earnest against Americans the Bashaw might capture. The ransom was paid before the Bashaw had taken a position on such an exchange. Morris and his four men left Tripoli on September 22 aboard a Danish vessel for Algiers, escorted by a chiaus of the Bashaw.

Captain Andrew Morris' experience was significant as disclosing the nature of Commodore Richard Valentine Morris' blockade. The Commodore had been ordered to employ his best efforts to keep the enemy's vessels in port, for which he was to lay his entire force before Tripoli, unless it should be necessary to detach a vessel to watch Morocco and the outlet to the Atlantic at Gibraltar. Finally Morris sailed from Gibraltar on August 17 for Leghorn with a convoy of American merchantmen. The year was advancing without much action in front of Tripoli. He tarried along the way and did not reach Leghorn until October 12, where he met the *Constellation,* which was going to Toulon for repairs.

Eaton at Tunis was stirred to one of his emotional outbursts by reports that the American squadron was leisuring along the coasts of Spain, France, and Italy, the officers enjoying social affairs in honor of the Commodore and his wife, who appeared to be feted despite Midshipman Wadsworth's comment that "she looks very well in a veil." Eaton in one of his excesses drew a comparison between the pleasures of Morris and the frivolities of Anthony and Cleopatra, then noted on the margin of his letter-book, "I would recommend to the government . . . to station a company of comedians and a seraglio before the enemy's port."

Eaton, never of robust health, had left Tunis for a vacation in Leghorn at the end of 1801, sickened further, quite obviously, by the continued arrival of tribute from the United States. While at war with Tripoli, the United States nevertheless was fulfilling its treaty obligations with the other Barbary regencies. The *George Washington* under the command of Lieutenant John Shaw—before she was laid up in the naval reduction program which involved the older ships—made a return trip with a store of naval goods for Algiers and convoyed a tribute ship of arresting name, *Peace and Plenty,* to Tunis. The naval surgeon of the *Philadelphia,* Dr. William Turney, was chargé d'affaires during Eaton's absence. The significance of Eaton's sojourn was that he set up arrangements in Sicily and with the King of Sardinia by which American warships, which were finding the British port of Gibraltar too remote a base for operations against Tripoli, could use the southern Italian ports.

While elements of the fleet were at Leghorn the first of two fatal and disconcerting duels occurred, which distracted the officers and caused Eaton to observe that blood was shed in personal quarrels though precious little could be found on the Barbary shore. The affair of honor was between two Marine Corps officers. Captain James McKnight, known as a famous duelist, was killed by Lieutenant Richard H. L. Lawson; both were from the *Constellation*. The fated meeting attracted such widespread notice in the early naval service that the circumstances should be reviewed briefly.

What they clashed over originally does not appear in the extensive correspondence, but the quarrel began some time before the *Constellation* was in Leghorn Road. Captain McKnight, who commanded the Marine detachment on the frigate, and was regarded by Captain Murray as a "deserving officer . . . tho rather irritable," sent the challenge. Lawson, less skilled and not looked on as the aggressor, accepted on condition the distance should be three paces. McKnight's second, Lieutenant Jacob Jones (later commander of the *Wasp* in her brilliant victory over the British sloop *Frolic*) refused to assent to such terms and declared Lawson was an assassin for proposing the distance, and dubbed him a coward.

Nothing further happened until the *Constellation* reached Leghorn Road, when the controversy was renewed with added spirit. Lawson, now taking the offensive, circulated a paper among the *Constellation* officers saying he had "proved the famous Duellist a coward." The paper was described by Captain Daniel Carmick, of the Marine Corps, a friend of McKnight, as containing many other aggravating statements. McKnight conferred with Carmick, who told him the world would concede neither Lawson nor he was a coward. He had passed his word of honor to his second that he would agree to any arrangement the second might make, and that, Carmick explained, was a sufficient demonstration of his courage. Moreover, said Carmick, if he had been the second he would not have allowed the Captain to fight at three paces because he could never have justified himself for bringing a friend to certain death, nor would he have cared to run the risk of being hanged for his part in such an affair.

Captain McKnight returned to the *Constellation* from his talk with Carmick and there the dispute broke out with fresh violence—"to the highest pitch," as others described the stormy session. Captain Murray, being deaf, heard and knew nothing of the angry exchange. An agreement was reached to fight, advancing at six paces with a brace of pistols, and should both antagonists fail, then they would resume the combat with cutlasses. They met under the proper requirements of the code and fired simultaneously. McKnight missed but Lawson's ball went through the exact center of the famous duelist's heart.

Captain Carmick was nearby and rushed to his friend, who had been killed instantly. Carmick had the body taken to the American Hotel, where it was learned that the law required transfer to a vault near the cemetery so the coroner might make his investigation. When all was in legal form the coroner's surgeon cut the heart from the body. Carmick remonstrated vigorously. As he reported it, he "even threatened to make a corpse of the surgeon," if it developed, as he suspected, the surgeon was cutting the body merely for the instruction of his students.

When finally convinced that everything being done was the law of the land, the Marine captain said he "left them up to their Armpits in blood." On the next morning they buried Captain McKnight's body with as many officers present as could be spared from the ships, but neither of the ship commanders then in the harbor, Morris and Murray, would attend, nor would they permit the Marine Corps detachment to fire a funeral salute. The burial was in a plot in the English cemetery, near the grave of Tobias George Smollett, the Scotch sailor-novelist who in Leghorn had completed his life and *Humphrey Clinker* together.

Lieutenant Edward Hall, a Marine Corps officer on the *Constellation*, in reporting about the duel to Lieutenant Colonel William W. Burrows, commandant of the Marine Corps, expressed sorrow but seemed to find nothing reprehensible in the event. "Both parties behaved with great firmness & presence of mind," he wrote proudly. As to Captain Mc-Knight, "fate has given him what the world calls an honorable death." He reassured the commandant that the dispute did not arise from any cause relating to the Marine Corps, but instead, they clashed "as private gentlemen."

Deaf old Captain Murray, who had not known until after the fatal bullet that there had been even an altercation on board his ship, placed both Lieutenants Lawson and Jones, his second, under arrest. Nor had he known that another duel had earlier been fought between two of his officers. This had been so carefully hushed that all the facts even now cannot be ascertained, but Lieutenant Hall, who had found merit in the McKnight-Lawson duel, had been wounded. It, too, apparently was fought at close range, for Hall was advancing, intent on blowing his adversary's brains out, when he was stopped four feet short by a ball in his groin and another in his wrist. Captain Carmick, who referred to this duel, did not give the other contestant's name.

After the fleet had gone to Malta it was electrified that winter by the excitement of still another duel, this the most spectacular of all because it involved British and American officers. The American principal was Joseph Bainbridge, younger brother of Captain William Bainbridge and a midshipman on the *New York*, a ship which had taken refuge in Valletta Harbor from a storm. The American officers obtained liberty. Experienced old Commodore Dale was not at hand to warn them not to get into "any scrapes with the People on shore." But British warships were in the harbor and the Americans thought they detected a sneering attitude. According to the American version, one of the British officers was heard to remark, "Those Yankees will never stand the smell of powder."

The group of Americans drew off to the hotel lobby to confer about their course of action and unhappily the British officers followed. Then the officer who had made the insulting reference collided somewhat roughly with Midshipman Bainbridge. He was Mr. Cochran, a resident of Valletta, and secretary to the governor general of Malta, Sir Alexander Ball, who was a friend of Nelson and had been commander of the *Alexander*, and victor over Bruey's flagship the *Orient* in the Battle of the Nile. After Cochran had bumped into Bainbridge three more times, apparently for emphasis, the young midshipman hauled off, caught the secretary a good blow, and dropped him to the floor. That, at least, is the American version.

Cochran was an experienced duelist and the Americans thought he was merely trying to set up a little easy practice. On the following morning Bainbridge received a challenge, delivered to him on shipboard. At that point Lieutenant Stephen Decatur, who recognized that the young midshipman had never fought a duel and knew nothing about the code, and was not even a good pistol shot, stepped in as Bainbridge's second. He accepted the challenge but, to test the secretary's mettle, chose pistols and specified a distance of four paces, instead of the ten paces proposed by the second for the challenger.

When Cochran's second said, "This looks like murder, Sir," Decatur replied, "No, Sir, this looks like death, but not like murder. Your friend is a professional duelist, mine is wholly inexperienced with the use of the pistol. If you insist on ten paces I will fight your friend at that distance."

But the challenger would not allow the substitution, nor would Decatur modify the distance. The duel was fought with pistols at the deadly distance of four paces. On the signal the two fired simultaneously. Bainbridge's ball went through Cochran's hat. Perhaps the Englishman was not such an experienced duelist after all, or was nervous about the distance, for his ball missed entirely.

This exchange would have been sufficient to satisfy the requirements of the code, but it was the prerogative of the challenger to so signify. Cochran, the challenger, did not feel that he had obtained satisfaction. Another fire was requested. Decatur is credited with cautioning Bainbridge to fire lower, but that should have been obvious to anyone who had hit his adversary's hat. On the second fire the British duelist again missed but Bainbridge's ball hit Cochran below the eye and he fell, mortally wounded.

The grieved Governor demanded that both Bainbridge and Decatur be turned over to the civil courts for trial. Fleet commander Morris' flagship, the *Chesapeake,* was scheduled to leave in the winter for the United States. Bainbridge and Decatur were suspended and ordered home. Apparently they were secreted carefully for a considerable period, because word came from London to the British authorities that they should be apprehended and charged. In the United States, an investigation led to the conclusion that there were no grounds against them. Midshipman Wadsworth, who was in the harbor at the time, seemed to reflect the American attitude when he said, "Mr. Bainbridge was clearly in the right & behav'd honorably throughout the affair." On reaching the United States the following spring, Decatur received from the Navy Department two weeks' leave. He and Bainbridge returned to the Mediterranean four months later on the new brig, *Argus.*

It is a point of interest that the commander of the *New York* at Malta during this affair involving his midshipman was Captain James Barron, who nineteen years later would kill Stephen Decatur in an equally deplorable duel.

Commodore Morris had been in the Spanish, French, and Italian ports and finally Syracuse and Malta, in the last seeking protection from the storms. The year of 1802 had now ended, but he had not yet appeared in front of Tripoli, which had experienced a good autumn because of unusually heavy grain crops. The pinch felt when Dale was off the city had passed under the softer blockade of Morris.

Captain Murray had returned home with the *Constellation.* Considerable shifting occurred among the officers, and some of the frigates had to be laid up for caulking or repairs. But the main feature of Morris' conduct of the squadron was that it could not quite make the final leagues to the capital city of the enemy. The suggestion has been made that Morris did not want his wife shot at, but he might have advanced while she was in Leghorn or Malta.

"Who but an American," Eaton asked, "would ever propose to himself to bring a wife to war against the ferocious savages of Barbary? The circumstance carries conviction to the enemy that the object is not fighting."

One incident disclosed to Mediterranean shippers that patience is required in pressing a claim before the American Congress. It involved the capture by the *Enterprise* of a Turkish ship, *Paulina,* with a cargo from the Levant consigned partly to the Isle of Jerba, a possession of Tunis, and partly to Tripoli. The *Paulina* stopped at Malta, then sailed for Tripoli, intending, according to the Bey of Tunis, merely to land two passengers. When Commodore Morris learned she had sailed he sent the *Enterprise* in pursuit. Lieutenant Sterrett caught the *Paulina* on January 17, 1803, and brought her back as a prize. The Bey of Tunis demanded immediate restitution but Morris contended that the owner of the greater part of the cargo was a Tripolitan and that the cargo was destined for Tripoli. He sent the papers to the admiralty court at Gibraltar for a disposition of the case, and instructed that whatever belonged to Tunis should be restored. The case became of interest not only to the Ottoman consul at Malta but eventually the Navy Department and President Jefferson.

The principal owner of the cargo, it developed, was David Vallanzino, a Jew who was alleged by the Americans to be a subject of Tripoli and by the Bey a subject of Tunis. When Vallanzino could obtain no satisfaction he went to the United States to prosecute his claim for restitution and damages. The Secretary of the Navy prepared a letter for him saying that if a court of justice found in his favor his property would be restored and damages allowed, and offering to pay his fare to Philadelphia and expenses while in the United States should he desire to return to the Mediterranean. But he remained and submitted his case to Congress. The House Committee on Claims held hearings. Then, apparently discouraged over the ponderous processes of government, Vallanzino committed suicide in the Capitol lobby. War, even a little war, had trodden over him and crushed him down.

Finally on January 30, 1803, Commodore Morris got his squadron out of Malta intending to display his strength at last in front of Tripoli. Cathcart was charged by the government with conducting peace negotiation with the Bashaw, and Morris sailed with the object of offering the Bashaw terms. But before he cleared Malta a gale rose and blew for eleven days, making it impossible to approach the Tripolitan shore. The *Chesapeake* came near losing her masts. Morris was using the *John Adams* as his flagship and with her on February 10, 1803, made Malta, where on the next day he was reunited with the *New York*. He sailed again on February 19, this time in the *Chesapeake*, and for Tunis instead of Tripoli. Eaton had summoned him and he went.

In Tunis, Morris encountered more trouble than he likely would have experienced had he sailed boldly into Tripoli Harbor. Instead of enter-

ing Tripoli in triumph he had the humiliation of being arrested in Tunis.
First he was plunged into the midst of the *Paulina* case, over which the
Bey threatened to declare war. But he and Eaton were able to persuade
the potentate that the case would be handled equitably, though Morris
yielded in agreeing that whatever belonged to Tunis would be returned
it, and approved the commercial agent's list, though obviously much was
lugged in. Then Morris prepared to leave the port. Perhaps it was his
oversight in not paying a farewell call on the Bey which led to his dis-
comfiture. He cut short his conferences with the Bey's commercial agent,
Hadgi Unis Ben Unis, and then ignored the carriage held in readiness
to take him to the palace for an official departure. Attended by Captain
Rodgers of the *John Adams*, Cathcart, and others, he went to the Marina,
there to be transported to his ship in the outer harbor.

But the Bey, feeling that the Commodore had not shown the proper
manners, had his guards at the Marina ahead of them. The seasoned
Commodore Dale would never have allowed himself to get into such a
position ashore in a hostile city.

When Eaton had written Morris about the Bey's unruliness he had put
in a phrase which should have placed a prudent commander on guard.
"Affairs of incalculable moment to the United States here," he said, "require the assistance of your counsel, perhaps your force." Forewarned,
Morris was not forearmed.

The subordinate officers were allowed to leave the mole for their vessels but Morris, Rodgers, and Cathcart were placed under arrest and
notified by the commercial agent that they could not leave Tunis until
they had paid $34,000. The fleet commander had permitted himself to
be made a hostage. The sum had been promised to the Bey by Eaton
in repayment of a loan which he had expended in what he regarded
the interests of the service. The commercial agent claimed repayment
was due as soon as the first American warship should reach Tunis. Now
a powerful fleet, the *Chesapeake*, the *New York*, the *John Adams*, and
the *Enterprise*, was on hand and the crafty Bey had rendered it impotent by seizing its commodore.

Eaton had used the money mainly in furtherance of a scheme to install
a new bashaw as regent in Tripoli. In this activity, the major developments from which were to come later in the Tripolitan War, he had the
sanction of the Washington government and Commodore Dale. He denied that he had made an outright promise of the money by the next
American ship, but had said only that he *hoped* he would be able to
pay when the squadron arrived. This minor point led to a great deal
of bad blood between Morris and Eaton. The Commodore, who thought

he had been trapped by Eaton into coming ashore, reported to the Secretary of the Navy that Eaton was "an accessory to my detention."

Eaton's conduct did not bear out the complaint. He was never devious. He was forthright, a man of direct action, a hitter and not a plotter. He stormed at the Bey for breaking faith with him after promising safe conduct for the American Commodore on shore. The argument continued for days, until Eaton finally made himself so obnoxious that the Bey impetuously demanded his recall.

Relations between the two had grown increasingly fretful and were at last at the breaking point. The Bey had been saying he wanted a less obstinate consul, one whose attitude would be more congenial with his own interests. And Eaton likewise was thoroughly disgusted over the succession of demands, the continual controversy, the angry exchanges. He had written Secretary Madison, "I cannot serve another summer in this station." Again, he told Madison that Siberia or Botany Bay would suit him better than Tunis.

Before the events leading to his formal dismissal Eaton traded a good many invectives with the Bey's commercial agent, Hadgi Unis, who held his bond for the $34,000. Again the parley was moved to the Bey's palace, where a volcano of charges and countercharges erupted. Eaton reiterated his denials, said he had some money of his own which he had intended to throw into the pot if his government would give some relief, then demanded to know whether he had ever yet deceived the Bey.

"No," Bey Hamouda Pacha replied. "You have a good heart but a bad head." He went on to lecture Eaton, lapsing into Oriental serenity, saying those entrusted with important affairs must be endowed with a great deal of forbearance, which he was obliged to exercise himself, and which he recommended to the American consul.

Eaton's reply was characteristic: "No wonder my head is bad when I am surrounded by so many imposters." Then he shifted his ground and claimed he had been robbed by the Prime Minister, who happened to be present.

The argument grew so heated that Cathcart, who had been serving as dragoman, asked the Bey to supply another interpreter, but this the potentate declined, though Commodore Morris joined in the request. "You are mad," shouted the Prime Minister at Eaton. "Yes, you are mad," the Bey agreed loudly.

Cathcart in quoting said the Bey "stuttered it in a Phrenzy," and at the same time curled his whiskers. "I will turn you out of my kingdom," he added. Then, addressing Cathcart, he continued: "Tell the commodore this man is mad." He went back to the incident of Eaton knocking down Famin, the Frenchman, on the street and allegedly bulldozing others, whereupon Eaton declared if he had Famin and some of the others somewhere else they would receive a lot worse treatment.

"You might do as you please in your own country," said the Bey, "but if you had killed a man in mine I would have had you hung at your door."

While such a passage of ill humor between a minister and the head of the government to which he was accredited might seem incredible by later day standards, such was the tough-fibered American diplomacy of 1803 as conducted by William Eaton.

At this stage Commodore Morris broke in and asked Cathcart to inquire of the Bey whether he was really determined to dismiss Eaton.

"Yes," said the Bey. "He shall no longer remain here. Inform him."

Morris said he had no power to name a new consul but under the treaty the Bey did have a right to have a consul changed, therefore he would appoint an officer to act in Eaton's place until the will of his government could be known. The heated exchange seemed at least to have cleared the air. Morris asked if any impediment remained to his going aboard his ship.

"None at all," the Bey answered. "Settle with Hadgi Unis and I wish you a good voyage."

That evening they worked out a settlement. A credit of $7,000 was agreed to as representing the value of the ship Eaton still owned at Leghorn, the *Gloria*, which would be sold. Eaton had owned two small vessels, the *Morning Star* and the *Gloria*, and it is not clear what had happened to one of them. He had written to his wife Eliza, who remained in the United States, about his hopes from these ships: "as valuable and handsome as any on the ocean of their size." He intended to keep them employed at cargo-carrying until he could increase his capital to $30,000, on which, he told his wife, they could live decently in a country town. Now whatever portion of the $30,000 he had accumulated was about to be obliterated. He promised an additional personal payment of $5,000, apparently all the cash he could raise. His cargo-carrying had languished. This reduced the obligation he had contracted to pay—for a variety of purposes but always, he felt, in the interests of the United States—to $22,000. For that amount the Danish consul, Captain Holch, agreed to stand security and Morris was allowed to return to his flagship. But Hadgi Unis insisted that someone of responsibility remain on shore until all the ends of the deal were tied together and Captain Rodgers and Cathcart remained.

When the Commodore got on board he sent the $22,000 from the *Chesapeake* by Dr. George Davis, surgeon of the *Enterprise*, whom he

designated chargé d'affaires. Before the money was turned over to Hadgi
Unis, Eaton gave Morris as security an assignment of all his property
to the U.S. government. He was never much concerned about his personal fortune where the interests of the United States were involved.
He had employed the money in furtherance of the scheme that would
have a later flowering. He had reported the expenditure to the State
Department, and had every reason to believe it would be authorized.

Back on the *Chesapeake* the detention of the Commodore many days
on shore had caused wonder, then blame of Eaton, whose personal
finances were held to be involved. Midshipman Wadsworth wrote scut-
tlebutt in his journal March 10: "The cause of the Com^rs detention is
REPORTED to be this 'Mr. Eaton entering into large speculations, became
involved in debt: this debt amounted to 34,000 dollars & was owing to
the Bey: Not being able to pay it he gave his Consular Seal as a security:
the debt of course became a public one.' "

Though in the instance of the Danish vessels Eaton had ignored the
opportunity to engage in speculations and pad his own pocketbook, he
was nevertheless being charged in shipboard rumor with the offense. He
was not mad; he was amply able to hand back contempt and scorn with
interest.

Now his service at Tunis was ended, and to all appearances his career
as a factor in the Barbary Wars. Pitifully he wrote Madison: "I am now
totally destitute of funds and credit here, and do not know where to
obtain the means of daily subsistence." But his spirit was unbroken, as
his subsequent career in North Africa disclosed.

Mordecai M. Noah, who was United States consul to Tunis a decade
later, and who left an entrancing account of his experiences, fully appreciated his predecessor's trials. Eaton was "in a state of constant irritation, subjected to the insolent demands of a nest of pirates, which he
resisted with a firmness bordering on indiscretion."

Eaton, Rodgers, and Cathcart shook off the dust of unfriendly Tunis
and went out to the fleet, which at 8:00 A.M., March 13, 1803, sailed for
Algiers. There it picked up Consul O'Brien, who was retiring. Affairs
there were in bad shape, also. The Dey was quarreling because the
United States had sent him $30,000 in money instead of in stores. He
demanded the stores but refused to yield the money. Cathcart had been
designated consul general at Algiers to replace O'Brien, but the Dey
refused to receive him on the ground that he was unsuited by character
for the position. His character should have been known in Algiers but
it had been good enough when he served as secretary to the preceding
Dey. Perhaps the Dey was referring to his temperament, and criticism
would have been justified on that score.

The fleet went on to Gibraltar. Tripoli was far behind and after more than a year Morris had never reached it. But he concluded he would have to do some face-saving, and the result was the first spirited fighting along the Tripoli shore.

Eaton returned to the United States on the merchant ship *Perseverance.*

CHAPTER TEN

The Battle of the Feluccas

MORRIS, after a year of dallying, decided to make a final descent on Tripoli and ordered his ships back from Gibraltar. He shifted his broad pennant to the *New York*. Accompanied by the *John Adams* under Rodgers and the *Enterprise* under Hull, he sailed by way of Leghorn and Malta, to be joined by the *Adams* under Campbell off Tripoli in May, 1803.

Enroute one of the ghastly accidents of the Barbary Wars occurred on April 25 aboard the *New York*, when a quantity of powder exploded in the gunner's storeroom in the cockpit, not far from the main powder magazine. To those on board it seemed that the ship was blowing apart; then that she would burn to the water's edge. The boats were hoisted and distress signals were fired. But the officers formed the men, allayed the consternation, and all hands were put to work with wet blankets, swabs, and buckets. After a stubborn fight for an hour and a half, the flames were extinguished and the vessel saved. Later investigation indicated the fire resulted from the carelessness of a gunner's mate in returning signal lanterns to the storeroom in the early morning.

Fourteen were killed outright or died from their burns. The dead included the chief gunner, two midshipmen, the surgeon's mate, the commodore's secretary, the purser's steward, the marine sentinel at the magazine passage, and the loblolly boy. Many were burned shockingly but recovered. The ship seemed to be saved almost miraculously because the explosion burst open the door leading to the main powder magazine and it was mere chance that neither the force of the explosion nor the flames reached quite that far. Two young lieutenants, already famed under Truxtun and Sterrett, David Porter and Isaac Chauncey, both of whom became squadron commanders in the War of 1812, distinguished themselves charging the flames when that called for probably more courage than boarding a corsair.

Morris' first task when his squadron reached Malta, May 1, 1803, was to put carpenters to work repairing the *New York*'s fire wounds. This, together with recoppering the bottom of the valiant little *Enterprise*, required three weeks, a period during which Captain John Rodgers with the *John Adams* was having a fresh experience with the old flag-ship of Murad Reis, the *Meshuda*, now the property of Dey Muley Soliman of Morocco and named, according to the Moroccan listing, the *Meshouda*. The ship had been blockaded for two years in Gibraltar, though the members of the crew had long since worked their ways back to Tripoli. Emperor Muley Soliman laid claim to the vessel at the time he was soliciting permission to ship wheat to Tripoli. How the title passed is not clear from the records except that he issued a proclamation September 17, 1802, asserting ownership and announcing that the ship's captain was Arraiz Omar, a native of Tetuan; that he had manned her with forty mariners and that "she carried Our Victorious Flag, and goes on the fulfillment of Our Orders and intentions."

In the extensive correspondence exchanged among American officers and the Barbary governments over the status of this ship, which every-one seemed to have forgotten was the old *Betsey* out of Boston, an officer of the Marine Corps, Lieutenant Presley N. O'Bannon, destined for a great deal of hard service and glory on the Barbary Coast and in American history, made his first appearance. Writing to Lieutenant Colonel Burrows, Marine Corps commandant, about the pleasing pros-pect of being able to leave the "wretched Hole" of Gibraltar, he told how the Moorish ship was being fitted out, it was generally believed, for the purpose of war against the United States. With foresight he suggested that if the *Meshouda* got out of the harbor she would be back again under American guard. But he could see as clearly as did Jefferson and the State and Navy Departments, that war with Morocco was to be dreaded and avoided. Whereas the other Barbary States operated in the Mediterranean, Morocco faced the Atlantic as well and could dis-patch her corsairs—if she ever got a navy together—to the Atlantic shipping lanes.

The *Meshouda* was being guarded by the *Adams*, commanded by Captain Campbell. O'Bannon confided to his superior, "I am sorry to have it in my power to tell you that Capt. Campbell has conducted him-self in such a manner as to forfeit all the respect of his Officers on Board his own Ship and I believe it extends to all who know him." Campbell was not ordered home until the next year. With such examples as McNeill, Morris, Murray, and Campbell, it was clear that the ships were not being officered in a way Jefferson had a right to expect. And as for judges of proper conduct, events were to show that there was scarcely anyone in the Mediterranean better qualified to judge than Lieutenant O'Bannon.

For seven months the Moroccan Emperor had demanded the right to take the *Meshouda* out of Gibraltar. Finally, with the assent of Commodore Morris, and in order to minimize the threat of a Moroccan war, Consul Simpson issued the required passport, but stipulated that the ship should not trade with a port under the American blockade. The Moroccan consul at Gibraltar promised she would not go to Tripoli. Meantime the brig which had accompanied Murad Reis and the *Meshouda* from Tripoli had been sold and her guns had been loaded on the *Meshouda*. Who bought her and who got the money from her sale do not appear in the records but she ceased to be a factor in the war.

Captain John Rodgers cruised from Malta with the *John Adams* on May 8. On the afternoon of the 12th, off Tripoli, he sighted a sail which on examination proved to be the *Meshouda* making for the Tripoli Harbor. Rodgers, who understood the purpose of a blockade and was given to direct action, chased and overhauled the vessel at sunset, boarded her, took the forty seamen and fifteen passengers prisoners, examined the cargo, and towed the ship back to Malta. Her passport was no safeguard against Rodgers. She had not only her own twenty-eight guns and the brig's cannon, but also a variety of naval stores she had picked up enroute, either at Algiers or Tunis, for she had put into both ports. Her agents described them as nothing more than "provisions and necessities" but when Captain Rodgers' men made an examination they proved to be cutlasses, guns, hemp, and other contraband articles not a part of her authorized cargo when she cleared Gibraltar.

When the prize was towed back to Malta, arriving May 18, Commodore Morris wrote to Consul Simpson at Tangier that the captain of the *Meshouda* would be punished if he were trying to run the blockade with this contraband on his own responsibility, without the orders of the Emperor of Morocco. But he summed it up: "This whole business appears to be a detestable fraud." Reports became current in the fleet that Morris disapproved the capture and held that if there were blame it should attach to Rodgers. He did comment that he was getting under way for the Tripoli coast and sincerely wished to avoid a war with the Emperor.

Leaving the *Meshouda* at Malta to be picked up later, the fleet, consisting of the *New York*, the *John Adams*, and the *Enterprise*, sailed May 20 for Tripolitan waters, there to be joined six days later by the *Adams*. Morris at last had a presentable squadron in front of the city and might enforce his demands for peace. He chose to handle the negotiations in person. Cathcart, who had been entrusted with the responsibility by the administration, had been left in Leghorn. Morris merely ignored him.

Almost at the moment the fleet reached the Tripoli coast, the swift

little *Enterprise* was sent in pursuit of a sail the *John Adams* espied
west of the harbor. Lieutenant Hull, running parallel with the coast,
was fired on by the land batteries and replied from the *Enterprise* with
a broadside, which caused the Tripolitan ship, a felucca of 25 to 30
tons, to run ashore. Her crew abandoned her and scampered up the
beach, leaving their red flag still flying. (A felucca was a common
Mediterranean sailboat, slim, fast, and lateen rigged.)

Hull now waited for the *New York* to come up with Commodore
Morris, who wavered whether or not to launch his small boats and take
off the prize, but at last determined against it. While the American
vessels were close by the shore a body of cavalry came charging out
from the city and began firing with a two-gun battery, but at too great
a distance from the ships to inflict damage. The officers of the *New York*
were much disappointed at not being allowed to capture and pull off
the felucca and to test themselves against a cavalry detachment which
came close down to the shore to guard it, but Morris was not disposed
to fight.

The *Enterprise* fired a broadside in an unsuccessful effort to hull the
felucca; then the Americans drew off, leaving the red flag of Tripoli
flying on her. Observation showed she was an unarmed oyster boat and
in the opinion of the Commodore, ventured perhaps in self-justification,
not worth much effort. But the incident marked an inconclusive exchange with the enemy on the very day the Morris squadron arrived.
Midshipman Wadsworth noted in his journal: "Thus ends the narrative
of the first day. Twelve months pass'd after I entered the Straits before
I saw Tripoly. The *Chesapeak* returned to America without seeing her
enemies' Port."

Five days after the squadron arrived, a small ship and nine gunboats
were sighted close to the land five miles west making for Tripoli Harbor.
There they were protected by the battery which had been engaged the
day the fleet arrived. The *New York*, the *John Adams*, and the *Enterprise*
made after them with a gentle wind blowing onshore and seemed certain to cut them off. But the wind and sun died down together. Though
the Americans were able to get in range they had to fire in darkness at
the flash of the enemy guns. Young Wadsworth complained: "Had there
been anyone on board who like Joshua of Old could have commanded
the sun to stand still, The Gun Boats would have been our[s], Tripoly,
& thy people our Slaves." He gave a picture of this first extensive night
bombardment directed at the seacoast batteries five miles west of
Tripoli:

"It was a most elegant sight. the frequent flash and heavy report of
the gun boats: the still more frequent broad Sides of our squadron

form'd the most sublime scene you can imagine. The shot from the Gun boats whistl'd over us & struck all around—none hit us."

The Americans engaged at a disadvantage, since the enemy on land was under a dark shade and could not be seen, whereas the fleet was silhouetted against the western horizon and made an excellent target. The American ships hauled off in a near calm, but the midshipman could not refrain from the remark: "Now had their Gun boats been manned by Americans, they would have rowed out & completely wrecked our three ships." In just such a situation, oars were better implements than empty sails.

On the next morning the gunboats were sighted near the mouth of the harbor, while the ship they had been escorting already had entered. Among the charges of mismanagement later lodged against Morris was that he failed in this instance in the disposition of his ships, but he pleaded the lightness of the wind and the coming of darkness as the reasons for the enemy's escape. The Americans suffered no casualties. A few days later a French sloop leaving Tripoli for Messina gave Morris the information that the Tripolitans had three killed and five wounded, among the wounded being the Bashaw's brother-in-law, who lost his right arm.

Nicholas C. Nissen, the Danish consul to Tripoli, noticed on May 31 that the *Enterprise* made the signal offshore which had been established a year earlier by Commodore Dale as indicating he wanted a boat to come out for a parley. Nissen asked the Bashaw to send off a boat but he replied he had nothing to talk about to the Americans. He did instruct the Dane, in what was obviously an attempt at a friendly gesture, that if the Americans desired fresh provisions, Nissen had permission to take them out. Nissen sent off the boat under the stipulation to the Americans that he was responsible for it and that under the law of nations it must be permitted to return. The boat, manned by six Turks, ran under the stern of the *Enterprise* and that schooner then took the emissaries out to the *New York*. The two officers of the Bashaw, described as "Tripoline gentry," came on board and advised Commodore Morris that the Danish consul had been authorized to send fresh provisions but had declined to receive any; that the Bashaw had nothing to communicate; and, haughtily, that "were the Rock of Gibraltar abreast him he knew how to defend himself." But Morris wrote a letter through Consul Nissen offering to negotiate peace and the two "Tripoline gentry" returned to Tripoli with it, declining the polite offer of Lieutenant Hull of the *Enterprise* to tow their boat close to the city.

Morris wrote his peace letter because the Bashaw a few days earlier had been thrown into a fury by the receipt of a letter from Commodore

Rodgers, given to the French sloop when she entered the harbor, before
Morris arrived, suggesting negotiations. The Bashaw felt insulted, perhaps rightly, that he had not been addressed by the commanding officer
of the squadron, and told Nissen he would not talk to the Americans
except to their top commander.

Sporadic firing continued between the vessels and shore batteries. On
June 1 Lieutenant Hull came near the *New York* with the *Enterprise*
and reported that ten or twelve enemy feluccas had been caught in a
small bay about thirty-five miles west of Tripoli, where the *Adams* was
watching them. They were grain boats and four of their skippers had
gone aboard the *Adams* to claim they were Tunisians. Morris on arriving directed the skippers to haul the feluccas alongside else he would
burn them. Crowds rushed down to the eminences that afternoon to witness the threatened attack by the American ships, and young Wadsworth observed Bedouins on Arabian horses "riding full speed flourishing their guns over their heads & cutting Capers." Every now and then
the *Adams* in the spirit of the occasion threw a shot at them.

Near where the boats were grounded a stone house served as a for-
tification. That evening Morris determined to make a reconnaissance.
Lieutenant Porter, Midshipman Wadsworth, and five sailors, each armed
with cutlass, musket, and a pair of pistols, put off in the jolly boat and
were joined by a boat from the *Enterprise* with five seamen commanded
by Lieutenant James Lawrence. They rowed to within pistol shot of
the grain boats and heard those on board talking, but were discovered
and the crews set up a yell and fired on them. The shot went overhead
and struck all around and the American patrols returned the fire briskly,
but the moon, shining from the land, lighted up the small American
boats as had the sun the frigates during the earlier exchange, and they
pulled off. Porter's detachment landed on a large rock about a quarter
of a mile offshore, where the frolicsome Wadsworth raised his hand
toward heaven and took possession of the tiny island in the name of
the United States. For souvenirs the men put some of the earth in their
pockets and at midnight responded to the signal from the *New York* to
return.

Porter requested permission to undertake a night attack in force but
Morris decided to await daylight.

Porter had been a midshipman serving with that select set of officers
when the *Constellation* under Truxtun defeated the French *Insurgente*,
and, as has been noted, was in the shrouds and foretop. With a handful
of seamen he picked off the enemy on the deck of the *Insurgente*, but
won his distinction when the foretop mast was hit and shattered by a
French shot early in the battle. The mast swayed as the ship pitched

and the fore topsail bellied in the wind, and threatened to come crashing down on the forecastle. Porter in an instant saw the danger, and while the battle was raging and the air was filled with bullets he ran up the ratline, cut the slings that held the shattered spar and let it down, thus removing the menace to the men on the forecastle. Probably it was in recognition of this service that Porter was selected among the midshipmen as the one to accompany Lieutenant John Rodgers, the executive officer of the *Constellation*, and the eleven seamen who boarded the *Insurgente* after she struck, and who saved her as a prize during the heavy gale that followed the battle. For his conduct Porter won promotion to lieutenant. That gave him the rank to head the reconnaissance and then the daylight attack Morris now contemplated.

Next morning preparations were made to take the dozen feluccas or destroy their cargoes, ranging from twelve to twenty-five tons of wheat. The attack flotilla was made up of small boats: three from the *Adams* under Lieutenant Charles Ludlow and Midshipman Francis Wise; two from the *New York* under Porter, who was in general command of the venture, accompanied by Lieutenant Enoch S. Lane of the Marine Corps and Midshipmen Wadsworth, James S. Higginbotham, William S. Lewis, and John Downes; and two boats from the *Enterprise* under Lawrence and Lieutenant Jonathan Thorn. Lawrence was named second in command. The entire detachment consisted of about fifty men. Two additional boats were loaded with combustibles with which to fire the grain ships.

At 8:00 A.M., under the cover of a cannonade from the ships, the little flotilla put out for the shore. As the boats swept forward it was noticed that none of the enemy force was yet drawn up along the beach where the grain boats rested, but that a barricade had been built of sails and yards reaching out from the corners of the stone house, while other parties of defenders were posted behind rocks and small hills. According to Wadsworth, they kept up an annoying fire while some of the Americans piloted the two fireboats into the midst of the grain ships under cover of the musketry of the others and the fire from the ships. In the distance pranced the Tripolitan horsemen. Some of the bolder would make circuits and join in the firing. Wadsworth noticed one in particular on a black horse, who made his circuit at a gallop and waved his carbine over his head, but when he came in good range several Americans fired. He plunged forward and, in Wadsworth's colloquialism of that day, "bit the dust."

Midshipman Wadsworth, ordinarily the best chronicler aboard the *New York,* was in this instance a more conservative recorder of the battle action than the events justified. The spirited onslaught of the small

American assault party was worthy of more adjectives. The attack had all the aspects of a modern landing on a hostile beach—the artillery cover, the quick approach, the establishment of a beachhead, the hand-to-hand collision with the defenders, who rushed down to the beach, where it was more clashing steel than sounding muskets—all of the aspects of a present-day beach assault except that the propulsion was muscular instead of mechanical, with oars, which the sailors cast aside for cutlasses and guns as quickly as the keels grated on the sand.

This was the first onshore test between seaman and corsair, Western republican against Arab, Berber and Turk, and the seamen, vastly outnumbered, at every step held the initiative. Splashing through the gentle surf, with cutlasses held between their teeth, some with muskets and others with pikes or axes, and a few with pistols, they clashed against the defenders thrown down to the shore from the barricade. A few minutes of din and uncertainty, the air filled with Moslem imprecations and seamen's oaths, with the sharper bark of muskets and pistols sounding above the roar of the big guns from the battery and the ships, and always the sickening whir of the scimitar and ring of steel on steel, and the Tripolitan army began to give ground. Porter and James Lawrence were at the head of the assault party, leading the men by showing them. As the first line of Americans moved up the beach, others overran the feluccas, loaded the combustibles, and lighted the fires.

Perhaps the most trying period of the short engagement was the retreat. Here Porter was wounded by bullets in both thighs. The two balls hit him almost simultaneously. Others were wounded in fact who could not properly be entered on the casualty lists. The Moslems were using an ancient weapon—but new to the Americans—sand, which they scooped from the desert and threw into their assailants' eyes.

Porter when hit simply sat down in his boat and continued to direct, but soon had to pass the command to Lawrence, who was ablaze with fervor as he slashed at the Mussulmans. When the Americans had expended their ammunition and reddened all their swords, and the feluccas were burning merrily, though it was difficult to ignite the wheat. stored in bulk in the holds, the detachment drew off to the big ships. They noticed that as soon as the Tripolitans saw them clearly out of range, crowds rushed down and began putting out the flames, though they were still subjected to a heavy cannonade from the two frigates and the *Enterprise*. It was estimated that only about half of the wheat was destroyed. The Americans were back on their ships by 10 o'clock, and at 11:00 A.M. the fleet sailed to a position farther offshore.

Guesses of the number of Tripolitans defending the barricade and hills ranged from one to several thousand, the larger being Commander

Morris' opinion, who placed the enemy cavalry force at a thousand. This army he supposed was waiting for the detachment to advance farther inland, upon which it would try to surround and pocket the Americans. Wadsworth judged that "from the Number of heads popping up from behind the Mounds & hillocks: the stone house, &c, &c, there were about one thousand in all." But he conceded that the Commodore's opinion might be more accurate. His only souvenir was an earthen jug he brought from one of the boats. He noticed that when the ships sailed the defenders of the feluccas began to throw handfuls of sand into the air in exultant defiance.

The *Adams* appeared to take the gunnery honors by making several direct hits with 12-pounders on little defending parties who exposed themselves. Wadsworth reported that some of the groups were buried in the desert sand by near-hits, then could be seen digging out and scampering for safety.

" 'Twas good sport I must confess," he wrote in his journal. "Yet they might with justice join the Frogs in the Fable & say what is pleasure to you is death for us—Yet they had no right to complain when with fifty men we attacked them on their own shores—for there if we gave death, we likewise expos'd ourselves to receive it."

The American loss is uncertain and is placed by some reports as high as fifteen killed and wounded. Wadsworth said none of the American detachment was killed. He mentioned as wounded, aside from Porter, one Marine and three sailors.

Porter and Lawrence were entitled to great credit for the skillful manner in which they planned and executed the attack. Each displayed the qualities which went to make him a great ship commander at a later date. Each showed a boldness which inspired the men and gave them confidence that they could handle anything they might encounter on the Barbary shores. Long were the details of the battle of the feluccas discussed on the American ships.

Commodore Morris resumed negotiations with the Bashaw after the affair. He wrote in French, and on June 4, 1803, the Tripolitan ruler answered that he was not averse to peace but that someone should be sent onshore to meet with him. Sweden had made peace with him at a price long since, and since America was now his only enemy, his conditions were not likely to be moderate.

Nissen, who followed the negotiations, reported the impression existing in Tripoli that the Bashaw would not settle for less than half a million dollars. In a letter to Cathcart in Leghorn he asked leave "candidly to observe that Tripoli this year is well provided with provisions by a rich harvest." Plenty of European goods were on hand, brought by

several ships which had run the blockade. Since the Bashaw had the
money obtained from the Swedish treaty, which was sufficient for his
current expenses, he was not in a mood to be easy. Nissen regarded the
type of blockade maintained by the Americans during the preceding
year as useless.

After considerable correspondence Captain Rodgers and his aide went
into the city of Tripoli under a flag of truce, where they met both the
Prime Minister and the Bashaw and arranged a guarantee of safety from
the French consul for Commodore Morris to come ashore. Despite his
arrest at Tunis, Morris was willing to stake his fate on a French guarantee. He requested the protection of three nations, but had to be
satisfied with the French. He experienced no unfortunate consequences.

Morris and his suite left the *New York* at 10:00 A.M., June 7, under
a truce which allowed any ships to enter Tripoli but none to depart
while it was in effect. The Americans gained information through the
French consul during this truce that in the first of the two engagements
between fleet and shore defenders, on May 27, one of the Tripolitan
guns was dismounted and a large number were killed, but the defenders
—they were now being called "Tripos" by the sailors—were keeping it
secret.

The seamen learned also that some of Captain Rodgers' shots on an
earlier occasion had been more impressive than anyone suspected. When
Rodgers first appeared before the city ahead of Morris, he ran along
the coast close in and tossed some shots over the town and into it. He
took the fire of the harbor batteries but since he was moving briskly
sustained no hits. One of his shots, it was now learned, went through
the Bashaw's palace, which stood on the waterfront, causing his favorite
wife to faint. The city was thrown into confusion, with much running
about. Rodgers brought the *John Adams* close to the shore on the next
day and the information now gained was that the Bashaw's regular gun
crews balked and he had to expend a considerable sum hiring substitutes
who would man his batteries. The regular Tripolitan army appeared
none too steady.

On shore, Morris was conducted to the home of Sidi Mohamed Dghies,
Secretary of State of Tripoli and one of the most tolerant men in the
regency. The Commodore remained on shore three days, one of which
he passed at the house of Danish Consul Nissen. But the negotiations
were abortive. The Bashaw had scaled down his figure from that cool
half million reported by Nissen to Cathcart, but he demanded what was
equally impossible, $200,000 in cash. On top of this the United States
must pay him $20,000 a year in tribute and indemnify him for all the

expenses of the war to date. Then he would require an unspecified quantity of naval stores annually.

Morris had the spirit to reply that if the combined might of the world made such a demand against the United States it would be treated with contempt. Jefferson, always more frugal with the public money than with his own, would probably as leave have torn up his treasured Declaration of Independence as to yield to more of this kind of international blackmail, added to what the treaties already called for.

Again it was becoming clear that talking with Tripoli was getting nowhere. The Bashaw's favorite wife may have fainted, but he had not learned how much louder cannon spoke than words. He was thrown into a rage by Morris' refusal of the $200,000. That night the white flag which had been hoisted as a symbol of the truce was pulled down, though Commodore Morris was still on shore. The mere lowering of the flag was a violation, which aroused the French consul, who sent word to the Bashaw stressing that he had guaranteed the Commodore's security and bringing in some references to Napoleon and the awesome power of France.

Whatever he said was impressive, because the next morning the white flag was raised again, and under its protection Morris came off to the *New York*. All he had offered was that the United States would make a consular present of $5,000 on the arrival of each new consul, plus $10,000 payable after five years provided the treaty had not been violated by Tripoli in that time. This was too much but it was as unacceptable to the Bashaw as his sums were to Morris.

Morris left Tripoli with the *New York* June 10 and reached Malta June 14, where the ship was subjected to a quarantine for fourteen days. On the next day Malta was in a stir, for Lord Nelson arrived on the British frigate *Amphion*, 32, to be saluted by the Valletta forts with seventeen guns and by the American flagship with the same number. England was at peace with Tripoli but a short time before a Tripolitan xebec with 18 to 20 guns encountered the British sloop-of-war *Termagant* and mistook her for the American frigate *Adams*. Without hailing, the xebec fired, but did not count the cost, because the Britisher answered with such spirit that the xebec quickly struck.

Morris found his new son awaiting him, five days old. The suggestion has been made that he hastened from Tripoli because of the expected event.

Cathcart, left stranded in Leghorn, was incensed that Morris had undertaken single-handed the negotiations with Tripoli which had amounted to nothing.

He protested to both the Commodore and Secretary Madison, pointing out that Morris acknowledged in a letter to Nissen that he was "unacquainted with the usages of Barbary." Cathcart's complaint continued: "How extraordinary then doth it appear that at the moment
he contemplated a negotiation he should refuse to accept the assistance
of a person legally authorized by the government for that purpose &
who was perfectly acquainted with their usages and intrigues."

The high-spirited Captain John Rodgers, thirty years old, remained
on patrol off Tripoli after Morris departed.

Born on a farm near the lower Susquehanna River ferry, later the
town of Havre de Grace, Maryland, he was one of the group of bold
adventurers drawn to the sea and later to the Navy by the threatened
war with France, where as executive officer under Truxtun he won his
captaincy by courage in combat. But even before the quasi-war with
France, Rodgers was becoming a legend in the service. That was mainly
because of an incident in Liverpool in 1796, involving a personage notorious in America, Sir Banastre Tarleton.

Tarleton, who had commanded Cornwallis' cavalry and lost the battle of Cowpens, was more celebrated in England than his legion had
been in the Carolinas, and had been elevated to major general in 1794.
He was running for re-election to Parliament in 1796 when Rodgers and
a party of young Americans were dining at a Liverpool inn. Looking
down from their place on the second floor they saw Tarleton being
carried through the street at the head of a parade of aroused partisans—
a "howling rabble" according to an American recorder—one of the dis-
plays being a huge banner depicting the cavalryman charging and dis-
persing a band of Americans. That was all right, except that the American flag was on the ground being trampled into the dirt by the hoofs
of Tarleton's spirited steed.

When he saw this Rodgers leaped down the stairway, elbowed his
way through the crowd, and landed a blow on the chin of the unsuspecting flag-bearer. Then before anyone could attempt punitive measures
he rushed back into the hotel, armed himself with a saber and a brace
of pistols, and went again into the street, this time to confront Tarleton
in person. The general disclaimed any knowledge of an insult to the
United States and said he would be glad to meet Rodgers should he call
at campaign headquarters that night.

Rodgers went and the question was discussed in cooler mood. Tarleton and his campaign committee took exception to the banner themselves and agreed to destroy it. When that decision was announced,
Rodgers suddenly became a hero among the Tarleton supporters. Instead of a howling rabble they had become a discerning set of honorable

citizens. As they had carried Tarleton, so they now carried Rodgers on their shoulders. They admired what his sailors later came to admire, his spirit. Perhaps that quality and the response it aroused gave Rodgers an enviable record during his long service in the Navy and merchant marine. He never lost a vessel. He never ran a ship aground.

Now he was in command off Tripoli, and on the night of June 21 a movement of the gunboats inside the harbor put him on guard. He concluded that the Bashaw, now that the peace talks had collapsed, meant to send out some cruisers that night or that he expected vessels to enter. Rodgers disposed his ships as best he could to cover the approaches, the *Adams* under Captain Campbell to the west of the city, the *Enterprise*, Lieutenant Hull, on the east side, while he with the *John Adams* watched directly in front of the harbor. Nothing occurred during the night but at 7:00 A.M. Rodgers saw the *Enterprise* flying a signal flag for him to come. He stood toward her with the *John Adams* and when alongside Hull told him a large enemy vessel was anchored close to the beach. The *John Adams* shortened sail and at 8:30 o'clock discovered the enemy ship anchored in a deep narrow bay about twenty miles east of Tripoli, in a position judged by the American commander to be most advantageous for defense.

Rodgers then observed the other defensive elements. Nine gunboats were moving close along the shore, coming to the assistance of the cruiser, which was found to be a well-armed polacre of 22 guns, more than twice the size of the *Enterprise*, though she had taken refuge from that schooner in the bay. She had been cut off trying to slip into Tripoli at night undetected. Rodgers saw also cavalry and infantry, "a vast number," he said, ranged along the beach. He began firing seven minutes before 9 o'clock, and the enemy ship replied. For forty-five minutes the American frigate lay at what Rodgers termed "Point Blank shot" and threw her heavy cannon balls into the Tripolitan, which replied as best she could. In that time her response weakened and at length she was silenced. Suddenly her crew abandoned her, "in the most Confused and precipitate manner." Those who could not crowd into her boats jumped into the water and swam ashore.

Rodgers meantime noticed he had the frigate in shallow water, through which rocks could be seen jutting from the bottom in every direction. He judged it prudent to lay his ship's head off the shore but ordered Hull to close with the *Enterprise* as near as was safe, watch the abandoned warship, and divert the enemy on shore until he could hoist the small boats of the *John Adams* and send boarders and take possession. At 9:45, while engaged in hoisting the boats, he noticed one of the enemy boats returning to the abandoned ship, upon which he tacked and renewed his cannonading. Soon the enemy colors were hauled down and the ship fired both its broadsides. Then suddenly she blew to pieces with a heavy explosion. The hull of the ship burst into bits. The main and mizzenmasts, with all their yards, shrouds, and stays, were hurled perpendicularly into the air 150 feet or more.

The explosion of the polacre was an extraordinary sight. Rodgers described it as "awful," but "one of the Grandest Spectacles I ever beheld." From his description one sees a small likeness to those of later-day atomic blasts: "After a Tremendous Explosion there appeared a Huge Column of smoke, with a Pyramid of Fire darting Vertically through its Centre interspersed with Masts, Yards, Sails, Rigging, different parts of the Hull &c and the vessel in an instant dashed to Attoms."

The polacre, termed by Rodgers a fine vessel, had a crew he estimated at 200, judging by the number he saw leaving the boat. That large a force, taken with the advantageous position of the ship in shoal water, should have been able to annoy the Americans considerably. But Rodgers reported that "to the disgrace of Tripoli, we have received no injury." Not a casualty was sustained. He estimated the Tripolitan loss as heavy. All who returned to the ship were killed and he believed this group included the captain. Numbers must have been killed or wounded before the ship was abandoned, while others were felled on the beach.

In compliance with orders from Commodore Morris, Rodgers left the Tripoli blockade five days later, taking the *Enterprise* and the *Adams* with him. His squadron was at Malta June 30. He had no apprehension of hostile measures by the Bashaw, who had only one small boat at sea, cruising in the Gulf of Venice. He sailed close to the town the day before he departed and found the cruisers there in what appeared to be an inactive state. He thought the loss of their most valuable warship in the explosion would be felt by them severely.

But the responsibility for raising the blockade was Morris's, whose operations against Tripoli had accomplished not one thing of permanent value. The Americans had fought with great spirit when they had a chance. But the Bashaw was secure in his castle with coffers and granaries full and European imports aplenty, and had in fact suffered no hurtful chastisement except to his sailors since he cut down the American flagpole.

After the departure of the Morris squadron from Tripoli, American merchant ships went into hiding. The London *Times* reported (Dec. 23, 1803) that the Austrian was the flag seen most frequently in the Mediterranean. Tripoli was left entirely unguarded. Since Sweden had made peace her warships no longer gave protection to the Americans. British and French privateers occasionally put into Tripoli, but the main result of the lifting of the blockade was a spurt in Tripolitan exports, going to Leghorn, Trieste, Malta, and the Levant.

Though Nelson got his provisions and sailed June 17, being in the Valletta Harbor only two days, Morris did not get away until twenty-seven days had passed. He always seemed to like the towns. The terms of enlistment of the crews of the *New York*, the *John Adams* and the *Adams* were expiring and they would soon be going home.

Morris' squadron sailed from Malta July 11, 1803, depending on no more than Captain Rodgers' hope that the Tripolitans would remain inactive, despite the fact that the summer was their favorite season for forays on unprotected shipping. But there were not enough vessels for an effective, round-the-clock blockade. The *Meshouda* which Rodgers had captured was under tow when the ships cleared Messina and doubled Cape Pelorus, the *New York* in the lead. Here an American squadron had its first experience with the treacherous currents in the haunts of Scylla and Charybdis. Around the cape the head of the fleet encountered a dead calm, in which the current drew the leading vessel sharply—"violently" was Wadsworth's word—upon Scylla, the cliff on the Italian side of the Straits of Messina, at this point from three to four miles wide.

The *New York* was almost on the rocks from which Scylla was supposed to have snatched the sailors of Odysseus out of his homeseeking ship. But before the frigate touched, a saving breeze arose and she made it across to the Sicilian side and anchored. The *Adams*, being in the rear and witnessing the danger to the *New York*, already had made a safe anchorage. But the prize was whirled about two or three times by the eddies, then was caught by a vein of the current and swept along the Calabrian coast, at length to be allowed to make the center of the channel once more. There she was again seized and carried down the coast of Calabria, but this time, after she struck off for the middle of the channel, she was able to make an anchorage on the Sicilian side.

The *John Adams* had an experience not unlike that of the *Meshouda* but after whirling out of control for a while gained the anchorage. No anchorage existed on the coast of Calabria but eventually all the vessels were safe and able to continue their voyage to Naples. There was not a doubt in the American fleet but that Homer was reciting about these very straits when he told the story of the perils of the Greek wanderer, even though he did not name the precise locale of the wily Odysseus' misadventures.

Midshipman Wadsworth found the *Meshouda* a novel exhibit to the people of Naples. Neapolitan vessels were seized often by the pirates but rarely was a Barbary vessel brought captive into the southern Italian port.

Though Morris had accomplished little to distinguish himself, he again brushed shoulders with greatness. Off Málaga on September 9, 1803, the *New York*, enroute from Leghorn to Gibraltar, passed a British fleet of six ships of the line and one or two frigates. Wadsworth was thrilled when the *New York* sailed close to the stern of a majestic man-of-war, the *Victory*, which, soon to be the flagship at Trafalgar, was to become the most famous warship in the world. Nelson was at the rail and exchanged greetings with Morris. "We had a full view of him," the midshipman wrote. But unhappily neither he nor others on the *New York* made a record of the words spoken, or left their impressions about Nelson's manner and appearance.

Morris was suspended and called back home by order of the Navy Department dated June 21, 1803, which placed Captain John Rodgers in temporary command of the Mediterranean squadron. Morris was censured by a court of inquiry. President Jefferson stripped him of his commission without a court martial, which some thought was his due. Then Morris published a long defense. Probably the most valid charge against him was that while he was the commodore nothing much had happened.

Information about Morris' lethargy reached naval officers in the United States well before his recall. Lieutenant Richard Somers, preparing the *Nautilus* at Baltimore, wrote to his brother May 23, 1803: "The Secretary is much displeased with the conduct of Commodore Morris. His wife it is said commands, so much as to lay five months in a port."

Late that summer he had opportunity to observe the state of the blockade. He took the *Nautilus* to the Mediterranean, looked for American ships, found none at Malta, and wrote to his brother: "From thence I proceeded to Tripoli, saw none of our ships there—and but only two small Tripolitan boats close in. I went close in to the Batteries & fired a shot at them. I hove to for a short time, but I saw no gunboat make any appearance. I then bore away for Malta again." After searching about he finally found the flagship at Málaga.

Morris was singularly soft in at least one respect. In the autumn of 1802, always apprehensive of an attack by Morocco in his rear, and with the American consuls being bombarded constantly with complaints over the stoppage of the North African wheat trade with Tripoli, he had reversed his earlier position and the position taken by Commodore Dale, and had authorized Consul Simpson to issue passports for wheat vessels sailing to Tripoli from Morocco. Even the paper blockade was thus lifted, though Tripoli and the United States remained at war.

The order which recalled Morris stated that a new squadron would leave the United States about August 1, 1803. Jefferson and Madison were growing impatient with the handling of affairs in the Mediterranean. In the list of ships and officers who would go out, one name was to mean more than all others in the entire war. The new squadron would be commanded by Edward Preble. An American naval power was about to rise out of the western ocean and the dawn would be like thunder.

CHAPTER ELEVEN

Preble Enforces Peace with Morocco

P REBLE had about him the atmosphere of old Portland—Longfellow's beautiful town of a few years later with its bearded-lipped Spanish sailors, black wharves and slips, its beckoning streets with their shadowy lines of trees—a town which breathed the "beauty and mystery of the ships, and the magic of the sea."

Born there in 1761, when the seaport was called Falmouth, Preble became the friend in later life of its most distinguished public citizen, Lawyer and Congressman Stephen Longfellow, the poet's father, though he never came close enough to politics to become involved in Stephen's views which led to his part in the Hartford Convention affairs. His father was Brigadier General Jedediah Preble, who had fought alongside Wolfe when that general fell on the Heights of Abraham. He was recommissioned brigadier general by the Provincial Congress in 1774, one of the three of that rank appointed for the Minute Men.

These distinctions did not give him nearly the fame he had obtained in New England for being, by common acceptance, the first man to climb to the summit of Mount Washington. The tradition was that "Brigadier Preble had gone up and washed his hands in the clouds." But he tired of soldiering and retired to farming and put his boys to work in the Maine potato rows.

Edward, the third son by his second marriage, was a lad who could have understood Washington's injunction of later date, to reflect on matters carefully but execute swiftly. One day when sixteen he hurled down his hoe at the end of the row and announced that he was through with farming forever, and from that time he was scarcely ever on clods or off boards again. A privateer out of Newburyport was in the harbor. Young Preble walked to the Neck and got a job on her for a rough trip across the Atlantic and much shipboard drudgery, but he loved it all. His father, seeing he was hopelessly lost to the farm, got him a midshipman's warrant in the Massachusetts state navy in 1779, where he cruised with the *Protector*.

Preble got his first taste of pent-up shipboard fighting when the *Protector* met the more powerful British letter of marque *Admiral Duff*. The ships battled so furiously and evenly that for a long time the issue was unsettled and when powder became scarce the crews hurled cannon balls at each other from their decks. Finally the British ship struck her flag. Preble was about to lead a boarding party when the vessel suddenly exploded and blew to bits.

On the *Protector's* second voyage he was captured, and was thrown into the hold of the prison ship *Jersey* in New York Harbor. There he sickened and probably would have died along with the many others had he not been paroled on account of his fever and then released through the intercession of one of his father's old friends. He became a lieutenant of the splendid sloop-of-war *Winthrop* and served on her until peace came. He had little time on shore, even when incarcerated.

When he was discharged from the Massachusetts vessel in 1783, he was a sea veteran at the age of twenty-two. He had been athletic in his youth but the prison ship apparently had weakened him. In his later years an intense, burning spirit was housed in a frail body, though his physical weakness brought no prompting to enter sedentary pursuits. The sea held him, first as a supercargo in the merchant service, then ship captain, and eventually owner of his own vessel. When the Navy was organized and the country was casting about for good officers, Preble, who was known to keep a "tight" ship and to be a disciplinarian without peer in the merchant and the Revolutionary War services, was a natural choice for a responsible command. He did not have the maturity or naval background yet to be on Washington's top list of six captains, but in 1798 President Adams made him a first lieutenant.

He gained early seniority by a mere chance. He was assigned briefly to the *Constitution*, of which Samuel Nicholson was commander. The first lieutenants were given rank according to the captains under whom they served. Since Captain Nicholson was ranked only by John Barry, Preble was second on the list of first lieutenants. Soon he was given command of the brig *Pickering*, 14, and with her served under Barry in the West Indies.

His captaincy came in 1800, when he stepped on board the *Essex* (the frigate a Massachusetts county had built) as supervisor of the later part of the construction, and took her as an escort for American merchant vessels on the year-long voyage to and from the Pacific Ocean. The *Essex* under Preble was the first warship to carry the American colors around the Cape of Good Hope, as she later would be the first, under Captain David Porter, to carry them around Cape Horn.

But the voyage to the Orient enervated him and when in early 1802 he was asked to take the command that went to Morris, he was forced to decline. The tuberculosis from which he would die three years after his grand exploits in the Mediterranean was apparently already setting in.

Only an innate shyness could explain the letter he wrote to the widow Mrs. Dorcas Deering, of Portland, during the time he was at Salem, just after the completion of the *Essex*—a pitiful letter and one of those touching personal missives that ought never to become the common property of biography and history. It was addressed not to his beloved Mary Deering—for he, though a man of thirty-eight, did not know how to speak to that fair young lady directly—but to her mother. He told the widow that when he had last seen her son, James, in Salem, he had sent her a snuffbox by him, which he besought her to accept as a token of his respect. Then he broke the news that he was ordered to sail to Newport on the first fair wind and thence to the East Indies. He said the order grieved him exceedingly because it would separate him from the society of her family for a year. It never seemed to occur to the seafarer that he could become a chandler or harbor director or merchant or even a farmer and have plenty of courting time. The Deering family had money and land; Longfellow told in his nostalgic verse of Deering's Woods. Then the full burden of his missive came to be unloaded.

"You know how very dear to my heart your amiable daughter is," he wrote, "but I beg leave to assure you she is infinitely more dear to me than my existence. I love her with the tenderest affection, and would sacrifice my life to promote her happiness."

But Preble did not seem to recognize that she was not as dear to him as the sea!

"For heaven's sake, Madam, plead for me, and if she should consent to be mine on my return, my whole future life shall be devoted to a tender and delicate attention to her happiness and your own . . ." Then the emotion swept on:

"If I possessed the world I would give it freely to pass one hour with your amiable family before I go, but that alas is impossible. Adieu."

Even then he added a wail of anguish, saying if Mary loved another, "I am lost forever," and again, "for heaven's sake, plead for me."

These delicate sentiments, obviously sincere, might seem inconsistent in one already being known as the sharpest-tongued, highest-tempered, hardest-bitten disciplinarian of the Navy—a captain hated even as was

Truxtun. He was frail but tough, with fire in his heart—a sort of an Andrew Jackson of the ocean, though Jackson was quicker to win his men's affections. Those came to Preble at length, but more from a sure recognition of his competence than from any warmth rising above his New England sternness.

Lovely, wealthy Mary Deering was waiting for him when he came back from the far seas, as she would be waiting when he returned from the Barbary Wars. She was not favored, as was Mrs. Morris, with an order to accompany her new husband in campaigning against the pirates. And she was in the funeral procession only two years after his triumphant return, when he who had never kneeled to a Barbary satrap bowed to the slow bombardment of tuberculosis.

Hearses were not used then in old Portland, but the bier was carried on the shoulders of the pallbearers. On the black velvet pall was laid his commodore's sword. The band played the Roslyn Castle march. All walked to the cemetery—all but Mary Deering Preble. She collapsed in the cortege and had to be taken into a house on the funeral route. She could treasure only two or three scant marriage years with him, for nearly always he was at sea.

The men came to like Preble because he could not be intimidated. That was clearly demonstrated when he reached Gibraltar on his flagship *Constitution*. In the darkness she was unexpectedly alongside a large unidentified ship. Preble took the megaphone and, with a courtesy not always practiced in either land or marine intercourse, first identified himself and his ship. Then he asked the identity of the stranger. He got no answer. With emphasis he now demanded the name and stressed his sharpness by saying he would fire a shot unless he received a reply.

"You fire a shot and I'll return a broadside," came a response in English from the ship that loomed beside him. Preble was not cowed, only angered. He took the trumpet, jumped into the mizzenmast rigging, and shouted:

"This is the United States ship *Constitution*, a 44, Commodore Edward Preble. I am about to hail you for the last time. If not answered I shall fire into you. What ship is that?" Then he told his gunners to blow their matches.

This time he got an answer: "This is his Brittanic Majesty's ship *Donnegal*, a razee of 60 guns."

Preble was soothed but not fully satisfied. He replied that he doubted the statement but would lie alongside until daylight, when he would discover for himself the nature of his neighbor. Soon the British ship put out a boat and an officer came over to apologize. The ship was not a razee but the frigate *Maidstone*, of lesser power than the *Constitution*.

The American ship had come upon her unawares. She was not sure who the American was and sought to gain time to clear her decks and get her men to stations for action.

Preble's conduct was approved all along the rail, where the young officers said that "if he were wrong in his temper, he was right in his heart."

These young men came to be known as "Preble's Boys" and his squadron as the "Nursery of the Navy." Few of the officers were acquainted with Preble at the beginning. He had been in the merchant service until the French war threatened and then had been on the long voyage with the *Essex*. After that he had been ill nearly a year, at a time when these midshipmen and lieutenants were coming into the service owing to the Barbary disturbances.

Youth was an asset not to be scoffed at in just such a war. The Preble squadron had plenty of it. Most of the young men who had been with Morris remained on the rosters and to their names were added others who became distinguished.

As a teacher Preble excelled, but most of his lessons were demonstrational. He knew ships and he knew fighting. He was an excellent instructor in the use of small arms, with which he gained early proficiency. A story told about him when he attended Dummer Academy was that he brought down five swallows with five successive shots! That kind of marksmanship would have astonished Daniel Boone or Daniel Morgan's best Virginia rifleman. The story sounds apocryphal. There was nothing soft about Preble. Though severe, he was known to be just. His was the first great name in the American navy after the adoption of the Constitution, and after the passage of nearly a century and three quarters, there are few indeed entitled to a place above him.

The smaller craft built at the beginning of the Tripolitan War were now coming into commission and augmented tremendously the effectiveness of the squadron both in combat and blockading work. Preble's fleet —though all the ships were rarely if ever brought together—consisted of the frigates *Constitution, Philadelphia, John Adams,* and *New York,* all of which had been out to the Mediterranean except the *Constitution;* and the brigs and sloops *Nautilus,* 12; *Vixen,* 14; *Siren,* 16; *Argus,* 16; and *Enterprise,* 14. Not a ship commander except Preble was over thirty years of age and that was the top age for most of the subordinate officers. The captains of the American navy in the War of 1812 were here mostly as junior officers and their schooling was to be aggressive, and still more aggressive.

Accompanying Preble on the *Constitution,* Tobias Lear went out to be consul general at Algiers as a substitute for the rejected Cathcart.

The Dey of Algiers had not made the decision against Cathcart impetuously at the time when the former slave appeared off the city with Commodore Morris, but had earlier communicated his decision to Secretary Madison. Lear had just returned from Santo Domingo at the request of Napoleon's brother-in-law, General Charles V. Le Clerc, who apparently wanted no interference in his effort to reconquer the island, and because of his splendid service in that war-torn situation was a promising selection for the principal diplomatic post in North Africa.

Lear would be the man on whom the Jefferson administration relied to negotiate the proper treaties and re-establish more stable relations with the Barbary States than had been achieved under the pacts of the Washington administration.

Lear was a native of Portsmouth, New Hampshire, son of a prosperous shipmaster, and such a good scholar at Harvard that he continued his studies abroad—altogether an ideal preparation for the job which was suddenly opened to him as George Washington's personal secretary. He began this work when he was twenty-three years old, in 1785, at the time Washington put aside his uniform to resume life as a Virginia planter. With breaks for travel and other duties, he was with his chief at Mount Vernon and during the presidential terms in New York and Philadelphia, until 1799, when, bowing over the Mount Vernon bed, he caught the last words spoken by the expiring Washington, whose hand was clasped to Lear's as he died.

As secretary to Washington—the exacting position which had been filled competently by Alexander Hamilton, John Laurens, and David Humphreys—Lear was not only inspired by the General's character and integrity, but learned industry, evidenced by an eagerness to splice in writings about the Potomac River area, and gained some military background as well. When war with France threatened and Washington was recalled to active duty, Lear was commissioned colonel and became Washington's military secretary. Jefferson came to know him well, gave him letters when he traveled abroad, and imposed confidence in him.

While Preble was preparing his flagship and his ships were sailing, going out as they became ready—the *Nautilus* first under the devout young Lieutenant Richard Somers, then the *Philadelphia* under Captain Bainbridge, and last of all, the *Enterprise* under Lieutenant Isaac Hull—crises were shaping themselves for the new commodore in the Mediterranean. The first was the *Meshouda*, claimed by Morocco, which Rodgers was bringing back to Gibraltar as a prize.

An equally nettlesome problem was the case of the Moroccan vessel *Mirboka*, commanded by Reis Ibrahim Lubarez, who, even though quite obviously a pirate, came to charm the Americans and to be regarded by Tobias Lear "a sensible, considerate and well informed man."

Lubarez and the *Mirboka* were picked up by the *Philadelphia* red-handed, with an American merchant brig they had just captured. The *Philadelphia* under Captain Bainbridge, coming out early in Preble's new squadron, touched briefly on August 24, 1803, at Gibraltar, where Bainbridge heard of the presence of two Tripolitan cruisers off the southern Spanish coast. News in the Mediterranean seemed almost to be wafted by the soft breezes. While information moved a bit more slowly than today, it passed with facility and with about equal reliability as after the coming of the marine radio, which sped fancy quite as readily as fact.

When Bainbridge heard of the enemy vessels he investigated immediately. He came on two sails that night, running before the strong wind off Cape de Gata, Spain. Arriving alongside the larger vessel, Bainbridge hailed her, and when he received a jumble of answers, he sent a boarding party. Her papers and a passport from the American consul confirmed her commander's statement that she was Moroccan. Since everything appeared to be in order, Bainbridge was about to dismiss her. She was a small frigate of 22 guns with a crew of 100. Only then did Bainbridge determine in the darkness that the brig was in her company. When the answers about the brig were even more jumbled than they had been about the cruiser, he examined the smaller craft.

Lieutenant David Porter led a boarding party which discovered that the brig was the *Celia*, under Captain Richard Bowen, out of Boston. Captain and crew had been sent below decks. The *Celia* had been captured off Málaga, after which the *Mirboka* had made for Cape de Gata, the promontory which vessels sailing from Marseilles and North Mediterranean ports skirted enroute to Gibraltar. There the *Mirboka* was lurking for other merchant craft. Bainbridge took possession of the two ships and amid the difficulties of heavy weather brought them to Gibraltar, where the *Celia* was turned back to her master, Captain Bowen, and allowed to continue her voyage. The Moroccan cruiser was detained as a prize.

Reis Ibrahim Lubarez, her commander, was a person of parts in Morocco, having been ambassador from the Moorish Emperor to Spain. He was well known in Gibraltar, where the incident of his capture of the American brig and the American charges of either war by Morocco or piracy by the ex-diplomat raised considerable excitement. When he was examined by Commodore Preble and Consul General Lear he produced orders from the Moorish governor of Tangier, Hadge Alcayde Abde-Rhaman Hashash (usually termed by the Americans Alcady

Hashash), directing him to capture vessels of the United States, Sweden, Denmark, Holland, Russia, and Prussia and bring them into Moroccan ports. It appeared that Morocco was taking on as enemies a sizable part of the world. The orders he exhibited were not signed, but the Moroccan consul at Gibraltar, Hammet, said the handwriting was either that of Alcady Hashash or his secretary, since he had letters from the Governor in the same handwriting. The commander Lubarez certified that the orders had been received sealed from the Governor and were not to be opened until he was at sea. He declared that when he left port he had no idea he was being ordered to cruise against American commerce.

The capture of the *Celia* and the breach of faith with the voyage of the *Meshouda* to Tripoli put a different complexion on affairs with Morocco. It was well known that the Emperor had another formidable cruiser at sea. On September 6, when the *Constitution* was sailing from Cape St. Vincent to Cape St. Maria along the southern Portugal coast, she encountered the frigate *Maimona*, 30, carrying 150 men, belonging to Morocco. Nothing about her excited hostility or suspicion. Perhaps it was to emphasize the illusion of friendship that she took the initiative and sought to speak with the American, then requested an examination of her papers to impress them that all was well. Lear, who was acquainted with Consul Simpson's handwriting, went aboard with a detail and found things in order. Her papers showed she was proceeding to Lisbon from Sallee, the Atlantic port now identified as Salé but a notorious seventeenth-century rendezvous of corsairs. It and Mogador were regarded great danger points by the Americans because these ocean ports could not be bottled up by a single frigate cruising in the Strait of Gibraltar. The *Constitution* permitted the *Maimona* to proceed, but the attitude was best expressed by Lear in his report September 26 to Secretary Madison:

> Altho' everything appeared so clear & correct on board this Vessel, that there could be no pretext for detaining her, and the Commodore was fully satisfied that he could not do it with propriety; yet, such was his anxiety & uneasiness lest there should be some deception, that might operate against the Am. Commerce, that I really believe, had she been in sight next morning, he would have ventured to detain her.

Now, with the examples of the *Meshouda* and *Mirboka*, it was clear that Morocco was not to be trusted with cruisers loose from her ports. This was confirmed when the *Constitution* approached the strait and stood into the Bay of Tangier, where Preble fired a signal gun to call the American consul on board. He could see the consular flags of seven other nations flying but not the American, nor did a boat put out from the shore. Strongly impressed that peace with Morocco was strained or ruptured, he continued to Gibraltar and anchored at 3:00 P.M., September 12, 1803. Captain Bainbridge came on board promptly and reported his affair with the *Mirboka* and the brig *Celia*.

Preble had never been in the Mediterranean. His first experience with a Turk was when his father devised a heavy-handed prank to test his courage, when he was a boy of ten and entitled to some punishment. He was told that a Turk would carry him away in a bag. Then a Mussulman from a ship came at the father's contrivance, carrying the bag. When the dark-complexioned man with his peculiar hat and trousers appeared in the darkness, Edward bristled. "I am not afraid of you," he shouted, then caught the tongs, seized a hot brand from the fire and stabbed it at the strange invader's face. The son of the Prophet was the one to make the retreat before the son of the General. The senior Preble, observing from the next room, was mightily pleased.

The incident remained with him. None could have expected him to be instinctively enamored of the Mussulmans.

He and Lear paid their respects the next day to the British governor of Gibraltar, Sir Thomas Trigge, who, Lear wrote, met them with "great cordiality & politeness." In a "delicate manner" he expressed anxiety about the apparent rupture between the United States and Morocco because the Gibraltar garrison was wholly dependent on the Moors for fresh provisions from across the strait. His fear was that if the United States began bringing in their ships as prizes the Moroccan small craft would no longer venture forth. But he merely stated his problem without intimating any course that would disrupt the amicable relations between Great Britain and the United States. That day the *New York* came in from Malta and Naples and the schooner *Vixen*, which would play a notable part in the blockade of Tripoli, arrived from Baltimore under Lieutenant John Smith. The fleet was gaining strength. When the *New York* anchored, Preble went on board to meet Captain Morris, the retiring commodore returning to the United States.

On the following day, September 14, Captain John Rodgers, commanding the frigate *John Adams*, arrived with the *Meshouda*. For two years she had been blockaded in Gibraltar and now she was back before she had completed a single cruise. Rodgers had been designated acting commodore and was senior to Preble, but since Preble had been appointed to the command and Rodgers had been ordered back to the United States, Rodgers waived his rank and accompanied the new commodore in the plan he now promptly formulated. This was a descent on Morocco in force to ascertain from Muley Soliman in person what kind

of a peace, if any, he was intending to maintain thereafter with the
United States. Clearly no attack on Tripoli was feasible as long as Morocco remained a potential belligerent in the rear. Simpson, though his
consular flag had not been seen, was still at Tangier, but by one of the
Emperor's whims, which exerted themselves on occasions to show the
potentate of Morocco did not have to bow to the common practices of
nations, he had been under arrest as a result of the capture of the
Meshouda.

When Simpson learned that the *Meshouda* had been caught making
for Tripoli he lodged a sharp protest with the Emperor and informed
him that Alcady Hashash had disavowed ordering the voyage. As he
was writing he learned of Bainbridge's capture of the *Mirboka* and the
recapture of the *Celia*. He demanded that the Emperor withdraw the
authority the captains of his cruisers possessed to seize American ships.

He likewise denounced the seizure of his person by Governor Alcady
Hashash of Tangier, a detention following the lodgment of his protest.
The circumstances were that the Governor had summoned him to come
to the official palace at 11:00 P.M., an unlikely hour, but one at which
the Moslems sometimes conducted business. On receipt of a third summons he went, only to be informed that the Governor was asleep but
that he would be detained personally until the frigate *Meshouda* should
be liberated by the Americans. The attendants closed the doors and held
him until 10 o'clock the following morning, when Alcady Hashash gave
him partial release after a protest against his detention had been lodged
by all the other consuls in Tangier. They were required to assume the
responsibility that he would not leave the country without the Emperor's
permission. The consuls then made representations to the Emperor
against the detention, but when Simpson wrote to Consul Gavino in
Gibraltar two weeks later he said guards continued at his door.

Meantime reports reached Gibraltar that the Moroccan frigate *Maimona*, which the skeptical Preble had allowed to proceed to Lisbon,
had captured four American merchantmen in the Atlantic—reports later
followed by accurate information that she had reached Lisbon without
making any captures whatever—and another, which proved true, that
an American vessel had been seized while unloading at Mogador. This
was the *Hannah*, under Captain Joseph W. Williams, out of Salem, with
a cargo of seventy-five bales of cotton, ten chests of tea, iron, and bales
of piece goods.

Preble was a commodore of sharp action and blunt words. Writing
to Secretary of the Navy Smith on September 23, he denounced the
Moors as "a deep designing artfull treacherous sett of Villains" and
said the Emperor had no doubt been meditating war but awaited only

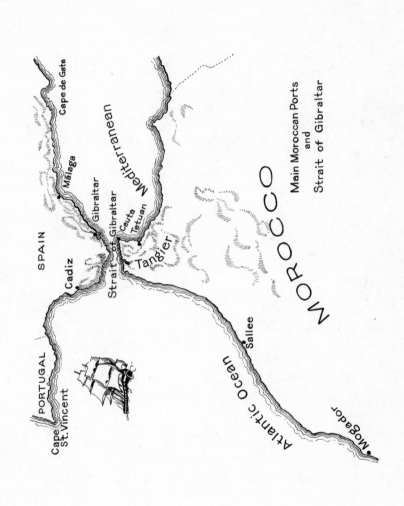

SPAIN

Cape de Gata

Málaga

Gibraltar

Mediterranean

Ceuta

Tetuan

Strait of Gibraltar

Tangier

Cadiz

PORTUGAL

Cape
St. Vincent

Sallee

Atlantic Ocean

MOROCCO

Main Moroccan Ports
and
Strait of Gibraltar

Mogador

some pretext. That, he supposed, had been provided by Captain Rodgers' capture of the *Meshouda*. He reported likewise his meeting with
Captain Campbell of the frigate *Adams* and Consul Cathcart. They
came to Gibraltar, where Cathcart reported that the Bey of Tunis positively demanded a frigate.

"Should that demand be acceded to," said Preble, "it will require
another Frigate on our own account to watch her motions. I suspect
the demands of the Barbary Powers will increase . . . all of them except-
ing Algiers appear to have a disposition to quarrel with us unless we
tamely acceed to any propositions they chuse to make."

On September 16, 1803, after receiving a letter from Consul Simpson,
still under surveillance in Tangier, Preble and Rodgers decided to sail
immediately with the *Constitution* and the *John Adams* to Tangier Bay.
Lear, who had been appointed consul general to Algiers, had no authority in Morocco, but the two captains persuaded him to accompany
them and take charge of the negotiations, at which they intended to
bring to a head the exact condition of affairs between that country and
the United States. The frigates weighed anchor at midnight and at daylight came into the bay and anchored about two miles from the town.
They carried on board the *Constitution* the captain and six officers of
the *Mirboka* who had been captured by Bainbridge, and, on board the
John Adams, both the Moroccan captain and the Tripolitan officer taken
by Rodgers on the *Meshouda*.

Soon a boat came out rowed by four Spaniards bearing a note from
Consul Simpson written on an open slip of paper which said merely that
the boat might bring on shore any letters the American commodore
might have to send. Preble was sending something else, either himself
or lead. Rodgers came over to the *Constitution* and the two captains
wrote a letter saying they were in the bay to see if the differences could
be settled by negotiation. They told of the presence of the officers of
the Moorish ships, the possession of the ships' papers showing everything
in a true light, and urging the necessity of a personal interview with
Simpson, who was told to come out to the ship.

Late that afternoon another set of Spaniards with a different boat
brought word that Simpson could not come aboard, that he had guards
over him in his own house, that the Governor was in Tetuan and that
he had sent an express to the Emperor, who was expected in Tangier
on the following Friday, the 24th. He recommended against sending any
boat ashore from the ship. He advised Preble of the seizure of the *Hannah* in Mogador. In a separate letter answering a note sent by Lear he
said that when they met he would open "a scene of deep deceit" at
which Lear would be astonished.

On the strength of this information Preble sent the *John Adams* on a cruise down the Atlantic coast as far as Mogador and took the *Constitution* back to Gibraltar, there to give directions to Bainbridge with the *Philadelphia*—orders which through no fault of Preble's would lead to the doom of that noble frigate—and to prepare to return to Tangier on September 24. Both frigates were sailing away at 8 o'clock that night, the *John Adams* to Mogador and the *Constitution* back to Gibraltar. When off Tangier Preble offered to set on shore the Moorish officers captured by Rodgers and Bainbridge, that they might tell how they were captured and relate the manner of their treatment, but they declined the privilege of liberty. At night the waterfront was lighted with great fires, some built along the mountains to alarm the country about the coming of the American ships, and some nearer at hand to light the beach and prevent landings.

Preble had examined the harbor forts and judged that while they appeared formidable they were not such as to daunt him and his zestful young officers. From the information he and Lear gained they were in bad condition and their guns were not well manned. That night the wind was light and the *Constitution* made little progress. At 11:00 P.M., September 18, she met the *Philadelphia* and the *Vixen* standing out for the Mediterranean, convoying the *Port Mary*, a merchant ship bound for Messina. Bainbridge and Lieutenant John Smith, commanding the *Philadelphia* and the *Vixen*, came aboard the *Constitution*, where Commodore Preble gave them their final orders. They were to cruise along the coast looking in nooks and bays for any Tripolitan craft, then make for Malta, where they were to remain no more than one day unless required by necessity, and go on to Tripoli. Off that city they were to maintain the most effective blockade they could accomplish with such a force, and were to "annoy the enemy with all the means in your power." They were to detain any Moroccan vessels and send them back to Gibraltar, and were not to suffer the vessels of any nation to enter Tripoli. They were to treat as an enemy anyone attempting to enter the harbor or carry anything to it without their permission. If Tripoli were to be blockaded, Preble wanted it done tellingly.

On the following evening he and Lear held a long conversation with their Moroccan prisoners and were especially attracted to the urbane Reis Ibrahim Lubarez, the Emperor's former ambassador to Spain. They stated the American position: a desire for peace, but, if war were forced on them, the ability to make it terrible for Morocco. Their ability might be seen from the strength of their flotilla, though they did not emphasize it was already being scattered! The gentle treatment the Americans had meted out to the prisoners did not result from fear, but, as Lear stated it, "from the principles of humanity and manliness," always exercised by Americans toward their captive enemies. They went on to demonstrate how much more the Emperor could gain from peaceful commerce and American friendship than from a war in which his vessels would be destroyed and every seaport city in his empire would be battered down.

The Moors appeared to be impressed. Lubarez placed the blame for the rupture on Alcady Hashash who had issued the orders for the capture of the American ships, though this Alcady subsequently denied. He said the Emperor was "one of the best princes they ever had . . . just and considerate," but surrounded by bad advisers, the worst being the governor of Tangier. He said he would see the Emperor and tell him the facts face to face. He felt the generous treatment he had received would make an impression, for he was persuaded that the Emperor only wanted to be justly informed.

Preble and Lear declared the conduct of Alcady Hashash had been so outrageous and wicked toward the Americans and unfaithful to the Emperor that they would not negotiate with him or with the Emperor either until the Governor, if he had acted without orders, had been punished. Lear reported that the Moors spoke so feelingly that tears came to their eyes. Later, when Preble thought it would be more convenient for four of them to go aboard the *New York*, his own cabin and table being crowded by so many captive officers, whom he treated as guests, the four selected wept, and Preble was so touched he allowed them to continue his fare in the cabin of the *Constitution*.

On the 21st, Preble was along the African shore off Cuta, when an incident allowed him to cement more cordial relations with the British, whose port, because of the Moroccan disturbances, the Americans continued to use as the base for their Mediterranean operations, in preference to south Italy harbors, as by Eaton's arrangement. A British brig was struck by a sudden squall with all her sails set. Both of her topmasts were snapped and carried away. Preble at once hauled up to give assistance. The British sent an officer to the *Constitution* with the information that the brig was His British Majesty's *Childers*, Sir George Bolton commanding, carrying dispatches to Lord Nelson. Preble offered every possible help. Sir George wanted to go to Tetuan, where a British frigate was anchored, and as they were now in sight of that place Preble sent a boat with a hauser and began to tow the *Childers* at a rate of ten knots in the freshening wind. Then, as suddenly as the squall had struck, the wind calmed. Sir George came aboard the *Constitution* to acknowledge with the warmest thanks the American's assistance. Seamen were brothers in battling the adverse elements. In the pleasant weather Sir George was able to raise other topmasts and make sail without going to Tetuan. Preble offered him spars, rigging, or anything else he might need, but as the sun was setting he was making off under a light western breeze with one topmast in place and the second going up.

Two other American ships arrived the next day, the doughty little *Enterprise* under the command of Lieutenant Hull, and the frigate *Adams* under Captain Campbell. Cathcart, arriving with Campbell, reported he had left consular presents of watches and jewelry valued at $11,000 at Leghorn, plus $24,000 in currency he had raised on his own security to use for the government in the abortive negotiations with Tunis, of which he gave an accounting to Preble.

One result of the preliminary operations in the strait was to impress Lear with Preble's competence. In filing his long report with Secretary Madison covering the period to September 27, 1803, he included this comment:

> Permit me to add, that the Zeal of Commodore Preble to promote the interests of our Country, can be equalled only by his activity and diligence . . . I flatter myself the President will find in this Officer prudence & good judgment, joined with firmness, activity and a real wish to promote, all in his power, the best interests of the U. States.

Preble continued cruising off Tangier until the date set for the Emperor's arrival. The Moroccan Secretary of State wrote Simpson on September 30 acknowledging receipt of the papers and orders found on the two captured Moroccan vessels and saying that when His Majesty reached Tangier "he will only do all that is good with your Nation." Preble wrote Secretary Smith on October 1 that he had been in Tangier Bay three times in the week and ventured the Moroccans would find themselves so closely watched they would want peace. The Emperor had now set October 4 as the date of his arrival. Heavy rains had retarded his journey from the provinces. The Alcassar River was flooded and could be crossed only on rafts supported by goats' skins filled with air. But the Emperor had sent a message earnestly requesting that the American commodore bring the *Meshouda* into the bay. Simpson suggested to Preble that he stand off with the fleet and merely send in a brig with a message, upon which the consul would acquaint him with the situation on shore. He warned that if Preble arrived without the *Meshouda* "we shall have a violent dust with him, for His Majesty is allowed to be as positive a Gentleman & strong headed as any Man can be."

Preble placed a detail of eight seamen commanded by Lieutenant Joseph Tarbell (later commander of the gunboat flotilla defending Norfolk in the War of 1812) to navigate the *Meshouda* to Tangier, while the other Moorish vessel, the *Mirboka,* was left at Gibraltar as a prison ship for the two crews.

Finally on October 5 Preble brought the *Constitution* and brig *Nautilus* to anchor in Tangier Bay. As he approached the shore, now aboard the *Nautilus,* the other available vessels of the fleet came into the harbor, the frigates *New York* and *John Adams,* and the schooner *Enterprise.* They gave Preble enough firepower to crumble the dilapidated stone castle that guarded the bay and loomed above the shrine of St. Augustine, and to sink every Moorish craft in the hook-shaped harbor of Tangier. Then, at the time he had arranged through Consul Simpson, now relieved from his house arrest after the arrival of the Emperor, Preble went ashore.

Preble did not stalk blindly into a trap as did Commodore Morris at Tunis. He gave positive orders, and there was not a man in the American force who did not know he would break him or throw him out of the fleet unless the orders were obeyed implicitly. If the Commodore should be detained forcibly, the frigates and the lesser craft were to bombard the town. No compact or understanding whatever was to be engaged in for his release. No consideration was to be given to his personal safety, a matter over which Preble had exclusive jurisdiction.

Before he left the ship he called a final conference of his officers so there might be no mistake. The words handed down are a bit stilted but they show his purpose: "Comrades: The result of the approaching interview is known only to God. Be it what it may, during my absence, keep the ships cleared for action. Let every officer and seaman be at his quarters, and if the least injury is offered to my person, immediately attack the batteries, the castle, the city and the troops, regardless of my personal safety."

Tobias Lear went with him. This devoted and unusual man, whose patriotism appeared to be accompanied by an equally ardent fervor for peace, had no concern over his personal safety. He had passed unshaken through the bloodshed and terror of the slave revolt of Santo Domingo and staunchly maintained American rights during the chaotic conditions that attended the rise of Toussaint L'Ouverture. Now, though not directly responsible for peace with Morocco, he was eager to share any dangers attending the effort to establish it.

Two young midshipmen completed the party, going as Preble's aides. They took the small boat of the *Nautilus,* the broad pennant of the fleet commander flapping gaily and proudly in the breeze, and landed at the mole, from where they were escorted to the Castle. There they passed through a double file of soldiers to the presence of the Emperor.

Few events since the coming of the Koran under Acbad the Conqueror had created more excitement in Morocco than the arrival of the

American squadron from afar over the Atlantic and the landing of the
Yankee admiral on the Moslem shore. Towers, terraces, and mosques
were loaded with the faithful, who relished the spectacle of not only
the ships, but the military display of thousands of their own picturesque
horsemen, and the sight of the Emperor sitting on his fresh, gleaming
carpet, awaiting homage, but manifestly not wholly expecting it.

Preble by his dauntlessness and the sheer force of his personality retained control of the situation from the start. As he entered the presence,
the attendants asked him to turn over his side arms. His starchy refusal
left no doubt about his intention to retain them and the matter was not
referred to again. Then the Emperor had the presumption to ask him
to kneel. This, too, he emphatically refused.

"Are you not in fear of being detained?" the Emperor asked.

"No, sir," Preble answered firmly. "If you presume to do it my squadron in your full view will lay your batteries, your castles, and your city in
ruins."

The Emperor grew apologetic. He regretted the breach between the
two countries. His earnest hope was for peace. He had given no orders
provoking the hostilities to American shipping and agreed that any
vessels taken should be restored.

The meeting was best described by Midshipman Ralph Izard, Jr., of
Charleston, South Carolina, one of the two junior officers who accompanied Preble and Lear. His impressions of the Emperor who had just
come down to the seacoast leading an army of 15,000 were recorded in
a letter written to his mother October 11, 1803. He considered the
potentate docile indeed in the presence of the American commodore:

> We were introduced to his Majesty with very little ceremony. I had
> connected with the idea of Emperor of Morocco, something grand,
> but what was my disappointment at seeing a small man, wrapped up
> in a woolen *heik* [haik] or cloak sitting upon the stone steps of an
> old castle in the middle of the streets, surrounded by a guard of very
> ill looking blacks with their arms covered with cloth to prevent them
> rusting. We stood before the Emperor with our Caps in hand & the
> conversation was carried on by means of an interpreter. The Emperor
> said he was very sorry that his Governor had behaved so much amiss
> & said he would punish him "more than to our satisfaction." That
> was his expression. After having assured us of his ignorance of Hash
> hasha proceedings, he promised not only to ratify & confirm the treaty
> . . . but to write the President of the U. S. that altho' the treaty made
> by his father was to have effect but for 50 years he will consider it
> as binding for ever.

Another midshipman, Wadsworth, was able to reduce the situation to its simplest terms. Addressing a letter, facetiously to Miss Hash Tash, he wrote that the Emperor, taking no prizes and finding the American fleet on his coast, blamed it all on Governor Hash Hash. "Hash denies giving the captains orders to go out, & and Captains declare that Hash did give the orders, but it is thus—Hash gave the Capts Sealed orders, & when they arrived at the place where they were to be opened, there was no signature on the orders. Why then did they obey the orders by taking the Brig? I think we may conclude them all to be in Plot . . ."

More pacific reassurances than the Emperor's could scarcely be stated. The guns of the *Constitution* looked large and angry indeed.

Preble and Lear then talked to the Prime Minister, whom Izard described as intelligent and to all appearances a friend of the Americans, and with him the details of the new rapport were put into effect. The *Meshouda* was restored to the Emperor, who issued an order to all his ports calling for the release of any American vessels which might have been detained, including the *Hannah* at Mogador, and instructing that they be received thereafter as those of a favored nation. That day, October 11, the monarch left Tangier, and Governor "Hash hash" was supposed to be in his entourage. The Americans thought he was being taken away to be executed, but when Captain Rodgers delivered the *Meshouda* on October 19 to Arraiz Omar, of Tetuan, who had been captain of the cruiser when she was captured, Omar was bastinadoed severely, Simpson reported, then was loaded with chains. Simpson received this intelligence from Governor Alcady Hashash himself, who said the punishment was inflicted at the Emperor's orders because the captain had received on board the naval stores and Tripolitan passengers at Algiers and Tunis. Thus the captain who went out with his forty seamen by the Emperor's proclamation, carrying "Our Victorious Flag" in fulfillment of the ruler's "Orders and intentions," appeared to be the one to receive the onus for the untoward turn in events. He was Alcady's scapegoat. "I forbear comments on such conduct," wrote Simpson to Preble, "as you are too well acquainted with circumstances not to see it in its true light."

Then Alcady Hashash left Tangier for Tetuan and disappeared from the Barbary Wars. It is anyone's guess how he fared with Emperor Muley Soliman—probably not so severely.

But Muley Soliman did appear serious in his desire for peace. No doubt the frigates ranged off his capital and port city were the eloquent persuaders, but now the Americans were assuredly the Emperor's choice friends. On Saturday, October 8, he marched to the beach with his court and musicians to view the American squadron, composed of ships which for the grace of their lines, their trimness, orderly decks, and what might almost be regarded their greyhound readiness to leap before the wind, were the handsomest in the world. The spirit of the master architect Humphreys was in the craft riding the northeast winds of early October in Tangier Bay.

Most of the populace of Tangier took a position where it could watch the Emperor and the fleet. Behind him was ranged the 8,000 of his army's imperial guard, extending for three miles along the beach, light horsemen all, but dismounted for the ceremonies. They were Moors and Tuaregs with beautiful Arabian steeds, probably as accomplished a body of cavalry as Murat could lead past Bonaparte, though scarcely as suited as the French for heavy battle action. Whoever entered the matter in the log of the *Constitution* was aroused to say: "The hole shore was crowd^d with the inhabitance as fair as the Ey could Extend."

Salutes were fired—twenty-one by Preble from the *Constitution*, returned in like number by the fortress. Then the Emperor's band struck up the march of Olestor, used to signify peace and friendship. To emphasize the new cordiality he sent out to the *Constitution* a gift to Preble of ten bullocks, twenty sheep, and four dozen fowls. Preble took four bullocks, six sheep, and a dozen fowls for the more heavily manned flagship and sent the rest to be divided equally on board the *New York*, the *John Adams*, and the *Nautilus*. When Captain Malamorta, the Moorish officer who with twenty men brought out the two lighter loads of fresh meat, turned back to the shore, the American flagship expressed her thanks with a three-gun salute.

Peace was now so all-pervasive that that night the *Constitution,* which for four days had been cleared for action, piped down hammocks so the men might have normal sleep, and re-established a cautious routine.

Back in Gibraltar on October 15, Preble wrote to Secretary Madison announcing a renewal of peace between Morocco and the United States, a re-ratification of the treaty of 1786. He sent the papers relating to the affirmation together with a letter from Emperor Muley Soliman to President Jefferson. Preble said the Emperor had been a little hurt in not having heard from the President and suggested a letter once a year.

But when he sailed from Tangier to Gibraltar and on to Lisbon for supplies, then to Algiers to drop Consul Lear at his new post, Preble left no presents for the Emperor or any of his numerous functionaries. Preble was not the present-giving sort. The only gifts he carried were the round shot in his lockers.

If Jefferson had made a mistake with Morris, he had more than compensated for it by the selection of Preble.

CHAPTER TWELVE

The Tripolitans Capture the
Philadelphia

J UST as Preble was about to strike at Tripoli after the pacification
of Morocco, his fleet suffered a shocking and unparalleled disaster,
which not only severely crippled its offensive power, but threatened
to throw the ascendency to the Tripolitan navy and give to the corsairs
one of the finest, fleetest frigates on the seas.

The loss of the *Philadelphia*, the second largest vessel of Preble's fleet,
resulted from one of those plays of chance which entered not infre-
quently into the naval warfare of the sailing era, and before the coasts
of the continents were adequately charted; and while the calamity may
have involved no reflection on the nautical skills of the ship's captain,
William Bainbridge, it did bring into question his discernment and
capacity in the larger responsibility of conducting an effective blockade.

Bainbridge, as has been seen, received orders from Preble off Gibraltar
September 16, 1803. He was to convoy American merchant vessels eastward from Gibraltar, stop at Málaga no more than twenty-four hours,
pick up such other ships as were there, and conduct them as far to the
east as was deemed advisable. Preble assigned the *Vixen* under Lieutenant John Smith to accompany the *Philadelphia*. As she was smaller
and of lighter draft, her duty would be to look into the bays and "snug
places," as Preble called them, as the two ships worked their way along
the coast, and if no cruisers of Tripoli were encountered, to go to Malta.
There, by Preble's orders, the ships were to remain no more than twenty-
four hours unless the necessity of refitting required it. The new commodore wanted no repetition of the Morris practice of hanging around
the harbors.

From Malta, Bainbridge was to take a position off Tripoli and maintain, as long as the season permitted, as effectual a blockade as could

be accomplished with his two ships, annoying the enemy by all means in his power. The orders were clear and left little ground for misunderstanding. The port of Tripoli was to be blockaded.

Bainbridge responded with the promptness called for by the time limits Preble imposed. He remained in Málaga only five hours—just long enough for the *Vixen* to take in water—then continued along the Spanish coast, speaking with all vessels he encountered to get information on possible Tripolitan raiders at sea. He passed south of Majorca and Minorca and dropped down to the Bay of Tunis. Here he ordered the *Vixen* to cruise separately for a brief time and went into Malta with the *Philadelphia,* where he obtained the permission of the governor to use the harbor, store spare spars, and land his sick, numbering thirteen. He was forced to exceed his time limit in Malta by some hours—the weather had been rough on the voyage up from Tunis—but on October 3, again in company with the *Vixen,* he sailed for Tripoli.

The *Vixen* was a new schooner of 14 six-pounders, launched early in the summer in Baltimore. Lieutenant John Trippe, her second in command, was one of Preble's brilliant young officers, as the fighting at Tripoli soon was to disclose. She was on her maiden voyage, serving as a needed companion of the larger *Philadelphia,* which could not navigate safely amid coastal reefs or in the smaller bays. The two ships reached the coast of Tripoli October 7, and on the 22nd Bainbridge reported to Preble that he had been "on this solitary station" two weeks without seeing anything of the enemy except behind well-fortified works. He said that, weather permitting, he would remain until November 20, after which cruising would be dangerous. Then he added grandiloquently, but somewhat in keeping with his times, that he conceived the weather to be dangerous already, "but fervent zeal in the cause of my Country and desirous of giving you satisfaction in my conduct will induce me to persevere to the last."

Even before this report, Bainbridge spoke on October 19 to an Austrian brig sailing from the harbor and gained intelligence that two Tripolitan cruisers were at sea. At this point the American captain exercised questionable judgment. Believing it most likely that the raiders were westward (if indeed they were out at all), he ordered Lieutenant Smith to take the *Vixen* and cruise off Cape Bon as the most likely place where they might be intercepted.

Cape Bon, the land's end of Tunis, which projects the continent of Africa to its far northern point into the Mediterranean, was three hundred miles from Tripoli. Bainbridge later had the additional explanation that the gale season was advancing and the *Vixen* would have a safer position off Cape Bon than off Tripoli. But the chances of intercepting

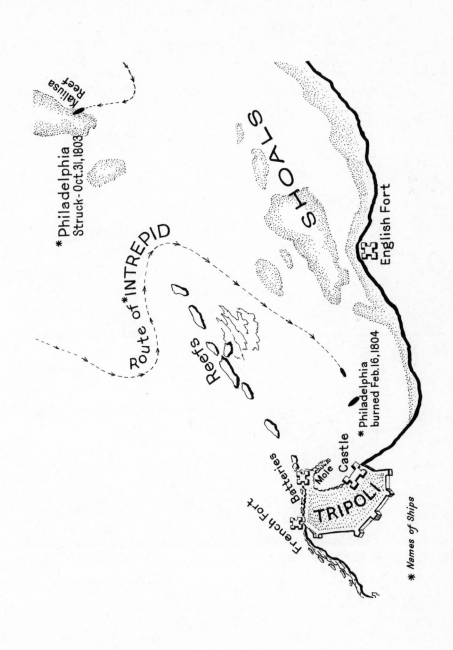

Kallusa Reef

* Philadelphia
Struck - Oct. 31, 1803

Route of * INTREPID

SHOALS

English Fort

Reefs

* Philadelphia
burned Feb. 16, 1804

Batteries

Castle

Mole

French Fort

TRIPOLI

* Names of Ships

the corsairs would seem to be greater by maintaining a close watch for them at the Tripoli harbor than groping for them at sea, even off such a promontory as Cape Bon. The best place to watch for the mouse is at the mousehole. But an even weightier condition was that Bainbridge was dividing his force, already too scant for a full-scale blockade, and subjecting the *Philadelphia* to the hazards of battling single-handed off Tripoli any force which might be sent against her; and a frigate was always vulnerable to attack by gunboats propelled by sweeps in a calm. He was, in effect, virtually opening the port to small craft which might hug the shoreline, find haven in the bays the *Philadelphia* could not enter, and gain the harbor under cover of darkness. With an ample squadron, Cape Bon certainly should have been patrolled. But the main consideration with as limited a force was that the vessels could support one another if held together. Since they were in the presence of the enemy, a division under any circumstances might be adjudged hazardous.

The *Vixen* sailed westward on October 20 and two days later a heavy northwest blow carried the *Philadelphia* east of Tripoli about eighteen miles. There, at 9:00 A.M. on the 31st, she sighted a sail standing westward close to the shore. Giving chase, she came within gunshot two hours later, by which time the two ships were approaching Tripoli. Since the soundings taken continuously of the depth of the water would not permit the *Philadelphia* to venture close in, she followed a zigzag course, firing repeatedly with bow guns, hauling on and off shore as permitted in depths of from seven to ten fathoms, or roughly from 40 to 60 feet. Her draft was from 18½ feet forward to 20½ aft. Bainbridge's hope was either to disable the enemy craft with his fire or drive her ashore so she might be captured and destroyed by a boarding party.

About four and a half miles east of the city the chase became hopeless, and at 11:30 A.M. the *Philadelphia* ceased firing and hauled off shore. The soundings showed 48 feet of water. The ship, as explained by her second officer, Lieutenant David Porter, constantly had three leads going, one known in naval parlance as a dipsey, tended by a lieutenant, and two hand leads, or ropes, each tended by either a midshipman or a masters' mate. Bainbridge showed no lack of caution while so near the mainland. The *Philadelphia* was sailing at about eight and a half knots. He had ordered Porter to the mizzentop to take a view of the harbor of Tripoli, the city being now about four miles distant, and Porter had climbed halfway up the mizzen rigging when suddenly the water shoaled and the ship, to the amazement of all hands, struck.

Bainbridge had been seeking an offing into what he judged to be deeper water, but at this location in the eastern approach to the harbor

of Tripoli, he had hit what the Barbary mariners knew as the Kaliusa
Reef. Where the *Philadelphia* struck they were not reefs in the sense of
jutting rocks, because there was no penetration of the ship's hull, but
rather a shelving or ridge of sand on which the vessel merely rose and
bottomed. The impact was more a mounting than a collision. Bainbridge
saw that the ship rested on the shelf to the afterpart of the fore chains,
and that the stern was free and clear. His bearings showed that Tripoli
was 4½ miles southwest by west from the grounding.

No such reef was shown on any of Bainbridge's charts and he had assumed he was safe in making directly for the open Mediterranean. Tripolitan vessels knew how to get through this barrier; informed piloting
was the only thing required, because the reef was divided into two parts
with an open channel between them. Had Bainbridge continued a short
distance farther toward Tripoli before he hauled off shore he would have
passed through this channel; and, of course, had he continued after the
Tripolitan xebec until he was close to the harbor entrance and then
turned to sea, he would have encountered no difficulty. But unhappily
he veered at the wrong place and struck the eastern part of the shelving.

His first recourse was to crowd on all sail in order to force the ship
over the bank. This happened to be exactly the wrong procedure, for
the bank was wide and the ship could by no means be carried across it
by the wind or any other method.

Bainbridge then turned to Porter, who had come to the deck from the
ship's rigging, and the Lieutenant suggested that the officers generally be
consulted, which led the Captain to call a hurried council. Meantime it
was noticed that the stern lifted and fell with the waves and was still
clear of the shoal, a fact which was confirmed when a small boat was put
out to make soundings entirely around the ship. The deep water was
astern. The judgment of the council naturally was that efforts should be
made to back the ship off the reef. The anchors were cut from the bows,
only one being retained, and all the guns were run abaft. The sails were
then laid aback to gain the assistance of the wind, which was blowing
strongly from the northwest. But the sea, running heavy waves, only
lifted the ship farther on the reef. She listed to the port to the extent
that her larboard sills were at the water's edge. Her decks sloped so
much that her guns could in no manner be aimed or worked accurately.

The consensus then was that the ship should be lightened. All hands
set to work throwing overboard the heavy articles. The pumps were
started to drain the water casts. The guns were heaved overboard except
the minimum necessary on the decks and in the bow to defend the ship
from the enemy gunboats which already could be seen putting out from
Tripoli Harbor. Finally in desperation the foremast was cut away to

lighten the front of the ship. But the *Philadelphia* was stuck fast on the shelf, a gentle incline on the bosom of the sea. When the measures taken to save her were being reviewed at the court of inquiry convened nearly two years later on board the *Constitution,* the witnesses were questioned on whether there were not sufficient boats to carry out an anchor, by means of which the ship might have been kedged off the reef. Bainbridge covered this in the statement he laid before the court when it opened, saying he had no boat capable of carrying an anchor. If such a boat had been available, he further explained, it could not have been employed because the enemy gunboats by that time had come close enough to command the area where it would have had to be placed. The ship grounded only a mile and a half offshore and on the water between were now ranged nine enemy gunboats.

When the enemy opened, it was obvious they meant to capture and preserve the ship. Their fire was directed at the rigging. Bainbridge replied in such manner as he could, considering the degree to which the ship had heeled over to the port side. He had a part of the stern cut away but even then could not run his guns out far enough to prevent setting the ship on fire by their discharges. They did once set the ship ablaze but the flames were extinguished without much trouble. He fired the guns he had retained on the main deck and the three carronades on the quarterdeck, but ineffectually because of the great heel of the ship. Even cutting away the mainmast made the management of the guns no easier, though it was never made clear why, if the carronades could be fired at the target at all, they could not in some manner have been given a degree of effectiveness.

The soundings showed the *Philadelphia,* after she listed, had 12 feet of water forward and 17 abaft, whereas she drew, by the calculation made the day before by Lieutenant Theodore Hunt, 18½ feet forward and 20½ feet aft. She needed roughly five feet more water. As every expedient to move her proved futile and as she apparently could not be defended, Bainbridge despaired of further effort. It was now 4:00 P.M. and all aboard had been laboring desperately since she struck at 11:30 A.M. The enemy had been firing but not attacking with resolution, though five additional gunboats were now seen issuing from the harbor. Bainbridge called another council of his officers, apparently his third, to lay before them the question of surrendering. As he stated it:

> Upon a deliberate consideration of our situation, it was the unanimous opinion that it was impossible to get the ship off, and that all further resistance would be but unnecessarily exposing men in a situation where neither perseverance nor fortitude would be of any benefit

to our Country or ourselves; and it was unanimously agreed that the
only thing left for us to do was to surrender to the enemy.

Perhaps the deciding factor, brought out by Porter rather than Bainbridge, was that one of the Tripolitan gunboats had crossed through the
erratic fire from the *Philadelphia* and taken a position on her starboard
side, perfectly safe from the frigate's guns because of the sharp heel of
the ship to the port. The starboard guns could shoot only at the sky.
Still, there is no evidence from the testimony that the ship was under
more than desultory attack. No casualties had been suffered and certainly there had been no effort at boarding.

Here was the juncture at which Bainbridge urgently needed the missing *Vixen* which could have stood off the gunboats and very likely sunk
enough of them to demonstrate that an attack *en masse* on the *Philadelphia* and an effort at boarding would be costly. If it had at length been
necessary to abandon the *Philadelphia* she could have taken off the crew
and saved upward of 300 officers and men from long captivity and suffering. But the *Vixen* was off Cape Bon, 300 miles away, meeting not the
missing Tripolitan corsairs, but heavy seas which buffeted her severely
and finally drove her back into Malta.

Neither Porter nor Lieutenants Jacob Jones and Theodore Hunt in
their testimony confirmed Bainbridge's statement that the officers were
unanimous for surrender but neither disputed it either, and Porter did
absolve him from any remissness. He said that on the contrary "I noticed
in Captain Bainbridge great coolness and deliberation."

Preparations were then made for the surrender. Midshipman Daniel
T. Patterson, by order of Bainbridge, destroyed the code signal book.
The Captain had ripped out the pages and torn them himself before
handing them to Patterson to be burned or tossed overboard. Gunner
Richard Stephenson obeyed the order to open the cock and flood the
powder magazine, and when the water was running he locked the door
and went on deck with the keys in his hand and reported compliance.
Articles on board judged to be useful to the enemy were destroyed. Cannon shot were thrown into the pumps to block them.

Then Bainbridge directed that the ship be scuttled. He ordered the
carpenter, William Godby, to let in the water and Godby, acording to his
own testimony, summoned his two mates. The three pierced the bottom
with chisels and augers in a number of places, sufficient in his opinion to
fill the ship. Godby said he reported to the proper officer. But Godby
obviously did his work poorly. The ship did not fill. In his testimony he
contended the Turks got possession in time to stop the holes. Sailing
Master William Knight was certain the forward part of the ship was

pierced by the carpenter because he had heard the water running through the auger holes. He was vaguer in his opinion as to why the ship did not fill, venturing only that the auger holes "must have been stopped in some manner." The question was of the first importance because on the failure of the ship to fill rested the ability of the Tripolitans a little later to float her.

When all was supposed to be in readiness, the flag of the *Philadelphia,* the beautiful 38-gun frigate the people of the City of Brotherly Love had built by public subscription and presented to the government, a striking vessel designed by the versatile Josiah Fox, which was worthy of a great name, was hauled down. The sun was setting in the western sea as the colors were struck.

Only once before in the history of the U.S. government had a warship struck. By a whim of chance the ships were under the same commander. In the quasi-war with France, Bainbridge had surrendered the *Retaliation,* the former *Croyable,* recaptured by the French off Guadeloupe.

In the several letters he wrote about the *Philadelphia,* on November 1, 1803, the day following the surrender, addressed to the Secretary of the Navy, to Commodore Preble, to Lieutenant Smith of the *Vixen,* and to his wife Susan Bainbridge at Perth Amboy, New Jersey, he did not deviate from the general outline of his story that he worked to his limit to save the ship, but he did tell his wife that his agony was not from his confinement but because of his absence from her and "an apprehension which constantly haunts me, that I may be censured by my countrymen."

There was, in fact, a minimum of censure. In his letter to Preble he acknowledged the misfortune in dispatching the *Vixen* to Cape Bon: "Had I not sent the Schooner from us," he said, "the Accident might have been prevented: If not we should have been able to have extricated ourselves from Barbary Prison, but my Motives of ordering her to Cape Bon, was to grant more efficient protection to our Commerce, than I could by keeping her with me." He hoped the Commodore would regard the dispatch of the *Vixen* judicious, however unfortunate it proved to be. In another letter to Preble he gave more details about the loss and stressed that there was no chance to offer resistance.

"Some Fanatics," he asserted, "may say that blowing up the ship would have been the proper result. I thought such conduct would not stand acquitted before God or Man, and I never presumed to think I had the liberty of putting to death 306 Souls because they were placed under my command."

(Varying totals have been stated as the number of Americans captured. This writer's count of the ship's roster at the time shows 235 seamen, 41 marines, and 33 commissioned and non-commissioned officers, a total of 309. The number reported to be housed as captives in Tripoli was 307. Two appeared to be absent and unaccounted for, a small discrepancy in such a circumstance.)

Bainbridge was indeed despondent at this hour: "I have zealously served my country and strenuously endeavored to guard against accidents, but in spite of every effort misfortune has attended me through my Naval life—Guadeloupe and Algiers have witnessed part of them, but Tripoli strikes the death blow to my future Prospects."

When Preble finally replied, he assuaged the distressed man with words not of condemnation but of comfort. William Ray, a marine, who wrote the most graphic and sympathetic account of the captivity and suffering of the crew of the *Philadelphia* during the nineteen months they were in Tripoli prisons, contended after the war that some of the crew believed at the time the ship could be floated and pleaded with Bainbridge not to surrender her. Always there was some question. Bainbridge lost no standing among the officers or future opportunity at the hands of the Department by the surrender; but taken with his surrender of the *Retaliation* and his submittal to the impressment of the *George Washington* by the Dey of Algiers, he did lose prestige among the seamen.

When Ray, the marine, came to reflect after the war on the officers of the *Philadelphia,* he judged many of them competent but felt Bainbridge lacked the inspirational qualities of Preble or the dauntless flare of Decatur which made anyone who sailed under his flag willing to sacrifice his life for him. Bainbridge was rated a good officer by many of the seamen, but Ray thought he "trusted to implicitly to his subordinate myrmidons." Lieutenant Richard B. Jones he considered a "calm, mild and judicious officer, beloved by all seamen." He spoke well of Lieutenant Theodore Hunt, and Midshipmen Robert Gamble and James Gibbon, and of his own officer, Lieutenant William B. Osborne, who commanded the Marine Corps detachment. The omission of the names of Lieutenants Porter and Jacob Jones gave evidence that their strict discipline, which went to make them great ship captains of a later decade, did not meet with universal approval. The attitudes between officers and men are of more than ordinary interest because they all had to endure a long imprisonment under the most trying circumstances in a hostile city.

Jacob Jones, who would rise to command formidable American squadrons in both the Atlantic and Pacific oceans, was above the average in age, education, and intelligence among the junior officers of 1803, and certainly was among the ablest. A native of the Smyrna, Delaware, area, he had studied at the Lewes Academy and had taken the medical course at the University of Pennsylvania. This, together with four years in a doctor's office in Dover, eminently qualified him for the practice he began in his home state. When patients did not come in sufficient numbers he shifted to clerk of the Delaware Supreme Court, but neither that nor medicine could retain him when in early 1799 hostilities erupted with France. Though he was then thirty-one and many other midshipmen were still in their teens, he took the low rank on the *United States.* Two years later he became a second lieutenant on the ill-fated *Philadelphia,* where he was unobtrusive but firm, respected both for his seamanship and his breadth of learning. His greatest moment was to come in the War of 1812, when in command of the *Wasp* he outfought and captured the well-matched *Frolic.* One of his lieutenants in that fight was James Biddle, a midshipman with him on the *Philadelphia* when she struck. Biddle became one of the most skillful navigators of the service, whose long naval career was filled with notable events. Among the most important was taking possession of Oregon Territory for the United States.

Whether the Tripolitans had been timid to approach the American craft because of the punishment they had taken in the battle over the grain polacres, or did not appreciate fully the helpless condition of the *Philadelphia,* or had not been boldly led, or did not want to damage her, is not clear from their action, but they well understood what was meant by the lowering of the American flag. Grand Admiral Murad Reis had come out personally with the last wave of gunboats and now directed the boarders. He gave primary attention to the seaworthiness of the frigate. His first act was to see that the auger and chisel holes were securely plugged.

The wave of Mussulmans swept across the frigate's deck intent mainly on looting. They began stripping the Americans of items of worth, watches, chains, trinkets, rings, and money and continued the process with officers and enlisted men alike while the crew was being removed from the ship and taken in boats into Tripoli. The seamen were robbed of their bundles of clothing, or what in later American colloquialism came to be known as duffel bags.

Night had fallen but the dark city, lighted here and there by torches, was alert to the great stroke of luck which had given the Bashaw hostages, quantities of stores the Americans had been unable to destroy, and a splendid frigate which, if she could be dragged off the shoals, could be pressed into service. With the Tripolitan xebecs and gunboats, this vessel would raise the regency to the status of a presentable maritime power. No other African nation except envied Algiers had such naval strength. So swift a raider loose in the Mediterranean could play havoc with merchant shipping from Gibraltar to the Levant, and stand off or destroy the lesser craft that made up the bulk of the American fleet. Other frigates which had been with Preble at Tangier were going home. The *Constitution* remained at the moment his only frigate in the Near East, and the only warship that might challenge the *Philadelphia* on reasonable terms.

The boats were rowed across the rough waters at night and reached Tripoli about 10 P.M., and by the time they landed, few of the prisoners had any personal property remaining. Bainbridge was stripped of his watch, money, gloves, cravat, and epaulets. The only thing he saved was a miniature of his wife which he wore as a pendant around his neck. Being more attached to it than anything else, he threatened personal combat when an enemy boatman tried to tear it from him. Most of the seamen were deprived of their clothing except shirt, trousers, and hat. They were drenched by the spray as they were rowed into the harbor, and by having to wade ashore.

Officers and men were landed at the Bashaw's castle, which stood on the waterfront, a great fortress that had been reared bit by bit over the ages, with almost innumerable chambers and labyrinths, half splendid, half decayed, which overlooked the magnificent arch of Marcus Aurelius, the only remaining vestige of Roman glory. Crowds were at the waterfront and some took advantage of the opportunity to spit on the contemptible infidel prisoners. They passed through two rows of armed men extending from the beach to the castle gate. Inside the fortress, they were conducted along one of the dark, winding passageways, described as dismal, and came into a paved avenue lined by some of the Bashaw's guards whom Marine Private Ray regarded as "terrific janizaries, armed with glittering sabres, muskets, pistols and tomahawks." Some of these spit on the Americans as they passed. Eventually after more winding about they reached the inner chamber where the Bashaw in person was awaiting their coming.

The inlaid mosaic throne, raised four feet above the floor, was richly covered with velvet, fringed with gold, and speckled with brilliants. Heavy Oriental carpets covered the floor of gleaming, ornate marble. Behind the throne were walls of porcelain through which ran designs that seemed fantastic and rococo to Americans accustomed to the simple homesteads of the New World. There, decked out for the great occasion of his reign, wearing an embroidered robe of cerulean silk wrought with gold, with a diamond-studded belt holding a golden-hilted saber and two gold-mounted pistols, sat a corpulent, black-bearded man, with strikingly handsome countenance that reflected curiosity mixed with proud disdain, Bashaw Yusuf Karamanli, usurper of the throne of Tripoli.

CHAPTER THIRTEEN

Tripoli and the Karamanlis

RIPOLI was then as now a city of enchantment. Its buff and white houses stood against a background of olives and palms. The abundant flowering hibiscus showed against gleaming sand, and before and almost on three sides—for the old town occupied a small peninsula—was the usually gentle Mediterranean with its variegated blues and greens.

City of cloudless skies, of the sweet jasmine and the white and purple oleander tree, of the soft onshore breeze which often in the late afternoon of the mellow autumn, and in the blossoming spring, whitened the crest of the sea waves with its brisk, envigorating blow.

Secluded behind the rocky reef which formed a harbor and accounted for its existence—together with the bounty of eight inches of annual rainfall—Tripoli had been protected for centuries from the winter storms, and almost hidden from rovers along the flat African shore. What was noticed first, when sighted from the sea in the 1800 era, was not the flat-roofed houses nor the low mosques, nor even the disorderly walls or the pile of the Bashaw's waterfront castle, but the unusual verdure of the coast. Groves of date palms stood in orderly rows, and here and there pomegranates and aloes, behind which were fields of tobacco, millet, and barley. Watermelons seemed to thrive in the Tripolitan sand and drink from the drought, for there were stories before the coming of the Americans that they sometimes reached the weight of one hundred pounds.

One of the most entrancing of the Tripolitan products came from the neighboring island of Jerba, the ancient Meninx, at times a part of the regency's possessions. This was a fruit of a pod, with bright yellow flesh not unlike the mango or pawpaw, which is supposed to have been the enervating delight of the ancient lotus-eaters. The hard seed of this fruit, which was distinctive from the ordinary carob tree of the Levant, was termed by the Moors *karroob* and by the Arabs *quirat*. They used these seeds as balances for weighing precious stones. Thus a diamond might balance a number of karroob seeds and hence weigh that many karroobs or, in the evolvement of the word, *karats* and now *carats*. The seeds were light; 2,300 made a pound.

Behind the town was the sandy plain, called the Messea, stretching away toward the Sahara. One of the visitors at this era spoke of the desert to the east of Tripoli, which reached to Egypt, as involving "a journey more dreadful than can be conceived." It could not be undertaken without a knowledge of astronomy and the aid of a compass, because the landscape was constantly undergoing change from the shifting sands. They might raise a mountain in an area that had been a valley or level off the land where a mountain had once stood.

Even in the immediate region of Tripoli, the verdure noted from the distance was somewhat illusory, because the green tops of the inviting palms, seen at an angle on the approach, rose out of the sand and afforded only a thin shade, and in the outcountry especially, the greenness disappeared. Given water, as it must have once had in abundance, the soil is fertile. The Romans, who never worshiped leisure, solved the water problem to an extent with their great aqueducts and cisterns. In later times an easier method was attempted by seeking to appease the gods who withheld the needed rains.

John D. Leyden, the British physician who visited the country twelve years after the American war and left an engaging account of his travels through North Africa, told that in time of severe drought the first effort of the populace was to bestir the powers by clamor, importunings, and exhortations. Children were sent to run through the streets screaming the entire night long, often for eight successive days. If the heavens were still unready to exchange rain for quiet, the saints and seers took a hand and finally even the King added to the entreaties and unholy din. Persecution never has its humorous side, but at times its ludicrous aspect, and such was the case here. When all else failed, the distraught people assembled and exiled the Jews of the city, and told them not to return until they brought rain with them.

Still, there was meager animal fare on the rim of the shimmering desert. Wild beasts roamed the Barbary shore during the era of the American war. The most common was the hyena, called the *dubbah*. There were panthers, wild boar, ostriches, and antelopes, while snakes and scorpions abounded.

Though the harbor was commodious, it was shallow and could not grant ingress to vessels drawing more than five or six fathoms, or from thirty to thirty-six feet. The dominating structure of the harbor was the gray old Castle (now neatly restored) which, partly in ruins, loomed above the shore. It was a formidable stronghold in appearance, while inside it was composed of a series of splendid chambers, arched colonnades, and circling courts, brilliant with mosaics. Beneath was a labyrinth of subterranean passages where captives were imprisoned and the condemned were executed. In those days a wide, circular beach stretched in front of the town and toward the east, and much of the city was built in a crescent extending eastward from the tip of the peninsula, and westward for a distance facing the Mediterranean beyond the reef which formed the harbor.

In this city of flat-topped houses, sometimes built from and on heaps of ancient rubble; of mosques, narrow streets, of baths with their clustered cupolas; of fruit trees and date palms giving their scant shade, but with the soft afternoon breeze often coming pleasantly from the Mediterranean, lived a population of extremes in poverty and opulence.

For the more consequential men the coffee bazaar was the place of assembly and, in the absence of newspapers, the forum where information was exchanged. These bazaars were strictly for coffee and no other refreshments were served. Inside they were smoky kitchens, and Arabs of distinction never entered them, but sent their slaves, who brought the coffee in vessels to the arbor-covered marble benches outside. These were in effect couches, richly draped with carpets and mats, on which the chief men would sit cross-legged—"bear-like," as Eaton described the posture in Tunis—and sip their beverage leisurely. Sometimes the females of the castle might prefer their coffee flavored with cinnamon, nutmeg, or cloves, but the men at the bazaar drank theirs black, thick, and straight.

As these patriarchs of wealth sipped, behind them stood their slaves, often three to one master. One held his pipe, a second his kerchief, and the third his coffee cup, thus releasing his hands while he conversed. Any distinguished Tripolitan Arab required both hands to emphasize and illustrate his words. Often he would do this by jabbing or drawing designs with the finger of one hand on the palm of the other.

On state occasions the chief officials and wealthy men appeared in flowing, gold-embroidered robes of satin and velvet, and, when seasonal, in rich furs. They wore shawls of the finest texture, jewels, and long silver pendants that served as charms. At noon, which British Consul Richard Tulley's sister observed to be "an hour when no Moor of distinction leaves his house," the city napped.

Beggars were common on the winding streets. In sharp contrast with the ornate garb of the wealthy was the wretchedness of the poor and of even the ordinary-run citizen, who was covered with a piece of dark brown homespun cotton, no more than an age-ripened blanket. Blindness was common among the beggars. The glaring sun of the summer months, taken with the sand particles which filled the air when the ghibli blew from the desert, induced an eye-soreness or ophthalmia, which became aggravated by the presence of numerous busy insects.

Dr. Leyden, who studied social and moral conditions of North Africa, and noticed that games of chance were prohibited as strictly as was alcohol, found the time of the average man occupied with "eating, drinking, sleeping, women, horses and prayers." Apparently cock-fighting, which thrived, was not regarded a game of chance, or else no wagers were laid. Ostrich-racing was another sport.

He reported too that the saints were venerated, but, "any extraordinary qualification—a remarkable crime, sometimes pure idiotism raised them to the rank of saint."

The women of the harem, usually Georgian or Circassian slaves who had been brought to Tripoli when young and trained for court or harem life, went out but rarely, and only to the mosques to fulfill a vow or make an offering; and then the journey was made from eleven to twelve at night in a palanquin enclosed with linen. They were accompanied by a large train of guards who showed lights and shouted their approach. This crying was a signal for all common people to clear the streets, for none could look on the females from the seraglio without grave risk to his neck.

Such was the city and society the United States was fighting, by no choice of the Jefferson administration, in its first formal war under the Constitution.

The name Tripoli is a combination of the Greek words *tri* and *polis,* employed by the Romans to designate the province of the three cities, the ancient Oea of the Greeks, Sabratha, and Leptis Magna. The title came into use during the Vespasian dynasty in Rome.

Sabratha, about fifty miles west of Tripoli, was destroyed when the Vandals and Saracens swept across North Africa and never was rebuilt. Leptis Magna, seventy miles east of Tripoli, is one of the imposing ruins of antiquity, with remnants of the Arches of Trajan and Septimius Severus, lavish, marble, colonnaded Hadrianic baths, Doric temple, forum, and great amphitheater.

Oea, the only survivor of the three cities, is the present Tripoli. Its life extends back into the dim days of early Phoenician trade and exploration. There is a tradition that the city once was farther north, and moved southward as the land fell into the sea; that the whole indentation of this part of Africa was once fertile soil, reaching directly across what is now the Gulf of Sidra and the Gulf of Gabès, from Cape Razat to Cape Bon. But though the harbor of Tripoli is shallow, the sea outside is deep and gives no evidence of a receding shore.

Nevertheless, the mystery of the ancient productivity and present barrenness of much of this area remains to perplex students. The legend of the receding shore is one effort to explain where the fertile soil went long before history was written. Even in historic times, Nero is supposed to have marveled over the country's yield of barley, and something must have accounted for the great "corn wells" noticed by the Consul Tulley, which were huge, man-made, storage caverns where surplus grain is supposed to have remained dry and in an entirely serviceable state for as long as a century. These wells, it is averred, were filled in an era when Tripolitan corn was exported about the world and "prized almost above any other." But today much of the land is drifting waste except for the tufts of esparto grass, of heavy texture like hemp or linen, which for more than a century has been exported to the Scottish paper mills and has provided a revenue perhaps as large and certainly more stable than piracy. Oea became Tripoli when the Saracens conquered and mistook the name of the province for that of the city. The Moorish name Trablis is the way the Arabs pronounce Tripoli.

A transition in the modern history of the principality occurred in 1714, when Hamet Karamanli seized power by surprising and massacring the entire Turkish garrison of the palace fortress. The city had been walled, except on the north so as not to exclude the sea breezes, by Dragut the pirate, Suleiman's Grand Admiral, and after his passing the Porte had appointed the governor, known to the Turks as the Sangiac or the Pacha. Since the Tripolitan-Arabian tongue did not accommodate a p, (a Phoenician-Greek letter) the Turkish term Pacha, or Pasha, became in Tripolitan usage the Bashaw, often spelled Basha. After Hamet's bloody coup the Porte tolerated a hereditary rule, which had become a petty despotism, passing to the eldest son, but the Karamanli family was not so reliable in this respect as their remote Turkish masters and the succession became the cause of continual intra-family intrigue and violence. Hamet's ascension marked the passage of government from the Turks to the home people—Arabs and Berbers, though in the naval reports of that day they were usually called Moors, a term more properly applicable to the Moroccans. The tie with Turkey could be detected only by the payment of the annual tribute.

Hamet raised an army and brought the outlying provinces under his control, and extended the domain of Tripoli across Cyrenaica and beyond Derna to the borders of Egypt. He overran Fezzan, the great desert tract to the south with its scattered oases, which gave him control of the caravan routes bringing from central Africa rich products like ivory tusks to add to the carpets, coffee, and spices that came across the great caravan routes from the east. These conquests rewarded Hamet with the title of "the Great" in Tripolitan history.

His end was far from imperial. The Bedouins, Berbers, and Arabs, with their abiding faith in portents, necromancy, prophecies, and spells, told the story that Allah had punished Hamet the Great because of his tyranny and stricken him blind. The awful retribution resulted from his lust for a beautiful native girl he had seen near the city, who was the daughter of the Marabout, or holy man of the region. Hamet told him to dress his daughter richly in keeping with her beauty and send her to the royal chamber that night, else the holy man would be cut into ribbons. The Marabout sent her. Hamet the Great came eagerly to the room, there to view her as a corpse.

The Marabout—a Moslem term for an anchorite—had procured poison and she had taken the potion just before going to the tryst. Then he besought Allah to strike Bashaw Hamet the Great with blindness. Whether for this or other cause, Hamet had grown blind. His power weakened, he could gaze no more on the fair maidens and covet them for his harem. The faithless subjects who had knelt to him now treated him with contempt. Life lost its value and in 1745, after a reign of thirty-one years, Hamet the Great put a pistol to his head and blew out his brains.

Hamet's second son, Mohammed, emerged triumphant in the succession squabble and for twenty-one years gave Tripoli a relatively stable rule, the memorable feature of which seems to have been that he allowed his seven brothers to survive him. That did not assure them natural deaths, for Mohammed's son Ali, on ascending to the caliphate, quickly got six and possibly all seven out of the way. The claim was made in Tunis that the youngest of the seven brothers escaped; and a pretender long resided in that city. Tunis would have liked Tripoli as a dependency and was not indisposed then or later to sponsor reasonable aspirants to the Tripolitan throne. Ali grew mellow with the years, had but one wife, and maintained the ornate court described by Consul Tulley's sister in her inimitable letters which are referred to from time to time in this account.

Travelers came and went but none ever left so engrossing a story of Tripolitan life and manners as this sister of Tulley, who was never given any more satisfactory identity than that. Her name does not appear on her publication nor among the many British and American references to it. But she was a gifted observer. Her compilation of anecdotes about the Bashaw and palace personalities and her letters about the customs and habits of the Moors, Arabs, and Turks were published in London in 1816. They give the best available pictures of the city and its people at about the time of the American-Tripolitan War, which followed the reign of Ali.

Ali designated the eldest of his three sons, Hassan, as his successor and there was every prospect that he would become a beneficent autocrat because his early life was marked with generosity and fidelity to his associates and much activity for the public good. He was neither lazy nor greedy, but alert and dedicated. Bashaw Ali gave him the title of Bey, entrusted to him the army command, sent him on expeditions to quell mutineers, and prepared as well as he could for an orderly transfer of power when he died. Ali's second son was Hamet, amiable, gentle, judged to be indecisive. Even before their father passed, he and Hassan quarreled. The elder brother was charged with sending an improper message to Hamet's wife and they armed themselves against each other.

But the third son, Yusuf (Joseph), the handsome Bashaw who fought the Americans, was both ambitious and ruthless. When he became sixteen he decided that he, and neither of his elder brothers, should rule Tripoli. Boldly he announced his intentions to his friends. Hassan, the eldest, discounted his threats as the vaporings of youth and did not appear concerned even after Yusuf allied himself with Hamet and together they denounced Hassan's right to the throne. That was while the father, Ali, still lived. The country was thrown into such a state of discord and civil strife that the Porte ordered the Capudan Pasha to go out with a fleet, and Tunis likewise prepared an army of intervention; but before the fleet could sail it was given substitute orders to suppress the Mamelukes in Egypt, and without the aid of Constantinople, the Bey of Tunis never risked the march across the desert.

Tripoli had to work out its own affairs, and this the ambitious young Yusuf did with dispatch. In 1790, before the old Bashaw died, Yusuf, now twenty, arranged an ostensible reconciliation with his eldest brother, Hassan, in the apartment of their mother, Lilla Halluma. She, a cultivated woman and friend of Tulley's sister, had been their father's sole wife and her great hope was that she could pacify her three embittered sons. The trusting Bey Hassan came armed with his sword, which his confident mother induced him to unbuckle so he might meet his brother unarmed. Yusuf likewise appeared unarmed. He called for the Koran to give religious validity to the reconciliation, but that request proved to be no more than a signal to his Numidian escort. One of his attendants handed him two pistols instead of the book, and with one of them he put a bullet into his brother's body, while his horrified mother was looking on.

Hassan, grievously wounded, struggled to get to his sword, but before he could secure it another bullet into his vitals laid him on the palace floor. (The murder occurred in a room of the palace, or Castello, now used as the Library of Antiquities, a part of the Tripolitan museum.) Bey

Hassan thought his mother had betrayed him. To her his dying eyes were turned. "Mother," he said, "is this the present you have reserved for your eldest son?" Yusuf's bodyguard of Negro slaves was then ordered to complete the work of the pistols and they stabbed Hassan, by some accounts a hundred times. To these last atrocities his wife also was a witness, because she had been drawn to the reconciliation chamber by the sound of the pistol shots. Yusuf went out to celebrate the achievement with a feast.

When Hamet, the second brother, arrived in Tripoli from the country, Yusuf consented that he be designated Bey, and for a time they worked together resisting the squadron of a Turkish freebooter Ali-ben-Zool, who captured Tripoli in the summer of 1793 and ousted old Bashaw Ali and his wife Lilla Halluma, who fled to Tunis. Both of them died as expatriates in 1795. Hamet and Yusuf, raising a force in Tunis, marched back to Tripoli and the pirate Ali-ben-Zool evacuated the city on their approach. The Porte sided with the Karamanli family. When it came to proclaiming a new Bashaw, Yusuf was on the ground and took the honor, and Hamet, who had been sent on another trip into the country, found the gates closed when he confidently was returning home. Though he was the elder, the pitiless Yusuf was on the throne. Hamet retired to Tunis, where for a time he had the sympathy and support of Bey Hamouda Pacha, though that satrap was a usurper himself; and where, as one of the most fateful events in his career, he was thrown into an acquaintance with the fretful but dynamic American consul William Eaton. Yusuf, meantime, in November, 1796, as the ruling Bashaw, signed the treaty with Joel Barlow establishing peace between the United States and Tripoli. He had just ascended his bloody throne and needed time to consolidate his power. Then, five years later, when he felt more secure, when he wanted ships and loot, and when the Scotch renegade Murad Reis provided a competent commander of his xebecs, he had the American flagpole cut down.

Eaton had appreciated that Yusuf's weakness was more in his sanguinary usurpation than in the crumbling walls of his city. Cathcart had advised him of the possibilities inherent in Yusuf's usurpation and Eaton had taken fire to the idea when he noticed Hamet's pliability and learned of Yusuf's lack of popularity with his subjects. He became convinced that by taking Hamet with it, the American squadron might go to Tripoli as a force of deliverance. Cathcart had written from Leghorn, June 29, 1801, that they must effect a revolution in favor of Hamet, "for as long as Joseph Bashaw lives our commerce will not be secure."

Yusuf at this stage set a trap. He offered Hamet the governorship of Cyrenaica with Derna his seat, and sent a forty-man escort to Tunis to conduct him to his new post. But Eaton, who had begun to supply Hamet with money borrowed on his personal credit from the Sapatapa of Tunis, warned him against acceptance in a letter saying, "Remember that your brother thirsts for your blood." Eaton added persuasion to his cautioning with a fresh gratuity of $2,000. "I have learned from a certain source that his project of getting you to Derna was to murder you," he said for emphasis, then added that the only way Hamet should enter the basha-lick of Tripoli was in the character of the true sovereign. Eaton's borrow-ings on behalf of Hamet made up at least $22,000 of the $34,000 he had owed Hadgi Unis, the commercial agent of the Bey of Tunis, concerning which the controversy occurred at the time Commodore Morris went ashore there—the quarrel leading to the dismissal of Eaton by the Bey. Part of the $12,000 balance had been spent by Eaton in the quixotic ransom of a beautiful Sardinian maiden, Countess Maria Anna Porcile, who was about to be assigned to the harem of the old and creaky Tuni-sian Prime Minister, one of Eaton's especial dislikes. The expenditure might have been looked on as in the interest of humanity but scarcely of the United States.

Hamet had anything but clear sailing even with such a persevering advocate as Eaton pressing his cause. When Eaton was on his Italian vacation the Sapatapa of Tunis, Side Yusuh, another controversial char-acter with whom Eaton had to match wits at every turn (he had come to Tunis as a slave from the slopes of the Caucasus Mountains and had grown wealthy in the service and it appeared at times the disservice of the Bey) had joined his ruler in momentarily siding with Yusuf, in un-dertaking to induce Hamet to take the Derna assignment. Eaton heard of this and rushed back from Leghorn, and on his return promptly broke up the plan. He promised the Sapatapa $10,000 if Hamet won the throne; notified American ships to intercept any vessel transporting Hamet toward Derna; and finally induced the prince to feign to go to Derna but to slip into Malta enroute and remain there in greater security than he was enjoying in Tunis, where the Bey had cut off his supplies. In Malta, Hamet dismissed the escort which had been supplied to him by Yusuf, and which could scarcely have been expected to allow him to reach Derna in one piece, and awaited assistance from the Americans. The Sapatapa had confided to Eaton that Yusuf's plan was to get pos-session of Hamet and destroy him as he had his elder brother Hassan.

Commodore Morris did not feel that his instructions authorized him to try to set Hamet on the throne and advised Hamet's agent to take up the matter with the U.S. government—a very roundabout process for one seeking quick action. Captain Murray earlier was even more outright in his rejection of the entire Eaton project. Opposition came also from Captains Bainbridge and Barron. The only American ship commander who appeared sympathetic with Eaton's plan was the erratic Captain Daniel McNeill of the *Boston* and at the time he was being recalled to the United States. McNeill met Hamet in Malta and told him to hold fast to his purpose. Eaton learned that the escape of Hamet to Malta had excited brother Yusuf, who had called up the Arabs from the desert to help defend the city against an expedition he supposed would be launched forthwith to install Hamet on the throne. "This fact, together with the solicitude of the usurper to get possession of his brother's person, go to demonstrate the correctness of our calculations," Eaton wrote.

Both Jefferson and Madison were impressed with Eaton's proposals and the possibilities they opened to place in power in Tripoli one who avowed he would "always remain the faithful friend of the United States."

Eaton all along had taken violent exception to the attitudes of several of the naval officers for tending to block him in the Hamet project. Perhaps they were doubtful more of Eaton than Hamet, because Eaton had been so intemperate and unrelenting in his criticism of the ship captains for what he regarded their lackadaisical prosecution of the war. Now he was even more incensed. In June, 1802, he wrote Secretary Madison protesting against the severe criticism of Captains Barron and Bainbridge, saying he had been "by them reprobated in a stile of most illiberal censure," and that under their influence his measures for the rightful Bashaw had been rejected by Captain Murray "in an air of authority and reprimand which I should not expect from the highest authorities of the government."

But the opposition of the ship captains was not shared by the careful Secretary of State. Writing on August 22, 1802, after consultation with President Jefferson, he gave Eaton a guarded assent to proceed with the Hamet project, and added a reassurance for Hamet that he would be dealt with fairly if the plan to put him on the throne failed:

> Although it does not accord with the general sentiments or views of the United States, to intermeddle in the domestic contests of other countries, it cannot be unfair, in the prosecution of a just war, or the accomplishment of a reasonable peace, to turn to their advantage, the enmity and pretensions of others against a common foe. How far success in the plan ought to be relied on cannot be decided at this distance, and with so imperfect a knowledge of many circumstances. The event, it is hoped, will correspond with your zeal and with your calculations. Should the rival brother be disappointed in his object, it will be due to the honor of the United States, to treat his misfortune

with the utmost tenderness, and to restore him as nearly as may be to the situation from which he has been drawn, unless some other proper arrangement should be more acceptable to him.

This, Madison explained, was President Jefferson's wish, which would be communicated to the commodore of the fleet and to Consul Cathcart, with a suggestion that if peace should be declared with the ruling Bashaw, an attempt should be made to insert a provision in the treaty favorable to his brother.

But Captain Murray, who was in Malta at about the time Madison was writing from Virginia, held a meeting there with Hamet and shifted his view from the opposition he had expressed when the project was Eaton's. He wrote to Commodore Morris that Hamet was "a mild, amiable man, & would be perfectly friendly and Peaceable toward us." Hamet thought he could assemble a large army at Derna if the Americans would co-operate. Murray followed this with a letter to the Secretary of the Navy saying he thought the plan was feasible. Murray reported another crime of Yusuf, that to get the throne he had poisoned his own father. So Murray, at a greater risk than Eaton was prepared to take, gave Hamet a passport to go to Derna. He sailed with a few followers in a chartered British brig, but he went not as a governor for the seated Bashaw, but in his own right, as Eaton had demanded, as one entering a country he intended to rule.

Hamet landed at Derna late in 1802. On January 20, 1803, he addressed a letter to President Jefferson direct, in which he explained his claim to the throne:

> After the death of my father, I became the lawful Bashaw of Tripoli. I continued so only five months when one unfortunate day my brother advised me to go Pleasuring in the Country, but I was no sooner out of the gates of the City than he shut them against me and I was obliged to go to Tunis, where I remained seven long years, untill my brother more from fear than love wrote to me that he would give me back part of my dominion Viz: the territory of Derna also my wife and five children whom he kept prisoners all this time—I accepted the offer and engaged an English Brig called the Salamine to take me there. I afterward sent the said Brig to Tripoli for my family but he would not let them come away. Therefore I am determined to go there with an hundred thousand men and take him and them too.

He said that to complete the expedition he would need guns, powder, and an advance of forty thousand Spanish dollars.

Hamet's welcome in Derna was all a returning monarch might desire.

Bedouins came in from the desert and a nephew who had been living in Egypt espoused his cause with a body of followers. He won a small brush with some of Yusuf's partisans. So elated was he with his prospects that he meditated an advance overland against Tripoli and dispatched a message to Eaton urging that the assistance expected from the Americans be sent forthwith. All this was at the approximate time Commodore Morris was trying to negotiate a treaty with Bashaw Yusuf at Tripoli. But the Bashaw, fortified by ample food stocks and an army he had been recruiting ever since Hamet landed at Malta, was making excessive demands for tribute and stores before he would listen to the Americans. When the peace talks failed, none seemed to pay much further attention to Hamet.

Hamet held resolutely to his isolated city. Morris went back to Gibraltar, and Eaton, dismissed from Tunis, sailed for the United States, mainly to re-emphasize to the government that Hamet's cause had been left dangling when it offered the most favorable means of establishing permanent friendly relations with Tripoli.

Then the *Philadelphia* was captured. The loss of that frigate appeared to doom American prospects in the eastern Mediterranean. Hamet's followers gradually fell off and disappeared into the desert. Deserted by his own people and apparently forgotten by the Americans, and likely at any time to be picked up by Yusuf's agents, who were seeking him, he abandoned his pretensions to the throne of Tripoli and fled into Egypt. Fearful of the Turks who ruled that country, he went up the Nile and disappeared among the Mamelukes.

Nobody on either side of the Atlantic except Eaton would have been likely to think Hamet would ever be a factor in American relations with Tripoli again. Yusuf sat happily on his throne, where by a great stroke of luck he had become possessed of three hundred hostages and a frigate. So elated was he that he counted the prisoners personally, then sent them off to an outdoor piazza with tiled floors, where they were given some dry clothes—mostly rags which they wore thenceforth because their own clothes were never returned. There they slept that night without covers and without supper.

Bainbridge appears to have been remiss in not ascertaining that his men were fed, though he did send a messenger on their behalf to the Danish consul Nissen. The officers were given supper and blankets and mats to sleep on, after having to answer almost endless questions from the Bashaw about the United States and the strength of the American squadron in the Mediterranean.

Forty hours after the *Philadelphia* had struck, a heavy wind blew from the north and northwest, raising the sea. Murad Reis already had segregated the technicians from the balance of the crew and on the first day after the surrender had them at work repairing the vessel, stopping the leaks more securely and manning the pumps. About noon November 2, the *Philadelphia* suddenly loosened herself from the bed of the sea and floated free. She was towed prettily by a flotilla of small boats into the deep water between the Kaliusa Reef and the shore. "This still adds to our calamity," wrote Bainbridge, but he again emphasized that the crew, in the situation they faced, could not have done what the wind and the Mussulmans accomplished, and he found consolation in the fact that "it is not the first instance where ships have been from necessity [of running aground] oblidged to surrender, and afterwards got off by the enemy, which could not have been effected by the ships company." He cited the cases of the *Hannibal* at Algiers and the *Jason* at St. Malo, both apparently British vessels, and said there were several others.

The members of the *Philadelphia* crew were astonished and in large measure horrified when on the second day after their surrender they saw the Tripolitans towing the frigate from her resting place, where she had seemed so unresponsive to their efforts, into the harbor roads and to a haven near the castle under the protection of the city forts. The refloating of the ship was viewed in Tripoli as a consummate reflection on Bainbridge's seamanship. At the instigation of the Bashaw, Murad Reis, the principal go-between because of his ready command of both languages, came with a group of Tripolitan officers to the window at the back of the prison where the crew was housed temporarily, and questioned the American sailors inside.

The Grand Admiral asked a loaded question: whether the men thought their captain was "a coward, or a traitor?" When they replied that he was neither, Murad Reis continued: "Who with a frigate of forty-four guns, and three hundred men, would strike his colors to one solitary gunboat, must surely be one or the other."

The conversation was recorded by Marine Private Ray. The sailors answered that since the *Philadelphia* was fast on the shoal and they had cast their guns overboard, they had no chance to defend themselves. They conceded that their danger was not immediate except from the one gunboat, but they feared, as Ray reported it, that after nightfall the enemy "would surround and cut us to pieces, giving no quarter." At this the Admiral asserted there had been no need for Bainbridge to throw the guns overboard, "that he might have known she would be got off, as soon as the wind shifted."

The proof was that the *Philadelphia* was afloat in the sight of all. He said that if the Americans had not struck his men would not have ventured to board. That was no doubt a truthful statement, for the prospect of carrying the heavily manned deck of the *Philadelphia* against the

Americans desperate and at bay would have been remote, and, as had
been noted, the Mussulmans, once repulsed, did not ordinarily return
to a second hand-to-hand encounter.

Murad Reis then taunted the sailors by ridiculing their captain and
charging him with cowardice or something worse, as Ray reported the
incident:

> He persisted in the idea that the ship was given up by design; for
> he said, the captain not bringing a pilot with him, and leaving the
> brig, when he acknowledged himself unacquainted with the harbour,
> and then running so nigh in so precipitately, were circumstances
> weighty enough to overbalance all doubts of his treachery, or at
> least, indubitable evidences of his want of judgment, and proofs of
> his pusillanimity.

Murad Reis's case against the American captain's decisions—fortified
by hindsight—was not without some persuasiveness, though the charge
that Bainbridge might have acted treacherously was of course preposterous. Treachery on whose behalf? Bainbridge's character was enough
to refute that charge. The only question was whether he acted with the
proper discretion, and on that, opinions might vary. Clearly his judgment
was not sufficiently erratic to make him culpable in the opinion of the
court of inquiry, the members of which unanimously gave him a clear
verdict.

Another matter of recurring concern to the Bashaw was the latent
strength of the United States, about which he had already interrogated
Bainbridge. Though Murad Reis had been in America as a seaman, Yusuf
wanted him to inquire of the sailors the number of vessels the Americans
possessed and the general strength of the country. To these questions
the sailors gave him fanciful statistics, and he must have been able to
detect the misrepresentations.

The meager power of Tripoli to wage war with the fresh young
Western nation, even when the United States was fighting with scant
forces and at arm's length, must have been apparent to the captives and
to anyone who visited the regency. The city itself had a population of
only around 30,000 Moslems and 2,000 Jews or about one-third that of
Algiers. The entire kingdom of Tripoli, extending indefinitely into the
desert, embraced a population estimated at a million, composed of
Arabs, Berbers, Moors, Negroes, Turks, and Jews. From the whole the
Bashaw received a revenue of not more than $100,000 annually, not
much of an income for waging warfare in any times. This explains why
he felt tempted to pad out his purse by piracy.

Apart from a main reliance on Murad Reis, Yusuf had other ministers, some able, the most outstanding of whom, and the only friend of the Americans, was Sidi Mohammed Dghies, the Secretary of State. He was educated and enlightened about world affairs and possessed neither the Bashaw's rashness nor his tendency to gloat. His Minister of Marine, before that post was taken over by the Scotch renegade, was Hamet Rais, a warlike spirit hostile to the Americans because their merchant vessels offered rich loot. Another of his sea captains, regarded by American sources as a "desperate ruffian," was Rais Amor Shelly—a name suggestive of English nationality, but little more is known about him than the name, though he seems to have been more a commerce raider than a fighter. The Bashaw's treasurer, as nearly as that office was filled, was the Jewish banker Leon Farfara.

The Moslem hatred of the Jews was supposed to exceed their hatred for the Christians, yet the American consul Mordecai M. Noah, referring at a later date to the service of Farfara as the Bashaw's commercial agent, pointed out that with all the supposed oppression of the Jews, "the sovereigns of the Barbary States confide important negotiations to their care and discernment."

The conversation between Murad Reis and the sailors seemed to be mainly a diversion for the Grand Admiral and his coterie and a part of the gloating in Tripoli over the intoxicating possession of more than three hundred hostages and one of the handsomest frigates on the seas.

The Tripolitans procured other items of value. The *Philadelphia*'s guns had been rolled overboard in shoal water. Murad Reis had his men grapple for them and pull them up. They were a neat addition to Tripoli's defensive power.

CHAPTER FOURTEEN

The Captives

AT 8 o'clock on the morning after the capture, the American seamen were visited by a bent, squawlike old sorceress, "ugly by nature, and rendered frightful by art." She pitched into a harangue of meaningless chants but mainly a shrill bu-bu-bu-bu, accompanied by striking her staff on the stone floor. She went among the Americans scrutinizing them closely. She selected one crewman, a Negro, and it was assumed she was going to take him, but she had merely picked him to be one of the cooks for the Castle attendants. This aged crone had forecast the capture of the *Philadelphia* and more than one person in Tripoli, the Bashaw seemingly among them, believed the ship struck because the old witch had put a spell on it. The Bashaw venerated her as an enchantress and prophetess.

Even on the first day the sailors ran into a little trouble which was to prove a recurring point of friction between them and the Tripolitans. The good Moslems were opposed to alcohol and their abstention was no mere lip service, while the seamen were by no means averse to a touch of toddy or grog whenever it could be obtained, or even *aguardiente,* a whisky distilled from dates, and more easy to come by. The Neapolitans and the Jewish merchants, not being Moslems, sold the liquor. One outlet was through the Neapolitan slaves of the castle, the long, flowing Oriental robes being better for concealment than a frontiersman's boots. Some of the Americans who had managed to secrete their money and had been chilled on the November night, sleeping with a single cotton shirt, traded their money for aguardiente and rum. Because they knew nothing about exchange values, they unwittingly gave the Neapolitans—"villainous, mercenary knaves," Ray called them —four times the normal payment.

An early assignment for the unskilled captives was to make their own prison, or bagnio. They were marched to a malodorous warehouse filled with a hodgepodge of supplies—lumber, corn meal, sacks of grain, com-

bustibles—which they had to carry to another building, leaving the
warehouse clear for prison use. In this first labor they could feel they
were in an ill wind. The fierce Mussulman slave-drivers established their
authority by beating the men who showed a flicker of independence or
failed to step lively to orders.

The building, which had once held some captive Swedes, was 50 feet
by 20, with a roof 25 feet high. There was a skylight in the top and two
grated windows in front. This poorly lighted, forbidding old building,
characterized by the scholarly Marine Private Ray as "fuliginous," was
to be the home of around 300 men for nineteen months, except when on
bad behavior they were housed in even more depressing surroundings.
This meant a space of about 1 foot by 3 per man. All the while, on this
first day, clearing the heaps of rubbish from the building, they were not
given a bite. They had had nothing to eat since their capture. Finally at
evening each got a small loaf of coarse bread weighing about twelve
ounces.

The jailers had a practice common in all armies and navies of all time,
of lining up the men and counting them at regular intervals. Perhaps
this was done more frequently here out of fear of escapes. When they
were counted into the prison those who refused to take off their hats
to the jailer were bastinadoed. Ray told how they slept:

> We had nothing to keep us from the cold, damp earth, but a thin,
> tattered sail-cloth; the floor of the prison was very uneven, planted
> with hard pebbles, and as we had nothing but a shirt to soften our
> beds, and nothing but the ground for a pillow, and very much crowded
> in the bargain, the clouds of night shed no salutary repose.

Danish Consul Nissen, who had called on the sailors as well as the
officers the night of their capture, came again the next morning, and
after he had the opportunity to make arrangements for a supply of fresh
food—which he did at the request of Bainbridge—provisions came fairly
regularly. The men had room for a little exercise, walking on the roof
much as a captain would on a New England harbor-town house, or on
a terrace, both overlooking the harbor and the deep blue Mediterranean beyond. They could look down on the *Philadelphia*, at first still
fast to the ledge, and see the boatloads of Mussulmans going and coming
bringing into the city the stores of provisions from the warship—plunder
as plentiful as ever a corsair was likely to bring into a Barbary harbor.
Then they could sweep their eyes over the city and see among the
white-robed, burnoose-swathed crowds, persons wearing American
naval garments. They were not American seamen, but the Tripolitans
who had stripped the Americans of their uniforms on the frigate or on

the boats coming ashore. One of the Bashaw's cabinet said he would collect as much of this stolen clothing as possible and restore it to its owners, but there is no report of what he brought in.

On the second day the prisoners received assignments, the carpenters, blacksmiths, coopers, and other skilled workmen being appointed to appropriate tasks with the xebecs and gunboats on the waterfront. The general run of seamen were organized into labor gangs, mostly to carry stone, dirt, and mortar, and work on the fortifications. Ten others were taken out of the line, apparently by no more careful a selective process than the sorceress used with the Negro crew member, to be cooks at the Castle. As there was a reference in Ray's manuscript to men on the *Philadelphia* who "were called cooks," the crew could not have expected the Bashaw's staff would eat heartily of the American cuisine if any of the shipboard cooks were among the ten. Others were assigned to bring water from a well a quarter of a mile from the work site. The main project on which they labored was a rampart on the waterfront east of Tripoli commanding the entrance of the harbor, which because it was built by the *Philadelphia* sailors came to be known as the American Fort, just as a nearby bulwark was named the Fort English and one west of Tripoli the French Fort.

One common item of diet, called *coos-coos*, was made of barley coarsely ground and boiled in oil, a viand not unlike but probably not so palatable as the Carolina hushpuppy. Sometimes the bread was black, made of barley nobody had taken the time to clean, the loaves being full of chaff and straw. One black barley loaf of twelve ounces, sometimes sour, was the food allotment for twenty-four hours. For a time the details brought from the frigate stores of pork and beef, which the hungry prisoners ate raw. There is no further mention of meat, usually a scarce item in African diet, and apparently the prisoners later received scant protein fare. Those who had money could purchase vegetables and fruits in the public markets in the old city. Private Ray described these marts:

> On each side of the main street in the town, commencing at the principal gate, a long string of low mud-wall huts on each side of the way, is all the market they have; at the doors of which, seated cross-legged on the ground, and a blanket wrapped round them, the Turks retail pumpkins, carrots, turnips, scallions, oranges, lemons, limes, figs, &c, &c. with a thousand trinkets and haberdashers' wares.

While the unskilled men labored on the fort the artisans were put to repairing the frigate, and though many resented the task, they had no alternative than being lashed, a punishment which in a case of active rebellion undoubtedly would have meant death. Manifestly there was not ample sleeping space on the floor for so many prisoners, and those who dropped off first were generally allowed squatter rights, while those who stayed up late talking or drinking had to sleep standing. The spirit of these American sailors living under the most rigorous and squalid conditions, poorly fed, miserably housed, driven at work with lashes by slave masters, and not looked after very solicitously, it appears, by their commanding officer, was nothing short of amazing. Even when things were most trying and many would have despaired they would sing sea ditties and joke with each other, and when there was space because of some being away, caper about their bleak little prison room much as they would on leave in Boston or Charleston.

They had many off-job assignments, some that led them into peculiar situations. Four, including Private Ray, were taken as pack horses and had glimpses ordinarily forbidden of Tripolitan femininity. Led through dirty, crooked alleys and streets, they were taken along a dark passage into a large courtyard, where they suddenly found themselves amid a group of scantily clad females, described as beautiful, who sported themselves on the piazzas above the courtyard. Private Ray's own description is best:

> As the women in the streets are constantly wrapped and muffled up in blankets which conceal their shapes and faces, except one eye, this to us was a novel sight; for the ladies were exposed to view, as much as the half-naked belles of our own towns. They were fantastically wrapped in loose robes of striped silk; their arms, necks and bosoms bare, their eyelids stained round the edges with black, their hair braided, turned up and fastened with a broad tinsel fillet. They had three or four rings in each ear as large in circumference as a dollar. Several of them were very delicate and handsome. They brought us dates, olives, oranges and milk. They expressed or manifested great surprise at our appearance, and, like other ladies, were full of giggling and loquacity.

The prison slave-driver ended the brief party and Ray never did explain what kind of a place they had happened into, whether the seraglio of some Tripolitan of consequence, or a more commonly available establishment, but their job was to take a large copper kettle and carry it half a mile to another house with more women. Here they were less hospitably received. One woman would have slaughtered them if not prevented by their guard, who made it known that her husband had been killed by the fire of the *Philadelphia* when it was on the reef. They left the big kettle here—a four-man kettle must have been of considerable size and may have been used to boil down sugar cane—and walked back to prison over streets which Ray noticed were "not paved, never swept, and full of sharp pebbles," the last causing discomfort to their bare feet.

Lesser characters among the Americans began to drop off obsequiously and seek the favor of the Bashaw and his officers. The first to turn against his companions was John Wilson, a quartermaster of the *Philadelphia,* who fabricated a story for the Bashaw that before Bainbridge struck his colors he had tossed overboard nineteen boxes of dollars and a large bag of gold. Yusuf summoned Captain Bainbridge, who denounced the story as a lie and said the ship's money had been left in Malta. The Bashaw chose not to believe Bainbridge, though the Captain swore on his word of honor, and tried to elicit the truth from the Captain's servant boy by having him flogged. The staunch lad adhered to Bainbridge's version and the Bashaw at length desisted, but Wilson was put in the role of overseer.

When Bainbridge learned of his quartermaster's tale about the money boxes he went to Wilson and demanded an explanation. The man could not make an outright denial but was trying to explain mitigating circumstances when Bainbridge cut him off and declared he would be hanged as a traitor if they ever got back to the United States. The Captain was so enraged he threw a chain at the culprit.

Wilson carried to the Bashaw repeated false stories, including one report of a supposed escape plot. Though the sailors had signed a parole which gave them freedom to go into the town, they were now by Wilson's treachery confined to their warehouse. When Wilson mingled with the other prisoners, they shunned his association. That whipped up his anger and before the first month of the captivity was ended, he renounced his Christian faith, embraced Mohammedanism, and put on the habiliments of a Mussulman. Another lad, Thomas Prince, seventeen years old, proved pliable and after twenty days of captivity became a Mohammendan, causing great anxiety to his mother in Rhode Island. Others abandoned Christianity from time to time until the apostates numbered five, but Wilson alone seems to have been guilty of outright treachery to his former shipmates. One of the other apostates was a carpenter, Peter West, who "turned Turk," as the prisoners described the metamorphosis to the Koran, on December 7, 1803. West was put to work directing a gang building gunboats and repairing gun carriages for harbor defense. Nobody knew such terms as "brainwashing" in those days, but the percentage of defections, five out of three hundred, could not be regarded large, considering the methods of assembling crews in the early years of the nineteenth century.

One day when the Bashaw rode with his retinue through the city he passed the prison. Apostate Wilson had announced his coming and told the Americans he would have to be greeted with three cheers. Wilson lined up the prisoners in single file. Some, to the disgust of others, became "silly asses" who "swung their hats and brayed like the animal they impersonated," but most of the sailors looked on with disdain, unwilling to play the role of sycophants. The Bashaw traveled in medieval state. Foot guards moved ahead of him at a distance, followed by the high constable on a handsome gray Arabian steed, carrying the elegantly ornamented, three-pronged scepter. There was no doubt Yusuf played the role of a king, not a mere Turkish satrap. He rode a horse as white as Napoleon's, caparisoned and decorated with gold and glitter. His robe was white and came to a tasseled hood.

One of his chief staff officers was a large Negro who rode on his right and was reputed to be the man who had finished Hassen, the Bashaw's eldest brother, who, it will be recalled, died from two pistol wounds followed by a hundred hacks. Three or four of Yusuf's younger children rode on mules, while on his left was his vizier, or chief of state. At his rear were Mameluke bodyguards who sought his attention by feats of horsemanship. But the noteworthy feature of the procession was the mule with two boxes slung across its back led by a Neapolitan slave. The animal carried the Bashaw's richest treasure, which went where he went. Government could not be very stable in Tripoli, if the ruler could not leave his castle without taking his jewels and gold with him.

A consideration entering into the imprisonment of the *Philadelphia* crew was that a substantial number were not Americans at all, but British subjects. How many cannot be determined precisely but Bainbridge placed the number of British (they may all have been "English," as he termed them) at more than half the crew.

"The greater part of our crew," he wrote to Preble on December 5, 1803, "consists of English subjects, not naturalized in America; Suppose Lord Nelson was to claim them, and to enforce his demand, would it not be the policy in the United States, to accede to such a measure? Interest, and Humanity, would (in my opinion) sanction an acquiescence."

Possibly he was building up his estimate to get as many as possible qualified for Nelson's attention. A British source has placed the number at about one-third. The presence of so many British subjects on an American vessel throws interesting light on the question which was already creating an issue between the United States and Great Britain and would become a leading factor in bringing on the War of 1812. The roster of prisoners showed two members of the *Philadelphia* crew who claimed French citizenship but the British were not designated. British Consul Brian McDonough made no effort to secure their release, as he had done with the two British subjects on the American merchantship *Franklin* at the time she was captured by Tripoli.

Seamen of that period took merchant ship berths freely without much regard to the nationality of the vessel, especially as between British and American ships, where language was no barrier. What occurred with the merchant vessels happened to a lesser extent with the warships, but there the pay ordinarily was lower and it was more difficult to fill out the crews. Preble undoubtedly had a good many British sailors in his Mediterranean fleet. Beyond question quite a number were on the *Philadelphia,* just as there were American sailors on the *Victory* with Nelson at Trafalgar, though scarcely enough, as some Americans liked to contend, to throw the decision in Nelson's favor.

Whether they were Americans or British, the sailors enlisted on the *Philadelphia* were waging war against Tripoli and no intercession by McDonough, however much he may have enjoyed the Bashaw's favor, would have been likely to free any who might have claimed primary allegiance to the British standard. The problem, while it might intrigue those dealing with British impressments and re-impressments of this era (and impressment was about the only method by which the British home government could satisfy the British navy's ravenous demand for sailors) did not reach the point of an issue in Tripoli during the captivity of the *Philadelphia* crew. British Consul McDonough never raised it.

One surprising encounter on the street was with a Moslem who spoke English well and French better, who, it developed, had been Lafayette's servant during the American Revolution, then had remained in America two years after the General departed. He had been stranded as one of Napoleon's soldiers left behind in a hospital in Egypt, where a kind Mussulman saved his life and gave him such attentions that he became a Mohammedan. He was enroute to Tunis when he met a group of the Americans carrying faggots, and asked "a thousand questions" about America, which he regretted ever having left.

Eventually the prisoners settled down to a variety of humdrum tasks. Some were boring cannon, one of the hardest jobs of all. Others carried mortar. A detail was set at coining buckaseens at the Castle mint, the coin being worth twenty-five to the Spanish dollar. All lived on black barley bread and three-fourths of a gill of oil a day.

Tripoli was building new vessels at feverish pace because of the American war. Spanish carpenters were employed and American prisoners helped, and when they launched a xebec salutes were fired amid public acclaim.

About half of the *Philadelphia* captives were assigned for a time to the task of raising an old ship half-buried in the sand, and though the waters of North Africa are cold in late December, they had to work near naked in water to their armpits, shoveling sand from the bottom and carrying it in baskets to the shore. They labored from sunup until 2:00 P.M. before being given food, when they received some bread and a shot of aguardiente and were allowed to sun themselves a bit. But they had no change of clothing and had to sleep after their labor in their wet breeches, on the floor, without covers. Illness was frequent; deaths occurred. Two seamen who died in early January, 1804, were buried on the beach at the western part of the city.

William Godby, the ship carpenter, was given special work and delicate treatment and was so boastful about it that some of his messmates, among them a Marine sergeant, a purser's steward, and a ship's cook, beat him up. He carried his complaint tattlingly to the Bashaw, where he had the support of the apostate Wilson, who likewise had exchanged blows with Marine Sergeant Erving. The three men were taken to the Castle and given an unmerciful lashing in the customary method of bastinadoing, across the posteriors and then across the soles of the feet. Wilson directed the whipping of the Marine to be sure he would not be spared. Then the three lacerated men, though it was not to be supposed they could move after such a flogging, were heavily chained on each leg. Wilson a little later indiscreetly quarreled with Murad Reis and received 500 bastinados for his insolence. Not even the turncoats were secure from the Grand Admiral's dislike of Americans.

Possibly the imprisonment was not as cruel and heartless as that suffered in earlier years by the American slaves in Algiers. The moderation was due to the presence of Consul Nissen and the consideration of the Secretary of State Sidi Mohammed Dghies, but the suffering in Tripoli was sufficient to inspire John Greenleaf Whittier to one of his passionate outbursts against slavery. He described the captives

> Rough-bearded men, whose far-off wives,
> Wear out with grief their lonely lives;
> And youth, still flashing from his eyes
> The clear blue of New England skies.

Meantime the officers received much more considerate treatment, due to the attentiveness of Sidi Mohammed Dghies. He set aside for them the house Cathcart had occupied when American consul and though it had been stripped of furniture, it was spacious enough for their requirements. Danish Consul Nissen gave every possible attention to their comforts. He sent the officers beds from his consulate, and bedding, other furniture, and articles that made living easier. He handled their letters and provided them with fresh fruits and vegetables from the markets. He called almost every day to learn what service he might perform. What was of the highest value, considering the time on their hands and their despondency over the loss of their vessel, he brought them books.

He remarked knowingly to Bainbridge that "leisure without books is the sepulcher of the living soul." He first sent two large basketloads of books that had been worth transporting all the way to Tripoli—English and French classics, and books of mathematics. The appetites of the incarcerated officers for literature were so insatiable that after he had given them his own volumes he purchased the books which had composed the frigate's library. The price was low because nobody wanted these volumes in English, but they were of the highest worth to the Americans and sufficient to give a fair amount of learning to the younger men. With the aid of Lieutenant Porter and the well-educated Lieutenant Jacob Jones, the Captain set up a sort of a naval academy for the junior officers, where they had school hours, studied mathematics, tactics, navigation, and other subjects, and obtained some value out of the nineteen months which otherwise would have been wasted in idleness.

The old American consulate was sufficiently commodious to allow Bainbridge a separate room for his headquarters, where he wrote much, especially words of advice to Preble, who had some ideas of his own. Bainbridge carried on a double correspondence with the Commodore, the first part the ordinary run of news and the second confidential intelligence written at the beginning in cipher and later in invisible ink— usually known at the time as sympathetic ink—and sent by Consul Nissen along with the diplomatic dispatches going to the Danish consul at Malta, by whom they were transmitted to Preble. Bainbridge is reputed to have written in lime juice, though the more common method was with the juice of lemon or onion, diluted with three parts of water to one of juice, as the pure juice corroded the paper. This sort of ink would seep into the paper and remain invisible until subjected to heat, at which time the writing could be discerned, though more heat was required for juice-ink, to which Bainbridge was reduced, than some other types. The Captain had found that the Bashaw objected to cipher and decreed that no papers should go forth unless written in understandable language.

That led Bainbridge and Nissen to develop the scheme of putting the letters between the pages of the books loaned by the Dane, or on the wrappers in which the books were returned. Nissen managed to explain to the Danish consul at Malta that the papers contained more than met the eye, and how the letters were to be made legible, and this information was passed to Preble. The flourishing secret correspondence came to be important because it had some bearing on Preble's later activities off Tripoli.

Officers and sailors alike were impressed with the Fast of Ramadan and the Biaram festival, the first a strict religious rite and the second a festive observance of the release from the abnegation and penance. The fast lasted thirty days and the restrictions imposed were severe. The faithful were required to be hospitable and charitable to their enemies. They had to observe restraints summarized as:

> To taste food or drink, to smell perfumes, or swallow spittle, to vomit, bathe, or even breathe the air too freely, from day-break till sunset, would render the sacred ordinance null and void. But from evening till day-break, the faithful are allowed to refresh nature.

So austere a discipline for that length of time was rewarded at the end by the Biaram festival, of from three to six days' duration. The fast ended with the new moon which appeared in mid-January. The only significance to the imprisoned sailors was that they noticed "the Turks were all looking at the moon, and muttering some kind of prayers or thanks." Then the feast began on January 15, 1804, and the sailors observed that "joy seemed to brighten the gloomy visages of all the Tripolitans." Every gun in the harbor was fired to acclaim the occasion and "the Turks all appeared arrayed in new suits." The markets were loaded with fresh goods.

For the top officers the feast became a more notable event. Bainbridge and Porter, the senior Americans, were escorted to the Castle by Minister Sidi Mohammed Dghies, conducted into the audience chamber of the Bashaw, and presented to him before what might properly be termed his chair of state, but more realistically his throne, where he sat with the counselors of his Divan, his children, and his bodyguards. The ottomans scattered through the chamber were covered with elegantly embroidered scarlet cloth; the Bashaw and his attendants were richly attired in robes the seamen would have termed their "new suits," and the air was permeated with the fragrance of frankincense and rose-scented perfumes.

The Bashaw invited Bainbridge and Porter to be seated, had sherbet and coffee served to them, treated them as the faithful should to be hospitable to enemies at this season. When they departed, the Americans did not kiss the regal hand, but gave the military salute, in conformity with their own customs.

As Bainbridge passed from the festive scenes and returned to his prison quarters, he noticed three woebegone lads who had taken no part in the Biaram festival, sitting on a stone bench. Their faces, according to the Captain, were handsome but marked by sadness. The Bashaw's object seemed to be to degrade them and exhibit them in their dejected, helpless state. Bainbridge asked who they were. They were the three sons of Hamet, the rightful owner of the throne. More than the children of Yusuf seated in the festive party, they were the true heirs of Tripoli. But even then, their father, advised of the capture of the *Philadelphia*, was fleeing through Egypt and up the Nile, seeking safety from the Turks and the Bashaw's agents sent in pursuit of him.

In February, when spring was softening the winds of the North African coast and making the countryside resplendent with olive trees and fields of barley and the oleander tree was giving promise of its rich summer blossoms, the officers through the courtesies of Sidi Mohammed Dghies were allowed to ride out a few miles from town and take liberty in the country. Unhappily no such privileges were given the sailors, who labored at the forge and carpenter's bench, and at carrying stone and mortar, in the unending task of strengthening the city's fortifications.

Then about 11 o'clock on the night of February 16, 1804, the city was filled with excitement. Great crowds rushed from the houses and raced about, uttering shouts of fright and dismay. They looked weird and ghostlike with their white garments in a flickering light that danced in the streets and illuminated the entire city. Soldiers hurried to the Castle walls, where the Bashaw's Divan was gathered. Above the confusion the prisoners could hear repeated in startled shouts the word *"Americano! Americano!"*

In order to know what had happened, it is necessary to go back to Commodore Preble who, after dictating the new peace with Morocco at Tangier, had gone to Cadiz—Gibraltar being stripped of provisions by Lord Nelson's fleet—to replenish his supplies and then sail to a new base at Syracuse.

CHAPTER FIFTEEN

Preble's Preparations

AFTER pacifying Morocco, Preble replenished his water in Cadiz, reprovisioned, procured a new cable to replace the one that had parted in Tangier Bay with the loss of an anchor, and sent his invalids back to the United States in the returning *John Adams* and *New York*. Then on November 6, 1803, he turned toward Syracuse and Tripoli.

On the following day he arrived in Gibraltar Bay where he ordered Lieutenant Stephen Decatur, who had come out on the *Argus*, to take command of the *Enterprise*, which had been in company with the *Constitution* at Cadiz. This amounted to no more than an exchange of ship commanders, for Lieutenant Isaac Hull, who had commanded the *Enterprise*, and was the senior, took the *Argus*, a larger ship. Preble assigned her to the highly responsible but less exciting work of patrolling off Gibraltar.

Preble was elated by his view of the *Argus*, the arrival of which he reported to the Secretary of the Navy on November 9. She was "without exception the handsomest vessel of her rate that I have ever seen. She is very much and very justly admired by every Officer." The orderly condition of the brig after her passage of the Atlantic did great credit to Lieutenant Decatur, he told the Secretary. Decatur delivered $30,000 in cash, which Preble would need in his vigorous operations. He promised the Secretary: "You may rest confidently assured, there shall not be an idle Vessel in my Squadron." Referring again to his delight over the *Argus*, he said he would like to have her in front of Tripoli and urged that a frigate be sent to the Straits of Gibraltar and the Moroccan coast, so as to release this splendid new ship.

At the conclusion of this letter to the Secretary, Preble made a statement as prophetic perhaps as any in American history: "I have on board the *Constitution* many remarkable fine young men whose conduct promises great things for their country."

Corporal punishment was resorted to frequently in the U.S. Navy as in others at this period. Preble's severe discipline could be seen from the log book of the *Constitution*. One unruly marine, who had been received in irons from the *Argus*, was punished with forty-eight lashes on November 16 for refusing duty, contempt of a commissioned officer, and insolence to a non-commissioned officer, and trying to desert. He was put down in the log book as a "very Notorious character." On the same day a seaman was given thirty-six lashes for drunkenness, neglect of duty, and insolence to a superior; while still another got twenty-four lashes for drunkenness and neglect of duty.

The transfer of Decatur to command the *Enterprise* was the beginning of a series of events which opened to him unusual opportunity and a glorious naval career. The *Enterprise* sailed eastward November 9 as an escort to the provision ship *Traveller*, which Preble was sending to establish a base at Syracuse, from where he might conduct at closer quarters a more spirited war against Tripoli. Then Decatur was to join the *Philadelphia* and the *Vixen*, presumed to be off Tripoli. He was to continue to cruise off that city until the coming of the stormy weather made it dangerous, but even in the worst season he was to go out occasionally and show the *Enterprise* off the hostile harbor as a reminder to the Bashaw that his craft were not safe at any time in the year. The spirited blockade Preble had in mind with the single schooner could be seen from his orders to Decatur:

> You are to capture all Vessels belonging to the Bashaw of Tripoly, or his subjects, and to annoy the enemy by all means in your power, you are not to Suffer the Vessels of any nation to enter or have commerce with Tripoly, But if any Vessel bound in, who might not have been informed of the Blockade, it would be well to order her off, and if detected in making a second attempt, you will send such Vessel into Syracuse for adjudication.

He issued a circular on November 12, 1803, proclaiming a blockade of Tripoli and notified the leading European powers through the American consuls at London, Paris, and Madrid.

Preble, after many delays, reached Algiers with the *Constitution* and the *Nautilus* on November 19. Consul Tobias Lear was put on shore amid salutes exchanged between the *Constitution* and the garrison batteries. While the Dey of Algiers was sending out presents of bullocks, sheep, fowls, and vegetables, Preble went ashore. He reported to Washington that he was treated with politeness and attention, and believed the United States stood as high or higher in Algiers than any European nation. He sailed on the 22nd.

Lear, left behind in his new post as consul general at Algiers, arranged for the gift of $20,000 in consular presents and for bringing the tribute up to date, which was being paid at the rate of $30,000 a year. The Dey received him "with great apparent satisfaction," as Lear reported to Secretary Madison. He expressed strong friendship for the United States and continued with personal flattery for Lear, saying he liked a consul "with a clean face." He examined the consular presents, appeared highly gratified and again expressed happiness at being on good terms with the Western republic.

This last feeling was mutual, because the Dey of Algiers had built up an impressive naval force. He had sent nine cruisers on a voyage along the coasts of Naples and Sicily on October 3 and they had returned December 1, the day before Lear's audience. They had brought 150 prisoners taken from a small coastal craft but no prizes. Lear reported to Madison that the Dey's flotilla consisted of a frigate of 44 guns built at Algiers; another frigate, 44, captured from the Portuguese; the handsome *Crescent*, built in the United States; three xebecs of from 20 to 30 guns, and the brig and two schooners built in the United States. This was a formidable navy in the hands of a piratical ruler, and one created in large measure by the United States as a result of the expediency which had earlier controlled American policy in the Mediterranean. The Dey was friendly at the moment, but still, he was a pirate.

On the early morning of November 24, 1803, the *Constitution*, sailing from Algiers with the *Nautilus* in company, spoke off Sardinia to the British frigate *Amazon*, whose captain told Preble the full and depressing story of the loss of the *Philadelphia*—how the vessel had been caught on the reef, then had been got off in the succeeding days and towed by the Mussulmans into Tripoli Harbor. Three days later the flagship was off Malta and a boat brought out a letter from Bainbridge giving the details of the disaster.

Joseph Pulis, American consul at Malta, whose activities, it developed, had to be watched because for some unexplained reason he impeded intercourse between Bainbridge and Preble, had other and to a degree reassuring information. The Bashaw had written from Tripoli trying to arrange through his consul a sale of the *Philadelphia* because he did not have the power to man her properly. Consul Pulis also stated that the vessel the Spanish shipbuilder had under construction at Tripoli was a schooner that would carry 16 guns; that Tripoli was about to send out a brig, a polacre, and a xebec; and finally that the Bashaw's brother Hamet had fled from Derna, had been seen passing through Alexandria, and that the Bashaw had sent troops overland to capture him. The news had come four days before on a vessel reaching Malta from Tripoli. It brought Preble up to date on affairs at Tripoli.

The report that the Bashaw might be trying to sell the *Philadelphia*

was not for Preble a weighty factor. He possessed her and she remained
a great potential danger to American commerce in the Mediterranean,
or, if she could pass the Straits, on the high seas. Preble did not tarry
at Malta. On November 29, he was at his new base at Syracuse. He
called on the governor, who obligingly offered him the free use of magazines for the deposit of provisions and stores and said he would be
pleased to have the Americans use the harbor as a rendezvous since it
would protect the coast from Barbary depredations. The store ship
Traveller was there and her escort, *Enterprise*. The *Nautilus* had arrived
a little ahead of the *Constitution*. After acquiring necessary articles and
stores, the *Enterprise* sailed for her assignment off Tripoli.

Syracuse offered another great advantage, apart from its proximity
to Tripoli. There was less opportunity for the seamen to desert. At Gibraltar they would sometimes jump overboard, swim to a British vessel
and enlist, and there was no means of compelling the British to return
them. Lord Nelson eventually put an end to the practice of shielding
American deserters. A good deal of negotiation and controversy had
arisen without anyone being able to explain why some British seamen
.deserted to take American berths and some deserted the Americans for
the British. Perhaps a ship merely looked better from the exterior. The
beautiful harbor of Syracuse was not being employed by the British in
fighting Napoleon as were Gibraltar and Malta, so the Americans had
full control. Preble continued his strict disciplinary measures. On the
day the *Constitution* reached Syracuse he had punishments inflicted for
"breach of trust and Drunkenness," as he worded it. One seaman got
three dozen lashes for drunkenness, neglect of duty, and stealing rum
from the ship's stores. This last offense appeared to be a party affair,
as four additional seamen were punished for stealing the ship's rum.

While he was making toward Syracuse, Preble had received some interesting and rambling advice from Consul Cathcart at Leghorn on
peace and war with Tripoli:

> We had better be at war with all the Barbary States at once than
> to be treated by them as a subdued nation, which We certainly shall
> be, if we condescend to comply with the Bashaw of Tripoli's demands;
> all Europe as well as Barbary has view'd our conduct in silent expecta-
> tion, since the war with Tripoli commenced, the former with inten-
> tion to follow our example if worthy imitation, & the latter to know
> how to rank us among the nations of the earth, whether to class us
> with Great Britain and France the only nations who make themselves
> respected, or with the northern nations whose miserable pusilanimous
> aconomy has so far preponderated in their Councils as to induce them
> in many instances to sacrifice their national dignity. . . .

Cathcart offered to procure gunboats, saying that with two mortars and eight or ten gunboats Preble's force would be sufficient to reduce Tripoli to ashes.

From Syracuse Preble wrote to Secretary of the Navy Smith a roundup report on December 10, 1803, in which he gave his reactions to the loss of the *Philadelphia*. He told of receiving the particulars in a letter from Bainbridge. There was a strong odor of censure in his statement that the *Philadelphia* was captured "without a man on either side having been killed or wounded." He told how the affair "distresses me beyond description," and said it would very much derange his plans. He feared the American character would be injured along the Barbary Coast. "Would to God," he exclaimed, "that the Officers and crew of the *Philadelphia*, had one and all, determined to prefer death to slavery; it is possible such a determination might save them from either." He transmitted to the Secretary Bainbridge's account, saying belatedly, "I will not forward an opinion on the subject of the loss. You can form as correct a one from Capt. Bainbridge's own letters . . . as it is possible for me to do."

Preble undoubtedly would have fought it out on the decks of the *Philadelphia*, and might have held the vessel until the coming of the succoring wind, but he never said quite that much, nor went beyond the tone of this letter in any criticism of his fellow captain. But he did put his finger on one defect in Bainbridge's operations, when in a general observation to the Secretary he said: "One Ship never ought to cruise alone on the Coast of Tripoly, if it can be avoided. If two Ships are in company, and an accident of running on shore happens to one, the other can protect her whilst getting off—and the same protection would be wanted, in case of losing a Mast."

Then he expressed the belief that the *Philadelphia* would never be of service to Tripoli because "I shall hazard much to destroy her." He went on to say, "it will undoubtedly cost us many lives, but it must be done. I am surprized that she was not rendered useless, before her Colours were struck."

Cathcart, writing Secretary Madison from Leghorn, implied a censure as severe as Preble's:

How glorious it would have been to have perish'd with the Ship, but how apt are we to prefer a precarious, nay an ignominious life of slavery to a glorious death which would transmit our names to posterity & have establish'd a national character which time could not efface; while humanity recoils at the idea of launching so many souls into eternity, every thing great glorious & patriotic dictates the measure, & our national honor & pride demand the sacrifice.

Another of those minor events which come to have great bearing on an individual's career and through him on history occurred when Preble reached Syracuse. Midshipman Thomas Macdonough, lately a lad from The Trap, Delaware, was regularly assigned to the *Philadelphia* and under normal circumstances would have been a prisoner with the other officers of that frigate in Tripoli. But he had been left by the turn of events in Gibraltar as prize-master of the *Mirboka* which the *Philadelphia* had captured off Cape de Gata; then when the prize was returned to Morocco during the pacification arrangements, he had taken passage east on the *Constitution*. Preble now assigned him to the *Enterprise* under Decatur. The distinction he won with Decatur gave him the propulsion in the Navy that led eventually to his command of the American squadron on Lake Champlain in one of the most significant triumphs in American naval history. What would have happened had he either remained with the *Philadelphia* and been captured, or continued aboard the *Constitution*, would have been another story—possibly a great story, but certainly a different one.

Preble at once glimpsed the significance of the capture of the *Philadelphia*. "Were it not for that loss," he wrote Secretary Smith, in another letter, "I have no doubt we would have had peace with Tripoli in the Spring; but I have now no hope of such an event." He had forecast a spring peace in a letter he wrote Smith from Cadiz, October 23, 1803, before sailing for Malta and Syracuse.

The Department itself did not get the intelligence until five months after the frigate had been surrendered. The news fell on the United States like a Bull Run or a Pearl Harbor. Jefferson's response was immediate. He decided to put back into the Mediterranean service the *President*, the *Constellation*, the *Essex*, and the *John Adams*. Only the last was on hand in time to help Preble in front of Tripoli and it, though due in April, did not arrive until August, 1804, but the squadron was given later strength.

The *Vixen*, which Bainbridge had sent to Cape Bon, had learned of the loss of the *Philadelphia* in a letter from Bainbridge; had headed toward Gibraltar, been buffeted by storms, and eventually joined the fleet at Syracuse December 12. In a dead calm she had to be towed into the harbor. Upon the wind's rising, Preble sailed in the *Constitution* in company with the *Enterprise* for a look at the Tripoli coast, which he had been struggling to reach since entering the Mediterranean. On December 23, off North Africa, nine miles east of Tripoli, the *Enterprise* at 8:30 A.M. signaled a strange sail to the southwest and the two ships, both flying British colors, gave chase. At 10:00 A.M. the chase was brought up by the *Enterprise*. Decatur sent an officer to board the ship; he found about twenty men on the deck conferring and waiting the turn of events. They were thrown into great confusion when their captors hoisted the American flag.

The prize was a ketch of sixty to seventy tons, rigged after the Tripolitan fashion but flying Turkish colors. She was the *Mastico* sailing from Tripoli to Bengazi and thence to Constantinople. An examination showed she was armed with two cannon and had two others in her hold; she had muskets and pistols, was commanded by a master claiming to be Turkish. She had on board seven Greek and four Turkish sailors, two Tripolitan officers, and ten Tripolitan soldiers; and forty-two Negro men, women, and children, all slaves who according to the master were being sent as a present from Bashaw Yusuf to the Grand Seignior and the Capudan Pasha at Constantinople. In her locker was $1,000 in Tripolitan money. She carried no passport from any consul at Tripoli except that a Turkish officer on board had a British passport as a passenger but with no vessel named. Preble, coming up, directed that the *Mastico* be taken as a prize. He appointed Midshipman Hethcote J. Reed as prize-master and directed him with another midshipman and seven sailors to take her into Syracuse, under convoy of the *Enterprise*.

An Italian doctor, who had served the Bashaw as a surgeon, and who later came aboard at Malta, told Preble he had been in Tripoli when the *Philadelphia* was captured. He identified the Tripolitans aboard the *Mastico* as high-ranking officers of the Bashaw, and the Tripolitan soldiers as members of a gunboat crew which had helped capture the frigate. He said the master was among the first to board the *Philadelphia* after she had struck.

Preble took the crew, passengers, and Tripolitan officers on board the *Constitution*, leaving two Tripolitans to cook for the Negroes. Preble gave the Tripolitan officers the courtesy of taking them at his own table during the voyage back to Malta and Syracuse. Strong winds encountered over Christmas separated the *Enterprise* from the *Mastico*, and when they subsided Preble told Decatur to tow the prize into Syracuse. There the squadron was reunited December 30.

At Syracuse the commodore obtained verification that the *Mastico* had been highly active in the capture of the *Philadelphia* and looting of the crew, and that the Turkish captain had led a party of boarders. The master of a British-Maltese vessel, Salvador Catalano, of Palermo, who had been in Tripoli Harbor at the time told almost exactly the same story Preble had received from the unidentified surgeon and other sources. This led him to hold the vessel. He released the Turkish officer, who was in the diplomatic service, and had the slaves set ashore, where he obtained housing and appointed cooks and caretakers and supplied provisions.

Salvador Catalano was a valuable witness as to the activities of the

Mastico in the harbor of Tripoli when the *Philadelphia* was captured. Catalano appeared in the Vice Admiralty Court in Syracuse in February, 1804, and testified that the ketch, commanded by Mustapha Rais, was flying the Ottoman colors, but after the *Philadelphia* hit the shoal she took them down and hoisted the Tripolitan flag. Then a crowd of Mussulmans armed with firelocks and sabers went on board the *Mastico*, which made sail toward the frigate. She anchored nearby, and that evening sent over to the American ship a wave of boarders headed by Mustapha Rais, who "with great eagerness" assisted in the removal of the American sailors and personally conducted them into the presence of the Bashaw in the castle.

With such testimony the *Mastico* was condemned and taken into the service of the United States, where she was given a name that was to become famous, the *Intrepid*.

Bainbridge in Tripoli had not acted with much vigor in trying to check work being done by skilled Americans which would redound to the great advantage of their enemies. His attitude on this important question can be described as nothing short of weak. He wrote Preble on December 13, 1803, explaining the nature of the crew's labors and saying the head carpenter Godby had been ordered by the Bashaw to build a gunboat. He told Preble that unless a positive order should be given to the crew stopping such work, "Tripoli will receive great advantage from their labour and they cannot receive much worse treatment than they do." Then he showed his own timidity: "I do not conceive it policy in me to give the order, and was I to do it; it would not have the same weight as if come from you."

Manifestly Bainbridge did not want to meet the Bashaw's displeasure by commanding his sailors to stop building warships for Tripoli. But he more than Preble was the officer to do it because, being on the ground, he could exert pressure and observe those who failed to comply. The prisoners were whipped unmercifully for infractions and disobedience, to be sure, but the Bashaw would stop short of having them killed for failure to work because he would lose their immense value as hostages in a peace settlement with the United States. It was likely too that beatings were administered mainly for defiance and might not follow a general refusal by all prisoners to work against their own country when their captain forbade it.

Still, Preble did not want the matter to go unnoticed, and on January 4, 1804, directed a message, which he signed as "your friend," to all warrant and petty officers, seamen, and marines lately of the *Philadelphia*, telling them that though the fortunes of war had made them prisoners, they were not slaves. He said their determination not to work would be proper, and if the Bashaw punished them for refusal, "I shall retaliate on his Subjects which I now have, and which may hereafter come into my possession." He told them that if they conducted themselves properly they in due time would be redeemed and restored to their friends. Meantime they would be given clothes and kept as comfortable as circumstances would permit. Then he gave a warning: "But should any of you voluntarily engage your services to the Enemy, and afterwards fall into the hands of your justly incensed Country Men, you will undoubtedly suffer death agreeable to the laws of the United States." He told them they should obstinately demand treatment as prisoners, not slaves.

As something of a clincher he said he would inform the Bashaw immediately that Americans who suffered themselves to be compelled to work for Tripoli would be regarded as having alienated themselves from the United States and the government would not feel obliged to ransom them.

Preble kept his brigs and schooners busy all winter cruising along the African coast but could not risk the *Constitution*, his only frigate, being driven ashore by the high gales which blew out of the northwest during the cold season. But on January 6 the Commodore, intending to go to Malta on business, ordered Lieutenant John H. Dent to equip the flagship with water and provisions and everything necessary for a cruise of at least four months: the rigging to be completely overhauled and repaired or replaced; the ship and gun carriages to be scraped and painted; a set of hanging shot lockers to be made for the guns on both decks; the boats to be repaired and painted; the sails to be attended to; the rigging to be tarred lightly where needed. He wanted the ship in readiness for an active campaign. During his absence no officer was to sleep on shore or be on shore on any pretense whatever after 9:00 P.M.

Leaving Dent in command of the *Constitution*, Preble shifted his broad pennant to the *Enterprise* and on January 10 sailed for Malta. Just out of the harbor he met the *Vixen* with dispatches; and after returning to Syracuse, and finding from a survey made at Decatur's request that the *Enterprise* badly needed repairs to be seaworthy, he shifted his pennant to the *Vixen* and reached Malta January 14.

Preble's relations with the British in the Mediterranean continued most cordial. In Malta he granted the request of Governor Sir Alexander Ball that a British vessel be permitted to transport from Tripoli 1,000 bullocks which were needed by the Malta garrison and the inhabitants of the island. He reassured Sir Alexander of the wish of the United States "to cement more strongly the present Friendship and good understanding with Great Britain."

He took advantage of the dispatch of this ship to send letters and bundles of clothing to Bainbridge, and he also wrote British Consul Mc-Donough requesting his kind attention to the needs of the prisoners and asking him to learn what the Bashaw would require for the ransom of the officers and crew. Along with the clothing he sent bundles of French and American newspapers. These were read by the American sailors and, in turn, by the Bashaw (with the aid of a translator for those from the United States). These papers, and others which followed, Yusuf studied with care. From them he gained some impression of the tremendous resources of the United States.

Preble was gratified by the friendly attention shown not only by the governor of Malta, but also by Admiral Richard Bickerton of the Royal Navy, who disapproved the protection two of the British captains had given to American deserters and said he had no doubt Lord Nelson would order their return. He promised there would be no recurrence and offered the Americans every assistance that could be provided by the ports in British control.

Back in Gibraltar Strait, Lieutenant John Johnson of the Marines, on board the *Argus*, heard that 140 members of the *Philadelphia* crew, claiming to be British subjects, had petitioned Lord Nelson for their release. Johnson reported to Commandant William W. Burrows of the Marine Corps that Nelson replied, as the Marine worded it, that "If he done anything in the Business, it would be to have the Rascels all hung." It was not clear whether Nelson was irked by their leaving the British service for the American, or because they had surrendered the frigate without a fight. Both considerations probably were involved in his disgust.

Preble's purposes in Malta were to forward supplies to the prisoners in Tripoli, to get a translation of the documents in Arabic he had taken from the *Mastico* which would disclose her true ownership, to see about procuring small craft that would serve for gunboats, and especially to straighten out his correspondence with Bainbridge, who had been complaining on all sides that his letters to the Commodore had gone unanswered. The distressed Captain had languished in Tripoli for nearly three months, had addressed eight to ten letters to Preble, two of them written with his sympathetic ink, and had never received one word of acknowledgment. Each day he awaited a letter that never came, and all the while Preble had been writing him words of sympathy and encouragement.

The cause, it developed, was the American consul at Malta, Joseph Pulis. Either indifferent or treacherous, he had allowed the mail from both Syracuse and Tripoli to accumulate in his office and paid no attention to forwarding it. Pulis was fluent in his native language, Maltese, and in Italian, but unable to speak English, and Preble had to deal with him gropingly through an interpreter; but he was a weak link in any language. Preble called on him with four other officers and found he had received a large number of letters from the United States addressed to individuals in the squadron, and from officers of the squadron to friends in the United States, London, and Mediterranean ports. Quite by chance Preble was able to bring out in their conversation that the letters had not moved out of Malta.

When the Commodore asked to see the letters Pulis had on hand, the Consul hesitated, but on Preble's stern insistence produced them. They were in four large packages, directed to the care of American Consul Gavino at Gibraltar to be forwarded to the United States. Pulis at first said they were his own letters and those of friends directed to America, but Preble ripped open a bundle and found letters addressed to the Navy Department by officers of his own squadron. Another bundle was an accumulation of letters to the captives in Tripoli, which the Consul had readdressed to be returned to the United States. Nothing could have been more heartless. Not one letter in all the mass was from Pulis, as he had claimed. He was merely a hoarder of mail, for what purpose Preble did not undertake to fathom. But he told Secretary Smith that Pulis formerly had been consul to the Bashaw of Tripoli and "has no respectibility attached to his character."

Not being able to speak a word of English, he was an unlikely representative of the United States in Malta. Preble did not have the authority to dismiss him, but circumvented him by appointing William Higgins, a respectable merchant, to look after his interests and be the agent for the squadron at Malta. One of his first acts was to get off a fresh letter to Bainbridge to show that his unintentional silence suggested no ill will: "Keep up a good heart and for God's sake do not despair. Your situation is bad indeed but I hope ere long, it will be better." He sent Bainbridge a new suit of clothes by British Consul McDonough. He asked that Porter be advised that he had recovered the Lieutenant's sword and belt "in bad hands"—that is, on the *Mastico*.

Preble learned in Malta that the Bashaw was scaling down his peace demands. He talked with the Bashaw's agent, who consented to peace on these terms: no tribute; no consular presents except a small one from the first consul; a schooner in exchange for the *Philadelphia*; ransom of $500 each for the officers and crew, with credit for the Tripolitans captured on the *Mastico*. The balance in favor of Tripoli would be about 240 prisoners, who at $500 each would mean a ransom of $120,000. Preble thought the figure would be lowered if the *Philadelphia* were destroyed. He had written Tobias Lear for advice on these terms.

Then he showed his repugnance over negotiations of any character:

"If it was not for the situation of our unfortunate Country Men, I should be sorry to have peace with the Bashaw, until we could oblige him to beg for it as a favour, and sign any treaty that might be dictated to him." He awaited only a favorable season when he might blockade Tripoli ports closely, fret their coast, and destroy their commerce.

Preble, being a hard-hitting naval officer not especially versed in statecraft, had overstepped a bit in his notice to the European powers that he had placed Tripoli under blockade, without having a fleet immediately at the harbor. The first cautioning came from Talleyrand, who had earlier conveyed Napoleon's sympathy to the Americans over the loss of the *Philadelphia* and the imprisonment of the crew. But when the French minister read the blockade notice he advised Robert R. Livingston, U.S. Minister to Paris, that it was not sufficient to have a single frigate cruise off Tripoli in order to declare a blockade, but that the port must be under attack by a number of vessels proportionate with its defenses. The French, never partial to naval blockades, nor recognizing those which were vague or of a paper nature, held that the coast of a country had never been included in a blockade, and that to include it would be a violation of the rights of neutrals.

Five days later, by coincidence, Jefferson, a close student of the niceties of such matters, had Secretary Smith write similarly from Washington, saying that the trade of a neutral nation not contraband could not be rightfully obstructed from a port not actually blockaded by a force "so disposed before it as to create an evident danger of entering it." When Preble had formed that kind of blockade he would have a right to prevent vessels from entering. But he was not to take as a prize any vessel attempting to enter which did not have knowledge of the existence of a blockade. If the vessel made a second attempt he could take her.

In Malta, Preble was able to catch up on events respecting Hamet, the elder brother who was a contender for the Tripolitan throne. Hamet's representative came to him with a request for fifty barrels of powder, six brass 4- and 6-pounders, and eighty to ninety thousand dollars with which to wage war against younger brother Bashaw Yusuf. This, with the assistance of the American squadron, would, he believed, put him in possession of Tripoli. He offered to give hostages and to allow the United States to hold the principal fort at the entrance to Tripoli Harbor; to release the Americans and all other Christian prisoners; and to ratify permanent peace as quickly as he took possession of the government.

Clear-sighted Commodore Preble was impressed that use could be made of Hamet and wondered at the indifference others had shown him. "I wish earlier notice had been taken of this man and his views," he wrote to Secretary Smith from Malta on January 17. "In fact I am astonished that the first and second Squadron did not oblige the Bashaw to sign any treaty they pleased."

Now he was confronting Tripoli with a much weaker squadron than either of his predecessors had commanded in the Mediterranean. Of this he was fully cognizant. In his letter he referred to the earlier fleets: "I have less force than either with ten times the force to contend with. The Tripolines by May will have 19 Gun Boats and unless we have boats to fight them in their own way we shall not be likely to succeed." He requested money with which to procure gun and mortar boats, with which he would attack Tripoli under the protection of his cruisers.

With the *Philadelphia* lost, Preble had remaining only the single frigate, the *Constitution*, 44, two brigs, *Siren* and *Argus*, each 16, and the three schooners, *Enterprise*, *Vixen* and *Nautilus*, each of 12 guns. Compared with the frigates Morris had commanded, it was not much of a squadron, though it was stronger in smaller ships, which had a place in this type of warfare.

Meanwhile Preble was casting about for gunboats in Leghorn and Naples. He wrote to Leghorn for the purchase of two or three mortar boats with 10-inch mortars and three or four gunboats. He wanted boats large enough to carry a long 24- or 32-pounder plus 300 shells and 500 solid shot. He desired also one or two good bombardiers and about fifty "Men of different Nations" to mix with his Americans in manning these boats against Tripoli. He continued his quest for gunboats while in Malta.

While this search was in progress, Preble, believing that action would be more conducive toward ending the war than words and negotiations, put into excution the plan he had been formulating ever since he learned of the loss of the *Philadelphia*, which he had suggested to Secretary Smith in his letter of December 10, 1803. This was to capture the *Philadelphia* by a quick surprise dash into the harbor of Tripoli and burn her. He had told Smith he would "hazard much to destroy her" and now that the season was opening, the opportunity was at hand. The little ketch *Intrepid*, the former *Mastico*, would be the covert attack vessel because she was a Barbary craft in every line, sail, and spar, and would excite no suspicion entering Tripoli Harbor.

Both Bainbridge's and Decatur's biographers like to give their subjects credit for suggesting the plan for the destruction of the *Philadelphia*, but it was mentioned by Preble in dispatches before he had heard a word from either of them. No doubt it grew out of one of his Revolutionary War exploits. While he was serving under Captain George Little on the *Winthrop*, of the Massachusetts navy, cruising off Maine, the officers learned that a brig which the British had taken from the colonists was at anchor off Castine under the guns of the British fort. Few would have thought the brig could have been assailed, but Little formed the plan to run the *Winthrop* alongside her and carry her by boarding.

Preble led the boarding party of forty picked men dressed in white frocks for the purpose of identification. The *Winthrop* came alongside the brig, as planned, but she was sailing too rapidly and only Preble and fourteen followers managed to jump to the brig as the *Winthrop* passed. Little called to him and asked if he needed the remaining twenty-six.

"No," Preble shouted back. "We have more than we need. We stand in each other's way."

That may have deceived the British into believing they had been boarded in force. They offered slight resistance. Some jumped over-board. Preble rushed to the cabin and assured the officers they were trapped and could save their lives only by surrender. But then came the difficult part of the operation, getting the prize to sea. Shells and bullets were rained on them from the British on shore. Still, Preble got her off under the fire of the batteries and took her into Boston safely. The ease with which the ship was carried but the hazards of taking her out were points which must have remained with Preble, for they controlled the orders he was now about to issue to Lieutenants Decatur and Stewart for the recapture of the *Philadelphia*.

While Preble had the plan in mind, it was occurring to others. Almost as soon as his *Enterprise* captured the *Mastico*, Decatur began to think in terms of using the ketch to sail into Tripoli and seize the *Philadelphia*. He went to Preble with the suggestion. His bold conception was the turning point of his career, for Preble was casting about for the ideal man to head the enterprise he, too, had been projecting, and none was better suited for it than Stephen Decatur.

Bainbridge's friend and biographer Thomas Harris attributed the plan to Bainbridge, who in a letter written in sympathetic ink on December 5, 1803, described the lay of the harbor and the position of the frigate. He related that the gunboats which had captured the *Philadelphia* were beached. He had been able to observe only one small battery of poorly mounted guns outside of the Castle. He wrote:

Charter a small merchant schooner, fill her with men, and have her commanded by fearless and determined officers. Let the vessel enter the harbor at night, with her men secreted below deck—steer her directly on board the frigate, and then let the officers and men board, sword in hand, and there [is] not a doubt of their success, and without any very heavy loss. It would be necessary to take several good row boats, in order to facilitate the retreat.

He went on to say the frigate was a powerful defensive factor for the Tripolitans in the harbor, but he thought she could not be recovered:

Though it will be impossible to move her from her anchorage, and

thus restore this beautiful vessel to our navy; yet, as she may, and no doubt will be repaired, an important end would be gained by her destruction.

The letter is no longer extant, nor Preble's supposed reply, which, according to Harris, accepted the idea. He tested it with other officers and when they approved wrote Bainbridge he was preparing to carry out the plan, for which Lieutenant Stephen Decatur had volunteered to take the lead. Harris said he had his information about the content of both letters from Bainbridge direct.

Bainbridge repeated his suggestion in a letter to Preble dated January 18, 1804, which is a part of the records. He was thinking in terms of sending into the harbor the ship's small boats, which could enter after sunset unnoticed. It is not clear when this or other of Bainbridge's letters reached Preble, because of the mishandling and slowing of the correspondence by Consul Pulis.

Preble on January 31 issued orders at Syracuse for the *Siren* and the *Intrepid*, commanded by Lieutenants Charles Stewart and Stephen Decatur, respectively, to sail on the following evening. Events were shaping which would cause the frenzy of excitement noticed by the American prisoners on the night of February 16, 1804, in Tripoli.

CHAPTER SIXTEEN

Burning the *Philadelphia*

YEARS after the Tripolitan War, Stephen Decatur, commander of the *United States*, would send the flag of the British frigate *Macedonian* to Dolley Madison by a young lieutenant—the son of Paul Anderson, Secretary of the Navy at the beginning of the War of 1812.

When the lieutenant, arriving during the Naval Ball of the Christmas festivities of 1812, laid the trophy at her feet, the usually self-controlled Dolley, the center of warmth and witticisms, conceded that she blushed like a schoolgirl.

The reason has never been well explained. But one is privileged to believe it was because the enemy standard had been sent to her by one of the most intrepid and certainly the most handsome officer of the U.S. Navy, whose physical strength and virility were in such contrast, as the bewitchingly feminine Dolley must have observed, to the frail delicacy of her beloved but diminutive Jimmy Madison, the President.

If Dolley was not stirred by Decatur's magnetism she was different from virtually all other women who met him, and most men also, because few could be indifferent to this graceful, athletic officer whose broad shoulders, slim waist, curly crown hair and warm, dancing brown eyes, usually tender in conversation but alert and piercing under the excitement of action, made him distinguished physically in nearly any gathering. His biographers—and quite a number have written of him in sympathetic and none in disparaging vein—seem to agree that he drew the notice of ladies wherever he appeared, and the allurement went much beyond the appeal of the resplendent naval uniform of the day; while the seamen and others who kept journals dealt with him in terms ranging from admiration to reverence. Said Marine Private Ray: "The intrepid Decatur is as proverbial among sailors, for the good treatment of his men, as he is for his valour. Not a tar, who ever sailed with Decatur, but would almost sacrifice his life for him."

There was something more mystical about Decatur than his vivid personality and the stimulating glow of his presence, for when he married Susan Wheeler, daughter of Luke Wheeler, wealthy merchant and Mayor of Norfolk, Virginia, his union was with a young lady who had fallen in love with him desperately before she had ever seen him, merely from looking at an Italian miniature of him. And it was characteristic of his devotion to the United States and to its naval service that he told the beautiful girl, when he proposed, that he had already made vows to his flag which had precedence, because if not steadfast to it, he would not then be worthy of her. Somewhere along the line he had read Richard Lovelace.

With some others, such zeal might seem affected or touched with chauvinism. That was not the case with Decatur, who was never heard by his fellow officers to boast. The spirit was the same as moved him in his famous toast, spoken at the public entertainment in his honor at Norfolk, reported with some variations in the press, which summed up to: "Our country. In her intercourse with foreign nations, may she always be in the right. But right or wrong, our country!"

This fervor shone also in his response to Captain John S. Carden, commander of His Majesty's frigate the *Macedonian*, when they were together in Norfolk just before the War of 1812 and talked lightly about the possibility that they might meet in battle. Decatur answered Carden's playful remark by saying that if the forces were near equal the battle would be desperate, but that "the flag of my country on the ship I command shall never leave the staff on which it waves as long as there is a hull to support it." He was not able to make good that promise in one instance, when after the longest and one of the hardest fights of his embattled career he was forced to surrender the *President* to a British fleet of several frigates supported by the mighty man-of-war *Majestic*.

This young man—and he would never live to be an old man—was generous and unpretentious, but so dutiful and exacting that it was the common practice of superiors to commend him, from the hour when he became a midshipman on the *United States* under the personal eye and friendship of the rugged Irish sea captain of Revolutionary War fame, John Barry. Stephen Decatur was a Philadelphian, though born in the village of Sinepuxent, in Worcester County on the east coast of Maryland, whence his family had fled when Lord Howe occupied the Pennsylvania city during the Revolution. His mother returned soon and he was reared on the Delaware waterfront. His birth date was January 5, 1779, at a time when his father, Stephen, a patriot sea captain, was commanding the *Fair American*.

The senior Stephen, in turn, was the son of a lieutenant in the French navy who had gone to Newport, Rhode Island, to escape a yellow fever epidemic in the West Indies. This French officer—the junior Stephen's grandfather—fell in love with Priscilla Hill, a comely Newport girl, whose parents adamantly refused to assent to her marriage unless he would quit the ocean, which he did. But he died soon after his son was born in 1751. Though the French father had been debarred from the sea by his wedding agreement, the son took to it quickly and by the time he was twenty-two was master of the sloop *Peggy*; then, on the outbreak of the Revolution, after he had married a Scotch-Irish girl, Ann Pine, and was living in Philadelphia, he turned privateersman, fought the British, and became a friend of Barry, who was later to take the son as a protégé and give him a naval training which could not be excelled.

Stephen the elder captured some British vessels during the Revolution but his top command came in 1800, when as a captain in the new navy, he commanded an American expedition of thirteen ships sent into the Caribbean, with his flagship the *Philadelphia*—the same vessel that was now occupying the attention of his son. He captured the French cruiser *Croyable*, 14, renamed the *Retaliation*. The father left the naval service in 1801, the year his son, then twenty-two, became a lieutenant on the *Essex* and sailed with Dale for the Mediterranean.

Stephen, Jr., had made his first sea voyage with his father to Europe when he was eight years old, but he mixed a thorough education on shore with his early sea journeys. The customary stories were told about him later of how he led the boys in adventures and combats, being given the name of "Captain Dick" for a reason not now ascertainable. He swam the Delaware and skated on the Schuylkill as did Philadelphia boys of many earlier generations, attended the Episcopal Academy, made good grades at the University of Pennsylvania, and all the while the parents sought to dissuade him from a sea career. They even put him to work in a counting house, from where it was fairly certain his ardent spirit would liberate itself, but meantime he spent much time drawing designs and building ship models. Finally, when his preoccupation with ships was thoroughly manifest, his employers at the counting house assigned him to supervise production of the keel pieces for the frigate *United States*, then building at Philadelphia. The transition to the role of midshipman under Barry was prompt in 1798 when the quasi-war with France threatened.

Robert T. Spence, who like Decatur would gain distinction in the Mediterranean, met a group of gentlemanly, pleasant young officers in the Caribbean during the French disturbances. They had the air of sailors. "But in Decatur," he wrote, "I was struck with a peculiarity of manner and appearance calculated to rivet the eye and engross the attention. I had often pictured to myself the form and look of a hero, such as my favorite Homer had delineated; here I saw it embodied."

Just then, as Spence told the story, someone shouted, "Man overboard!" While others launched the boats, he noticed Decatur jump without hesitation from the mizzenmast, rescue the lad, and hold him afloat until help came. One of the peculiarities of this hard-fighting early U.S. Navy was that it had a great many seamen, and officers likewise, who could not swim. An example was Captain Bainbridge. Decatur, able in most of the sports available in that day, was at home in the water. One of his regular swims with some of the other Philadelphia lads had been the circuit of Windmill Island near the far side of the Delaware off the northern end of the city.

On his first ship, the *United States*, he made solid friendships with the lovable Richard Somers and staunch Charles Stewart, junior officers of the first capability, who were with him much in the Mediterranean. One of the singular aspects of the career of this relatively modest, always courteous young man was the frequency with which he was drawn into duels, and now, in his first, Somers and Stewart were his advisers. When a fourth-lieutenant, Stephen had been sent to Philadelphia to recruit a new crew for the *United States* while she was being reconditioned, but some of his best recruits, prime seamen, jumped their compacts and arranged to ship on an Indiaman in the harbor, whither the young officer followed them. The first mate of the merchant vessel was enraged at having his deck invaded and in offensive language denounced not only Decatur but the whole American naval service. Decatur controlled his own emotions and looked for his men. It is not clear how many he got back, if any at all. When he told his father about the incident, the senior Decatur felt his son had been remiss in tolerating the mate's language and declared the man should be required to make an accounting.

Somers carried the demand for an apology, which the mate refused, then conveyed the challenge. Before he left the deck of the *United States* for the duel, Decatur, already an expert pistol shot, told his friend Stewart that, since he presumed the mate of the merchantman was not adept with the pistol, he would not take his life needlessly, but only wound him in the hip. That is where his bullet struck. He would not find the last of his dueling adversaries, Captain James Barron, so magnanimous in his aim.

With all this dueling, which implied quarrelsomeness, John Quincy Adams, who knew the early country and its great men as well as any did, would say: "He was warm-hearted, cheerful, unassuming, gentle in deportment, friendly and hospitable, beloved in social life, with a soul all devoted to his country . . ." And his epitaph would bear the words, chiseled twenty-six years after his death: "The pride of the Navy, the glory of the Republic."

The exploit on which Decatur was now embarking would be one of the reasons why twenty American towns, some of them now thriving cities, and quite a number of counties would bear his name.

Preble's orders were specific. Decatur was to take seventy-five officers and men and go into Tripoli Harbor. Seventy were to be from his own ship, the *Enterprise*, if that number could be assembled through volunteering. Preble augmented this force by sending five midshipmen from the *Constitution*. Decatur was to proceed to Tripoli in company with Stewart, who received separate orders for his role in the adventure, enter the harbor at night; board the frigate, burn her, and retire with the *Intrepid* if possible, unless she might be converted into a fire ship to destroy other vessels in the harbor. In that case the men were to retreat in their small boats or those of the *Siren*, which was to be the covering ship for the operation.

He was to take all necessary combustibles. The list the Commodore provided is now missing. Usually gunpowder and pitch were employed. Preble emphasized that the object of great importance was the destruction of the *Philadelphia*. He directed that when the frigate was on fire, two 18-pounders should be shotted, pointed down the main hatch, and fired to blow out the bottom of the ship. Anticipating that they would meet with resistance in boarding the vessel, he directed that they carry her decks with the sword so as to prevent alarming the city.

In his orders to Stewart, Preble directed that before approaching the shore the *Siren* be disguised with paint of another color and that her sails and rigging be altered to give her the appearance of a merchant vessel. The ships were to remain off the harbor until night, but not so far but that they could reach it by midnight. The *Intrepid*, being rigged after the Mediterranean fashion, and therefore less likely to arouse suspicion, was to be sent in ahead, and her men would be the ones to board the frigate.

As soon as the *Intrepid* entered the harbor, Stewart was to stand in and anchor at the position judged best to assist in the main object, to cover the retreat and do as much destruction to the enemy cruisers as possible. Preble added another order. They were to destroy the *Philadelphia*, not try to bring her out of the harbor. On that point he was positive.

Decatur piped his crew to the deck of the *Enterprise*, explained the service ahead and called for volunteers to step forward. The entire crew moved up a pace. He had to reduce the number by about one-half and selected sixty-two men carefully, being governed by the stalwart bearing and the hard muscles of the men, because the task would be one of hand-to-hand fighting.

Among those rejected was a slender Quaker youth of nineteen, who had been guilty of some minor dereliction and taken a berth on a warship. He went to Decatur and complained he had been overlooked. The Commander said the detail was complete but the lad would not be put off. He returned and insisted and finally Decatur put him in. Curious as to his persistence, Decatur asked why he wanted to go. The gently reared Quaker lad would not say he wanted to share in the excitement of the combat, but blushed, looked down, and answered that he wanted to see the city. That was his mild manner of saying he wanted to take part in the fight. Eight of the enlisted men were marines, going to the "shores of Tripoli," never suspecting how famous they and other marines a bit later would make that phrase.

For his lieutenants, Decatur selected James Lawrence, Joseph Bainbridge, the Captain's brother whom he had supported in the duel at Malta, and Jonathan Thorn. Louis Heerman, surgeon's mate, went as the medical officer. The five midshipmen Preble sent from the Constitution were Ralph Izard, Charles Morris, Alexander Laws, John Davis, and John Rowe. One midshipman of the *Enterprise*, Thomas Macdonough, and one from the *Siren,* Thomas O. Anderson, who joined later, when at sea, completed the roster of officers. To this party was added one of the most important members of the entire enterprise, the ship captain Salvador Catalano, of Palermo, Sicily, who with his British-Maltese craft had been in the harbor when the *Philadelphia* struck, who knew every shoal, reef, and headland, and who served as pilot.

Thus to the sixty-two petty officers, seamen, and marines were added Decatur and three lieutenants, six midshipmen at the outset, one surgeon, and one pilot, making a total of seventy-four aboard the *Intrepid.*

"This evening, my Dear Mother," wrote Midshipman Ralph Izard, Jr., "I sail for Tripoli . . . for the purpose of burning the Frigate *Philadelphia* . . . We are certain of success." Then young Izard dreamed, "Before this day week I am in hopes we shall see the *Philadelphia* in flames—We shall astonish the Bashaw's weak mind with the noise of shot falling about his ears. Perhaps some shot 'more lucky than the rest may reach his heart' & free our countrymen from Slavery."

The *Siren* took on board a pilot, Lewis Jourvass, from the *Constitution,* and at 5:00 P.M., February 3, 1804, the two ships stood out to sea. Not until they were at sea, at 9:00 A.M. the morning after they sailed, was the crew of the *Siren* piped on deck and told exactly what they were setting out to attempt. When Lieutenant Stewart divulged their mission he was answered by three cheers. The journal kept by Midshipman F.

Cornelius deKraft of the *Siren* showed that the voyage was begun with fine breezes and pleasant weather.

Preble had been encountering much spoilage in the meat he had received from the United States on the supply ship *Traveller*. He called the consignment from Georgetown, D.C., "miserably poor, and badly put up," and said nothing but "absolute necessity" would induce people to eat it. The fault seemed to have been that the beef was packed in fish barrels that were poorly hooped. The pickle leaked out and some of the barrels were so foul they could not be kept on board and had to be tossed overboard. The pork, rice, and flour were in better shape. He recommended that superior beef could be procured in Boston or Connecticut.

Decatur's *Intrepid* by evil chance had been supplied with some of this bad beef, which was offensive beyond eating even in "absolute necessity." So while they were out, the seventy-four men had to live mainly on biscuits and water.

The *Siren* and *Intrepid* were off Tripoli in late afternoon on February 7. The lateen-rigged *Intrepid*, the type of ketch familiar to every harbor along the North African coast, went ahead, while the *Siren*, fully disguised and looking like an ordinary merchantman, followed at a distance of about a mile. They gave no evidence of being associated. The weather was pleasant, the wind gentle. Everything seemed auspicious for the consummation of the plan. Night came on and the two ships were about to move in for their respective roles in the fort-rimmed harbor of the enemy city.

Just after darkness the weather turned. One of the quick winter squalls common on the North African coast whipped up the waves and tossed the little ketch, which was still beyond the harbor. Decatur, keyed for the attack, his men instructed in their various parts, was reluctant to postpone the affair, fearing that delay might bring in new elements, lead to detection, or in some manner frustrate his hopes. But Catalano, the pilot, with his intimate knowledge of the harbor, advised him of the danger of venturing through the rocks that guarded the ingress they had selected, while the sea was breaking heavily against them. Unwilling still to be baffled, Decatur sent out Midshipman Charles Morris and the pilot in a small boat with muffled oars to report on the condition of the sea at the harbor entrance. They drew close to the entrance on the western side, saw the waves roll high and break across the reefs into which their small vessel might be carried by the high wind, and reported back to Decatur that it would indeed be risky beyond reason to try to go in and utterly impossible to sail the craft back out against the wind and sea.

Then the storm which had been blowing a gale turned into a winter tempest which confirmed with emphasis the findings of the reconnoitering party. The small boat Morris and Catalano had rowed was battered and broken before it could be hoisted back on the Intrepid. They weighed anchor but found that the anchor had been broken. Knowing that it would not be well for them to be seen near the harbor after the coming of daylight, and fearful of being dashed against the rocks, they sought safety in the lashing wind by making for the open sea. So violent was the weather that they could not communicate with their companion craft, but fortunately the Siren saw their ship's lantern departing, felt the same force of the angry storm, and understood that the venture had been abandoned for the moment.

More difficulty was experienced by the Siren in her retreat than was by the ketch she escorted. While the weather was still calm the Siren had put out and manned her small boats with the details which were to cover the withdrawal of the Intrepid's crew. When the weather turned the boats had to be hoisted, but she had anchored off the harbor and a long and vain effort was made to get her anchor up. She was rolling in the trough of the sea and in the end the anchor had to be abandoned. They had worked so long through the night to bring up the anchor that dawn was drawing on, so they cut the anchor cable and sought an offing before being detected. Lieutenant Stewart was injured but not so severely as to be forced to surrender the command.

For seven days the gale continued. They were most hazardous days for those crowded aboard the little ketch, which was constantly in danger of foundering. The two ships were reunited off the coast but were of no comfort to each other in the tempest. The wind shifted and blew from the north and finally drove both ships into the Gulf of Sidra far to the southeast of Tripoli. Not until February 15 did the weather moderate. During the period of the storm great hardship was imposed on the Intrepid's crew more by the conditions on board than the turbulent weather. Surgeon's Mate Lewis Heerman thought officers and crew had grown despondent because of the putrid provisions, the frail construction, and small size of the Intrepid, and because of the gale, which had prevented early success and brought on apprehensions of eventual failure. A lingering fear was that the two vessels might have aroused suspicions by being anchored near the port and that a lookout would be maintained for their return.

Midshipman Morris told how the commander, Decatur, the three lieutenants and the surgeon's mate occupied one small cabin, while the six midshipmen and the pilot slept on a platform placed on top of the water casks. They were on what was in effect a shelf, so narrow that they could not sit upright without striking their heads against the deck above them. On the opposite side of the vessel the eight marines had the same kind of sleeping quarters. The sailors slept in the hold and did not have any more room, if as much, as the officers. All being vigorous young men, they suffered from lack of exercise, which could be taken vertically only, and there was no room for drill or calisthenics on deck.

Another and perhaps the most grievous difficulty was that the ketch had been knocking about the Mediterranean and seemed to have taken on vermin at every port, and the supply was ample for everyone on board.

They made their way westward on the 15th but could not get near enough the city to undertake their enterprise that evening, so lay off until the next day. On the night of the 16th Decatur called a council of his officers, which determined that since the *Siren* was not yet up, the crew of the *Intrepid* should proceed on its own responsibility and take its chances about withdrawing after the frigate had been fired. The rendezvous had been scheduled for 10:00 P.M., but the wind now was dying and Decatur feared that if he delayed he might not have enough in his sails to reach the *Philadelphia*. Certainly no plight could have been more tantalizing than being becalmed in the harbor with the rich morsel of the frigate just out of reach. Therefore the little *Intrepid* with her seventy-four men pointed her head toward the harbor of Tripoli. The watchword given out was easy for anyone to remember. It was "Philadelphia."

Decatur, dressed in loose Maltese garments, stood on the bridge with Catalano, similarly dressed. Half a dozen seamen, seemingly Mediterraneans, showed themselves on deck. The wind had been light, but to avoid an arrival too early in the inner harbor, the *Intrepid* had towed buckets astern to slow her progress; now as the breeze died these were hauled in. To any watcher on the shore she might seem to be a small craft eagerly seeking to make the harbor before darkness. As daylight died they could see the surf still running along the western entrance, which gave Catalano knowledge that they would have to make their way through the eastern channel, at that time a devious course between reefs and shoals. The night came on clear and serene with a crescent moon, the moon of the Ottoman flag, providing just enough light to give them assuredness in their progress, but not enough to permit them to be studied closely.

Meantime the *Siren*, coming toward the shore, saw the *Intrepid* standing for the harbor and followed her, and at darkness prepared her boats. At about 8:30 P.M. the wind subsided and the *Siren* anchored three miles distant from Tripoli, put out her boats, and sent them with about thirty men under Lieutenant James R. Caldwell to row to the *Intrepid* and place himself under Decatur's command, to add to nine men sent to Decatur under Midshipman Anderson the day before. Anderson had gone on board the *Intrepid* with his men, who thus increased the number in the attack party to eighty-four. The brig remained on the scene ready to give what other assistance was necessary.

Gently the *Intrepid*, flying British colors, moved through the channel and into the harbor underneath the castle walls. In this small craft on a desperate mission in a far sea were four of the great characters of American naval history: Decatur; Lieutenant James Lawrence, second in command, whom Theodore Roosevelt would call the "Bayard of the Seas," and who in his death hour would give to the Navy its greatest watchword, "Don't give up the ship"; Midshipman Thomas Macdonough, victor on Lake Champlain, in the peculiar yet all-important battle fought at anchor in Plattsburg Bay; and Midshipman Charles Morris, a captain after his heroic part in the battle of the *Constitution* and the *Guerrière*, whom David Farragut, one of his junior officers when he was a commodore, would call "the ablest sea officer of his day."

Their approach had not been unnoticed. People in Tripoli saw the two ships off the harbor, and thoughts about them varied without anyone suspecting that they were disguised Americans on a raid. Jonathan Cowdery, surgeon's mate of the *Philadelphia*, whose journal, kept during his captivity, is of equal interest to that of Marine Private Ray, had been pressed into service as a physician by the Bashaw. He later became an established practitioner and eventually the chief surgeon of the Navy, and he was certainly the best doctor in Tripoli, among the sorcerers and medicine men. He had been on a professional call that afternoon to the ailing Bashaw's eldest daughter—apparently the daughter who married the Grand Admiral Murad Reis—and he noted down that the husband "offered me many civilities," a rarity to an American from the Scotch apostate. After his call he recorded he was informed that two English merchantmen were standing in for the harbor. It was then 5:00 P.M.

Another opinion about the vessels was that of Private Ray, who saw them and hoped they were Americans, perhaps coming to negotiate peace. Neither he nor Cowdery wrote down any further impressions until after the *Intrepid* reached the *Philadelphia* and threw consternation into the city.

Decatur had drilled his men into a responsive team. Each officer had a detachment and knew exactly what to do. Complying with Preble's orders, the frigate was to be captured with cold steel. Only in the most urgent circumstances were firearms to be employed. The first task was to carry the spar deck and then the gun deck beneath. While a group held the spar deck against the possibility of counterattack, others would scatter in details and place the combustibles at vital points in the frigate from which the flames would spread and devour her.

Decatur, with Midshipman Izard and Rowe and fourteen men, would hold the spar deck; Lawrence, Laws, and Macdonough, with ten men, would go to the berth deck and forward storerooms; Bainbridge and Davis and ten men to the wardroom and steerage; Morris with eight men to the cockpit and storerooms abaft. To Lieutenant Thorn and Surgeon's Mate Heerman went the irksome assignment of staying behind and guarding the *Intrepid* with fourteen men. The final duty went to Anderson and his nine men from the *Siren*, who were to watch the *Philadelphia*'s boats and cut off any enemy trying to reach shore in them or by swimming. The hope was to sever contact between the frigate and the shore and prevent the city from becoming alarmed until the destruction was certain. The assignments of the few remaining men are indefinite.

Decatur entered the harbor at 7:00 P.M., but it was not until 9:30 that the *Intrepid* was alongside the *Philadelphia*. The frigate was moored within what Decatur called half a gun shot of the Bashaw's castle, where the main battery guarding the city was mounted. She was bare of sails and the foremast that had been hacked down to lighten her forward so she might get off the shoal had not been replaced. She had her guns loaded, double-shotted, it developed, for the purpose of augmenting the forts. From her position commanding the main approach to the city, she was the Bashaw's strongest protection against attack, with half of her forty guns aimed toward the sea. The others pointed toward the city were loaded also, though the frigate could not have been readily maneuvered.

Decatur's main force of officers and men were now lying on the deck of the ketch, behind the bulwarks, but a few were about the deck much as they would be on a small merchant craft. Decatur and Catalano, who would have to answer any challenge from the vessel, were still standing together. It was now nearly 10:00 P.M. Harbor and city were in silence. Two cable lengths, or less than a quarter of a mile, off the frigate's starboard quarter, were two cruisers against which the tide lapped softly, while considerably closer, within gun shot, Decatur noticed, two gunboats were off her starboard bow. Here and there a block creaked and a tackle groaned, and the breeze flapped a canvas crisply as they edged slowly toward the big ship which now loomed above them. Suddenly a voice from the frigate hailed them, demanding that they keep off. Catalano by Decatur's orders answered in Maltese that they were a trading boat from Malta which had suffered during the recent gale, lost their anchor, come near to shipwreck, and now besought permission to make fast to the frigate and ride beside her during the night.

This was the critical moment for Decatur because a refusal would have vastly increased the difficulties of boarding. But the Tripolitan officer, reassured by the explanation and appearances, let the conversation drag along while Catalano told what his ship was carrying and other things. One question asked was the identity of the other ship, which Catalano declared to be the *Transfer,* a Tripolitan vessel due to arrive at any time from Malta, where she had recently been purchased. All the while Catalano talked, the *Intrepid* was edging closer to the *Philadelphia,* but suddenly her situation became critical when the wind dropped and she lay becalmed only twenty yards from the frigate and directly underneath her loaded guns. Decatur could not know it until a little later, but during this time the Tripolitan gun crews had taken the tampions from the frigate's cannon and made ready to fire. Any misstep or disclosure at this moment would have been fatal.

Decatur's cool courage commanded the situation. Without haste he had the boat from the *Siren* which had brought Midshipman Anderson and his men, and which the *Intrepid* was towing, manned with a detail which started with a rope to the *Philadelphia,* to be met halfway by a boat coming out with a rope from the frigate. The ropes were tied and the small boats returned to their respective ships. The crew lying on the deck of the *Intrepid* hauled on the rope and gradually drew the vessels together. It seems incredible, but it was a fact that not until they were alongside did the *Philadelphia*'s Tripolitan crew suspect foul play. Then, as the ships touched, someone more wary than the rest shouted "Americanos!" a cry which a short time later was resounding through all Tripoli. The doubt had been stirred by the *Intrepid*'s anchor, which someone saw, clearly giving a lie to Catalano's story that the anchor had been lost in the storm.

Decatur had intended to be the first on the frigate's deck and would have gained that distinction had he not lost a few seconds when his foot slipped as he was going up the side. He was waiting with Laws and Morris, and as the ships met the three leaped forward. Laws was held back an instant when the pistols he wore on his boarding belt caught in one of the frigate's ports. Morris was up without mishap and ever after had the fame of having been first on the deck of the *Philadelphia.* The sailors who manned the frigate are called Turks in contemporary American accounts and some of them may have been Turks or Janissaries from Constantinople, but most were likely of the Arabic-Berber stock who made up the bulk of the Tripolitan population and the Bashaw's naval force. Whoever they were, they were not interested in stubborn resistance. It is true that the surprise was complete, but when Decatur and his front detachment came storming across the spar deck, their cutlasses flashing, the defenders gave way hurriedly in front of them, rushed to the starboard side, put up a half-hearted fight there, and then those who were not killed threw themselves overboard. A few in the stern had no more stomach for the steel than had the main body, and on the approach of the Americans, leaped into the water.

Following Decatur's party and all along the ship's rail a gang of desperate boarders armed with cutlasses, knives, and pikes sprang up and swarmed over the frigate's deck. They divided quickly into little groups who hastened off precisely as Decatur had planned, some to the forward storerooms, some to the cockpit, some to the steerage. Nothing could have been more inspiring than the performance of the midshipmen, mostly lads in their late teens or early twenties, executing their tasks in the near darkness with exactness and steady courage. The Quaker youth who had prevailed on Decatur to include him among the volunteers was directly behind his commander when they boarded and fought lustily with the rest across the deck to the forecastle.

Turmoil arose from the fighting despite the fact that the boarders did not fire a gun. The clash of steel reached the nearby shore. The fight on the gun deck, where gun crews had been maintained to man the pieces and guard the harbor, was more protracted than on the spar deck above, but in ten minutes the noble frigate was restored to American hands. In that time the waterfront was resounding with cries of alarm.

Several have speculated on Decatur's thoughts at this minute. He had the frigate, an experienced pilot, a fair breeze, a moonlight night, double-shotted guns, and no opposition worthy of notice from the cruisers and gunboats beached along the shore. Did he have bitter regrets that his orders to destroy her were peremptory? Some have thought so. The pilot Catalano, writing years later, said the ship could have been taken out. The state of the wind, added to his own knowledge of the currents and soundings of the harbor, convinced him that she could have been saved. He made an affidavit twenty-one years after the event, after Decatur had been killed, saying that he had made this recommendation to Decatur at the time, as they stood on the deck they had won, and strongly suggested that Decatur would have made the attempt were it not for his orders. He added that this was the opinion of all nautical people to whom he had explained the situation existing at the time.

Jacob Jones, one of the Bashaw's *Philadelphia* prisoners, held a like view, and on such matters he was a most competent judge. Long after the event, he said:

I know of nothing which could have rendered it impractical to the captors to have taken the *Philadelphia* out of the harbor of Tripoli. The water was sufficient, and I believe the wind was favorable; consequently nothing but the want of skill in the pilot who was with them, was likely to have prevented such a result, if it had been attempted. The brig *Syren,* which lay off the harbor, would have been sufficient to have protected her the moment that she had cleared the port.

But these opinions appear not to have taken into consideration the condition of the frigate when Decatur boarded her and the time at his disposal. She was stripped of sails and had no mainmast. She was anchored directly beneath the castle guns. Time was of the essence. Could this great ship have been towed by the little *Intrepid* or by the *Intrepid*'s boats? The progress would have been slow indeed and it seems as likely that Decatur and his eighty-four men would have died in the waters of Tripoli harbor as that the frigate could be brought under the protection of the *Siren* and gain the open sea.

The Tripolitan gunboats could have been launched and the harbor batteries would have played on her. Still, one may believe that peremptory orders are rarely advisable in a situation like this. Though the main reason for Preble's command to burn, not save the frigate may have been his memory of the Revolutionary War incident on the Maine coast, he was no doubt strongly influenced on this point by Bainbridge's letters. Bainbridge had cautioned him repeatedly against trying to take the frigate out of the harbor. "It would not be possible to take the frigate out, owing to the difficulty of the channel," he had said in his recommendation of Dec. 5, 1803. Again: "Let the boats be well prepared with combustibles to set her on fire, the only thing to be attempted."

Decatur executed his orders exactly. His details put the combustibles in the predetermined places in the frigate. Though Morris had been first on board, he was last to receive his combustibles, which he had to place in the cockpit and after storerooms. Already flames were breaking out when he reached his position but he did not hurry. He had his own fire blazing before he and his men made their way through the smoke to the spar deck. They were just in time, for the great flames were beginning to roar and mount. When every detail had reported back to Decatur, the lines which held the ketch to the frigate were severed and the Intrepid began to glide away in the brilliant light illuminating city and harbor. Decatur was the last to leave the burning ship. Had he slipped as he did in boarding he would have encountered disaster, for he jumped to the rigging of the ketch as she slid away.

The hazards of the enterprise were far from ended. The ketch still had on her deck quantities of combustibles which had been reserved for possible use with other enemy craft. The barrels holding them were covered with tarpaulins. The proximity of the burning *Philadelphia* put the *Intrepid* in acute danger of catching fire or of having the combustibles ignited. At the same time the castle and shore batteries, now fully aware of what was happening, opened on the ketch. Fortunately for the Americans the aiming was poor. "They commenced to fire on us from all their Batteries on shore, but with no other effect than one shot passing thro' our Top Gall^t Sail," said Decatur. He gave also another surprising bit of information: "Many boats filled with men lay round, but from whom we rec^d no annoyance."

Another difficulty was that the great rush of air caused by the mounting flames tended to draw the ketch into the vortex, but the *Siren's* small boat which had been used by Anderson's party and one of her own boats began towing, and quickly sixteen sweeps were being manned by the crew, and soon the *Intrepid* was clear of the flaming furnace. None on board paid much heed to the roar of the harbor guns once there was no longer danger that the combustibles might ignite.

Lieutenant Stewart and the *Siren's* crew were elated when they saw the ketch returning accompanied by the boats the *Siren* had sent out to cover the withdrawal. These did not appear to be necessary but they met the *Intrepid* at the entrance of the harbor and escorted her to her companion vessel.

The flames at their height burned the frigate's cable and she broke loose from her mooring, drifted closer to the Castle and blew up, rocking the city with a fearful concussion. It had not proved necessary to blow out her bottom. The wreck burned on through the night and her red glow could be seen far at sea by the brig and the ketch sailing happily back to Syracuse. What happened to the frigate's Tripolitan flag none knew. The Americans returned without this trophy.

The feature causing not surprise but amazement was that Decatur had sailed into the harbor, captured a prized frigate beneath the Castle walls, cleared her decks, routed her crew, destroyed her, and retired in good order without suffering the loss of a man, and with only one being wounded. In his report to Preble, he praised his officers but spoke with especial gratitude about the enlisted personnel, "the brave fellows I have the honor to command, whose coolness and intrepidity was such, as I trust will ever characterize the American Tars."

He was unable to judge the number of enemies on board when he attacked. He placed their dead at twenty, said a large boat got off and that many jumped into the sea.

Decatur's report probably did not tell the full story. Midshipman

Anderson, whose assignment was to cut off contact between the frigate and the shore, fought it out with one of the frigate's boats which had been lowered after the attack, and according to Surgeon's Mate Heerman, the entire crew of this boat was killed. These bodies were lost in the water.

The episode from the moment of boarding to the time the ketch shoved off with all hands on board did not require half an hour.

Midshipman Izard, who fought beside Decatur, wrote to his mother: "The Tripolitans . . . were dreadfully alarmed when they found who we were. Poor fellows! About 20 of them were cut to pieces & the rest jumped overboard. . . . It is a miracle that our little vessel escaped the flames, lying within two feet of them & to leeward also. Our men were in high spirits . . ."

Sublime indeed was the scene to those on the shore as the yellow flames licked out of the dry frigate's hatchways and ports and went up into the rigging, where the tar on the ropes sent out bright, darting lights. Few in Tripoli, or aboard the *Intrepid* or *Siren*, had ever witnessed a scene so spectacular. From the forts on the waterfront and the Bashaw's castle the ineffective cannon flashed and roared, notifying the countryside for miles in all directions that Tripoli was under attack. Then as the flames heated the double-shotted guns of the frigate, they suddenly unloosened a broadside directly into the town, which Decatur did not doubt did damage, though he had no means of knowing the extent. The other broadside spent itself in the direction of Fort English some distance east of the town.

Heerman, the surgeon's mate, told a story which varied in minor details from Decatur's. He said the *Intrepid* was under a continued fire of small arms from two xebecs lying near the *Philadelphia*. "The whooping and screaming of the enemy, on being boarded and defeated" drew this fusillade. All of the din which aroused the Castle was not the clash of arms.

Midshipman Morris grew near poetic as he contemplated the scene:

> While urging the ketch onward with sweeps, the crew were commenting on the beauty of the spray thrown up by the shot between us and the brilliant light of the ship rather than calculating any danger . . .
> The appearance of the ship was indeed magnificent. The flames in the interior illuminated her ports and, ascending her rigging and masts, formed columns of fire, which, meeting the tops, were reflected into beautiful capitals; whilst the occasional discharge of her guns gave an idea of some directing spirit within her.

There were claims for a share in the credit made on behalf of other officers, and, as has been noted, especially as to the inception of the idea, but in the end the honor went to Decatur, where it belonged, and to Preble, who never cared much about credit so long as the work was done. But Charles Stewart, who as commander of the *Siren* witnessed the entire exploit, and had earlier asked permission to execute it himself, only to find Decatur ahead of him, asserted in later years that Decatur had had the idea from the moment he learned the *Philadelphia* had been surrendered.

Stephen Decatur's widow wrote to him saying her late husband had given her to understand that the project of burning the frigate had originated with him.

> This understanding [Stewart replied] was perfectly correct; it did originate with your late husband, and he first volunteered to carry it into effect, and asked the permission of Commodore Preble, off Tripoli, (on first discovering the frigate was lost to the squadron) to effect it with the schooner *Enterprise,* then under his command. The commander-in-chief thought it too hazardous to be effected in that way, but promised your late husband that the object should be carried into effect on a proper occasion, and that he should be the executive officer when it was done.

Where another might have been jealous, having coveted the assignment, Stewart was unrestrained in his commendation of Decatur. After the event, he could remember vividly the perils of approaching the coast and all that transpired:

> ... the recollection of the difficulties and dangers he had to encounter in that expedition, of which I was an eye witness, excites more and more my admiration of his gallantry and enterprise, and although the result shed a lustre throughout Europe, over the American character, and excited an unparalleled emulation in the squadron, in our country alone is where it has never been duly estimated, or properly understood.

On the day after the destruction of the frigate, Dr. Cowdery wrote in his journal that "the Turks appeared much disheartened." As with others, "Turks" signified all Mussulmans. He told how a strong guard was placed at the door of the officers' prison and they were refused permission to go out. This may have been partly to protect them from the hostile mobs which were venting their wrath against Americans. Cowdery was restrained from visiting his sick patients. The information he got was that eight Turks were in charge of the *Philadelphia* when the Americans boarded. Two Turks escaped and told the news of the fight. Six had disappeared and were supposed to have been carried off by the Americans.

The Bashaw apparently did not want to make known the full extent of his casualties. A guard of twenty stood over the American officers and two days later Cowdery reported: "A gloomy aspect continued over the faces of the inhabitants for the loss of the frigate." Four days later he was allowed to resume his sick calls. Soldiers had been summoned from the back regions and scattered posts and he reported the town "full of country militia." Tighter restrictions were imposed on the American mail, all of which was censored.

About two weeks after the burning, Bainbridge was reprimanded severely by the Tripolitan government on the allegation that the Americans had been cruel in their attack. Three bodies of missing Turks had been washed ashore. The claim was made that they had been murdered by the Americans after they surrendered. Cowdery did not elaborate on the basis for this complaint. But for a long time the prisoners received much more rigorous treatment, partly out of fear that they were going to rise and try to take over the Castle, and with it the city.

Private Ray provided the best scene of the city when the Americans were in the harbor. He was alarmed at about 11:00 P.M. by the hubbub, "screeches of women, clattering of footsteps through the prison yard, and the harsh loud voices of the men, mingled with the thundering cannon from the castle which made our prison tremble to its base." He described the terror which struck the city: "Tumult, consternation, confusion and delay reigned in every section of the town and castle, and it was verily believed that if we had been at liberty and armed, we might with ease have taken the castle and every fort in the town."

Most of the population believed, in fact, that the prisoners had risen and captured the Castle. The prisoners, in turn, hoped a landing party was coming ashore to rescue them. But their situation was made more grievous by the spectacular raid. Their doors were bolted and the jailors expressed the town's anger by spitting in their faces and, according to Ray, "hissing like the serpants of hell." All the time the prisoners in their confinement did not know exactly what had happened, but when the word came at length that their old vessel had been utterly consumed by fire, they shouted in their elation. For a long time every boy would spit at them as they passed along the street and throw stones at them.

Decatur was honored fittingly for his great achievement. As soon as the ships returned, Preble wrote to Secretary of the Navy Smith saying he was too valuable an officer to be neglected, declaring that the crews of the enemy corsairs which surrounded him "stood appalled at his intrepidity and daring." Preble recommended that as a stimulus to the service Decatur be given "instantaneous promotion" to the rank of captain. Jefferson complied just as soon as the dispatches reached Washington.

Thus the commander of the *Intrepid* was appointed captain, then the highest official naval rank, at the age of twenty-five. None so young had attained that rank. Congress presented a sword to him. The country resounded with praise for the *Intrepid's* officers and crew. The *National Intelligencer* in Washington found room for the story and the list of the participating officers along with accounts of the trial of the Duke de Enghein and the biography of General Moreau. More than normal attention was given to President Jefferson's prompt response to Preble's recommendation and Decatur's promotion, but the entire Tripolitan War was soon swept out of the press by stories in July of the mournful death of Alexander Hamilton in the duel with Aaron Burr. The eulogies were profound.

Most of the junior officers were promoted and several were merely at the beginning of brillant naval careers. Secretary of the Navy Smith conveyed President Jefferson's thanks to Decatur and asked him to thank in the name of the President "each Individual of your gallant Band." And applause came from an unexpected quarter. Lord Nelson, who knew about such things, and who at the time was off Toulon blockading the French fleet, said when he heard of the feat that it was "the most bold and daring act of the age."

Mrs. Decatur in after years tended to confirm the judgment of Jacob Jones and the pilot Catalano that the *Philadelphia* might have been saved. She gave it as her late husband's opinion that the frigate could have been towed out by the *Intrepid,* that the shore batteries would not have been effective in the darkness, and that what made the mission perilous was the burning of the ship and the lighting of the harbor.

But if this were Decatur's studied opinion, it must have had an unconscious element of hindsight in it, because on his return to the fleet the commodore gained the impression that the frigate could not have been saved. In his first report to Secretary Smith, dashed off at 10:00 A.M., February 19, 1804, the day the *Siren* and *Intrepid* returned to Syracuse, Preble said: "The frigate was moored in a situation from whence she could not be brought out." Decatur and Stewart reported to him on board the *Constitution* after their ships had passed through the cheering fleet and Preble must have gained the information from them.

Almost a century after the burning of the *Philadelphia,* the charred ribs of the frigate were located by Charles Willington Furlough, an American working in 1903 with a detail of Greek divers and a glass-bottomed boat. Among the relics they brought up from her timbers was an 18-pound cannon ball, fired from a shore battery on the night Decatur captured the ship. When the present-day breakwater was built during the period of Italian occupation of Libya, the rocky islands which early formed the harbor were united and the mole extended to cover the site where the *Philadelphia* went down.

CHAPTER SEVENTEEN

The Battle of the Gunboats

P REBLE needed small gunboats which could go into the harbor, engage the Tripolitans at close quarters, and bombard the town, and not until he procured them could he strike effectively against the enemy stronghold.

His ships made seizures from time to time. In February, the *Nautilus* under Captain Somers captured the *Crocifisso,* a merchant brig with Fortunata Barbara as master, which was taken a few miles east of Tripoli trying to slip into the harbor under British colors. She was loaded with hemp, spars, sails, plank, and building stone, and had nine Tripolitan passengers on board. Preble notified the British governor of Malta, Sir Alexander Ball, that he intended to make the ship a prize, but he nevertheless sent her to Malta for investigation so Sir Alexander would be satisfied about the propriety of the proceedings.

On March 17, 1804, Stewart, with the *Siren,* captured the Tripolitan brig *Transfer* which the Bashaw's agent in Malta had purchased from the British. She had been plying back and forth as a blockade runner. As she was being expected in Tripoli on the night Decatur burned the *Philadelphia,* the pilot Catalano had reported her as being the ship off the harbor, when the vessel inquired about was the disguised *Siren.*

Now that she was indeed off Tripoli, and caught in her proscribed activities, Stewart took her easily with the *Siren,* which he was using as his flagship. She carried a crew of eighty men, mounted ten guns and was a sturdy, fair-sized vessel, once a British privateer. Her part owner Gaetano Andrea Schembry of Valletta made a plea to Preble for her return but the latter took her into the U.S. service, equipped her with sixteen 6-pounders, rechristened her the *Scourge,* and assigned her to Lieutenant John H. Dent, who had commanded the *Enterprise* while Decatur was absent on the *Intrepid.* The name *Scourge* was to recur on the naval lists, and was that of a schooner of Commodore Chauncey's Lake Ontario fleet in the War of 1812. If Preble could not get warships from the United States he could acquire them by his own efforts, first the *Intrepid* and now the *Scourge*, both cruisers suited for coastal fighting.

The fleet officers seemed pleased that two popular young midshipmen, Izard and Wadsworth, were appointed acting Lieutenants and assigned to the *Scourge* under Dent. Wadsworth wrote to his Cousin Nancy: "I have been so long in the Mediterranean that I have acquired an habitual hatred of the Bashaw our enemy, & I feel as much interested in punishing him as if he had personally insulted me."

The *Scourge* was sent to join the blockading cruisers off Tripoli. Another happy reinforcement arrived at about the same time. The *Argus*, the patrol ship off Gibraltar, had been scouring the western Mediterranean following reports that a Tripolitan cruiser was at large, but when she could find no trace of any piratical craft, and in view of the increasingly effective blockade Preble was maintaining with the advent of spring, the Commodore ordered Hull to bring the *Argus* to the main squadron. She came by Syracuse and was off Tripoli in April. Midshipman Wadsworth confirmed Preble's judgment about her. Writing to his Cousin Nancy, he was ecstatic:

"The *Argus* is universally allowed to be the finest vessel floating in the Mediterranean. The envy & jealousy of the British officers is excited by our fine ships and handsome manoeuvring."

While Preble was busy in different Mediterranean ports assembling a flotilla and preparing systematically for his campaign, the blockading vessels off Tripoli, the *Siren* and the *Vixen*, joined, as the season advanced, by the *Argus* and the *Scourge*, were commanded by one of Preble's most faithful and competent subordinates, Lieutenant Charles Stewart, who had been the senior officer and commander of the *Siren* on the raid to burn the *Philadelphia*.

Stewart, who would become one of the outstanding ship captains of the War of 1812, and commander of the *Constitution* during part of that conflict, was twenty-five years old in the spring of 1804, when at intervals he had the responsibility of directing the blockade. He had won his way up in the merchant and then the naval service. Born in Philadelphia of Irish parents, July 28, 1778, just after Lord Howe evacuated the city, he was youngest of eight children. His father, an Irish sailor, died when he was two, leaving his mother with the large family to care for. For a time he was Decatur's schoolmate. He got a job on a merchant vessel at the age of thirteen, rose from cabin boy to the master of an Indiaman, and when war with France threatened, he offered his services and was appointed a lieutenant.

He performed brilliantly in the Caribbean as commander of the schooner *Experiment*, and among other feats captured in ten minutes the French schooner *Two Friends* without losing a man. Now, in the Mediterranean, he was one of Decatur's closest friends.

Of all the officers who fought in the quasi-war with France and perhaps of all who fought in the wars against the Barbary powers, Stewart was the only one who survived to witness the naval innovations of the Civil War, such as the advent of the ironclads, and to see that war won in large measure by naval strength and a blockade. He devoted more than sixty years of active service to the Navy, then lived during his late years on the Delaware River at Bordentown, New Jersey, where he met numerous callers and told stories of the sea.

Preble, while awaiting procurement of the gunboats, took the *Constitution* down to the Tripoli blockade on a peace feeler in March, not with any thought of paying tribute or indemnity, but in the hope of effecting the ransom of the *Philadelphia* prisoners. For them the peace-seeking Lear was willing to pay $600 a head, but Preble firmly declined to go higher than $200. Nothing short of his humanitarian instincts could have compelled him to offer the Bashaw any ransom at all, and nothing would satisfy him except outright and complete victory before talking terms. He wrote to Secretary Smith the day he learned of Decatur's success, saying of the Bashaw: "My heart is fixed on obliging him to sue for Peace and I hope yet to make him consent to sign a treaty as favorable as ours with Morocco without a cent for Peace or Tribute. I had rather spend my life in the Mediterranean than we should ever consent to either."

In March Preble was expressing hope for more ships so he could take Derna and Bengazi and deprive the corsairs of rendezvous, and strip the Bashaw of revenues collected from that beylic.

Preble went to Tripoli largely through the hope that Napoleon, then First Consul, who had seemed to interest himself in the unfortunate plight of the *Philadelphia* captives, might have enough influence in Tripoli to cause the Bashaw to listen to reasonable ransom terms. The First Consul's interest resulted from an approach made to Talleyrand. When the *Philadelphia* was captured some of the American diplomats in Europe, moved by humanitarian considerations but without a full appreciation of the niceties of the situation confronting the independent and presumably self-reliant United States, appealed to different governments—France, Russia, Spain, etc.—asking them to intercede with the Tripolitan government.

When Jefferson learned of it, he was deeply chagrined, since he believed the United States should show the resolution and power to protect its own citizens. He wrote to Secretary Smith: "I have never been so mortified as at the conduct of our foreign functionaries . . . they have

hawked us in *forma pauperis* begging alms at every court of Europe."
Later when Secretary Madison thanked Russia for the friendly inter-
position on behalf of the prisoners, after the Russian ambassador at the
Porte had employed his good offices, he made it clear that "the measures
taken by the Gov^t of the United States, in consequence of the accident
at Tripoli, and which will be followed up with the requisite vigor, promise to repair the loss, and to bring the Bashaw to proper terms of peace."
He appreciated the friendly attention of the Russian Emperor in the
matter, but wanted it understood the United States was taking its own
measures.

Bonaparte grasped the matter of the prisoners more vigorously, being
concerned at the time with American friendship during the period of
the Louisiana treaty and ratification. Robert R. Livingston, U.S. minister
to Paris, solicited his mediation to establish peace and release the unhappy men. The First Consul was, as Talleyrand put it, "touched with
the most lively commisseration for their misfortune." Talleyrand directed Citizen Beaussier, French chargé d'affaires at Tripoli, to "put all
in train to alleviate their situation, and to obtain their deliverance." He
told the chargé to tell the Bashaw that Bonaparte desired "a solid and
advantageous peace to both parties."

Livingston sent Preble the reply he received from Talleyrand, which
was accompanied by the instructions to the French chargé, and suggested that he should see that these instructions were safely delivered.
Preble was to give them to the chargé. "I doubt not that the Consul's
recommendation will have much weight," wrote Livingston to Preble,
and added: "I shall feel myself extremely happy if with that aid you can
effectuate anything for our brave but unfortunate fellow Citizens."

Preble, who relied more on gunpowder than words, could not have
been highly impressed with the prospects of peace through the intercession of a far-distant First Consul, though he expressed admiration of
Napoleon's genius, but he took the letter and sailed from Syracuse. On
March 26 he was off Tripoli in the *Constitution,* where he joined Stewart
with the *Siren* and *Nautilus* on the blockade. Under a white flag Lieutenant Izard went ashore to deliver the letters to Citizen Beaussier and
to see Captain Bainbridge, the only officer the Bashaw would allow him
to meet. Unhappily, Izard did not write a letter to his mother about it
and the story has to be taken from the less graphic naval reports. Bainbridge did not look hearty, which led the Commodore to write him expressing concern over his health. Bainbridge in truth was showing the
effects of his captivity, and his sturdy character at times appeared from
his correspondence to be on the verge of breaking.

"Mr. Izard's report is true," he wrote to Preble March 29, "I am quite thin; your sympathy I justly estimate . . . but in spite of every effort of my own, and your good advice, I cannot prevent sad reflections; my character; My loss of services to my country! And my Family, are painful subjects to contemplate on in a close Prison in Tripoli." The distressed man seemed to require sympathy but Preble was not close enough to solace him. The sterner Preble no doubt would have kept his lamentations to himself.

When the Bashaw's minister complained that Decatur's men had been heartless in their capture of the *Philadelphia,* though it was never explained how the bodies washed ashore could have given evidence that the men were killed after they had surrendered, Preble wrote Bainbridge about the complaints sharply, indicating a scant number of Americans had attacked a great many Tripolitans. The officers had reported to him no act of massacre or inhumanity.

"People who handle dangerous weapons in War, must expect wounds and Death," he indirectly advised the enemy leader.

But he declared he would never countenance wanton acts of cruelty.

Sailing Master Nathaniel Haraden, who was keeping the log of the *Constitution,* noted down his impressions as he waited four miles out for the return of Izard's boat. "The Town of Tripoli," reads the log, "is situated at the bottom of a circular Bay with Groves of trees to the Eastward and a sandy desert on the S.W. & W N: W as far as the Eye could reach— A long reef of black rocks to the Eastward of the Town—Nine Gun boats within them—The Entrance is defended by Batteries from the North shewing 72 Cannon."

Izard carried a letter to the Prime Minister also, suggesting an exchange of prisoners. It was rejected without discussion. The Bashaw was rarely concerned about his captured subjects. On the following day the French chargé d'affaires came out to the *Constitution* and told Preble he would do anything he could to rescue the prisoners, but he named a ransom figure out of line with Preble's thinking. What it was is not certain because Preble in his report to Secretary Smith put it at $200,000, whereas the French official, in a letter he sent to Preble after returning to the shore, thought that the "Bashaw's pretensions" would come to $500,000. Preble had indeed written earlier that the first expectation after the prisoners were captured had been $3,000,000. The sum he still had in mind was around $60,000, or $200 a head for the three hundred prisoners.

The Frenchman told Preble he had warned the Bashaw of the impending descent of an American flotilla against his shores and had cautioned also that Hamet was to be brought back and placed on the throne. But Bashaw Yusuf, unalarmed, responded that his brother Hamet was a drunkard, without means, and was incapable of acquiring partisans. "All these assertions are truths," the French representative affirmed, adding that the conference fatigued the prince, so he took his leave pending Preble's reply about the "pretensions" of half a million.

With this Preble broke off the negotiations, being satisfied that Citizen Beaussier was more friendly to the Bashaw than to the Americans. The Commodore's conclusions were entered in his diary that night: "I am confident that the French, English and Swedish Consuls are all in the Bashaw's Interest, That the Danish Consul is the only respectable character among them, and he is not permitted to visit us. We must therefore depend wholly on our own exertions . . ." In that he was concurring with Jefferson. He added in his diary that he required gun and mortar boats to batter down the Castle and city. That night, March 28, he sailed back to Italy to get them.

Possibly he had been unduly severe on one or two of the foreign consuls in Tripoli, but he was certainly correct in affirming that the United States must rely on its own efforts.

Procuring the type of gunboats he wanted was a toilsome operation. Preble had the assistance of the King of the Two Sicilies, who was just as much at war with Tripoli as was the United States, though he was doing much less about it. Here was an instance where the monarch could be of service, so Preble dropped the *Constitution*'s anchor in Naples harbor on May 9 and called on Sir John Acton, the British peer who had become Prime Minister and commander in chief of the Neapolitan army and navy under King Ferdinand IV. This monarch, the son-in-law of Maria Theresa and brother-in-law of Marie Antoinette, held precariously to his throne, by the aid of Lord Nelson and the British minister Sir William Hamilton, being assailed by the French and by revolutionists in front and by the Barbary powers behind. Napoleon two years later would shake him off of it.

On the next day Preble presented his formal request to Sir John in writing for eight gunboats and two mortar boats. He adhered to the specifications he had mentioned earlier. He asked also for eight long brass cannon, either 24- or 32-pounders, with carriages, for use on floating batteries which would go into the harbor of Bengazi and bombard that town, where, he was advised, the Bashaw intended to build gunboats while Tripoli was being blockaded. He told Sir John he wanted also to destroy Derna and all other Tripolitan seacoast cities. He requested supplies of powder, shot, shells, muskets, and sabers. If the gunboats could be loaned to the United States, they would be returned in good order or be paid for at their just value.

Because he did not have enough men, Preble also asked for ninety-six

Neapolitans to supplement his American crews and serve as bombardiers, gunners, and sailors, and while thus engaged they were to enter the
United States naval service.

Preble by his personal force and diligent leadership and the example
he set of devotion to the American cause had been able to get an extraordinary response from his own seamen, many of whose enlistments had
long since expired. The crew of the *Enterprise* had sent him a rather
pitiful petition at Messina on April 5, 1804, pointing out that they had
discharged their duties to the utmost in faithfulness in support of the
rights and independence of America, but solicited his attention to their
own rights as freemen. They had served six months over their time.
Some had been two years and three months away from home, some
longer. Their wives and families had been left in a distressed state for
want of support, which their absence had rendered impracticable. They
asked relief and Preble was compelled to give it to them just as soon as
a new crew could be brought out on the *John Adams* from the United
States. The *Enterprise* and some of the other vessels had to be laid up
in the late spring or early summer for repairs.

Sir John Acton notified Preble on May 13 that the King had acceded
to his request for the gunboats, the two mortar boats, or bomb ketches,
and the munitions, as a loan, but had reduced the number of gunboats
from eight to six. The flotilla was to be assembled at Messina. According
to the Neapolitan orders they were to be manned by from five to fifteen
sailors each, aside from the masters, while "two cannoneers most skilled
in the use of the mortar" were to be embarked on each of the bomb
ketches. Though Preble was compelled to discharge part of the crew
of the *Enterprise,* he used those who would remain, plus the crew of the
Nautilus, to man the gunboats and mortar boats, the Neapolitans being
used as auxiliaries. American officers were put in command. He received
the boats at Messina on May 20, 1804, and hoisted the U.S. flag on each
of them. Not until July 14 were the mortar boats and the balance of the
flotilla ready, and on that date Preble sailed for Tripoli.

The gunboats were shallow, flat-bottomed and heavy, almost barges,
not suited for navigation; but they were equipped with sails and oars.
Preble said that "they do not sail or row even tolerably well." They were
of about twenty-five tons and they had one good piece of equipment, the
long iron 24-pounder mounted in the bow. Each had a complement of
thirty-five men. The bomb ketches were larger, of thirty tons, and carried 13-inch brass sea-mortars and forty men. The eight long brass
cannon, 24-pounders, which he borrowed in the same requisition for
eventual use at Derna, were mounted on the spar deck of the *Constitution.*

Meantime the blockade was being maintained by the *Argus,* the *Vixen,* the *Siren,* and the *Scourge,* with occasional exchanges with the enemy forts. On July 7 the four vessels gave chase in a fine breeze to a large galiot caught at dawn trying to enter the harbor, but she was able to make the shore nine miles west of Tripoli where she began unloading. Stewart, who commanded, sent Lieutenant James R. Caldwell with the *Siren's* launch and a 12-pounder carronade and a barge with a heavy swivel under Midshipman John S. Dorsey. They advanced to a reef where for a time both boats were grounded and exposed to heavy cannonading, but they soon got off and kept a steady fire of their two pieces playing on the galiot. The *Vixen* sent boats to cover them and the enemy vessel and its boats, in the words of Stewart, were "cut to pieces." The galiot could not be taken because she was grounded on the reef. Stewart expressed great satisfaction to Preble over the conduct of the small American force which opposed about one thousand Tripolitans stationed in strong positions on the shore. He estimated the enemy's loss as severe. The Americans lost one killed and three wounded, one of them mortally. All were marines.

This was the only ship action of consequence before Preble brought up his gunboats. They came July 25, accompanied by the *Constitution,* the *Enterprise,* and the *Nautilus.* At last an effective fleet was off Tripoli; not as powerful as those which preceded and immediately succeeded it in terms of guns and frigates, but effective in its leadership, because Preble was there not to listen to complaints that the tributes were in arrears or that a frigate was due because some other country had been given a frigate, but to fight a war. The squadron consisted of one frigate, three brigs, three schooners, two bomb ketches, and six gunboats; and the entire force of officers, sailors, marines, and Neapolitans numbered 1,060. The ships and their armaments were:

SHIP	CLASS	NO. OF GUNS	TYPE OF GUNS
Constitution	Frigate	44	24-pounders
Argus	Brig	18	24-pounders
Siren	Brig	18	18-pounders
Scourge	Brig	16	6-pounders
Vixen	Schooner	16	6-pounders
Nautilus	Schooner	16	6-pounders
Enterprise	Schooner	12	6-pounders

The fleet had 140 guns to which were added the six long guns and two mortars of the gun and mortar boats and the eight additional brass cannon mounted in the waist of the *Constitution's* spar deck, making a total armament of 156 guns.

The city he was attacking was walled and protected by strategically located forts—"batteries judiciously constructed," in Preble's words—which mounted 150 pieces of heavy artillery. The firepower of fleet and city artillery was fairly equal. The city was defended by an army of indefinite size but placed by American calculations at 25,000 Arabs and Turks, while the harbor was protected by nineteen gunboats, two galiots, two schooners, each with eight guns, and a brig with ten. The ships gave the defenders a heavy superiority in artillery. The fleet was commanded by Murad Reis, who, despite his Scottish antecedents and British and American seaman services, had not in his preliminary battles with the Americans proved himself much of a combat leader, however he may have excelled as a mariner. He had his protecting fleet drawn up in the harbor in a line of battle two miles long, with vessels moored inside the long range of rocks and reefs which in that day protected Tripoli. This ridge of rocks, now connected into the long breakwater or mole, was what made the harbor of Tripoli, which is situated on a stretch of coast providing practically no other protection against the northern storms. Because of these rocks it was difficult for a warship as large as the *Constitution* to approach close enough to blast the defending gunboats out of the water.

The Tripolitan gunboats were more heavily armed than the American. Each had a heavy 18- to 26-pounder in the bow and two brass howitzers on her quarterdeck. Their crews ranged from thirty-six to fifty men. Their galleys, brigs, and schooners carried crews of about one hundred each.

Because of the gunboats, which, being unseaworthy, had to be towed, Preble's was a good-weather flotilla, and at the outset he encountered bad weather. He managed to get an anchorage off the city on July 28, three days after his arrival, but within two hours the wind, which had been from the east, shifted to the northwest, and soon it was blowing such a gale and setting so heavy a sea against the shore that Preble signaled for the fleet to gain an offing so as not to be carried against the rocks. The gunboats were in great danger of foundering but the squadron got sea room and weathered the heavy blow until it subsided August 1. Some damage was suffered. Preble pointed out that the sea did not rise in proportion to the strength of the gale, else all the gunboats would have been lost.

Preparations were again made for the attack. On August 3, in pleasant weather, the squadron stood in toward Tripoli and by noon was within two to three miles of the batteries. As Preble noticed some of the Tripolitan gunboats and galleys had advanced in two divisions to positions outside the rocks, he determined to punish them for their venturesomeness and at once signaled his ship commanders to come within hailing distance of the *Constitution*. At 12:30 P.M. he announced to them his intention to attack the ships and batteries at once.

The gunboats and mortar ketches cast off as prearranged, the gunboats in two divisions. The order of the gunboats and their officers was:

BOAT NUMBER	COMMANDER	OFFICER'S SHIP
	First Division	
No. 1	Lieutenant Richard Somers	*Nautilus*
No. 2	Lieutenant James Decatur	*Nautilus*
No. 3	Lieutenant Joshua Blake	*Argus*
	Second Division	
No. 4	Lieutenant Stephen Decatur	*Enterprise*
No. 5	Midshipman Joseph Bainbridge	*Enterprise*
No. 6	Lieutenant John Trippe	*Vixen*

Some of these officers already had been promoted by the Navy Department but notice of their new ranks had not been received. The mortar ketches were commanded by Lieutenant John H. Dent of the *Scourge* and Master Commandant Thomas Robinson, Jr., of the *Constitution*.

Preble gave the signal for general battle at 2:00 P.M., and the mortar boats began the action by tossing shells into the city, upon which the Tripolitan batteries opened all along the shore with a heavy cannonade—"tremendous," Preble called it—joined by the guns of their naval vessels. The American squadron was now sufficiently close to throw grape, which was scattered over the enemy shipping and town. Under this cover the American gunboats went forward. The first detachment to get into action was a part of Stephen Decatur's. His three boats, using both sail and oars, advanced on the far eastern enemy detachment of nine gunboats, lying farthest from the city and Castle, outside the end of the mole, where they were covering the harbor entrance.

Long had the Barbary corsairs been the terror of the Mediterranean because of their boarding tactics, in which black-whiskered screaming men, brandishing scimitars and dirks, and supported by phalanxes with boarding pikes, quickly overran the object of their attack and won it by hand-to-hand encounter. Terror was their weapon almost as much as steel. Lieutenant Sterrett had first brought into question the invincibility of the Barbary boarders when he captured the *Tripoli* with the *Enterprise*, and now the matter was to be brought to a more convincing test. Decatur headed straight for the nine Tripolitan gunboats with his Division Number Two, and since Somers, who headed the other division, had a more sluggish boat, speedily outdistanced him. One other boat of

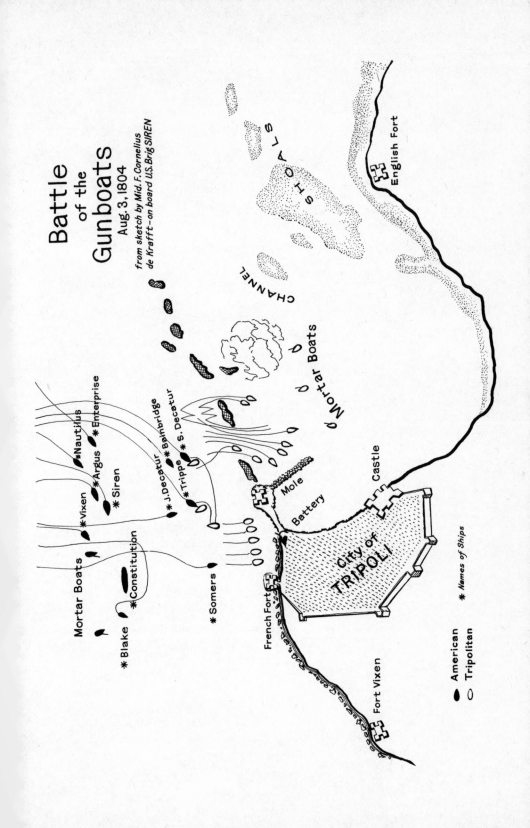

Battle
of the
Gunboats
Aug. 3, 1804

from sketch by Mid. F. Cornelius
de Krafft—on board U.S.Brig SIREN

SHOALS

CHANNEL

English Fort

Mortar Boats

Mortar Boats

* Nautilus
* Vixen
Argus * Enterprise
* Siren
J.Decatur * Bainbridge
Trippe * S. Decatur

* Blake
* Constitution

* Somers

Mole
Battery

French Fort

Fort Vixen

CITY of
TRIPOLI

Castle

● American
○ Tripolitan

* Names of Ships

Decatur's division, that of Sailing Master Trippe, and one of Somers' boats, No. 2, commanded by the younger Decatur, kept abreast of him and joined in the first wave of the attack. Midshipman Bainbridge's No. 5 boat grounded for a time and maintained a steady fire but did not get into the front action.

When they were close to the harbor entrance and concealed by the smoke of the enemy guns they no longer had the protective cover from the American squadron, which necessarily ceased firing and left them on their own. Stephen Decatur showered the boats in front of him with grape and musketry. Being in the leading boat, he closed on and grappled the largest of the Barbary gunboats, and almost before the Tripolitans were aware of it their deck was overrun by a desperate band of fifteen American sailors headed by Decatur, Lieutenant Thorn, and Midshipman Macdonough, armed with cutlasses, axes, dirks, pistols and tomahawks. Step by step, the compact band of Americans, though heavily outnumbered, forced the enemy back until they reached the large open hatchway in the center of the gunboat, where they tried to make a stand. Here the Americans divided, pressed around both sides of the hatch, and renewed the slashing and hacking as they pushed toward the stern of the boat. But before they reached it, the few survivors of the Tripolitan crew surrendered. The fighting had lasted only ten minutes. One reason why the Turks were overcome so speedily was that their captain had been wounded fourteen times by grape and musket balls before the Americans boarded, and the boat was leaderless. On this one gunboat, thirty-six of the Bashaw's sailors had gone into the action. Sixteen were killed, fifteen wounded and five made prisoners. The American loss was three wounded.

Decatur took the gunboat as a prize and turned to the next in the line of enemy craft, a smaller vessel with a crew of twenty-four, but carrying three guns and led, it developed, by a huge Turk who did not intend to yield an inch of his deck while he could still wield a weapon. Though no longer fresh after their first heavy encounter, Decatur and Macdonough again stormed the gunboat with the eight sailors of their own crew who remained in fighting condition or were not manning the prize. Decatur battled with five of the enemy; then as the other Americans came up he made directly for the big Turkish leader. The fight which ensued was so protracted and desperate that it became a favorite theme of the historical artists and remains perhaps the most frequent illustration of the hand-to-hand fighting in the Tripolitan War.

Decatur was met by the Turk with a jab by a boarding pike, a weapon more often employed in the past on Christian than Barbary decks. In parrying the thrust he broke off his cutlass at the hilt. He had actually tried to strike off the head of the pike and his blade snapped. He parried a second thrust with his bare arm and received an unpleasant wound, but before the Turks could withdraw the weapon for a final jab, Decatur, now unarmed, clutched the pike, and wrested it from him, then clinched with him, grabbed his throat and wrestled with him around the deck. Either by chance or by his athletic prowess, the American dropped his opponent to the boards and remained on top. The success was almost a fatal success for Decatur, who was down with his back exposed as he struggled locked in the Turk's embrace. Other Americans and Tripolitans were battling all around them intent on their own frantic strife, but at an unfavorable moment one of the Turks broke loose and raised his scimitar directly above Decatur's head. Another two seconds and the Commander's skull would have been split. He was saved by a noble act of heroism by one of his men. Daniel Fraser, a young seaman, seeing the blow aimed, and being wounded in both arms and unable longer to fight, jumped quickly in front of the Turk and took the blow on his own head. None would have given him a chance of survival, but the blow, aimed at Decatur, glanced when it caught Fraser and while it laid his scalp open it did not kill him. Before the Turk could aim another blow he was felled by a musket ball.

But Decatur was still in furious personal combat with the Turk beneath him on the deck. That stalwart fighter, the larger of the two, whirled Decatur underneath, then wrested his arm free and drew from his sash a poniard about a foot long having a rhinoceros tusk for a handle. Before he could sink it home Decatur grabbed his hand and held it aloft. The American with his other hand reached into his coat pocket and drew out a pistol, which, by wrapping his arm around his adversary, he held to the Turk's back and fired. The bullet might have penetrated his own body after killing the Turk but the urgency of the crisis did not permit hesitation. The bullet did pass through the Turk's body, but it lodged, spent, in Decatur's clothing. The Turk crumpled. Decatur rose from the bloody deck and extricated himself from the bodies strewn about it, which except for chance and Fraser's self-sacrifice would have included his own.

Seaman Fraser survived the affray and the war, drew in later years a pension, and long told the story of the battle of the gunboats. Decatur presented the rhinoceros-tusk poniard to his friend Stewart, who treasured it throughout his long naval career and exhibited it in his late years to callers at his home in Bordentown.

In these first two Tripolitan gunboats which Decatur captured, aided by the well near unbelievable courage and dexterous hand-fighting of Thorn and Macdonough and their handful of followers, were heavily superior forces of enemy seamen and gunners. When the fighting was over, fifty-two were known casualties, killed or wounded, and eight not wounded were taken prisoners. The others either had jumped overboard or had been killed and their bodies had fallen into the sea.

How spirited a fighter the Tripolitans faced in Macdonough might be seen from an incident before the fleet sailed from Syracuse. The town was beset by robbers who grew so bold at times as to attack American naval personnel. They would fall on a victim in the dark, put a dagger into him, and take his money and watch. Three of them ganged up on Macdonough one night but the young midshipman managed to get his back against a door and his sword into play, and wounded two of his assailants. The third turned and fled. But Macdonough was not content with merely escaping. He pursued the man around the barracks and finally to the rooftops. There the bandit, when he saw his pursuer coming on, was thrown into such a fear that he jumped from the roof and killed himself.

The good naval officers of the day seemed innately self-reliant and most of them a little overly bellicose. They were on the lookout to find, not avoid, a good fight.

By the time he had won the second boat, only four Americans of Decatur's original boarding party remained uninjured.

Decatur at this instance received grievous information about his younger brother, James. When Somers' lead boat of the first American detachment had been held back by being a dull sailor, James Decatur, who had a faster boat, had gone ahead and attached himself to his brother's No. 2 division. Selecting an enemy, he riddled it with musketry and grape, then went alongside it to board. The Tripolitan commander, according to the preponderance of American accounts, immediately surrendered. The younger Decatur unsuspectingly stepped to the enemy craft to take the boat as a prize, when the enemy captain pulled a pistol from his sash and shot him in the head. He died that afternoon on the *Constitution* and the next day they buried him at sea. Said Preble in his report: "Lieutenant James Decatur was the only officer killed. . . . He was a young man who gave strong promise of being an ornament to his profession. His conduct in the action was highly honorable, and he died nobly."

The missile with which the Tripolitan captain killed James Decatur was supposed to have been a peculiar type of chain shot adapted to small-arms use. Two bullets were linked by a heavy wire and were fired from the same chamber. The wire caught Decatur in the forehead and bent and the two bullets entered his temples.

When Decatur received news that his brother had been shot—and he was believed to have been killed instantly—he summoned as many men as he could gather quickly, and eleven responded to his call. He made after the Tripolitan captain, who was fleeing with the gunboat he had saved by treachery. Never has it been certain that Decatur positively identified the boat but the odds seemed strongly that he did. He overhauled the suspected craft, fought a sanguinary battle for twenty minutes, killed the captain outright, and took this gunboat, his third, as a prize. His retribution was immediate and complete. In his vengeance at least was ground for Spence's comparing him with a Greek god.

Preble had no question about the manner in which James Decatur met his death, though some have tended to demand more verification. Said the Commodore's official report: ". . . he was treacherously shot through the head by the captain of the boat that had surrendered, which base conduct enabled the poltroon (with the assistance he received from the other boats) to escape."

Stephen Decatur's own account of his fight with the first two gunboats is perhaps the best summary of the many written. It was contained in a letter to his friend Purser William Spence of the *Philadelphia*, one of his early sponsors in the service. Purser Spence was a prisoner in Tripoli during the action of the gunboats in which his son, Midshipman Robert T. Spence, fought gallantly. Decatur said:

I found that hand-to-hand is not child's play—'tis kill or be killed. You no doubt recollect the conversation which we had when in the city of Washington. I then informed you that it was my intention to board if ever I had an opportunity, and that it was my opinion there could be no doubt of the issue. You will not doubt me, I hope, when I say that I am glad the event has proved my ideas were correct. I always thought we could lick them their own way and give then two to one. The first boat, they were thirty-six to twenty; we carried it without much fuss. The second was twenty-four to ten; they also went to the leeward. I had eighteen Italians in the boat with me, who claim the honor of the day. While we were fighting, they prayed. They are convinced we could not have been so fortunate unless their prayers had been heard. This might have been the case; therefore we could not contradict it. Some of the Turks died like men, but much the greater died like women.

Stewart thought it typical of his good friend to take the chance of firing the bullet into the Turk's back when his own body was underneath. He heard the details of the fight from Decatur direct. "The chances were ten to one the bullet would pass through both their bodies," Stewart said, "but luckily it met a bone and the huge barbarian rolled off dead." He was a defender of Tripoli who died fighting like a man.

But Decatur's was not the only spectacular battle of the afternoon. His No. 6 gunboat, commanded by Lieutenant Trippe, had fighting as sanguinary and experiences as varied and hazardous as any other.

Trippe was comparatively small but compactly built and strong. That accounted for his ability to wage one of the most desperate combats of the war, of which the *Naval Chronicle* said "a more extraordinary action was probably never recorded." It will long be remembered in naval annals, as will the circumstance that one of Oliver H. Perry's vessels in the Battle of Lake Erie bore Trippe's honored name, as others of Perry's ships did, equally appropriately, the names of *Lawrence* and *Somers*.

Trippe held his fire and poured it at close range into one of the largest of the enemy's gunboats, then, following the tactics of Decatur, came alongside to board. He, Midshipman John Henley, and nine others of his crew jumped to the Tripolitan craft, but just then the ships fell apart and none of the other Americans could get on the enemy deck. Eleven Americans faced a crew of thirty-six Turks and Arabs, and, as Preble pointed out in his report, it was "conquer or perish."

Trippe had happened to pick an enemy boat commanded by one of the most resolute leaders in the Tripolitan navy, an athletic captain, strong, standing well above six feet, twenty-four years old, and quickly admired for his gallantry by his enemies, the Americans. With the spirit of the old conquerors who had overrun North Africa, he had sworn on the Koran before the battle that he would either win or die. But the eleven Americans, fighting in formation and supporting each other, slashed into his crew and gradually overcame them, battling with a frenzy the Turks had not experienced in the Mediterranean wars. They pushed the defenders relentlessly across the deck of the gunboat. The dexterous Trippe, an able swordsman and pikeman, was in front, Midshipman Henley fighting by his side.

Trippe was well near cut to pieces but he battled on, picking the big Turkish captain as his especial antagonist. Henley came to his assistance and they called on the Turk by word and signal to give up the fight. His men were falling all around him and the two American officers, admiring his gallantry and resolution, wanted to spare him. But he scorned indignantly their repeated requests that he surrender and seemed to fight the harder because of them. Those who witnessed the combat considered that Trippe survived only by his agility and complete self-possession. He fought on coolly with the captain while his men were still at work subduing the enemy sailors who battled on.

While the hand-to-hand fight between the two leaders was at its merriest, another Turk came up in Trippe's rear and was about to cleave his head open when Sergeant Jonathan Meridith of the Marine Corps passed a bayonet into the Turk's body. None had time to reward Sergeant Meridith for his alertness. He was killed in the fighting two days later.

Trippe and the Turk were covered with blood. Both had numerous wounds. The Turk's method was to advance and bring down his scimitar as Trippe was trying to get in a pike thrust, and both were therefore momentarily exposed. Trippe had taken eight saber wounds on his head and two on his chest when the Turk by a quick dash suddenly struck him heavily on the head again, giving him his ninth head wound and bringing him down to his knee. But the fleeting success was fatal to the Turk. Trippe, fighting with a short pike, got in a quick jab into the man's vitals and the Turk reeled and collapsed on the deck. Trippe always felt he killed the captain in self-defense, but he did it so regretfully that in later years when he spoke of it his eyes would fill with tears. He lamented the necessity of putting out the life of such a stalwart fighter.

Even as he was expiring, the Turk put his last flicker into the struggle. Henley, believing he was dead, stepped over his body, which the prostrate man seemed to recognize as an indignity. He grabbed Henley's ankle, twisted it violently in a final defiance, then fell back dead. With his death, his crew quit the fight and surrendered.

Trippe, with his eleven wounds, some severe, had displayed courage which might be remarked about as emphatically as that of the Turkish captain. He accepted the surrender of what turned out to be probably the largest gunboat of the Tripolitan navy. Though Preble placed the number of its defenders at thirty-six, none could be certain how many may have jumped or been pushed overboard in the fighting. Twenty-one were found on the deck dead or wounded, while fifteen others surrendered.

The engagements of Trippe and Decatur were demonstrations of early American courage at its height, the sort that had made the nation and was now winning for it world respect.

When Trippe's victory was witnessed by the Tripolitans all along the line, they withdrew their remaining gunboats behind the shelter of the rocks. For Trippe there remained one more nerve straining situation. He had won a good gunboat by fair combat and now he put some men on it and sent it back as a prize to his ship, the *Vixen*. In the excitement of the battle and amid the blood and bodies on the deck, nobody had thought to haul down the Tripolitan flag. Much of the battle of the gunboats had been fought in the smoke. Out of this cloud now appeared before the *Vixen* a Tripolitan gunboat flying her flag jauntily. The *Vixen* did what was normal; she let loose a broadside. This did not chance to be one of the few instances of poor firing by an American vessel in this war, because the broadside riddled the gunboat's rigging, brought down the enemy flag, and felled the mast and yards, but happily did not injure anyone aboard. That was probably because the boat was lightly manned by the prize crew. She identified herself before risking a second broadside.

Part of the first division of American gunboats, commanded by Lieutenant Richard Somers, did splendid service but did not turn up such spectacular boarding episodes as did Division Number Two. One of Somers' boats, No. 3, commanded by Lieutenant Blake, took little part. She kept to the windward and fired some rounds. Preble thought that had she gone with Lieutenant James Decatur at a time when Somers' own boat was failing to make headway, or with Somers later, several more enemy boats might have been captured. When the expenditure of ammunition came to be checked it was seen that Blake's boat had fired but two 24-pound round shot and six discharges of grape.

Blake was rated by some as the failure of the engagement, though he felt he acted with good judgment. When the *John Adams* came in a short time later, Purser John Darby, who kept a journal, gave an account of the battle as he picked up the information from the fleet:

It is said the Tripolians fought very desperately in the first engagement, and never Did the American officers & men act with more bravery and enterprise than on this occasion every one being anxious to distinguish themselves in the glory of there Countrys cause, with one exception only, which is a Lieutenant Blake who it is said, did not conduct himself in the manner which he ought to have done, and is now publickly called a coward by the officers of the Squadron.

Blake wrote Preble four days after the battle requesting relief from the gunboat assignment rather "than to continue under a Suspicious Eye." He claimed his boat was placed and kept in close action as long as the signals and prospects of helping in the battle justified. He continued his service under Hull on the *Argus*. He had no further prominence.

Somers himself was not able to join with the detachment of enemy craft attacked by Decatur but he used his sweeps and bore down alone on five Tripolitan gunboats at the western end of the line outside the reef. There, single handed, he engaged all five of them at pistol-shot range, battered and shattered them, and drove them back behind the rocks, inflicting heavy casualties. In this fire Somers had the support not only of the two mortar boats, which did effective work throughout the afternoon, but of the fleet.

Preble felt that the fire from the *Constitution* kept the enemy flotilla inside the harbor in check. "Our grape shot," he said, "made great havoc among their men, not only on board their shipping, but on shore. We were several times within two cables length [400 yards] of the rocks, and within three [600 yards] of their batteries, every one of which, in succession, were silenced, so long as we could bring a broadside to bear on them." As soon as the *Constitution* passed a battery it was reanimated. Everywhere the fort and batteries fired when they could not be fired at. Thus when the flagship was wearing or tacking and could not present a broadside it suffered most severely and it was then, Preble said, that he felt most sensibly the need of another frigate. Not until some days later did Preble learn that the enemy navy and the forts and batteries had suffered severe punishment during this battle of the gunboats, at times called the battle of August 3, 1804.

Although continually under the enemy fire, the *Constitution* came through the battle in excellent condition. Only two hits inflicted severe damage. One 24-pound shot went through the center of her mainmast twenty-five feet above the deck and a 32-pounder made a direct hit on a gun on her quarterdeck and shattered it into bits. The rigging and sails were laced by enemy grape and round shot and the main royal yard and sail were shot away. The only casualty was one marine wounded when the quarterdeck gun was hit.

At 4:30 P.M. the wind shifted toward the north and since the remaining enemy gunboats had gone behind the reef, and none had come out to their relief, Preble signaled an end to the action. He gave orders to the ships to tow off the gunboats and prizes and this work was executed handsomely under the covering fire of the *Constitution*.

When he had a chance to survey the results, he knew he had fought a highly successful battle, though his report of it was free from evidences of self-satisfaction.

Reports of enemy casualties vary and could not be precise. Preble's account of the battle was succinct. He entered it on the journal of the *Constitution* on the day after the battle:

We captured 3 Gun Boats two of which carried each a long Brass 24 pounder & two Brass Howitzers and thirty six men with a plenty of muskets pistols pikes sabres &c, the other mounted a long Brass 18 pounder & two Howitzers & 24 men. 44 Tripolines were killed on board of the 3 Boats and 52 made prisoners, 26 of which were wounded, 17 of them very badly 3 of which died after they were brought on board, the Enemy must have suffered very much in Killed & wounded among their shipping and on shore, one of their Boats was sunk in the Harbour several of them had their decks nearly cleared of men by our shot, and several shells burst in the Town, which must have done great execution.

Later it was learned that most of the Tripolitans went into the country soon after the shelling was begun.

Before the battle the Bashaw was confident. According to the information going to the *Philadelphia* prisoners he had expected the customary display of naval force in front of the city and little more. When the Americans came in close, the rooftops, towers and castle walls were crowded with spectators, who looked to see the impertinent Preble soundly chastised. After a broadside from the *Constitution* the roofs were cleared.

One of the wiser, observant Tripolitans was quoted: "The English, French and Spanish consuls have told us that they [the Americans] were a young nation, and got their independence by means of France; that they had a small navy and their officers were inexperienced, and that they were merely a nation of merchants, and, that, by taking their ships and men, we should get great ransoms. Instead of this, their Preble pays us a coin of shot, shells and hard blows; and sent a Decatur, in a dark night, with a band of Christian dogs fierce and cruel as the tiger, who killed our brothers and burnt our ships before our eyes."

After the rest of the fleet had withdrawn, the *Constitution* took the two bomb ketches into tow, and at 4:45 P.M. Preble hauled off, the flagship being the last ship out of range from the shore. His commendation went to Lieutenant Charles Gordon and the other officers and the crew of the *Constitution* for the able handling of that ship. Preble attributed the slightness of the damage she suffered while under such heavy fire to two factors. One was that the flagship kept close in during the battle and the forts and land batteries overshot her. The other was that her scattering of grape into the city's defenses, which annoyed, dispirited and sent into hiding those operating the harbor artillery, gave her the security of fire superiority. But he could not avoid the comment, "They are, however, wretched gunners."

That was one of the lessons of the battle: that the Tripolitans had never mastered artillery firing, an exacting art calling for a great deal of study and practice, and one in which the fresh and spirited American navy of that period excelled. Perhaps the scarcity of powder along the Barbary Coast restricted test-firing of the guns, or possibly the ages-old experience of the Saracens and Turks with steel made it still the preferred weapon. They liked their lances and horses, and if the land could have yielded them a living, could have done better on it than taking to piracy in an era of improved gunnery.

Another lesson of the battle of August 3 was that it ended indisputably the legend of the invincibility of Barbary boarders. In no instance did the Tripoli corsairs attempt to board an American craft. The story was turned around the other way. Thereafter the Americans were the ones dreaded as boarders. Never again in the Tripolitan War did an armed vessel of Tripoli get close enough to the Americans to allow them to board.

American vessels suffered mainly in their rigging. The fleet took a position off the city and made repairs. When a check was taken it was found that the American casualties aggregated two killed and thirteen wounded. That was not much of a price for such an impressive victory.

CHAPTER EIGHTEEN

Preble Bombards Tripoli

P REBLE had nothing but praise for his followers, but he was not satisfied with the results of the battle of August 3, 1804, which he looked on as indecisive. He wanted to settle the issue with the Bashaw with a victory so clear and resounding that the usurper would forget tributes, indemnities, and ransoms and sue humbly for peace and relief on any terms.

While dressing the wounds of his ships, all of which yielded to the dexterous carpenters, mechanics, and sailmakers among his crews, he turned three prizes into serviceable American gunboats by altering them from lateen-rigged vessels to sloops. They could be used to augment the Neapolitan craft in the second attack he was planning. The fleet's position was only six miles off Tripoli, where a close watch could be maintained of the harbor. When the prize boats were ready for service Preble appointed to their command Lieutenants Jonathan Thorn of the *Enterprise,* William M. Crane of the *Vixen* and James R. Caldwell of the *Siren.* Thorn and Caldwell had been with Decatur on the night they captured and burned the *Philadelphia,* Thorn being among the first boarders. Thorn's boat was called No. 7, Crane's No. 8 and Caldwell's No. 9.

On the morning of the 5th, while most of the fleet was at anchor, they noticed a sail making to the westward, and the trim new *Argus* gave chase. She overhauled the vessel, a small French privateer which had gone into Tripoli a few days before merely to get water, and brought her to the *Constitution.* Preble there prevailed on her master, using coin that would amply cover his expenses, to turn back to Tripoli and deliver to the Bashaw fourteen severely wounded Tripolitan prisoners captured on their gunboats. He did this primarily as an act of humanity so the men might be cared for by their families and friends, but also in the hope it might be reflected in gentler treatment of the American captives. Their wounds had been dressed carefully by American surgeons. With them he sent a letter to the Bashaw's Prime Minister leaving open the question of whether the Bashaw might want to reciprocate "this generous mode of conducting the war" and send out an equal number of Americans. Preble in the report he wrote that day expressed doubt it would happen, and it did not.

The French privateer came out two days later carrying a letter to Preble from the French consul, who said the Bashaw was disposed to accept more reasonable terms. He invited Preble to send a boat to the rocks bearing a flag of truce. But Preble had an idea if the Bashaw wanted to sue he should be the one to put up a flag—a white one over his castle—and he paid no attention to the French consul's suggestion. Preble could look across and see that an enemy schooner and a brig in the harbor were dismasted. He learned from the Frenchman that the vessels had been so damaged in the battle that their masts had to be taken down. The Americans heard, apparently from some of the French sailors, that the fourteen prisoners returned by Preble told the Bashaw that "the Americans in battle were fiercer than lions," but gentle in the treatment of their prisoners.

Preble, on August 7, prepared to renew the assault and at 9:00 A.M. signaled the vessels to go into action. The two bomb ketches were directed to take a position in a small bay west of the city, where they would be secure from all but a few of the harbor batteries, and to toss shells into the town. The gunboats were to stand toward the west and in particular were to silence a battery of seven guns which guarded the approach to the city on the west. It is not clear which battery Preble had in mind but it was probably the French castle, a strong fort west of the Bashaw's castle, not far from Fort Vixen. Fort Vixen was so named because this battery had fired on the *Vixen* when she was patrolling close in before Preble brought up his main squadron. Though the *Vixen* was not damaged, the occasion seemed to the Tripolitans worth commemorating. Americans at times referred to the French castle as Battery Français.

Preble directed his brigs and schooners to give fire support to the gunboats and chase enemy vessels which might venture out of the harbor. Because of the lightness of the east breeze and a strong current which was running, he felt obliged to keep the *Constitution* anchored farther out, recognizing that should a chance shot bring down her mast she probably could not be got off, unless the wind blowing onshore should fortuitously shift. He could not hazard his only frigate unnecessarily. However, at 1:30 P.M., under a north-northeast breeze, he did come in closer, but not within range to engage the harbor forts.

By 2:30 P.M. the bomb ketches and gunboats were in position, the gunboats in two divisions, commanded by Somers and Decatur, and the bomb ketches again under Dent and Robinson. With a blast that might have seemed to flatten the waters and reverberated through the city and across the desert hills, the bombardment was begun.

Somers, heading the first division, was in gunboat No. 1. As she went into action he was leaning against the flagstaff, observing. He saw a roundshot coming his way and was able to dodge it, showing remarkable agility, because the firing was now at close range. The shot snapped off the flagstaff. Curious, Somers went back and stood beside the stump. He must have thanked his lucky stars, because had he not ducked the big cannon ball would have hit him directly in the chin.

The American fire was accurate and destructive. It fell on the shipping which undertook to reply from the harbor, on the walled castle where the Bashaw was sent hurrying to his bombproof cellar chamber, and over the city, where the exploding shells awoke a terror such as had not been experienced in the city since the days of Dragut. In the two hours during which the bombardment was sustained, six of the seven guns in the battery were silenced, their emplacements were demolished, and the walls were battered down. One gun kept on firing, though the fort was in what Preble termed "point blank shot"—a phrase common in warfare then, meaning within a range where the guns could be pointed directly and not inclined upward to fire in a trajectory. The term blank meant the white bulls-eye of a target. To fire point blank was to aim at the blank directly and not above it. Thus the gunboats were close in and Preble observed that their fire was returned by the enemy warmly.

The Tripolitan gun crews scored one effective hit, which brought tragedy to an American crew but gave opportunity for a demonstration of American steadfastness in this type of close naval fighting. After the fleet and forts had been blazing away at each other for an hour, a red-hot shot from an enemy battery made a direct hit on gunboat No. 9, carrying twenty-six officers and men and commanded by Lieutenant James R. Caldwell. The shot passed through her magazine, blowing her up and sinking her with startling dispatch. Caldwell and Midshipman John S. Dorsey, both described by Preble as "excellent officers" and both admired in the fleet for their parts in the burning of the *Philadelphia,* and eight enlisted men were killed instantly. The enlisted personnel lost were the boatswain's mate, a sergeant of the Marine Corps, a quarter gunner and five seamen. Six others were wounded, two mortally.

In the few seconds while a part of gunboat No. 9 remained afloat, there was time for an act of heroism. The boat was in Decatur's division and Decatur was near when she exploded. He saw, and later reported to

Preble, that Midshipman Robert T. Spence, son of Decatur's old friend, Purser Spence of the *Philadelphia,* was supervising the charging of the forward gun when the hot shot struck. In spite of the explosion, two of the gun crew, who luckily had not been killed in the blast, finished loading the gun; then, while the ship was sinking and only the prow remained above water, they fired their parting shot, yelled defiantly, and jumped into the water. The smoking muzzle was the last thing seen above the waves. Another fact not known to Decatur when he reported this incident to Preble was that young Spence did not know how to swim. But he grasped an oar and managed to keep himself up until rescued. The others swam to the closest boat and fought on through the remainder of the engagement. Twelve of No. 9's crew were saved.

Stewart, who was only 200 yards away with the *Siren* when Caldwell's gunboat was hit, immediately sent boats to rescue the survivors. The explosion caused a momentary cessation of the fire from the other gunboats, but Stewart noticed that when the firing was resumed, "it was redoubled on the enemy, so that it seemed to say for four hours we revenge our brave companions."

When Decatur learned the full story, he recommended to the Commodore that Spence be promoted. Preble made him an acting lieutenant on the spot. The captain of this gun, working under Spence, was a gunner's mate of the *Siren,* Edmund P. Kennedy, whom Preble admirously made an acting midshipman. Later Secretary Smith ratified the appointment. Kennedy went on to higher rank in the Navy, and eventually to fleet command, being one of the very few in the early Navy who were promoted through every grade in the service, from common tar to commodore.

Spence, writing to his mother, said he had just been aft before the shot struck but had returned forward and was sighting his gun. He was blown into the air but alighted by his gun, on the only part of the boat remaining. One man was by his side. "Around me lay arms, legs, & trunks of Bodies, in the most mutilated state." Though he was a little bewildered by the enemy shot and concerned by the prospect that he could not swim, he remembered not to quit while there was a remnant of his ship still floating. He fired the gun and loaded it again. Then they all went down together.

As he landed on the boat he saw Caldwell's body come down—"without arms, or legs; his face so mutilated that I could not discriminate a feature—by his dress only, I recognized him."

While the firing continued Preble noticed that the enemy gunboats kept in motion under the land batteries and he speculated that they might be intending to come out and engage the American gunboats at close hand. But Preble kept three of his ships, the *Constitution*, the *Nautilus*, and the *Enterprise*, to the windward of the harbor entrance so he could cut them off if they ventured out, while the *Siren* and the *Vixen* were in close support of the American gunboats. Obviously the Tripolitans had their stomachs full of boarding. The Tripolitan navy failed to distinguish itself in this second American attack on the harbor but fired a few shots and, as Preble stated it, thought it prudent "to retire to their snug retreat behind the rocks." He believed the town must have suffered severely and that the seven-gun battery lost many men.

At 5:30 the northeast wind freshened and Preble signaled for the bomb ketches to retire and their mother vessels to take them out. At 6:30 P.M. all the boats were in tow and the fleet stood off the harbor.

In the two hours of bombardment Preble had thrown forty-eight shells and about five hundred 24-pound shot into the town and batteries. The Americans had suffered damage. Gunboat No. 9 was lost; Nos. 4 and 8 had 24-pound shots through their hulls; the lateen yard of No. 6 was shot away; sails and rigging were cut up on all of them. The shot that hulled No. 8 killed two of her seamen. The total casualties were fourteen killed or mortally wounded and six wounded.

Charles Stewart, writing to the United States in a letter published by the *National Intelligencer* December 4, 1804, gave the American public the first details of the two battles of the gunboats. He described the prizes taken as excellent craft. Two mounted brass 26-pounders and the other a brass 16-pounder. The Tripolitans in the first engagement had loaded their guns with forty pounds of musket balls in lieu of grape and had met the Americans at twenty yards with these discharges which ought to have been devastating but were in fact singularly ineffective. In the second battle the enemy gunboats were not much of a factor, the contest being between the American fleet and the forts.

Stewart's description of the captured Tripolitan guns varied slightly from Preble's, who said two of the boats mounted 24-pounders and the other an 18-pounder.

Bainbridge seemed to play down the effectiveness of Preble's bombardment. Of the forty-eight shells thrown by the two bomb ketches into the town, he claimed that only one exploded. Another version was that "few" exploded. Some of these shells, procured in Naples, appeared to be what in wars of the next century were termed "duds." But how well Bainbridge could observe their effectiveness is a matter of doubt, and there is ground for wonder if his confinement and chagrin over loss of his frigate had not already begun to stir an introspection extending to jealousy which was noticed, in one quarter at least, in later years. In a subsequent bombardment he discerned that the shells fell short. Preble did not appear to be doing the best sort of a job of bombarding, in Bainbridge's eyes.

A suggested explanation of the bad shells was that they had been made originally for use by the Neapolitans against the French and that French agents or sympathizers had sabotaged them. When Preble examined them later he found lead stuffed into some of the fuseholes. The curious aspect is why someone had not inspected the ammunition when it was obtained, or possibly fired a trial round or two. Preble was impatient to get the fleet off to Tripoli and could not be expected to handle every detail personally, but the whole story of the "duds" seems to have doubtful aspects, and there probably were not so many as Bainbridge was led to believe. The bomb ketches would not have kept on firing indefinitely shells they could not see explode.

While the battle was at its height a strange sail appeared on the western horizon. Preble dispatched the swift *Argus* to investigate and she signaled that the sail was friendly. The two ships beat slowly against the northeast wind and not until 8:00 P.M. did the stranger anchor alongside the *Constitution*. She was the *John Adams*, out of Hampton Roads on June 26, long delayed by adverse weather. She was commanded by Master Commandant Isaac Chauncey, returning to the Mediterranean, where he had distinguished himself as much as one could during the Morris command and shown true heroism in putting out the fire on the *New York*. He was a product of the merchant marine service of John Jacob Astor and had entered the navy under Truxtun.

The *John Adams* brought much news, part of it being that it was the forerunner of a powerful squadron including the *President,* the *Congress,* the *Constellation,* and the *Essex,* which was sailing from the United States. There was welcome news about promotions, and letters from home fully as pleasant. But the doleful intelligence was that the fleet would be commanded by Captain Samuel Barron, who ranked Preble, and who would supersede him in command of the American forces in the Mediterranean. The unhappy notice apparently did not at once reach the men in the fleet—men who had hated Preble's stern discipline and had come to love him because nobody had ever cowed him or his fleet—and it did not immediately influence the fighting off Tripoli. The effect of the change was to be felt at a later season.

The melancholy fact of immediate intrusion was that the *John Adams,* the much-longed-for extra frigate which might allow Preble to batter Tripoli into quick submission, had come all the way from the United States to the firing line and was not then ready to give as much help as a Neapolitan gunboat. She had left her gun carriages on the *Congress* and the *Constellation* a day or two before she sailed, much as four years later the *Chesapeake* put to sea in troublesome times to encounter the British *Leopard* without being prepared to fight anything better than an Indian canoe.

The gun carriages had been taken out of the *John Adams* in order to allow more room for provisions, the theory apparently being that a navy as well as an army "fights on its belly." But it was even then a more realistic principle that guns and ammunition should have precedence over bread and beef, because a sailor cannot eat without surviving or survive without fighting, or fight without guns.

That night Preble wrote: "Had the *John Adams* brought out her gun carriages, I should not have waited a moment, and can have no doubt but the next attack would make the arrival of more ships unnecessary for the termination of the Tripoline war." He told Chauncey to keep the frigate at hand because her small boats would be useful! Nearly half the crews of the *Constitution* and the brigs and schooners had been assigned to man the gunboats and bomb ketches. The squadron was grievously short of sailors and could find duty for the fresh seamen of the *John Adams*.

Because the other ships of the new fleet were to sail from the United States five days after the *John Adams*, Preble expected Barron fairly promptly after the coming of Chauncey. He did not know the leisurely ways of some of his fellow captains. When the new Commodore failed to appear he determined not to sacrifice the gains already made against Tripoli but to press his campaign with vigor. Had the promised frigate power been on hand, "the fate of Tripoli must be decided in a few hours," but without it he would have to fall back on his brigs, schooners, gunboats, and ketches.

Good officer as he was, he reprovisioned the gunboats with ammunition and rations so they would be ready the moment Barron took command. His feelings were recorded in the line he included when he was detailing his activities of August 9: "I cannot but regret that our naval establishment is so limited as to deprive me of the means and glory of completely subduing the haughty tyrant of Tripoli, while in the chief command; it will, however, afford me satisfaction to give my successor all the assistance in my power."

That afternoon he made personal reconnaissance of the harbor on board the *Argus*, every timber of which gave him joy as he stood on her deck. They ventured in close and one of the enemy's heaviest shots made a direct hit, hulling her and all but sinking her, because the shot, which hit three feet from the water line, ripped the copper from her bottom and cut halfway through the planking. That night the squadron kept under sail but on the 10th anchored six miles northeast of Tripoli.

At 10:00 A.M. a white flag was seen on the flagstaff of the French consulate. Preble sent in a boat which brought back a letter with the uninteresting news that the Bashaw would settle for $500 a head for the prisoners with no tribute. That would aggregate about $150,000, which was $350,000 less than the figure the Bashaw had been talking about before the battle of the gunboats on August 3, but it was more than double Preble's offer of $60,000 plus a $10,000 consular gift. Preble begrudged any payment at all, being now joined in combat. But he was willing to make concessions on account of the prisoners. Chauncey had told him the expectation in Washington in sending out so strong a fleet as four frigates was that the prisoners could be had without ransom. That accorded with Preble's own thinking.

The agent who went in under the white flag was not his, in a sense, but Secretary Madison's. At Syracuse, Preble had picked up the old negotiator O'Brien, but he made it clear that the ex-Consul had no authority to deal on his own account with the Bashaw, that prerogative having been delegated by Lear, the Consul General, to the Commodore. O'Brien would be useful because of his knowledge of the Barbary language. Preble wrote this in a letter to Cathcart, who had warned him that the "iniquitous" O'Brien wanted to beg or purchase a soft peace. Said Preble: "I value the national character of my Country too highly, to consent to a peace which the most powerful Nation of Europe would blush to make."

Nevertheless, O'Brien carried a letter from Preble to the French chargé saying he would give the Bashaw $80,000 ransom for the prisoners plus a $10,000 consular present on the arrival of a consul from the United States. The terms would have to be accepted by 10 o'clock the next morning and the Bashaw could signify by flying a white flag over the castle. No flag was shown.

Water was running low, and on August 16 Preble sent the *Enterprise* to Malta with orders to his agent there to hire transports and immediately send water, food, and supplies. Some of the vessels had been in front of what he termed "this dismal coast" for more than five months without putting into a friendly port, and these ships and the gunboats had been drawing on the *Constitution's* water supplies, which were growing low.

By August 18, with no Barron yet in sight and the season suitable for fleet operations against Tripoli drawing toward its close, he was done with waiting and ready for action. He sent Decatur and Chauncey in small boats to reconnoiter the harbor again and see where the enemy vessels were disposed during the night. They found the fleet anchored in a formation known as line abreast, with their heads to the east, and extended between the Bashaw's castle and the mole. Thus they were defending closely the inner harbor and they could not be reached by the gunboats except by entering the harbor through the channels between the rocks. They could, of course, be shelled across the mole from outside the harbor. But the sea rose and the attack had to be postponed until August 24, at which time, though the *John Adams* had been with the fleet seventeen days, there still was no sight of the new Commodore.

Meantime a transport brought water and livestock; and the ketch *Intrepid* returned from Syracuse with another cargo of water, livestock, and vegetables—all of which lifted the spirits of the crews more than would have a mail ship from America. Scurvy was appearing and the first need was antiscorbutics. The *Enterprise* returned and reported she had seen no trace of Barron and the missing frigates.

Favored by a light northeast breeze, Preble took the squadron toward Tripoli in the early evening and anchored at 8:00 P.M. two and a half miles from the batteries. Bainbridge had recommended to him some time before that he bombard the city at night to frighten and destroy the morale of the populace. Persuaded either by that suggestion or by other considerations, among them a natural desire to protect his fleet by operating at night, he sent in the bomb ketches and gunboats at midnight, towed to their positions by their customary mother ships.

Whatever the city of Tripoli may have felt about earlier battles or earlier American fleets, that night it had occasion to wonder whether piracy pays, and whether some of the European consuls knew what they were talking about when they said of the United States what Napoleon said of England, that it was merely a nation of shopkeepers. From 2:00 A.M. on the 25th until daybreak the gunboats and mortar boats threw shells and solid shot into the town. Preble could not tell the effect in the darkness and reported it as uncertain.

Always it was difficult to know without close inspection the results of a bombardment because the city in that day was marred by heaps of rubble left over from the devastation of earlier wars and invasions. Much of the building was done with the loose stone scattered about and often a dwelling was mounted on heaps of rubbish and ruins. One would have to be closely acquainted with the buildings and streets to know whether a wall had been knocked down by Preble, the Knights of Malta, or one of the early human tides that swept across the desert sands.

But the target was fixed and there was later evidence that the damage was severe. This was the bombardment regarding which Bainbridge claimed the shot fell short. But it is curious how he could have entertained that view, because a 36-pound shot came crashing through his prison wall into the room where he was in bed, "sleeping," according to the *Naval Chronicle* account—though that is difficult to believe while the city was under such heavy bombardment. The big cannon ball flew across the room and struck the wall opposite its point of entry, then, its force near spent, rebounded and hit Bainbridge's bed, carried off the bedclothes, but missed his body. The debris from the shattered wall— stones that had probably been quarried by Carthaginian slaves and mortar made by Dragut when he fortified the port—was scattered around the room, across the bed, and over Bainbridge, who was found bruised and half-buried when his officers came running to his rescue. He was lame in the right ankle for months.

Tripoli was virtually emptied of people during the bombardment. The civilian population had learned to take to the country at the sound of the guns. One stalwart resident who did not stir from his post was Danish Consul Nissen. The prisoners admired him and testified to his hardihood. The American Congress later passed a resolution stating: "His house was much exposed in the attack Commodore Preble made on the town of Tripoli; but such was his zeal for the accommodation of the American prisoners, and his anxiety to be near them, that he refused to seek a place of security, although urged to do so; and by remaining at home greatly endangered his life."

Congress for one did not believe Preble's shot was falling short or that his shells were dead.

The shelling of August 25 was mere child's play compared to what Preble had in store for the city on the pleasant night of August 28-29. At 3 P.M. the fleet stood in for Tripoli and the *Constitution* anchored two miles north of Fort English, a short distance east of the town. The flagship was about two and a half miles from the Bashaw's castle. The smaller ships, going closer, remained in continuous motion during daylight hours, and at 8:00 P.M. preparations were complete. Since some officers and a great many seamen had been assigned from the *Constitution* to man the gunboats, Chauncey, some of his officers, and seventy seamen of the *John Adams* volunteered to serve on the flagship and were transferred to her.

The two bomb ketches had to be left behind; on one the bed for the mortar had collapsed, and the other had grown leaky under the strain of incessant firing. They were anchored in what might be termed the hospital department seven miles out in the Mediterranean, along with the transports which had brought food and water, the useless *John Adams,* and the *Scourge,* a covering ship. But Dent, the *Scourge* commander, boarded the *Constitution* and took command of the gun deck, bringing with him Lieutenant Izard of the *Scourge.* This expressive officer, who had been elevated from midshipman in April by Preble's appointment—a temporary rank until confirmed by Washington—is entitled to the sympathy of anyone reading about the Tripolitan War. He had written much, letter after letter to the United States, but finally, in his letter to his home a year and a half after the attack here being discussed—a letter dated January 9, 1806—he told his mother that since he had left America, years before, he had "not been blessed with one word from a human being in it." Recalling how Consul Pulis hoarded the mail, one might wonder how many of Izard's letters were scattered about the Mediterranean. Mail was a most difficult problem for the fleet. Of course, Izard's family or friends may not have written, though this would seem unlikely. But he was blithe and uncomplaining, a young man any captain would be proud to have on his ship. Later in the war he would sail a harbor gunboat, of a cut better than the Neapolitan barges but still a gunboat, from the United States to the Mediterranean and then again across the Atlantic to his beloved Charleston.

The gunboats again were arranged in two divisions with Decatur and Somers in command. Decatur had jumped ahead of Somers when intelligence of his promotion had come with the *John Adams* and now had over-all command of the front-line action. Lieutenant Charles Gordon of the *Constitution* was assigned to take the command of No. 2 gunboat which Lieutenant James Decatur had held when he was killed. Lieutenant James Lawrence was assigned to command No. 5 in place of the wounded Trippe. No. 3, which had been Blake's, was assigned to Sailing Master Samuel B. Brooks of the *Argus*. Two gunboats were added—serviceable prizes, under Lieutenants Wadsworth and Thorn.

Preble sent the two detachments forward at 1:30 A.M., August 29, to range themselves just outside the rocks where they would command the harbor entrance, and within grapeshot range of the Bashaw's castle. Though most of the supporting ships were small, the squadron was formidable, consisting of the *Constitution, Siren, Argus, Vixen, Nautilus,* and *Enterprise,* all of which put out their small boats with detachments of sailors who were to assist in boarding should the hostile gunboats and galleys venture from the harbor. Preble kept the brigs and schooners under weigh for the same service.

At 3:00 A.M. the bombardment was opened. A comment runs through the dispatches that Barbary Coast officialdom was accustomed to transacting business at night. Preble was falling into line nicely with their habits. "War is my business," the Bashaw had said, and he was now to be given some night office work. Preble's fire fell on the Bashaw's castle, the forts, batteries, the town, and the navy the boastful Murad Reis kept timidly behind the rocks in fear that the dreaded American seamen and marines might get near enough their decks to board. The Tripolitans returned the fire warmly from the shore but Preble found it was not well directed. The spectacle of the bombardment, with bursting shells and flashing cannon, made an awesome sight over the harbor and countryside. Still, Preble had to be content with nothing more than a bombardment. Having a naval force of little better than a thousand effectives even after the arrival of the *John Adams,* he did not possess the manpower to undertake landing operations at a time when it was fairly evident a relatively small body of troops under enterprising leadership could have captured the town.

Preble at daybreak concluded the gunboats had about exhausted their ammunition, so he stood in for the harbor with the *Constitution,* sailing directly into a heavy Tripolitan fire from Fort English, the Bashaw's castle, and the mole battery. This splendid frigate revealed to the city's defenders her full power, by boldly challenging the forts and throwing a destructive fire of round shot and grape into the enemy cruisers sheltered in the harbor. She sank one and disabled two others and caused them to run aground to avoid sinking.

The daring Preble took his big ship to within a musket shot of the mole battery and another fort, difficult to identify, which he called the "crown battery," being apparently close to the French castle on the waterfront west of the Bashaw's castle. Here, audaciously near to the city and its defenses, Preble brought up the *Constitution* and hurled three hundred round shot plus untold quantities of grape and canister into Tripoli, the Bashaw's castle, and the waterfront forts. The castle and the two near batteries were silenced, either by having their guns dismounted or from dread. The Barbary gunners did not like to keep their posts when under fire. Silent forts did not draw so many rounds of grape. Thus the flagship had discerned that her best protection was an energetic offensive. Her gunners were among the best and they worked at top speed.

In these early morning hours the ships and gunboats sank a large Tunisian galiot inside the mole, while a Spanish vessel which had come into the harbor to bring an ambassador from the Grand Seignior was battered up considerably. By 6:15 A.M. the gunboats, out of ammunition, were taken in tow behind the covering fire of the *Constitution* and the fleet hauled off. Preble found that the gunboats had fired upward of three hundred round shot plus canister and grape, he felt with good effect.

The Commodore was proud of the conduct of the fleet in what he judged to be an effective if not devastating bombardment of the hostile city. He commended Decatur and Somers for their handling of the

gunboat divisions, and their officers and men for their staunch performance. In his opinion the guns of the brigs and schooners were too
light to have done much execution but the ships were well handled and
kept in the action, blazing away with what they had. They suffered
damage to sails and rigging.

The crew of the *Constitution,* which was in hazardously close action
near the mole for three-quarters of an hour, received his praise, as did
Chauncey of the *John Adams* for his help on the quarterdeck of the
flagship during the battle. The ship was damaged, but mainly above the
hull, where stays, shrouds, trusses, chains, and lifts were shot away while
the sails showed a lot of cannon-ball holes and riddling by grape. Her
hull also had sprinklings of grape. One of the small boats of the *John
Adams* which was being towed by the *Nautilus* was hit by a double-
headed shot fired from one of the batteries. Three of the eight men
aboard were killed and one was severely wounded. Master's Mate John
O. Creighton, who commanded the boat, and four others were picked
up from the water.

The Spanish vessel at the mole which had received a drubbing was
able to make repairs and on September 2 she came out of the harbor
carrying the Grand Seignior's ambassador. The custom of the Porte was
to send an ambassador to the satraps every five years to reappoint them,
or confirm them in their rule. Largely a formality, it nevertheless gave
notice that the regents of the North African states ruled at the pleasure of
the Grand Seignior. This ambassador was now on his rounds, and did
not seem to have suffered from the American bombardment. The Spanish captain gave Preble his first information about the effectiveness of his
fire. He said the cannonade had caused great havoc and destruction both
in the city and to the shipping anchored in the harbor. He reported a
"vast number" of people killed.

If the Bashaw did not already have a stomach full of Preble, he was
now about to experience what was perhaps the most devastating
bombardment of all, this in full daylight, when the Commodore might
more readily observe the effect of his fire. Murad Reis brought on the
engagement on the afternoon of September 3 by sending his galleys
and gunboats to the east of the inner harbor about two miles, in the
region of Fort English and a new battery the Tripolitans had erected a
day or so before, just west of Fort English. The Tripolitan admiral was
risking his fleet at a distance from the Bashaw's castle and the protective
mole, though it was still behind the rocks and shoals where the *Philadelphia* had grounded. He had worked his ships eastward against the
wind, which Preble judged a judicious move for the enemy to make,

because should the Americans enter the harbor the Tripolitan craft would be in their rear and would possess the weather gauge and consequently the advantage in maneuvering.

Preble decided to attack the enemy galleys and gunboats with his own gunboats and at the same time bombard the town with the bomb ketches. At 3:30 P.M. his boats were in position. The mortar boats anchored off the mole and began to toss shells into Tripoli while at the same time the two divisions of gunboats, under Decatur and Somers, attacked the warships and Fort English and the new battery which protected them. Again the firing was at a range Preble termed "point blank shot."

Fort English and the new battery answered with spirit, but as quickly as Somers and Decatur got their gunboats within musket shot of the enemy galleys and gunboats, these gave way and scurried to the shore to get the cover of whatever rocks they could find and also the musket fire from Fort English. When the American gunboats advanced, behind them sailed the brigs and schooners *Siren, Argus, Vixen, Nautilus,* and *Enterprise.* They had to respect the reefs and rocks even more than the hostile shot but they moved close enough to augment the fire of the gunboats. They concentrated their guns against Fort English and battered it well near to pieces. One of the American gunboat divisions fired after the fleeing ships and disabled a number of them, though Preble received no count of how many.

While this fight was in progress the bomb ketches performed what the Commodore regarded splendid work, throwing their shells briskly and sustaining a heavy cannonade from the shore. This could not have been very effective else they would have been destroyed, for they were alone and exposed near the shore. When they opened they were out of danger from the enemy fleet, which was well to the east, but as the firing continued, Preble became apprehensive that they might be sunk, so he ran the *Constitution* between them to amuse the Tripolitans and draw the shore fire, and incidentally to add to the iron poundage that was being hurled into the city. The intrepid Commodore sailed and maneuvered the frigate under the muzzles of seventy enemy guns and passed out much more than he received. The *Constitution* fired eleven broadsides into the Bashaw's castle, which should have given the potentate notice that the United States was something besides a nation of shopkeepers. Her broadside silenced one shore battery and damaged severely the Castle, the town, and other batteries.

At 4:30 P.M. the wind freshened and inclined rapidly from out of the north, and an onshore wind always increased the hazards for the attacking squadron. Preble signaled a retirement. After the gunboats had been towed away by the brigs and schooners Preble retired with the *Constitution*, licking a number of wounds, but again mainly above the hull. Most of the other ships suffered damage to rigging and sails. Lieutenant Robinson's bomb ketch was rendered almost worthless, and though near sinking, was towed out with her mortar bed ruined and every shroud shot away. The beautiful *Argus* took a 32-pound shot in her forward hull, her second bad wound of the campaign.

That night the squadron anchored nine miles offshore, and at daybreak Preble signaled the fleet to prepare for action. Carpenters were at once busy making repairs, and fresh ammunition was passed out to the gunboats and the remaining mortar ketch. He was determined that as long as he had command the Bashaw would have no rest until he displayed a white flag over his castle.

CHAPTER NINETEEN

Somers and the *Intrepid*

SPIRITED as his attacks and bombardments had been, Preble was not convinced that they had brought Tripoli much nearer to capitulation and a request for peace on the terms of the Americans. He sought some quick measure by which he could terrify the Bashaw, cripple his remaining warships, and at the same time dismantle or destroy one or more of his main harbor forts.

The Commodore had been turning over in his mind the use of a fire ship—an "infernal," he termed it—against the enemy navy and castle, a recourse he had suggested first when Decatur went in to burn the *Philadelphia*. The galleys were customarily beached or anchored near the Castle, and the two targets might be aimed at with one "infernal." When he discussed it, Somers was immediately interested, and volunteered to take the fireboat into the harbor. Preble promptly appointed him commander of the enterprise.

For several days, in what time he could spare between the battles of the gunboats, Somers had been preparing the *Intrepid*, a ketch now celebrated in the Mediterranean and the United States alike as the boat which had taken Decatur's band to the destruction of the *Philadelphia*. The *Intrepid* would be the "infernal." When Lieutenant Henry Wadsworth volunteered to accompany Somers, Preble assigned him. No duty could have more perilous and no volunteering more risky.

The two supervised the transport to the *Intrepid* of 100 barrels of gunpowder and 150 charged shells which were disposed through the ketch in what Preble considered a prudent manner. Fuses calculated to burn fifteen minutes were laid to the powder, which would give the crew ample time to get clear of the ship. This was the arrangement as Preble explained it. The main cache for the powder was a magazine in the forward part of the hold below the mainmast, which was boarded over as a protection against an accidental ignition of the charge. In the after part of the hold another room was filled with a quantity of powder

323

and the two were connected by a tube or trench containing gunpowder.

A precaution was taken against the eventuality that the enemy might board the craft after the Americans had lit the fifteen-minute fuse, and manage to sever or extinguish it. A room was filled with shavings and splinters, possibly to help in igniting the blast, but more especially to cause boarders who saw the splinters burning to believe that the charge would explode at any instant and to beat a hasty retreat. Over the main charge of powder in the forward part of the hold were placed the shells —one hundred 9-inch and fifty 13-inch—and pig iron ballast, shot, and anything that would answer the purpose of a deadly missile.

Somers and Wadsworth looked over the rowing boats and selected the two judged fastest in the entire fleet, in which to make their getaway when they put the match to the fuse. Somers' boat would be manned by four seamen from the *Nautilus* and Wadsworth's by six from the *Constitution*. This made a dozen on the *Intrepid*, two officers and ten men. All of the seamen were volunteers.

Just before the *Intrepid* weighed anchor (she was often referred to as the *Infernal* after the event), Lieutenant Joseph Israel slipped on board, by stealth, as most had the story, and told Somers he had to go. Another version was that he boarded the ship to deliver a final message from Preble. Poor, gallant, foolhardy young Israel! (When Preble had recommended him and Ridgely to be lieutenants in April, he had said "they are certainly two of the smartest Officers of their rank in the service.") At first rejected, he won Somers by his ardent pleas, and seemingly, in some manner, either he or Somers gained the Commodore's assent. There is no certainty on this point but it is suggested by the Commodore's treatment of him in the reports as a regular member of the *Intrepid* detail. Israel brought the number on board to thirteen.

With all in good order aboard the craft, the crew calm, and with Preble and the fleet hopeful, the *Intrepid,* at 8:00 P.M., September 4, 1804, got under sail, bound for the inner harbor of Tripoli.

Somers, like most of the young officers of Preble's fleet, was gentle in deportment but terrible and unrelenting when aroused by a fight. He had had an experience similar to Macdonough's in Sicily, where it seemed as easy to find a battle with banditti as with pirates on the opposite Mediterranean shore. He was strolling in the twilight with two officers near Syracuse when they were set upon by five Sicilian soldiers with drawn swords who were anxious to share in the pay the American officers received, scant as it was for those who earned it at no slight risk of neck and reputation. The unhappy aspect of this incident was that the unsuspecting Americans were unarmed save for a single dirk, which one of Somers' companions possessed. He used it to good effect and quickly dispatched one marauder.

Somers, unarmed, had to procure his own weapon, which he did by taking a sword away from his assailant, at the cost of a bad hand wound inflicted on him when he parried the steel with his flesh. Still, the hand was good enough to allow him to thrust the sword through his assailant's body. Thereupon the other three rogues fled and were never apprehended.

Somers was a native of southern New Jersey, where he grew up with good salt water close at hand. He naturally took to the sea as a boy, then served in the Navy under one of the best of the captains, Barry, and one of the most irresponsible, Captain Daniel McNeill, with whom he had come to the Mediterranean on the *Boston*.

James Fenimore Cooper, who entered the Navy as a midshipman in 1808 after previous merchant marine service, knew personally many of the officers of the Barbary Wars period. Although not acquainted with Somers, he learned much about him, and described him as "a warm-hearted friend, amiable and mild in his ordinary associations, a trained seaman, and a good officer," and in the naval service a "conspicuous and favourite" member. He found much in the characters of Somers and Decatur which was unlike, though he did not specify what, but: "In a chivalrous love of enterprise, a perfect disregard of danger, and in a devotion to the honour of the flag, however, they had but one heart."

Somers was senior to Decatur by one day when they were lieutenants and they had become Preble's principal combat leaders, and rarely if ever did the Navy have two more dauntless officers on the front line.

Stephen Decatur, Charles Stewart, and Richard Somers were the closest of friends, having begun their service as midshipmen together on the United States under Barry. Because the relationship was something of a three-musketeers type, it was perhaps natural that others would seek to disrupt it, and such an occasion developed while the fleet was in the Mediterranean prior to the coming of Preble. Decatur, speaking loosely and indifferently, and apparently without anger or the vaguest thought of malice, used the word "fool" in relation to Somers. The remark had some reference to Somers' garments and could in no manner relate to his character, and was spoken in good spirit.

So high was the feeling—clearly an exaggerated feeling—among young officers over points of honor that the use of the word was analyzed and discussed and six companion officers decided they would not imbibe wine with Somers any longer on the ground that he had not recognized an affront in Decatur's language and demanded a retraction or satisfaction.

Somers, deeply disturbed, talked to Decatur about it and that surprised young man offered to clear the atmosphere by entertaining the whole group at dinner and stating to all the world that he had no purpose of insulting his good friend and old-time messmate. That might have ended the matter but Somers was not satisfied. He refused to assent, saying his courage had been suspected, that he would have to vindicate himself, and that the only course open to him was to challenge all six of the scoffers.

None appeared to appreciate the ridiculous extremes to which the affair was descending. Somers proceeded to challenge the six and Decatur, his closest friend, served as his second. The duels began on the Sicilian shore, which had witnessed vain and inglorious personal combat since the beginning of history and no doubt long before. Kindly, friendly, peacefully disposed, deeply religious Richard Somers, loved by nearly everyone in the fleet, took the first bullet in his right arm, which he would need for later duels. In the second duel he was hit in the hip and drained of some good blood. Decatur thought it time for him to quit and let his second take his place but Somers would hear nothing of it.

No man is in a good dueling condition with his right arm crippled and his left thigh so wounded he cannot stand; still, on Somers' insistence that the affair was not finished, Decatur sat by his side at the third duel, wrapped his arm around his friend's back, and supported Somers' wobbly right arm so he could fire. It might be suspected that Decatur's expertness with the pistol had something to do with the fact that the third adversary was wounded. Somers could scarcely have held up the pistol unaided.

Three duels were decided by the party to be enough to demonstrate that Somers was no coward, which, if they could all have waited a trifle longer, was to be demonstrated clearly for all to see. With that the felicitations were exchanged, the young men drank wine with Somers freely, and he recovered from his wounds in time not to miss the activities of the Barbary Wars.

The *Argus*, the *Vixen*, and the *Nautilus* escorted the *Intrepid* as far as the rocks sheltering the harbor, then watched her sail into the channel easily under an eastern breeze. When she was supposed by those on the three ships to be inside the harbor, some of the batteries opened and several shots were fired at her. The eyes of all aboard the three escorting craft were strained forward, following her as far as they could as she disappeared into the darkness. The *Nautilus* went closest in, perhaps because Somers had commanded her from the beginning. He had written from Baltimore to his brother about the ship when he first took her, saying the man who had sold her to the government "says he will be Damn'd if any thing that ever floated Can beat her Sailing." Her commander could not but have looked on her fondly as he sailed away from her into the night. Her famous name, like that of Somers, would resound through the naval lists of later years.

Then the *Nautilus* hauled off to avoid being seen from the shore. As she drew away Lieutenant Charles G. Ridgely on her deck tried to follow the canvas of the disappearing *Intrepid* through his night glass. He could see her vague outline as she went ahead and he thought he could follow her to the very end and see her constantly moving forward, but it may have been only an impression. The night was black.

Then, suddenly, at 9:47 P.M., the harbor of Tripoli, the town, the desert, and the sea were lighted by a great blinding flash, followed by the roar and concussion of a fearful explosion. In the light like the brilliance of day could be seen the *Intrepid*'s masts blown skyward. Then there were exploding shells in the air and a rain of debris into the water, shrieks and alarms from the town, and at length silence. Never, as the minutes passed, then hours, was there anything else but silence for the watchers. The three escort vessels waited outside the rock until the sun was up, scanning the waters for the small boats that would bring Somers and his men to them, or for some wreckage or clue to what had happened, but the story had ended in that one blinding flash.

Not a trace of the *Intrepid* could be seen on the calm waters of Tripoli Harbor or the blue Mediterranean outside. The question of what occurred should be examined in some detail because this was one of the mysteries of the early American Navy. Preble said that one of the largest Tripolitan gunboats was missing while three others, badly shattered, were observed as the enemy was hauling them on shore. These circumstances caused him to believe that the enemy had detected the approach of the *Intrepid* and had detached the four boats to intercept her. Not knowing she was a fire ship, the missing boat had boarded her, then: "The gallant Somers and heroes of his party, observing the other three boats surrounding them, and no prospect of escape, determined, at once, to prefer *death* and the *destruction of the enemy* to *captivity* and *torturing slavery*, put a match to the train leading directly to the magazine, which at once blew the whole into the air, and terminated their existence." The italics were used by Preble in his report and show his effort at emphasis.

One weak point in Preble's deduction was that it credited the Tripolitans with boarding an unknown American vessel on a dark night, which would have been a reversal of their attitude after the battle of August 3. Preble supported his theory by saying Somers, Wadsworth, and Israel had formed a compact never to be taken nor to allow the enemy to capture the powder on board. Preble's word cannot be doubted on this matter.

"They expected to enter the harbor without discovery," he said, "but had declared that, should they be disappointed, and the enemy should board them, before they reached their point of destination, in such force as to leave them no hopes of a safe retreat, that they would put a match to the magazine and blow themselves and their enemies up together; determined, as there was no exchange of prisoners, that their country should never pay ransom for them, nor the enemy receive a supply of powder through their means."

Lieutenant Spence, who had been picked out of the water when Lieutenant Caldwell's gunboat was sunk on August 7, gave a picture of the *Intrepid's* last voyage, which he observed from the deck of the *Constitution*. He had volunteered to accompany Somers, thought for a time he had been selected and was disappointed when he was not.

The Night came—She went in, all were anxious with expectation when Cannon announced her near approach to the Castle. Cannon were fired from all parts of the town. In a few moments she went up— How awfully Grand! Every thing wrapp'd in Dead silence, made the explosion loud, and terrible, the fuses of the shells, burning in the air, shown like so many planets, a vast stream of fire, which appeared ascending to heaven portrayed the Walls to our view—20 minutes elapsed, without seeing the signal agreed on, between Capt S[omers] & the Commodore. Guns were fired from the Commodores ship; signals repeated by the different vessels—our small schooners sent to reconnoiter the Harbour—but no Boat appear'd.

Spence told a story similar to Preble's conjecture: that the *Intrepid* within a half mile of the Castle was boarded by two gunboats. He placed their crews at fifty men each. Somers, he thought, touched the fire to the fuse himself, in keeping with his promise.

Preble's reasoning is impressive until subjected to close analysis, as it was by Marine Private Ray, who tried to fit it into the conditions in Tripoli as he observed them at the time. He was not trying to minimize the heroism of the men on the *Intrepid* but, he asked, if the Tripolitans had boarded the ketch would they not then have been destroyed also? Never was there a hint of any Barbary seamen—"Turks," he called them —being killed in such an affair.

The enlisted-men prisoners had become closely acquainted with the Neapolitan slaves, who looked to the Americans for eventual deliverance. These slaves were in attendance of the Bashaw and the principal men of the town. Ray said they brought "avidly" every scrap of information about the Bashaw's defeats, yet they never brought one word about any Turks being destroyed in the explosion. Many others communicated with them freely—Maltese, Jews, Greeks and disaffected Turks—but never a word about any loss to Tripoli in the blast of gunpowder.

The Christian consuls apparently never heard of such a loss, else the Dane Nissen, who communicated with them freely as a particular friend, would have mentioned it. Lewis Hexiner, one of the seamen who had "turned Turk" then regretted it, was in a position of enjoying the confidences of both sides. He never heard of any reports among the Turks about the loss of a crew. Surely, Ray thought, with all these channels of communication some intelligence would have reached the American seamen of such an extraordinary event as the destruction of one to two hundred Turks, the crew of one of their cruisers.

"It is therefore very evident that no Turks were destroyed," wrote Ray after reading Preble's version, "and if none were destroyed, is it not full as evident that the train communicated to the magazine sooner than was expected, and that the explosion happened before our men could possibly avoid a catastrophe so much to be lamented?"

A circumstance reported by Dr. Cowdery, the surgeon's mate impressed as the Bashaw's physician, would tend to support Private Ray's deduction. The Doctor noted that the exposion did so little damage that the Bashaw and his people held a thanksgiving to Mahomet. That would scarcely suggest that he had lost a cruiser with perhaps two hundred men.

The term thanksgiving as used by the Doctor may have been deceptive, because he said "the ceremony was prayer in a doleful tone, and singing, accompanied with the sound of an instrument made by drawing a skin over a hoop." That could have been a dirge as readily as a jubilee. The Doctor had been in the country with the Bashaw on the night of the explosion and was returning to town in his retinue. Suddenly they saw the great flash and heard the loud report. "We all wheeled about, and made for the place we had left; but the Bashaw soon altered his mind, and proceeded to town, while I went to the country palace and staid that night."

Dr. Cowdery reported that the Turks found ten dead men—he did not specify whether or not they were the bodies of the Americans—near where the vessel exploded. While the remnants of the *Intrepid* were lost to the Americans, who could not see a stick of her, they were not to the Tripolitans. What remained of her hull was discovered by the Turks grounded on the rocks near the western channel into the harbor. It was on the north side, which would be outside the harbor. Two Americans were in her bottom. Dr. Cowdery was wrong in his figures because the Bashaw's men found the bodies of all thirteen Americans who had been in the ketch when she put out. Six washed up on the beach southeast of the city, which would tend to confirm that she got inside the harbor, whereas the location of the hull would suggest that she did not.

One body was in a boat which washed ashore and four others were found floating in the water inside the harbor.

None of the bodies could be identified. Bainbridge and other officers of the *Philadelphia* were allowed to view them on September 6, two days after the explosion and probably the day on which they were found or washed ashore. The features were so horribly mutilated that none of the officers could make a single identification. The American captives held services and the bodies were buried by a gang of workmen under Dr. Cowdery's supervision.

Five graves are now marked in Tripoli as those of *Intrepid* volunteers, and 150 years after the ketch exploded a memorial marker was placed nearby and a wreath was laid. But there is no certainty that these are the authentic graves. They are in an old Protestant cemetery which was established by the European and American consuls in 1830. After Field Marshal Montgomery's British army had liberated Libya from Italy in 1943, five unmarked graves were found in the cemetery; and by conversations with living residents, who were supposed to have heard the story from their grandparents, these were accepted as the resting places of five of the brave sailors whose lives went out in the harbor blast. On each a marker was placed which admits of no doubt about the authentication. The site serves at least as a shrine.

Dr. Cowdery made an unsettling entry in his journal by saying he saw fourteen bodies, three of which appeared to be of officers. This was one body too many. He wrote that the Bashaw's son-in-law said six others had drifted up on the shore west of the town. That would mean twenty bodies altogether, and some of them, though they should have been distinguishable, would then have been Tripolitans. The only other explanation would be that the Bashaw's son-in-law was simply talking about the same six bodies found on the southeast beach. Cowdery did not make it clear, but his remark has been taken by some to mean that some bodies of Turks were found after the explosion. If so, the boarding story would have more weight. Cowdery said he could not ascertain the truth of the story told by the Bashaw's son-in-law.

Another element of doubt was introduced by Eaton, who wrote to Preble a little later from Beherah in Egypt. He said he had met in Alexandria an Arnaut Turk who had been in the Bashaw's service and who talked to him freely, believing him to be an Englishman. The Turk told of the Bashaw's heavy losses from Preble's fleet, and said the fire ship had been blown up after it had been boarded by the crews of two row galleys. Eaton reported that the Turk was so worked up over this loss that he wept. He repeated that the Americans had been called merchantmen but had proved to be "Devils, from whom nothing is to be gained in war." With no profits in sight, he therefore quit the Bashaw's service.

Bainbridge's close friend and biographer Harris, who got his material from his subject, adhered to the version that the *Intrepid* had been boarded. Whatever Bainbridge may have thought at the time, it is fair to assume that this became his judgment in later years else Harris would not have been so positive.

Curiosity naturally attaches to the method Captain Somers intended to employ to set off the charge. Ordnance of the day was fired with a match or portfire. The match was a long cord of hemp or cotton impregnated into a wick which would burn uniformly and not go out easily. The portfire, a term frequently used at the time, was an anglicizing of the French *porte* and *feu*, meaning "to bear fire," and was about the same sort of a wick as the match. While preparations were being made with the *Intrepid*, Preble experimented with a portfire in the cabin of the *Constitution*, with Somers present. The Commodore, a man of detail, was taking interest in every step in the "infernal" plan. He lit a portfire and timed its burning with his watch, and remarked as he was afterward quoted, that "it burned longer than was necessary, as the time might enable the enemy to approach and extinguish it before the train would be fired." Thereupon Somers replied in his soft manner, "I ask for no portfire." How then was he to fire the ship? Did he have some other methods in mind, which perhaps failed to give him and his followers enough time?

Midshipman William Henry Allen, later the bold commander who in the War of 1812 would sail the *Argus* around the British Isles and die on her deck, returned to the Mediterranean on the *Congress* with Barron's reinforcements. He had sailed with Bainbridge in 1800 on the *George Washington* to Constantinople. He took an interest in the *Intrepid*, made a study of her, and drew a sketch of her which he sent to his father, General William Allen, together with a detailed description. He said eighty barrels of powder were in the magazine built forward of the foremast and that the 150 loaded shells were placed in a position so that, on the supposition that the craft would be going in before the wind, they would be thrown forward by the explosion into the town.

The portfires which were to be used, by his account, were composition placed in gun barrels, which were calculated by test to burn eleven minutes. More than one gun barrel was used, apparently to guard against failure of a single portfire. Leading from these gun barrels, which were thrust through holes bored in a bulkhead, was a trough containing a train of powder leading forward and aft. All one had to do was touch a match to either gun barrel and then get off in eleven minutes, which was ample time to move to security. He adhered to Preble's version that the *Intrepid* was boarded and that Somers blew himself and his companions up, just as he had announced he would in such a case.

The more likely explanation is that the "infernal" was fired by accident before she reached her desired position, or else was hit by a red-hot shot. Preble's death-pact version is not convincing. He could easily have been mistaken in believing a Tripolitan ship was missing; one could have been hidden, or he might have miscounted, or one might have been scuttled or sunk because of damage in one of the battles.

Of one matter Preble had no doubt: "That she was blown up before she had gained her station is certain." He lamented the loss of three officers who were, in his words, "of conspicuous bravery, talents and merit." Gloom was indeed cast over the fleet by the sudden and ghastly death of three officers who had distinguished themselves in the battles and of enlisted men selected for their courage.

Henry Wadsworth's name would have an immortality he could never know about. Three years after his death a son would be born to his sister, Zilpah Wadsworth Longfellow, daughter of General Peleg Wadsworth and wife of Stephen Longfellow, of Portland, Maine. The Longfellows lived next door to the Prebles. They would name the baby Henry Wadsworth Longfellow in honor of the brave lieutenant.

The officers of the Mediterranean fleet collected a fund out of their own pay and erected at the Washington Navy Yard a shrine to the officers who died in Preble's fighting—Somers, Wadsworth, Israel, Caldwell, James Decatur, and Dorsey. Of white marble, with a shaft forty feet high, with symbolic figures, and surmounted with the American eagle and shield, it was an imposing memorial. When General Robert Ross's British army occupied Washington in late August, 1814, ten years after the explosion of the *Intrepid*, his soldiers, or Admiral George Cockburn's sailors who accompanied them, hacked at the monument—in vandalic reprisal because of the American naval victories, it was often said, but more probably for souvenirs. After the War of 1812 the mutilation was obscured and the memorial was placed for a time at the west front of the Capitol, then was removed to the Naval Academy at Annapolis, where it remains.

Decatur and Stewart were hit especially hard by the loss. Both had been Somers' early companions. Decatur had lost his brother only a month before, and now his closest friend was gone. For a time there was little satisfaction for him in his promotion to the captaincy. On the day following the explosion the fleet mournfully went about its work. The ships that had escorted the *Intrepid* returned with no explanation of her fate. The threat that bad weather was coming caused Preble to take the guns, mortars, shot, and shells out of the gunboats and bomb ketches and hoist them on board the *Constitution* and the *John Adams*. Repair work was begun on the bomb ketches preparatory to another attack. But the squadron had been through a period of prolonged action and ammunition was running low. Preble judged the ammunition the squadron had on hand was ample for only three of the vessels to keep up the blockade.

Still there was no intelligence about the expected reinforcements. As days passed the Commodore decided the season was so far advanced that the gunboats could not be hazarded longer in the open sea. He ordered the *John Adams*, *Siren*, *Nautilus*, *Enterprise* and *Scourge* to take them and the bomb ketches in tow and sail for Syracuse. He directed the *Argus* and *Vixen* to remain with the *Constitution* on the blockade. On September 10, 1804, two sails hove in sight. On nearer approach they were discerned to be the *President* with Commodore Samuel Barron, the new commander in the Mediterranean, and the *Constellation*, under Captain Hugh G. Campbell.

None could possibly have expected it at the time, but one wise in the affairs of man might have divined that the war against Tripoli had been fought largely in Preble's heart, and that with his departure, never again would an American broadside be thrown into the town. Henry Wadsworth Longfellow, the brave lieutenant's nephew, would say "great men stand like solitary towers," and while he did not do so, he might well have said it of Preble.

Preble made five attacks on Tripoli and employed the full firepower of his force in every instance where he could. His wooden fleet bombarded stone forts and protected land batteries and a navy of impressive strength. His casualties were thirty-two killed or mortally wounded and twenty-two others wounded. Rarely was more accomplished at so low a cost. Truly it might be said that the U.S. navy under Preble, as in its first faint traces under the fighting Truxtun, had a glorious beginning—a dawn like thunder.

CHAPTER TWENTY

The Passing of Preble

F EW events in the early history of the Republic caused greater shock than the recall of Preble. President Jefferson was as chagrined about it as anybody else and tried by his recognition of the replaced Commodore and the honors he gave him to soften the blow, but it fell heavily nevertheless on both the public and the naval establishment, where the Captain's great worth as a planner and fighter were just gaining recognition.

The reason for the relief of Preble in the face of a continued flow of enthusiastic reports from the Mediterranean about his able performance —though the action came before intelligence of his naval victories in front of Tripoli was received—was a snarl-up in naval legislation and regulations, resulting, broadly, from an unwillingness of a sensitive and pacifically inclined Congress to recognize the implications of the Constitutional provision that the President is commander-in-chief of the armed forces.

Congress put into the naval legislation a provision that a frigate should be commanded by a captain. Therefore, when Jefferson sent the four frigates to the Mediterranean after he learned of the loss of the *Philadelphia,* he had to select captains for the command of each vessel. The frigates which were either newly dispatched to the Mediterranean or returned after earlier service, and their commanding officers, were:

President, 44—Captain George Cox
Congress, 36—Captain John Rodgers
Essex, 32—Captain James Barron
Constellation, 36—Captain Hugh G. Campbell
John Adams, 28—Captain (acting) Isaac Chauncey

Commodore Samuel Barron selected the *President* as his flagship, as had Dale, because of her fleetness. He was allowed what had been denied Dale, or Truxtun, either, when offered the command: a captain under him on the flagship. He had also at his disposal most of the smaller ships which had been used so effectively by Preble. Never in its history had the United States brought together a squadron of such beauty and power as that which Samuel Barron commanded in the autumn of 1804.

Preble had been superceded in orders issued by the Navy Department May 22, in which the new squadron was enumerated, though the *John Adams*, used mainly now for dispatch service, was not mentioned. Possibly the omission was because she, not having a captain in command, but only Master Commandant Chauncey acting as captain, did not conform to the condition mentioned in Secretary Smith's letter to Preble, which was that the Department had been "unavoidably constrained" to supercede him, despite the altogether satisfactory nature of his service. As Smith explained, there were only two captains in the United States junior to Preble. They were James Barron and Campbell, and "as the Frigates cannot be commanded but by Captains, we of necessity have been obliged to send out two Gentlemen senior to yourself in Commission." These were Samuel Barron and Rodgers. The fact that the *John Adams* was a frigate and was commanded by a master commandant (who did not get his captaincy until 1806) was overlooked.

There is no doubt that Jefferson and Smith were sincere in their reluctance to replace Preble, though the full measure of his achievements would not be known in the United States until the passage of another half-year. But seniority, a god which had insinuated itself into the old British service as early as the War of the Roses, gripped the flowering navy tightly, and perhaps was a good system in a young nation where different sections would be alert to detect evidence of favoritism, and fragmentation was an ever-lurking danger, as the people would be reminded by the activities of Aaron Burr a bit later. Still, it is reasonable to suppose that a President as prudent and mentally flexible as Jefferson might have found a pathway around seniority had he been aware at the time of Preble's great worth. Here slow communication resulted in immense national loss. Possibly Congress could have been prevailed on to create a new rank of flag officer or admiral commensurate with what it had done for the Army in establishing the rank of lieutenant general on the threat of war with France.

Secretary Smith did soften the blow when he told Preble that no want of confidence was mingled with the considerations that made the change necessary: "You have fulfilled our highest expectations and The President has given it as an especial charge to me, to declare that he has the highest Confidence in your Activity, Judgment and Valour." He asked the Secretary to convey his thanks "for the very important services which you have rendered to your Country."

Preble was hurt but maintained his poise and dignity. Apart from the brief reference already noted in his report, he merely confided to his diary that his feelings were lacerated at being superseded at the moment of victory. But he wrote later his thanks to the President and for "the very obliging language" in which Secretary Smith informed him he was being replaced.

Preble, with the *Constitution*, reached Malta September 17. There he received a report that the gunboats and bomb ketches he had borrowed from the King of the Two Sicilies had reached Syracuse safely and had been returned to their owners. These were the only boats the American navy was able to borrow. French pressure stayed King Ferdinand. French opinion appeared to be hardening against the United States along the Barbary shore, possibly because of the friendly sentiments prevailing between American and British officers in the Mediterranean and the continued use of British harbors and repair docks by American warships.

Preble attributed the refusal of the gunboats to the French. Writing to Decatur from Naples, he related that General Acton, whom he had met at Palermo, had been quite agreeable to another loan, but that the King had discovered he wanted the boats to protect his own commerce. "Some more powerful Interest than ours has been the cause," Preble said. "I believe the French have had a hand in the business." Toward the close of his presence off Tripoli, the attitude of Beaussier, French consul at Tripoli (who had dropped the "Citizen" in his name after Bonaparte threw the French Revolution into history), had seemed to be more unsympathetic to Preble's warfare against the Bashaw. His reasoning was peculiar in his letter to Preble August 6: "The Fanaticism & fury of these Africans would be difficult to curb in case of total destruction." Good curbers had been appearing in such men as Decatur and Trippe. The letter seemed to be a loosely worded plea that Preble augment the sum he had offered for ransom, though M. Beaussier avowed he was not working in the interests of the Bashaw. This stiffening of the French would be detected in Egypt as the cordiality between the British and Americans became more noticeable in the Mediterranean.

Preble took advantage of the commendatory passages in the order superseding him to make certain that the true situation of his recall might be understood throughout the Mediterranean, where he had won not only many personal friends, but numerous admirers in the southern European ports who had never seen him. Every gun he had fired at Tripoli had added to his fame. He went to Syracuse on the *John Adams*, arriving September 22, thence to Naples, where he made the unsuccessful try to negotiate the loan of gunboats for next year's campaign.

On December 23, 1804, he sailed in the *John Adams*, which Chauncey was taking back to the United States with dispatches from various consuls. One of the intrepid young lieutenants of the Tripolitan War, James Lawrence, who had fought in nearly all the actions and been second in command when Decatur burned the *Philadelphia*, was first lieutenant under Chauncey. Ex-Consul O'Brien, Jefferson's old captain in the Virginia navy, no longer needed in either the fighting or negotiations in the Mediterranean, sailed with them. They reached Gibraltar January 6, 1805, and on January 10 while the *John Adams* passed through the Straits into the Atlantic, Edward Preble took his last view of the fading waters of the Mediterranean, where he more than any other had given an éclat and *esprit de corps* to the American navy.

Preble carried with him a document signed by fifty-three of his officers. Few if any who signed it had known him at the beginning of the campaign. Most of them had found his severity distasteful. But all had come to admire him deeply and devotedly, if not, in fact, to love him. Their letter testified to their high estimation of him as an officer and commander. They said they deeply regretted his "supersedure in a command in which you have acquired so much honor to yourself and country." They hoped that "our Countrymen may generously bestow on you that *meed* which your important services so richly deserve."

Quite appropriately the first name on the list was that of Stephen Decatur. Among the fifty-three were later great naval tacticians and fighters; Charles Stewart and Isaac Hull, commanders of the *Constitution*; Lawrence, Macdonough, the gallant Trippe who would die five years later while commanding the *Vixen* in the Caribbean; Burrows, who died on the *Enterprise* at the moment of his triumph over the British *Boxer*; Tarbell, Morris, Chauncey, Spence, Thorn, Joseph Bainbridge, and a host of others—those who at times referred to themselves as "Preble's boys." Hovering over the signing must have been the spirits of Somers, Wadsworth, and Israel, who could understand the meaning of devotion to country. And of course those who would have signed no doubt had they been free from the Tripolitan jail included other great naval names: William Bainbridge; Jacob Jones, captor with his *Wasp* of the *Frolic*; Biddle, a great seaman whose memorable deeds included the sinking of the *Penguin* while he commanded the *Hornet*, and David Porter, whom few excelled. Truly it might be said that if Humphreys were the "father of the navy," Preble was the early tutor who shaped its character.

Preble answered the officers with thanks for their support in a difficult and dangerous service and said he should "always consider my reputation as an officer secure while my views were seconded by that talent & intrepidity for which you stand so eminently distinguished." He acknowledged he would have been gratified to command them until the war had been concluded successfully, but it was an officer's duty to submit with cheerfulness and this he did, knowing they would serve their country with the same ardor under his successor.

Marine Private Ray summed up the enlisted man's feeling when he said: "The brave man is never a cruel one. The dauntless Preble is said to be as humane as he is brave; as just as he is humane; and as merciful as he is just."

Preble received many letters from friends he had made in the Mediterranean. Among the most cordial was that from Nelson's old sea-fighter of the Nile, Sir Alexander Ball, the British governor of Malta whom young Izard, like many others, had come to admire and mention in correspondence home, because he had been so helpful to the American squadrons. Sir Alexander observed:

I beg to repeat my congratulations on the service you have rendered your country, and the hair-breadth escapes you have had in setting a distinguished example. Their bravery and enterprise are worthy a great and rising nation. If I were to offer my opinion, it would be that you have done well not to purchase a peace with the enemy. A few brave men have, indeed, been sacrificed, but they could not have fallen in a better cause, and I even conceive it advisable to risk more lives rather than to submit to terms which might encourage the Barbary states to add fresh demands and insults.

Of all the messages he received or of the comments made about his operations, the most distinguished and frequently referred to was that of the gentle and able Pope Pius VII, the pontiff who defied Napoleon and was long held captive by the Corsican in later years at Grenoble and Fontainebleau. Pope Pius said: "The American Commander, with a small force and in a short space of time, has done more for the cause of Christianity than the most powerful nations of Christendom have done for ages."

When the ebullient Eaton read this remark he wrote to an army acquaintance on September 20, 1804, that: "If I could obtain as handsome a certificate, and as fairly, I should be apt to be very indifferent about an absolution for past sins, and should be in danger of being so about committing fresh ones." Eaton, who had denounced the earlier American ship captains, felt pride after Preble that "an American is no longer ashamed of an American Uniform." He gave one of the best estimates of Preble's service:

"The enterprize of this judicious and gallant commander has effected astonishment. . . . With the small force under his command he has stamped an impression on the Barbary mind which will not be erased this generation and has restored the character of our arms to its proper consideration among the neighboring nations."

Preble landed at New York after a difficult voyage on the *John Adams*, during which it was discovered the faulty water casks had leaked out most of the water supply and all had to go on short rations while the ship was headed for the closest port. He went first, as duty demanded, to Washington, before rejoining his family in Portland. He reached the capital on March 4, 1805, the day Jefferson was being inaugurated for a second term, and received ovations next in warmth and cordiality to those for the President himself. In these greetings and honors Jefferson joined heartily. The great man knew the qualities of a hero and gave every courtesy and distinction to the one who more than any other had graced his administration with martial splendor. The tall, slim, stately, reserved Preble had become the leading naval character of his times in the United States, and was attended, to his surprise, by ovations wherever he went.

Already, upon the receipt of intelligence about Preble's battles, the President had sent a message to Congress, dated February 20, 1805, commending "the energy and judgment displayed by this excellent officer" and "the zeal and bravery of his men," and saying they deserved well of Congress and their country.

Congress voted him thanks in the most generous terms, directed the President to have a gold medal struck "emblematical of the attacks on the town, batteries, and naval force of Tripoli"; that the President present swords to those who had distinguished themselves, and that an extra month's pay be granted to the petty officers, seamen, and Marines. Congress gave Jefferson an impossible task when it directed that he present swords to officers and midshipmen "who have distinguished themselves in the several attacks," because with one or two exceptions it would have involved the entire commissioned personnel. He let the matter drag along and it got lost in the War of 1812, a conflict in which most of them received individual honors and swords aplenty. The Secretary of the Navy presented the Gold Medal to Preble in 1806.

Congress did not neglect to name the officers who had given their lives: Somers, Wadsworth, James Decatur, Caldwell, Israel, and Dorsey. It asked the President to convey to their parents or other relatives the deep regret felt over the loss "of those gallant men, whose names ought to live in the recollections and affections of a grateful country, and whose conduct ought to be regarded as an example to future generations."

Jefferson was so admirous of Preble that shortly after his departure from Washington the rumor became widespread that he was to become Secretary of the Navy. Smith, diligent but rarely applauded in the job, was reported to be on the verge of retirement in the spring of 1805, and the word went to the country and the fleet that Preble might have Cabinet rank. From the far-off Mediterranean, Stewart exclaimed that nothing could "give more real pleasure to his boys of the infant squadron." Chauncey was still more enthusiastic: "I pray God, that the President may have the good of the country so much at heart, as to make so judicious an appointment."

But Smith, who has been termed a "notorious gossip" and "beyond his depth even in tranquil waters"; who was subsequently forced out of Madison's Cabinet under charges of mishandling funds, brought by Secretary of the Treasury Albert Gallatin (but who has had defenders as well as detractors), decided to remain. Had Preble's health permitted he would have given much abler service in the post, for Smith was not in character above viciously attacking Madison, his old associate and then his chief, after leaving Madison's Cabinet. He was a politician upon whom the niceties of the naval service were lost.

Preble left Washington March 17 on an assignment to procure gunboats, which he had recommended as an essential need for the prosecution of the Tripolitan War. Arriving in Philadelphia enroute for Boston and Portland, he was persuaded by George Harrison, the naval agent there, to sit for a profile likeness by Rembrandt Peale, a portrait which shows his strong features, alert eyes, and thorough self-possession. It recalls the comment of a clergyman who saw Preble and a distinguished Indian chief walking on the Boston street, and thought "they were the noblest specimens of the human race he had ever observed." He had about him the aura of command. There were some who thought that had he not been a great sea captain, he could have become a celebrated singer. His voice was as strong and melodious in song as it was crisp and compelling in shipboard orders.

Straight, stalwart, and commanding as he appeared, Preble was unwell and his action-crammed career was drawing toward a close. He had one other important service, the gunboats. When he found he could not procure them in Naples, he knew the only alternative was to build them in the United States, for nearly all Europe was at war and intent on its own affairs. That meant an alteration of design from what already were being built, so that they might make the long journey across the Atlantic, hazardous for such small craft, unaided. He hurried about the crowded New England shipyards and had the boats designed and built, but none reached the Mediterranean in time to be a factor in the languishing Barbary Wars.

Nevertheless, the gunboat, once introduced, struck Jefferson's fancy. They suited his pacific intentions because they were instruments of defense in the harbors of America and not essentially those of aggression. By the end of 1807 he had authorization from Congress for new construction that would bring the total number of U.S. gunboats to 257. The gunboat idea fitted also into Jefferson's earlier "mothball fleet" conception. They could be laid up until a crisis made it actually necessary to man them. Few matters brought Jefferson more ridicule than the gunboats, to which the historical artist John Trumbull, among many others, took scornful exception. Well before he was attacked for the embargo, he was scoffed at for the gunboats. They were in a measure a heritage of Preble's successful operation with the much more unwieldy, borrowed craft in Tripoli Harbor, and they had a very distinct place in harbor fighting, where they could use sweeps when the larger vessels were becalmed. The ridicule of Jefferson did not end the era of the gunboats, which under steam propulsion came into their most effective employment on the rivers during the Civil War.

Preble understood naval warfare: how to be audacious, how to find security in boldness, how to test the enemy before deciding he is too strong to venture near him, how to demand rights from a position of strength instead of treating for wants from a position of weakness.

His success was in his restless energy. He followed George Washington's injunction to plan carefully but execute swiftly. He knew what was so well expressed by Lieutenant Henry Wadsworth's nephew in his translation of Dante, that "Seated upon down, or in his bed, man cometh not to fame."

He did not know it at the time of his recall, but he, perhaps more than any other, was the sea captain who ended the age-old policy of paying tribute, though tribute was to linger a bit on the Barbary shore after his passing from the Mediterranean.

When his vitality began to weaken he took to the sea air again, but the voyage failed to give him his old buoyancy and he died in Portland August 25, 1807, just three years after his battles in Tripoli Harbor, at the age of forty-six years.

Samuel Barron, the new Commodore, was the elder brother of James Barron, one of his ship captains. They were the sons of Captain James Barron, commander of the Commonwealth of Virginia navy in the Revolutionary War, who had performed a signal service at the outset by intercepting in Chesapeake Bay a letter from Lord George Germain, British secretary of state for the colonies and directing head of the war to retain the colonies, addressed to Governor Robert Eden of Maryland. The letter discussed the plan of Sir Peter Parker to strike the southern colonies with an impressive fleet, and the disclosure caused the colonists to prepare for the blow, which they repulsed when Sir Peter attacked Sullivan's Island at Charleston, South Carolina.

The Barron boys learned seamanship under their father and had their first naval experiences in the quasi-French war, where James won more attention, but remained subordinate to his brother Samuel. James seemed destined for a distinguished naval career until at his great moment, when in command of the *Chesapeake*, he truckled to a haughty British captain, Salisburg Pryce Humphreys, commanding the *Leopard*. He was convicted by a court martial of neglect of duty and suspended from the service for five years, and never given sea command again. Much has been written in his vindication but the sentence still seems light.

Commodore Samuel Barron's fleet was delayed more by weather than procrastination, though he was never hurried. He made the passage from Hampton Roads to the Azores in the remarkably rapid time of fifteen days. This was usually regarded as two-thirds of the crossing but it required twenty-two days to make the other third to Gibraltar because of unfavorable winds. The *President* went by Mogador thence up the West African coast, and reached Gibraltar August 12, 1804, the day of the arrival also of the *Constellation* and the *Congress*. The weather was beautiful during the entire voyage, "not a day but a ship's barge might have lived at sea without danger," but too calm for rapid progress. The *Essex* arrived the next day. The fleet took on provisions, the *Congress* and the *Essex* sailed in two days to show themselves off Tangier, and the *President* and the *Constellation* continued toward Tripoli by way of Malta, which the *President* reached September 5, 1804, the day after the explosion of the *Intrepid* at Tripoli.

Between Gibraltar and Malta, when off Cape de Gata, the *President* and *Constellation* had such a singular experience that Commodore Barron made a detailed report on it to Sir Alexander Ball, British governor of Malta, mainly as a bit of news but perhaps also in a vein that the British, who with Nelson's fleet were in substantial charge of the Mediterranean, ought to take control over natural as well as human disturbances. The American ships were sailing in an uncommonly smooth sea under a light westerly wind at about three knots when suddenly the *President* seemed to strike heavily, as on an uneven, rocky bottom. Barron was at dinner in the cabin with the ship's officers, having as his guest Captain Campbell of the *Constellation*, which was sailing nearby. For about forty seconds the violent shock, which came in a succession of quick strokes, lifted the ship about a foot out of the water at each stroke, then let her fall back again.

Barron and his officers rushed from the cabin, believing the ship aground, in the same plight as had been the *Philadelphia*. On deck they saw no evidence of a shoal nor had the vessel been retarded in her progress. But they heard the crew of a cutter which the *President* was towing cry out in what Barron described as "great consternation," saying the cutter had struck something.

Campbell signaled to his ship, a mile distant, to come in speaking distance, and when alongside she reported she had struck on rocks. As her officer described it, her experience had been precisely the same as the *President's*. When the time was ascertained it was the same instant the shock was felt on the *President*. Barron soon spoke to a Spanish ship which had been about five miles away and the master informed him his ship had felt the same shock, and described it as very violent. Next morning, fifteen miles farther on, the two frigates moving a mile and a half apart felt another violent shock, accompanied by a rumbling noise which sounded like a vessel grating over a shoal. This shock lasted a minute.

"The effect which these singular occurrences," Barron reported to Sir Alexander, "seemed to have on the feelings of the ship's people was also remarkable: the alarm, agitation, and amazement appeared much greater than would have been created, I believe, had the ship been actually aground."

Earth-shaking events were occurring all about: Napoleon was being crowned Emperor, Alexander Hamilton was being killed by Aaron Burr, Immanuel Kant was at Königsberg expiring by degrees, Spain was declaring war on Great Britain, and Preble at that time was blazing away at Tripoli, but nature seemed placid where its creatures were turbulent. No violent volcanic eruptions or earthquakes were reported except on the otherwise unruffled waters of the Mediterranean off Cape de Gata. But was it a portent that Barron's mighty squadron would meet continually with circumstances over which it had no control?

Possibly it was what shook up the new Commodore's liver, which soon got out of hand and kept the distressed man on shore leave more persistently than had Commodore Morris' wife restricted the navigation of the second squadron. Never in American history did a single organ have more bearing in frustrating the purposes of a naval force than did Commodore Samuel Barron's liver. But he was able in early September to go on from Malta and, as has been noted, reach Preble's squadron off Tripoli September 10.

Barron brought with him a passenger from Hampton Roads who would be worth as much to the American cause in the Mediterranean as all the newly arrived frigates combined: the haughty, domineering, ever-talking, ever-doing, deeply patriotic William Eaton, now possessing the new and somewhat ambiguous title delivered to him in a special commission by the Secretary of the Navy with the assent of the Secretary of State and the President, of Navy Agent of the United States for the Several Barbary Regencies.

If the soul had been taken out of the Tripolitan War by the departure of Preble, a dynamo had been put into it with the return of William Eaton.

CHAPTER TWENTY-ONE

Eaton's Quest for Bashaw Hamet

W ILLIAM Eaton's stern nationalism—an eagerness to undergo any type of hardship or toil for the American cause, and his proclivity to haul up sharply anyone of any rank not giving what he regarded top performance to the country—was a heritage of his army service on the Northwest frontier, where he formed an almost idolatrous affection for General Anthony Wayne.

Wayne was his type of American: able, resourceful, but above everything else, diligent. The lesson of the "Paoli massacre" in the Valley Forge campaign had never been lost on him.

> He endured fatigue and hardship with a fortitude uncommon to men of his years [Eaton wrote]. I have seen him in the most severe night of the winter of '94, sleep on the ground like his fellow soldier; and walk around his camp at four in the morning, with the vigilance of a sentinel . . . When in danger, he is in his element; and never shows to so good advantage as when leading a charge. His name is better in an action, or in an enemy's country, than a brigade of undisciplined levies.

The last sentence could at a later time be applied with equal pertinence to Eaton himself, and certainly he had Wayne's attentiveness and sleeplessness, but in the general settling-down of his character, or more properly the boiling up of it, he was nearer to becoming a small Andrew Jackson than a duplicate Mad Anthony. The emphasis he developed was, in the main, that of some of Jackson's less winning traits, of quick-tempered combativeness or a chip-on-the-shoulder attitude, and an intense partisanship that utterly blinded him to anything but his own decisions and predetermined course. If Jackson could be regarded a moderate alongside anyone else in the formative years of the nation, it was Eaton.

Eaton's pugnacious trait first proclaimed itself in his military career

347

when he was on maneuvers during the time Wayne was preparing his army in Ohio for the Fallen Timbers campaign against Little Turtle and Bluejacket. Eaton, a captain, had a violent wrangle with the adjutant general of the maneuvers, who merely countermanded one of his marching orders. That threw Eaton into a seething rage because he knew he was correct—"I was positively right" he said—and the adjutant stupid; but the adjutant, Captain Edward Butler of the 4th Infantry, had his boiling point also and it looked for a time as if the Indians would be forgotten. Friends of the two officers reconciled them. Fort Recovery was built and Wayne went ahead to establish United States authority in the Northwest Territory.

Eaton, restless, enterprising and adventurous from the beginning, had, much earlier, his first army experience as a dishwasher for a battalion of Connecticut troops in the Revolutionary War. Born in Woodstock, in northeastern Connecticut, February 23, 1764, the second son of a farmer and schoolteacher who had thirteen children, he found in his youth, as did Preble, that there was nothing alluring in the hoe. But he read under the trees, and from the allusions in his later voluminous writings it is clear that he read voraciously. When William Tryon, the royal governor of New York, began to make raids into Connecticut and the state was aroused, Eaton, sixteen, "eloped from home," as he put it, and enlisted for a year, but found his duty was not fighting the British but waiting on the major's table. At the end of the year he returned home sick, but he quickly re-enlisted and served out the war, being discharged at the age of nineteen, in 1783, as a sergeant.

Penniless but yearning, the first a frequent condition and the second one that would follow him to the grave, he walked to Hanover, New Hampshire, to enter Eleazer Wheelock's thriving college, where he found himself, already self-educated in Greek and Latin, pleasantly received and ably instructed by John Wheelock, the founder's son and successor. After being graduated he taught school in Vermont and became clerk of the House of Delegates of that state, and seemed to be entering a routine sort of life when the old army days began to call louder than the Bachelor of Arts degree. Through the agency of Senator Stephen R. Bradley of Vermont, a fellow native of Connecticut and veteran of the Revolution, he gained a captain's commission, got married, and left almost at once for Pittsburgh, where Wayne was assembling his troops.

After the Ohio service Eaton went to Georgia, and controversy went with him. He reached Savannah at the end of 1795, and with 160 regular army soldiers from Virginia, using his Fort Recovery building experience, he built a fort on the St. Mary's River that would come to play a part in Spanish border affairs. Quickly he clashed with his commanding officer, Lieutenant Colonel Henry Gaither of Maryland, veteran of William Smallwood's celebrated Maryland Brigade in the Revolution, but described by one of his subordinates and Eaton's partisans as "an ignorant, debauched, unprincipled old bachelor," who seemed willing to "sacrifice the purest character to gratify the spleen of his soul."

The crux of the matter was Eaton's reports, and he always wrote them in abundance. The Lieutenant Colonel, according to a plausible version, ordered him to stop making them, not wanting the War Department to know too much, and was quoted as saying, "We must get rid of Eaton." The clash is worth examining briefly because it was typical of the voluble Eaton's quarrels, in which, though they were frequent, he never appeared to be entirely wrong, if, indeed, he were wrong at all. In this instance he claimed the commandant was deliberately trying to discredit him by giving him oral orders, then reprimanding him for allegedly disobeying them, even after he had objected to receiving them in verbal form.

There is an implication that the Marylander did not like Eaton's Connecticut origin or Dartmouth erudition. In the long letter Eaton wrote to Secretary of State Pickering about the friction, he maintained that Gaither owned a tract of the Yazoo purchase land and offered to sell Eaton on his arrival 500,000 acres for $35,000. Eaton inserted an aside in his letter, saying that the commanding officer had not supposed he had informed himself already that Gaither's title was no good.

Gaither had Eaton arrested and preferred court martial charges of disobedience of orders, selling public corn and unjustly defrauding the troops of rations and putting them in the garrison store. The charges sounded worse than the case, and it developed that no fraud was involved. Despite the fact that one of the members of the court claimed Eaton was merely the object of the Commander's jealousy, as another captain had been before him, he was convicted and sentenced to suspension from the service for two months. Rallying to Eaton's defense were the residents of the neighborhood, who sent word to the War Department that he had given great satisfaction to the people. But the Lieutenant Colonel confined him for a month in Fort Pickering and it appeared that his military record was stained. However, when he was transferred and reached Philadelphia he learned that the War Department had declined to confirm the sentence of the court martial. At about this time, on the recommendation of Timothy Pickering, who had taken a fancy to his spirit, he was appointed consul to Tunis and sailed on the brig *Sophia* in company with Cathcart, who was going to Tripoli. His service in that post and his return to the United States on the *Perseverance* have been dealt with in foregoing chapters.

While in the United States after being dismissed from Tunis, Eaton went first, in the spring of 1803, to see the wife in Brimfield, Connecticut, from,whom he had been separated four and a half years. Then he journeyed to Washington to adjust his accounts and to denounce again the conduct of the fleet commanders in the Mediterranean. He flailed about in Washington over the manner in which the Barbary War should be conducted. His presentation of a claim to Congress for $22,000 of the personal funds he had advanced to Bashaw Hamet gave him the opportunity to place his views before the legislators with his customary vehemence. Some thought him merely bombastic. Few things are more indicative of Jefferson's perception than that he saw Eaton was not all wind in the sail but had some good ordnance on the gun deck. He had ransacked the history of the ages and must have known that sometimes eccentrics make the best generals; that ruggedness and confident assertiveness are often better military attributes than respect for the conventions and usages.

Jefferson determined to send a thousand stand of small arms, some field artillery, and $40,000 on loan to Hamet. Then when word was received that Hamet had fled to Egypt, the prospects of advancing the American cause through aiding him appeared more doubtful. Enthusiasm waned. Secretary of State Madison was cautious. While Eaton was given his novel commission as naval agent, he was entrusted with no original authority and had to be governed by Commodore Barron's decisions. Eaton declined any remuneration for his services unless the expedition proved successful, and then only if the "enterprise in the estimation of my country should entitle me to it."

Barron, it will be recalled, was the ship captain who along with Bainbridge took pointed exception to Eaton's proposal to put Hamet on the throne of Tripoli as the surest means of gaining and preserving peace, when it was first advanced. But Eaton treated Barron with rare consideration during the voyage on the *President* and eventually imparted some of his own enthusiasm to the reluctant Commodore.

Barron had instructions from Secretary Smith which dealt with Hamet in a most indifferent vein and left to his judgment the entire matter of supplying assistance. Eaton was merely a person who might be "extremely useful." This section of his general orders read:

> With respect to the Ex-Bashaw of Tripoli, we have no objection to you availing yourself of his cooperation with you against Tripoli—if

you shall upon a full view of the subject after your arrival upon the Station, consider his cooperation expedient. The subject is committed entirely to your discretion.

By the time the fleet reached Malta, Eaton had the Commodore in a fairly co-operative mood. On arrival Eaton wrote to Secretary Smith saying Hamet was in Egypt still awaiting American assistance. This information he received from Consul Pulis. The advantages of co-operating with Hamet he found as inviting as they ever had been; discontent prevailed among the Tripolitans, who were ripe for revolt against the usurper, and an uprising would be accompanied by release of the *Philadelphia* prisoners. As Eaton put it: "The enemy may be taken from his sofa at the same instant that our fellow citizens are rescued from chains."

Barron with his bad liver at times did not seem to have the kidney either for bold measures and mulled over the Hamet project. Eaton said he was not decided "whether any construction of the President's instructions extends to a discretion of procuring and furnishing [supplies for Hamet]."

Despite Eaton's softening of the Commodore the prospects of cooperation with Hamet did not yet seem bright. Few more muddled and indefinite situations can be found than those preceding the dispatch of Eaton to find Hamet. In order to understand the transactions it is necessary to follow the movements of Commodore Barron and Eaton, and of the *Argus*, the little brig that was to become a key factor in this dramatic episode.

Barron after his arrival at Malta went for a short time, as we have seen, to the blockade off Tripoli, arriving September 10, 1804, and relieving Preble. Eaton still was with him in the *President*. Off Tripoli Barron ordered the *Vixen* back to Malta to be converted from schooner to brig, then sent the *Constitution* and *Argus* to convoy three captured blockade runners as prizes to Malta. While at sea off Tripoli, before the departure of the *Argus*, Barron held a conference with Hull and Eaton on board the flagship *President*, September 15, 1804. This conference had crucial bearing on the development of the Eaton-Hamet plan.

Barron at the conference issued both written and verbal orders to Hull. No report from Barron giving the content of these orders exists. The text appears to have been lost. But Hull and Eaton made a memorandum respecting them and were in agreement. Their attestation as to the purport quotes Barron as saying to Hull:

> Sir, the *written* orders, I here hand you, to proceed to the port of Alexandria or Smyrna for the purpose of convoying to Malta any vessels you may find there, are intended to disguise the real object of your

expedition; which is to proceed with Mr Eaton to Alexandria in search of Homet Bashaw, the rival brother and legitimate sovereign of the reigning Bashaw of Tripoli; and to convoy him and his suit[e] to Derne or such other place on the coast as may be determined the most proper for co-operating with the naval force under my command against the common enemy; or, if more agreeable to him, to bring him to me before Tripoli—

Should Hamet Bashaw not be found at Alexandria, you have the discretion to proceed to any other place for him which the safety of your ship can be, in your opinion, relied upon.

The Bashaw may be assured of the support of my squadron at Bengazi or Derne; where you are at liberty to put in, if required, and if it can be done without too great risque. And you may assure him also that I will take the most effectual measures with the forces under my Command for co-operating with him against the usurper, his brother; and for re-establishing him in the regency of Tripoli. Arrangements to this effect with him are confided to the discretion with which Mr Eaton is vested by the Government.

Attest Isaac Hull
William Eaton

As the wording of the memorandum is either Hull's or Eaton's, it is perhaps more positive in tone than Barron would have made it in committing his views to writing. But he was apparently impressed with a memorandum Eaton submitted to him described as "an opinion of the probable advantages" that would accrue from cooperating with Hamet. Eaton set down also the possible disadvantages, which were clearly outweighed. Still, subsequent delays indicated that Barron did not remain as enthusiastic about the expedition as the memorandum indicated, though the general accuracy of its contents is not to be doubted. Barron was in the company of Consul Lear for ten days in early October and Lear was always an opponent of Hamet.

Barron sailed via Malta to Syracuse. He arrived September 27, 1804, and that port became his headquarters, where he remained except for an occasional journey to Malta when his health permitted. Lear visited him in Syracuse from October 3 to 13, then went to Malta. The busy little *Argus* was here and there about the mid-Mediterranean during the autumn weeks. Eaton went in her from the Tripoli station when she convoyed one of the prizes to Malta. At Valletta Eaton met O'Brien, who was enthusiastic about Hamet and thought the plan to set him on the throne of Tripoli could be effected easily.

Eaton went to Syracuse and took a room at the house of the American

naval agent George Dyson. The *Argus* sailed via Syracuse to Messina to
refit after arduous service off Tripoli under Preble, where she had been
one of his favorites.

October of 1804 was a month of irresolution and inactivity, except for
the *Argus*. Eaton, Stephen Decatur, and Preble made an overland journey to Messina and returned to Syracuse on the refitted *Argus,* arriving
October 19 after a stormy voyage. The *Argus* went again to Malta, where
one of the significant events of the Tripolitan war occurred. There, on
October 26, 1804, Lieutenant Presley Neville O'Bannon went on board,
having been assigned to command the Marine Corps detachment of the
Argus, relieving Lieutenant John Johnson, who was given what was regarded an elevation. He was transferred from brig to frigate service
after the hard weeks off Tripoli, and was assigned to the *Constitution*.
Whatever Johnson's merits may have been, and he never had opportunity to demonstrate them in any spectacular manner, it became clear
that no other Marine Corps officer in the Mediterranean was better
suited for the tasks ahead than O'Bannon.

The *Argus* was off Tripoli again on October 31, having been sent to
check on the condition of the blockading vessels, the *Congress, Constellation* and *Nautilus,* which had been buffeted in a heavy storm. Then
she returned to Malta and was back in Syracuse November 6. Eaton returned to Syracuse from Messina on November 3. Thus with Barron,
Eaton, Hull and the *Argus* finally together at Syracuse, the elements necessary to set the Hamet project into operation were on hand. Barron
received a letter dated November 1, 1804, from Salvatore Bufuttil, consul for Hamet at Malta, telling him that the rightful Bashaw was awaiting in Egypt the promised American assistance. He said Hamet had "a
great number of Troops Engaged for the Purpose of Cooperating with
the U.S." and would "repay all money advanced and give over all prizes
that may be taken in Derna, Bengazi, or Tripoli, and always remain at
peace and friendship." He thought $10,000 would cover the costs of
taking Derna and Bengazi. He explained that the winter season was the
best time for the troops to march from Egypt.

Barron soon after reaching Syracuse became so ill he had to go ashore.
Even after the Commodore's verbal orders to Hull, Eaton was not sanguine. He wrote to Secretary of the Navy Smith in late October suggesting that Barron be given more positive instructions and saying that the
Commodore appeared neither physically fit to command nor mentally
resolute about the Hamet project:

Information [Eaton said] will be undoubtedly communicated by
the ordinary reports of the very imperfect state of the health which

has compelled Commodore Barron to take lodgings on shore—His physician, Doc. [Edward] Cutbush, has been under serious apprehension of alarm for him, and, it seems, is not yet wholly relieved from them. It appears to me very improbable that he will be able to keep the sea this winter—And, I much fear, will not have sufficient health to transact the business necessaryly preparatory to operations of next spring and summer—Much is to be done which requires health and assiduity.

But despite the delays and uncertainties, the Commodore had been won to the Hamet project, temporarily, to a greater degree than Eaton suspected.

There appears to be no precise statement by Barron of his plans (most of Samuel Barron's papers were lost when fire destroyed his home at Hampton, Virginia), but on November 7 Richard Farquhar, an English resident of Malta who wrote frequently in the interest of both Hamet and the American cause, confirmed to Barron that, by the Commodore's instructions, he had informed Hamet's consul that aid was coming. Barron would send a vessel to Alexandria with powder, money, and assistance. The *Argus* on that date was burying a smallpox victim at sea and sending ten marines and six seamen to the hospital ketch infected with the disease. The loss of these marines from the *Argus* force would be felt severely. By November 10 Hull had orders from Barron to take Eaton to Alexandria.

But the aid which was to be given Hamet had simmered down to scant help indeed. In the end it was left to the resources and discretion of Master Commandant Isaac Hull, who happily was of the fighting type but had a small force available on the *Argus*. Barron told him that upon his arrival in Egypt "if it should be found necessary" to furnish any stores, ammunition, or money to Hamet, "you are hereby Authorized to supply Mr. Eaton with such as may be wanted for that purpose, and can be spared from the *Argus* . . . taking his receipts & Vouchers for the Same." Eaton went on board the *Argus* November 14 and she stood out of Syracuse harbor that evening under light winds. Ralph Izard, Jr., commanding the *Scourge*, watched her go. The generous Sir Alexander Ball sent Eaton letters of introduction to the British consuls at Alexandria and Cairo, "who will have great satisfaction in any occasion of being useful to you." Sir Alexander's letter to Samuel Briggs at Alexandria explained that Eaton was going to Egypt "to transact some affairs of a temporary nature for his government." A similar explanation went to Major E. Missett at Cairo.

From Malta, where the *Argus* stopped, Eaton sent a letter to Barron explaining why he was not taking Hamet's consul Bufuttil with him, the reason: "there is too much wood about his head and beef about his ancles either to advance or retreat handsomely." Eaton now elucidated for the Commodore a new phase of the plan. Barron's idea was that Hull with the *Argus* should pick up Hamet and his followers and transport them from Egypt to the shore of Tripoli, land them, give them aid and let them conquer Bashaw Yusuf by force of arms and popular uprising. Eaton now was thinking of a possible land expedition. If, on Eaton's falling in with the friendly Bashaw, Hamet could raise a sufficient force to march across the desert and take Bengazi from the rear, Eaton would accompany the expedition. His hope was to capture the Bey of the Derna beylic, one of whose wives was Bashaw Yusuf's favorite sister. He apologized for not calling on Barron and taking leave, saying he had tried twice to find the Commodore's house in Syracuse but had fallen to the right on one trip and the left on the other. A third try for the middle was prevented by the sailing of the brig. Barron was gingerly on record, and one wonders about the diligence of Eaton's search for him. There seemed always a possibility that Barron might call off the entire project.

They reached Alexandria November 26 with a heavy sea setting on the shore, and in better weather the next day entered the harbor, saluted the Admiral's flag flying on a Turkish frigate, and the commandant of the town, both of whom replied. Egypt at the time was in a state near chaos. Though presumed to belong to the Ottoman empire, the country had been in the last few years the tramping ground of French and British armies, then had passed in large measure from the control of the Porte to that of the Arnaut Turks, essentially Albanians, and the Mamelukes. France had been ousted by the British and they in turn evacuated their army in 1803 and the conflict now rested between Mohammed Ali, leader of the Albanians, who would rise slowly to rule Egypt for nearly four decades, the Turks, and the Mamelukes. The last were embittered by the treachery of the Turkish leaders in attacking and killing many of their leaders after inviting them to a social engagement on the Admiral's flagship.

At the time of Eaton's arrival the shifting fortunes and the excesses of the conflicting parties plagued Egypt more than did an inadequate inundation of the Nile, followed by a scant harvest. Food was difficult to obtain. Starvation was a menace about as real to the Nile dwellers as in the seven years of famine. Eaton on arrival described it: "Nothing can be more fluctuating and capricious than the government in this Country, except the disposition of the slaves over whom it dominates."

On arrival at Alexandria, Eaton and Hull waited on both the Turkish admiral and the English consul. The Turk treated them to sweetmeats and coffee and the commandant of the town, a Turk, was equally hospitable. "In fact," wrote Hull to Barron, "every body appears happy to see us, the people of the country, the Consuls of the different Nations, *French* and *Spanish* excepted." Neither the French nor Spanish consuls paid the *Argus* the courtesy of hoisting their flags when the brig went in—the first American warship, it seems, ever to enter that port. Neither did these consuls call, though all others did. The friendship between the English and Americans was having its very decided reaction on representatives of the French and their Spanish allies in Egypt.

At Alexandria the Americans were advised that Hamet had gone up the Nile a considerable distance above Cairo and joined the Mamelukes, taking a handful of his Tripolitan followers with him. The situation presented the greatest embarrassment because the Mamelukes were fighting the Turks and had been driven up the river, and how Eaton was to extricate a portion of their army under Hamet and bring it back to the *Argus* at Alexandria, passing through the Turkish and Albanian forces which Hamet presumably had been fighting, was a problem that taxed even Eaton's resources.

He set out for Rosetta on November 29, having in his party Farquhar, an Englishman from Malta; two midshipmen from the *Argus*, George W. Mann and Eli E. Danielson, his stepson; and finally a composed, twenty-nine-year-old Virginian, First Lieutenant Presley Neville O'Bannon, of the Marine Corps, whose family was a century removed from Tipperary County, Ireland, and had been embraced as early settlers in the heart of Fauquier County in the Blue Ridge foothills. There his mother owned land among the headwaters of a rivulet which would become famous in another war, Bull Run. Back in Winchester he had left his bride, Matilda Heard, granddaughter of General Daniel Morgan.

Undoubtedly Eaton would have failed at the outset had it not been for the friendly assistance of the consuls to whom Sir Alexander Ball had addressed letters of introduction. Eaton found Major Missett, who had moved to Rosetta from Cairo, to be a "frank, open hearted, generous soldier" and disclosed to him without reservation the purpose of his mission, and Missett did everything he could to help the American in it, notably in making arrangements for his passage up the Nile.

They chartered a *marche* at Rosetta, the particular type of craft used on the Nile, and set our for Cairo—Eaton, the Marine lieutenant, the two midshipmen, Farquhar, a Janissary named Selim Comb, and a dragoman named Alli, along with six servants, all well armed; and in another boat escorting them, the British consul's secretary, Captain Vincents, and Dr. Francisco Mendrici, a member of the British mission in Egypt and chief physician of the Turkish viceroy in Cairo, whom Eaton had known when the doctor was serving as chief physician of the Bey of Tunis. Eaton commented wryly that he had been expelled from Tunis for lack of congeniality with the Bey, while Dr. Mendrici had been expelled for too much geniality with the Bey's wife.

The escort boat was prepared against river pirates or "the predatory attacks of the wild Arabs" who infested the banks of the river "during this general suspense of justice." Government in Egypt was indeed impotent outside the cities. They mounted two swivels and had muskets, pistols, and sabers, and about the same number of servant retainers as accompanied Eaton. The first *marche* flew the American flag, the second the British.

Eaton was now embarking on one of the strangest and boldest adventures of American history. British Consul Missett, having heard in advance of the American's coming, had already written Hamet about it but the problem remained to gain the assent of the Turks to get in touch with him and proclaim him the rightful Bashaw of Tripoli. Sailing tranquilly along the beautiful Nile in early December, they reached Bulac, just downstream from Cairo, on the 7th, near where they saw a predatory band of Arab marauders strip a village of its camels, buffalo, and cattle amid the shrieks of the people. Eaton's party sent up fusillades of musketry aimed ostensibly at great flocks of ducks nearby, and this formidable firepower dissuaded the Arabs from attacking them, though the bandits did stop and rob several boats which followed. Eaton found an almost universal prayer among the villagers for the return of the British and the restoration of order to Egypt.

Eaton in his best Dartmouth rhetoric wrote Sir Alexander Ball a graphic description of this river voyage and the despair of the people over the war and factional strife. "Grand Cairo," he said, "differs from the places already passed only as the presence of the tyrant stamps silence on the lips of misery with the seal of terror. Pale Wretchedness and dumb melancholy stalk here! . . . Egypt has no master, though the most frightful despotism. The Turkish soldiery, restrained by no discipline sieze with the hand of rapine, everything for which passion creates a desire."

On the next morning the Turkish viceroy, Kourschet Ahmet Pacha, sent horses and carriages to transport the detail to the Palace, and at 9:00 A.M. the American party entered the ancient city, attended by great crowds brought together by curiosity to see officers of the Army and Navy from the distant republic of the West such as had never been in the city before. Eaton noticed that the onlookers stood "at that respectful distance peculiar to the people of the East toward strangers of distinction." Avowedly the party was a group on a sightseeing visit to Egypt during the winter lull in operations around Malta.

Two days were devoted to receiving state visitors and returning visits. The Viceroy's dragoman brought assurances that it was agreeable to his highness to have them wait on him at the third hour of the night of the next day, an hour fixed because the fast of Ramadan was being observed and refreshments could not be taken in the daytime. Eaton looked about meantime and found Hamet's former Secretary of State Mahmoud and two of his followers whom he termed ex-governors, "destitute of everything but resentment, for every hope had abandoned them." They told him that Hamet "after a series of vicisitude and disasters" had been reduced to joining the Mamelukes and was then being besieged with them at Miniet, a village in upper Egypt. Three thousand Mamelukes were confronted by eight thousand Arnaut and Levant Turks. He still had a few of his followers, which pleased Eaton, but there appeared to be no possibility of gaining personal access to him. Then he would have to be parted from the Mameluke army and Eaton would have to procure for him a firman which would give him free passage through the army of the Turks.

With all the disorder in the country, there was still splendor in the Viceroy's trappings of power. At 8 o'clock on the appointed evening he sent six ornately caparisoned Arabian horses with a heavy escort to the British consulate to convey Eaton's party to the Palace. Captain Vincents and Dr. Mendrici were in their British uniforms. Eaton was not yet in his role of general, an official office from Hamet and a complimentary American title he was to wear for the rest of his life. Ahead of the processions went bearers with flaming torches lighting the dark streets while for a mile and a half the way was "margined with Spectators, curious to see *the men who had come from the new world.*" Guards and grooms were at the Palace gate and a parade of troops was drawn up, while the stairs to the grand saloon were flanked with richly uniformed, well-armed Turks. Nothing Eaton had seen along the Barbary shore touched in magnificence the surroundings of the Turkish viceroy of Egypt, shaky as his power might be.

The Viceroy—"His Highness"—proved to be an affable, companionable, even jolly sort of a despot, interested in affairs, curious about the United States, eager for intelligence about Bonaparte's wars. He took Eaton by the hand, led him to the sofa of embroidered purple damask, and seated him on the luxurious cushions on his right hand, while the others he seated on his left. He inquired about the status of the conflicts in Europe, of the date of American independence, where the country was situated, and how far it extended. Finally by a signal he dismissed his own court attendants except his interpreter, then commented that the coming of the Americans at such a critical time must have other implications than mere sightseeing.

Eaton felt that the best approach was one of utter frankness. Speaking in French, he told the Viceroy candidly what he was up to—the difficulties experienced by the United States in dealing with Tripoli and Bashaw Yusuf's faithlessness, and the progress of the war, not omitting to insert a heavy load of flattery by commending the habits and customs of the Ottoman empire while deprecating those of the regents of the Barbary States. Then he injected a thought which had helped Bainbridge at Constantinople, by touching on "the affinity of principle between the Islam and American religion," both being founded on the supremacy of *one* God. Eaton explained in his Navy Department report the stress he placed on the *one* God, saying "*triune* Christians" should not be startled by the numerical adjective, which was not meant to imply that unity could not "be composed of congregated members." Both religions, he told the Viceroy, "enjoined the universal exercise of humanity: and both forbade unnecessary bloodshed."

Progressing with his story, he said he sought the legitimate sovereign of Tripoli to restore him to his rule, thereby to show the world that the Americans did not unsheath the sword for spoils but to vindicate rights, and were willing to employ any honorable means to prevent a further effusion of blood. The war against Yusuf was falling on the innocent people of Tripoli, "deluded victims of his avarice and hypocricy." The Americans desired to end it by putting the true sovereign on the throne.

At this stage the Viceroy broke in and said he knew Hamet Bashaw, had given him supplies, and approved the resolution of the Americans, but he added that he did not know where Hamet was at the time. Eaton by his able presentation had won him completely. He said he would do all he could to serve a purpose so manifestly humane. But he threw cold water on Eaton's hopes by saying that in case Hamet had joined the Mamelukes, a possibility to be considered, it might change the complexion of things. Eaton forestalled a decision on that point by asserting that an object of distress like Hamet could not be the cause of resentment to an exalted mind like that of Viceroy Kourschet. He brought in that it was Godlike to pardon, not to punish, a repenting enemy.

Thereupon the Viceroy nodded his assent and said he would send couriers to search for Hamet. Writing to Secretary Smith after this interview, Eaton said he had no doubt about obtaining permission for Hamet to embark with his followers, but the embarrassment remained of how to get him away from the Mamelukes without making them suspect treason, which would mean his death on the spot. The Viceroy granted

a firman which would give him amnesty to pass through the Turks besieging Miniet, though he reproached Hamet for joining the Mamelukes
when he heard of it.

Eaton needed urgently to communicate with Hamet, to tell him, first,
that the Viceroy was sending couriers after him; and second, that if he
could free himself from the Mamelukes and keep his head on his shoulders, Eaton could give him clearance through the Turks. He had already
written asking Hamet to mention a favorable meeting place from which
they could proceed to Alexandria and board the *Argus* for Tripoli, but
had no knowledge whether the courier sent from Alexandria had gotten
through.

At this stage an extraordinary stranger was thrown by circumstance
into Eaton's arms; apparently a Mussulman who could speak Coptic,
Arabic, English, and about everything else, including fluent German and
French. He had been in Alexandria shedding one of his wives when he
heard that a party of Americans was in Egypt and that their leader Eaton
could use a good man. When they talked, Eaton swore him to secrecy on
the Koran, never knowing then that this itinerant soldier of fortune could
shed religions as easily as he could uniforms or wives. He was a native
of the Tyrol, now using the name of Eugene Leitensdorfer. Behind him
was a rambling career that would have made the roving of a restless
gypsy band look like the buzzing of a fly in a bottle or the thrashing of
a fish in a minnow bucket. None would have expected that this sun-
darkened itinerant picked off a Cairo street would live for years in
the United States Capitol and sleep and cook his breakfast eggs in an
upper chamber behind the old Senate gallery, or that he would become
chief of staff (in name at least) of what (again largely in effigy) would
be an army of the United States, engaged (and this beyond all question)
in one of the most difficult campaigns ever conducted beneath the Stars
and Stripes.

Because of the novel nature of his duties and the spectacular aspects
of the campaign, Leitensdorfer's past history as soldier of fortune, peddler, dervish, and man of many resources should be related, though only
in outline; for the account, fully developed, would fill volumes.

Leitensdorfer was born Gervasso Prodasio Santuari near Trent in the
Tyrol in October, 1772. In studying in the province schools he devoted
his time uncertainly between literature and mechanics and agriculture,
thereby laying the basis for his versatility. He broke from his parents'
intention that he prepare for the priesthood, quit theological studies, got
married, worked as a surveyor, then entered the Austrian army under
Laudun and Wurmser, fighting the Turks at Belgrade and the French at
Mantua. When Mantua capitulated he deserted and a little later enlisted

under Napoleon under the name of Carlo Hossondo, only to be suspected as a spy. He poisoned his prison guards with opium and escaped to a Swiss village, where he first assumed the name he always bore with the Americans, Leitensdorfer. His mistreated family sent him money and he peddled watches for a season impudently through France and Spain, a deserter from two armies.

Entering Toulon with his wares, he was lured by the prospects of the French invasion of Egypt, served under Menou, undertook agricultural projects for the learned French scientific commission which had accompanied Bonaparte, and since desertion was now becoming a pattern, he quit the French and joined the British in Egypt. Being encouraged by the British officers, he opened a coffee shop for them, prospered, bought a house in Alexandria, forgot his wife in the Tyrol and married a Coptic maiden, and helped to conduct a theater at which the British gave dramatic productions. But when the British army was withdrawn he forgot his second wife and reached Messina broke, there to hearken back to earlier years and under a fresh name became a novice in a monastary of Capuchin friars. He deserted them, too, and sailed for Smyrna, thence to Constantinople, where, being destitute again, he begged a pistol and a deck of cards from a Capuchin and with these is supposed to have made money performing tricks, though one wonders about the part played by the pistol in his rising fortune.

Incidents crowded in on Leitensdorfer in hot haste. The French commander, Marshal Brune, from whom he had deserted in Milan, now turned up as French ambassador to the Porte, so for security he enlisted in the Turkish army and was sent back to Egypt, where he saved himself in a defeat by fleeing to the desert and hiding among the Bedouins. He worked his way back to Constantinople, and being rejected by the Russians and unable to try military service again, and being adept in tricks and conjury, he became a dervish, renounced Christianity, and accepted Islam as the true faith. To manifest his sincerity he circumcised himself with his own razor while the faithful of Allah observed. His name now became Murat Aga, under which he traveled to Trebizond on the south shore of the Black Sea selling small excerpts from the Koran written on bits of paper. He sanctified these papers and greatly increased their value by touching them to the shaved spot on the top of his head.

Here he found the old Bashaw of Trebizond sick and growing blind. Faced with the necessity of prescribing, the new dervish went in boldly with much ostentation, saw that the Bashaw's eyes were inflamed and his body wracked with fever, went through mouthings and display and proclaimed pompously that Allah had decreed the man would be healed. He had caustic lime blown into the Bashaw's eyes in order to "eat the films away," then washed them with milk. Not wishing to be held accountable for the results, he took his rich gifts and hurried eastward, leaving the Bashaw in the midst of a sweat cure, wrapped in blankets and filled with warm liquids. He joined a caravan loaded with goods for Persia, and when robbers beset them and they chose to purchase safe conduct instead of fighting, he overheard one of the marauders telling of how a wandering dervish had cured the old Bashaw of Trebizond of blindness. He decided to go back and was received in state and loaded with presents.

On and on went his wanderings, with nothing exactly suiting him. He fell in with pilgrims and reached Mecca after a journey replete with dangers and escapades, thence traveled to Jedda on the Red Sea, where he dropped his dervish attire and became an interpreter to Lord Gordon, a gentleman Scot on a tour. They toiled through Abyssinia (the modern Ethiopia), Nubia, and other areas, and returned to Cairo, where Lord Gordon gave a grand dinner, entertaining the foreign consuls and gentlemen of the city. Leitensdorfer had charge of the arrangements in the hall, which he decorated with fruits, flowers, leaves, and elegance.

Still, the Tyrolese seemed to tire of everything. He quit the gentleman's service. Going back to Alexandria after an absence of five years, he found his deserted wife in hiding, but she had apparently wearied of him; they separated in law as well as in fact and she married one of her own nationality. He, casting about, learned that Eaton could use a confidential agent. Thus the American was soon to have as his chief of staff a former soldier of the Austrian, French, British, and Turkish armies, but one who had never yet been through a campaign like what they were about to undertake. Once hired by Eaton, Leitensdorfer, whose heart was in adventure and not wives, sorcery, or trimming tables for Scottish noblemen, left on December 20, 1804—on Eaton's directions for him to find the missing pretender to the Tripolitan throne.

The new agent carried a letter from Eaton, written in Cairo December 17, to Hamet, whom he addressed as the Bashaw of Tripoli: "Excellence, God ordained that you should see trouble. We believe he hath ordained also that your troubles should now have an end." He told of the amnesty he had obtained from the Viceroy and advised Hamet to meet him at the house of Major Missett, the British consul, in Rosetta.

Leitensdorfer sped through the night out of Cairo and across the desert by day. He took a single attendant along and outdistanced the Viceroy's couriers. They rode on dromedaries and, as the story was told to Eaton, traveled with the swiftness of the wind, feeding their animals on balls of meal and eggs, sleeping only on the backs of their rolling beasts whose strides Leitensdorfer knew well from his long caravan journeys, until finally they reached the Mameluke camp in upper Egypt. There the sheik in command, impressed with the man's bearing and address, gave them welcome and coffee.

Eaton could not have found in the length of Egypt anyone more adept than his new agent in the art of desertion. While he conversed now and then with the sheik, he arranged with Hamet that he should go out one night with his 150 Tripolitans on what appeared to be a normal expedition or reconnaissance and simply never come back to the Mameluke camp again.

That is the way it happened. Over the shifting sands, their tracks obliterated by the winds, they marched toward the meeting with Eaton. The Turkish viceroy had been told by one of his young scouts that Hamet had 20,000 Barbary Arabs at his call. This was a disturbing number, but when the ruler learned that Hamet was approaching with a scant force, reported to him as consisting of a suite of forty, he called Eaton to him, praised him for his frankness in the discussions, and gave him a good meal.

Hull had written to Eaton on December 16 that he was holding the *Argus* at Alexandria, hopeful of the success of Eaton's project. "Tell Mr. O'Bannon all his shipmates are well and very anxious to hear his description of the Nile," Hull added, not knowing some of these shipmates were in for adventures with their lieutenant ashore more desperate than were likely to be found along the Nile, infested as it was with bandits.

Hull wrote to Barron on December 23 saying he expected to be ready to sail by January 10 or 15, 1805, but would have to remain until the uncertainty about Hamet's whereabouts and intentions was resolved. Already Hull was out of funds and Eaton was calling on him for credits to push Hamet's cause. Then Hull, one of the capable men of the fleet and no slouch on boldness, gave his opinion about the project Eaton had been discussing: "The plan you have formed of taking Derne, I think rather a Hazardous one, unless the Bashaw can bring into the field from Eight hundred to one Thousand Men, particularly as we are destitute of every article necessary for an expedition of the kind."

Hull was willing to grant him that a small force could capture and hold Derna but an army, even a small one, must have supplies and these were beyond his power to give. "I think the most we can do, is to get the Bashaw, make as many friends in this Country as possible, and make the best of our way to Syracuse, get some little addition to our force, and make arrangements for our being supported, when we have got possession, and set off anew for Dern or Bengane [Bengazi] as may appear most proper."

His was the practical view, though he conceded Eaton might have information in Cairo he did not possess. But he returned to this assertion: "I say as I have said before, that I do not see that anything more than getting the man can be done—should we be fortunate enough to get him, I think it will be doing a great deal." With only a little vessel, without friends and without authority to act, he could see no prospects. At Rosetta, whence he went from Alexandria, he left Eaton's trunk and small sword, plus articles for others in the party. He had put $1,000 at Eaton's disposal and in answer to a request for four or five thousand more answered "god knows where we shall get it."

Eaton himself was growing concerned waiting in Cairo. He reported to Hull by letter December 29 that he had heard no word from Hamet, and feared his messages, sent by different routes, had not reached him. Farquhar and Purser Robert W. Goldsborough of the *Argus*, who had joined Eaton, had a quarrel over the tally at a game of billiards, which progressed to a fist fight in which both got black eyes. "Good God!" wrote Eaton, "when will our Young Men learn the weight of respect which ought to attach itself to Uniform and Sword."

Eaton now experienced one of the most difficult periods of his career, pressed on the one hand by Hull, who wanted to return to Syracuse with the *Argus* in a reasonable time, baffled in his efforts to gain personal contact with Hamet, hampered at almost every turn by a sinister, behind-the-scenes influence which both he and Hull suspected to be French intrigue, and dealt with capriciously by the Turkish provincial governors and Arab sheiks, none of whom was prepared to recognize the prerogatives of another.

Back in Syracuse Barron was believed to be on the point of death from his liver ailment and Rodgers was conducting the blockade. But in early January the Commodore showed improvement, and by January 17, 1805, he wrote Lear saying "the long and painful illness which I have suffered and under whose effects I am still laboring" would explain his recent silence. Preble had returned to the United States and Lear, whose main aim was peace on presentable terms, but mainly peace, was left in virtual charge of American policy in the Mediterranean. His views and Eaton's were far apart.

Both Eaton and Lear assumed authority easily and accepted as much as they could get. Eaton's personality was dominant, often arrogant when he was trying to forward his plans, but not out of hauteur or supercilious self-esteem. He inclined toward a ruddy complexion which was accentuated in his late years by intemperance, though drinking never appeared to be a problem for him in North Africa. Among his striking features were his large, expressive, penetrating blue eyes that reflected authority, or as quickly, when that was the mood, impatience. He had a large mouth but lips that were not protruding, and his forehead retreated above the eyes, then rose craggily. This last feature is not shown with any emphasis in his profile portrait, but one gets a hint of his strong countenance possessing vigor and the ability to command.

Eaton was protected to an extent by having his agent Leitensdorfer with Hamet, but he did not yet know that the Tyrolese or other of his messengers had got through. On January 8 he wrote Hull that he was preparing to leave Cairo to put the "experiment" to a test—this being his method of telling Hull he was going to abandon his base at Cairo and go in search of Hamet personally. But later that morning a message came from Hamet at last, saying he had been disappointed in the delay of the Americans with help, which must have been for good cause; that he was leaving at once for Behera; and that he was still Eaton's friend just as he had been back in Tunis. Eaton, elated, wrote Hull by special courier. The ship commander was beginning to suggest that he should sail while Eaton completed his arrangements, and then return, because "it will certainly be improper for me to remain here while you work out the experiment." The Commodore would begin to wonder what had happened to the *Argus*.

Now that contact with Hamet had been established, the problem arose of Hamet's progress, which would have been blocked completely had it not been for the good offices of the two British consuls, Briggs and Missett, an assistance which still accounted for the hostility of the French, who spread rumors that Eaton and his Americans were simply British spies. At length, as Hamet came down from upper Egypt, Eaton went back to Rosetta and then Alexandria. An impulsive man, and badly in need of cash, his attitude in the midst of an impoverished people crushed down by despotic little chiefs and pillaged by raiders might be seen from an incident at Damanhur, where at the end of January he was waiting for Hamet. A boy of eleven whom he described as beautiful came to the house of the Americans and looked in sadly. Eaton found it had been his house but that his father, being one of the wealthy men of the village, had been plundered of all his possessions by the local chief, then had had his head cut off. The boy, his mother, and five other children were starving a few houses away. Eaton was so touched that he emptied his pockets, giving the lad every cent he had. The boy kissed his hand and wept. That night Eaton entered in his journal, "God, I thank thee that my children are Americans!"

Eaton's low acquisitive instincts were explained by a line in a letter to his wife: "There is more pleasure in being generous than rich." That was a principle he followed through his career. What money he made he gave away paying ransoms and the like. Then he added a thought which has recurred frequently: "Man wants but little, and not that little long."

Hull had sent to Eaton a business representative, John Severac, whom Eaton had introduced to the Viceroy at Cairo. He returned with Eaton, bringing a beautiful sword, worth $200, to Hull. The Viceroy had made a similar present to every member of Eaton's Cairo party. The genial despot remained pleased with the Americans and held to his amnesty for Hamet when it was being challenged by governors and sheiks all along the line. Eaton had done a good selling job with the head man of lower Egypt.

While he waited he bought horses and tried to enlist volunteers. His recruiting activities were checked by the Turkish authorities, who claimed their good soldiers were deserting to enter the American service, and Eaton and Hull had to release those already obtained. Reports of the size of the force Hamet was bringing changed with every wind; it ranged from several thousand down the scale to a realistic forty. Eaton learned that when Hamet left the Mamelukes, thirty Arab chiefs were put in chains to prevent them from following him. Prospects appeared bright that a good force could be assembled. Finally at Damanhur Eaton and Hamet were reunited. Three of Eaton's messengers failed to reach him. They had been arrested and sentenced to death and escaped only by getting their custodian, a renegade from Europe, drunk. Leitensdorfer rejoined Eaton and soon became his adjutant.

Beyond Damanhur Eaton's plans were changed sharply, through the agency of the French. The Turkish admiral at Alexandria positively refused to allow Hamet to enter the city. When Eaton's party reached the passageway between Abukir Bay and Lake Mareotis on February 5, 1805, they were halted by a Turkish guard. The French consul had been to the Admiral and, in Eaton's opinion, reinforced his views with cash. Apparently he did not conceal his attitude. Eaton wrote Secretary Smith: "The french Consul excuses himself for this intrigue, as he does also for the open indignity he has offered our flag, by saying his 'Zeal for the interest of the Emperor will justify his conduct, and save him from reproach.'" Recalling Preble's difficulties with the French consul at Tripoli, Eaton thought it not clear whether Napoleon had a design against American interests or whether his Mediterranean consuls were acting with unwarranted freedom. "But this impediment does not stop our progress," said the undeterred Eaton.

Hamet favored going to Derna by land instead of water—a startling choice because it involved marching across the great Libyan Desert. He thought that if he and his personal suite went by the *Argus* his Arab followers, left on the shore, would lose interest and disperse. Eaton approved his choice to march instead of sail. They moved around Lake Mareotis and took a station eleven miles west of Alexandria. Hamet requested of Barron 100 stand of arms, 2 brass fieldpieces, and 100 marines for the *coup de main* on Derna and estimated that the expedition would cost $20,000.

Eaton had told Hamet in one of his letters: "Do not think about money because the occasion demands heavy expenditure. It is a matter of making war, and war calls for money and men." Hamet on the same day wrote to his minister for money for horses, camels, saddles, clothes, and provisions, saying, "Whoever wishes to make war must spend without thought and take no account of the money." Money was the need and hard to lay hands on.

Eaton negotiated a convention with Hamet by which the intended Bashaw pledged the tributes to Tripoli from Sweden, Denmark, and the Batavian Republic to cover the expedition's disbursements. That provided a little doubtful credit. Another obstacle was a messenger from Bashaw Yusuf to the Turkish admiral beseeching him not to allow Hamet to leave Egypt. The private secretary of the governor at Alexandria, with whom Eaton had tampered, told the Americans confidentially about this messenger, and Eaton summarized the burden of his story about conditions in Tripoli:

"The subjects of Tripoli were getting weary of the war with these new Infidels; they could not learn from their movements, their intentions; and were attacked unaware: The Bashaw believed he could resist them upon his batteries—but if they made a descent with his brother, his people would all leave him."

Eaton (Hamet's followers were now beginning to address him as "General Eaton") at length found that the firman issued by the Viceroy at Cairo would allow Hamet to enter Alexandria, but Hamet declined to avail himself of it. Farquhar, who was sincerely interested in Hamet's cause, laid down certain conditions under which he would accompany the land expedition, "Viz. that Mr. Eaton shall be *more reserve* in his manner of speaking," followed by some others about the size of the army and its equipment. A hopeless condition! None from President Jefferson down to the camel drivers could have bridled Eaton with any sort of reserve.

The adventurous young Englishman, a stalwart in a pinch, is one of the mystery figures of the Eaton expedition. There were two Farquhars, Richard and another variously termed Percival or George, though the naval correspondence treats them as one. Richard was the elder, an English merchant of Malta, and there is a strong supposition that the younger man who accompanied Eaton, probably Percival, was Richard's

son. The confusion results because Eaton accused a Farquhar of pecula-
tion and dismissed him, and yet a Farquhar was one of his most resolute
supporters on the march.

The misundertanding about money seems to have come from Richard
Farquhar's initiative. Eaton charged him with being delinquent $1,350,
or not making an accounting for it, but Farquhar contended he had spent
everything, including some of his own money, in Hamet's cause, doing
recruiting work in Alexandria. British Consul Briggs explained this to
Eaton, and certainly money had to be used in these efforts. He had also
chartered a Greek boat with the intention of bringing Bashaw Hamet's
children from Tripoli to join their father. He intended also to take supplies along the coast to help the expedition, but after the quarrel he
returned to Malta and stopped by Syracuse. There he asked Barron for
an order requiring Eaton to settle accounts with him, indicating he
thought money was owed his way, not Eaton's.

The younger Farquhar who accompanied Eaton was likely the "Mr.
Fahr" whom Hamet addressed as his friend "like my son." How ably he
performed might be seen by Eaton's offer to him of what must have been
the greatest honor the American commander could think of, a recommendation that he be given a commission in the Marine Corps.

Hamet addressed a letter to Barron in which he revealed that he had
appointed Eaton "my General of the Army" and said he had agreed on
a plan of operations; that Eaton had suggested he go to Syracuse to meet
the Commodore but business of the camp prevented it; and that he was
sending his Secretary of State, Mahmoud, to represent him. He requested
powder, field artillery, muskets, and money. Eaton put gold epaulets on
his shoulders, wore a cocked hat with plume, and took on the attitude
of a general.

Finally, on February 19, the expedition which had survived in its formative period enough internal and external difficulties to baffle any
ordinary commander was shaping up. Farquhar had been busy collecting supplies. Recruiting had been halted officially but men were coming
in. On that date, under orders of Hull, Lieutenant O'Bannon, who had
returned some time earlier from Cairo, left the *Argus* with a detail of
marines, six enlisted men and a sergeant. Eaton, who had made final
arrangements with Hull, debarked from the brig in company with Midshipman Pascal Paoli Peck of the *Argus,* who would accompany him.
They had an understanding with Hull that the *Argus* would go to Syracuse and return to meet them at the Gulf of Bomba, on the other side of
the desert near Derna. Instead of the one hundred Marines Eaton had
requested, he received a lieutenant and seven. They were all Hull could
assign from the small force on the brig, and he did this much on his own

responsibility. Recruiting was continued at Hamet's camp eleven miles west of Alexandria until March 6, when the strange little army commanded by General William Eaton and Bashaw Hamet Karamanli—titles dependent for permanancy on the success of the expedition—composed of men of eleven different nationalities, consisting of 300 superbly mounted Arabs, 70 Christians recruited in Alexandria, a midshipman, a lieutenant, and 7 marines, and a baggage train of 107 camels, moved into the desert.

Eaton's novel army—and it was quite clear at once who was in command—was linked together by the weak ties Hamet held over a few Arab chiefs and their halfhearted followers, and by the adventurous spirits of the chance volunteers Eaton's helpers had been able to collect, mostly by stealth, in Alexandria. John Gordon, probably the Scotch gentleman Leitensdorfer had served, sent Eaton his Mameluke saddle, his bridle and accouterments. O'Bannon at once proved his mettle. On March 2 an alarm had spread through Hamet's camp at the approach of an armed Turkish force and the Arabs were on the point of fleeing into the desert when O'Bannon by his "decided conduct" stopped their stampede. The trouble was that Eaton had neglected to purchase the influence of the collector of revenue. A day of effort and the influence of the British consul were required to get the collector's clearance.

Almost on the day Eaton was moving out, Dr. Cowdery in Tripoli reported that Bashaw Yusuf had appointed Hassen Bey, his chief Mameluke, to command an army which would move toward Egypt to protect the eastern dominions of Tripoli. Prisoners from the *Philadelphia* were put to work packing the provisions. The Bashaw accompanied the army, of unspecified size, out of the town to receive absolution and assurances of victory from the holy men. On the same day British Consul Briggs and Dr. Mendrici visited Hamet's camp to witness the formal signing of the convention concluded between Hamet and Eaton. Briggs wrote to Eaton on the day after the march was begun telling him that the elder Farquhar, whom Eaton in a hasty petulance had dismissed, had hired a small Greek boat and would join the party down the coast with provisions. This move Eaton heartily approved but it did not eventuate.

When Eaton took stock of his force at the first halt he found it to include only 10 Americans: the marines, Midshipman Peck, and himself. He had a mixed company of 25 cannoneers, mostly soldiers of fortune, commanded by Selim Comb, his Janissary and interpreter, and Lieutenants Connant and Rocco, about whom little appears to be available except their names. He had 38 Greeks—Christians he had enrolled in Alexandria and who turned out to be staunch troops indeed—commanded by Captain Luco Ulovix and a Lieutenant Constantine. Leitensdorfer served as adjutant and "chief of staff," but there was no staff. The Bashaw's personal following—Eaton called it his "suite"—consisted of 70 men. The parties of Arab cavalry were commanded by Sheik el Tahib, a malcontent, and Sheik Mahomet. The footmen and camel drivers brought the whole number to about 400. The baggage caravan, which moved more slowly and came up in the nights, consisted of 107 camels and a few asses. A doctor accompanied the party but it was not Dr. Mendrici, who stayed behind.

Bainbridge had suggested that a land army of 5,000 should co-operate with the fleet against Tripoli. Eaton had asked for men and munitions from the beginning. Now he was starting out across a forbidding desert waste to conquer Tripoli with an undisciplined little force of 400, the backbone of which was a handful of Greek mercenaries and a lieutenant and 7 marines.

CHAPTER TWENTY-TWO

The March Across the Libyan Sands

THE U.S. Marine Corps was born in 1798, when the act of July 11 authorized that a major, 4 captains and 28 lieutenants be commissioned, and 720 privates be recruited. But the tradition of service and glory which has abided with it to the present day, the soul which has made the corps something to die for and never disgrace, was first breathed into it by the hot blasts of the Desert of Barca in March and April, 1805.

Some spectacular desert marches were in the public mind of that day, much discussed and honored, and in France especially, justly celebrated as events that would be recorded in the history of heroism.

Such had been the story of Bonaparte's general Caffarelli, who, when the French army was debarked in Egypt and before the horses could be landed, had tramped across the desert at night to Alexandria, stumping along through the sand on his wooden leg. Napoleon had used the incident to jest with and inspire his troops: "Caffarelli fears nothing. He always has one foot in France."

Lieutenant O'Bannon and his seven marines did not have any feet in America but they had their hearts in the work assigned to them as a sort of headquarters guard, and the main reliance to get Eaton's motley army over hundreds of miles of burning waste, jutting rock, and shifting sand.

At the step-off, they were a thousand miles from Tripoli, their ultimate objective, and half that distance from Derna, the heart of the most prosperous and productive area of Bashaw Yusuf's dominions, their first aim. Derna was five hundred miles across the Desert of Barca, the northern part of the Libyan Desert—a part, in turn, of the great Sahara.

There was a trace also in their leader Eaton's dominance and driving will which paralleled Kléber's fierce spirit after Napoleon had raised the siege of Acre a few years before. In the withdrawal of the French army with its wounded across the parched desert the litter-bearers mutinied.

The tall Alsatian rushed among them, denouncing them in his high anger: "You think that to make war is to pillage, and rob, and kill, and do all one's pleasure. No, I tell you. To make war is to be hungry and thirsty, it is to suffer and to die, it is to obey." Cowed by his fury, the soldiers of the Republic took up their litters and continued the retreat.

Eaton and O'Bannon and a few other rugged characters had to impart this same kind of lesson about the tough side of war to undisciplined Arab bands devoted to no particular nation and interested in campaigning only for what little money and booty they could get out of it. Eaton and his lieutenant were to learn that in the desert the human being often is less stable than the sands.

Crossing the northern arm of the Libyan Desert even with modern motorized equipment and tractors, jeeps and supply trains is no small military accomplishment and much was rightfully made of it as late as World War II, but Eaton did it with his army partly on horseback and

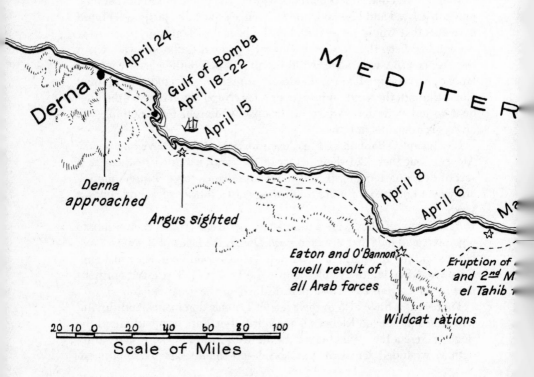

Derna
approached

Argus sighted

April 24

Gulf of Bomba
April 18-22

April 15

MEDITER

April 8

April 6

M

Eaton and O'Bannon
quell revolt of
all Arab forces

Eruption of
and 2nd M
el Tahib

Wildcat rations

20 10 0   20   40   60   80   100
Scale of Miles

Derna

partly afoot, and with a slow-moving baggage train of camels and asses tended by reluctant drivers. A camel had to be slaughtered for meat to supplement the wildcat fare which at one period was the main protein allowance. Lions had not disappeared from North Africa at the time of Eaton's march, the last noted in Tripoli having been killed in 1823, but unhappily none was encountered by the little army, which had to get its meat by chance in smaller portions or do without.

Eaton's time of marching in April and May was advantageous because he escaped the midsummer heat, but it took him into the season of the "winds of fifty days," which customarily blew before and after the equinox. Though the blasts were more sporadic than constant, they were accounted hazardous by travelers and inhabitants of the caravan routes; they blew out of the south and seemed to be accompanied by a murkiness of the sun and a dark, violet cast through the atmosphere. The peculiar, even frightening hue of the air and sky resulted from the particles of

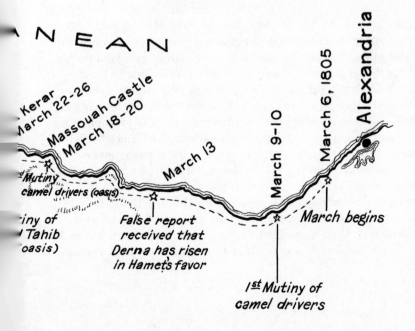

Route of
Eaton's March
with
Hamet Bashaw

fine sand whipped along by the wind, the grains often being imperceptibly small, but penetrating and cutting and affecting the lungs even to causing death.

Sometimes the sandstorms obscured the sun, though Eaton's party does not apear to have encountered any of this violence. The winds whipped up racing columns of sand. Some explorers of that era, notably the Scot James Bruce, seemed to see in them, when they were lighted by the rays of the sun, moving pillars of fire.

The whirlwinds of Egypt, vividly described a few years after Eaton's march by Giovanni Belzoni, Italian explorer and antiquarian, occurred by his reckoning especially at the time of the fifty-day winds. These winds were termed by the desert people the Khamsin (Arabic for "fifty") and were out of the southwest. They raised a great cloud which overhung the country and in that day stopped the caravans and at times the boats plying along the shore. They penetrated everything and even made eating difficult, because the journeyer found that, despite precaution, the sand managed to get into his mouth and mix grittily with the food.

Still, Eaton's main problems were not with nature's unruliness, but man's. Confident and zestful at the outset, and with the most cordial relations appearing to exist through their small force, he and Hamet got their followers into a loose marching order on the caravan route leading west along the Mediterranean shore. Midshipman Peck gave an account of the first day's march. They pushed ahead rapidly, expecting to reach a good well at the campsite that night, but here at the very beginning they found the well dry and no other water within six hours' marching time.

"Here commenced the first of our sufferings," the Midshipman wrote to his father. "After marching near 40 miles in a burning sun, buoyed up with the idea of finding water at the end of our march, we found on encamping, not the least sign of water, nor was a green thing to be seen."

They set to work to clear out the well, though fatigued from the long journey. Some of them must have recalled the story of the foolish virgins. "For myself," said the midshipman, "not having taken the precaution to procure a small skin of water to carry on my horse, had it not been for a few oranges I had, I should hardly have been able to move next morning. I laid myself down on my bed to sleep, but I could not, being for the first time in my life almost dead with thirst."

Their story of the first day was a sample of much worse things to come. The Arabs did not like the prospect and on the second day refused to resume the march. They were disturbed not by lack of water, but lack of money. Eaton had hired 190 camels at eleven dollars a head, presumably for the full journey, but as no time limit was specified, the sheik who owned them thought he should be paid additional sums now and then. Eighty-three camels had failed to appear and the loads for the 107 were heavy. But mainly the Mohammedans put no trust in Christian promises and demanded pay at the beginning instead of at the end of their employment.

Eaton thought he would have it out with them at the start, not yet knowing how irritating and persistent these Arab sheiks could be. He about-faced his men and declared the entire expedition would be abandoned at once and on the spot if he could not get compliance with his orders. The revolters relented. Then the marines collected some money out of their own pockets to put a little more rattle into the army strongbox and the march was continued.

During the delay the efforts of a squad of diggers brought water into the well, but it was "worse, if possible than bilge water." Let Peck continue his unexcited story: "We moved on the 8th and continued our march, by irregular stages, until the 22nd, halting whenever water was to be procured, and frequently suffering very much from the want of it; our only provisions a handful of rice and two biscuits a day, and every day perplexed and harassed by the Arabs for money, who finding us in their power, endeavored to extort everything from us."

Few campaigns in American history—even Morris' two years before—have been more incompetently handled than Barron's against Tripoli in 1805, and the most shocking evidence of it was that Eaton was being compelled to march his little army across the desert without adequate money and with rations of two biscuits a day and a handful of rice, when Barron had plenty of provisions available at his base, a great squadron at his command, supply ships, frigates, brigs, schooners and a sloop, and adequate personnel to man them. No doubt he was the victim of circumstances and of his unfortunate illness and it is not to be expected he could have foreseen all the trials to which Eaton and his marines would be subjected. But the failure was in sending Eaton out to hunt Hamet without the money and manpower to do something when he found him. If Hamet's army were to be the main reliance, as Barron appeared to believe, the American co-operating force still might have been larger than a mere squad, and that gained by the grace of Hull and not Barron. And Barron was showing an utter lack of familiarity with the Barbary War when he thought an attack on Tripoli might succeed without the Americans providing a great deal of stiffening for the assaulting army.

Frequently Eaton was accounted by those of his day, as he often has been in history, a swaggerer deserving of little applause for his effort. Scoffed at by John Randolph and Henry Clay, called jibingly a modern

Alexander or Scipio, his campaign to seat Hamet nevertheless was the soundest advanced for ending the Tripolitan War. Preble could see its merit, and so could Jefferson. Eaton, it has been noted, was not the instigator of a march in lieu of a sea campaign. Hamet had declined to go by ship and desert his followers. Eaton either had to accompany him or lose him; and having his person so as to be able to proclaim him the rightful Bashaw, which he was, was the heart of Eaton's purpose to restore peace without ransom or tribute, a lasting peace on terms favorable to the United States.

Barron could have sent Eaton to Egypt with stronger resources of men and money, confidently and not doubtingly. He should have been sent with enthusiasm or not at all. Eaton was serving without pay and putting every cent of his own money into the venture. The plan had merit on its face. These considerations ought to have been enough to cause a spirited and daring commander to back it to the limit. The proof that it was the superior strategy is seen in the fact that this march of a motley army held together by a squad of marines did more to bring peace than any other factor after the passing of Preble.

By March 10 Eaton was well out into the desert. He moved along the route taken by the conquerers, from ancient days up to the passage of Field Marshal Montgomery's army in the pursuit of the Germans under Rommel in 1943, but he saved time by cutting behind the peninsulas and promontories and was often deep in the desert and far from the shore.

After the first few days Eaton was moving his army at a rate of twenty miles a day without incident worthy to note down in his carefully kept journal. Consul Noah, Eaton's successor, thought the expedition "had more the appearance of a troop of wandering Arabs, with their tents and camels, than a regular organized force." They passed low sandy valleys and rocky plains. About ninety miles west of Alexandria they reached a castle of Greek architectural design. Eaton with his classical education must have recalled, though he did not record it, that Alexander the Great had passed this way 2,136 years before, going to the Temple of Ammon—a march the triumphant Macedonian made in January and early February, when the weather was at its best. Alexander had his sandstorms and thirst but he endured them in the belief that he went on the pilgrimage as a god, where Eaton had to rely for security on the earthly fortitude of a handful of marines.

On this day a courier reached Hamet from Derna and reported falsely that the city had risen in his interest, had shut Yusuf's governor in his castle, and was awaiting his coming. The news caused a wave of elation to pass through the Arab force. Whatever they used for fuel is a question but they managed to light a bonfire in front of Hamet and his suite, then

prance about exhibiting feats of horsemanship, and wasting good ammunition by shooting off their muskets recklessly like so many Western
cowboys of a later day. The celebration had unhappy repercussions. The
foot Arabs who brought up the rear, toiling along with the camels and
baggage, thought the firing meant the caravan was being attacked by
desert tribesmen. Their first reaction was not to go to the help of the forward party under attack, but to turn on the few Christians with them in
charge of the rear, and try to disarm and kill them. Any emergency
seemed like a good time to kill Christians. But one sensible Arab told
them they had better first find out what the firing was about. The entire
army, still lifted by the false tidings of an uprising in its favor ahead,
camped that night on the seashore near many wells cut to great depth
through solid rock, and pouring forth water which Eaton rated "a pretty
good quality."

They had water but they were short of food. Had it not been for the
careful guard kept by Eaton and O'Bannon over the provisions, the army
would have eaten itself bare of rations in the first few days, and then
starved, just as countless others had starved along this barren desert
shore.

By March 14 Eaton had advanced to a ridge which he judged to be
the dividing line between Egypt and Tripoli. He consequently looked on
himself after that date as an invader. The route had led past ruins of
ancient forts and over another rocky, barren plain. Before him stretched
the vast desert of Libya. The army marched twenty-five miles the next
day and camped in a ravine where rain water had been captured in great
natural wells cut out of the underlying bed of rock by cascades that
gushed to the sea during the rainy season. High winds—not those from
the south announcing the Khamsin, but bold winds from the northwest
accompanied by rain and heavy thunder—kept them in camp for a day,
then drove them from it to higher ground. The idleness permitted ideas
to form in the minds of the disgruntled Arabs, who again refused to move
without money and money was scarcer here than water. Promises had to
suffice and Eaton was generous with them, and emphatic enough in
this instance to have them accepted.

By March 18, after the army had been out twelve days, they reached
Massouah, a castle which appeared to be the principal remaining splendor of a city that had perished long ago. It had reigned in its splendor
over an extensive plain cupped with hills. Those to the north, being of
drifted sand, rose to great height and obscured the view of the sea. Eaton
surveyed the scene of ancient grandeur: the traces of gardens, mansions,
and what he termed "pleasure houses," and evidences of fields and
meadows suggesting that the area had once been productive of grain.

The desert had reclaimed it all except a few patches of poorly tended barley and wheat. The castle, a roughly constructed building occupied by the tribal sheik, was the community center for a few families scattered about the plain, and served also as the storehouse for their produce. Eaton found food for sale—cattle, sheep, goats, fowls, skins of butter, dates, and milk—but the price was high indeed for the purse of his near-destitute orphan army.

The crisis here was again over wages more than food. Hamet had employed his Arab carriers to go only as far as Massouah, and although Eaton had put up the eleven dollars a head for the camels presumably for the entire journey, the drivers looked to Hamet as their chief and told him the families they had left in Beheira required their attention more urgently than he did. Sheik el Tahib, who missed few opportunities to foment discord, upheld the camel men and for the better part of the day they remained adamant. No persuasion seemed likely to induce them to go on to Bomba.

Finally Eaton prevailed on them to continue for two days until he might hire another Arab caravan to replace them. They agreed, but for cash on the line. Eaton took all the money he had remaining except three Venetian sequins, worth about $2.25 each. Then he borrowed what was left in the pockets of the Marine Corps members, the Greeks, and other Christians, and raised a fund of $673.50. This was about all the money the army possessed which the Arabs had not already exacted from him. He gave it to Hamet who gave it to the caravan chiefs, and they in turn agreed to continue for two days.

Faithless indeed was their promise. That night all but forty stole away for Egypt and those who remained declined to move forward. Hamet suggested that the army leave its baggage in the Massouah castle and then camp with different tribes as they marched ahead, but Eaton felt that since he was now destitute of cash, it would not be well to march ahead destitute of provisions also. On the following night the forty camels whose drivers had remained steadfast pulled out for Egypt. They left through the connivance of Sheik el Tahib, Eaton discovered, and he even began to suspect the irresolute Hamet of wanting further resources of men and money before moving farther into his brother's realm.

One thing which alarmed the Arab force was a pilgrim journeying from Morocco to Mecca, who had come through Tripoli. He told what was essentially true, that an army of eight hundred cavalry and numerous foot was on the march from Tripoli to defend Derna. The numbers may not have been exact, nor was his information true that this army, which Dr. Cowdery had seen leave Tripoli, had already reached Bengazi.

The reactions of the two leaders showed their innate characteristics. Hamet thought the news should cause caution and delay. Eaton insisted that, if true, the intelligence was all the more reason why they should hurry ahead and capture Derna before Bashaw Yusuf's troops got there. But the sheiks talked and eventually concluded that they would stay in camp until a runner could go to Bomba and return to make sure the promised American vessels were awaiting them.

The fervent Eaton, angered at the indifference of the Arabs and Hamet's listlessness, decided to hit them in the only vital spot where he could, and cut off their rations. He prepared to barricade his faithful marines and Christians inside the Massouah castle until he could get word to the ships and summon a larger detachment of marines to their relief. Then he would extract his staunch supporters and leave the Arab tribesmen and their sheiks to make their own way out of the desert.

He served notice of this intent on Hamet and the chiefs at a meeting held in Hamet's tent, which must have been stormy and quite evidently was protracted, because it was after midnight before the American commander returned to his own tent to reflect. Never at a loss for words or the energy to get them on paper, he set down his feeling at that hour in his journal:

> We have marched a distance of two hundred miles, through an inhospitable waste of world without seeing the habitation of an animated being, or the tracks of man, except where superstition has marked her lonely steps o'er burning sands and rocky mountains, whence the revelation of one of her most hypocritical fanatics trains her wretched victims a tedious pilgrimage to pay their devotion at his shrine. But while we reproach the imposter we cannot but ascribe some good to the effect of the imposition: it has here and there opened a water source to its votaries, which now allays the thirst of pilgrims, bound across this gloomy desert on pursuits vastly different from those which lead to Mecca; the liberation of three hundred Americans from the Chains of Barbarism, & a manly peace.

Eaton was a man without tolerance, but so it is with zealots. While tolerance was one of the warmest of Jefferson's attributes, it was not a common possession of either the leaders or the ordinary run of people of that day. Neither side had much of it in this war. At about the time Bashaw Hamet's Arabs balked, Bashaw Yusuf was receiving pleasant news in Tripoli. He told Dr. Cowdery he had heard his elder brother Hamet was dead. "He seemed highly pleased at such news," Cowdery observed. But to solidify his position Yusuf brought in from the country the sons and dearest friends of the chiefs in the outlying districts. He held them hostages in his castle to guarantee fidelity to him against Hamet.

Eaton, stonily adamant, won over the vacillating chiefs and on the day after the midnight meeting fifty camels came back to the camp prepared to continue the march for two days more. The army did not move until 11:00 A.M. and covered only thirteen miles that day.

Bashaw Yusuf had heard also that Commodore Barron was dead but the day he was telling Dr. Cowdery about it, and on which Eaton was winning this latest brush with the Arab chiefs, Barron, far from dead, was writing Eaton a letter. The *Argus* had reached Malta, and Hull had given him the reports. Eaton was not to receive the letter until three weeks later but it contained pleasant passages of commendation for his perseverance in hunting and finding Hamet. Barron said he had not lost a moment in arranging to send relief. Hull would go to Bomba with supplies and $7,000, which would be placed at Eaton's discretion. The *Argus* would be accompanied by a sloop. Barron did not name her, but she proved to be newly arrived from Baltimore, the *Hornet,* as trim a vessel of her type as the Navy possessed. Lawrence later would win fame with her in his spectacular defeat and destruction of the *Peacock,* the ornate show-ship of the British navy. John H. Dent, who commanded her for a time in the Mediterranean, would say that she was "one of the finest vessels of her class in any service."

Eaton would have ships, food, and money, but nothing in the long letter promised any more marines to augment his woefully small army. He was warned that if he encountered unexpected difficulties which made his success precarious, he should not commit the supplies and money out of his control. About this Barron wrote: "Indeed in the point of view in which I regard the measures already pursued as well as the subject of cooperation [with Hamet] generally, I conceive you ought to tread with the utmost circumspection." Then Barron tried to give Eaton some advice about how campaigns are won and lost. He doubted Hamet's character and the advantages of the convention Eaton had made with him and withheld approval of any agreement committing the United States to place him on the throne.

Whatever Barron may have thought of the elder brother, and questions about him were beginning to multiply in the Commodore's mind, Hamet was as redolent as a lily of the valley compared with the stench emitted by the faithless and tyrannical usurper, Bashaw Yusuf. Still, he emphasized in this letter that no engagement with Hamet should be allowed to stand in the way if favorable peace terms with Yusuf could be obtained. With a good many promises made to Hamet over a period of years and with Hamet already in the field, with a sort of motley army to be sure, but still the best he could summon forth, it was late in the day to be telling him that the United States would leave him high and dry if it had a chance to negotiate a satisfactory treaty without him.

Yet, that was the point stressed by the Commodore. Hamet could not stand in the way of any "terms of accommodation which the present Bashaw may be induced to propose," said Barron. "Such terms being once offered and accepted by the representative of Government appointed to treat for peace, our support of Hamet Bashaw must necessarily be withdrawn."

Jefferson had given Barron full discretion over Eaton's movements. Still, it is not to be supposed that the government, in this first play of the United States in the affairs of another country, would want Hamet used and then cast aside like an old shoe, as Barron intended.

Perhaps the most revealing line of Barron's letter was: "If by your energy and exertions added to the supplies now sent forward, you succeed in getting possession of Derne & Bengazi . . ." Did not the Commodore recognize that a few more marines would be of immense help? The marines could play little part in any bombardment of Tripoli by the ships, if Barron ever got around to that. But they could add highly useful bayonets to the resolute little army—resolute as far as Eaton's own part of it was concerned. Instead of thinking of reinforcing Eaton, although some recruiting work had been carried on by Captain John Hall of the Marine Corps in Catania, Barron was thinking of recalling the lieutenant and midshipman he already had. Barron took this attitude:

"I beg leave to mention to you that as we are short of officers the services of all will be called for on board the respective ships as soon as we enter upon offensive measures. Should you conceive however that any serious disadvantage may result from withdrawing those with you, I have no objection to their remaining as volunteers, but it is impossible for me to comply with your requisition for one hundred marines to be sent to the coast."

He did say he saw Eaton's need of field artillery, which could not be procured where he was, but he had sent the *Congress* to Messina in hopes of obtaining four fieldpieces which might be sent to the coast. Barron wrote to Hamet at the same time telling about sending the supplies and looking for the field artillery but making no mention of what he emphasized most to Eaton, that if the United States made peace with Yusuf it had no responsibility for Hamet.

In giving Hull his orders, Barron told him to learn the posture of affairs, and the prospects of success and land the provisions. "Should it be determined to persevere, you are authorized to afford him every support & assistance, consistant with your means and situation." Still there was no order about landing seamen or more marines. Barron expressed a desire to keep closely informed and apparently told Lieutenant Samuel Evans, commander of the sloop *Hornet*, to accompany the *Argus* mainly for purposes of communication.

The *Argus* loaded a good assortment of supplies for Eaton's army, including thirty hogsheads of bread, twenty barrels of peas, ten tierces of rice, a hogshead of brandy and two of wine, one hundred sacks of flour and, of equal importance, seven thousand Spanish dollars.

Meantime, if Dr. Cowdery's observations are to be given weight, Tripoli under Yusuf was becoming a hollow shell of a country which might be pushed over readily by Hamet and Eaton and one hundred additional marines. Yusuf had sent his son-in-law into the country to gather recruits but he found the people refusing to fight because of the Bashaw's heavy demands for money, which extended to stripping the women of their jewels. The son-in-law returned empty-handed. Then it was reported that a muster of ten thousand troops would be held on the beach so the Bashaw could address them and inspire them to fight against the Americans and Hamet. Cowdery went to see the proposed assembly but wrote that "to my disappointment not one of them appeared." The best of the army had marched toward Derna under Hassen Bey.

Eaton was now at a high point on his march, having reached at noon March 22 a great encampment of Bedouins, friendly to Hamet's interests, while about them was a plain described by Midshipman Peck as "spacious and barren," but it must have provided some food because 50,000 head of sheep and 10,000 camels were feeding on it. Eaton gave the Arabic name of the community as *Oak Kerar ke Barre* and placed the number of the tribe at between three and four thousand. They owned "vast herds" of cattle as well as horses, camels, goats and sheep. "We were the first Christians ever seen by these wild people. We were viewed by them as curiosities. They laughed at the oddity of our dress; gazed at our polished arms with astonishment." Eaton found that they were deferential to those they distinguished as officers. They brought goods to sell, including ostriches. Eaton's men had no cash and could only exchange some rice for a few items. The dates had been brought from the interior a distance of five days' journey, and were excellent.

The happy cirmumstances of this halt of five days was that Hamet received substantial reinforcements. Eaton placed the number at 80 mounted warriors who appeared attached to the Bashaw. Later forty-seven tents of Arab families joined the march with 150 fighting men. Here Eaton's and Hamet's horses had good feed and water, though the soldiers were reduced to hard bread and rice. "From Alexandria to this place," said Eaton, "there is not a living stream, nor rivulet, nor spring of water." Using credit, Eaton hired ninety camels at eleven dollars a head to complete the journey to Bomba.

Just when all seemed in readiness for a resumption of the march, Sheik el Tahib excited another mutiny, this time an insurrection of the newly hired Arabs. Winning half of them to his standard, he began a march back toward Egypt, though it would seem at this point that Bomba might be just as easy going. Hamet, concerned, sent a messenger to Eaton asking him to send an officer after el Tahib to "request him" in his name as general to return. Eaton well understood his prerogatives. He sent back word to Hamet that under no consideration would he ask as a favor what was due him as a right. He had paid for the chief's services and was entitled to them. Hamet feared the sheik would turn against them and use his influence for Yusuf.

"Let him do it," said Eaton. "I like an open enemy better than a treacherous friend."

El Tahib, as Eaton told the story, raged and swore vengeance against Hamet and "his Christian sovereigns," as he termed Eaton's Americans. Eaton ordered that the march be begun without him and at 7:30 A.M. they moved, but at noon a messenger arrived from el Tahib saying he would rejoin the army "if the camp halt seasonably." Hamet wanted to stop and await him, so they halted at 12:30 and he arrived at 2:00 P.M., chagrined, according to Eaton's impression, but with the boldness to go to the American tent and boast: "You see the influence I have over these people!"

"Yes," replied Eaton, "and I see also the disgraceful use you make of it."

El Tahib delayed the army so that it made only five miles that day. Eaton now noticed that Bashaw Hamet was again growing reluctant. As he neared the showdown with Yusuf's troops he seemed to think more earnestly of Egypt. Yusuf's forces had "seized on all his nerves." He had loaned horses to some of Eaton's officers for the desert march and these he now reclaimed for assignment to some of his own party who had walked. The parting of the ways appeared at hand, for none could trifle with Eaton. When Hamet drew his followers aside and seemed undecided, Eaton denounced him stormily for his want of perseverance, and demanded the horses be returned to his officers. Angers flared. Eaton moved forward toward Bomba and Hamet started back toward Egypt. Taking the baggage, the little American army with its Greeks and mercenaries of many lands, its dervish adjutant and sturdy little group of marines, continued the march toward Bomba alone.

In about two hours Hamet caught up with them, congratulated them on their devotion to the task of getting him a throne, and tried to explain that he was forced to dissemble his position in order to make his followers manageable. They camped shortly after noon and that night discovered that the Arabs who had joined from the big encampment a few days before had again retreated at the instigation of troublemaker Sheik el Tahib. Hamet sent one of his top officers, Hamet Gurgies, to induce them to return.

While Eaton was marching toward Bomba and Hull was loading the *Argus* with supplies, while Preble was sitting for Rembrandt Peale in Philadelphia and Barron was ever planning to descend on Tripoli, President Jefferson at Monticello, whence he had returned following the inaugural events, was reflecting on the course of the Tripolitan War and laying down some general principles. According to his information from the American consuls, the other three Barbary States were awaiting the outcome of the war with Tripoli as a guide for their conduct. If the United States paid tribute to Tripoli, they would expect the same treatment.

If peace were made, Jefferson believed it would still be necessary to keep a frigate in the Mediterranean to overawe potential enemies or else the market would have to be abandoned. Morris had been sent to try coercive action and had failed. "Having broke him," as Jefferson put it, "we try the same experiment under a better commander." Then he asserted that if in the course of the summer of 1805 the naval force could not produce peace he would recall all except a frigate and two small vessels which would keep up a constant blockade.

"Such a blockade will cost us no more than a state of peace," Jefferson wrote, "and will save us from increased tributes, and the disgrace attached to them. There is reason to believe the example we have set, begins, already to work on the dispositions of the powers of Europe to emancipate themselves from that degrading yoke. Should we produce such a revolution there, we shall be amply rewarded for what we have done."

The important point in the statement was that the Navy would have to win the war that summer or Jefferson would recall it and try to do the patrol work with a frigate and two brigs or schooners. Eaton's expedition became more important because there would be no other land army. Taken with what Barron might be able to do, it was a last chance to humble Tripoli. Whether the American public would have been satisfied with curtailing the war effort instead of fighting it out to a decision was an unanswered question, but it was quite apparently, in the spring of 1805, Jefferson's decision.

Eaton wondered like many others about the circumstances of a country, already becoming a world power, sending as an army mainly a squad of marines to invade a hostile foreign nation. Certainly the blame could not be placed against Jefferson, who had been won to the Hamet proposal. Barron, the squadron commander, either ought to have resigned when he became ill or delegated authority to someone to conduct the war on his own responsibility and free from his approval. Eaton asked later some pertinent questions when he was commenting on the fact that the Commodore was too ill to take part in the expedition. "But was he so destitute of energy of mind as to be incapable of directing its operations, and had he no commander in the fleet to whom he could confide the conduct of an expedition under his own direction?" Eaton went on to say that if he were destitute of these capacities himself, counselors must have had them "and it would have cost them no more exercise of mind to encourage than to derange Plans."

Since the theater of the war had been shifted to the eastern provinces, "Why not then support us there with the means of subsistence and detachments of Marines?" That this would have exceeded the Commodore's authority was ridiculous. "What!" Eaton exclaimed. "A commander in chief without authority to make discretional dispositions of his forces and the means of subsisting them?" As to the marines, Eaton remarked on their zeal and said it did not require greater discretion on the part of Barron to "indulge them the permission to fight at Derne than to furlough them on parties of pleasure at Catania." There was irony in his remark that they could have been subsisted more cheaply on the desert coast than in any port of Italy. Eaton's requirements for more men were not excessive. All he wanted was one or two hundred additional bayonets like those of O'Bannon's. All factors considered, Eaton's march is both one of the most glorious and one of the most shocking of American history.

On March 29, 1805, the day Jefferson was writing at Monticello, Eaton was issuing a Napoleonlike proclamation addressed to the "Inhabitants of Tripoli" and saluting them as "Brothers; Sons of Abraham; true believers of the true messengers of the truth!" While Napoleonic in its effort, the appeal had one marked difference. Napoleon's addresses were succinct; Eaton's rambled on for about two thousand words. He began with the history of the United States and its aims. He denounced Yusuf "the traitor, usurper of the throne of Tripoli, a bloodthirsty scoundrel." He paid his respects to Grand Admiral Murad Reis, "a renegade thief from his youth up and a brutal drunkard." He called on all to rally behind Hamet through whom they could secure peace.

Eaton waited that day at an oasis, and while his proclamation brought in no recruits from the desert wastes, Hamet Gurgies did return in the

late afternoon with the Arabs who had been induced by el Tahib to
desert. The reunited army assembled at 6:00 A.M., March 30, just in time
for one of the major emotional explosions of the campaign. Sheik Mahomet had learned that el Tahib had defrauded him. Bashaw Hamet had
given el Tahib $1,500 at the beginning of the march to be split equally
between the two, but el Tahib, the most treacherous of the party, had
kept the heavy portion. Mahomet, enraged, found three lesser sheiks
siding with him and they all left the camp and moved hurriedly toward
Egypt.

The distressed Hamet, reliant as usual on Eaton, rushed to him at the
head of the column, fifteen miles advanced from the camp with the baggage, which was transported under the Marine guard. Hamet already
had dispatched Hamet Gurgies to try to win back the deserters and he
now decided, after consultation with Eaton, to go himself with an escort
of twelve horsemen and Eaton's dragoman Selim. Eaton halted and
while they were gone gave free play to his wrath in his journal entries:

> This will detain us until tomorrow. From Alexandria to this place
> we have experienced continual altercations, contentions and delays
> among the Arabs. They have no sense of patriotism, truth nor honor;
> and no attachment where they have no prospect of gain, except to
> their religion, to which they are enthusiasts. Poverty makes them
> thieves; and practice renders them adroit in stealing. The instance the
> eye of vigilance is turned from an object on which they have fixed a
> desire, it is no more to be found.

Then he did find some characteristics to deal with less harshly:

> With all their depravity of morals they possess a savage indepen-
> dence of soul, an incorrigible obstinancy to discipline, a sacred ad-
> herence to the laws of hospitality, and a scrupulous pertinancy to their
> religious faith & ceremonies.

He told how he had been admitted as a special honor to the castle they
had passed some distance back and that every Arab in the tribe crowded
about him to touch curiously the lace on his cap, his epaulets, buttons,
spurs, and sidearms. The gleaming articles they took to be gold or silver.
They were amazed, Eaton said, "that God should permit people to
possess such riches who followed the religion of the devil!"

While Hamet was gone seeking the return of Mahomet, Sheik el Tahib
determined to take control. Putting himself at the head of five minor
chiefs, he went to Eaton's marquee and demanded an increase in the
ration, which Eaton refused. When he grew menacing Eaton unloaded
on him a storm of vituperation and anger which made him pause.

The American leader told him he had engaged to bring four hundred mounted Arabs to Bomba in fourteen days, yet now had only twenty-eight men who had been out twenty-five days covering half the distance. The sheik had impeded the progress at every turn.

When el Tahib complained about Hamet and the other Arabs, Eaton told him they were better men than he was. He in turn cautioned Eaton about a revolt: "Remember you are in a desert, and a country not your own. I am a greater man here than either you or the Bashaw."

"Leave my tent," shouted Eaton, "but mark! If I find a mutiny in camp during the absence of the Bashaw, I shall put you to instant death as the fomenter of it."

El Tahib mounted his horse and rode away with the others but the Bashaw's *casnadar*, or treasurer, who apparently had been drawn to Eaton's tent by the commotion, rode after him and induced the lesser chiefs in his following to maintain peace until Hamet's return. In the afternoon el Tahib went to Eaton with profound apologies, which he emphasized by returning three hours later to swear eternal fealty to Eaton and his cause. That night Eaton was deeply concerned because Hamet failed to appear and the expedition was worthless without him.

Hamet rode in at 3:00 P.M. the next afternoon bringing Mahomet and the other rebellious sheiks, whom he had overtaken fifty-nine miles back on the route to Egypt. The Karamanli heir had on this occasion displayed energy and courage, and a resolution which inspired Eaton, for he had ridden all night and all day in a chilly rain and high winds of the Khamsin with nothing to eat except milk and dates given to him by desert Arabs. That night, April 2, 1805, Eaton had a meeting of all the chiefs in his tent, admonished them for their disagreements, and tried to impress on them that their strength was in unity. All pledged their faith to the cause. When Eaton ordered the march the next morning he had an army of seven hundred fighting men, who, with their families and the camp attendants and followers, made a party of twelve hundred, a fairly sizable host to be leading across the desert without a cent of money and with only a meager store of rice and biscuits.

Surely never in American history—in the long and difficult conquest of the West or in the grueling War Between the States; in the toiling advance of Benedict Arnold and Daniel Morgan through the Maine forests to Quebec or Washington's flight across New Jersey; in the tramp of Doniphan's thousand across the waterless sands of Northern Mexico, or anywhere in conflicts which have now been fought around the world —has so long a march been made over worse country or attended by greater hardships than Eaton's, yet never once did he appear to lose confidence in his final triumph.

After early April the progress became increasingly difficult, more on account of shortages than terrain and weather. The very next day after they had pledged their fidelity the chiefs halted until they could send a detachment to Siwah, an oasis five days by caravan, to procure dates. Eaton induced the main party to continue the march and let the date detachment rejoin it at Bomba. Each day brought new problems. Eaton's dragoman, Selim Comb, now a captain, and one on whom Eaton could rely, ran down a wildcat with his greyhound, "color sable, brindled about the body; black ears and nose, and dark brindled tail," but the point to Eaton was "it was cooked, and it eat very well."

Meat was in such short supply that Hamet soon had to slaughter a camel for food and trade another for a sheep. While this hungry little army was living on a meager hand-to-mouth diet consisting mostly of wild fennel roots and sorrel leaves gathered from the desert, reports going to the United States were giving a more attractive coloring to the campaign. A letter from an officer at Malta dated April 5, the day after Selim Comb caught the wildcat, though not published by the *National Intelligencer* in Washington until four months later, described Eaton's meeting with Bashaw Hamet:

> He was received with much attention, and appointed generallissimo by the Bashaw; he is now at the head of about six thousand men on his march for Tripoli, a distance of 1000 miles, he is supposed by this time to be at Derne, a province of Tripoli, about half way from Alexandria . . . The reigning Bashaw is much alarmed . . . Commodore Barron continues very ill yet.

Past the sites of other ancient cities Eaton marched along, covering from twelve to twenty-five miles a day. One expanse of rubble reminded him of the ruins of Carthage. Here one of his officers picked up and presented to him two copper coins with badly effaced Greek inscriptions. A great mountain rose to the west which the Arabs called *Auk bet Salaum,* and the guides said the distance was 150 miles to Derna and 90 to Bomba. He was apparently at the present-day border between Egypt and Libya, at the modern Salum, then the French Cape Luco. He walked along the beach with Farquhar, and though they had no water that night, he seemed satisfied with his situation and the state of his balky army.

Still, the greatest test of his ability to dominate the headstrong Arab chiefs lay just ahead. Two days later, on April 8, they descended the mountain and came to a cistern of good water, and while the men of all ranks and races were refreshing themselves, Eaton went ahead to reconnoiter the route along the seacoast. When he returned he was surprised to find that although it was only mid-morning Bashaw Hamet had ordered that the camp be pitched. The purpose, soon revealed, was that he intended to send a courier ahead to Bomba to make sure American vessels were there before he would march farther. The confidence Eaton had in the army's power was not shared by the presumptive monarch of the realm.

Delay was out of the question because Eaton had no bread or meat remaining, none of what he described as "small rations," nothing in fact except a six days' supply of rice. Hamet insisted his chiefs needed rest, and Eaton replied sharply that "if they preferred famine to fatigue they might have the choice." He ordered the ration supply cut off. The Bashaw packed up and began to move his men on another retreat to Egypt. Eaton, determined to show no concern, let him go. But he soon discovered that the Arab chiefs planned to seize the food supply, and he had a drummer sound the call to arms. The marines, Greeks, and other Christians responded and with them he drew a line in front of the supply tent, while the Arabs drew up opposite them, and for an hour both parties glowered at each other over possession of the food. Hamet, seeing Eaton's determination, induced the Arabs to fall back and pitched his own tent again, and the rupture appeared to be healed.

But Eaton at this stage made a false move by ordering the marines in a display of their discipline to go through the manual of arms, at which the Arabs, not understanding, took alarm, remounted, and shouted that the Christians were preparing to fire. Even the Bashaw had that impression. He put himself at the head of the Arabs, and showed that if the discord had degenerated into actual conflict, he would be on the side of his fellow Mohammedans. Then two hundred Arabs advanced. Eaton said they were "in full charge," but he did not specify if Hamet led them. Whoever commanded them, the line of American marines and mercenaries did not budge. The Arab horsemen wheeled before reaching the Americans, withdrew a short distance, took aim, and someone ordered, "Fire!" But none was quite ready to fire the first shot. Some of the Bashaw's more sensible officers saw the disaster of open warfare and cried out, "For God's sake do not fire! The Christians are our friends."

Eaton was at the front, with O'Bannon, Peck, and young Farquhar alongside him. The marines, the officers of the cannoneers, and the Greek officers stood fast but some of the mercenaries wavered. If he did not always have discretion, he made up for it with a superabundance of courage, and now he marched forward to the Bashaw, in the face of a line of muskets aimed directly at his breast, and warned him not to sanction the desperate mutiny. The irresolute man appeared so distracted he scarcely knew which side he was on or what to do amid the clamor raised against Eaton. Just then a group of more moderate Arab chiefs rode between the mutineers and the Americans, and while they were restoring some order, Eaton was denouncing Hamet for his weakness. His treasurer, a prudent man, asked Hamet if he "were in his senses." What the casnadar intended was anyone's guess, but Hamet, enraged by the train of events and anxious to vent his anger against something, hit him with his naked blade.

In the hubbub which followed it appeared that a battle would still be joined, but Eaton managed to get Hamet dismounted, took him by the arm, led him out of the press of his followers, and asked him if he knew who his friends were. He softened, said he was too prone to anger, gave orders for the Arabs to disperse, and went with Eaton to the General's marquee. The Arabs were, in fact, desperately hungry. Hamet said that if Eaton would issue a rice ration the revolters would be pacified, and Eaton agreed to do so if Hamet would promise to march toward Bomba at reveille the next morning. Hamet agreed and Eaton had the rice distributed.

Eaton was generous in his commendations after the clash: "The firm and decided conduct of Mr. O'Bannon, as on all other occasions, did much to deter the violence of the savages by whom we were surrounded, as well as to support our own dignity of character." When tranquillity had been restored, the Bashaw embraced O'Bannon with an enthusiasm generated by respect and called him "The Brave American," words which Eaton wrote with capitals and underscored in his journal.

A reminder of Lieutenant O'Bannon's sturdy courage remains with the Marine Corps to the present day. Hamet, who came to admire his steadfastness and respect his leadership, gave him when they parted one of the most personal and valuable things he possessed, his jeweled sword. It was a blade he had obtained in upper Egypt and it had a Mameluke hilt. This blade with its Mameluke hilt was to become the pattern for the official sword of the Marine Corps. It is carried by officers on formal occasions today. It commemorates the march of the eight brave marines across the Desert of Barca in 1805.

For long the names of the Marine Corps enlisted men who accompanied Eaton were not known to American history. Though diligent searches were made through the early records of the corps, the quest was unsuccessful until 1952. In that year the names of six of the seven enlisted men were discovered, then verified and published in the November, 1952, issue of the Marine Corps magazine, the *Leatherneck*. They were Arthur Campbell, acting sergeant; and Privates Bernard O'Brian, David Thomas, James Owens, John Whitten, and Edward Stewart. One name is still missing.

At times it is stated that the detail contained only six enlisted men, the sergeant and five privates. But Midshipman Peck said that when it began its march from the *Argus*, on which he accompanied it, it consisted of O'Bannon and seven other marines. This was verified by Eaton on March 8, after he had already moved into the desert. He said nine Americans were in his army, "including Lieut. O'Bannon and Mr. Peck, a non commissioned officer and six private marines." He was obviously not including himself in his count, for he brought the number of Americans to ten.

Uncertainty has remained about the identity of the doctor who accompanied the army. He was not Dr. Mendrici, Eaton's Tunisian friend. Eaton's letter of March 7, written the day after the march was begun, refers to the doctor as though he were present, but the reference is not positive and there is no other mention of him in Eaton's journal of the campaign. There is also some indication in a letter of Consul Briggs that he was left behind. The doctor who did accompany Eaton did not stand as steadfast in this emergency as Eaton would have liked. "My Doctor behaved decidedly like a coward, and a base one," Eaton wrote, with reference to the April 8 incident. That did not seem to fit his old friend Dr. Mendrici.

Eaton paid high tribute to Farquhar, who conducted himself "with manly firmness." Undoubtedly the fortunate outcome of the incident turned on a misfire. An Arab pointed a pistol to Farquhar's breast and snapped the trigger. By chance the powder did not ignite. Had it done so the young Englishman would have gone down and the result would have been a scene of carnage, the likely extinction of the vastly outnumbered marines, and the failure of the expedition.

They marched ahead with fresh trials each day. Mutiny was imminent for a time in the ranks of Eaton's own mercenaries but was quelled by his promise to shoot the first mutineer. Soon thereafter a messenger came dashing in with the heartening intelligence that American warships were at Bomba. Neither food nor water could have been more refreshing to the played-out little army nearing the final stages of its punishing journey on half-rations or less, across nearly four hundred miles already of one of the most difficult stretches of the earth's surface.

Much distance remained to be covered and there were other crises. The Bashaw became ill. Threats of mutiny recurred. The Bedouin foot soldiers became so fatigued and emaciated they had to give up the march. The horsemen reached the Gulf of Bomba at length and were near despair when they looked out over the clear unruffled waters of the Mediterranean and saw no sail. At 4:00 P.M. on the afternoon of April 15 they reached the site of Bomba, once a town, but having no trace of human habitation. Eaton wanted to press on over the remaining sixty miles to Derna but his army was too exhausted to move. That night he had fires built on the hills. Next morning the Bashaw's casnadar went to a mountaintop and saw standing in to the shore a sail. As she came closer, those on the beach could identify her as the *Argus*. "Language is too poor to paint the joy and exultation which this messenger of life excited," Eaton said.

CHAPTER TWENTY-THREE

The Amazing Capture of Derna

ULL arrived with the *Argus* along the coast of Cyrenaica on April 2, 1805, and on the 4th passed within a few miles of Derna without detecting evidence of Eaton's force, then ran eastward along the coast, passed Cape Razatin, and anchored in the Gulf of Bomba hoping to gain intelligence from persons along the shore.

So bleak and uninhabited was this sub-desert land that the officer and seamen who went ashore in the small boat could not find one Arab, and no sign of human molestation except traces of an old encampment eight miles back in the country. There the tracks indicated too small a number for it to have been Eaton's party. On the 9th the boat went ashore again and found its first Arab, whom Hull sent off eastward to find the American party.

Since the gulf did not provide safe anchorage because of the winds, Hull adopted a practice of hauling off and then calling in every two or three days. He wrote a message to Eaton, though it is not clear how he dispatched it unless by the chance Arab, saying he had a sloop loaded with bread, flour, rice, and money, while the *Congress* was hourly expected with fieldpieces.

Barron meantime changed his intention of sending the *Congress* to Bomba. He judged her too heavy to approach the shore and therefore substituted the *Nautilus* under Captain Dent, who had two brass field-pieces with trains, powder, and shot, which Barron directed him to deliver to Eaton as a substitute for the four guns he had expected to send on the *Congress*. Eaton was making his march of necessity without artillery, which he could in no manner have drawn across the desert with such animals as he had available, though he did have his company of twenty-five cannoneers, the mercenaries under Lieutenants Connant and Rocco, intact. Without artillery, an attack on Derna's walls, forts, and batteries would be near foolhardy.

The shore on which the army encountered the American ships was

393

not suited for landing provisions, so on April 18 and 19 Eaton marched around the gulf and found both an "inexhaustible" cistern of water and a good harbor. Before marching this twenty-two miles, he sent Midshipman Peck and Farquhar out to the *Argus* to give Hull the information of where he could be found, because this was a change in plans he had made when on board the brig the previous evening. Probably it was the excitement caused by the presence of these two wayfarers on the ship after their hazardous march which led Midshipman George Mann to petition Hull to be allowed to join the expedition. Eaton had requested him and Hull assented that he should leave the ship. He shared in the final phases of the expedition. He was from Annapolis, Maryland, but long before anyone ever thought of founding a Naval Academy there. Peck was retained on the *Argus*.

Lieutenant O'Bannon, who had been loaned to Eaton at Alexandria and might be subject to recall now that joint land and sea operations were imminent, took precaution against this in a straightforward letter to Hull: "Sir, Unwilling to abandon an Expedition, this far conducted, I have to request your permission to continue with Mr. Eaton during his stay on land, or, at least until we arrive at Derne."

O'Bannon and his handful of marines had given such security on this march of wrangles that it would seem almost necessary to quit the entire land operation should he be severed from it.

After the spirits of the American force and Hamet's followers had been revived with food supplied in such abundance that the desert hardships were all but forgotten, Eaton arranged plans for the joint land and sea attack on Derna sixty miles farther along the coast. Word reached him on April 20 that Mustifa, commandant at Derna, had received reinforcements from Tripoli, but from what Eaton could learn from the Arab who brought the information, he judged the garrison did not exceed five hundred. "We have great need for field artillery," he wrote to Hull. "Besides the terror that Cannon impress on the undecliplined Savages we have to dispute with, they will be our best resort against the Walls of Derne, and surety in case of reverse." He expressed regret that the *Congress* had not arrived and asked for two carronades from the *Argus*, along with muskets, powder, ball, and flints. On April 20, the *Hornet* landed sufficient provisions at Bomba to take the army to Derna.

Eaton requested of Hull that, should his army reach close enough to the town to attack it, the *Argus* and *Hornet* should engage the batteries, which he understood to be poorly built of bad materials and not likely to withstand a bombardment. Then he asserted to the captain of the *Argus* what should have been obvious also to Barron and Tobias Lear, who were getting their heads together on peace negotiations: "I have no reason to alter the opinion long since adopted, of the importance to our affairs which the possession of Derne will have . . . and hitherto nothing has appeared to discourage our calculations of success from the Cooperation formed with Hamet Bashaw."

He could not repress a cynical remark, directed more at the world in general than Hamet's part of it. Hamet's followers seemed attached to his interests, he said, because it was to their own advantage to support him, and: "Notwithstanding their religious scruples and aversions, I find them like the rest of mankind, moved by a present good. Cash will carry them; with this the Gates of Tripoli may be opened."

He expressed hope that Hull would come in as close to shore as the safety of his ships would permit. Knowing that fighting was ahead, he gave directions for distribution of the few effects he had left on board, among them his small sword and Damascus saber, "in case I see you no more." He would fight with a gun instead of a blade. His arrangements made with the ships, he resumed the march toward Derna, and after laboring on April 23 over ten miles up a rocky mountain, came to flowing water on the very top, the first natural spring he had encountered since leaving Egypt.

The aspect of the country began to change. Cultivated fields appeared. The local dwellers must have looked with apprehension on the approach of such a host, for a herald was sent through the camp near the water, crying out this warning: "He who fears God and feels attachment to Hamet Bashaw will be careful to destroy nothing. Let no one touch the growing harvest. He who transgresses this injunction shall lose his right hand!"

Soon the country was covered with greenness. The army entered into a stand of large, beautiful red cedars—"the first resemblance of a forest we have seen in a march of nearly six hundred miles." On the night of April 24 they camped in the verdant valley of a rivulet scattered along which were fields of barley. They were five hours' march from Derna.

Just as Eaton appeared on the verge of winning some reward for his long toiling march across the wasteland, the army was thrown suddenly into one of the severe crises of its sullied history, resulting neither from lack of food nor money, but more from a dearth of fortitude. A courier came into camp from Derna with confirmation of the earlier reports that Hassen Bey's army of relief which Bashaw Yusuf had sent out from Tripoli was approaching Derna and probably would reach the town by forced marching ahead of Eaton and Hamet. The Arab sheiks were seized with "alarm and consternation" while Hamet was overcome with despondency.

Hamet, as was to be demonstrated in the final phases of the campaign, was not a coward, nor innately as hesitant as was at first believed by Eaton, who wrote of this incident in his journal, but he had quite obviously hoped to capture Derna and establish himself in command of that area without the final showdown of battle with Yusuf's army. The reason was less weakness than a concern over his wife and children, who were Yusuf's captives in the Tripoli castle, hostages just as were the three hundred American sailors from the *Philadelphia*, and Hamet was fully aware of the cruelty of which his younger brother was capable. At a time when Bainbridge was writing to Barron that the espousal of Hamet's cause might so inflame Yusuf that he would direct his vengeance against the *Philadelphia* prisoners and slaughter them, Hamet had a right to some anxiety about how his family would fare when he became more threatening to Yusuf's throne.

All night the Arab chiefs and Hamet held their parleys apart from Eaton. They wanted none of the American's counsel, which they knew would be an urgency to press ahead. At 6:00 A.M., indifferent to the parley, Eaton had the drums beat. Immediately Sheiks el Tahib and Mahomet rebelled, put themselves at the head of their Arab horsemen, and started on the long road back to Egypt.

Their defection caused the mass of stray Bedouins, who had attached themselves to the army from time to time, to remain in their tents, which they refused to strike until it was determined whether the army would go back or forward.

Money, even in the barren desert country where it can be little used, can assuage in most cases the emotions of fear and prejudice, and Eaton now had on hand a goodly sum he had received from Hull three days before, entrusted to the keeping of the marines. After much argument and some reproach, he used $2,000 to still the alarm caused by the courier from Derna. One suspects that the fright was self-engendered by the sly sheiks, who were well informed that Eaton now possessed cash where he once had only promises. Late in the morning this last of the mutinies was quelled, the sheiks returned, and at 2:00 P.M. the little desert army reached the shoulder of the mountain set back from the sea, looked out over the verdant coastal plain and down at last on the walls, batteries, and forbidding fortress of the city of Derna, richest and most beautiful of all Bashaw Yusuf's outlying possessions. Alexandria was fifty days and 520 miles behind them.

Much of that 520 miles' expanse was desert; much sub-desert; much indescribable desolation which once had been a populated, thriving Roman countryside, but reclaimed for the wilderness by the shifting sands of nature and the more surely effacing processes of human neglect.

Now that the march was at an end the qualities Eaton exhibited on it could be examined. That he reached Derna without a single casualty among his Christians and none reported among Hamet's Arab followers remains one of the marvels of American history. He was a clearer thinker on the march than around the table of compromise in a diplomatic role. There was no bargaining with the desert. Being a man of direct action was what got him and his army across the sands. He was described by American Consul Noah, who followed him to Barbary, and the characteristics Noah saw in his diplomatic career were in full play on the desert march: "Possessed of a fiery and ungovernable spirit, he obeyed his first impulse. If a Turk insulted him, he knocked him down . . . if the Bey and his officers treated him cavalierly, he retorted bitterly; he maintained a proud and sullen independence, which could not in all cases be judiciously exercised in Barbary."

In all his march he did not truckle once to Hamet or an Arab chief. He never took orders; he gave them, unhesitatingly, imperiously. Clearly he possessed the ability and self-assurance to handle a much larger army if he had had a chance.

Derna and Bengazi, which is 225 miles farther west, were the principal towns of Cyrenaica, the first being the ancient Darnis and the second the Berenice of the Ptolemies, names that recur through the history of antiquity. Derna, when visited by the British naval officer, geographer, and explorer, Frederick William Beechey, who with his brother surveyed this coast sixteen years after Eaton's expedition, was a flourishing center of date groves and irrigated gardens, one of the attractive areas along the hundreds of miles of forbidding shore. The town was set back on a bay a mile from the sea, on a point of low land extending from the mountains, which were the eastern end of the Jebel Akdar, or Green Mountain, bountiful here because the range gushed forth a torrent of water, a river called the Wadi Derna, to the sea. That was the source of Derna's strength and beauty—water.

Derna, often at that time called Derne and so referred to in American naval dispatches and earlier histories, but then, as now, more properly Derna, had been built, like most of the other coast towns thriving at the time of the Barbary Wars, by quarrying from the ancient Greek and Roman ruins. Where the stone came from originally is a matter of considerable speculation. The cultivated land around the town produced melons, grapes, figs, bananas, oranges, greengage plums, and other fruit, the yield, as Beechey found it, being abundant. The fruit trees and extensive groves of date palms gave the town a perpetual shade and made it the most comfortable of any in the Bashaw's realm. An earlier bey had run the water from the mountain stream through the town so that it irrigated the gardens, and at times of freshets—this area was fortunate enough to have a rainy season—inundated the streets. The inhabitants were good Mohammedans in most respects but did not resist the temptation of sipping the delicious wine they made from the luscious grapes grown in this coastal oasis.

From Eaton's vantage point he could look down on the narrow, winding streets characteristic of the old Mediterranean towns, on a beautiful mosque, but of more importance to him, on Governor Mustifa's defenses.

Against attack from the sea the town had a water battery of eight 9-pounders. Temporary breastworks had been thrown up augmenting the walls of old buildings, and these served as defensive positions on the northeast. The houses of the town were utilized as lines of defense along the southeast and along the waterfront. The inhabitants had put loopholes through the walls of houses and terraces—those, at least, who were in sympathy with Bashaw Yusuf, whom Eaton calculated were not more than a third of the population. Governor Mustifa had as his main palace defense a 10-inch howitzer mounted on his terrace. His palace was on the western side of the Wadi Derna, across from the main gardens and the harbor fort.

Eaton made no advance that afternoon. In the evening a number of sheiks from the town rode into Hamet's camp to pledge their fealty and to say that two of the three sections of the town favored his cause, but they brought a word of warning. The governor had a combat force of eight hundred. Being on the defensive behind his batteries and walls, he could not be dislodged easily. The army coming from Tripoli was close at hand. Eaton had been fortunate in reaching Derna ahead of this succoring force. He felt that the one most disappointed by this circumstance was not among the town's defenders, but the very individual for whom all the effort and agony were being suffered, Hamet himself. "I thought the Bashaw wished himself back in Egypt," Eaton wrote that night. But Hamet was in the hands of a tough, courageous and desperately resolute commander, and now that the army was at its objective, Eaton had no intention of allowing him to falter. More than likely he misjudged Hamet, or exaggerated his apprehensions.

While Eaton scanned the town he kept watch also on the horizon. Not a sail appeared on the 25th, the day of his arrival. On the next morning he made fires and sent up smoke columns from the high point of the mountain behind the town. At 2:00 P.M. a sail appeared, then exchanged signals with the shore, and at 6:00 P.M. Eaton and her commander spoke to each other. She was the *Nautilus* under Captain Dent, newly arrived, but not with the two brass fieldpieces Eaton urgently needed. He advised Dent that if the other ships arrived as expected he intended to attack the town in the morning. In the early morning light of Saturday, April 27, 1805, the *Argus* and *Hornet* could be seen standing in to join the *Nautilus*.

The *Argus*, it developed, had transported the fieldpieces. After Hull learned from Dent of Eaton's intent to attack as soon as he had artillery, he had the boat of the *Argus* hoisted and the guns and ammunition put on board to be landed. On approaching the shore the boat crew found that the guns would have to be hauled up an almost perpendicular cliff twenty feet high. With much effort by the detail from the *Argus*, one gun was hauled up the rock. So much time was consumed that Eaton, anxious to begin the action, decided he could not wait for the second piece. While the gun was being landed the enemy appeared in force outside the town as though contemplating an attack, which caused Eaton to order Lieutenant Samuel Evans, commanding the *Hornet*, to stand as close as he could to the shore and give fire coverage to the combination American-Arab-Bedouin army as it advanced.

Eaton had sent on the day before a letter to Mustifa under a flag of truce, demanding access through the town. His summons, brief and direct, said:

> Sir, I want no territory. With me is advancing the legitimate Sovreign of your country. Give us a passage through your city; and for the supplies of which we shall have need you shall receive fair compensation. Let no difference of religion induce us to shed the blood of harmless men who think little and know nothing. If you are a man of liberal mind you will not balance on the propositions I offer. Hamet Bashaw pledges himself to me that you shall be established in your government. I shall see you tomorrow in a way of your choice.

He received a blunt answer. The Bey merely wrote on the bottom of the note: "My head or yours. Mustifa."

Evans anchored the *Hornet* within one hundred yards of the water battery of eight 9-pounders, and at that close range, which Preble would have regarded "point blank" indeed, opened a heavy fire. The *Nautilus* meantime had come in to the east of the *Hornet*, and at a range of a half-mile offshore, opened on both the battery and the town. The *Argus*, farther out and east of the *Nautilus*, opened on the same targets with her 24-pounders. Thus Derna was suddenly brought under the fire of the 38 guns, the *Argus*, 16, *Nautilus* 12, and *Hornet* 10. The battery answered briskly and maintained the exchange with spirit, but the destruction inflicted by the accurate fire of the American ships began to have its effect, and in an hour the waterfront fort was silenced, then abandoned by the Tripolitan gun crews. Most of them ran back into the town and to the gardens behind the terrace walls, there joining the defenders facing Eaton.

Eaton divided his little army so as to approach in two columns, the first, and his main reliance, consisting of the marines; Selim Comb's 25 mercenaries of all nations and the 38 Greeks, both companies under their regular officers; and some lightly armed Arab foot soldiers. This skeleton battalion was under the immediate command of Lieutenant O'Bannon.

The other division consisted of Hamet's horsemen, numbering about 1,000, who advanced on Derna from the south and southwest on the west side of the Wadi Derna and deployed across the plain between the town and mountain. Hamet's sheiks seized at the outset an old castle overlooking this approach, a development which provided Eaton with some security should advance elements of Hassen's relief army arrive at the very moment when he was joined in battle with Bey Mustifa's Derna garrison.

O'Bannon opened his musket fire on the town about 2:00 P.M., April 27, just after the fleet began its bombardment. Only two participants' accounts of the battle which ensued appear to be extant, Isaac Hull's, relating mostly to the fleet action, contained in his report to Commodore Barron, and Eaton's, and both are scanty. But the essential features were that when the three ships silenced the water battery, the artillerists and musketeers who rushed back to join the Bey's forces confronting Eaton, who already was outnumbered, threw the odds heavily in favor of the defenders. These Tripolitans had taken a position in a ravine behind the temporary parapets, which provided natural cover. O'Bannon's men blazed away with their single fieldpiece. At the critical moment, just when the opposing line was being reinforced by the refugees from the waterfront fort, the rammer of the fieldpiece was shot away by the cannoneers-of-all-nations and the firepower of the Americans was severely crippled.

Eaton, in general control, noticed that the musketry of the defenders was warm and increasingly effective. The attacking line, an undisciplined aggregation except for the few marines, was thrown into confusion and he feared it was about to break. At this instant the audacious quality which seemed to distinguish this unusual man came into play. Unable to recognize failure, which now stared at him; unwilling to order a retirement, though many a leader would have done so, he quickly determined that the only way to steady his wavering little force was by boldness. He daringly ordered a charge. He called it "our dernier and only resort." The marines had worn their regulation blue uniforms all

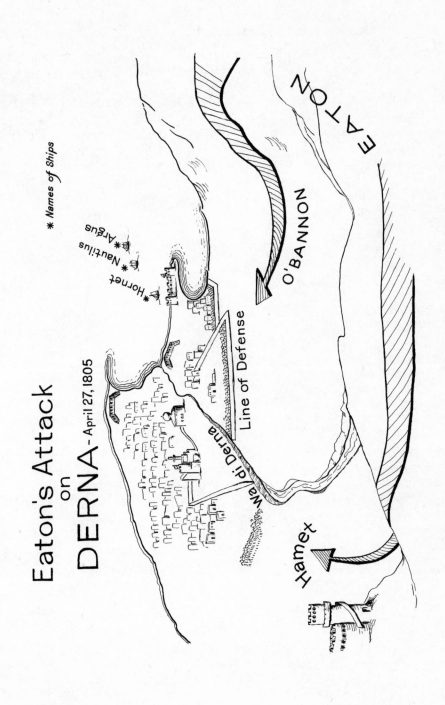

Eaton's Attack on DERNA – April 27, 1805

* Names of Ships

* Hornet
* Nautilus
* Argus

Line of Defense

Wadi Derna

O'BANNON

EATON

Hamet

the way across the desert. Eaton did not specify whether they were of wool or cotton, but the navy blue coat of the time was buttoned across the vest with two rows of heavy navy buttons on each side, and a collar and trimmings of scarlet. They made a striking picture as the thin line sprang forward at the bugle call. As Eaton described the charge: "We rushed forward against a host of Savages, more than ten to our one."

Then what might have been altogether unexpected happened. The army of Bey Mustifa broke. Some of them kept up a sporadic fire retiring from palm tree to palm tree. Most of them ran out of their cover in the ravine or abandoned their loopholes and fled across the Wadi Derna. Eaton, rushing forward with his men, took a musket ball through his left wrist which permanently impaired the use of his arm. He had left his saber and was carrying a more effective weapon, a rifle. His use of the term "rifle" in his report indicates that this newer type of firearm, carried by some units in the Revolution, had been introduced to his little army, though muskets were still the regular issue in the services. The marines, Greeks, cannoneers, and Arab footmen took over the defensive positions the Tripolitans had vacated, then pressed toward the waterfront battery.

Hull, Dent, Evans, and the other officers watching the charge from the fleet saw at 3:30 P.M., an hour and a half after the beginning of the combat, the Tripolitan colors flutter down from the fort and Lieutenant O'Brannon, with Midshipman Mann by his side, raise the American flag over the city of Derna.

Much mopping-up work remained. A surprising discovery was that the gunners had deserted the waterfront battery so hurriedly that they had not taken time to fire a departing shot, though the guns were primed and loaded. O'Bannon's men turned them about on the town and the ships resumed their bombardment. Then Hamet's cavalry units, riding in from the south, cut off the enemy fleeing to the plain and worked their way up to the Bey's palace, which Hamet occupied. As the town was being overrun the ships stopped their fire and sometime after 4:00 P.M. the last of the enemy musketry from the houses and terraces ceased. The city of Derna was won.

The motley little army which had marched upward of five hundred miles across the desert, plagued by mutinies, often without water, living on scant rations and compelled to scatter and dig roots for food, attended by a half-reluctant Bashaw Hamet and by desert sheiks who had little more interest in the cause than the cash it might yield them, driven ahead by the resolution of its dominating leader, had captured one of the most important and certainly one of the most productive and beautiful cities of the Libyan coast; and the main element, apart from Eaton, had been the steadfastness of a lieutenant and seven marines. Truly it was an attack of desperation and a victory of marvels!

When Midshipman Peck summarized it for his father and told of the companionship of desert tribesmen "who would shoot a man for the buttons on his coat," and of the vast stretch of territory behind them on which he thought no Christian had ever before set foot, a tone of amazement was in almost every word:

> Certainly it was one of the most extraordinary expeditions ever sat on foot. We were frequently 24 hours without water, and once 47 hours without a drop. Our horses were sometimes three days without, and for the last 20 days had nothing to eat except what they picked out of the sand. The country was a melancholy desert throughout, and for the space of 450 miles [to Bomba] we saw neither house nor tree, nor hardly any thing green, and, except in one place, not a trace of a human being.

And after such a journey, to have come up to Derna and attacked it without a moment's hesitation or a vast amount of reconnoitering or approaches by regular stages, such as the military conventions of the times demanded; to have charged right in against heavy odds and to have won, was an achievement of which Eaton, the Marine Corps, and the young American republic might indeed be proud.

Whittier, in his poem "Derne," told grippingly of the attack:

> What dark mass, down the mountain-sides
> Swift-pouring, like a stream divides?
> A long, loose, straggling caravan,
> Camel and horse and armed man.
> The moon's low crescent, glimmering o'er
> Its grave of waters to the shore,
> Lights up that mountain cavalcade,
> And gleams from gun and spear and blade
> Near and more near! now o'er them falls
> The shadow of the city walls.
> Hark to the sentry's challenge, drowned
> In the fierce trumpet's charging sound!
> The rush of men, the musket's peal,
> The short, sharp clang of meeting steel!

Considering the size of the three small companies commanded by O'Bannon, the loss was heavy. Fourteen Christians were killed or wounded. Of the seven enlisted marines, one was killed, one mortally wounded, and a third wounded. The rest of the casualties were mainly among the Greeks, who, according to Eaton, "in this little affair well supported their ancient character." The losses of the defending Tripolitans must have been heavy, but were unreported.

Eaton in his report to Barron said it was out of his province to comment on the conduct of the navy officers, but they could not have stationed their vessels in better positions nor managed their fire more skillfully. Then he added: "The detail I have given of Mr. O'Bannons conduct needs no enconium, and it is believed the disposition of our Government has always discover'd to encourage merit, will be extended to this intrepid, judicious and enterprising Officer. Mr. Manns conduct is equally meritorious."

Eaton put in his report words of unstinted praise for "the young English Gentleman, Mr. Farquhar" who had volunteered "and in all cases of difficulty, exhibited a firmness and attachment, well deserving my Gratitude." With such praise, it is not surprising that Eaton recommended for Farquhar a lieutenancy in the Marine Corps.

One wonders about Eaton's failure through the later phases of the campaign to make any mention of Leitensdorfer, who must have been giving resolute service by his side, as the story was unfolded in later years. An explanation might be that the soldier of fortune and man of many languages was the one who was keeping Eaton's journal and was not advertising himself. But the entries are so characteristically Eaton's that this is doubtful. Leitensdorfer was there, and apparently as steady as one who had served in the leading armies of Europe would be expected to be. His role is a matter of guessing.

Whittier found an explanation for the victory in the cause for which Eaton and his marines fought:

> Vain, Moslem, vain thy lifeblood poured
> So freely on thy foeman's sword!
> Not to the swift nor to the strong
> The battles of the right belong;
> For he who strikes for Freedom wears
> The armour of the captive's prayers,
> And Nature proffers to his cause
> The strength of her eternal laws. . . .

Bey Mustifa, cousin and brother-in-law of Bashaw Yusuf, seeing his army disintegrate, fled to the refuge of a mosque, but apparently not regarding that a safe haven against the infidels who had carried his town, sought firmer sanctuary in the harem of one of the leading men of Derna, an individual who, it chanced, strongly sympathized with Hamet over Yusuf. He had afforded precisely the same asylum to Hamet about two years before, when Bey Mustifa, who was trying to seize him at the instigation of Yusuf, forced him to flee from Derna into Egypt. But the inviolability of the harem was so established among the Mussulmans that Eaton's measures to drag him out of the refuge met the immediate and stern opposition of Arabs of all groups. The harem's master said he would die before being so disgraced.

So Eaton desisted in his plans to storm the seraglio, eager as he was to gain possession of the Bey's person. He wanted to use this favorite of Yusuf as an exchange for Captain Bainbridge. He undertook one or two stratagems to beguile Mustifa from his safe and not unpleasant retreat, but they failed and the refugee Bey finally escaped to join parties of his followers who were collected outside the town awaiting the arrival of the Tripolitan relief army under Yusuf's Mameluke, Hassen.

Eaton set about at once to prepare Derna for an attack. While Hamet occupied the Palace, he installed his marines, Greeks, and Selim Comb's mixed company in the waterfront fort, the strongest position in the area. The Arab tribesmen under Shieks el Tahib and Mohamet were brought closer into the town, partly to prevent them from getting independent notions on the plain. Supplies of ammunition were replenished. He had little time. He captured Derna in the late afternoon of April 27, and on the morning of May 1 Hassen Bey with the army which had marched from Tripoli, and with recruits he had picked up on the way, numbering two and three thousand in all, was before him.

Most of Hassen's reinforcements were the horsemen of the Beys of Bengazi and Ogna. His cavalry was under the command of another leading Tripolitan, Hadgi Ismain Bey. They came down from the Jebel Akdar, over much the same terrain Eaton had crossed in his approach to the town, and camped two miles out, near where he and Hamet had first looked down on Derna. But unlike Eaton, Hassen did not favor immediate assault. He required the better part of two weeks for his reconnaissance and preparations, and it was not until May 13 that he moved his army down from the heights for the attack.

One of Barron's main shortcomings as commodore was that he seemed to have his ship officers impressed with a necessity of returning at every shift of the wind to the Syracuse base, or keeping in close contact with it, much as though he would rather have the ships out of action than be uninformed. Hull, who had been deeply disturbed by the duration of his stay in Alexandria Harbor while Eaton was up the Nile seeking Hamet, now felt it necessary to apologize, almost, for retaining the *Nautilus* a few days longer off Derna. Immediately after the capture of the town he dispatched the *Hornet*, whose guns had been disabled because the plank-sheers of the vessel's deck had collapsed, to carry the tidings of the victory. He understood Barron wanted to convert her into a bomb vessel that summer and no doubt would be anxious for her return. Then he felt compelled to send back the *Nautilus*.

Hull said the force at hand could keep possession of the town with one vessel cruising offshore, but he thought reinforcements of three to four hundred Christians would be required to continue the expedition to Bengazi and Tripoli. He manifestly was not concerned about Hassen Bey's approaching army as long as the weather permitted the *Argus* to keep the town under her guns.

That army, led by a spirited Mameluke, was much more formidable than the hesitant force with which Bey Mustifa had defended the town, and had it arrived a few days earlier Eaton and Hamet would have had vastly greater difficulty, if, indeed, they had been able to capture Derna at all. Still, the little fleet with its 38 guns and, in Isaac Hull, a commander who was not afraid to use them was a tremendous asset and could have rendered the town uninhabitable to Mustifa and Hassen combined.

After his thorough preparations, Hassen launched his attack up both sides of the river valley, directed first against Hamet's outpost of cavalry about a mile from the town. To the astonishment of the Americans, Hamet's Arabs put up a stiff resistance. Being outnumbered, they at length gave way, then fled in wild confusion into the town. The Tripolitans and Arabs, fighting each other, showed much greater resolution than when either had faced the Americans, especially when under artillery fire. Hassen's men drove into the town and reached Hamet's headquarters at the Palace. They showed marked fortitude in the midst of musketry fusillades from the houses and terraces and occasional firing from the water battery and ships, which had to await opportunities when Hamet's men would not be endangered.

Eaton preferred to hold his small Christian garrison in the fort in preference to undertaking a sortie in Hamet's favor, his numbers being so few. It was imperative to keep the fort garrisoned and he was not likely to make an impression against the horde of Tripolitan horsemen charging about over the plain.

Sometimes a chance shot in a battle is as consequential as a random word in politics or diplomacy. Just when Hassen seemed about to scatter Hamet's Arabs, who were falling back and beginning to show signs of breaking into fragments, Eaton was able to play the guns of the battery against the oncoming Tripolitans. One gun fortuitously—perhaps a well-aimed gun—tore into a group of attackers and killed some, wounded others. Never at their best against artillery, the Tripolitans wavered. Then, suddenly overcome by panic, they turned and fled out of the town. Eaton ceased firing, and the Arab horsemen followed in swift pursuit.

Hassen's Tripolitans lost heavily, eighty being left dead or severely wounded in the town or its environs. Hamet's men, having the protection of the houses and the cover of artillery, had casualties of only twelve. But mainly, they established a morale superiority over the enemy, who were so unnerved by the repulse that all of Hassen's efforts could not induce them to make another advance into the town. Brave enough in the old-time warfare with lances and scimitars, the Mussulmans were much like the American Indians of the same period when it came to confronting cannon, though their Moslem associates, the Ottoman Turks, had been among the first to employ modern-type artillery in a major campaign, when they captured Constantinople in 1453.

Hassen kept to his camp two miles out and tried to substitute stratagem for battle by offering $6,000 for Eaton's head and twice the amount for him alive. The price for the ordinary-run Christian was only $30. Here again, it seemed, those experienced enough to undertake a venture to bag or kill Eaton were experienced enough to want payment in advance. According to the story, Hassen tried to bait the trap for Eaton with two handsome female Arabs, but the American, forewarned, was forearmed and cautious against poison. Then, with the passage of days, when memory of the first repulse faded, Hassen was able to organize an approach to the town by using camels much as tanks came to be employed in later warfare, as cover behind which his foot soldiers could advance. When the advance was begun it developed quickly that his men prized the lives of their camels almost as much as they did their own. Rather than have the faithful beasts shot by the American gunners, they began to steal away with them into the desert.

During this fighting Eaton deployed his Christian battalion outside the fort under O'Bannon's command. On June 3, when the townspeople were alarmed by one of Hassen's feints, O'Bannon marched his marines through the city and virtually the entire population gave them a surprisingly cordial ovation. They shouted in words which Eaton, the only American in the group with a passing fluency in Arabic, interpreted as "Live the Americans! Long live our friends and protectors!" Young and old, and "even women from their recluses," shouted their welcome.

Eaton detected the weakening of Hassen's force and commented that with a little money—money which, of all things, had proved about the most effective weapon in desert warfare—he could end the campaign. He wrote: "We want nothing but cash to break up our enemy's camp without firing another shot."

But behind the town still hovered the Tripolitan forces. The least resolute element, it was seen, was part of the cavalry under Hadgi Ismain Bey, which on June 7 abandoned Hassen's army and moved off with Hassen's money box to Egypt, thereby showing that Yusuf's Mameluke Hassen had as many problems with the temperamental Arab chiefs and horsemen as Eaton had experienced with el Tahib and Mahomet on the long march to Derna. Hassen held the town under desultory attack from May 28 to June 3, retired for a time, and then, on June 10, despite the defection of Hadgi Ismain Bey, his prospects suddenly brightened.

While Eaton was calling on Barron for more marines—and from the success in hand there appears little doubt that a force of five hundred Mediterranean Christians, including the unemployed marines in the fleet and such seamen as could have been spared from the idle frigates, supplemented by Hamet's thousand Arabs and Bedouins, could have marched into Tripoli—Hassen was receiving such a large reinforcement from Yusuf that he felt strong enough to undertake another full-scale attack on the obstinate Derna defenders. The action was begun when Hassen tried to cut off Hamet's cavalry outpost. The fighting was stubborn. Both Hassen and Hamet sent out reinforcements and soon a full-scale cavalry clash involving about five thousand white-robed horsemen on their splendid Arabian steeds—a sight which must have been thrilling to those on the *Argus* and in the fort who enjoyed the wheeling, din, and carnage of a typical cavalry clash, where swords and scimitars were more handy than cumbersome muskets—was raging on the plain between town and mountain. Eaton still thought the place of his meager army of Christians was inside the battery, which would be the only security in case of Hamet's reversal on the plain.

Again the Americans were highly gratified by Hamet's conduct in battle. Where Bashaw Yusuf had gone into hiding in his bombproof shelter during Preble's bombardments of Tripoli, Hamet, declared to be timid and the weakling of the Karamanli family, whom Bainbridge and Barron distrusted and some dubbed a coward, and about whom Eaton himself had been uncertain, was leading his men in a rough-and-tumble affair where there were no marine marksmen or big guns from the ships and battery involved.

Eaton began to have more respect for his ability: "I have lately had good reasons to correct the unfavorable opinion at one time entertained of his military enterprize," he wrote in his report. Though not a great general, Hamet was, in the opinion of Eaton, and his officers also, fully capable of ruling the kingdom.

The *Argus* in the harbor did stand by in the hope of getting an opening through Hamet's men, and managed to fire an occasional shot at long range, but it was essentially an all-Arab battle which could not have been much different from those fought when the Saracen hordes were sweeping across North Africa more than a thousand years before.

For four hours this combat raged between Hamet's one thousand and Hassen's army of indefinite size, but probably, due to the reinforcements, much the superior force. What determined the outcome in such a melee went unrecorded, but the main factor seems to have been the superb fighting and staying powers of Hamet and his men. Hassen finally gave way. His loss was heavy in men and horses. Some women brought in a report from his camp that he had between forty and fifty killed and more than seventy wounded. Hamet's casualties were between fifty and sixty. Hamet was satisfied with repulsing the attack. With his army tired out after long and hard fighting, he did not try to pursue.

Inside the fort O'Bannon was restive not to be taking part. He asked Eaton's permission to take out his marines and Greeks, leaving the mixed company to man the battery. But Eaton thought it would leave the fort inadequately defended in case of a reverse. Perhaps of more bearing, he had learned that Tobias Lear was negotiating with Bashaw Yusuf and he doubted if in that case he would be justified in using his few Americans in an offensive. "Had the aids come forward seasonably which we hoped to receive here," he said, "we might now have been at Cape Mensurat and in fifteen days more at Tripoli."

Hull witnessed the battle from the *Argus* and entered some of the details in the ship journal. At 12:15 P.M. he espied the enemy advancing down the hill behind the town, and forty-five minutes later he saw the two armies engaged warmly, at this stage firing briskly with muskets. Both the *Argus* and *Hornet,* which had returned from Malta, fired when they could, the *Hornet* hauling in closer to the beach than the *Argus* could venture. About 4:40 Hassen's men began retreating "in all directions." By 5:00 P.M. the Tripolitans were back on top of the hill and Hamet was in possession of the field, which he had retained from the very first of the action. "Several Charges were made and a great number must have been Killed and wounded." Hull sent three casks of powder to the fort to replace what it had fired, and a little later Eaton came on board to request that the ship's doctor be landed to care for Hamet's wounded.

On June 11, the day after the cavalry battle, a sail appeared. She was the magnificent American frigate, the *Constellation,* commanded by Captain Hugh G. Campbell. When Hassen's Tripolitans behind the town identified her as an American, bringing no doubt more men, guns, and supplies to assist Eaton and Hamet, they were thrown into something approaching a panic. Nursing their wounds from the cavalry action, they were in no position to sustain a war that might now be conducted with renewed vigor. Hassen broke his camp overlooking Derna and retired fifteen miles into the country. Rejoicing filled Hamet's followers, who saw their campaign for Derna at last triumphant and the road to Tripoli opened.

But the *Constellation* brought a message of a different character. On June 4, after Bashaw Yusuf had been shocked by news of the loss of Derna and well near terrorized for his throne by the threat of Hamet's army, Tobias Lear had negotiated a treaty with him and the war between the United States and Tripoli was ended. The American flag had been raised again in front of the consulate where the pole had been chopped down. The *Philadelphia* prisoners had been released and were going home. One of the provisions of the treaty was that Eaton and his Americans must evacuate Derna and restore the hard-won province to Bashaw Yusuf.

Eaton read the dispatches with consternation. He had already received something of a warning in a letter from Barron brought by the *Hornet* when she returned, ordering the *Argus* and *Hornet* recalled and giving intelligence that peace discussions were being held. In this letter, dated May 19 at Malta, Barron said that he was "still too weak for the exertion of Letter Writing" and that his secretary wrote with difficulty because of an inflammation of the eyes. It would have been better had they both been completely instead of partially incapacitated, for he wrote that Hamet "must be held unworthy of further Support and Cooperation." He voided any arrangement Eaton might have made with him. He pleaded lack of funds and means to help Hamet. But his main complaint rested on Hamet's character. Without adverting to any pleasant traits he might have found in Yusuf, he wrote of the elder brother: "His want of those qualities so essential in the Character of a Commander, & especially to a Prince, contending for his Throne, is a serious obstacle to the advancement of his cause." He served notice that he was cutting off all supply of arms, money, and provisions to Hamet, who must thereafter rely on his own resources.

Then this ardor-dampening message had been followed by the arrival of the *Constellation*. The devastating orders that Eaton must withdraw his Christians and abandon Derna struck like a point blank broadside on his hopes. There seemed almost to be a sneer in the message from Captain Campbell, one of his several old dislikes in the Navy, saying his ship had been sent to assist in withdrawing the Americans with all possible dispatch, and adding that "a cot" had been provided for Eaton on board. Not the promise of a gracious welcome, or praise for heroic deeds, but a cot. Eaton might have said that, accustomed to sleeping with his men on the desert floor, he would not require more than the generosity of the gun deck or a hammock with the seamen.

Could Eaton have looked down the years ahead, he would have known that this would not be the only instance in which timid diplomacy surrendered what gallant American arms had won.

Eaton was a soldier and orders were his master. Still, the evacuation of Derna was a touchy problem. While Hamet's followers were celebrating the arrival of the *Constellation*, laden presumably with the sinews of war and carrying the portents of final victory, Eaton adopted his only possible course, which was imparting the distressful news to Hamet frankly, without apology or dissembling. This sensible prince said at once that to abandon him was to co-operate with his brother. He recognized that without Eaton and American support he could not march overland and capture Tripoli. He was deserted—lifted up to the mountaintop of promised triumph, then suddenly dropped over the precipice of despair by those in whom he had put his faith. He was mindful of the fact that if he remained after Eaton departed he would quickly fall into the hands of Yusuf. He said without hesitation that he would have to accompany the Americans on their ships.

Eaton had to disengage his men by stealth. He made preparations as though he planned to attack Hassen's army in the back country. He had his troops inspected, passed out ammunition and rations to the Arabs, and sent Arab spies to reconnoiter the enemy force. That night he stationed all his marines to cut off communication between the town and the waterfront fort where the Christian elements of the army were concentrated. A messenger was sent to summon Hamet as if to an interview, and he came with his personal suite. Under the cover of darkness, all of the *Constellation's* boats came to the wharf at the fort. The Greeks and mercenary company under Selim Comb were embarked, much to their surprise, because they had no intimation of what was intended. Then Hamet and his retinue were carried out to the frigate, leaving on shore only Eaton and his marines.

Meantime, cloaked as were the intentions and cautious the movements, the Derna townsmen and Hamet's Arab followers sensed that something untoward was transpiring. The impression grew to conviction and they crowded down to the waterfront fort. They called out for Eaton and Hamet. The marines were boarding the last boat. As the soldiers and citizens rushed down with din, shouting and cursing, raging at finding themselves being deserted by the faithless infidels with whom they had journeyed, Eaton, the last man, stepped on board.

The agonizing march, the desperate assault and the triumph at Derna

—a saga which survives in the opening stanza of the Marine Corps hymn, in the hilt and blade of the Marine officers' sword, and as a little part of the esprit de corps of a great fighting organization—belonged to the chroniclers.

Campbell brought Yusuf's grant of amnesty to the people of Derna who had upheld Hamet, that being a treaty provision, but none would be likely to trust in the Bashaw's promises. Yusuf's agent carried the paper but the townspeople sent him back to the ship in disdain.

It was 2:00 A.M. before all of Hamet's and Eaton's parties were on board the *Constellation,* and by that time their tents and the property they had left on shore had been pillaged and the Arabs from Egypt already were heading for the hills. Then, as daylight came and the *Constellation* made for the open sea, Eaton wrote these lines in his report to Captain Rodgers, now the acting commodore:

> In a few minutes more we shall lose sight of this devoted city, which has experienced as strange a reverse in so short a time as ever was recorded in the disasters of war; thrown from proud success and elated prospects into an abys of hopeless wretchedness. Six hours ago the enemy were seeking safety from them by flight—this moment we drop them from ours into the hands of this enemy for no other crime than too much confidence in us! The man whose fortune we have accompanied thus far experiences a reverse as striking—He falls from the most flattering prospects of a Kingdom to beggary!

Then Eaton requested that he be returned to the United States:

> The duties understood to be annexed to my appointment in the Navy Department having ceased with the war, I have no reasons for remaining any longer in this sea; I request therefore you will have the goodness to allow me a passage in the first ship of war of your squadron which you may dispatch to the United States.

He had joined Preble—in retirement and in history. As Preble had shared in the thunderous dawn of the Navy, so Eaton had helped the Marine Corps to a glorious awakening.

CHAPTER TWENTY-FOUR

Tobias Lear and Peace at a Price

WITH his kingdom tottering from dissention at home, growing sympathy for Hamet's cause in Tripoli and in the provinces, and the startling loss of Derna and repulse of the succoring army sent under Hassen, his best Mameluke, Bashaw Yusuf's problem was to win peace and salvage the best ransom he could obtain for the *Philadelphia* prisoners without more haggling.

His confidential go-between with the Americans had become the Spanish consul general, Don Joseph de Souza, who was thoroughly distrusted by Eaton as he had been by Cathcart, and whose interests clearly were with the Bashaw and not the United States. No doubt it was his conception of his duty to thwart the Americans, at a period when relations between the United States and Spain were strained over the Florida border after Jefferson's purchase of Louisiana. Eaton could not forget that De Souza had advised the Bashaw to go to war against the United States in the beginning, and he described him as "the confidential man of the Bashaw." Eaton had heard him remark in Tunis that "the Americans miscalculated if they thought of forcing a peace without paying for it."

The Don's sympathies might be seen from the entry in Dr. Cowdery's journal of April 12, 1805, when it was well known that Eaton was marching on Derna and the war was drawing toward a decision, that the Don had presented three hundred stand of arms and a number of pistols to the Bashaw and advised him to continue the war and force the Americans to meet his terms. Cowdery gave an interesting incidental bit of information that the Bashaw had determined to keep his women and children in the Castle during the summer of 1805, the custom being to send them to the country in the hot season. They had told him that if they were to be captured they would rather fall in the hands of the Americans than the Arabs.

Yusuf's growing concern was shown by his questioning of Dr. Cow-

415

dery a week later, when he asked how many marines the United States "kept in pay." Cowdery told him ten thousand. How many soldiers? Eighty thousand, all ready to march, plus a million militia. "At this, his highness assumed a very serious look, and I returned to my room," said the doctor.

The Spanish consul general had written Tobias Lear, American consul general at Tunis, in December, 1804, proposing that he come to Tripoli under a flag of truce to negotiate. Lear waited about three months, then replied that earlier proposals for peace had been rejected by the Bashaw and any new one must come from him. Lear promised that the considerable American force at sea would act "with decided Vigour," but that negotiations for a peace "Compatible with the rising Character of our Nation" would not be rejected.

Lear's instructions from Secretary Smith gave him broader powers while Barron was commodore than he enjoyed while Preble was in the Mediterranean. Where Preble's authority over negotiations was supreme, Lear was vested, on June 6, 1804, in the long circular of general instructions given to Barron, with "full power and authority to negotiate a Treaty of Peace with the Bashaw of Tripoli," and to adjust terms and conciliate with the other Barbary States.

The verbal campaign being carried on against Hamet by Americans in the Mediterranean in late 1804 was bitter and persistent. Bainbridge on November 24, in one of his sympathetic ink letters to Dr. George Davis, American chargé d'affaires at Tunis, gave the intended Bashaw so severe a raking-over that one wonders if the target were not more Eaton than Hamet—Eaton who had never spared criticism of do-little ship captains in the early phases of the Tripolitan War. Bainbridge pointed out that Bashaw Yusuf's "right" to the throne had been approved by the Grand Seignior and all the nations of Europe and he hoped the United States was not involved in "such an impolitic & extraordinary measure" as backing Hamet, who was pusillanimous and never popular, and unable to hold Derna when given that province. Bainbridge persisted in the notion that Hamet had gone to Derna from Tunis by Yusuf's appointment, and could not hold the job. He had gone as his own master and had been driven to Egypt by Yusuf's agents. When the question is looked at dispassionately there is every indication that Hamet would have made a much more humane and enlightened ruler than the usurping Yusuf, and that the weakness detected in his make-up was gentleness and respect for the rights of others. He was considerate where Yusuf, already a murderer of one brother, was despotic.

But Bainbridge's attitude respecting Hamet, communicated to the American officers in both consular and naval services, became Barron's settled policy and it was therefore easy for Lear, who had never met Hamet but had been unimpressed from the beginning with the plan to seat him in Tripoli, to drop him. Lear went by Syracuse, called on Barron, and set up headquarters at Malta in October and thereafter took virtual charge of American affairs in the Mediterranean, bringing Commodore Barron under his complete domination. The Commodore's illness appeared to have other symptoms than the liver complaint. Lear was expressing doubt in November that Barron ever would recover. The suggestion has been made that he was suffering from the low fever picked up in Malta, which weakens mind and body alike.

Perhaps the best statement about Barron's condition was made by Master Commandant John H. Dent, who as commander of the *Nautilus* was in close communication with fleet headquarters at this period. He said that during the winter and spring of 1804–1805, and until after the peace negotiations, Barron's health was such "as to disqualify him from transacting any business, his mind being so much impaired as scarcely to recollect anything that transpired from one day to another." Dent found that on going to him for instructions he would frequently forget during the conversation what they were talking about.

As to Lear, Dent, prior to taking the *Nautilus* to participate in the capture of Derna, frequently heard the consul general say he thought the Eaton-Hamet expedition would be fruitless and would fail before reaching Derna. Dent had transferred to the *Hornet* and had carried the news of Eaton's triumph. On May 13 he arrived off Tripoli not only with this intelligence, but with a communication from the Secretary of the Navy, apparently picked up at Malta enroute, notifying the Commodore that reinforcements would join him about July 1 and that the attack on Tripoli should be suspended until after their arrival.

Lear, who was off Tripoli, commented, according to Dent, that "we did not want the assistance of Hamet Bashaw's army to bring the enemy to terms," because the Navy had sufficient power to do it. "It was generally believed," Dent stated, "by the officers in the Mediterranean, that Mr. Lear had a great ascendancy over the commodore in all his measures relative to the squadron, and from frequent observations of Mr. Lear's intimacy with the commodore during his debilitated state, I am of the same opinion." Dent made his statement in 1806 to a Senate committee investigating the relations which had existed between the United States and Hamet.

Lear's opposition to the Hamet enterprise had been consistent and no doubt sincere, though perhaps suggestive that little of Washington's military perception had rubbed off on his secretary. In November, 1804, Lear wrote to Madison from Malta his presumption that the Hamet expedition would not be undertaken because the naval force would be sufficient without it, and it was doubtful in any event if Hamet could be of service, being, as he had heard, a man of no force or influence. "Indeed," wrote Lear, "I sh^d place much more confidence in the continuance of a peace with the present Bashaw, if he is well beaten into it, than I sh^d have with the other, if he should be placed on the throne by our means."

Thus Lear swung toward Yusuf instead of the more tractable Hamet. When the *Argus* took Eaton to Egypt, Lear wrote to Barron expressing doubt that any ultimate good would result from it. All along, the case against Hamet appears to have been prejudged, without ever a conversation with him, by the supreme American negotiator in the Mediterranean, who fully dominated the ailing Commodore. Lear in turn was being told by Bainbridge in invisible ink that no good would result from dealings with Hamet.

Lear, after his belated reply, received another feeler through the Spanish consul general, the Bashaw's terms being that he should receive $200,000 as a ransom and peace payment, and that all Tripolitans be returned to him and restitution be made for their property losses. Bainbridge thought a figure of $120,000 could be reached without any of it being regarded a purchase price for peace, and Danish Consul Nissen confirmed Yusuf's desire to negotiate. Lear on May 1 wrote to Captain Rodgers, commanding the blockade off Tripoli, saying that it appeared the Bashaw wanted peace but would not suggest acceptable terms because of the example it would set before other nations.

All the while Rodgers, who had the spirit of Preble of wanting to enforce peace instead of purchasing it, had been anxious to resume the naval attack on Tripoli which had been suspended since the departure of Preble. Lear advised him on May 1—and one wonders about his injection of his views into strictly naval matters—that "I see no prospect of our forces being concentrated and ready to act against Tripoli sooner than the beginning or middle of June; so that I must regret that you will not have your just and sanguine wishes accomplished of seeing us ready to attack before that time."

The situation seems to have created surprise and some amusement throughout the fleet. Decatur wrote to Preble at that time congratulating the ex-Commodore on the report that he was to be made Secretary of the Navy, and dropped in a reference to the peculiar condition of affairs. Preble in his reply said "That a Col. [Tobias Lear] should command our Squadron as you inform me must be a matter most of surprise . . . abroad as well as at home."

Lear, much as would a commodore, told of the stations of the different vessels and said there was no prospect that Barron, whose health was not improved, would be able to take an active part. Then he gave the latest calumnies that were being passed around the Mediterranean about Eaton: "We have heard from Mr. Eaton by a man of the name of Faquier [Farquhar] . . . who has returned to Syracuse, having quarrelled with Mr. Eaton, and left him. He writes to the Commodore, that Mr. E. is a madman—that he has quarrelled with the Ex-Bashaw &c &c &c, we are in daily expectation of more authentic accounts from that quarter, but I make no calculation in our favour from that source."

Much of the correspondence passed about among the higher officials and some of the naval officers in those days appeared to relate to how little could be expected from Hamet and Eaton and what truly terrible people they were proving to be, when the fact was they were setting an example of patriotic zeal which might well be emulated by the top command. Barron wrote to Lear on May 18 that he had changed his mind about Hamet and "I must candidly own that I have no longer the same expectations which I once entertained of the result of the Cooperation with him." Hamet's want of military talents, the great expense already incurred, and the amount that would be necessary to continue the expedition were advanced as reasons for the want of confidence. Barron, in this strangest letter written during the Tripolitan War, was arguing that, while he had sent Eaton to Egypt in Hamet's favor in the beginning, he could not now put faith in the expedition, though it had captured Derna, an achievement of no small significance in the war. He summed it up thus:

"Indeed on mature reflection I am of the opinion, that if the Ex Bashaw, having received the first impulse from our strength and being put in possession of Dern, the province where his interest is supposed to be the strongest has not in himself sufficient energy address & Courage, and cannot command sufficient means to move on with firm steps toward the Usurper's Residence whilst we second his operation by sea. He must be considered no longer a fit subject for our support and Cooperation." The punctuation was Barron's, whose illness was no doubt affecting his correspondence.

But Barron could not ignore the fact that the capture of Derna must have had "a powerful effect" on the reigning Bashaw and "will have its influence to moderate his pretensions and to think seriously of peace."

Lear and Barron were together in Malta in mid-May, and Lear answered the Commodore the next day saying he had reviewed the situation and conceived it his duty to open a negotiation for peace. He

did not mention Eaton but was generous enough to say that the "un-
daunted Bravery and perserverence of the few of our Countrymen at
Derne" would be proof of what the Americans could do alone.

Barron wrote to Eaton on the day of his letter to Lear. He washed his
hands of Hamet by saying that he was now in possession of Derna and
if he did not have the means and talents to proceed with his project "he
must be held as unworthy of further support and the Cooperation as a
measure to expensive & burthensome & too little pregnant with Hope or
advantage to justify its further prosecution." He held that Madison's
conditions that he should not be left in a worse condition than when the
United States undertook its co-operation had been met when he was
placed in control of Derna.

Thus the processes were set in motion for treating with Yusuf and
dropping Hamet, with Bainbridge, Barron, and Lear mainly accountable, though it must be recognized that Barron, influenced by Lear, was
not the dominant factor. Those who opposed the peace which followed
tended to excuse the Commodore because of his physical weakness or
mental lapses. Nevertheless, it was clear then that he was unfit to command and quite apparent that rarely if ever in American history, and not
even in the case of Morris, was an American squadron overseas subjected to such enfeebled leadership. For while Rodgers did command
the operation of the blockade, Barron still issued general orders and
controlled policy from his couch at either Syracuse or Malta.

Lear in his zest for a treaty conveniently forgot Madison's opening
statement in his general circular of June 6, 1804, that with the sea power
being entrusted to Barron it was hoped peace could be negotiated "without any price or pecuniary concession whatever." Such was the government's position as imparted to Preble when the *John Adams* brought the
first word of the coming of the heavy squadron. Lear was authorized to
pay ransom if it were unavoidable, but Madison limited the amount to
$500 per prisoner, the payment to be made preferably in installments
over four or five years. Writing on April 20, 1805, after he knew of
Preble's bombardment of Tripoli but before news of Eaton's expedition
had reached the United States, Madison was thinking even more emphatically of peace without a price tag. This was more likely, he felt,
because of "the spirited attacks made on the enemy by Commodore
Preble" and the possibility of a repetition of them on a larger scale when
the season reopened.

Madison announced in this letter of April 20, 1805, the coming of other
strong reinforcements, to augment the fleet of frigates Barron already
commanded. The new force would consist of the *John Adams* and nine
American-built gunboats, eight of them with 32-pounders and one with

a 24-pounder, and all with crews of about twenty men. They would sail by May 1. Two bomb vessels with 13-inch mortars would sail by June 1. While small, they would venture to cross the Atlantic, and all but one did make it. What Preble would have done with such power is an easy speculation, but even without the reinforcements, Barron had more than ample strength to reduce Tripoli and with a few broadsides to refresh Lear's memory about Madison's first request for peace without pecuniary concession.

Lear without much consistency found in Eaton's capture of Derna, after the expedition on which he had frowned from the start, what he considered the happy moment to recognize the Bashaw's peace feelers and join the blockading squadron off Tripoli in order to open negotiations. It chanced to be the moment when the Bashaw also was in a most receptive mood.

One reason why the Bashaw trembled after the loss of Derna was the misleading information he received about Hamet's force. Bey Mustifa of Derna knew the only way he could justify his loss of the place was to magnify the strength of the attacking army. The army of less than two thousand with Eaton and Hamet became several times that number.

Bey Mustifa dwelt also on the valor of the Americans, whose fighting qualities were well-known in Tripoli from Yusuf's experiences with Decatur, Trippe, and any number of others. The prisoners from the *Philadelphia* detected no menace against them because of Eaton and Hamet, such as Bainbridge reported to Barron, but they did get word through Dr. Cowdery that the Bashaw had collected his jewels and his women to be ready on the approach of immediate danger, to take them and the American captives and retire into the Desert of Barca. The prisoners thought Lear opened his negotiations at the moment "an awful alarm struck into the Bashaw's heart." They said Yusuf "trembled for the safety of his dominions."

About the only person in Tripoli who feared the Americans would be slaughtered if Hamet approached appears to have been Bainbridge, for when the prisoners came to relate the story in an interview on reaching Richmond, Virginia, after their ransom, they thought they were the very last thing the Bashaw would sacrifice.

Apart from the loss of Derna, the other factor weighing heavily on the Bashaw was his continued reading of the American newspapers being sent to the prisoners. The story which struck his eye especially was the enactment by Congress of the revenue measure termed the "Mediterranean Fund," which was to be continued until the end of the war with Tripoli. Secretary Gallatin estimated it would produce a revenue of $550,000 annually, which by the Bashaw's calculations, and in comparison with the piddling revenue he was able to raise in taxes, was a tremendous sum. He had not anticipated the Western republic possessed such resources or would go to such ends.

Commenting on this point, the *Republican Advocate* of Frederick-Town, Maryland, a newspaper then circulating freely in the capital city, said the Bashaw saw in the tax the spirit of the American nation, and:

> He saw that they were determined to carry on the war until they could bring it to an honorable accommodation. What efforts could he expect to make in opposition to a nation, which would thus contribute "millions for defense but not a cent for tribute"? Such were the reflections that passed through the Bashaw's mind, and such, according to the opinion of our captive countrymen, were the first inducements that prompted him to make preparations for peace.

There was no doubt in the first accounts reaching the United States about who was responsible for the peace. The merchant brig *Belle-Isle,* under Captain Leach, made Salem, Massachusetts, August 28, 1805, after a voyage of sixty-six days from Naples. She brought a highly garbled account of the Derna fighting which had reached Naples eight days before she sailed. The story was published next day in the Salem *Register:*

> It is said that General Eaton's army suffered most severely, and that every American was killed, except Mr. Eaton, who was wounded in the shoulder.
>
> The effect of the battle, however, was an immediate negotiation for peace, to assist at which Col. Lear went from Malta to Tripoli; and two days before Captain Leach sailed, dispatches were received from Col. Lear at Naples, bringing the important and glorious intelligence, that a PEACE highly honorable to the U.S. had been concluded, and of course the Americans who have been so long suffering in captivity released.

Thus the first news received was that the peace was "highly honorable." That impression has never been wholly erased. A great deal more had to be accomplished before the United States could take satisfaction in a truly honorable peace, but that did come, through the blunt efforts of a determined Navy officer, Decatur, rather than a diplomat looked on as a skilled negotiator, Lear.

Captain Leach carried dispatches for the government in Washington and the newspapers, which reprinted the Salem story, knew they would soon get from Washington an official statement on the end of the Tripolitan War.

Lear went to Tripoli on the *Essex,* under Captain James Barron, and joined the frigates *Constitution* and *President* off the harbor on May 26. Lear and James Barron went first to the *Constitution* and gave Captain Rodgers a belated letter in which Samuel Barron at last surrendered command of the squadron and turned it over to the next in rank, Rodgers. Then Rodgers returned with them to the *Essex* and they sailed close enough to the city for their white flag to be seen. Soon the Bashaw showed a white flag from the Castle and a little later a boat came out bearing the Spanish consul. Lear informed him that the latest peace suggestion he had made—a lump-sum payment of $200,000 covering peace, ransom, and indemnity—was unacceptable.

Lear would not have come so far merely to register a rejection, which must have been obvious to the Spaniard as he returned to the Bashaw. Three days passed without more word, but the delay resulted from rough weather instead of any reluctance by the Bashaw to come to terms. Lear meantime returned to the *Constitution* and Don Joseph was rowed out to the flagship on May 29; he advised the consul general that the Bashaw was willing to settle for $130,000 ransom, with no sum for peace, and the delivery of all Tripolitans held captive by the Americans. The total would have been under Madison's maximum allowance of $500 a head for the prisoners but it was still far above what Preble would have been prepared to pay to free the captives, and Lear, too, objected to the amount. Lear then reduced to writing what he referred to as an "ultimatum," which was that he would restore the Tripolitan prisoners numbering about 100, and Tripoli should free the 300 Americans, and that the United States would pay $60,000 for the excess of Americans.

On May 31, 1805, Bashaw Yusuf agreed to take the $60,000. No doubt he knew it was more than he had a right to expect, but it was the small portion of the peace, indeed, when he reflected that peace with Lear meant American recognition of his right to continue on the throne of Tripoli. He stipulated that he would not release the American captives until his Tripolitans were delivered to him in Tripoli. At this stage Bainbridge came out to the *Constitution* under parole with further explanation of the Bashaw's attitude, and Lear consented to negotiate a treaty, though he dismissed the Spanish consul general as a go-between. Nissen, the Danish consul, took over the negotiations, boarded the *Constitution* June 2, and attended Lear in the drafting of a treaty. Lear went on shore the next day in the *Constitution's* barge, flying the American flag, and was met by the American officers of the *Philadelphia* and a great crowd of Tripolitans who appeared overjoyed that peace was at hand.

Lear appeared to have a distorted notion of what he was accomplishing, for on June 4, two days after his landing, he sent a letter back to

Rodgers declaring "our peace will be so unusually honorable, that we must not expect it to be fully relished by all the Representatives of the European Nations here, which is already manifested . . ." He was not altogether collected because he told Rodgers that his party had forgotten to take the colors out of the barge when they came ashore, so he requested a large ensign and a small one for the boat, then added: "When the American Colours are hoisted on the Cons^r House there will be a salute from the Castle &c of 21 Guns, which you will be so good as to have returned from your Ship." Another salute, this of nine guns, should be answered when he called on the Bashaw. He requested two or three officers to come ashore because "it would give a degree of parade to the Business, which will have a good effect here."

The *Philadelphia* captives, he said, would not be ready to leave until the next afternoon "as the intoxication of Liberty & Liquor had deranged the faculties as well as dresses of many of the Sailors and Cap^n B. wishes them all on board quite clean and in Order."

The treaty, which has generally been looked on as favorable to the United States, was in fact a compromise, in which the Navy and Eaton's marines were stripped of the rewards of a great deal of hard fighting, and it left the relations with the Barbary powers in a disturbed state for another decade. The treaty did have some merits. The United States received the guarantee of most-favored-nation treatment. Her merchant vessels would not be seized. The provisions for exchange of prisoners and the payment by the United States of $60,000 were incorporated. The force at Derna was to be withdrawn and the United States would give no supplies to Tripolitan subjects in rebellion against Bashaw Yusuf. An effort would be made to persuade Hamet to depart but his family would be restored to him. In case of war, prisoners would be exchanged and not enslaved. These were the principal items.

But Lear allowed Yusuf to insert what can only be described as a "sneak clause" unbeknown to the officers of the fleet and unreported to President Jefferson, by which Yusuf was allowed four years in which to restore Hamet's family to him. The poor elder brother, the rightful Bashaw, who had been lifted up by Eaton's treaty and shown the mountaintop, was not only being tossed down, having his claim to the throne rejected and his person ousted, if possible, from Derna, but was being deprived of a family for whom he manifestly had a great deal of affection—enough to give him concern about their safety all the while he was marching across the desert.

The crafty Yusuf thought that if Hamet had his family he might renew the rebellion. Under the sneak clause Yusuf could hold them as hostages, and four years would be time enough for something to happen to Hamet or for him to consolidate his own powers beyond challenge.

Captain Rodgers had to stand by and see the $60,000 paid, and give lip service to the transaction, though it was clear he had no stomach for it. Barron had directed him, at least by implication, in the letter surrendering the command to him—a long, wandering discussion of Barron's health and affairs—to give his "activity and zeal" in co-operating with "a Gentleman of such ability experience & moderation as Colonel Lear." Rodgers co-operated, but he told Lear that if Yusuf would deliver the captives without making peace, he would pay him not $60,000, but $200,000, and not of public money, but of cash he could collect from among the officers of the fleet, who would give it with the greatest satisfaction. That is, if the prisoners were out of the way, they would pay $200,000 in their own money for a chance to get at the Bashaw and continue the war so there would be no uncertain conclusion. But as is often the case, the Navy had the spirit, the diplomats the authority.

Lear's explanation of the treaty to Eaton was a bit apologetic and not entirely truthful:

> I found that the heroic bravery of our few countrymen at Derne, and the idea that we had a large force and immense supplies at that place, had made a deep impression on the Bashaw—I kept up that idea, and endeavored, from thence, to make an arrangement favorable to his brother, who, altho' not found to be the man whom many had supposed, was yet entitled to some consideration from us. But I found this was impractical, and that if persisted in, would drive him to measures which might prove fatal to our countrymen in his power.

Then, after telling more about the peace, he added the deception: the Bashaw engaged that "if his brother withdraws himself quietly from his dominions, his wife and family should be restored to him." The inference here is that the delivery of wife and family would be made forthwith, upon Hamet's withdrawal, and not after four years. This letter was no doubt influential in causing Hamet to leave Derna with Eaton, in anticipation of the reunion which had never been intended.

Lear sent the *Constitution* to Syracuse for the Tripolitan prisoners and the $60,000, and on June 10, 1805, all of the preliminaries for peace were completed. When the treaty was ready for ratification, Lear and his attendants called at the Castle and witnessed the ceremony. Lear sat on the Bashaw's right hand and said "great order and solemnity were observed." He handed the treaty to the Bashaw who passed it along to his first secretary, Mohammed Dghies, to read aloud to the assembled Divan. When questions arose about some of the articles the Bashaw explained the provisions. At the end the seals of the Bashaw and his Divan members were affixed to two copies and the Bashaw delivered one to Lear "in a solemn manner, and with many expressions of friendship."

President Jefferson submitted the treaty to the Senate December 11, 1805, and it was ratified April 17, 1806. The receipt attached to the English text for the $60,000 specified that the sum was for "two hundred americans," the other hundred presumably being counted against the hundred Tripolitans exchanged.

Yusuf in truth was indifferent about these one hundred Tripolitan prisoners. He accepted the exchange because it saved his face with his own people for reducing the ransom from the fantastic figures he had first talked of to a mere $60,000, but he was heard to comment that he "would not give an orange a piece for them."

A revealing incident occurred before Bashaw Yusuf parted with his three hundred Americans. He summoned those who had "turned Turk" to an audience, explained to them that peace had been concluded, and said they were free to depart or remain as they chose. Of the five who had become Mohammedans, only John Wilson, whom Bainbridge found treacherous from the very beginning, elected to persevere in his adherence to the Crescent and Koran. The other four, one of whom had a wife and four children in Boston, decided they wanted to discard the turban and put on their old seamen's uniforms.

When Wilson swore renewed fealty to Islam and Tripoli, he was felicitated and made over by the Bashaw and his Divan. The other four were put under close guard, sent into the country, and were never heard of again. "We had a glance of them," said Private Ray, "as they passed our prison, and could see horror and despair depicted in their countenances." Technically it might be regarded a violation of the treaty but none ever seemed to express concern about the fate of the four faithless Americans who had turned on their comrades to ease their own lots.

The healthful climate along the arid African shore, which was indicated by the lack of illness in Eaton's army, was further evidenced by the fact that out of a crew of more than three hundred only six had died during the cruelties and hardships of nineteen months of captivity and slavery. Private Ray attributed the good health to the oil the men mixed with their food. The night the treaty was signed they were kept in their old prison but had a new set of guards. Gone were the drivers—the Moor they called "Captain Blackbeard," the chief jailor; "Scamping Jack" Soliman, a fierce Tunisian, "more furious and less vindictive" than Blackbeard; Tousef, a querulous Frenchman whom the Americans called a "quid," a term of that day synonymous with a later-day "square" or "drip." Others were a crooked-legged Greek whose deformity won him the nickname of "Bandy"; a mean sort of Algerine doctor they called

"Blinkard"; and finally a Tripolitan, "the most barbarous villain of the whole," they dubbed "Red Jacket." He beat them whenever Preble's squadron fired on the town. Never would the sailors and marines of the *Philadelphia* have to suffer under them again. That was the most pleasant aspect of the peace.

Ray summed up his opinion of "these wretches," who sought only the Bashaw's favor: "Mean, fawning, mercenary and cruel, they were held in as much contempt as slave drivers in our own country, as jail-keepers in all countries, and as boatswains' mates of a man of war. I have often seen the citizens of Tripoli hiss them as they walked the streets."

Now the long captivity was ended, and while Rodgers was enroute to Syracuse to get the Tripolitan prisoners, the Americans were transferred to the fleet.

Rodgers in the end came out of the negotiations with a bad taste in his mouth. Even while Lear was negotiating for peace through Don Joseph and Nissen, Rodgers—a much bolder commodore than Barron—wanted to have the talks broken off so that the new naval support expected to arrive momentarily from the United States might be exercised to save the ransom and, of greater importance, chastise the faithless and bloody Yusuf for arrogantly chopping down the flagpole, seizing American merchant vessels, and making war against the United States when it had appeared defenseless in the Mediterranean.

But Lear would not hear of delay, claiming that the main consideration was to relieve the *Philadelphia* prisoners. About them, Rodgers affixed a line to his report: "I never thought myself that the Lives of the American Prisoners were in any danger." In any case, lives were scarcely as important as the nation's honor.

Peace in order to save the prisoners had quite obviously become Bainbridge's main objective also. The fire of his youth, when he was as ready to fight with his fists as with his side arms, appeared to be cooling. The peace thus promoted by Bainbridge and executed by Lear, without ever once soliciting the opinion of the hardy warrior Eaton, proved to be as shaky in its influence throughout Barbary as it was illy conceived and impetuously concluded.

Rodgers was incensed also at Captain James Barron, who commanded the *Essex*, whom he suspected of contriving against him with his brother, the ailing Commodore, while at the same time feigning friendship and claiming that he was doing everything in his power to persuade Samuel Barron to turn the squadron over to Rodgers, the next in rank. What the facts were cannot be ascertained, but James Barron in character seemed to be a cut below his brother Samuel. Rodgers, a straightforward fighter and one of the noble characters of the early Navy, suspected that James

Barron was at the seat of slanders circulated against him in the United States.

When Rodgers returned home from the Mediterranean in mid-1806, he felt sufficiently aggrieved to issue a challenge to James Barron. It is a pity the duel was not fought, because it might have meant that Barron would not have commanded the *Chesapeake* in her disgraceful performance when overhauled by the *Leopard*, or that he would not have been in a position to provoke a quarrel with Decatur and kill him, after Decatur had been a member of the naval court which held Barron culpable in the *Chesapeake-Leopard* affair. But Barron became ill for a sustained period, during which Rodgers' anger subsided, and in the end others interceded and patched up the affair without resort to weapons.

Commodore Samuel Barron had achieved one thing during his command of the American squadron in the Mediterranean. He had managed to keep the ships always separated and never once concentrated in a show of force off Tripoli Harbor, where Preble had seemed to think the war was being fought. And in all his tenure his fleet had never fired an angry shot at Bashaw Yusuf's stronghold. His hostile words were addressed mainly against his principal Moslem ally, Hamet Karamanli.

Here and there it was being demonstrated again in this age that a fleet, like an army, depended on something more than its material substance. A fleet was not only its wooden decks, canvas sails, iron guns, and cannoneers and seamen, but just as truly the fervor of its leadership. While Lear was negotiating with Bashaw Yusuf, he received a message that the big French fleet under Villeneuve had put to sea from Toulon. It was destined to encounter the glowing ardor of a great sea captain. It was sailing to keep an appointment off Cape Trafalgar.

Rodgers had a single chance to show his mettle. The obstreperous Bey of Tunis, who had ousted Eaton and made a nuisance of himself by continually demanding the gift of a frigate when with half the effort he might have built or purchased one, was becoming temperamental again. Rodgers, while blockading Tripoli, on April 24, 1805, had caught a Tunisian xebec with 8 guns convoying two prizes into Tripoli Harbor. They were captured Neapolitan ships. Rodgers sent the three vessels to Malta under convoy of the *President*. A month later he became commodore in the Mediterranean and therefore could use his own judgment in dealing with Tunis, which was demanding of the American chargé d'affaires, Dr. George Davis, a restoration of the three ships.

When the American fleet was released from the patrol off Tripoli by Lear's peace treaty, Rodgers showed his power to Bey Hamouda Pacha at Tunis. He dispatched the *Congress* and the *Vixen* and followed with the *Constitution, Constellation, Essex, John Adams, Siren, Nautilus, Franklin, Enterprise, Hornet,* and part of the flotilla of gunboats which were now arriving from the United States—sixteen sail in all. What Barron could have done with such a fleet in front of Tripoli would have cost less than $60,000 and perhaps given Tripoli a more gentle rule than it was due to experience under Yusuf and his rebellious sons. Rodgers had picked up most of the vessels at Syracuse or Malta. They made an imposing sight when they rounded Cape Bon and stood into Tunis Bay on August 1, 1805. Then Rodgers wrote a letter asking the Bey if he wanted peace or war and giving him the generous time of thirty-six hours in which to reply.

Davis informed Rodgers that Barron earlier had authorized him to give the Bey the impression that the vessels might be restored, but he had refrained from doing so "even at the risk of war." The Bey now refused to receive Decatur, whom Rodgers sent ashore, and the Captain started back to the ship. The Bey told Davis that Rodgers' letter amounted to a declaration of war.

But Bey Hamouda Pacha had no appetite for the big guns of the frigates anchored off his city, and on quick reflection he sent a messenger to Rodgers in such hot haste that he reached the waterfront ahead of Decatur and got a conciliatory reply to the Commodore before Decatur could report how he had been snubbed. Lear eventually went ashore to assist Davis in the negotiations, but he could not have put any indemnities or weasel clauses into this arrangement even had he desired because Rodgers was watching. To the Bey's complaint that the entire American fleet had descended on him, Rodgers gave assurance it was not so, because a frigate, a brig, eight gunboats, and two mortar boats had not yet arrived. Davis wrote to Rodgers suggesting a suspension of any hostilities until a communication could be had with the President of the United States.

That was not Rodgers' way of doing business. He replied that unless Bey Hamouda gave a guarantee of the maintenance of peace and signed it in the presence of the British and French consuls, he would seal the port so tight that nothing could get in or out. Then Rodgers sent a copy of the wording he wanted in the guarantee. Lear and the Bey went into a round of letter-writing during which Rodgers' patience was wearing thin. In a letter of August 15 he declared that the Bey must give a guarantee of peace and then he could send an ambassador to Washington to treat if he desired. Then Rodgers let loose to Lear an opinion about this petty tyrant:

"His prevaricating with you in particular, induces me to believe, that he is now more than ever the Scoundral, I had thought him before, and I have only to repeat, that if he does not do all that is necessary, & proper, that even at the risk of my Conducts being disapproved by my Country, he shall feel the Vengeance of the Squadron now in his Bay."

In the face of such force and persistency Bey Hamouda capitulated. He gave notice that the United States would be placed on a most-favored-nation basis and that he would send an ambassador to the United States to deal with any complaints. Rodgers answered cordially, said he had a frigate returning, and asked to have the ambassador make ready at once. The ambassador was Sidi Suliman Mellimelli, who sailed with Decatur on the *Congress*, and was to become a startling figure, during the winter of 1805–1806, in the American capital where he lived luxuriously at the expense of the American government and pressed a claim for tribute and indemnity. Decatur carried a letter from Rodgers to Secretary Smith, saying of the Bey of Tunis that if his late hostility should be overlooked, "I can with almost certainty say that he will never again attempt to behave in a similar manner."

Mellimelli took four beautiful Arabian stud horses with him as a gift to President Jefferson, one having been a gift to the Bey from the Dey of Algiers. The scrupulous Jefferson would not accept them for himself but the Treasury sold them as part payment of Mellimelli's expenses. But first they were kept in the President's stables and the stud fees went to the collector of revenues. The ambassador was accompanied by a suite of eleven, including an Italian band. He was short on women, for whom he had a ravenous appetite. The prim little Secretary of State Madison had to have concubines supplied at public expense, and wrote about it later, saying: "Appropriations to foreign intercourse are terms of great latitude and may be drawn on by very urgent and unforeseen occurrences." Madison never lacked the ability of choice expression.

Mellimelli did not know the tightness of the American farmer-congressman. He was unable to exact a single coin from Congress or Secretary Gallatin, but the more freehanded Lear did make an adjustment with the Bey two years later by paying $10,000. After much difficulty and some revolts among his followers, Mellimelli, whose main argument for tribute appeared to be that he would likely be killed if he returned without it, was packed off home in a ship from Boston.

The United States continued its payments of tribute to Algiers through the years, but learned what other powers had long known, that it was best to be in arrears. Then the sum owed became so considerable that the Dey could not risk losing it by seizing ships or declaring war.

The United States was at peace in the Mediterranean at last, but it was not a pleasant or satisfactory peace. In a few years, by one pretext or another, some of the Barbary States began to lapse into their old piratical ways. Peace at a price was not the proper method. Still, none of them wanted outright war with the United States. Along the Barbary shore the memories of Preble and Eaton, of the storming of Derna and the blazing ships in Tripoli Harbor, lingered.

CHAPTER TWENTY-FIVE

Reward and Neglect

TEN years were to elapse before hostilities between the United States and the Barbary powers were renewed by a declaration of war against Algiers. Before dealing with these developments it is necessary to get some of the actors of the 1801–1805 conflicts off the stage.

Lear's treaty with Tripoli evoked a storm of dissent which came to be directed against Jefferson, though he was the last person responsible for either dumping Hamet or paying a cash ransom to Bashaw Yusuf. But it was peace, and peace was what the country wanted, and it was generally believed to be a favorable peace.

Among the first to reach the United States were the *Philadelphia* prisoners, who sailed in July and landed at Hampton, Virginia. They made their way to Washington via Richmond and Fredericksburg, Virginia, being received enroute with generous applause and warm sympathy. Bainbridge for some reason was feted as a hero. Fredericksburg held a parade and the master of ceremonies commented: "We gave our departed friend a welcome to his native shores, which potentates might have envied. Such was the enthusiastic welcome which was manifested by our citizens, that he was completely overcome, and could not refrain from shedding tears."

Among those who came to the dinner tendered the captain of the late *Philadelphia* was Colonel William Washington, the gallant cavalryman of the battle of Cowpens.

When the extent of the kindness of the Danish consul at Tripoli, Nicholas C. Nissen, was reported by members of the *Philadelphia* crew, Congress adopted a resolution of thanks. From beginning to end, he had been a true friend of the United States. Bainbridge went on to spend some months with his family, became commander of the New York Navy Yard, then returned to the merchant marine service until the War of 1812, when he re-entered the Navy. He deeply resented Private Ray's book on the *Horrors of Slavery* in 1808 and attacked Ray for having ap-

proached him for a subscription before the manuscript was published.
He called Ray "an ungrateful wretch with no character to lose" and
wrote to the Secretary of the Navy a complaint against the "infamous
publication," which he claimed was "replete with calumny & falsehood."
What angered Bainbridge was the charge of neglect of the crew, and it
did seem that at times the ship commander could have exerted himself
more energetically in their behalf.

In any event, the Marine Corps private had a right to his side of the
story and he gave the most graphic description available of the life and
suffering of the captives during their long incarceration. It would have
been a tragedy had Bainbridge been able in advance of publication to
moderate the text. His own account is readily available in his voluminous
correspondence and his Navy Department reports. He had little else to
do except write and the naval correspondence was loaded heavily with
his advice, information, and opinions.

An unhappy circumstance of his return to the naval service in 1812
was that due to his seniority he took over command of the *Constitution*,
thereby replacing Isaac Hull, the gallant captain of the *Argus* and sup-
porter of Eaton at Derna. Hull had commanded the *Constitution* in one
of the greatest and perhaps the most sensational of all American naval
victories, the triumph over the *Guerrière*, which gave notice to the world
that Great Britain had met a match, frigate for frigate, on the seas. Hull
turned over the ship generously and Bainbridge did go on to defeat and
capture the British frigate *Java*.

After the evacuation of Derna, Eaton and Hamet sailed on the *Constellation* to Syracuse, where Hamet undertook to gain possession of his
family, but encountered only Yusuf's rebuffs. Upon Eaton's solicitation,
the Commodore gave Hamet a temporary allowance of $200 a month to
defray his expenses and those of between fifteen and twenty dependents
of his suite who had accompanied him from Derna. He was not a whiner.
When he wrote to Eaton on June 29, 1805, after intelligence about the
peace had been received, he addressed him as "friend and brother" and
"late General & Commander in chief of our allied forces in our Kingdom
of Tripoli." He expressed at their moment of final separation "the deep
sense of gratitude I feel for your generous and manly exertions in my
behalf." Wherever God placed him, he would "always bear this impression of gratitude on my heart."

Hamet seemed to consider himself more at fault than anyone else for
the failure of their plans.

It is true my own means were small. I know indeed they did not
answer your reasonable expectations. And this I am ready to admit is

a good reason why you should not chuse to persevere in an enterprise hazardous in itself, and, perhaps, doubtful in its issue. I ought therefore to say that I am satisfied with all your Nation has done concerning me—I submit to the will of God; and thank the King of America and all his servants for their kind dispositions towards me.

What he requested as another expression of friendship was that the terms be fullfilled of "your treaty with Joseph Bashaw, my perfidious brother." He wanted his family restored to him. He hoped also for some small assistance in repairing to some country where he might spend the rest of his days in peace. Later he wrote to the People of the United States, dated September 1, 1805, telling how Yusuf had won the throne by murder and had driven him to Egypt, where he had obtained rank under the Mamelukes and ceased to repine the loss of the kingdom. Then Eaton had arrived and given him hopes of better fortune, and they concluded a treaty stipulating recovery of the throne for him and containing provisions advantageous to the United States. Should he have believed that engagements entered into by an American agent would be disputed by the agent's government?

Then Hamet summed up about the strongest case made against the Lear treaty:

> General Eaton and myself with our joint followers had already advanced 600 Miles into the Kingdom of Tripoli; and a general defection had seized my brothers army, and all things prepared the protected of America to be hailed Sovereign of his usurped Throne. At this juncture a peace is concluded in which a Throne, acquired by rapine & murder, is guaranteed to its usurper, and I the rightful Sovereign, the friend and ally of America, am left unprovided for. No article in my favor, no provision for me and my family, and no remuneration for the advantages I had foregone in trusting to American honor.

He said that when the expenses of his retinue were paid out of the $200 a month, he, a sovereign prince, was reduced to $1.50 a day. Had it not been that Eaton had assisted him with his own finances in Syracuse, his lot would have been hard indeed. Eaton with his generosity could not realize that he would come to experience straitened circumstances himself. Hamet then asked that the United States take interest in his case, and at least send him back to Egypt indemnified for the comforts lost in uniting his fortunes with the Americans.

When Eaton returned to the United States he undertook some lobbying for Hamet. President Jefferson submitted the appeal to Congress in a special message January 13, 1806.

Clearly Hamet had fared poorly from the Americans in the Mediterranean. Still, neither Jefferson nor Madison can be fairly charged with bad faith. They had recognized from the beginning that they were too remote from the scene of action to appraise accurately a shifting situation or an individual's worth and had left to Barron the decision of what use might be made of the ex-Bashaw.

The only formal compact with Hamet was the one executed by Eaton at the beginning of their march from Egypt, which Barron disavowed. It contained a clear provision that Hamet would be restored to the throne and that the United States would supply the means of placing him there, but there was a safeguarding clause which limited the government's exertions to what comported with its own interests. The final article provided that the convention should be submitted to the President for his approval. This gave the document a tentative and not a permanent binding effect, though it was provided that while ratification was being awaited operations against Tripoli should be continued.

Madison's instructions, it will be recalled, were guarded, and so was the correspondence of the Secretary of the Navy to Barron and Lear. But it was never made clear to Hamet that the United States might deal with his brother at any instant it chose, and he was quite obviously proceeding under the impression up to the very minute of Eaton's recall that he was engaged in a co-operative endeavor which would be pursued by both parties to the end.

Opinions might differ as to whether a breach of faith were involved somewhere along the line of negotiation and command. But if so, the changed attitude was not that of the administration in Washington, but of Barron, who controlled in the field. Lear could scarcely be credited with turning on Hamet because he had been against the enterprise from the start. But Barron had sanctioned it, then dropped from under it.

Apart from Eaton's conditional treaty, which was witnessed by Lieutenant O'Bannon, Midshipman Peck, and Dr. Mendrici, the only other commitment to Hamet might be found in Barron's oral instructions to Captain Hull of the *Argus*, expressed on September 15, 1804, with Eaton present. He was quoted as saying: "The Pasha may be assured of the support of my squadron at Bengazi or Derne . . . and you may assure him also, that I will take the most effectual measures . . . for cooperating with him against the usurper, his brother, and for reestablishing him in the regency of Tripoli." What Barron said to Hull in the presence of Eaton—and Hull agreed as to the substance—could not be regarded a compact binding on the nation. Eaton maintained nevertheless that the term "cooperation" was tantamount to "alliance" and that he had never heard one syllable about peace from the President on down, "which did not look forward beyond an effort to chastise the enemy," and "I always felt a confidence that such an effort, well conducted, would dethrone him."

Then, in his communication to the Secretary of the Navy upon his return home, he summed up:

> On entering the ground of war with Hamet Bashaw. M^r OBannon and myself united in a resolution to perish with him before the walls of Tripoli, or to triumph with him within those walls. In the former event we should have acquitted our duty—in the latter glorified our country. . . . And to encourage Hamet Bashaw to perserverence, and in order to move understandingly with him I induced the convention which has been made the base of our treaty with his rival.

In submitting to Congress the appeal from Hamet, President Jefferson analyzed the responsibilities of the government closely. He said concerted operations by those who had a common enemy had been regarded entirely justifiable, and possibly favorable to both, "without binding either to guarantee the objects of the other." He thought Barron's instructions and letters showed that "a cooperation only was intended and by no means an union of our object with the fortune of the ex-pasha." He adverted to the safeguards in Eaton's convention against any ill effect to the United States. He said it was never contemplated to put a land army into the field or raise, pay and subsist an army of Arabs. He explained that Lear thought the best moment had arrived to listen to overtures of peace and that he did gain the restitution of Hamet's family. Jefferson pointed to his own difficulty: "In operations at such a distance it becomes necessary to leave much to the discretion of the agents employed." Clearly he felt that nothing was owed to Hamet. He had to deal with accomplished actions and could not go back to Derna six months after it had been evacuated, nor to war without grave provocation after Lear had signed the peace. In an age of slow communication, he had to rely on the judgment of his subordinates, faulty as it might sometimes be, and support them unless they were in marked error. Had Barron sent Eaton and Hamet ahead from Derna, and then attacked Tripoli, and ended the war in outright victory, none would likely have been more pleased than Jefferson.

Largely through Eaton's efforts, Congress in April appropriated $2,400 as an "immediate and temporary relief" for Hamet but that was all he got, aside from the monthly allowance, the aggregate of which was $5,895. When Hamet received the $2,400, Naval Agent George Dyson in Syracuse cut off his monthly allowance. A year later he was still appealing for the restoration of his family, and it was then discovered that

Lear had permitted addition of the sneak clause which gave Yusuf four years in which to return the captive wife and children.

The discovery came when Dr. George Davis, formerly chargé d'affaires at Tunis, was transferred to be consul at Tripoli, replacing Dr. John Ridgely, surgeon of the *Philadelphia* when she was captured, who had taken the post when the treaty was signed. Dr. Davis reached Tripoli May 7, 1807, on the *Hornet*, and by Jefferson's instructions made an immediate demand on Yusuf for the release of Hamet's family. Only then was the secret clause disclosed. But pressure from Davis made Yusuf release the captives, and on May 12, five days after taking his post, Davis wrote to Hamet that all the members of his family would be ready to embark in twelve days except his married daughters, who desired to remain with their husbands. Davis did not give the number, but one had married her cousin, Yusuf's eldest son, Bey Mahomet. Hamet, who in his correspondence was invariably deferential to the Americans, wrote appreciatively to Davis that "I shall always preserve the memory of how much you have assisted me."

That strained relations still existed between Tripoli and the United States might be seen from the fact that two Tripolitan officials, unidentified by Davis, refused to receive his consular gifts. He took the rejection as an affront and complained about it to Sidi Mohamet Dghies, the Secretary of State. While he awaited transportation for Hamet's family, which was slow to arrive, Davis studied the condition of the regency and reported to Secretary Madison that "this Kingdom has been on the decline for many years, and the American war has given it a more severe blow than was believed."

Davis observed Bashaw Yusuf: "There are certain moments in which timidity marks every action, and others in which he is alike deaf to reason and blind to his own interest. When under the influence of the latter he is cruel and sanguinary, and, at such a moment, no exertion of mine could save the unfortunate children of the ex-Bashaw."

The regency in 1807 was being torn by revolts attributed to friends of Hamet, and these caused Yusuf to remain suspicious of his elder brother. Davis found that Hamet possessed many friends of significance. The report gave further evidence that had strong naval pressure been exerted by Barron and had Eaton been reinforced, Tripoli could have been taken readily and Yusuf toppled from his throne.

Time dragged on and in October Davis was still trying both to arrange transportation and get possession of Hamet's family. Finally Yusuf relented and on October 7, 1807, Davis was able to write to Hamet saying his wife, three sons, and one daughter were on the vessel which carried the letter, and that Yusuf had promised such remittances from time to time as he would judge necessary for Hamet's support. Yusuf would be guided merely by "the dictates of his own breast." Then Davis finally washed his hands of Hamet on behalf of the United States: "Should the provisions allowed you by your brother be unequal to your expectations, or should it at any future period be totally discontinued, you are not thence to found any claim upon the American government. The United States did not feel themselves authorized to demand such a concession from Yusuf and they never will insist upon its performance."

Hamet passed slowly into obscurity. Yusuf agreed to an allowance provided he would settle in Morocco but this the elder declined, and demanded instead the governorship of Derna. Yusuf at length consented and Hamet governed Derna for two years, only to be expelled again by Yusuf for reasons which do not appear, and compelled to flee to Egypt much as he had done before the coming of Eaton. Twenty-five years after the restoration of his family to him, in October, 1832, a Mahommed Bey presented himself to the American consulate in Alexandria and said he was Hamet Karamanli's eldest son. Hamet had died long before and his destitute family was living in Cairo. The son would have liked aid but there is no indication that he received any. Possibly Hamet would have died in poverty if he had never met Eaton. One thing seems clear from the records: he was a gentle, courteous, honorable man.

Jefferson was much chagrined when he learned of the secret clause in Lear's treaty. The President adverted to it in a special message to the Senate November 11, 1807, saying it was a "declaration" signed by Lear the day after the treaty was executed, allowing four years for the restoration of the family. Jefferson, in submitting the papers the Senate requested, said that upon receipt of the information from Davis about the clause he had caused Lear's correspondence to be re-examined carefully and that no reference to this declaration had been found. The President thought it was due the Senate and the Bashaw that he make a candid statement of the facts. Much indignation arose over the deceit, but Jefferson stated that the family had probably been reunited by the time of his message and consequently no legislative action followed his remarks. Congress did not pass out money readily in that era, though a House committee did go so far as to recommend another grant to Hamet.

After Eaton and Hamet had returned to Syracuse from Derna, Eaton's little army of mercenaries and Greeks was disbanded and scattered about the Levant, perhaps never to understand fully just what a glorious page they had helped to write in the early history of the Western republic.

While in Syracuse Eaton had made out his accounts and had found that the entire cost of the expedition from Alexandria to Derna, including the pay of all the troops, was $39,108. Much was accomplished on little; but rations for a considerable time had consisted of roots, wildcat meat, and wild fennel!

Adjutant Leitensdorfer, according to a contemporary account, witnessed on the ship enroute to Syracuse the "mortification of the ex-Bashaw and the ravings of his lieutenant general" Eaton. Though a colonel in the recent polyglot army, he took off his insignia, and in his American clothes began working his way toward the Tyrol to see what had happened to the son of his first marriage. In Albania the Turks identified him as an apostate Mohammedan and made him a slave. His career for a time was almost as checkered as before he met Eaton; he raised himself from slavery by healing Turkish sailors, married again temporarily in Palermo, and finally in 1809 reached Salem, Massachusetts, as a seaman, to throw himself on the hospitality of his old commander Eaton, who was then retired at nearby Brimfield.

Eaton sent him to Washington loaded with commendatory letters. There, because of his skills in surveying, draftsmanship, and engineering, he obtained employment under Jefferson's chief architect, Benjamin Henry Latrobe, and became known as the surveyor of public buildings. The job may have amounted to little more than janitor service but he did make maps and shoes and do a variety of tasks, and guard the Capitol as a night watchman. Congress rewarded him for his African service with a grant of 320 acres in Missouri and, twenty-four years after his arrival in the United States, with the pay of a colonel for the time he served under Eaton, plus (of all things!) mileage allowance for his march across the desert.

Though Eaton had not seen fit to give him much mention during the campaigning, but dwelt on O'Bannon, Peck, Mann, and Farquhar, Leitensdorfer fared best of any in the desert army at the hands of the U.S. government. Being janitor in the Capitol must have given him advantageous lobbying opportunities. Senator Stephen Row Bradley of Vermont, Eaton's old patron and a distinguished Revolutionary War veteran, sponsored legislation in his behalf.

He was an unusual man. His career was made the theme of a Vienna theatrical production. He passed at different times as Christian, Jew, and Moslem, and worked in thirty different occupations with ability and craftsmanship, not including deserting, at which he excelled. The contemporary writer Charles Prentiss said of him:

> He can utter the Hebrew words almost exactly like a rabbi in the synagogue. He can recite the Latin prayers and homilies of the Christians after the manner and in the tone of the Capuchins; and he can

pronounce the religious sentences of the mussulmen in Arabic, with the earnestness and emphasis of a mufti. All these he performed for me one morning with singular readiness and skill.

Lieutenant Presley Neville O'Bannon continued his service on the *Argus* and in October, 1805, maintained communications between Hull and the American chargé d'affaires in Tunis, James Dodge. After that his name disappeared from the reports of naval activities in the Mediterranean until his resignation from the Marine Corps was accepted by the Secretary of the Navy March 5, 1807. It has generally been supposed that he resigned from disappointment over the recall of the Eaton expedition. But that remains no more than a presumption. Very likely his action resulted from a natural desire to set up a family and enjoy a normal life after such arduous service and long absence from home.

Virginia awarded him a jeweled sword with the Mameluke hilt inscribed on one side, "Presented by the State of Virginia to her gallant son Priestly [sic] N. O'Bannon," and bearing on the other side reference to the assault and capture of Derna, April 27, 1805. Beneath an eagle's head on the hilt was a plate showing O'Bannon holding the flag in one hand and a sword in the other. The curve of the present Marine Corps sword has been moderated from O'Bannon's Mameluke blade. He went to Richmond in the autumn of 1811 to receive the sword, which he considered "the most pleasing reward for my service." That, in fact, was all he received, other than the satisfaction from a duty well performed.

O'Bannon and his wife migrated to Kentucky in 1809, at the recommendation of his brother, John, who earlier had set up a distillery in Woodford County, near Versailles. Their son, Eaton, apparently died young, causing O'Bannon deep grief. He served in both houses of the Kentucky legislature and died at the age of seventy-four at Russellville, September 12, 1850. His remains were removed in 1920 from Russellville to Frankfort. There a memorial to him states: "As Captain of the United States Marines he was the First to Plant the American Flag on Foreign Soil."

Naval vessels have been named for him, the first a destroyer in World War I by Secretary of the Navy Josephus Daniels, and another in World War II, which sank a Japanese battleship at Guadalcanal and earned sixteen battle stars. These honors to the early Marine Corps lieutenant were richly deserved. The name O'Bannon has been propitious in American history.

Eaton, the dominant personality in the Mediterranean after the departure of Preble, served as judge advocate of the court of inquiry on board the *Constitution* in Syracuse Harbor in the summer of 1805, which vindicated Bainbridge of blame in the loss of the *Philadelphia*, then sailed for the United States on the brig *Franklin*, an old Tripolitan and Tunisian craft being used as a supply ship. He had written a long report to Secretary Smith on the voyage and flayed about especially at Lear, whom he termed

> A colonel . . .
> Who never set a squadron in the field
> Nor the division of a battle Knows
> More than a spinster.

Captain Samuel Barron took offense at Eaton's letter and began to talk about "some remarks which cannot pass unnoticed as it seems to reflect on a Character which hitherto the Breath of Slander has never dared to Sully." He apparently was thinking in terms of a duel, though how he could have fought one is a question. What kind of a duelist or pistol shot Eaton would have made is also uncertain, but he would have been an awkward hand in a tavern brawl.

Barron read Eaton's report in a newspaper and wrote both Chief Clerk Goldsborough and Eaton asking an explanation. But Eaton's target was Lear, not Samuel Barron. He wrote to Barron that he had no intention to traduce his character, but ascribed his failure to fight with the squadron "to the general debility of your system over which you could have no control." Then of Lear he added: "The bad management, which no sophistry can veil, and the reproach due to the inglorious manner of finishing the war with Tripoli, I meant should affix to our commissioner of peace. I then believed, and still believe him the author and the Agent of our national disgrace." He went on to charge Lear with duplicity and intrigue. He seemed more than generous in his attitude toward Barron, who impeded victory just as clearly as did Lear. None could believe the war would have been delayed had he retired much earlier and given the command to Rodgers. In another memorandum, presumed to have been written by Eaton, Rodgers was quoted as having said that "his name should be written in blood on the walls of Tripoli before he would consent to pay a cent for ransom and tribute."

Probably Eaton had not expected an ovation on his arrival home, yet few returning soldiers ever received a more hearty, admirous greeting. There was something fresh and spectacular in the march of the little band across hundreds of miles of wasteland and the triumphal storming of Derna when nearly everyone had thought the expedition was hare-brained. He landed at Hampton, Virginia, in early November and began his progress toward the capital.

After the applause of Richmond he reached Washington November 18 and the *National Intelligencer* of two days later commented:

On Monday arrived in this city, our gallant and distinguished countryman, GENERAL EATON, in good health. His achievements merit, and we entertain no doubt will receive, the respectful attentions of his fellow citizens in every part of the union. The glorious and joyful events, in which he has so gloriously participated, entitle him to the gratitude of every man, who feels an interest in the honor of his country, and who properly appreciates the liberation of three hundred captive citizens.

His reception in Washington was most cordial. Officialdom did not then know what a stormy petrel he could turn out to be. Not only was he dined by Jefferson at the Executive Mansion, but also publicly at a dinner held in his honor by the city, attended by the great of the capital from Chief Justice John Marshall down. Jefferson's message to Congress delivered on December 3, 1805, spoke warmly of his part in the peace:

In a government bottomed on the will of all the life and liberty of every individual citizen become interesting to all. In the treaty, therefore, which has concluded our warfare with [Tripoli] an article for the ransom of our citizens has been agreed to. An operation by land by a small band of our countrymen and others, engaged for the occasion in conjunction with the troops of the ex-Bashaw of that country, gallantly conducted by our late consul, Eaton, and their successful enterprise on the city of Derne, contributed doubtless to the impression which produced peace . . . Reflecting with high satisfaction on the distinguished bravery displayed whenever occasions permitted in the late Mediterranean service, I think it would be useful encouragement as well as a just reward to make an opening for some present promotion by enlarging our peace establishment of captains and lieutenants.

Clearly Jefferson, though a peace man, was not indifferent to the navy which had its full burst of glory under him in a far distant sea.

Unhappily the cordiality of the reception was short-lived, and the blame could be assessed against none but Eaton himself. Destined to controversy, he became a central figure in the political embroilment attending discussion of the Tripolitan treaty, in which he drove for the impeachment of Lear and compensation of Hamet. Being irreconcilably opposed to the treaty, which the Jefferson administration espoused, Eaton was thrown to the Federalists, which was a natural affiliation because of his early attachment to Timothy Pickering, who as Secretary of State had first sent him to Tunis, and now was a senator from Massachusetts and a nettlesome leader of the Jefferson opposition, though scarcely as odious a character as many Republicans believed him to be.

Eaton's main trouble was the boisterous nature of his assaults on Lear and the treaty in the Washington barrooms, where in the short space of a few weeks he undertook to compensate for the aridity of his long African journey. He was loud to the extent of bombast in recounting for imbibing officials, congressmen, and capital hangers-on the fantastic tale of his desert march and belaboring Lear for undercutting him and his men at their hour of triumph. Perhaps the most disturbing element of his tirade was that it held a strong vein of truth. Eaton's career shows that he clearly was not a drunkard, but there appears agreement that at this and other periods he sought to drown his disappointment and chagrin. Instead of gaining sympathy, he was shunned by those who had heard his story repeatedly, and given ample drinking room. Though one may never be justified in seeking solace in drink, if ever it were warranted in public affairs the instance might well be judged to be Eaton's.

After Eaton's return, Senator Bradley of Vermont, who long since had gained for him his commission in the Army under Anthony Wayne, introduced a resolution on March 18, 1806, to commemorate the achievement of Eaton, O'Bannon, and Mann, and their marines and other forces, "who for the first time spread the American eagle in *Africa*, on the ramparts of a Tripolitan fort, and thereby contributed to the release of three hundred American prisoners from bondage." The resolution would set aside a township six miles square to be called Derne, as a memorial to the conquest of that city. Each of the three officers would be given 1,000 acres, while the surviving Marine Corps enlisted men would receive 320 acres each. Like the resolution to present him with a medal and a sword, this effort of Bradley's was defeated by being postponed from time to time and allowed to die. There are a number of towns in the United States called Eaton, and two tiny O'Bannons, but no Derne or Derna.

Eaton went to Massachusetts in early 1806 to be reunited with his family. In Philadelphia, enroute, he took time to write Preble. Arrangements had been made to receive him at Elizabethtown, New Jersey, and in New York, New Haven, Hartford, and Springfield—attention indicative of the public enthusiasm generated by his return. But he looked for a chance to meet the former commodore, who, he hoped, would call on him at Brimfield: "Besides the gratification I shall have in waiting on you in my own homely cottage I may profit of your advice whether it would be most suitable for me to go to tending mill (I have a village mill) or to preaching the gospel." A bit later he contemplated starting a newspaper and also writing a history of the Tripolitan War. He did neither.

Congress in 1807 at last got around to considering Eaton's accounts and authorized the State Department to recognize those considered valid, and the amount was squeezed down to $12,636.60, which was probably as good a settlement as he could expect in view of the freedom of his remarks. But considering that he had dissipated his private resources in the service of the country and of Hamet, it was a trifling allowance and scarcely more than the pay he would have had a right to expect as naval agent for more than two years—a post from which he resigned upon reaching Boston in 1806. No longer did he have his little merchant ships or the nest egg he had begun to accumulate but which he had pledged in behalf of Hamet in Tunis and lost.

More valuable than the treasure he had expended in the nation's interest were the words of the clear-sighted Preble, who wrote at about the time of his return, saying that his arduous and dangerous services "have justly immortalized your name and astonished not only your country, but the world." Then Preble expressed disappointment that he and Eaton had not been able to co-operate: "I have often regretted that you did not leave the United States with me. An earlier acquaintance might have given greater reputation to our arms, while I was on the station, but could not have increased your glory beyond its present zenith."

Nobody around the Washington bars was recording how much Eaton drank or what he said and the tenor may be judged only from the reaction to it, but the bitterness of his writing in his more reflective moods suggests that orally he was a personage the administration always would like to have out of town. He met in John Randolph a greater master of sarcastic invective than he could ever hope to become, and while he did win the sympathy of committees, his great service to the nation went essentially unrecognized, as did that of O'Bannon, by the federal government of their own day. Eaton's home state of Massachusetts, though not that of his birth, gave him more generous consideration than the federal government, and on February 26, 1806, it rewarded him with 10,000 acres in Maine and with lavish praise. The tract must have been a wilderness for he never lived on it. He settled down to a life of gentle frugality in the small New England town, where his fellow citizens bestowed on him enough respect and confidence to make him a justice of the peace and send him to the Massachusetts legislature.

When he learned in 1807 of the death of Preble, he wrote a letter of deep regret. He lamented poverty of language to express his feelings but was able to say:

The world has lost a *man*—America a *pillar*—and I a *friend*! I would not arraign the dispositions of God—but why he should let *ordinary death* kill such a genius, dismantle such a frame, chain such a patriot, and freaze such a heart, can only be explained in his own mysterious cabinet. But that Preble is gone makes to me the terrors of the mighty king less terrible, and a futurity more wished for—if there be a heaven of the just, he is there!

Once opportunity seemed to be pointing a finger at him again. When Aaron Burr was casting about for aids in his scheme to take over the Southwest, and was toying with names like Truxtun and Eaton who might have legitimate grievances against the Jefferson administration, he approached Eaton with a request that he lead the army he planned to send against the Spanish provinces of North America. Such an operation was exactly to Eaton's fancy, and if there were an American of that day who could take an army through the wastes of western Texas and northern Mexico, Eaton was that man.

But Eaton was intensely patriotic. His devotion to his country was, like O'Bannon's, the impulse, more than any desire for personal gain (and there was scant promise of loot on the desert), which drove him to his unpopularity in the consular service and to the completion of his extraordinary march. When he came to believe that Burr planned not the conquest of Spanish North America but the dismemberment of the United States, he went to the Connecticut congressmen John Cotton Smith and Samuel Dana. They failed to take Burr's scheming seriously and felt that if Eaton talked about the plot Burr would be able to destroy him. But Eaton, undeterred, knowing how much can be accomplished by a few, gave the full story to Jefferson.

After Eaton's exposure, General James Wilkinson hastily turned state's witness. When the Burr trial was held in Richmond, Eaton put on his old desert sash and at times baggish Turkish trousers and appeared in the barrooms, and must have had an enjoyable time outside the courthouse, though inside it Burr's able counsel, Luther Martin, no mean tippler himself and fully as garrulous as Eaton—"a man of fine parts and ardent spirits"—undertook with some success to destroy his credibility as a witness. Martin went back to the old Georgia court martial case, showed Eaton's prison sentence, though the War Department had not upheld it, and brought out that his claim, long pending, had but recently been honored, and that he was therefore a paid witness for the Jefferson administration. After the trial and his tavern diatribes, he returned to Brimfield with his reputation even more frayed nationally than after his round of Washington drinking.

Ardent for the country, he was lukewarm as a partisan in politics. When his neighbors asked him to run for Congress on the Federalist ticket, he explained his refusal to be a party candidate by saying both Federalists and Republicans had become too closely adhered to *party*;

that a pledge to either would cramp his freedom of deliberation. "We want more union, more energy . . . The *names* Federalism and Democracy, which, at this moment, split the affections of our countrymen, ought to be lost in the proud name of *American*."

Consul Mordecai M. Noah gave a fair estimate of him when he said: "Eaton was an honorable, generous man, sincerely devoted to his country, and ardent in his zeal for its glory; had his temper been more mild and persuasive, and his character and services more correctly estimated, he would have ranked among our most distinguished citizens." Still, had he been as gentle as Hamet or as compromising as the legislators who deprived him of recognition for his achievement, he would never have got his army across the desert.

He maintained a correspondence with ex-Bashaw Hamet and the two remained cordial friends, after their many desert quarrels, until death parted them.

His last years in Brimfield appear to be those of a disillusioned, impoverished man, and when he died in 1811, ostensibly of rheumatism and gout, at the age of forty-seven, "heartbreak" could have been the only valid diagnosis. He left two sons and three daughters.

When the United States came during the next year to fight its War of 1812 with Great Britain, Preble and Eaton had passed, but a good number of Preble's boys survived to give the nation a creditable showing in that unhappy conflict.

If the Battle of Waterloo was won on the playing fields of Eaton, it is not too much to say that the spectacular naval victories of 1812–1814 were won on Preble's training ground in the Mediterranean and in the spirit of Eaton's driving march across the desert.

CHAPTER TWENTY-SIX

Decatur and Peace Without Price

G RADUALLY the naval forces of the United States were with-drawn from the Mediterranean. The prosperous merchant shipping that had carried American produce under Yankee sea captains into virtually every southern European port began to disappear, though from other causes than Barbary interference.

The *Leopard* and *Chesapeake* affair in 1807 signaled the approaching conflict between the United States and Great Britain, after the navies of the two countries had enjoyed years of harmony and, in general, cordial relations between officers and sailors in the British-held Mediterranean harbors.

Jefferson's Embargo of 1807–1809 laid a withering hand on American maritime enterprise. Then in 1812 the United States and Great Britain finally drifted into war, which neither nation wanted. Neither peoples understood clearly what the fighting was about. The peculiar War of 1812, costly and viciously fought, a war of disgrace and heroism, of poltroons and patriots, still produces long treatises in which students analyze the relationships between the two countries and undertake to determine the cause of the conflict, and generally arrive at conflicting explanations.

The war brought a more abrupt stoppage, following the leaky embargo, to American merchant shipping. Instead of trading vessels, the Atlantic coast ports sent out privateers to prey on British commerce. Concern over the Barbary shore waned. Even had there been situations warranting attention, the United States did not possess the means to approach them.

By the time of the general pacification of Europe in 1815, violent change had occurred in some of the Barbary governments.

In Algiers, the Dey's throne had been so saturated with blood and littered with corpses that ruling had become the most hazardous occupation in that distressed land. The American tribute, together with the payments still wrested from other Christian powers, formed so rich a take that they promoted avarice and revolution, not stability and national development. The Army, continually alert for plunder, found it in 1805 by cutting down Dey Mustapha, and this obese monarch felt a dagger thrust and went to his fathers.

Achmet, who succeeded him, tried the expedient of war with Tunis to divert attention from his throat, but because it was more difficult to fight across the North African land route than on the Mediterranean waves, soon forgot the treaty stipulations between Algiers and the United States and sent his corsairs out in search of American merchant vessels. This was in the period of 1806–1808, one of diminishing American shipping, due to the British Orders in Council and the Napoleonic decrees, when cargo ships were being seized and when Jefferson was experimenting with the embargo. The embargo, effective from December, 1807, until March, 1809, kept American merchant vessels in their harbors, except the venturesome smugglers, and these could not expect to enjoy the protection of the United States when violating its laws.

Still, some American merchant craft plied the Mediterranean and Achmet of Algiers was able to lay hands on a few of them. When in 1807 the United States fell two years in arrears with its tribute to Algiers— partly by design and partly because it had few vessels willing to sail past Gibraltar and risk almost certain seizure by Britain or France in the Mediterranean or its ports, and therefore no means of delivering the ransom—Achmet, late in 1807, at about the time the embargo was being applied, sent out his considerable Navy with orders to take American craft. The fact that the Tripolitan War had not been carried to a conclusion, and that the walls of Tripoli had not been battered down, had its very pronounced bearing on the willingness of other Barbary States to risk American displeasure. Dey Achmet had the effrontery to tell Tobias Lear, then consul at Algiers, that the depredations contemplated should not be regarded as hostile measures against the United States nor circumstances which ought to disturb cordial relations! He would like to enjoy the pleasures of piracy and have the tribute remain undisturbed.

After this notice the piratical vessels were again unleashed as of old and they did seize three vessels, two of which they convoyed back to Algiers and condemned. With the third American, the schooner *Mary Anne*, out of Boston, they got a stomach full. The crew was led by Ichabod Sheffield, a master of the Preble or Eaton mold. No sooner had the corsairs boarded, overrun and captured the vessel, and put her under a prize crew, than the old crew suddenly rose, drove this prize crew across the deck, killed four, dumped their bodies overboard and put the

other four in an open boat and sent them out to fare the best they could
and make land if possible. Then Ichabod and his Americans sailed their
own vessel back to Naples.

Achmet did not seem at first disturbed because Lear was paying the
arrears in tribute. He released the other vessels; all seemed tranquil.
But in March, 1808, after three months of indifference, he changed his
tune and whimsically set a price of $16,000 on the lives of eight subjects
—the four in the open boat did not seem to have won their way back to
Algiers—and served notice that unless Lear produced the money at once
he would be looking from behind the bars of the bagnio. He declared
also that he had any number of warships which he would send out
against American commerce.

Lear paid. Perhaps it was a fortunate circumstance that Preble was
dead and could not know of it. Lear put in a protest of mere words when
some of Preble's grape was needed, and squared up the entire amount
of the tribute due to that date. But Dey Achmet did not enjoy the fruits
of his statesmanship long. He began a clamor of "More! More!" and like
his predecessors, wanted naval supplies instead of cash, and naval supplies he obtained when the *Leonidas* made her way to Algiers by special
dispensation from New York. Lear and Achmet were elated but the Dey
failed to recognize that where there was treasure thieves would break
in. On November 7, 1808, while he was in the full enjoyment of money
and gifts from the United States, tendered to protect a commerce which
legally under the embargo terms had no right to be on the seas, the
Turkish soldiery slipped a knife into his vitals and put on the throne
an obscure keeper of a little mosque, named Ali, who should have tended
to his religious duties and not undertaken to carry scruples into North
African politics. Within less than five months he failed to awake one
morning because a silk cord had managed to get twisted around his
neck.

The Turkish soldiery now had Algiers under their full sway and followed the procedure customary in such situations of putting one they
regarded a humble tool on the throne. He was Hadji Ali, old, decrepit,
and mean, but it developed that in his sunset he wanted to see the sunrise
of a new and glorious Algiers, with much booty, to which all the Christian nations would pay tribute or feel the sting of his cruisers. Though
neither Great Britain nor France nominally paid tribute to Algiers, Great
Britain, at a time when most commerce had ceased in the Mediterranean,
sent him provisions, consular gifts, and naval supplies to keep him in line
as an ally in the war against Napoleon or any other enemies Britain might
encounter.

That was the situation at the outbreak of the War of 1812 between

Great Britain and the United States. Hadji Ali was plundering away, his corsairs seizing mainly Portuguese vessels, though that nation was an ally of England. Reis Hammida, his feared and daring corsair, became a plague to the Mediterranean and it appeared that all the noble efforts of Preble, Decatur, Eaton, Rodgers, and the many others for the suppression of the curse of piracy had amounted to little.

Algiers, making a reasonable gamble, sided with Great Britain and against the United States during the War of 1812. Great Britain sent an able diplomat, Lord Haytesbury, to keep Hadji Ali in line, and the Prince Regent buttered him with an obliging letter, their main object being to fill him with the dread of Napoleon's dream of universal empire, and incidentally to picture the United States as weak in naval resources and not much to rely on as a traveling companion in the Mediterranean.

Unhappily it was an accurate picture, if American naval power were compared with Great Britain's. Just after the United States declared war on Great Britain, on June 18, 1812, the American ship *Alleghany* reached Algiers with tribute of naval stores as provided for in the 1796 treaty and the pleased Dey ordered the cargo put ashore. Then the unloading was suddenly stopped, and the fierce old ruler informed Lear that the goods were not of the quantity or character called for under the treaty. He made a calculation using Moslem instead of Western time and concluded that the United States had fallen in arrears six months by the proper calendar. The sum thus due, plus the value of the stores required in place of the *Alleghany*'s rejected cargo, would have to be paid in cash by Lear else he would be put behind bars. The distressed, peace-loving Consul felt he had no choice but to pay, so he raised the money from the banking firm of Barci, which had been called on in earlier years.

When the Dey had the money, he severed relations with the United States and ejected Lear and all other Americans from the regency. They sailed for Gibraltar on the *Alleghany*. The Dey followed his break by ordering his corsairs to go out and seize American ships. The toll would have been heavy, except that the War of 1812 was taking American merchant shipping off the seas. The British were now seizing American ships and took the *Alleghany* when they learned that war existed and Lear did not get home until the next April.

From 1812 until 1815, the war years, the Algerines were able to lay hands on only one small American ship, a brig out of Salem, the *Edwin*, whose master, George E. Smith, and ten seamen were robbed of all they owned and put at hard labor on the mole just as had been the crew of the *Polly*, which, as Seaman John Foss wrote, had been subjected to the most enervating labor prior to the American treaty of 1796. Relations between the United States and Algiers were back exactly as they were at their miserable beginning when the North American colonies became an independent nation.

President Madison noticed this break with Algiers in sending Lear's reports to Congress on November 17, 1812, but being engaged in a desperately fought war extending from the Indian lands in the West and South, all along the Canadian border to the high seas and eventually to New Orleans, he could give no attention to the Barbary Coast. The main development there was that in 1814 Dey Hadji Ali was assassinated and the Prime Minister, who took over the power, followed him in two weeks to the grave, bringing to the throne an arrogant Turk, Omar the Aga. Names were becoming meaningless now in the quick succession from Dey to dust, but Omar the Aga, a native of Lesbos, was alleged to be a bit more intelligent and humane than some of the pride-bloated despots among his predecessors. Hadji Ali had refused to listen to private entreaties for the release of the captives, though a handsome ransom was then a standing offer from a group of American merchants in Cadiz. He said he wanted more prisoners, not fewer. Omar the Aga, taking the throne when America and Great Britain were about to terminate hostilities, never had an opportunity to realize the ransom, because after the murder of Hadji Ali, the offer of the American merchants was not renewed.

Thrifty, punctilious, sensitive President Madison had a long memory. As quickly as the Treaty of Ghent was signed and American warships were released from their duty against Great Britain, he put his finger on the map at Algiers. Happily he had better resources of naval officers and men than were available to Jefferson after the recall of Preble. The War of 1812 had developed and given further assurance to the officers who as young men had demonstrated their courage and capacity in Preble's fleet. Among them were Stephen Decatur, Oliver H. Perry, Thomas Macdonough, David Porter, James Biddle, and Jacob Jones, while among the seniors, Bainbridge, and especially Rodgers, were regarded with favor.

Madison had ample ships also, for though the War of 1812 had been costly to the Navy, some of the early stalwarts, including the *Constitution*, the *Essex*, and the *Constellation*, remained. To them could be added a number of British prizes, such as the handsome frigate *Macedonian*. Among newly built vessels was one bearing the name of the unhappy *Guerrière*, which Nelson had first captured from the French and Hull had sunk in the Atlantic. The new *Guerrière*, 44, was built in Philadelphia in 1815, at a cost of $306,158, and was one of several powerful vessels being commissioned as the war ended, including the *Wash-*

ington, 74; the *Independence,* 74; the *Franklin,* 74; the *Java,* 44; and the *Fulton,* 30. The last was a strange, heavily protected vessel with a ram, planned by Robert Fulton, Decatur, and others, and built in New York, which was a forerunner of the later ironclads. She was the first steam-propelled warship and thus marked a transition in naval warfare and attracted the attention of the world. These ships put to sea in 1815, though the Treaty of Ghent was signed December 24, 1814, and the United States thus emerged from a difficult war with satisfactory naval strength.

Madison did not await further protracted negotiations with Algiers. Having accepted the Preble doctrine that round shot had a louder thud than words, he sent a message to Congress February 23, 1815, only ten days after the text of the Treaty of Ghent reached the United States, and six days after it had been ratified by the Senate, asking Congress to declare war on Algiers. His recommendation was simple and direct. He referred to the reports from Lear he had submitted to Congress in November, 1812, which told of the Dey's hostilities:

> These have been followed by acts of more overt and direct warfare against the citizens of the United States trading in the Mediterranean, some of whom are still detained in captivity, notwithstanding the attempts which have been made to ransom them, and are treated with the rigor usual on the coast of Barbary.
>
> The considerations which rendered it unnecessary and unimportant to commence hostile operations on the part of the United States being now terminated by the peace with Great Britain, which opens the prospect of an active and valuable trade of their citizens within the range of the Algerine cruisers, I recommend to Congress the expediency of an act declaring the existence of a state of war between the United States and the Dey and Regency of Algiers, and of such provisions as may be requisite for a vigorous prosecution of it to a successful issue.

Congress a week later agreed that a state of war existed and empowered the President to take the measures he deemed necessary. The declaration of war actually had been made in the first instance by Algiers, when the Dey dismissed the American consul and ordered the seizure of American ships. Madison was well prepared. Commodore Stephen Decatur organized his squadron of ten splendid vessels, three frigates, three brigs, two sloops-of-war, and two schooners, with the gleaming new *Guerrière,* just completed by the Philadelphia yard, the flagship.

Commodore Decatur had a captain on his flagship, William Lewis, who as a midshipman had served on the *New York*, the *Constitution*, and the *John Adams* during the earlier phases of the Barbary Wars, and then on the *Argus*, and had sailed the bomb vessel *Vengeance* across the Atlantic. The other frigates were the *Constellation*, 36, Captain Charles Gordon; and the *Macedonian*, 38, Captain Jacob Jones. The sloops-of-war were the *Epervier*, 18, and the *Ontario*, 16; the 14-gun brigs the *Firefly*, *Spark*, and *Flambeau*; and the schooners the *Torch* and *Spitfire*, each with 12 guns.

Another squadron was organized under Commodore Bainbridge in Boston. Decatur made ready and sailed first, leaving New York May 20, 1815. He lost the *Spitfire* after a few days; she dropped her masts in a gale and had to put back, but rejoined the squadron later.

Lear had changed his ultra-pacific disposition and had expressed hope on leaving Algiers that the place could "be humbled to the dust," but he was superseded by William Shaler to whom Secretary of State James Monroe had given directions to negotiate a treaty and, in effect, to allow no nonsense to enter into its terms. In Monroe, Decatur and Shaler had the backing of a tough-fibered Secretary of State who still carried in his body the Hessian lead he had taken at Trenton and in his heart the emotional wound of the Bladensburg campaign, in which the British army the summer before had captured Washington. He had been one of the most resolute of the city's defenders and had demonstrated again the personal leadership, at a time when most other people were losing their heads, which was to make him President. None could anticipate softness to the Barbary powers with Decatur commanding the squadron and Monroe in control of the treaty-making.

At Cadiz and Tangier, before entering the Mediterranean, Decatur inquired of the American consuls to learn if the Algerine pirate Reis Hammida chanced to be in the Atlantic, where he had ventured from time to time to build up his warlike reputation and capture unarmed Portuguese merchant craft. Their information was that he had passed inside the capes and might be found in the Mediterranean. Clearing Gibraltar on June 15, 1815, after a rapid passage from New York, Decatur picked Cape de Gata as the likely place to encounter the Algerine. Without tarrying in Gibraltar lest warning of his arrival be communicated to Algiers and its fleet, he sailed at once and, in the Mediterranean, scattered his ships to some extent to make sure the Algerine craft would be intercepted.

On June 17 the *Constellation* espied twenty miles southeast of Cape de Gata a large frigate under topsails and identified her as the piratical flagship. Captain Gordon, who had commanded one of the gunboats in Preble's attack on Tripoli, and knew how to fight, signaled the *Guerrière* and the American ships closed in. Decatur had hoped to conceal the nationality of his squadron, but a quartermaster on the *Constellation,* through either mistake or pride, hoisted the American flag and Reis Hammida, taking immediate alarm, crowded on all canvas and sped toward his home port. His flagship was the *Mashuda,* 46, not to be confused with Murad Reis' old *Meshouda* which Morocco had purchased from Tripoli, but a larger, more formidable ship. She alone, at this period, would have made Algiers the leading seapower on the Barbary Coast.

Reis Hammida had his rise to fame in the Mediterranean during the period between Lear's peace with Tripoli and the return of an American squadron to that sea under Decatur, but it was altogether by his own ability and courage, for he had come down to Algiers from the Adrar Budfel (Mountain of Snow) as a poor Berber lad, one of the Kabyles who inhabited the Jurjura range. Being an inlander, he probably was naturally attracted to the sea. From a common sailor he made his way up by his own talents under a variety of none-too-competent Deys to become the Grand Admiral of the Algerine fleet—a more worthy route to the honor than that in Tripoli of the Scotch renegade Peter Lisle, by marrying the Bashaw's daughter.

The battle which ensued was fought as could have been expected from the talented Decatur, mercilessly and swiftly. Closest to the speeding Algerine ship was the doughty *Constellation,* being about a mile away when the *Mashuda* saw the American ensign and took fright, but she was a good sailor and soon opened. On the *Constellation*'s starboard was the *Guerrière* and astern was the sloop *Epervier,* won from the British in the War of 1812. On her port was the sloop *Ontario,* built in Baltimore in 1814. The other vessels of Decatur's squadron were either on scouting duty or were well astern when the *Mashuda* was sighted.

When the Constellation began the battle at long range, the *Mashuda* replied. At the very opening, one of the *Constellation*'s shots wounded the Algerine commander. Then, obviously judging that he could not outrun the Americans and make Algiers on the other side of the Mediterranean, Reis Hammida suddenly wore ship and made for the security of any neutral port on the Spanish coast. This allowed the *Guerrière* to draw nearer and the *Ontario* to cross her bow. Decatur's flagship drew close enough to receive musketry from the corsair's decks but he did not reply, being intent on coming alongside, where he suddenly let loose a devastating broadside that shivered the Algerine ship and swept her deck. The *Guerrière*'s carronades were 42-pounders. A 42-pound shot found the wounded Reis Hammida sitting on his quarterdeck, from where he was giving orders to his crew and directing the battle. The big ball cut his body through the middle.

The death of their celebrated captain appeared to dispirit the Algerine gunners, who had not been effective against the Americans from the beginning. Before they could answer Decatur's first devastating broadside he was alongside again and sent a second broadside into the *Mashuda*'s hull and across her decks, this time driving every Algerine sailor and gunner to greater safety below deck, except for a few with muskets, who had been wounding some few Americans on the *Guerrière*'s spar deck. Seeing the defenseless condition of his adversary and being a chivalrous contestant who did not want to take life unnecessarily or merely for the sport of it, Decatur sailed ahead and out of range of the *Mashuda*, which had not yet struck. Then the *Epervier* drew near on her starboard and, gaining the impression that she was trying to escape from the *Guerrière*, threw into her broadside after broadside. Captain John Downes of the *Epervier* had been one of Preble's boys. He played dexterously about the *Mashuda*, taking musket fire indifferently, until his sloop-of-war with her eighteen guns had put nine broadsides into the hostile craft. These were more destructive of morale than of life. They were enough for the big corsair. She hauled down her flag and surrendered.

Her deck was a scene of fearful carnage but she had plenty of manpower remaining. The bag of prisoners was 406, many of whom were wounded. Her decks were littered with 30 killed. The killed and the large though indefinite number of wounded were casualties mainly from the *Guerrière*'s two broadsides because the Mussulmans had gone below decks by the time the *Epervier* began her pounding. The American loss was trifling, and was confined to the *Guerrière*. One was killed and 3 wounded by the *Mashuda*'s musketry, but 3 others were killed and 7 wounded when one of the flagship's guns burst on discharge. The *Macedonian* now came up under Captain Jacob Jones and Decatur assigned her to convoy the Algerine flagship into Cartagena as a prize.

While combing the seas in his progress toward Algiers with his reassembled fleet, Decatur, on June 20, picked up an enemy brig off Cape Palos, the *Estedio*, 22, which sought safety in flight but was overtaken after three hours. She ran into shoal water where it was dangerous for the frigates to venture but some of Decatur's alert smaller craft, the *Epervier*, the *Torch*, the *Spitfire*, and the *Spark*, made after her and gave her a shelling while some of her crew were trying to get ashore in small boats, one of which was battered and sunk. Helpless and grounded, the *Estedio* surrendered. The prize crew which went on board found that the fire of the American brigs and schooners had been most effective. Twenty-three bodies were on the deck. The eighty survivors were taken with the prize into Cartagena.

The resolute American commodore now announced to a council of his ship captains an intention to enter the harbor of Algiers and bring the warring Dey to terms or batter down the walls of his strongly guarded city, and sink whatever ships he might have in the harbor as well. On June 28, 1815, the splendid American squadron of frigates and lesser craft stood into Algiers Harbor flying a flag of truce denoting a parley and the Swedish flag signifying that the Swedish consul, John Norderling, in whose hands American affairs had rested since the ejection of Tobias Lear, was the agent desired on board. He came with the captain of the marine, a sort of secretary of the navy for Algiers, just as that functionary fifteen years before had arrogantly given the score to Bainbridge in the same harbor.

This time the message was imparted by Decatur, whose information was that the renowned Reis Hammida was dead and his flagship captured; that an additional brig was an American prize, and that a letter from the President of the United States was at hand for the Lesbian Dey, Omar. (The term "Aga" meant to the Ottomans the chief military or civil officer.) Madison's letter advised Omar that the United States had declared war against his regency and that he could choose either peace or war; but if peace, then it must be durable, founded on stipulations mutually beneficial, and with neither party claiming anything it was not prepared to give in like measure to the other. Simply stated, Madison and Monroe were washing their hands of the iniquitous tribute the United States had been paying Algiers from the time of Donaldson's treaty of 1796 until the dismissal of Lear, which had been a considerable financial drain on the infant republic, and not one penny of which had contributed to good will or had even been appreciated, any more than a highwayman feels affectionate toward a victim whose pocketbook he has extracted.

Decatur and Shaler wrote a joint communication making it clear from the start that no negotiations would be entertained except on the principle that the United States would enjoy a most-favored-nation status with Algiers and that the fountain which had for so long spouted out the tributes from America was drier now than the Sahara sands. When the captain of the marine wanted to beguile the Commodore and the new consul on shore to discuss terms, and promised an amnesty, Decatur informed him that the negotiations would be held on the *Guerrière* and nowhere else. When he suggested an amnesty during which any Algerine ships at sea might return unmolested into their home port, Decatur said it was war, and that if any Algerine craft showed before the Dey ratified peace, she most certainly would be taken by the Americans.

Gradually it began to dawn on the rulers of Algiers, who had long received favored treatment and bountiful gifts from the United States,

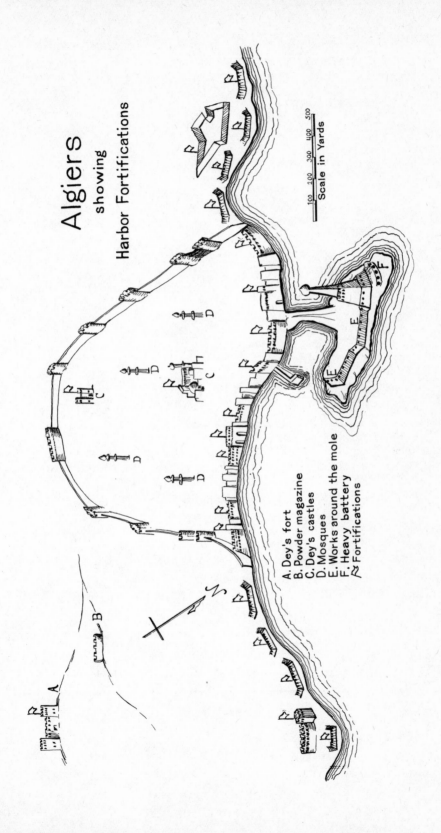

Algiers

showing

Harbor Fortifications

A. Dey's fort
B. Powder magazine
C. Dey's castles
D. Mosques
E. Works around the mole
F. Heavy battery
⚔ Fortifications

100   200   300   400   500

Scale in Yards

including the beautiful frigate *Crescent* which embodied the best New England workmanship and never should have sailed except under the American flag, that a different sort of negotiator was at the doorstep. No soothing words were here, but firm tones spoken while an arm rested over the muzzle of a gun. The generous Swedish consul Norderling and the captain of the marine were kept busy going back and forth, but on June 30 they returned to the *Guerrière* with authority to negotiate a treaty.

The terms were laid down by the American consul Shaler and the meaning was as different from the treaty of 1796 as an eagle's scream from a dove's coo! No tribute, no presents, ever, under any pretext; most-favored-nation treatment; all prisoners to be released immediately without ransom; return of consular property left by Lear; and compensation to American citizens of $10,000—this mainly for the *Edwin* crew. In war, prisoners were to be exchanged and not made slaves.

Other provisions were included such as would make for normal peaceful relations between civilized nations. When the captain of the marine looked at the provisional draft, he shook his head doubtfully. Algiers had never stooped to any such treaty, which would sacrifice the long-standing method of financing the state by leeching on the other powers. Tribute was ingrained in the Algerine system. But when the captain of marine contended that the two Algerine ships Decatur had captured ought to be returned to their owners, the American commissioners were not severe on this point because the ships were of utterly no value to the United States.

Then the captain asked for a truce during which the Dey might reflect on the terms. As easy would it have been for him to stay the hand of the grim reaper as to get more time from Decatur. The American Commodore would not grant a day, or an hour, or even a minute! If any Algerine ships appeared while the Dey meditated, most surely they would be taken or sunk. The reply was precisely that: "Not a minute. If your squadron appears in sight before the treaty is actually signed by the Dey and the prisoners sent off, ours will capture it."

Only one concession would Decatur make: that if the reply boat returning to the *Guerrière* from the shore flew a white flag, hostilities would cease at that moment. The concession was not material because Consul Norderling gave assurance that the boat would not show the flag unless it had the American captives on board and the Dey had signed the treaty.

Speedy as was the transaction on shore, it was sufficiently protracted as to almost lose Algiers a cruiser. While the Dey was reading the articles and signing the treaty a returning Algerine warship appeared and Decatur gave chase with the *Guerrière*. But before he got alongside, the boat was seen leaving shore flying a white flag, which signaled that the two nations were at peace and that the American prisoners were being carried out to the squadron. Ten Americans who had been enslaved by Hadji Ali and kept in the bagnio of Omar the Aga were in the boat. Most of them were from the *Edwin* but two of that crew had been liberated when ransomed by an American business man as British subjects, a means employed to save the Dey's face, and two others had been picked up as passengers on a ship under the flag of Spain.

Poor, hapless American seamen! After their long incarceration, when they were beginning to enjoy the blessings of freedom and were about to be restored to their own families in the United States, they were placed aboard the *Epervier*, commanded now by Lieutenant John T. Shubrick. He had entered as a midshipman in 1806 and therefore had been too late for service under Preble. He carried also the official copy of the treaty with Algiers. Worthy of note was the fact that just six weeks after Decatur's squadron sailed from New York, the *Epervier* cleared Algiers Harbor with notice that the major part of Decatur's work had been accomplished. How different was the conduct of the Mediterranean squadron under the determined Decatur from that of earlier squadrons under the slothful Morris or the physically ill and mentally irresolute Barron!

The *Epervier* sloop-of-war of 477 tons, an English-built brig captured in the War of 1812, has been described as "tubby" because she was shorter by ten feet, though of the same beam, than some of the other vessels of her class. She passed Gibraltar with her load of information and repatriated captives on July 12, 1815, made for the open Atlantic, and was never heard of again. The Atlantic was being swept by a heavy gale about the time she would have been approaching the North American coast and the assumption was that she foundered.

Apart from the tragedy of the liberated seamen of the *Edwin*, there was another poignant story in the disappearance of the *Epervier*. To Captain William Lewis, who had commanded the flagship *Guerrière* under the Commodore, was entrusted the mission of delivering to Secretary Monroe the treaty with the Dey. A veteran of both the quasi-war with France and the Tripolitan War, he had but recently married and Decatur gave him the assignment as a favor that would take him home. Lieutenant Benedict I. Neale, who had served as a midshipman aboard the *Congress* but had not reached the Tripolitan conflict, had married the sister of Lewis's bride. He, too, was granted leave and the two officers sailed for a homecoming as passengers on the *Epervier*. No doubt Decatur was thinking at the time of his own young wife back in Baltimore, and, needing a responsible courier, selected the young men whose return would mean happiness. The two brides waited for them in vain.

Decatur in a message to the Secretary of the Navy explained the reason why he restored to Algiers the frigate and brig. The Dey earnestly sought them as a means of saving face with his own people. Decatur judged them unsafe to send across the Atlantic. "It was determined by Mr. Shaler and myself that, considering the state of these vessels, the great expense which would be incurred by fitting them for a voyage to the United States, and the little probability of selling them in this part of the world, it would be expedient to grant the [Dey's] request."

Shaler reported to Secretary of State Monroe receipt of the $10,000 indemnity—the unfortunate members of the *Edwin* crew who were to enjoy much of it never had that opportunity—and 120 bales of cotton, a useful commodity since it was just coming into fuller production in the United States.

Decatur, who had seen his brother shot down by treachery, placed no faith in the durability of the treaty. When he wrote Secretary of the Navy Benjamin W. Crowninshield about it he told how the peace had been agreed to at the mouths of his cannon because Algiers feared even greater losses than those she had already experienced. "And I beg to express to you my opinion that the presence of a respectable naval force in this area will be the only certain guarantee for its observance."

The day the treaty was signed Consul General Shaler went ashore to set up his office and to receive the $10,000 indemnity. He found that resentment existed not so much against the Americans as the British, who were charged with informing the Dey and his ministers that the Americans would be "swept from the seas in six months," when in fact they were making war on Algiers with the very vessels they had captured from the British. That was in part the case, though the Dey's minister who so complained must have mistaken the new *Guerrière* for the vessel Isaac Hull battered into a wreck and then blew up when she was nearly sinking. But apart from the *Epervier*, the once proud British frigate *Macedonian* was there. Decatur, who in battling her with the *United States* demonstrated his mastery in rapid firing, had brought her a prize into Newport on December 6, three years before.

Decatur was wrong in a sense about the durability of the treaty. Never again to the present time did Algiers in any form or by any device demand tribute from the United States and never did she enslave another American seaman. The Dey balked when the brig Decatur had captured was not returned promptly because Spain claimed the ship as having been captured in Spanish waters. After some negotiation and a near-resumption of hostilities, she was restored to her Algerine owners.

Meantime Decatur, after the treaty with Algiers, went on to Tunis, leaving to squadrons which were to follow him from the United States the duty of impressing on Algiers the power and attentiveness of the United States to her Mediterranean shipping interests. The golden era of American merchant shipping, merging into the reign of the clipper ships and the ocean steamboats, was coming on. Two years after Decatur's peace with Algiers, the *Savannah*, the first trans-Atlantic steamboat, made the crossing. Certainly in the age of expanding trade and closer international ties—in the decades of peace which followed Napoleon's fall—piracy had become an anachronism. It had no place in the scheme of modern human affairs. None deserved greater credit than the U.S. Navy for ushering it out, and the demise was accompanied by a resounding funeral gun.

Tunis had been torn with internal strife and murder after the death of Bey Hamouda in 1814, who strangled on a cup of coffee taken after the long fast of the Ramadan. Revolutions followed, in one of which the Sapatapa with whom Eaton had quarreled was seized at the chess table and his body was dragged through the streets.

Controversy had arisen between Tunis and the United States over the disposition of prizes taken by an American privateer in the War of 1812 and the treaty was looked on by Mahmud, the latest Bey, with indifference. Decatur anchored in Tunis July 26, 1815, conferred with American Consul Noah, and after ascertaining the facts about the compensation due the American ship which had been robbed of her prizes, demanded as their fair value the sum of $46,000, payable immediately. Here again the Bey tried to inveigle Decatur ashore but it was a foolish endeavor. He was not dealing with a Commodore Morris. Then he even more foolishly requested delay, a word Decatur did not understand. The guns of the fleet looked big and the $46,000 was paid to the American consul.

Two prizes captured by the American privateer likewise had been taken into Tripoli and Bashaw Yusuf had allowed the British to recover them in violation of the treaty with the United States. Decatur sailed from Tunis August 2 and was in Tripoli Harbor demanding $30,000 for the two ships on the 5th. Yusuf blustered and talked of war again with the United States. But Decatur had crossed his path before and was known. Word of what had happened when the American squadron was at Algiers had run like wildfire along the North African shore and Yusuf concluded that there was prudence in compliance. In negotiations held on board the *Guerrière*, the American consul at Tripoli, Richard B. Jones, felt that a fair value of the two ships was $25,000 and Decatur agreed to that figure, but he stipulated that the Bashaw release ten Christians he held as slaves. Two were Danes and their liberation was a gesture in recognition of the many kindnesses of the Danish consul Nissen to the prisoners of the *Philadelphia*. Decatur must have been thinking fondly of Preble at the time. He demanded liberation of the other eight, all Neopolitans, in recognition of the loan by the King of the Two Sicilies of the gunboats with which the intrepid Commodore had bombarded Tripoli in 1804.

In all his undertakings Decatur liked to follow through, and the liberation of the Neapolitans was not completed until they were set on their own soil. He took the fleet by Syracuse and on to Messina, where the pilot declined to take the *Guerrière* into the harbor under an unfavorable wind. Decatur was unwilling to order Captain Downes to go in without the pilot and assume the responsibility for the ship under such a circumstance. He studied his charts, then piloted the ship in himself. The King of the Two Sicilies thanked the American commodore for the consideration shown his subjects. The Danes he landed at Naples, under their consul's care.

Bashaw Yusuf enjoyed tranquillity in Tripoli for a time. Checked in his naval and piratical career, he turned to the interior and reconquered Fezzan, the vast desert country to the south. An account of him was given by Consul Noah who from his post in Tunis visited Tripoli and studied the country. He judged Yusuf a "man of shrewdness and sagacity, not unmixed with some liberal traits." He had three wives, one white and two Negro, and a number of children.

Murad Reis, while now "of little note," remained an inveterate hater of Americans. Noah found that to his original dislike he had added an intolerance born of zest for his new faith. He quarreled with the Bashaw, was banished to Egypt, then was restored but acted mainly as an interpreter. The once impressive Tripolitan navy had shrunk to "a few vessels, poorly equipped and armed, and not calculated to do any essential injury to the Christian powers."

But Bashaw Yusuf suffered from a faithless son. Even as he had turned against his father, so his eldest child, Bey Mahomet, procured arms, revolted, and was ordered to Bengazi. Returning, he made an attempt on his father's life and again was banished to the outer provinces. Then the land was torn by a cruel civil war between Mahomet and Yusuf's second son, Ahmed. So bloody and heartless did this strife become that the Porte, at the request of the British and French consuls, intervened, and ended the rule of the sanguinary Karamanli family. The dynasty's best representative appears to have been the gentle and forgotten Hamet. The Grand Seignior issued a firman, and after 1835 the country was governed as a Turkish satrapy until it was occupied by the Italians in 1911.

Decatur, touching at various ports, worked his way back to Gibraltar, where he met Bainbridge with the second squadron from the United States intended to show American power in the Mediterranean. A third squadron was made up a little later under Commodore John Shaw, and for some years American frigates patrolled the sea. Bainbridge had as his flagship the powerful *Independence*, the first of the Navy's new 74s. He had frigates, sloops, brigs, and schooners—among them the gallant old *Enterprise*, on which Sterrett had fought so handsomely in the early stages of the Tripolitan War. But not least in importance with the fleet was a fourteen-year-old midshipman from Tennessee, a veteran already of the remarkable voyage of the *Essex* under David Porter in the Pacific, whose name would occur in another war, David G. Farragut.

Decatur reached New York November 12, 1815. He had often been a national hero—when he had destroyed the *Philadelphia*, when he had commanded the front line in Tripoli Harbor, when he had captured the *Macedonian*, and on lesser occasions—but he was now taken into the heart of the American people because he had finally handled the task in the Mediterranean with firmness, efficiency, and dispatch; in the way which reflected honor on the United States and gave security to the nation's shipping; in short, in the way the American people wanted it done. Congress, once reluctant in appropriating funds for ships but now glorying in the achievements of the American naval officers and sailors and marines, appropriated $100,000 to indemnify Decatur and his personnel for the prizes they had taken from Algiers, but which they had restored during the treaty negotiations.

Great Britain played the major role in ending the piracy of Algiers, as far as the European powers were concerned, though she was guided by Decatur's superb example. Such was the testimony of the Parliament debates and of the *London Annual Register*. Lord Exmouth (the Edward Pellew who fought Benedict Arnold on Lake Champlain in 1776) led a combined British and Dutch fleet to Algiers in August, 1816, and when he could get no satisfaction from the Dey, bombarded the town and reduced its defenses. The Dey signed a treaty with Great Britain totally abolishing Christian slavery. The situation was summed up by the British naval historian Captain E. P. Brenton, an authority on this period and brother of the distinguished American-born British Admiral, Sir Jahleel Brenton, when he said Britain would not tolerate a condition which the United States had shaken off in resentment.

Few in American history have been entitled to greater applause than the heroes of the Barbary Wars: Preble, Eaton, Stephen Decatur, O'Bannon, Sterrett, Trippe, Somers, Lawrence, Wadsworth, Israel, James Decatur, and the many others who in a far sea, in long absence from home, fought and endured so resolutely against an iniquity which other powers either had been compelled or were willing to look on with indifference, and who finally ended it for all time.

When confronted with the problem, the new and relatively feeble American nation, enervated and indebted after its long battle for independence, devoted more to local than national interests, and shunning international involvements, went in where others either had feared to venture or had failed, and in a great burst of power and courage, and over the handicaps of commanders at times ill-suited or incompetent, won, and left the world in a better state for its effort.

The peacefully disposed President Madison deserves some credit also for bringing Mediterranean piracy to a close.

While the wars with the Barbary Powers may be looked upon at times as a comparatively minor episode in the great American story, few events had greater significance, because they gave the United States a Navy, and the Navy a glorious beginning.

Acknowledgments

THE principal sources employed in writing this book are the letters and reports of the participants and other official correspondence contained in the seven volumes entitled *Naval Documents Related to the United States Wars with the Barbary Powers.*

Assembly of these papers was begun under the direction of Secretary of the Navy Claude A. Swanson in 1934, and the final volume was published in 1944. Compiled by the Office of Naval Records and the Navy Department Library under the supervision of Captain Dudley W. Knox, they are not only comprehensive, but are arranged chronologically, so that documents relating to a specific incident are readily located by the date on which the event occurred.

Thus the necessity of annotating this book has been largely obviated. The writer has used dates freely in the text. Since most of the material is from the Naval Records the source may be found easily in most instances without specific citations and the annoying use of supernumerals in the text. The writer has made his own interpretations and evaluations, which are clearly shown and should not be attributed to any of the individuals who have been most helpful in supplying information and suggesting sources.

The Naval Documents include copies of the pertinent William Eaton papers possessed by the Huntington Library at San Marino, California.

My appreciation is due and expressed to many who assisted me in the research for this book, among them several attendants at the Tripoli Library, who were most solicitous to give aid and who three or four times a day served a heavy, black, palatable demitasse coffee and honey, a veritable liquid bonbon, to break the routine.

The value of visiting Tripoli, more than from any library research, was in becoming familiar with the harbor where the principal fighting of the Barbary Wars was centered and where the *Philadelphia* was captured, and catching the atmosphere of past centuries in the old town, much of which remains as it was during the American bombardments. Splendid as has been the spread of the city along the waterfront and toward the interior, the old sections retain the small shops, the winding streets, and the imposing castle of ancient times. Wandering through this section, one feels almost transported to the era when Preble's squadron stood off the harbor and when the prisoners of the *Philadelphia* labored in slavery for Bashaw Yusuf.

In addition to the detailed information contained in the Naval Documents, material for Chapter Five, "The Building of the Ships," has been obtained from the excellent work by Ira N. Hollis, *The Frigate Constitution, The Central Figure of the Navy Under Sail;* Frederick Stanhope Hill's *Twenty-six Historic Ships;* James Fenimore Cooper's *History of the Navy;* Chapelle's excellent *History of the American Sailing Navy;* G. S. Laird Clowes's *The Story of Sail; Encyclopaedia Britannica* articles on ships and naval ordnance; Theodore Roosevelt's *The Naval War of 1812;* and Winthrop L. Marvin's *The American Merchant Marine.*

Other works which were helpful on distinct phases of the Barbary Wars are Ray W. Irwin's *The Diplomatic Relations of the United States with the Barbary Powers;* Louis B. Wright and Julia H. MacLeod's *The First Americans in North Africa,* dealing mainly with William Eaton's expedition; Francis Rennell Rodd's *General William Eaton,* an interesting biographical view from an English source; and, of much value as a guide to anyone dealing with this period, Gardner W. Allen's *Our Navy and the Barbary Corsairs,* a highly competent but comparatively brief study made at the beginning of this century.

The rank of naval officers as used in this book at the outset of the Jefferson administration—a list which did not contain the name of Captain Richard Valentine Morris—is from the Navy Department statement of June 11, 1801, in Naval Documents Barbary Wars, Vol. I, p. 488. The list differs from that used by Sabine and other writers, which was quite obviously of later preparation, and contained Morris' name. The point made in the text is that the original list was altered and Morris was accommodated.

With the early life and later activities of Stephen Decatur, assistance was obtained from Charles Lee Lewis' splendid biography, *The Romantic Decatur,* and the older biography by Alexander Slidell Mackenzie, who served in the Mediterranean in 1816 and wrote from Decatur's papers. In dealing with Commodore Bainbridge, the biography written by his friend Dr. Harris has been used for facts in many instances, and with Preble, the early work by Lorenzo Sabine. The biography by Eaton's contemporary, Charles Prentiss, gives a sympathetic picture, while another friendly early treatment is contained in Cornelius

C. Felton's work, which gives the history of Eaton's adjutant Eugene Leitensdorfer.

In this research the files of the London *Times* for the years 1800 to 1805 were covered to obtain the setting of the Barbary disturbances in the larger wars in Europe, while the research included also the available issues of a number of American newspapers for this period, especially those circulating in the Washington area, the *National Intelligencer* and the *Republican Advocate.* Hezekiah Niles had not yet begun his *Weekly Register.*

My thanks are expressed to others who supplied valuable help:

Lieutenant Colonel P. N. Pierce, Head of the Media Branch, Division of Information, U.S. Marine Corps, who supplied much information in the form of articles on the march of O'Bannon's marines.

William Bell Clark, Brevard, North Carolina, author of numerous works on the Navy during the Revolutionary War, now engaged in collecting and editing for the Navy Department the Naval papers related to that war—for the loan of copies of manuscript material and volumes of the Barbary Wars papers until the writer could assemble a complete set, and for conversations about early naval officers. Mr. Clark kindly read the galley proofs of this book and made suggestions of value.

E. K. Timings, Assistant Keeper of the Public Records, British Public Record Office, London, for assistance during a reading of the British consular reports covering the period of the Tripolitan War. In this work the writer was assisted by Mrs. D'Arcy Hart, an experienced research worker of London.

A. T. Smail, Scottish National Library, Edinburgh, in search for information about Peter Lisle, or Murad Reis.

Gerald D. McDonald and Mrs. Shirley Spangler, Room 315 (History), New York Public Library, for assistance during research.

Miss Alma Skinner and Robert Gross, Newspaper Room, Library of Congress.

Henry J. Dubester, Chief of the General Reference and Bibliography Division, and Alvin Moore, Jr., Stack and Reader Division, Library of Congress.

Florence Blakely, Reference Department, and Elvin Strowd, Circulation Department, Duke University Library.

Helen Rose Cline, Parish Recorder, Trinity Church, New York, for information on ransom collections in colonial New York for the ransom of American prisoners in Barbary. More detailed information on these collections was obtained from the study published by James G. Lydon, Associate Professor of History at Duquesne University, in the *New York Historical Society Quarterly,* July, 1961.

Mr. and Mrs. Joseph Sloan, Waynesville, North Carolina, former residents of Tripoli, of value for their information and in establishing contacts there.

William M. Goza, Clearwater, Florida, attorney. Charles F. Haywood, Boston, attorney and author, for information about Peter Lisle, alias Murad Reis. The librarians and curators at the British Museum and the Public Record Office, London. Mary Seagle, librarian, Hendersonville, North Carolina, for obtaining books on inter-library loan.

Finally I am indebted to my wife, Dorothy Thomas Tucker, for assisting me and taking notes during research trips to libraries in New York, Washington, Durham, London, Tripoli; for reading consular reports at the British Public Record Office in London, reading the manuscript, and making many valuable suggestions.

Bibliography

ABBATT, WILLIAM. "A Forgotten Hero." Reprint of William Ray's diary and story "The American Tars in Tripolitan Slavery" and his biographical note of General William Eaton, *The Magazine of History with Notes and Queries*, 1907 and 1911.

ABERNATHY, THOMAS P. *The Burr Conspiracy*. New York, 1954.

ALLEN, GARDNER W. *Our Navy and the Barbary Corsairs*. Boston, 1905.

———. *Our Naval War with France*.

BADGER, BARBER. *Naval Temple*. Boston, 1816.

BAILEY, ISAAC. *American Naval Biography*. Providence, 1815.

BEECHEY, F. W., and BEECHEY, H. W. *Proceedings of the Expedition to Explore the Northern Coast of Africa, from Tripoli Eastward, etc.* London, 1828.

BENNETT, MARION T. "Lt. Presley Neville O'Bannon, USMC," annotated manuscript about O'Bannon's career containing information supplied by the office of the U.S. Marine Corps Historical Archives and Library and other sources, and the O'Bannon Family Tree. Copy from Division of Information, U.S. Marine Corps.

BLYTH, STEPHEN C. *History of the War between the United States and Tripoli*. Salem, 1806.

BOVILL, E. W. *The Golden Trade of the Moors*. London, 1958.

BOYD, JULIAN P. (ed.) *The Papers of Thomas Jefferson*. Princeton, N. J., 1953. (Vol. 7.)

BRANT, IRVING. *James Madison 1800–1809*. Indianapolis, 1953.

BROADLEY, A. M. *The Last Punic War. Tunis, Past and Present*. 2 vols. Edinburgh, 1882.

BRODERICK, GEORGE C. and FROTHERINGHAM, J. K. *The History of England (1801–1837)* (The Political History of England Series. Vol. XI). London, New York, Bombay, and Calcutta, 1911.

CATHCART, JAMES LEANDER. *The Captives, Eleven Years a Prisoner in Algiers*. Compiled by his daughter, J. B. NEWKIRK. La Porte, Indiana, 1899.

———. *Tripoli—First War with the U.S.* Compiled by Mrs. J. B. Newkirk. La Porte, 1901.

Chapelle, Howard I. *History of the American Sailing Navy.* New York, 1949.

Chew, Samuel C. *The Crescent and the Rose: Islam and England during the Renaissance.* New York, 1937.

Clark, Thomas. *Naval History of the United States of America from the Commencement of the Revolutionary War to the Present Time.* 2 vols. Philadelphia, 1814.

Clark, William Bell. *Gallant John Barry.* New York, 1938.

———. Letters of Richard Somers to his sister. Copies from Barry Hayes Hepburn Collection.

Cleveland, Stephen. *History of the War between the U.S. and Tripoli.* Salem, 1806.

Clowes, G. S. Laird. *The Story of Sail.* London, 1936.

Collier's Encyclopedia.

Commercial Advertiser. Newspaper. New York.

Cooke, F. O. "O'Bannon in Libya." *The Leatherneck,* August, 1942.

Cooper, James Fenimore. *Lives of Distinguished American Naval Officers.* Auburn, New York, 1846.

———. *History of the Navy of the United States of America.* 2 vols. Philadelphia, 1839.

Cowdery, Jonathan. *American Captives in Tripoli—or, Dr. Cowdery's Journal.* Boston, 1806.

Cyclopaedia of American Biography.

Decatur, Susan (Mrs. Stephen). *Documents Relative to the Claims of Mrs. Decatur.* Pamphlet. Georgetown, 1826.

Dictionary of American Biography.

Dodd, William E. *Life of Nathaniel Macon.* Raleigh, 1903.

Eaton, Reverend Arthur W. H. *A Memorial Sketch of William Eaton.* Privately printed, 1893.

W. E[aton]. "Interesting Details of the Operation of the American Fleet in the Mediterranean." Comments in a letter from W. E. Esq. to his friend in the County of Hamshire. Springfield, Mass. (no date). (Pamphlet in New York Public Library.)

Elgin, Lord (Thomas Bruce). *Memorandum on the Subject of the Earl of Elgin's Pursuits in Greece.* 1810.

Eller, E. M. "To the Shores of Tripoli." *U.S. Naval Institute Proceedings* March, 1933.

Emerson, Edwin, Jr. *A History of the Nineteenth Century Year by Year.* New York, 1902.

Emmons, George F. *The Navy of the United States from the Commencement, 1775–1853.* Washington, 1853.

Encyclopaedia Britannica.

FELTON, CORNELIUS C. *Life of William Eaton* ("Sparks' Library of American Biography," 1st series, Vol. IX). New York, 1844.

FOLSOM, BENJAMIN. *A Compilation of Biographical Sketches of Distinguished Officers of the American Navy.* Newburyport, 1844.

FOSS, JOHN. *A Journal of the Captivity and Suffering of John Foss.* Newburyport, 1798.

FROST, HOLLOWAY H. *We Build a Navy.* Annapolis, 1929.

FROST, JOHN. *Pictorial History of the American Navy.* New York, 1845.

FURLONG, CHARLES M. *The Gateway to the Sahara.* New York, 1909.

FURMAN, BESS. *White House Profile.* Indianapolis, 1951.

GEER, ANDREW. "To the Shores," *The Leatherneck*, November, 1952.

GOLDSBOROUGH, CHARLES WASHINGTON. *The U.S. Naval Chronicle.* Washington, 1824.

GOOLD, WILLIAM. *Portland in the Past with Historical Note of Old Falmouth.* 1886.

GREEN, JOHN RICHARD. *History of England* ("World's Best Histories" series, Vol. IV). New York and London, (no date).

GREENHOW, ROBERT. *History and Present Condition of Tripoli.* Richmond, Virginia, 1835.

GUIZOT, M., and DE WITT, MADAME GUIZOT. *The History of France*, translated by ROBERT BLACK. New York and London, 1878.

HARRIS, THOMAS, M.D. *Life and Services of Commodore William Bainbridge.* Philadelphia, 1837.

HAYWOOD, CHARLES F. *Eastward the Sea.* A novel written from the Naval Documents of the Barbary Wars. Boston, 1961.

HILL, FREDERICK S. *Twenty-six Historic Ships.* New York, 1903.
———. *Romance of the American Navy.* New York, 1910.

HOLLIS, IRA N. *The Frigate Constitution, the Central Figure of the Navy under Sail.* Boston, 1931.

HOWLAND, FELIX. "Tripolitan Background of the War of 1801–1805," *The Marine Corps Gazette*, March, 1938.

HUNT, WILLIAM. *The History of England (1760–1801).* ("The Political History of England" series, Vol. X.) London, New York, and Bombay, 1905.

IRVING, WASHINGTON. *Life of George Washington.* New York, 1857.

IRWIN, RAY W. *The Diplomatic Relations of the United States with the Barbary Powers.* Chapel Hill, 1931.

JACKSON, G. A. *Algiers: Being a complete Picture of the Barbary States, etc.* London, 1817.

JOHNSON, EMORY RICHARD. *History of the Domestic and Foreign Commerce of the U.S.* 2 vols. Washington, 1915.

JOHNSTON, HARRY H. *A History of the Colonization of Africa by Alien Races.* Cambridge, England, 1930.

KNOX, DUDLEY W. *A History of the United States Navy.* New York, 1948.

LANE-POOLE, STANLEY. *The Story of the Barbary Corsairs.* New York and London, 1890.

Letters and Reports of Consuls Tully, Lucas, McDonough, and Lanford in Public Record Office, London.

LEWIS, CHARLES LEE. *The Romantic Decatur.* Philadelphia, 1937.

LEYDEN, JOHN, M.D. *Historical Account of Discoveries and Travels in Africa,* Edinburgh, 1817.

LINCOLN, C. H. *The Hull-Eaton Correspondence during the Tripoli Expedition of 1804–5.* ("Proced. of Am. Antiq. Soc.," Vol. XI.) 1911.

LOSSING, BENSON J. *The Pictorial Field Book of the War of 1812.* New York, 1869.

LYDON, JAMES G. "Barbary Pirates and Colonial New Yorkers," *New York Historical Society Quarterly,* July, 1861.

LYMAN, THEODORE. *The Diplomacy of the United States.* Boston, 1828.

MACLAY, EDGAR STANTON. *A History of the U.S. Navy from 1775 to 1894.* New York, 1894.

MACKENZIE, ALEXANDER SLIDELL. *Life of Stephen Decatur.* Boston, 1846.

Magazine of American History, Vols. II and III.

MARVIN, WINTHROP L. *The American Merchant Marine.* New York, 1902.

MARTIN, MARY. *History of the Captivity and Sufferings of Mrs. M. Martin, who was Six Years a Captive in Algiers.* Boston, 1807.

McDONOUGH, DR. BRIAN. *British Consul at Tripoli, Correspondence.* Public Records Office, London.

MERRIMAN, ROGER B. *Suleiman the Magnificent 1520–1566.* Cambridge, Mass., 1944.

METCALF, CLYDE H. *A History of the Marine Corps.* New York, 1939.

MINNIGERODE, MEADE. *Lives and Times, Four Informal American Biographies.* New York, 1925.

MORRIS, RICHARD VALENTINE. *A Defense of the Conduct of Commodore Morris During His Command in the Mediterranean.* New York, 1804.

National Intelligencer. Newspaper. Washington, D.C.

Naval Documents. *Barbary Wars.* 7 vol. Washington, 1939–1944.

Navy, Book of. New York, 1842.

NEFF, JACOB K. *Army and Navy of America.* Philadelphia, 1845.

NOAH, M. M. *Travels in England, France, Spain and the Barbary States.* New York, 1819.

Parton, James. *Life of Thomas Jefferson.* Boston, 1874.

PAULLIN, CHARLES O. *Diplomatic Negotiations of American Naval Officers.* Lectures at Johns Hopkins, in 1911.

———. "When Was Our Navy Founded?" *U.S. Naval Institute Proceedings*, Vol. 36. March, 1910.

———. *Commodore John Rodgers*. Cleveland, O. 1910.

PETERSEN, CHARLES J. *The American Navy*. Philadelphia, 1856.

PLAYFAIR, SIR ROBERT LAMBERT. *The Scourge of Christendom*. London, 1884.

———. *Travels in the Footsteps of Bruce in Algeria and Tunis*. London, 1877.

PRENTISS, CHARLES. *Life of the Late General William Eaton*. Brookfield, 1813.

RADFORD, ADMIRAL ARTHUR W. "The Constellation—The Ship America Forgot," *Family Weekly*, February 5, 1961.

RAY, WILLIAM. *Horrors of Slavery; or The American Tars in Tripoli*. Troy, 1808. (Reprinted in *The Magazine of History with Notes and Queries*.)

RENTFROW, FRANK HUNT. "To the Shores of Tripoli," *The Leatherneck*, December, 1929.

Republican Advocate. Newspaper. Fredericktown, Maryland.

RICHARDSON, JAMES D. *Messages and Papers of the Presidents*, Vol. I. Washington, 1896–1899.

ROBBINS, ARCHIBALD. *Journal of the Loss of the Brig Commerce, etc.* Hartford, Conn., 1842.

ROOSEVELT, THEODORE. *The Naval War of 1812*. New York, 1900.

ROSCOE, THEODORE, and FREEMAN, FRED. *Picture History of the U.S. Navy*. New York, 1956.

RODD, FRANCIS R. *General Wm. Eaton. The Failure of an Idea*. New York, 1932.

RUSSELL, REVEREND MICHAEL. *History and Present Condition of the Barbary States, etc.* Edinburgh, 1855.

SABINE, LORENZO. *Life of Edward Preble*. Boston, 1847.

Salem Gazette Office. *History of the War between the United States and Tripoli*. (No author.) 1806.

SCHROEDER, FRANCIS. *Shores of the Mediterranean*. 2 vols. New York, 1846.

SCHOULER, JAMES. *History of the United States under the Constitution*. ("World's Best Histories" series) New York and London, 1882 and 1894.

SCHUYLER, EUGENE. *American Diplomacy*. New York, 1866.

SHALER, WILLIAM. *Sketches of Algiers, Political, Historical and Civil*. Boston, 1826.

SHEFFIELD, LORD (JOHN BAKER HOLROYD, 1st Earl of). *Observations on the Commerce of the United States*. London, 1783.

SOMERS, RICHARD. Letters to his sister, Sarah Somers Keen, in Barry Hayes Hepburn Collection. Copies from William Bell Clark.

SOUTHEY, ROBERT. *The Life of Nelson* (Riverside Press edition). Boston, 1924.

SPARKS, JARED (ed.) *Life of William Eaton* and *Life of Edward Preble*. ("Collection of American Biographies.") New York, 1844.

STEPHENS, J. W. *History and Geography of Algiers*. Brooklyn, 1800.

The *Times*. Newspaper. London.

TUCKER, GLENN. *Poltroons and Patriots* (History of the War of 1812). 2 vols. Indianapolis, 1954.

TULLY, RICHARD (by his sister). *Narrative of Ten Years Residence at Tripoli, In Africa, From Original Correspondence.* London, 1816.

VILLIARD, HENRY SERRANO. *Libya, The New Arab Kingdom in North Africa.* Ithaca, N.Y., 1956.

WALDO, S. P. *Biographical Sketches of Distinguished American Naval Heroes.* Hartford, 1823.

WARD, CHRISTOPHER. *The War of the Revolution.* 2 vols. New York, 1952.

WELLS, H. G. *The Outline of History.* New York, 1925.

WILSON, THOMAS. *Biographies of Principal American Military and Naval Heroes.* 2 vols. New York, 1817.

World's Encyclopaedia of Wonders and Curiosities. New York, 1880.

WRIGHT, LOUIS B., and MACLEOD, JULIA H. *The First Americans in North Africa.* Princeton, N.J., 1945.

WRISTON, HENRY MERRITT. *Executive Agents in American Foreign Relations.* Baltimore, 1929.

WYATT, THOMAS. *Memoirs of the Generals, Commodores, and Other Commanders in the Army and Navy.* Philadelphia, 1848.

Index

477

George Washington Ryan, the Ameri... soldier of fortune; Sagaldo, the smi... sadistic commander of the Spanish force... Cuba; General Maximo Gomez, the "Old Fox," who armed a handful of peasants with machettes; Elmo Batson, who posed as a traveling salesman; the incredible Antonio Macéo, whose mixed blood had molded into a strange and fascinating creature, half consecrated fighter for liberty, half debauchee and rake.

As Mingo became more deeply involved in the plots and counter-plots of the insurrection, he was thrown into contact with the scum of Havana's state-policed waterfront. He became the intimate of harlots and remittance men, patriots and gentlemen-down-on-their-luck, the worthless spawn of Spain and all the Americas, as well as the downtrodden thousands for whom the flame of freedom burned brightest when tyranny was at its most intense.

In the pages of this lusty tale, you will walk arm in arm with Mingo Dabney and Antonio Macéo as they recruit their army of *insurrectos* under the eyes of the Havana police. You will follow the rebels through the vermin-infested jungle as they fight their running battles with Sagaldo's army of a quarter of a million men. You will thrill to the beat of native drums sounding the battle cry of the revolutionists: *"Venga Mambi!"*, meaning "Come on you dirt, and die!" You will see American heroes about to be hung on the gallows, walking their last steps with trembling limbs, yet stanch hearts. You will live on an island aflame, and you will know that you have watched history being made.

Mingo Dabney begins in 1895 and moves to a thunderous climax in 1896. It is a vigorous tale of swashbuckling, of men who lived and loved for the hour, knowing that the next might bring disaster.

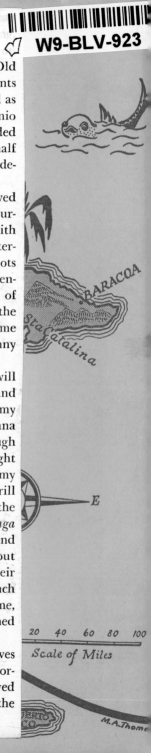

MINGO DABNEY

Other books by JAMES STREET
Oh, Promised Land, Tap Roots, By Valour and Arms, Tomorrow We Reap (with James Childers), Look Away, The Biscuit Eater, In My Father's House, Short Stories, The Gauntlet

MINGO
DABNEY

By

JAMES STREET

THE DIAL PRESS   1950   NEW YORK

For Jim Childers

who helped me so much in so many ways

To tell this story, I shifted the Virginius *episode from the Cuban Revolution of 1868-78 to the Revolution of 1895-98. I also took other liberties. I am, primarily, a story-teller and not an historian, and this book was written as a romantic adventure.*

I want to thank the following men for helping me:

Noel Houston of Chapel Hill, N. C., Dr. Fredrico Gil and Dr. Nicholson B. Adams of the University of North Carolina.

Dr. Emilio Soto Pacifico, René Abril and José Lamarque Bosch of Santiago de Cuba.

Dr. Louis A. Baralt of the University of Havana, Col. Cosme de la Torriente of Garcia's staff, and, particularly, Emilio Bacardi, former aide-de-camp to General Macéo.

JAMES STREET

Chapel Hill, N. C.
January 5, 1950

MINGO DABNEY

Chapter **1**   Mingo Dabney was leaving
the valley of Lebanon, riding a big white horse on a quest
for a woman he had known long enough to want, but really
did not know at all.

She was Rafaela Galban, a Cuban exile whose life was forfeit on her native island, and he knew not where to find
her; but on this frosty night of early 1895 he was hastening to Mobile, there to begin his search among her compatriots who were plotting to unshackle their homeland
from four hundred years of Spanish tyranny.

Mobile was a hard ride away even for a young man inflamed by a quest, and if she were not there then he must go
on until he found her, for such was the spell she had cast
upon Mingo, the first of the Dabney men ever to forsake
the family hearth.

He was the youngest of the Dabneys, not so tall as the
other men in his family, but stocky, thick-set in his shoulders,
and wiry. This was the restless Mingo, the impulsive one, and
his hat slanted at a rakish angle, covering his black hair
and shadowing his smoky brown eyes. Over the seepage of
the Mississippi swamp hung the mist, low, murky and heavy,
and pines massed on the ridges beyond. Here was Dabney
land, Dabney domain for a hundred years, and now the
youngest of his line was setting forth in search of a girl
whose hand was cold the day they met, and cold the day
they parted.

9

He remembered every moment he had spent with her, every mood; her eyes black and violent as summer storm clouds, then soft where the sun broke through. Above all, he remembered her hair, for Rafaela Galban's hair was white as frost, the gleaming silver of hair turned white in the beauty of youth. Quickened by his memories, he loosed the grip on his horse, a stallion named Shannon, and hurried through the night, over the road stretching dim in the moonlight, closing the door of his heritage behind him.

If she was not in Mobile, Elmo Batson was there and Elmo could tell him where she was. Ol' Elmo Batson. They knew him in Lebanon. Everybody knew Ol' Elmo, a drummer traveling the wilderness, peddling his wares and carrying spicy conviviality to the isolated hamlets.

It was Elmo who brought Rafaela—Rafaela Galban y Torres—into the valley of Lebanon on that rainy day months before, and he brought José Martí, her mentor; Martí the revolutionist, the prophet of Cuba's defiance, himself an exile from Spanish wrath.

The prophet was seeking sanctuary for the girl far from the cities where Spain's agents watched. Elmo brought them in and quickly took Martí out, leaving Rafaela in the protection of Lebanon, a guest of the Dabneys and their friends. She worked in the valley, seeking men and money for her country where revolution was boiling and soon must foam over. Then Martí sent for her and she returned to that communion to which she was dedicated—*Cuba Libre!*—liberty for Cuba.

And on this night when the frost on the sedge was as white as her hair, the gay young man was following her, as young men must; caring nothing for the revolution brewing among her people, thinking only of the revolution in his heart.

The white horse swept on down the road and the mist moved in from the swamps, blotting out the ridges of Lebanon. Ahead was Mobile where exiles plotted, and beyond Mobile was Cuba where shackled men spoke the name of

10

José Martí and whispered of a woman, *La Entorcha—La Entorcha Blanca,* the White Torch.

Mingo Dabney knew that Rafaela Galban was called *La Entorcha* in the flamboyant manner of the Cuban people, but he did not know she was answer to a prophecy, a symbol to the superstitious Cuban peasants, a girl consecrated to her country's death or deliverance.

She had not talked of this in Lebanon, convinced that provincial folk could never comprehend the mysticism of her dedication. She did not confide even in Mingo, whose songs and gallantry helped ease the days of her exile, because although he was the one man who might have understood, she had seen his eyes burn bright and feared a secret between them would embolden him to reach for her hand. And no man could reach for the hand of *La Entorcha Blanca.* . . .

Down from the ridges, skirting the swamps, Mingo Dabney hurried on through the night, his stallion's mane showing white in the moonlight while the pilgrim sang to keep himself awake, or hunched low over his saddle to relax his muscles; but never resting, never breaking the steady pace of the big horse.

He passed Minter's grist mill at dawn and the old miller was at his water wheel. Mingo shouted as he rode by, waving his black wool hat in greeting, then slanting his hat at such a jaunty angle that his hair rustled untamed around his left ear. The miller squinted at him in the hazy daybreak and shook his head. Bruce Dabney's young 'un was out helling again. Going to break his fool neck some day.

The sandy trace was two parallel paths curving through the forest and kept clear by the wheels of passing wagons. Mingo Dabney was a woodsman and read the story of the trail in the signs of the creatures that had passed that way; the coons, the possums, the big striding turkeys. Here a buck had stalked, there a shadow-footed doe. He read the signatures scribbled by the wild things and they kept him com-

11

pany, they and the white horse and his songs, for being a Dabney he was a singing man.

The sun came out bright before noon, melting the chill and quickening the land. The Chicasaway River was swollen and Shannon sniffed the stream and tossed his head, picking his way down the muddy path to the ferry. Mingo pulled the bell rope and sat back in his saddle and waited.

Handy MacLain came out of his shack on the other side, buttoning his coat against the wind that blew damp off the river. He brought his ferry over and Mingo led the skittish Shannon on to the flat bottom boat. Handy, a tall redneck, slow in his movements, eased the windlass and the ferry started crabbing back over the river.

"Been riding hard?" Handy asked, peering at Shannon's sweaty croup.

"Since midnight." Mingo leaned against the ferry's rail and watched the river sweeping down, silt-laden, churning yellow and red around the cypresses.

Handy held his ferry to the current and cut his eyes at his passenger, at the wide shoulders and knotty muscles showing under the tight-fitting coat. "Ain't you a Dabney?"

"I'm Mingo Dabney." The young man slouched against the rail in comfort; but even as he rested, his movements were quick and certain, his strength coiled. The river wind tingled his face, heightening the color in his cheeks and he grinned at Handy, the broad, friendly grin of Lebanon.

The riverman cranked his windlass. "Where you heading?"

"Mobile." Mingo straightened from his slouch. The ferry was approaching the bank. "You know Elmo Batson?"

Handy looked at him quickly, looking up from the cable drum. "Sure. Everybody knows Elmo."

"You seen him lately?"

"No." Handy tightened his windlass, sliding the ferry's bow into the soft bank of the river, squshing it into the mud. He might have said more, even wanted to say more, but

12

his ferry was swinging from the current and demanded his attention.

Mingo grasped Shannon's bridle. "I need to rest my horse and need a little rest myself."

"No trouble at all." The ferryman enjoyed company. He was a widower and his job was a lonely one.

"I aim to be in Mobile by sunup tomorrow. Reckon I'll have any trouble finding Elmo?"

"Not if he's in Mobile." Handy bent forward, hunching from the wind, and studied Mingo, a puzzle in his eyes. "Elmo's changed. Last time I saw him he warn't like himself a'tall. And I hear things —"

"What are you getting at?" Mingo demanded.

"I hear Ol' Elmo is messing around with them Cubans in Mobile. A good man like Elmo had oughta stay shed of them foreigners."

"Maybe you're right." Mingo was reluctant to discuss Cuba with the stranger because to him Cuba was Rafaela Galban y Torres, and he was determined to tell his plans to no man.

They led Shannon to a dry stall and to a feast of oats and timothy hay. Then Handy fed the traveler and showed him to a bed. "What time you want to wake up?" He looked closely at Mingo. For a Dabney he certainly was a quiet fellow. Most of the Dabneys were big talkers.

"Don't let me sleep much past daydown." Mingo slipped off his shoes and stretched on the bed, sighing in the luxury of the warm feather mattress.

It was dark when Handy aroused him and the moon was coming up, crawling through the black tangle of the woods. Quickly he drew on his shoes and followed the ferryman to the kitchen and to coffee. It was getting colder outside and there were creeks to ford, but he told Handy good-bye and went for Shannon. At midnight he crossed the Escatawpa River and was in Alabama. Frost was forming on the dry grass beside the road, gleaming like silver under the moon; the vivid frosty white of her hair.

13

At dawn Shannon stood upon Spring Hill, and Mingo Dabney looked down at Mobile, the first journey of his quest behind him.

The wind was cold across the hill and the pilgrim was tired and hungry. The stubble on his face was stiff, sticking his neck each time he turned his head. He wanted a shave, but more than that he wanted hot coffee and a big breakfast. First, however, he saw to Shannon's needs, quartering his horse in a livery stable near Dauphin Street. Then he found a café and ate eggs and sausage, batter cakes and syrup. Even the proprietor, accustomed to hearty eaters, marveled at his appetite, and later pointed the way down the street to a barber shop that opened early.

The shop was almost deserted and Mingo hung up his blue coat and the black wool hat and stepped into the chair, so drowsy after his ride that he almost went to sleep, the hot towels soothing him.

The barber pinched his nose, lifting it to shave the upper lip, and Mingo opened his eyes. "You know a man named Elmo Batson?"

"Hell, yes. Everybody knows Elmo. I bought this razor from him." The man held up the razor as though it was something special because Elmo Batson had sold it. "He ain't traveling for the Mobile Wholesale Company no more."

Mingo waited until his cheek was shaved. "What's he doing these days?"

The barber honed his razor, peering down at his customer's face, trying to identify him. "You know Elmo?"

"Uh huh. My folks run a store and we used to buy all our stuff from him."

The water in the cup was too hot and the barber jerked back his finger, then worked up the lather. "Elmo don't drop around any more."

"Maybe he started shaving himself." Anything to keep the conversation open.

"Maybe. But I hear talk." The barber stropped his razor one, two—three licks, the last a long one. "You hear a lot of talk around a barber shop."

Mingo touched his nose where the lather tickled him. "I hope Elmo is doing good, whatever he's doing."

"Heap of Cuban refugees around here these days. I hear Elmo is mighty friendly with 'em."

Mingo closed his eyes, enjoying the warm towel on his face, the clean tingling of his skin. "Reckon he's in town?"

"I don't know." The man leaned close. "Them Cubans might know. They hang out at Nick González' saloon."

Mingo stepped out of the chair, feeling his chin. "Where is it?"

"Down on St. Anthony Street. Just look for the sign of *El Delfín*. Nick González runs it. Customer of mine." The barber was cleaning his chair, slapping it with his cloth. "Nick is a Cuban, but he's all right. Them other Cubans around here would be in a hell of a fix if they didn't have Nick González to feed 'em and look after 'em."

Mingo buttoned his coat and put on his hat. "Maybe he'll know about Elmo, huh?"

"Maybe." The barber walked to the door with Mingo. "You can't miss Nick. Fat fellow. Talks hard but got a heart as big as a wagon."

The adventurer thanked him and went down to St. Anthony Street and the water front. His blood began pounding in anticipation of things to come and yet there was a tightness in his throat, for he was a woodsman from a little valley in Mississippi, and this was a city and there was the sea. He was a stranger and felt all the doubts that come to a man who finds himself away from home, adrift from his people. The rancid stink of crabs and shrimp and rotting wood along the water front, the puddled slime of sea water, told the wanderer how far he was from Lebanon, from the pines on the ridges and the willows bending over the creek.

He walked on down St. Anthony Street, glancing at the fish houses and the rickety old buildings, their fronts fading. He walked about three blocks and there was a wooden sign swinging over the sidewalk, a black dolphin arching out of a blue sea. The name at the bottom was *El Delfín*.

Mingo looked through the greasy, fly-dotted window and saw men inside. He breathed deeply to still the quick pounding in his chest and opened the door and went in, his eyes darting bright around the room, focusing every detail.

An old fire, its ashes spilled out of the hearth, burned dully in a grate at one end of the room and the air was stale with tobacco smoke, smelling of beer and wine and rum. A group of men was around a table listening intently to a small man, dark-skinned and wearing a sailor's jacket and a blue stocking cap, who was talking rapidly in Spanish, his hands making excited gestures.

No one seemed to notice Mingo except the bartender, and he left the table and walked behind his bar, waiting for the stranger to come to him. He was a short man and fat, exuding a proprietary air. Nick González. Bound to be.

Mingo nodded a quick greeting and the fat man smiled, two silver teeth gleaming in his lower jaw, accentuating the smile. His black hair shone with oil and his mustache was waxed and twisted tight, the two ends sticking away from his face like tiny spikes.

"We ain't open yet." He looked steadily at the visitor but kept his head tilted, listening to the story the little sailor was telling. "We don't open until ten o'clock." His English was good but there was an accent to his words.

"I'm looking for a man named Elmo Batson," Mingo said.

Nick González eyed him closely, carefully, then turned toward the men at the table listening to the sailor's narrative.

"I said I'm looking for Elmo Batson. . . ." Mingo Dabney repeated the words clearly, giving notice that he expected a reply.

The bartender frowned at him, scowling and signaling for

16

silence, and the little sailor went on talking until suddenly he hesitated and spat. All the men at the table spat and Nick González spat, blasting it out as if clearing his mouth of carrion. "Sagaldo," he growled. "Sagaldo the dog and blood brother of dogs."

Mingo leaned against the bar, waiting and watching, and the little sailor wearing the stocking cap began speaking again, talking on until his words trailed off and everyone started talking at once, gesticulating and speaking rapidly, their Spanish words running together and piling up into a wave of sound.

Nick González wiped his hands on the apron that stretched tight across his belly and eyed Mingo again. "You know Elmo Batson?"

"Sure. Friend of mine." Mingo said it quickly, almost abruptly. The pounding in his chest had subsided, but his spine was tingling as he looked from the fat man to the group at the table, suddenly silent and watching him. "My name is Dabney."

"One of the Dabneys from up around Lebanon?"

"That's right."

"Maybe I can put you in touch with Elmo." The bartender pushed a bottle of rum in front of the young man, never moving his eyes from the stranger's face. "What do you want to see him about?"

Mingo placed both hands on the edge of the bar and looked again at the silent group around the table, then at Nick González. "That, mister, is my business." He ran his fingers through his hair and adjusted his hat tight over his forehead, but still slanting.

Nick grunted his acceptance of the situation and pointed to a glass. "Pour yourself a drink." He turned to the men at the table and called, "Stockingcap. Go up and see if Elmo is still busy." The little sailor hurried up the stairs, anxious to do any bidding of Nick González.

Mingo concealed his surprise that Elmo was there and

poured the glass full of rum. He never had taken a drink so early in the morning and sipped it cautiously, eying the bartender.

Nick ran his hands over his bulging middle and again he smiled, a quick warm smile, his silver teeth gleaming. "If you're from Lebanon, you know José Martí, perhaps. Elmo took him up there once."

Mingo Dabney stuck his thumbs under his belt and hitched up his britches, showing off a little. "I met him." He almost mentioned Rafaela Galban, but this was no place to discuss her, no time to ask her whereabouts. "Do you know Martí?"

The fat man grunted his contempt for such a question and reached under his bar for a half-smoked cigar. "Hell, yes, I know him. Known José all his life." He touched a match to a cigar and puffed furiously. "I'm Nick González and if you want to know anything about José Martí just ask me." He leaned across his bar and tapped himself on the chest.

There were voices in the room above, the little sailor's excited tones high above the others. One of the voices upstairs was Elmo's. Mingo was sure of it.

Nick's cigar was out again and he balanced it on the edge of his back bar, then shook salt on a hard-boiled egg and bit it in half, smacking as he chewed. "Martí is about ready to begin the revolution back home and he needs all the help he can get." Nick slid his fingers along his mustache to the tip, tightening it. "Did he tell you that when he was up in Lebanon?"

"He said something about it." Mingo reached for one of the eggs and, like Nick, shook salt on it, bit it in half, and like Nick, he smacked, glancing at the steps and again hearing the voices upstairs; the jabber of the little sailor and Elmo's voice, then another, a heavy booming voice.

Nick González tucked the dead cigar in the side of his mouth, struck a match under his bar and held up the flame. "Martí raised a little money in Lebanon, didn't he?"

18

"A little." It came to Mingo then. Rafaela might be with Martí. "Maybe I'll get to see him while I'm around here. You know where he is?"

Nick was lighting his cigar, twisting the dead end in the flame, but watching his visitor. "José ain't hard to find. If a man's got proper business with him."

"I'd just like to see him again." The vague remark was deliberate, telling nothing, suggesting much.

The Cuban puffed out his cheeks, easing the smoke slowly from his nose. "He's over in Pensacola. Just across the bay —"

Mingo's heart leaped to his throat and he almost asked if she were with him, but again refrained from speaking her name in a saloon.

"—He's beating the bushes over there for nickels and dimes." The proprietor of *El Delfín* settled against his back bar and went on talking. "He's got to fight Spain with nickels and dimes and sticks. They've got gold and steel." He might have said more but the little sailor came down the stairs and nodded to him.

Nick straightened and motioned for Mingo to follow him. The newcomer brushed off his clothes, using the flat of his hand, and glanced at himself in the mirror. He smoothed his thick black hair, smoothing it away from the part on the left side. "You look all right," Nick said. They reached the bottom of the steps and the bartender turned. "Elmo is worried. We've had bad news from Cuba." He led the way up the stairs and pointed to the door at the end of the hall. "He's in there. And if you need anything, just ask for Nick González." Again Nick tapped himself on the chest.

Mingo went along the hall and rapped.

Elmo Batson opened the door, his bald head gleaming red within a half circle of straw-colored hair, his frayed cigar drooping in the side of his mouth. He was in his shirt sleeves, one suspender dangling below his hip. Same Ol' Elmo, paunchy and slouchy. "By God!" His haggard face lit up. "I'm mighty glad to see you. How you been getting along?"

He took Mingo's arm and led him into the room. "Shake hands with Cap'n Fry."

The young woodsman glanced toward the bulky man at the table, and crossed the room, offering his hand. He had heard of Captain Joseph C. Fry, an old man now, but once, so long ago, an unconquered commander in the Confederate Navy. His heavy black beard was flecked with gray and he looked like the pictures of a hundred Confederate leaders, Jeb Stuart and Stonewall Jackson; the beard, the huge frame, the deep eyes of torture and resolve. Captain Fry lumbered to his feet and accepted the handshake, his huge hand clamping hard. "Dabney?" It was a growled query, not a greeting.

"Yes, sir." Mingo was almost reverent in the presence of this old gallant who, so long ago, followed the Confederate mirage.

Elmo put his hand on Mingo's shoulder. "This boy's my friend, Cap'n."

The old man mumbled recognition and sat down again, easing his bulk into the chair. Elmo glanced at him, sensing his weariness. "Me and Cap'n Fry been up all night. He's a little tired —"

"Not tired at all," Joseph Fry snapped, bracing his sagging shoulders, trying to wipe away the years.

Mingo shifted from one foot to the other and Elmo slid his hand down his unshaved cheek, rasping the scraggly whiskers. "I'm sorta helping José Martí." There was nothing mysterious about the drummer; a blunt man without guile. "Cap'n Fry has joined with us. He aims to help Cuba fight —"

"Fight!" The commander growled the word, rumbling it in his beard. "There is no fighting in Cuba." He began pacing the floor, his hands clasped behind him, and the floor shook under his heavy tread. "Let José Martí preach and exhort, but there can be no revolution in Cuba until I get there." He stopped before the window, his feet apart, and glared. "I ask you to overlook my mood, young man. We've just had bad news."

"Nick González said as much." Mingo was awed by the towering old man and was anxious to be away from him off somewhere with Elmo. "I hope the news wasn't too bad."

Elmo nodded slightly, an indication of his approval of his young friend's behavior. "Hell, boy! We're used to bad news. Thrive on it. Get fat on it." He patted his paunch. "Let's me and you go get a drink. Will you join us, Cap'n?"

"No thank you, Batson. And don't talk about Sagaldo coming to Cuba. No use spreading bad news."

So Sagaldo was the bad news and Mingo had heard the name at the bar. "Excuse me." He wanted to say something helpful. "Those men downstairs were talking about Sagaldo —whoever Sagaldo is."

Elmo hooked his dangling suspender over his shoulder and lifted his coat from the back of a chair. Fry clasped his hands behind him and rocked on the balls of his feet, obviously a practiced gesture, a pose of dominance often rehearsed. "You never heard of Leopold Sagaldo?"

"No, sir. Should I?"

"Only if you choose to be an informed man." It was a pompous remark, spoken with the infuriating hauteur of an old man pontifically offering wisdom to the young. "Sagaldo is a soldier by training, a butcher by choice, and Spain is returning him to Cuba."

Elmo spoke out before the garrulous old sage could begin one of his long-winded speeches. "Sagaldo is a son of a bitch. The Cubans hate him so much they spit when they speak his name —"

"I saw 'em spitting," Mingo said, moving from the table toward the door.

The drummer picked up his derby and took Fry's hand. "I'll be in Pensacola by night. Anything to tell Martí?"

"Yes." The old man straightened, pulling back his massive shoulders. "Tell him to check on the whereabouts of my ship. I'm tired of waiting."

Mingo followed Elmo into the hallway and the drummer

closed the door, careful that it didn't bang or rattle. He rubbed the back of his neck to ease his fatigue, and smiled at his friend. "All right, son. What's eating you? What are you doing in Mobile?"

"I'm looking for Rafaela Galban. Do you know where she is?"

"Sure. She's over in Pensacola. With Martí."

And Pensacola was only fifty miles away, a day's journey on his white horse. Mingo grinned his anticipation and his surety. "Then I'm going to Pensacola."

"So-o-o?" Elmo rubbed his neck again and stretched. It gave him a moment to think. Here, perhaps, was another worry and the tired drummer had more worries than he could handle. However, he hesitated only an instant, then accepted the added burden. "I'll be going in a few minutes. You can go with me."

The pilgrim slanted his hat to the side of his head. A quick swagger was in his walk, and he grinned.

MINGO DABNEY

Chapter 2   Mingo was too excited to ask intelligent questions and Elmo was too tired to heed his pratings as they rode down to the ferry for the trip across Mobile Bay to Florida and Pensacola.

A few early stirrers glanced at them, at the rumpled, red-faced man slumping on a sorrel mare, almost asleep in his saddle, and the youth on the huge white stallion. Shannon was trembling his nervousness and Mingo's eyes darted along the water front, missing nothing. His hat was aslant on the side of his head and the wind brushed his black hair from his forehead.

They rode aboard the ferry, a grimy old steamer named *Glory Bound,* and Elmo hitched his horse, then almost stumbled forward, looking for a warm nook and sleep. Mingo had never been on salt water before and stood by the winches until the *Glory Bound* cast off for her first crossing of the morning. The north wind was blowing steadily down from the Alabama River and on south to the Gulf.

Mingo stroked the shoulder of his horse until Shannon no longer trembled his terror of the boat. The gulls hovered overhead, screaming as they dived for scraps, and Mingo stood by the rail, looking ahead, impulsively twisting a tuft of his hair around his right forefinger. He went forward, walking rapidly in his quick, agile way, a jaunty, confident stride. He was seeking Elmo, and found his friend sprawled on a stack of cowhides, his jaw sagging, breathing slowly in the sleep of the utterly exhausted.

Mingo returned to the rail and propped against it, watching the foam curl back. So Rafaela Galban was in Pensacola. What would he say? And how would he say it? Mingo Dabney felt a nervousness he never had known before. He had not declared his love to this girl, yet he had followed her and soon was to walk into her presence with no reason except the reason he dare not speak. How could he say that for her he had left his home and his heritage? How could he say that for her he would ride to the rim of the world?

His musings brought a vision of her in the curling foam, white as her hair, and the water dark as her eyes beneath the foam. Mist was rising, obscuring the land, swirling over the ferry and blotting out the shore.

The *Glory Bound* lazied on across the bay and chugged to its mooring, jolting Elmo awake. He yawned and scratched his whiskers, cursing the tribulations of a peddler turned revolutionist, mouthing condemnation of himself. "Plain crazy!" He sat on the cowhides, trying to wake up, blinking while the ferry was secured. "I was the best drummer between Mobile and Memphis. Now look at me!" His eyes were watering and he rubbed them. "Up to my neck with a bunch of Cuban galoots trying to start a revolution."

Mingo grinned at his friend, ignoring his habitual grousings, then fetched the horses and they rode off the ferry, traveling due east for Pensacola. The land was dreary stretches of scrub pine and bogs, desolate and foreboding. The snap of the winter air flicked the exhaustion from Elmo and he perked up, jolting awkwardly as his horse trotted. He questioned Mingo again, first about his family and happenings back in Lebanon. There was loneliness and longing in his voice as he recalled the days he traveled the backwoods, peddling his wares, telling his spicy stories. They rode the sandy trace on toward Florida and Ol' Elmo kept on talking until he noticed his companion was not listening, but staring off toward the south and the Gulf.

Only then did Elmo broach the question that troubled him. "What you aim to do when you get to Pensacola?"

"Find Rafaela." Mingo's reply was quick and certain. He slowed his stallion's stride, holding him steady on the trace.

"Then what you aim to do?" Elmo brushed past a scrub palm and reached out and yanked one of the pointed leaves. "After you find her, what you aim to do?"

There was a moment's pause and Mingo looked again to the south, over the sandy stretch that glistened white. "I'm not sure."

Elmo Batson knew all those things about Rafaela Galban y Torres that this man must learn for himself, and he slowed his horse, peering over at his companion, the restless brown eyes so bright in the morning sun, the muscles knotting firm around his shoulders. It was in Elmo's mind to speak the warning that *La Entorcha* was a living symbol to be seen and never touched, but the drummer was old enough and wise enough not to come between any man and his heart, and he kept his peace.

They ate lunch at a log tavern, then rode on out of Alabama and into Florida, the land stretching away in a wilderness of scrubby trees and isolated shacks. They crossed the Fish River and the River Styx and then, in late afternoon, Pensacola lay before them, hovering around the bay.

The fatigue of the journey went out of Mingo as they swung into a narrow street along the water front, and he gazed out at the harbor crowded with ships, nodding and bobbing, and the wind was strong off the Gulf, smelling of fish and salt. It all fascinated him for a moment, but for a moment only. Then he asked, "Where is she?"

"Keep your shirt on," Elmo scolded.

Mingo laughed and Elmo laughed, too, lifting his derby and scratching his bald head, chuckling as he jogged along the water front. They left their horses at the hitching rail in front of a chandler's and walked down a dirty alley. A heavy, pleasing odor of tobacco came from a rambling building at the end of the alley, close to the bay. The building was moldy, its balcony rotten and sagging, its windows smeared with grime and laced with cobwebs. "Cigar factory," Elmo said laconically. "If you want to find a Cuban always look for a cigar factory or a rooster fight."

"My God! Will she be here?"

"She'll be where Martí is."

They stepped to the crumbling porch and the drummer put out his hand, touching his companion and halting him. Then Mingo heard it, the low, vibrant voice inside, rising and falling like gentle surf. *"Cuba libre!"* The words came clear. "We shall be free or we shall be dead."

Elmo Batson's tired face, burnt red by the sun and leathered by the wind, lighted in a sudden fervor and he cocked his head toward the closed door, peering from under his thin, straw-colored brows. "Martí!" He whispered the name hoarsely. "That's him all right. That's Martí."

Mingo listened, his nerves tingling to the challenge of the voice. He had every reason to believe Rafaela Galban was just beyond that door and yet he hesitated to open the door, standing there on the porch and straining to hear the words of the prophet.

"Freedom! Freedom or the grave! It is our covenant!" The voice came stronger.

Elmo's eyes opened wide in a wonder he felt and could not explain. "That little man — he's why I'm up to my neck in this mess. Martí did it. Him and that preacher voice." He felt for the knob, turning it slowly and easing open the door. They stepped noiselessly inside so as not to disturb the meeting, and Mingo glanced around quickly, his eyes adjusting to the musty gloom, sun-streaked through the dirty windows.

It was a long room with a low ceiling and the pungent smell of tobacco irritated his nose and brought water to his eyes. Rows of workers, all Cuban exiles, sat on benches at each side of a wooden table, bending over, smoothing tobacco

26

leaves and rolling the fillers. Their eyes were on their work, but their ears were tuned to the words of the little man standing at the far end of the room, one hand on the table.

Mingo peered through the haze and the tobacco dust, staring for an instant at José Martí, the voice in the wilderness calling for a revelation from God or a revolution among men, calling the exiles to arms.

In a straight hard chair beside him sat Rafaela Galban, her black mantilla low on her forehead, hiding her white hair, concealing every strand of its silver beauty. The pilgrim's eyes sought her and found her, and she nodded her recognition. There was neither surprise nor delight in the gesture; a polite, casual nod and nothing more. He almost called out, but caught himself and stepped back into the shadow of the wall, waiting for Martí to resume his speech.

The evangel fixed his stare a second on Mingo, then took up his words again, rolling them in sonorous challenge. "It is better to die as free men in Cuban cities, or behind walls of Cuban farms, than to live as slaves on Cuban soil or toil forever in a foreign land."

Mingo Dabney heard the words, but saw only the girl, slender, her head high and her eyes like black water touched with fire. The late afternoon sun streaked in, gleaming on her mantilla, lighting her face in the gloom and the dust.

The prophet pulled himself erect, sweat on his high forehead, for the room was close and rancid with oil and tobacco. He shifted his weight, wincing as pain seared his right leg, injured forever by Spanish gyves. He wiped his brow with a linen handkerchief and smoothed his mustache, thick and tapering, black against his pale face. José Martí was so little, a puny body and a huge head, his smoldering eyes deep and wide apart. "The time has come for Cuba to strike again, to dare her life to gain her soul." His words reverberated through the room and the fingers of the toilers quickened.

"This time we shall tear Spain's grip from our throats." It was the fervid vow of the zealot. Here was the unconquered and unconquerable revolutionist, the poet in whom the love of Cuba and the hate of tyranny followed like the endless following of day and night. "Spain knows we will strike soon. And Spain has sworn we will be a mountain of bones before we are free." He leaned forward and hissed the curse, "Sagaldo is in Cuba."

Elmo mumbled and Mingo felt his blood rising slowly in his chest, filling it and almost choking him. His eyes darted from Rafaela to Martí, then to the workers bent over the table. A muttering, like far-off thunder promising the storm, passed through the room, but the exiles did not raise their heads from the rolling of the fillers, the swift wrapping of the leaves. And nine cigars they placed together. And one cigar they placed apart. Nine for the master for whom they toiled; one for Cuba.

"By your tithings —" Martí clenched his fists, color splotching his thin cheeks, creeping into the pallor of his face. "By giving one tenth of your toil you are buying weapons that will free your children."

The soft, sentient voice stirred Mingo, but he watched Rafaela. She was peering up at Martí, her mentor, and her eyes were transfixed. The evangel paused, leaning over the end of the table, his face near the wrinkled face of an old Cuban. "We have purchased a ship! Now Cuba owns a ship!"

For the first time the exiles looked up. "A ship? A ship for Cuba?"

"*Sí!*" Martí thundered the affirmation. "We have purchased the *Virginius*. She is ours and the weapons you buy she will sail to Cuba." Again he paused, looking about him, peering at the workers; and nine they put together and one they set aside. Rafaela Galban's breathing was quick and shallow. The tips of Mingo's fingers slid over the ball of his thumb and he moistened his lips and swallowed. Elmo leaned back against the wall and watched, his eyes slowly roving the room.

José Martí's hand rose, his finger pointing upward, trem-

28

bling as his hand moved higher and the prophet grew taller. "We have the *Virginius* and we have her master. He is Captain Joseph C. Fry, and he waits in Mobile."

The workers, their fingers endlessly moving, muttered and mumbled, *"Viva! Viva Virginius!"*

Mingo's throat was dry and he smeared his hand over his mouth. He had ridden from the ridges of Lebanon, the wind-clean ridges, into another world. He had come into a world where liberty was no man's heritage or freedom his birthright. Mingo shifted nervously and Elmo touched him, reassuring him.

"We will claw them with our hands and tear them with our teeth." The rhythm of Martí's voice was the pulse beat of the room. "There are no rules in revolution! Freedom or death!"

The room was hushed, the sunlight streaming low across the table as the day waned. Martí fastened his hands to the lapels of his black broadcloth coat, looking at the workers, at each of them. A Masonic emblem dangled from a heavy gold chain across his vest and he moved his hand to the emblem, holding it, his gaze intent upon the exiles. Then he turned slightly and bowed to Rafaela. *"La Entorcha,"* he said, and sat down.

The symbol rose slowly, accepting her role with practiced precision. She was tall and summoned her height to accentuate the drama of the moment. Her face tapered, thinning down to a tiny chin. She lifted her hand, forming it into the sign of a torch.

"Compadres!"

The word stabbed the silence and the room was tense, poised. She touched the edge of her mantilla with her long fingers, drawing it low, cowling her hair. Her eyes swept past Mingo and Elmo, and back to the workers.

"Children of slaves! Fathers of free men!"

The tobacco spilled from the shaking hands of an old woman and she stared up, her face enraptured, her eyes

29

brimming tears. *"La Entorcha!"* The old one mumbled the name. *"La Entorcha Blanca!"*

"The time of deliverance is upon us." Rafaela rested both hands on the table and flung the words at them, the lines she knew so well, the role she had played so often. "The embers of revolt smolder on Cuban plains and in the hills of the Oriente. Your sires lighted them and we will fan them into fire. Gómez —"

"Ah-h-h." The workers breathed their blessing, chanting in unison. "Gómez! Máximo Gómez —"

"He is in Santo Domingo." Her voice rose, trembling slightly. "He awaits the call. The *Grito!* The summons to arise and lead the people. Máximo Gómez, the Old Fox." She paused, then slowly, "Calixto García is in France, awaiting the call. Tomás Palma is in New York. . . ."

She was calling the roll of Cuba's idols, proclaiming the muster of men sworn to free a land from four hundred years of Spain's tyranny. She spoke the names and the workers bowed lower to their task, working more rapidly; nine for the master and one for Cuba.

Quintín Banderas and his hill fighters! Jesús Rabi! Pedro Díaz! The Ducasse brothers, Juan and Vidal, the black terrors! She listed them all, those to die and those to live, and all to live forever.

The names quickened Mingo's blood and he, too, was under her spell, feeling the hot fury of Cuban nights; gunfire in the hills and smoke on the plains.

The symbol rested her fingertips on the table, her black eyes blazing. "There is another who waits the *grito*." Her voice rose and sharpened. "Antonio Macéo —"

The workers shuffled their feet and their fingers stumbled as they reached for the leaves.

"Macéo waits in Costa Rica!"

"Macéo." They mumbled his name, their god of wrath and vengeance; their templar, their unsheathed sword.

"The sword of the revolution waits —" Rafaela drew back

from the table, her chin high as she loosed the mantilla around her temple, bestowing a glimpse of her white hair. "Antonio Macéo cries out for the *grito!*"

"Viva! Macéo!" They sprang up from their benches. The tears ran down the cheeks of the old men, and the young men screamed his name. "Macéo!"

"Let Sagaldo beware!" Rafaela spat the words. "Let Spain loose all her venom upon the trampled body of our homeland. We will stab them in our cities and burn them on our farms. Cuba shall be free!" She lifted her hands above her head and spoke the benediction. *"Cuba libre!"*

Again the people screamed and smote the table, and Mingo turned to Elmo Batson. The convert shook his head, for not even he could fathom the passion of those he had joined.

Rafaela's speech was ended and her shoulders sagged under the weight of her emotions. She turned from the table, walking toward the door, and Martí limped beside her. An old woman reached out and touched her, mumbling *"La Entorcha!"* The girl stooped and kissed the old cheek and swept out of the room, never once glancing at Mingo. Her head was high and her eyes no longer smoldered the tragedy of her people, but blazed with an inexorable fire.

The door closed behind her and the workers sat very still, then returned to their task, their fingers swift through the leaves; nine for the master, one for Cuba.

The rasp of tobacco was in Mingo's nostrils and his heart was pulsing in his throat. For almost a minute he stood there, the spell still upon him, and he stared at the spot where she had been. Then he shook himself free of the bewitchment and glanced at Elmo, and they walked out of the room.

Rafaela and Martí were standing on the sidewalk, under the balcony, and Martí came quickly toward them, his small hand extended. But the girl held back. Her eyes were closed and she was breathing deeply, relaxing from the strain of her exhortation.

31

"Ah, Mr. Dabney!" Martí's face lighted. "I am happy to see you again. And you, Elmo. How are you, *amigo?*" He shook hands warmly and his cordiality was unmistakable.

Rafaela did not move to greet them. The late afternoon was cool but there was sweat on her lip and she touched it with her handkerchief, glancing at Mingo and then quickly away, looking down the street, as if by ignoring him she might regain her composure. Her face was pale and her hands trembled. Her mentor understood her burning agitation and engaged the travelers, talking rapidly of trivia, until his glances convinced him she was free from the spell of her incantation. "Come, gentlemen. Señorita Galban is waiting to welcome you."

Mingo Dabney did not know this girl, this tragedienne in the role the revolution had cast for her. He was bewildered and frightened, and held back. This was not the girl he had known in Lebanon; this enraptured apostle of revolution was a stranger, and he was embarrassed and humiliated.

She came toward him and politely offered her hand. "Mingo." There still was no color in her cheeks. Her hand was cold.

And now that she was standing there, he knew not what to say. "You are looking fine, Rafaela."

She spoke to Elmo Batson, and turned again to Mingo, asking about the people of Lebanon. "They were all so gracious to me."

He answered her question, looking at her dubiously, still embarrassed and ill at ease. It was almost supper time and Martí suggested that Rafaela return to her boarding house and rest. He invited the travelers to accompany him to his hotel.

"May I see you after supper?" Mingo asked Rafaela.

Martí glanced at her, then at Elmo, but the drummer was watching the cigar workers file out of the factory. Rafaela turned from Mingo and addressed her mentor: "Is there any work for tonight, Don José?"

"No-o-o." A slight frown, a witness of doubt, passed over his face.

"Then you may call," she said to Mingo. They had been gracious to her in Lebanon and she could be no less. "But please come soon after supper as I must retire early. Tomorrow will be a busy day for me. Two rallies." One of the cigar workers passed and lifted his hat. She asked him to escort her home.

Martí motioned for his guests to follow him and the three men walked along the water front until they came to Palafox Street. They walked in silence, each thinking his own thoughts until they reached the hotel. Elmo followed Martí to his room to talk business, and Mingo took a room for himself. First he sent for Shannon and had him stabled near the hotel and then he bathed and shaved, shaving close. His skin was brown, tanned by the summer suns of Lebanon and the winter winds. He felt better. That wasn't really Rafaela Galban he had heard. It was a performance, a rally. True, she had shown no emotion one way or another at sight of him; but then ladies should be demure, particularly Cuban ladies reared in the sheltering protection of chaperons and nuns.

He put on a white shirt and a blue tie, and began whistling softly through puckered lips; then he grinned, the broad free grin of Lebanon. She had acted that way because so many folks were around and she was shy. That explained it. The whistling changed to a hum, and the humming eased into a song.

The Dabneys were singing folks, all of them, singing as they fought, singing as they played, and Mingo sang to himself as he carefully tied his tie:

> *Men are fools that wish to die!*
> *Is it not fine to dance and sing*
> *When the bells of death do ring?*
> *Is it not fine to swim in wine,*

33

And turn upon the toe,
And sink hey nonny no!
When the winds blow and the seas flow?

He joined Martí and Elmo at supper and the prophet stared at him, the frown back on his face. Mingo had a feeling they had discussed him in private and he resented the implication of Martí's frown. The drummer ordered whiskey and Martí took wine. The woodsman ordered coffee. He wanted a drink but was going to see Rafaela Galban, so he ordered coffee. Elmo sought to draw his young friend into the fellowship and winked at him as he grumbled. "José has been questioning me like a Philadelphia lawyer." He jerked his head toward Martí.

"Elmo is my purse." The frown passed from Martí's face and he smiled. "You will excuse us, Mr. Dabney, but there are many things I must know and the time is so short. Elmo assures me of your discretion." He sipped his wine and turned to his friend. "You are sure the *Virginius* has sailed from New York?"

Batson motioned for the waiter to refill his whiskey glass. "Dammit, José! I told you she sailed last week." His eyes were weak and he blinked them tight, drawing together his wispy, straw-colored brows. "She's falling apart, ain't worth a continental hooray, but she sailed last week. That old tub is so old her barnacles have whiskers —"

"Is Fry ready?" Martí snapped the question.

Elmo chuckled, his face reddening and his little paunch bobbing up and down. "Chomping at the bit."

"He understands we will rendezvous in Jamaica? That the *Virginius* must land us in Cuba before the *grito* is sounded? Before the call to arms?"

"Oh, good Lord!" Elmo grumbled. "Captain Fry knows his orders backwards and forwards."

How many *machetes* had Elmo bought? How many rifles? At that minute José Martí was not the impassioned counselor of revolution, but a shrewd man coldly calculating battle, scheming death for Cuba's enemy, already hearing gunfire in Cuba's hills. He spoke to Mingo only occasionally, addressing some courteous yet meaningless remark to him, then leaping back to his queries.

The drummer answered the questions until his patience was exhausted. Then he reared back in his chair and glared at Martí. "By God, José, lemme be." The red snapper on his plate was getting cold and the whiskey in his stomach was getting warm. "I aim to have my victuals."

The man from Lebanon shucked his oysters at the table and peeled his red snapper from the bone, feasting in the manner of a vigorous trencherman. Elmo lifted his ear to Martí, but was watching Mingo Dabney, envious of youth's dream, fearful of the awakening.

MINGO DABNEY

Chapter **3**   The Lebanon woodsman was
not aware of his song as he stepped from the porch of the
hotel and into the chilly night, his black hat on the side
of his head and an expensive cigar tilted high. He swung
down Palafox Street, walking rapidly in his restless stride,
his arms swinging and his shoulders flowing in the rhythm
of his strength and eagerness.

> *Men are fools that wish to die!*
> *Is it not fine to dance and sing*
> *When the bells of death do ring....*

The moon was climbing out of the bay, streaking a path
of silver to the shore. Rafaela's boarding house was only
two blocks away and he turned into the gate, breathing
deeply to gain composure. At that minute, he was almost
sure of himself again, a pilgrim hurrying to his shrine.

Rafaela herself answered his knock and they went to the
parlor and sat before a bright fire, she on a divan and he
on a chair near the hearth. The lamp was on a table near
her and Mingo looked first at the light, blinking at its brilliance, and then at her mantilla imprisoning every strand
of her hair. "They certainly have good fish in Pensacola."
It was an inane thing to say but he must say something. "I
ate a whole red snapper for supper. Did you have a good
supper?"

"Why, yes." She smoothed her dark blue skirt and folded

her hands in her lap. The sleeves of her silken blouse were loose and puffy above the elbows, the cuffs deep and tight-fitting. There was a cameo at her throat and she touched the cameo, sliding it on its thin gold chain. "We had a very good supper."

Mingo fidgeted a second, twisting a tuft of his hair around his right forefinger until the tuft stood apart.

Rafaela looked at his hair, almost stared at it, seeing it free and unruly. "What brings you to Pensacola, Mingo?" It was a conventional question and she asked it politely.

He might have told her then, but the words stuck in his throat, clinging there, and he retreated into petulance as an embarrassed man will. "Elmo was coming. I just came along with him." His voice was flat and he was staring at the fire.

His petulance was apparent. "It was a long ride," she said, adjusting her cuff, and her fingers were swift and deft. She waited a moment but he said nothing, and she excused herself and stepped to the door, glancing at the clock in the hallway. There was much work for the morrow.

Mingo rose when she returned, moving to the divan, but she crossed to a chair near the hearth. The light was full upon her, reflecting in a blood-red ruby on her finger. "How long will you be in Pensacola?" he asked.

"I?" There was puzzlement in her tone. "I will be here as long as José Martí thinks it is necessary." A log on the hearth fell apart and the sparks spurted from the break, darting and crackling. "How long will you be here?"

He crossed his legs and leaned back, again twisting the tuft of hair in a gesture that was part of him. "I don't know, Rafaela. I came down here to see you." The light was back in his eyes, the slow smoldering she had seen in Lebanon.

A sudden expression of incredulity tightened her face, but for an instant only, and then she was cold and distant. "You presumed to follow me?"

"It looks that way, Rafaela."

She stared full at him. He was a Dabney and the Dabneys

37

were powerful in Mississippi; and Cuba needed all the friends she could rally. "Perhaps you came to offer your services to my country."

"I came to offer my heart to you." It was spoken. His quest was told.

Rafaela Galban y Torres was dumfounded. Her hand was poised before her, motionless, then rose slowly to her mantilla, feeling for any exposed hair. "Are you completely mad, Señor Dabney?" There was no guile in her question, only bewilderment.

Mingo uncrossed his legs and leaned forward, accepting her stare and challenging it. "If I am mad, then you are to blame."

Blame! This man was daring to blame *La Entorcha Blanca* for his own impetuous behavior. "It is getting late —"

"It's just eight o'clock." He glanced at his watch and returned it to his pocket. He had come too far to be dismissed so abruptly. "You surprised me this afternoon. It didn't sound like you at all."

"So-o-o." The subject was the revolution and not herself, and her whole manner changed, her face brightening. "It is my work. I told you as much in Lebanon."

Mingo was twisting his hair again, his foot slightly swinging. "I knew you raised money and recruits, but I didn't know you were such a good actress."

"Actress?" She held the word, tasting it, and her indignation flamed. "Blessed Mother!" She flung the reproach at him, her chin rising disdainfully. "It was only a show to you. A performance." Her cheeks were almost scarlet and her eyes burned. "How unkind. How incredibly callow."

Mingo was startled. "Wait a minute. I didn't go to upset you —"

"Upset me?" She pressed her cheeks, glaring at him. "You Americans have no idea of Cuba's plight. You don't know and you don't care."

The vehemence of her tone enthralled him and he gazed

at her, the color suddenly draining from her face and sweat beading on her lips. She closed her eyes and her body trembled as she poured forth her litany—and Mingo Dabney saw the tragedy of her homeland, the island long and narrow, curving green in the Indian Sea, green on its plains and green in its hills, fat green in its tobacco fields and lean green in its cane fields, dark and somber under the pall of Spain. "The time has come for deliverance." She had said it before and she said it again, endlessly reciting her creed. "The time has come for the Cuban meek to strike for their inheritance." She opened her eyes, black and lustrous and defiant, daring him to desecrate her faith with talk of a performance.

He waited an instant and bent toward her, speaking softly. "How can I help you, Rafaela?" It was inevitable that he offer.

She looked at him a long time, studying him. Cuba needed men of strength. "It is for you to decide how you can help my country." She glanced down at the ruby on her right hand, twisting the ring that José Martí had given her years before, and the stone was deep red in the light of the fire. "In Cuba there is a place for every man." Her tone was a challenge. "There is a place for you, Mingo Dabney. Even your name is Cuban. Mingo —"

"No." He shook his head. "I was named for an Indian, a friend of my family's years ago. He was Tishomingo, and I was named for him."

Her mood changed completely, instantly, and she was almost friendly. "Mingo was a very common name in medieval Spain. A peasant name. Mingo —" The word drifted slowly from her tongue and she paused, a little frown on her forehead. "*Minguillo*," she whispered, whispering it because it was Cuban and therefore beautiful to her.

"What did you say?" Again he bent toward her.

"*Minguillo* . . ." The frown was gone and there was a shadow across her face, the light burning bright behind her and the fire softening to embers. "It means little Mingo." She had heard the name so many times as a child. It was a whisper of home. That, and nothing more.

"Me? Little!"

His words shattered her reverie. "Not small," she said, impatient that he had broken the lovely mood by referring to himself. "Little . . ." Her hands moved, groping, as she tried to find a way to explain; but she could not explain Cuba to this woodsman. So she lifted her shoulders, shrugging. "We Cubans often take a name and make it little. Sometimes we almost turn it into music. Mingo into *Minguillo*." And the way Rafaela said it, turned it into music.

The sound of the name, the way she rolled it in its Cuban beauty brought a quick gasp to Mingo Dabney, a boldness to his heart. "Come sit by me, Rafaela." He put his hand on the divan beside him, inviting her.

The look of bewilderment returned. *La Entorcha* went to no man. Men came to her. This one simply could not fathom the infinity of tradition and purpose that separated *La Entorcha*, the living torch of a people, and Mingo Dabney, a woodsman.

"You will go now." She arose from the chair and swept toward the door. Mingo hesitated by the fire, wondering how to call her back, and was standing there when a buggy wheeled to the gate. "It is Don José," she explained, speaking over her shoulder.

"And Elmo," he said as footfalls sounded on the steps. "I'd know that clomp anywhere."

Rafaela answered the knock and led the two men into the parlor, and Elmo walked to the fire and warmed his hands and then his back. Martí, however, stood by the divan, glancing from Rafaela to Mingo and seeing the light in his eyes. Elmo saw it, too, but seemingly saw nothing, holding his rough hands behind his back, and rocking on the balls of his feet. "I dropped by to say so long."

"Is the time so short?" Rafaela walked toward the fire, ignoring Mingo.

40

The drummer nodded. "Uh huh. Time's running out on us. And I got to be going." He turned to Mingo. "I'm heading for Connecticut, son. Collinsville, Connecticut. Got a chance to pick up a bunch of *machetes,* and I aim to grab it."

"Will I be seeing you again?" Mingo propped his elbow on the mantel, sharing the fire with his friend. Martí was in the shadows.

Elmo hesitated and his eyes sought Martí's face, but the prophet turned away. "Maybe you will." The drummer's tired old eyes were troubled. "So long, bud. Don't take any wooden nickels."

He went to the porch and Martí followed, and they walked together out to the gate. The Cuban leaned on the gate, taking the weight from his injured foot. "You saw it, too," he said. "You saw his eyes."

"You damn right," Elmo snorted, scratching the side of his nose in sudden agitation. "And I tell you sump'n, José. I helped raise that boy and I don't want him hurt."

The evangel braced himself in front of his disciple. "Are you implying that *La Entorcha* might forget her vows?"

"I ain't implying nothing, mister." Ol' Elmo backed against the gate, a frown ridging his forehead. "That girl may be a symbol to Cuba, but she's just a woman to him. And he's a Dabney."

Martí's anxiety swelled into alarm. "Mother of God! It could lead to tragic circumstances —"

"You mighty come a'right. The Dabneys don't take no shoving around. The sap is rising in that boy."

"Mother of God!" The prophet repeated it, reverently and fearfully. "She is Antonio Macéo's lodestar, his faith. General Macéo will kill the man who reaches for her."

Elmo Batson shoved his hands into his pockets and looked from Martí toward the parlor of the boarding house, the lamplight and the fire reflecting through the windows. "If Macéo messes with that boy, you might have to get yourself another general." He took his right hand from his pocket and

41

tapped the Cuban on the chest. "And sump'n else, José. If Rafaela don't tell him the truth about herself, if she don't give him a fair shake, then I'm counting on you to tell him."

"She will tell him," Martí pledged.

Elmo offered his hand and they rededicated their friendship in the clasp. "That's good enough for me. Just give him a fair shake."

"You have my word," Martí promised solemnly, and reached out both his hands and put them on Elmo's shoulders, embracing his friend. *"Adiós, compadre."*

Ol' Elmo blinked rapidly and ran his hand across his nose again. "So long, José. Don't you take no wooden nickels, neither."

He was gone up the road toward Alabama and railhead, up the sleeping streets, winter-wrapped and gloomy, heading north to buy *machetes* for Macéo and his desperate men. Martí stood there alone until Elmo was out of sight, and limped back into the boarding house. Mingo was waiting, his hat in his hand, smoothing the brim.

"Good night, *La Entorcha*," Martí said, bowing to her.

"Good night, Rafaela." Mingo bowed, too. "I will call tomorrow in case you need me to drive you to the rallies, or something."

"It is customary for Don José to escort me." She turned from them and, speaking a good night, started down the hall to her room.

Mingo slanted his hat on his head. "I'll drop by anyhow. Maybe I can help out." It was the persistence of the Dabneys.

All the way to the hotel Martí was moody, even sullen, and Mingo attributed it to the ordeal of his exile, never connecting the light in his own eyes with the scowl on the face of the prophet. Martí bade him good night in the lobby and hobbled to his room, the little man limping in agony, carrying the soul of Cuba in his soft, sensitive hands.

Mingo Dabney undressed slowly, thinking a thousand things. The magic of the evening was upon him, her valiant

42

words stirring his spirit. The fat green of tobacco fields and the lean green of cane fields. Gunfire in the hills. The sultry nights of the Indian Seas. The meek clawing for their inheritance.

Mingo went to the window and stared down toward the bay, looking south, and the wind was blowing toward the south and the waves were heading out into the night. The bay was dark, as dark as her eyes, blacker than shadows under the pall of the swaying Spanish moss.

The breeze died during the night and by morning the moss was still and the bay was gleaming smooth, broken only by the hulking grayness of the anchored ships and the foaming white ruff of the moving ships. Mingo slept past dawn, the salt air relaxing him. But José Martí was up soon after the sun, and, without waiting for breakfast, hastened to Rafaela's abode.

"Don José!" She answered his summons. "So early? Is there anything wrong?"

He opened the door to the parlor and it was dank, without fire or comfort. Rafaela drew her housecoat together at her throat and her mantilla tight over her hair. Even José Martí was not privileged to behold the white hair of *La Entorcha*. "I saw last night a thing that alarms me." The prophet did not bandy words and his tone was harsh, even peremptory. "I saw the ardor of Señor Dabney —"

She drew herself erect and was taller than her mentor. "It is unfortunate, Don José." She opened her hands in a little gesture, then dropped them in complete dismissal of the subject. *La Entorcha* had stirred the souls of many men, and the hearts of some bold enough to seek the woman within the symbol. "We have had these circumstances before."

Martí limped to the window, his back to her and his face toward the harbor and the open sea. "You will leave this afternoon for Guatemala." He spoke his command without explanation.

"Guatemala." There was no hesitation, no faltering. "And you?"

"I will take you as far as Tampa." He gave her no chance to reply and turned from the window and stood before her. "You will explain your position to that young man. I promised Elmo. Perhaps you saw only a spark in a reckless youth's eyes. I saw a fire in a dangerous man's heart."

"It will be done, Don José."

They walked to the door, Martí fastening his scarf against the cool morning. He touched her hand in reassurance, and left her, turning his steps toward the cigar factory. . . .

The town was stirring itself, street hawkers calling and carriages whirling by when Mingo woke up, glancing quickly at his heavy gold watch on the chair by his bed. It was not as late as he feared. He lighted the kindling in the fireplace and sponged himself. The water was cold and he caught his breath, blowing it out quickly in the invigorating shock. He breakfasted alone, wondering if Martí was up yet, wondering how far Elmo was on his way to Connecticut.

The sun was bright, but there was a nip in the air as Mingo went to the stables and made sure Shannon was well fed and curried. Then he walked by the bay, looking at the ships, curbing himself until the morning was half spent, then rang the bell at her boarding house.

Rafaela's dress was black cotton, her belt fastened through a white bone buckle. Her trunk was in the hallway near the steps and he glanced at the trunk, then at her. She did not offer her hand but slid her linen handkerchief through her fingers and nodded toward the parlor, leading the way into the room.

"Now what?" he demanded and moved toward her. "Don't tell me you are leaving again."

She withdrew before him, seating herself in a chair near the fireplace and indicating the divan across from her. He sat down slowly, watching her. "What has happened?"

44

This was the moment to shatter a pilgrim's illusions, this was the moment to end his hopeless quest and send him away forever. But they had been so kind to her in Lebanon. She had broken bread with this man's people, had shared their salt. She must not be abrupt. "I am leaving this afternoon for Guatemala —"

"I will go with you." It was an impulsive declaration, a straw to grasp.

She lifted her head in cold reproof. "I trust, Mr. Dabney, that your behavior is not as reckless as your words." She touched the ruby ring, twisting it, then locked her hands in her lap and spoke slowly, emphasizing each word. "I have no time and no inclination for frivolities."

"I haven't either, Rafaela."

His assurance startled Rafaela Galban, but did not disturb her. Her flaming words had sent a thousand recruits to General Antonio Macéo, and this man was needed in Cuba. She envisoned him at Macéo's side, perhaps on his staff; a Dabney serving the revolution. *La Entorcha* returned to her ritual: "The hour is approaching for the *grito*, the call." The words came in slow cadence. "Soon the call will sound and the children of Cuba will lift their shields and their swords to the motherland."

"When will you be in Cuba?" Mingo went straight to the point.

"The *grito* will send me to Cuba."

Mingo got up from the divan and propped his arm on the mantel, looking down at her. "I figured all along I'd wind up in Cuba."

She did not reply. Cuba was tomorrow, and tomorrow must take care of itself. Macéo would thank her for this recruit. Sagaldo was in Cuba, but a Dabney was enlisting for the revolution.

Mingo took two steps and was by her chair, still looking down at her and into her face, seeking something in her eyes and finding nothing. "I'll go back to Mobile and ask Captain Fry to take me to Cuba."

Martí's buggy pulled up in front of the house and he tied the reins and stepped out, reaching for the latch gate. Rafaela got up from her chair. "You will not mention that you are going to Cuba." It was almost a command.

"Why not?" Mingo was puzzled.

"If Don José knows you are going to Cuba, he will send you to Máximo Gómez —"

"Nobody is going to send me anywhere —"

"You must serve with Macéo." She hurried the words because Martí's steps were sounding on the path. "Macéo is the scourge. The lightning. But Máximo Gómez is the commander in chief and Don José will send you to him."

"But why?" Mingo persisted. "What difference does it make to Martí where I am?"

"Máximo Gómez is a white man. Antonio Macéo is a mulatto."

Mingo Dabney, a Southerner, understood the implication, and was provoked, but deferred to her request, assuming she had good reason. "I'll tell him nothing."

The knock came and José Martí limped into the room, glancing sternly at Mingo. "I trust you rested well last night, Mr. Dabney."

"Slept like a log."

"You are returning to Mobile? Perhaps to Lebanon?"

Mingo resented the questions, thinking them intrusive, but he subdued his annoyance. "I'm going back to Mobile this afternoon."

The little man tapped his Masonic emblem. "Give Captain Fry my regards." He nodded slightly. "And now *La Entorcha* and I have some arrangements to make. We are leaving immediately."

Mingo was embarrassed by the abrupt dismissal. He was not accustomed to such treatment and his resentment flared again. However, he swallowed his pride and said simply, "I must be going too."

Rafaela walked to the door with him and offered her

hand, and it was cold. He told her good-bye and stepped out into the sunlight, the door closing behind him.

Only once did he glance back, hoping she might be by the window, but she was not there and he swung out of the gate and on down the street. The sun was blazing into the bay and he blinked against the glare, hurrying to his hotel where he packed his saddlebag and went to the stable for Shannon.

The loiterers around the livery stable gawked at him as he mounted the stallion, his hat on the side of his head and his black hair showing below his hat. They stared at him as he rode away, a pilgrim beginning his quest again.

Back toward Mobile he hastened, back over the sandy trail, the River Styx and the pine thickets. Shannon felt the looseness of his master's grip and took the bit in his teeth and the miles in his stride, running free. There was gunfire in Cuban hills, fat green in the tobacco fields and lean green in the cane fields.

"Men are fools that wish to die. . . ."

MINGO DABNEY

Chapter 4 *El Delfín* was crowded to over-
flowing with Cuban exiles, and Mingo, pausing at the door,
was almost overwhelmed by the thick, stale air, the odor of
rum and tobacco and sweat. Nick González was behind his
bar, grandiloquently expounding the relative merits of
Máximo Gómez and Antonio Macéo as generals, and his audience was sipping black coffee and heavy wine. Stockingcap
was sprawled over a table, his arm a pillow, and he was cat-
napping.

Mingo stepped to the bar and Nick raised his head and
scowled, then smiled a quick greeting, his silver teeth flashing. He waddled forward, wiping his hands on his stained
apron, then wiped his mustache, tightening the black, oily
spikes.

"Good morning, Señor González," said the woodsman,
proud of his Spanish word.

The fat man nodded a welcome and reached to the back
bar for a bottle of rum. He put it in front of the boy and
shoved a plate of hard-boiled eggs toward him. "Did you
see Martí?"

"Uh huh." Mingo glanced around the room, hoping to
see Captain Fry; but he wasn't there.

"Martí cleared out of Pensacola yesterday, didn't he?"
Nick González grinned like a pleased Cheshire, proud to
exhibit his knowledge of events in the little world of the
exiles.

"That's right." Mingo was surprised at how rapidly the news had spread. He poured a small glass of rum and smelled it, making a wry face.

Nick picked his teeth with the nail of his little finger, still beaming. "*La Entorcha* left too, eh?"

Quickly Mingo was on his guard. "If you know so damn much, you ought to know she always goes with Martí."

"Not always, *amigo*." Nick's smile spread until his cheeks wrinkled deep. "Elmo Batson pulled out, too, didn't he?" He tapped his pudgy finger against his chest. "If you want to know anything, just ask Nick González."

"All right, Nick." The woodsman pushed his hat to the back of his head and leaned against the bar, sipping the rum and shuddering his distaste for the sweet concoction. "Have you got any plain, ever'day drinking whiskey in this saloon?"

The bartender was appalled and glanced around for a witness to the heresy, but the other men had drifted away, mulling over their drinks and gesticulating in feverish arguments; occasionally lowering their voices, and spitting. Nick sampled the rum and returned the bottle to his customer. "If you expect to hang around here," he growled, "you'll drink rum."

"But I don't aim to hang around here," Mingo replied airily. "I came back to see Captain Fry."

The fat man leaned forward, eager to be the first to receive a tidbit, a morsel of information. "What you want to see him about?"

The adventurer's finger went to his hair and he twisted the tuft unthinkingly. "Maybe I want to sell him a keg of nails. I understand he eats 'em for dessert."

"Only twenty penny nails, Señor." Nick's tier of chins melted into his chest as he lowered his head and stared at Mingo. "Perhaps Elmo sent you back to Fry? Or perhaps Martí?"

Mingo was annoyed by the questioning. "That's my business." He said it pleasantly enough, but he meant it.

Nick González was not offended and walked to the back of the saloon, returning with a pot of coffee. "How do you fellows expect me to be the post office if you don't let me in on things?" He was chuckling as he said it. "Joe Fry is eating breakfast upstairs. I'll take you up in a minute. How well do you know him?"

"I've met him." The coffee was thick and strong like the coffee they made back home.

"He growls like an old bear but he talks flowery like a politician." The fat man reached under his bar for a half-smoked cigar and jabbed it in the corner of his mouth. "But I'm his friend. I talked Martí into hiring him."

Mingo gave scant heed to the boast. The coffee was good and he was hungry, as usual. He reached for one of the hard-boiled eggs and cracked it on the bar. Only then did Nick's words really register. "Hire him?" He blew on his coffee and turned the words in his mind. "I didn't think Martí had enough money to hire anybody."

"If you want to call it hiring," Nick grumbled, then suddenly was bitter and his face flushed. "Joe Fry is a Confederate hero, but he was walking the streets of New Orleans when we found him." The Cuban reached out and tapped Mingo's arm. "The South had forgot him and he was damn near starving. We gave him $150. All we had." He shook his head slowly. "Fry sent a hundred to his family and used the rest to buy his sea gear. Old second-hand stuff."

Mingo debated a question, then asked innocently. "Did he join Cuba because he needed money, or because he believes Cuba is right?"

Nick González swelled like an angry frog and spluttered. "Well, I'll be pluperfect God damned!"

Mingo was a bit abashed but not apologetic. He glanced at the men around the tables, themselves quickly silent, and he turned again to Nick. "I didn't mean anything, but up where I come from one man has as much right to ask questions as the next. And, mister, you been doing a lot of question asking." He pushed his coffee cup aside. "I'll be obliged if you will take me up to Captain Fry."

The light in Nick's eyes, usually friendly and always inquisitive, was hard and his voice was sharp. "I'll take you up." He stepped from behind his bar. "And you better decide about Joe Fry for yourself."

"I aim to." Mingo moved away through the exiles and to the steps.

Captain Fry was gruff but mannerly and motioned for his visitor to take a chair. Nick González gathered up the dishes on the captain's table and went out, and Fry crossed the room, staring out at Mobile, at the bay and the ships. "What can I do for you, Mr. Dabney?" He asked it without looking around.

Mingo did not hesitate. "I want to get to Cuba."

"So do I." The old sailor wheeled quickly. "What's your business there?"

"I aim to get in the fight."

"I told you the other day there is no fighting in Cuba." He began pacing the floor. "There can't be until I land supplies." He peered out at the ships again. "You didn't say anything about Cuba when you were here before."

Mingo was disconcerted by this towering old man— almost afraid of him. But he grinned broadly, seeking refuge in his grin. "I made up my mind while I was in Pensacola."

"You must have heard Martí talk," Fry growled. "Martí can lure a starving man from a feast."

"Yes, sir. I heard him. And Señorita Galban, too. She was there."

"Ay!" The captain nodded. "*La Entorcha* is better at raising recruits than Martí."

Mingo rubbed his hands on his knees, grinning again. "I'll never get used to folks calling Rafaela by that name." He welcomed an opportunity for a casual remark, hoping to break down Fry's reserve. "She visited us up in Lebanon, you know."

The full meaning of the remark and the measure of this woodsman's ignorance was lost on the old man. He took a chair at the table and bowed his head, musing, considering the merits of his visitor. "You'll get used to it if you associate with Cubans. It's their tribute to their symbol."

"What kind of tribute?" Mingo tried to ask it casually, but the catch in his voice betrayed him and his infatuation was more apparent because he tried to conceal it.

Fry raised his head slowly, a veil of wonder upon his face as he saw Mingo's eyes, the bright light there. "Did Elmo Batson talk to you about Señorita Galban?"

"No, sir. Why should he?"

The old commander scowled, ignoring the question. "Elmo is a smart man and would not butt in, but didn't José Martí explain her position to you?"

Mingo flushed. "What is there to explain?"

Joseph Fry, bulwarking his sensitiveness behind gruffness, knew love as he knew the sea, and he understood instinctively the heart of this backwoods youth. He was distressed and showed it, indignant that the full truth about *La Entorcha* had not been revealed to a man who came so far to find so much. He growled his indignation. "It was unpardonable of them not to tell you—"

"Tell me what?" Mingo squirmed in his chair and bent forward intently, fear and doubt besieging him.

"That *La Entorcha* is almost a sacred symbol to the Cuban people." He banged his heavy fist on the table, resenting the obligation of disillusioning a pilgrim. He liked Mingo Dabney and sensed his embarrassment and bewilderment. "José is bound to have seen what I see." Fry felt for the words, then spoke them bluntly. "If he didn't tell you, she should have. No woman, saint or symbol, has the right to accept a man's honest look without returning an honest reply."

Mingo got up quickly from his chair and stood at the table, his face dark. "Let's quit beating around the bush. What are you talking about?"

Captain Fry walked over to the fire, walking ponderously

as he debated the things he must say. Then he paused and found the words, rolling his flowery pronouncement. "Rafaela Galban y Torres is the vestal virgin in Cuba's temple of hope."

The flush deepened on Mingo's face and he was angry. "I don't know what the hell all this means."

The captain leaned against the mantel, looking down at the fire and still resenting the duty imposed upon him. "Did she tell you she is the ward of Antonio Macéo?"

"No, sir." There suddenly was no life in Mingo's voice.

The room was still, so still that the drone of the voices below rose clear; a whispered hiss, a toast, a quick laugh. Fry gazed at the burning logs, spluttering and crackling. A moment, a minute, and the old man moved away, pacing the floor, groping for words to express the emotions within him.

"Rafaela Galban was a child when Spain scourged Cuba in the Revolution of '68-'78." His voice rose and fell with the rhythm of his tread. "Leopold Sagaldo butchered her family, then defiled the bodies."

The flush drained from Mingo's face, giving way to a pallor of horror.

Joseph Fry interrupted his slow walking and closed his eyes. "Cuba was bleeding to death and the people were praying for a sign, a burning bush, a pillar of fire. Antonio Macéo found the sign—a child crouching in a ditch."

Mingo gripped the arms of his chair and no words came. Fry opened his eyes and resumed his pacing, from the fire to the wall and back again. "It was Macéo who lifted her to his saddle, stilling her terror. She clung to him and through the cloudless sky the thunder rolled."

The old captain paused and held up his hands, himself enraptured by the miracle revealed to the valiant. "Macéo is an indomitable man, but he trembled as he lifted the child for all to see. It was he who proclaimed the sign of thunder in the sun. It was Cuba he held aloft. She was the sign, the pillar of fire, the living torch."

A tremor of solemn wonder passed through Mingo Dabney

53

and he was humble, remembering her as he saw her last, hallowing the memory.

Captain Fry pulled his chair near the fire and bent to the blaze. His voice was almost a whisper. "Her earliest recollections are two. Macéo the gentle one. Leopold Sagaldo the brute." The old sailor sensed the astonishment in Mingo and faced him squarely. "You have earned the truth and I will tell you all of it. *La Entorcha* is immaculate and dedicated. Macéo willed it so, and the Cuban people want it so. Her hair turned white before she was eighteen. The nuns who reared her taught her the graces, and she breathes for only one thing—*Cuba Libre!* Free Cuba."

Mingo felt like a man who had stumbled into a sacred place and reached for a sacred image. He was a woodsman from a little valley in Mississippi, a peasant yearning for Joan of Arc.

Captain Fry was tired and his head fell to his chest and he clamped his hands, locking his fingers. "Now, young man, do you still want to go to Cuba?"

The pride of his people surged strong through Mingo. She was the ward of General Antonio Macéo. Well, he was a Dabney. He knew nothing of white torches but he had ridden a white horse out of the valley of Lebanon. He had never heard thunder in the sun, but he had heard thunder over the ridges of his home. He got up slowly, resting his hands flat on the table. "I came here to go to Cuba. I aim to go."

Fry got up, too. "I'll take you to Cuba, son."

Mingo's face showed his gratitude. "When?"

"I don't know." The old man turned away. "I don't know where my ship is." He shook his head and pondered. "I am a captain without a command, a sailor without a ship."

It was Mingo's turn to sense bewilderment and confusion in the heart of another man. "Isn't the *Virginius* on her way from New York?"

Fry mumbled his uncertainty, clenching his huge fists, then opened them in exasperation. "She's at sea all right, heading for Kingston. I will pick her up there, God willing."

"But how will you get to Jamaica?" It was Dabney persistence again.

Now that Elmo was gone, Joe Fry must trust somebody, and he trusted this man. "On the first ship that leaves Mobile for the Caribbean. We all rendezvous in Jamaica. Martí. Macéo. Gómez —"

"Rafaela Galban?" Mingo asked eagerly.

"*La Entorcha.*" Fry nodded his massive head. "I will take them and the supplies from Jamaica to Cuba. God willing. There Martí will sound the *grito,* the call to arms, and Cuba will strike again for her freedom." He paused, and said slowly, "I will need a clerk on the *Virginius* if you care to sign on with me."

The captain's tone suggested delay and the woodsman was cautious. He had no desire to wait, and no intention of pledging himself to the *Virginius* and the sea. "Maybe I better think it over. I'm a land man, captain."

"Take your time." Fry stepped to the door and spoke to Nick González who, with Stockingcap, was sweeping the hallway to the captain's room. "Mr. Dabney has been offered a berth on the *Virginius.* Look after him."

Nick grunted his acceptance of the news and Mingo stepped into the hallway, and the door closed behind him. Nick glanced back at the door and snorted, "*Por Dios!* Didn't he bite you?"

Mingo spoke quickly. "He's all right. Just worried. He's got enough worries to run him crazy."

Again Nick snorted. "We're all crazy. My country has been under Spain since Columbus' time, and Spain has driven us mad." He held out his pudgy hands and shrugged. "Now Sagaldo is there to butcher my people. Sagaldo always leaves his mark on the dead. A slash into the belly."

Nick González introduced Mingo to the other revolutionists and they crowded before the bar, shaking his hand, telling him in English he was welcome, making fervent speeches in

Spanish. They pressed drinks upon him but he declined and set forth for the livery stable. The sight of his big white stallion thrilled him and he stroked Shannon, sliding his hand over the silken hair.

"That's a fine horse, mister." Mingo turned and the owner of the stable was standing by the entrance to the stall. "I like the looks of that horse."

"So do I." He saddled Shannon and rode him over the cobblestones, past square houses built so close to the streets that their galleries, enclosed by balustrades of iron lace, hung over the walkways.

The biting wind, down from the Alabama River and across the bay, tingled his cheeks and he debated Fry's offer, mulling over the problem. He smelled the sea and headed Shannon toward the water front, and the sight of the anchored ships, pitching lightly before the wind, nudging their hawsers, fascinated him. He held his horse tight, looking at the water, blue and flecked with gold by the sun, white-maned by the wind. He looked at the bay, long and narrow and stretching on to the south, pointing toward the open sea. Toward Rafaela Galban. He must go quickly. That he knew. He trusted Fry. That, too, he knew, but he must not pledge himself to any man or any ship. He must remain free on his quest to seek the girl and the grail.

He had heard the prophet's demand for the lowly to rise, and the symbol's plea for the meek to seek their own deliverance. There, with the wind white-maning the sea, Mingo Dabney kept a vigil with his soul and pledged his Dabney heritage to Cuban freedom, his honor to a white torch, his strength to the meek. There, in the quietness, he heard no thunder in the sun, only the lapping of water on an Alabama shore, but the air of a free land consecrated him and the resolve of a brave man dedicated him. His love was his sign, and his quest was his faith. His hope was substance not seen, hardly dared, but shepherding his spirit forever.

However, he must part with his white horse on the threshold of his odyssey, so he turned from the sea and rode rapidly to the livery stable and said to the owner, "You want to buy this horse?"

"Sure. I'll give you $140 for him."

Mingo was selling more than a horse; he was selling a gift from his family, a tie to Lebanon, and would not dicker. "All right. What'll you give me for my saddle?"

The owner looked up sharply. Was this country fellow a fool? Didn't he know the value of a horse? "I'll give you $18 for the saddle and chuck in $3 for the bridle."

"That'll be all right." Mingo accepted the money and walked out, stroking Shannon on the shoulder as he passed. Lebanon was infinitely far away and strangely long ago.

He swung down the streets of Mobile, striding long as a woodsman strides, and entered *El Delfin* with his head high and his hat aslant. The exiles waved a greeting and he saluted them with a flip of his hand, then took the steps two at a time. Fry's door was open and Mingo stood in the doorway, twisting his hair around his fingers. "I'll go with you, Captain Fry. You can count on me."

The old man laid down his pen, nodding his approval and Mingo crossed the room to the fire. "There's just one condition, sir. I must go as a passenger. I'll work as your clerk, but I aim to pay my way so I'll be under no obligations. When I get to Cuba, I want to be free to go and come as I please."

Fry smoothed his beard, clucking his merriment. "You'll pay in hard money, Mr. Dabney? You mean you have hard money?"

"Yes, sir."

Captain Fry threw back his head and his deep, tumultuous laughter rolled through the room. It was the first time Mingo had heard him laugh and he grinned back. "By George!" Joe Fry was a devout churchman, a good Catholic, and seldom swore, eschewing even the mild oaths. "A paying passenger on the *Virginius*! Believe me, young man, it can be arranged."

"Then it's agreed that I'll be under no obligations after we get to Cuba?" Mingo was insistent on that point.

The old sailor got up, still smiling his delight in having a clerk with brains and strength, and hard money. "It is agreed, and here's my seal." He offered his hand, gripping hard and walking with his clerk down the hallway. "We'll begin work tomorrow." He put his hand on the stair railing, peered into the room below and roared, "González!"

"*Sí.*"

"I'm sending my clerk below. Keep him sober and out of jail —"

"I'll handle him." There was mirth in Nick's tone.

"Pound a little Spanish through his skull."

"Anything else?" Nick came to the foot of the stairs and looked up.

"That's all." Captain Joseph Fry, himself a father, put a heavy arm around Mingo's shoulder for only a second, then pulled his arm away and stood erect, his hands clasped behind his back as though he were on the bridge of a ship instead of the rickety stairs of a water front saloon.

He had told Mingo Dabney the truth about Rafaela Galban and now, like Elmo, he must not butt in. However, there was one thing he should say and he said it emphatically. "Guard your tongue, son. Particularly about *La Entorcha*. A man is a fool to wish to die."

MINGO DABNEY

Chapter *5*   Mingo shared Nick's room at
El Delfiin, and took his meals downstairs with the exiles
except when he ate with Fry in the captain's quarters.

Word came from the Cuban committee in New York that
the *Virginius* was somewhere in the Bahamas, creeping south,
slipping toward the Antilles. She must make a port for
repairs, but the hand of Spain was so firm in the Indies that
the tiny republics dared not grant haven to a ship that was
a harbinger of revolution.

Any news, even meager news of his ship, bolstered Fry.
"Spain is watching her," he told Mingo. "But she's still
moving south. She'll skirt the west coast of Cuba for Jamaica.
Safer that way."

"When will we leave?" The pilgrim asked it every day.
He had been waiting in Mobile for more than a week and
was restless. Surely Rafaela had reached Guatemala.

"We'll leave on the first ship that sails for Jamaica." Fry
was patient with Mingo.

There was not enough work to keep Mingo busy and one
day flowed into another, and he grew restless. The promise
of adventure was not fulfilled and the black mood of the
Dabneys was upon him. He remained close to *El Delfín,*
though sometimes at night he and Fry walked along the
water front, visiting ships, seeking news from Cuba and
passage to Jamaica. A schooner or a barque in from the
Caribbean, smelling of mahogany and rum, hardly moored
before they went aboard. "Any news from Cuba?"

The answer always was the same. "No news. No news from Cuba."

"Any news of a ship named the *Virginius*? New York registry."

"No news."

"What is your destination?"

Puerto Rico. Santo Domingo. South America. Everywhere except Jamaica . . .

The azaleas of Mobile bloomed rich that spring and the city was chirping in the glory of its pink cape. Mingo himself began to feel like an exile, and still there was no information of the *Virginius*. Captain Fry shared his clerk's despondency, mouthing his impatience, sometimes storming it.

Mingo was in the captain's room one blustery afternoon and Fry was standing by the window, watching a vessel creep toward its mooring. "Come here, son. Who is she? Can you make her out?"

The clerk moved to his captain's side and glanced at the ship's bow. "The *Robert C. Turner*. A British barque."

Fry squared himself, clasping his hands behind him. "She's limping in. There's been rough water in the Gulf."

"Maybe she has news, Cap'n."

"Too late to make a proper call," Fry said stiffly. "We must wait until morning." The sight of the barque, fresh in from the islands, upset the old man and he stalked to the window and propped his hands on the sill, glaring toward the Gulf. His mood primed him for a long discourse. "If Cuba fails to free herself this time, the United States will have to kick Spain out."

There was a threat of rain outside and Mingo heard the exiles straggling into the saloon, coming for the free supper that Nick furnished, but Fry heard only himself, droning one of his lengthy monologues on Cuban history and Spanish perfidy. "The United States has never lifted a finger to help Cuba, but we can no longer tolerate Spain as a next door neighbor." He hesitated, scowling at Mingo. "Young man, are you listening to me?"

"No, sir." Mingo shook his head and grinned. "I was thinking about a little supper."

Fry threw back his head and his huge body shook with laughter. "I'm a garrulous old fellow. Mrs. Fry has told me so many times." He pulled his chair near the table and sat down. His laughter passed and his voice was gentle, immeasurably gentle. "Her name is Dita. We have seven children." He paused for a second, holding his memories close. "Maybe I've told you that before."

"Yes, sir."

The old man was silent and Mingo continued to watch the shadows gather over the bay. The *Robert C. Turner* had been warped into a dock, and there was no ship moving upon the bay. Suddenly Captain Fry looked up. "Why is everything so quiet below?" He listened a moment longer, got up and moved quickly to the door, then through the hall to the steps. Mingo was at his heels and they craned their necks, peering down the stairs into the smoky light of the saloon. The crowd was bunched around a stranger, listening intently. "González!" Fry bellowed. "What's up? Any news of my ship?"

"No." Nick walked to the foot of the stairs. "But this sailor is off a British barque just docked. He says Martí is in Santo Domingo."

Then where was Rafaela? Mingo almost shouted the question, but caught himself and looked at Captain Fry.

"Send him up here," Fry ordered and stalked back into his room.

The sailor was a Cuban, his black eyes sparkling at the honor of appearing before Joseph C. Fry who already was a hope for an oppressed people.

Yes, José Martí was in Santo Domingo with Máximo Gómez.

"What of *La Entorcha*?" Fry asked quickly.

"Guatemala, Señor. Recruiting in Guatemala. And Macéo is in Costa Rica."

"What is your next port?" Fry snapped the demand.

"Kingston, Señor. Kingston, Jamaica."

Mingo's heart bounced to his throat and clung there. She was safe and there was a ship in harbor destined for Jamaica. He excused himself and felt in his coat pocket for a cigar, a cheap one, and tilted it high, then swaggered down the steps and into the saloon. "Rum, *compadre*." He pounded Nick's bar and faced the room.

"What's going on?" Nick demanded, afraid he was missing something.

"I just want to treat the house." The pilgrim perked his cigar. "That's all, you nosy old gobbler."

Captain Thompson of the *Robert C. Turner* was a River Humber man, stern and easily irritated, especially by visitors so soon after breakfast when all men should be at work. Mingo sensed the Englishman's lack of cordiality and so did Fry, though he ignored it.

The master of the British barque offered refreshments, but said tartly. "I must get my repairs under way. We ran out a storm."

Mingo wished his captain would get straightway to the matter of passage, but knew Fry must do things his own way, usually slow and pompous and strictly according to the ritual and tradition of mariners.

"Are you going back to the islands?" Fry watched Thompson intently and tasted his whiskey. The old man was wearing his greatcoat, the coat so recently bought, and his cap. His beard was neatly trimmed.

The British master passed cigars. "I sail for Kingston in a few days. Then Venezuela." He did not sit down. "And now, what service can I be?"

His brusqueness annoyed Mingo, whereas Captain Fry

was patient and courtly. "We know you're busy, but have you any news of the *Virginius*, a paddle-wheeler of New York registry?"

Thompson took a chair. "She's poking around the islands somewhere." He was frowning. "Menace to navigation, that ship. Built thirty years ago as a Confederate blockade runner. She's old and breaking up."

Captain Joseph C. Fry put down his glass and got to his feet. "I was a Confederate naval officer, sir. I, too, am old, but the *Virginius* is my ship."

The Englishman glanced at the commander, then over at Mingo and his manner changed. He was a blunt man, but he knew pride when he saw it. "The *Virginius* is British built," he said quickly, "and there's a lot of life in her under a good crew. You gentlemen had breakfast?"

"Yes," said Fry. "And I apologize for taking so much of your time. But have you any news from Cuba?"

"Or from Guatemala?" Mingo asked.

Thompson looked at Fry's heavy boots, daubed with black stove polish, and at his new cap and coat. A new cap for an old man. "I suppose you know that Martínez Campos is returning to Cuba as Captain-General. Spain's greatest soldier."

"I thought Sagaldo was," Mingo said, showing his ignorance in trying to show his knowledge.

The host turned to Mingo and squinted. The stocky frame, the clear eyes, the strong hands; they, too, told their story and the master suddenly was sad. An old ship bought from the tithes of poor people. An old man coming back to the sea again. And a rawboned woodsman who never had been to sea at all. He understood and was patient with Mingo, smiling at him. "Sagaldo is a field general. He has been sent to the Oriente, the eastern end of Cuba."

Captain Fry cleared his throat to command their attention and pursed his lips, glancing up at Thompson's master mariner's license framed over his desk. "We have urgent

63

business in Jamaica, sir. I was wondering if it might be convenient for you to extend to us the courtesy of the sea."

It was the proud old commander's way of asking for free passage and Mingo resented the necessity of a man like Joseph C. Fry begging a favor of anyone. Mingo had money from the sale of Shannon, but it was not enough for both their passages. He could write home for money. That would take time, however, and time was precious. So he kept his thoughts to himself while a flush spread over his face, tingling to the roots of his hair.

Captain Thompson rose gallantly to the occasion. "My ship is yours, sir."

Joseph Fry reared back in his chair, proud of his calling and of the men it bred. He tapped his foot against the floor and rolled his cigar in his fingers. The old commander did not smoke and was saving the cigar for Nick González. "I hope, sir, that my gratitude is equal to your hospitality."

Captain Thompson bowed. "Your servant, Captain Fry. It will be an honor to have you and your friend as my guests."

Mingo blew his breath slowly between his lips and grinned, and he and Captain Fry arose, the old man stiffly and Mingo impatiently. Captain Thompson saw them to the gangplank and they walked off the *Robert C. Turner* and along the water front, walking rapidly back to *El Delfín*. Captain Fry was grinning, too, cutting his eyes over at his clerk. The old man had almost mastered the broad grin of Lebanon.

They were about a block from their lodgings when they heard shouts in the saloon. Fry looked quickly at Mingo and they hurried, almost running.

El Delfín was bedlam. The exiles were shouting and dancing and waving their glasses. Stockingcap was on a table, holding high a mug of beer and screaming, *"Viva Baire! Viva Cuba!"* Nick González was passing out drinks and the Cuban sailor from the *Robert C. Turner* was already drunk, pounding a mug and roaring, *"Viva Baire!"*

Fry stalked in and Mingo stood in the doorway, his mouth agape, looking from one face to another.

"What is it?" The captain bellowed above the tumult. He brushed his cap to the back of his head and put his massive fists on his hips. "What is it, I say?"

Nick ran from behind his bar, moving with amazing agility and pushing a path through the celebrants. "The *grito*!" He shouted. "The call has been sounded. In Baire!"

"No!" Fry's face was white under his beard and his beard trembled. "Who sounded it?"

"We don't know." Nick's big belly was bouncing his excitement and his face dripped sweat. "But the *grito* was sounded yesterday." He reached out and grabbed Mingo's hand and began pounding his back. "Cuba has sounded the call for her children to arise!"

Fry was glaring at the jubilant men, all of them in a frenzy and most of them drunk. "Come to my room, González," he ordered. "This call is premature. Any news from Martí?"

"No!"

"Macéo?"

"No!" Nick reached for his rum. *"Viva Baire!"* He held his glass high, gulped a part of it and handed the glass to Mingo.

"Viva!" Mingo shouted and raised the glass, emptying it. *"Si! Viva!"* The meaning of it all was beyond him but this was a promise of action and he grabbed another glass and drained it. "God dammit, hooray!"

"Dabney!" The captain's excitement was as evident as his clerk's but he retained his dignity. "González! Follow me." He pushed through the crowd. "What of Máximo Gómez?"

"I don't know," Nick spluttered. "We got a message from the New York committee that the *grito* has been sounded at the village of Baire."

"It's premature," Fry stormed. "Something has gone wrong." He stomped up the steps, his shoulders squared, his cap still on the back of his head. Mingo and Nick were behind him and grinning. In his room, Fry shoved two chairs around, nodding toward them, but nobody sat down. The tumult below still was deafening and the building shook.

"Shall I shut them up?" Nick asked.

"Leave them alone! I only hope they've got rum enough." The commander began pacing, his heavy shoes thudding the floor. "The *grito* was to come after the rendezvous in Jamaica. Cuban impatience again —"

"It seems to me," said Mingo, looking down the bay at the *Robert C. Turner*, "that somebody in Cuba got as tired of waiting as I am."

Nick González laughed. In spite of the tension, he laughed. "That's just about what happened."

Fry's hands were behind him and he beat his fists in his palm. "But we're not ready. Sagaldo can crush us."

The laughter passed from Nick González and his jaw, usually flabby, was hard. "Martí will move. He will answer the *grito*. José will take care of Sagaldo."

They heard a man running up the stairs, then along the hallway. Mingo opened the door and Stockingcap looked around frantically, saw Nick and hurried to him, handing him a dispatch on a yellow sheet.

"What is it?" Fry demanded.

The Cuban glanced at the message, then cut his eyes quickly at Mingo and gave the dispatch to Fry. The old man read it, and his hands shook as he rolled the paper into a little ball and tossed it into the fireplace. "It was from the New Orleans committee, son. *La Entorcha* left Guatemala last night. Heading for Jamaica."

Mingo paled and then his eyes were bright and Nick González looked at him, looking steadily at his eyes. The noise was swelling up from below, rising in waves and then subsiding into song. They were loud, defiant songs, Cuba's dare to Spain.

66

"Perhaps, González," Fry said graciously, "the men below need your steadying influence."

The proprietor of *El Delfín* started away and Mingo moved to follow. "They might need me, too cap'n."

"You stay here," Fry ordered. "And just a minute, González." He stepped to his sea chest, turning his meager belongings, and took out a treasure. "This is very old rum." He handed it to the Cuban. "I'd planned to save it for the medicine chest of my ship. But take it to the men."

Nick thanked him and waddled slowly out of the room, moving with dignity until he reached the head of the stairs. There he forgot his dignity and his bulk and dashed down, shouting and waving the bottle.

Mingo went to the window, gazing out at the *Robert C. Turner*, then down the bay to the south. "How far is it from Guatemala to Jamaica?"

"About eight hundred miles. They'll have to smuggle her across. Spain will be watching every rowboat."

"She's in danger?" A cold shock of fear crept into his stomach.

"*La Entorcha* has been in danger since Macéo proclaimed her thunder in the sun. Every breath in revolution is danger, Mingo." Fry closed his locker, then straightened and walked over to the mantel. He had a book in his hand and began thumbing the pages. "This is a book of prayers by Thomas Dekker, the Elizabethan. I ask your indulgence to read from it. The prayer is for Rafaela Galban y Torres, and for us." He began reading softly: "Be merciful unto us who are venturing into the deep. There shall we see Thy wonders, but let us not see Thy wrath. Set Thou an Angel at our helm, and charge him to guide us through the wilderness of waters, till we safely arrive on shore. Amen."

The devout sailor closed the book and put it on the mantel, and cocked his head to the roar rising from the room below. "I believe," he said slyly, "that González needs help. Suppose you go join him."

Mingo went below, in no mood for the celebration but

seeking easement in the company of his comrades. He arrived at the bar in time to share a sip of his captain's rum, then accepted a tumbler from Nick. The spirits burned his blood and spun his head and he began singing with the Cubans, singing the songs of Cuban seas, of the island itself—the Oriente and its mountains; Pinar del Río, its rivers and the tobacco fields.

It didn't trouble him that his voice was rising, drowning out the others as he sang in the wild, free way of a Lebanon woodsman. His comrades hushed, staring at him as he swung his glass to and fro, and sang. He drank and forgot where he was, forgot the sea and the gulls that swirled almost to the door of *El Delfín*. He forgot the exiles and their presence, remembering only Rafaela and his dream, snow on a green hill. The wanderer closed his eyes, tilted his head and the words sang themselves in the fervor of his longing:

"Men are fools that wish to die! . . ."

Stockingcap put down his mug softly. Others leaned against the bar and looked out at the bay. Nick González bowed his head. They were quiet, hushed by the voice, stilled by the ardor of their comrade. None heard Fry tiptoe along the hall and stand at the head of the stairs.

> *Is it not fine to swim in wine,*
> *And turn upon the toe,*
> *And sing hey nonny no!*
> *When the winds blow and the seas flow?*

None heard Fry walk back to his room and close the door. The old man reached again for Dekker's book of prayers. . . .

All that morning and into the afternoon the revelers drank and sang, but Joe Fry turned from Dekker's prayers to his rosary, telling his beads until his fears were calmed. At twilight he went downstairs and all the exiles cheered and some of them slapped him on the back. Mingo and Nick and Stockingcap were at the bar, singing a woodsman's ditty of Lebanon. The three still were on their feet, but unsteady.

"I'm going to the telegraph office," Fry said. "I'm going to get news."

"I'll go with you." Mingo's grin was out of control.

"You'll stay here! I'm ashamed of you, Dabney. I've been going to sea since I was twelve and I've never been overboard in my life."

"Viva!" Mingo said, and Fry hurried out, tucking his smile in his heavy beard.

They led Stockingcap upstairs and stretched him out on Mingo's cot. Nick stumbled toward his own bed and, because there was no other bed available, Mingo Dabney went to Fry's couch and fell asleep.

He had no idea of time when he woke and saw the captain at his desk, writing by lamplight. The lamp was turned so the glow would not disturb Mingo, but any light was painful as Mingo pulled himself to the edge of the bed and sat up, holding his head. There was no need for an explanation or an apology. He moistened his parched lips, munching them, and mumbled, "I wonder if you'd tell me the time, sir."

Fry didn't own a watch, but he glanced at the stars over the bay. "It's three A.M., or thereabouts. There's some hot coffee on the hearth. Can you make it, or shall I fetch it to you?"

"I can make it." He went to the hearth and drank the coffee black. "I hope the Cuban Navy is not going to discharge me."

"You will be a passenger, Mr. Dabney. A paying passenger. The Cuban Navy does not regulate the lives of passengers. Certainly not paying passengers." His smile was almost a grin, almost the warm grin of Lebanon.

Mingo began making up the bed, smoothing the blankets. "Any news of our ship? Or when the *Robert C. Turner* is clearing?"

"Oh! So you remember your duty." Then he was serious. "Yes, I have news —"

69

"My God! What is it —"

"This is no time for profanity, Mr. Dabney. The *Virginius* has been sighted at the eastern tip of Cuba. She is heading through the Windward Passage —"

"I thought she was going around the western tip." His head was clear and the cold shock was back in his stomach. Something had gone wrong again.

Captain Fry took a swallow of coffee and leaned back in his chair. "She's taking a short cut. Somebody on the *Virginius* got word of the *grito*, and my ship is running straight through the Windward Passage, daring half the Spanish navy."

"Who told you?" Mingo demanded.

"Elmo Batson," Fry said triumphantly. "I got a telegram from Elmo. He's heading out for Haiti. He said the *Virginius* would make Kingston within a week, or be a Spanish prize by morning. She'll make Kingston. God willing."

"God willing," the pilgrim murmured reverently.

Stockingcap was the first of *El Delfín's* exiles to answer the *grito*. The day after the call, as soon as he was sober, he announced his departure for his homeland. He bowed to Fry and shook Mingo's hand, but he embraced Nick González, weeping his gratitude for sanctuary and calling down heaven's blessings on the fat man who had fed him without stint. He expected to reach Cuba by way of Key West.

One by one the able-bodied exiles went away, leaving Mingo to moon over his delay, and Fry to scowl his impatience, and Nick to comfort them both that all would be well. The pumps on the *Robert C. Turner* were working day and night to clean her out, for Thompson, too, was impatient. Silence had swallowed the *Virginius*.

Three days after the call, news began trickling in to *El Delfín*. The *grito* was premature. A group of patriots had gathered at Baire to dedicate themselves to Cuban freedom.

Then it happened. No one knew how or why, but someone sounded the *grito* and the word spread like a thunderhead over the Windward Passage. A few patriots at Baire cried out and Cuba's Oriente, land of mountains and revolutions, was in ferment.

"Spain will crush them," Mingo said, speaking the fear in his own heart. "Spain will crush the revolution even before we get to Jamaica —"

"Where is Martí?" Nick wondered it aloud for the hundredth time. "José is the soul of Cuba. The people will wait for him to speak. . . ."

Mingo turned from the fat bartender and spoke his fears. "You know Sagaldo is already on the move —"

"I know nothing," Fry snapped.

But Sagaldo did not move. He was in Santiago de Cuba sending messages to Spain's government in Havana that the call was not important, dismissing the *grito* as a ripple; unaware that a ripple is the first pulse of a tidal wave. Leopold Sagaldo despised the significance of a few peasants calling from the hamlet of Baire. He was poised, waiting for a man he hated to madness, waiting for Antonio Macéo, the mulatto he called The Nigra.

A cry from a hamlet. A whisper among the hills. And a people were listening for the thunder in the sun. Sagaldo dismissed and Havana ignored, but Key West heard and Tampa heeded. *El Delfin* sifted the facts from the rumors and Mingo was posted at the telegraph office while Fry and Thompson made the rounds of shipping agents every day. Nick stayed at the saloon.

There came a bit of news from this source, a dribble from that. Rumors and wild talk, confusion and vague reports. A fishing smack was sighted off Grand Cayman, about five hundred miles from Guatemala. A Spanish ship spoke it, ordering it to lay to, but the little craft slipped into the fog and vanished, beating down toward Jamaica. Mingo clenched his fists and wiped sweat from his face, and waited.

Fry posted a map of Cuba in his room and, day after day, the remaining exiles of *El Delfín* crowded in, studying the captain's notations, wrangling about the news from the homeland. A band of hillmen attacked a Spanish outpost. Flor Crombet was killed in the Oriente. A dozen chieftains made ready to move in, to strike and draw back. Betancourt and Rodriguez, the clans of Nuñez and Céspedes. A Spanish remount station was raided near Monteverde and all the horses driven off. A sentry was killed, his throat cut.

The men at *El Delfín* slept fitfully, no longer counting the days, talking little and praying much. Skirmishes in the Oriente. Mumblings in Santa Clara. Uncertainty in Havana. And still Sagaldo dallied in Santiago de Cuba. And still the Cuban people prayed for the sign.

"Where is *La Entorcha?*" It was a wail in the mountains.

"Where is Macéo?" It was a plea from the plains.

"What of Máximo Gómez?" It was a demand in Las Villas.

"And where is Martí? Where is our soul?" It was a lament in all Cuba.

Nick González echoed the lament. *"Por Dios!* Where is José? Blessed Mother! Where is the prophet?"

A storm was raging over the Windward Passage, sweeping Baracoa where Columbus landed four centuries before, sweeping the sea between Haiti and the Oriente. The wind was howling down from San Salvador, swirling down through the hundred cays, churning the sea and driving it against the sands of Cuba.

On that night, in the storm from San Salvador, a little ship hove to in the Windward Passage. José Martí and Máximo Gómez slid over the side and into a waiting boat, a pitching boat manned by comrades who dared the tumultuous seas and rowed out from a hidden cove.

Where was Martí, the soul of Cuba? There he was, holding fast to the sides of the surging rowboat. Sought by all the armies of Spain, there he was, clinging to a rowboat in the

Windward Passage. The old man with him was Máximo Gómez, fox of the revolution; sixty-nine and pain-racked, yet coming again to fight Spain.

Máximo Gómez bent forward and took an oar. José Martí took an oar, bracing his festering leg as he pulled for the land he had pledged to liberate.

They rowed until suddenly a wave, thundering down from the cays, lifted their boat and flung it upon Cuban soil, crushing the boat and leaving them upon their knees to bow down and kiss the land they loved.

Before the sun rose, whispers sped through the island and Sagaldo ordered his soldiers to quarters and issued marching rations and bandoleers.

The prophet had returned, going straight into his homeland without waiting for the rendezvous in Jamaica. The premature *grito* was forcing his hand.

Nick González hung his apron on a peg behind his bar. "Now the war will start. I ain't too old to fight. I don't know how I'll get there, but I'll make it."

He put his hand on Fry's shoulder, then shook Mingo's hand and Mingo Dabney was sad to see him leave. He liked Nick. Everybody liked Nick, and the bartender bade them all good-bye, turned the keys to *El Delfín* over to a crippled exile and waddled out, heading for the bay and Florida beyond. . . .

It was raining hard in Mobile, a slushing rain that came on the heels of the Caribbean squall. Mingo Dabney could not sleep, but lay tossing on his cot, his mind darting to a dozen details. He heard Captain Fry pacing the room, pausing a moment, then pacing again.

Footsteps came along the hall, a soft tread and Mingo called, but there was no reply. He heard the door to Fry's room open, then close and he lay there, debating whether to go to his captain's room or try to sleep. A foghorn was growling in the harbor.

His own door opened and Fry was framed there, holding a lamp. "Dabney! Mr. Dabney!"

The formal manner brought Mingo to his feet quickly and he answered. The old man came in and Captain Thompson followed. Fry put the lamp on the table and Mingo squinted. "What is it, sir?"

The towering old mariner was trying to hide his excitement behind his dignity. "Captain Thompson has brought good news. *La Entorcha* has landed in Jamaica. She is safe and well."

"Thank the good Lord," Mingo said reverently after the full meaning of the words registered on his troubled brain. He glanced from Fry to Thompson. There was something else. He sensed it. Suddenly he demanded, "Where is our ship? Where is the *Virginius*?"

"Jamaica!" Fry's face lighted in the glow of the lamp. "Kingston, Jamaica! And the *Robert C. Turner* sails at daybreak." The old man took one step toward Mingo, braced himself a moment, then slumped to the cot and wept.

Mingo didn't know what to do. He looked at Thompson and the Englishman's face was turned. Mingo squeezed his fists and fought back his emotions. Then he stepped to the side of his captain and put his arm around the massive shoulders. "It's all right, cap'n. Everything's all right now. . . ."

"Yes. Of course, Mr. Dabney. Of course it is." Joseph Fry got up, leaning on the table for support, and turned to Thompson. "Captain, we will board your ship within the hour."

"We will sail on flood tide," the Englishman said.

They went to Captain Fry's room and the old man began checking his gear, the pitiful possessions in his sea chest, the greatcoat, his new cap, his book of prayers and letters from his family. "No medicine," he mumbled. "I must board my ship without a medicine chest."

"We can get medicine in Jamaica, can't we?" Mingo asked.

"With what?" Fry demanded. "I have no money."

Captain Thompson looked away. He must not meddle in this. He must not injure the pride of a fellow mariner and, more than that, a British sea captain must not contribute help to a ship dedicated to revolutions against a friendly power.

Mingo frowned slightly and remembered something. "Wait a minute." He reached for his purse. "I'd as soon pay my passage on the *Virginius* now as in Jamaica."

The captain closed his locker and pushed himself erect. "That would not be irregular, Mister Dabney."

"How much?"

Fry pursed his lips. "Well, it's about two hundred miles from Kingston around Morant Point to Cuba. I'd say $20."

The traveler was surprised. "Is that all?" He counted out $20 from the money he had received for Shannon and handed it to Fry.

"I'll give you a receipt —"

"Don't bother, sir."

"It is the proper procedure." The old commander sat at the table, moved the lamp closer and dipped his pen into the inkwell. "Rec'd, of Mr. Mingo Dabney twenty dollars ($20) for passage from Kingston, Jamaica, to Cuba." He signed his name and dated the receipt. Captain Thompson witnessed it as master of the *Robert C. Turner*.

Mingo accepted the paper and put it in his purse next to a few keepsakes from Lebanon. It was his receipt for his passage to Rafaela Galban.

Fry fingered the money. "Captain Thompson, there is an all-night apothecary on Bienville Square. Perhaps one of your men could make the necessary purchases. Morphine. Laudanum. Oil. Quinine. The usual things."

"I will see to it." Thompson accepted the money and took his leave. Fry looked around the room, then cupped his hand over the lamp and blew it out. Mingo followed his captain down the dark hallway, down the creaky stairs. *El Delfin* was sleeping.

75

"No need to get a hack," Fry said. "The walk will do us good. Save money, too."

There was a thin sprinkling of stars, an occasional pricking of the dark, as Joseph C. Fry and Mingo Dabney walked along the water front. The young woodsman, lonely and awed, watched the slow tilting, the rhythmic swaying of the masthead lights on the anchored ships. The stars were frosty cold, gleaming white, and so far away.

MINGO DABNEY

Chapter **6**   The sun was sharp off the port
bow as the *Robert C. Turner* made her run down the bay.
The sea was smooth and the breeze curved the sails full,
sending the barque skimming, rolling occasionally and dipping, curtsying to the sea.

Mingo never had been on a moving ship before and the
motion of the barque, lightly obeying wind and water, excited him. He was a man of trees and the steadfast earth,
and was pensive as he looked out at the undisciplined water,
remembering the surety of the oaks and pines of Lebanon.

He came on deck an hour before dawn, leaving Captain
Fry snoring in their cabin, and watched the sailors tidy the
ship and cast off. He stumbled over canvas and fouled the
lines and laughed for the joy of adventure, for now he was
away at last, bound for the Indies, for the *Virginius* and
Rafaela.

"Well, Mingo—" He turned and Captain Fry was behind
him, wearing his cap, and the winds of the seven seas were
blowing through his beard. "The bay is calm. Beautiful, eh?"

The woodsman looked out at the slow tilting of the sea.
"She's not steady. She needs roots to hold her down."

Captain Fry reared back. "Root the sea!" The old sailor
gazed beyond the puny bay to the Gulf, and beyond the Gulf
to the oceans, limitless, imperishable, no earth to mar
them. "Young man, you're a landlubber."

"We call 'em clodhoppers up where I come from." Mingo's

broad grin returned and he watched the men on the yard-arms clewing the canvas.

The barque skimmed out of the bay and Captain Fry pointed at Fort Morgan and Fort Gaines. "The defenses of Mobile."

There was a twinkle in Mingo's eyes. "So that's where the Yankees stomped the daylights out of the Confederate navy?"

Fry tightened his cap and tugged at his trousers. "It was a gallant action. Farragut's victory was praiseworthy; and the Confederate navy was magnificent, as always." He braced himself against the roll of the ship. "And I, for one, have never believed that Farragut said, 'Damn the torpedoes.' Pure humbug."

Mingo was not listening to Captain Fry, but was gazing at the sailors as they scampered through the shrouds and ratlines.

The *Robert C. Turner* steered past Dauphine Island, then full into the Gulf, dipping into deep water. There was an easy grace as she dipped, slowly leaning far to her side and hanging there, quivering; then gradually righting herself, pausing for an instant, only to fall away and begin the long roll to her other side. Captain Fry eyed his protégé closely, and hastened to Captain Thompson, requesting brandy.

"Is the landlubber sick?" Thompson asked.

"Clodhopper." Fry tried to imitate his clerk's grin. "He's going to be."

He stayed by Mingo, making him sip the brandy and wiping his face with a wet towel. The woodsman was too miserable to protest. "Go below and get some sleep," Fry ordered.

The pilgrim slept until mid-afternoon and felt better. His stomach still pulsed, but the hot threat at the back of his throat was gone. He ate a good supper and a better breakfast the next morning and gradually accepted the endless motion, but never liked it.

Swells and squalls began sweeping up from the islands and Captain Thompson veered his ship due east, hugging the Florida coast. Mingo mixed with the crew, sharing their tasks, and Captain Fry frowned. In his code it was improper for a passenger, dining at the captain's table, to mingle with the men; but Mingo Dabney learned more from the sailors than from the interminable talk of Captain Thompson and Captain Fry.

He learned about the ship, how to sail her and steer her, to caulk a pump and approximate time by length of the yardarm's shadow. In return, he taught the sailors to stretch rawhide and re-temper steel by heating it, then letting it cool in the damp air. He showed the English cook how to season the galley's scraps into palatable food. "He's a better cook than a Chinaman," one sailor said. "Wonder why a man like him is going to Cuba."

"There'll be a woman in it somewhere," said another. "Running from one, or running to one."

The sailors spoke much of Cuba, the only gem left in the Spanish crown that rested so precariously on the head of Alfonso XIII, the boy king whose mother spoke his mind. The island was Spain's last treasure house, and she was scheming and pleading to keep her most prized possession in the New World.

"But it don't make much difference what Spain wants," a sailor told Mingo as a group lolled on deck. "Sooner or later your country is going to step in. If you don't, England will. Or Germany. And you can bet your country won't stand for that. So it boils down to you and Spain."

"What about the Cubans?" Mingo asked. "Where do they come in?"

A few of the men laughed. "Oh, the *Mambises*."

It was a new word to Mingo, and the sailors weren't sure of its meaning. One said, "It's just a name for Cuban fellows. A Mambi is a poor Cuban who farms and fights and tries to live."

Another suggested, "Dabney, go ask Captain Fry about it. He knows everything."

"You ask him," Mingo said. He was in no humor for one of Fry's ponderous lectures.

They sent one of the group for the information, and he was grinning when he returned. "You're loony! *Mambi* means dirt. Just common clay. The Garlics started it and now the Cubans are proud of it."

"I'll be damned!" Mingo said. "Sort of like the Yankees starting Johnny Reb, and wishing they hadn't." He got up and headed for the galley. "I'm hungry."

"You always are," one of the sailors called after him.

The barque put in for a few hours at a fishing village near the mouth of the Suwannee River and refilled her water casks. Mingo and Fry went ashore, seeking information, but the natives knew nothing of the Cuban revolution and cared less.

The wind was from the northeast and the *Robert C. Turner* clapped on all canvas, running like a white cloud before the wind until a fog crept in, shrouding the coast, hiding the island pearls of Florida's necklace.

Captain Thompson cursed the fog and lifted only enough canvas to stay underway, nosing slowly south until he raised the light of Terra Cela and Tampa Bay. There he ordered all hands to the rigging. The fog be damned! The *Robert C. Turner* had a mission and Captain Thompson was in a hurry. There was gunfire in Cuba's hills and an old ship was waiting in Jamaica for an old man. Even Mingo went aloft, climbing the rigging and hauling at the sails. The fog be damned! There was a girl in Jamaica.

The barque curved her bow into the Gulf and ran out of the fog, skimming down from Terra Costa to Saddle Bunch Keys, past the Ten Thousand Islands. The beacon at Key West was sighted in darkness and next morning Cuba was visible, low on the horizon and misty. "There she is," Captain Thompson said.

The sea was blue-green and the sun was behind them, slanting golden spears deep into the water. A light wind sped down from the north and Mingo watched the island, wishing the mist would shift. The lookout cried a ship to port, a Spanish patrol boat blockading the island.

Fry strode forward and took his place beside Captain Thompson, and Mingo hurried to them. His old black hat was slanted and he leaned against the rail, squinting across the water, gazing at the dot of boiling smoke. "Will she bother us?"

The Englishman glanced back at his flag and shrugged. "Spain has crossed my country's course before. She will not repeat the error." He cupped his hands and shouted to his helmsman. "Hold her as she is."

"Steady as she is, sir," the helmsman answered.

The blockader disappeared.

Their course took them into the Channel of Yucatan, shearing the western tip of Cuba. Mingo's heart was as gay as the sailors' ditties and his stride was jaunty. He worked with the crew or stood by the rail, watching the gulls balancing and the dolphins at play, arching their gleaming backs.

The barque sailed under full canvas into the Caribbean and Mingo's pulse quickened. Captain Fry impatiently walked the deck in long, swinging strides or stood by the helmsman, his hands clasped behind him, his feet well apart, checking the flick of the compass and the swing of the wheel.

A thunderhead was puffing up in the south, boiling and bulging, and the *Robert C. Turner* heeled to starboard, shook herself and dipped on toward home. Captain Fry glanced at the sun, then back at the knot line.

"We'll raise Kingston around four bells," he said.

Captain Thompson corrected him. "It will be a bit later."

"Four bells," said Fry testily and stalked to the bow.

The bell of the *Robert C. Turner* was striking four as the barque, every sail billowing, climbed over the sea and

81

there was Kingston, the king's town, a British port for a British ship.

Somewhere in that haven the *Virginius* waited. And Rafaela Galban.

The buttons of Captain Fry's jacket were bright and his shoes were shined with polish borrowed from his host. His new cap was adjusted properly and he peered ahead, seeking first glimpse of his ship.

A pilot boat came alongside and Captain Thompson waved it away and stood by his helm, guiding his barque into the channel.

"Where is she?" Mingo asked. "Where's the *Virginius*?"

"I don't see her yet," Fry replied irritably.

"Is that her?" Mingo pointed toward a steamer moored near the entrance of the harbor.

"No. German merchantman —"

"How about that one —"

"Portuguese schooner —"

"Then where's our ship, cap'n?"

Thompson came up and they searched the harbor, gazing along the wharves, at schooners and barques, steamers and sloops. Fry puckered his lips, his eyes sweeping the harbor from buoy to dock. Suddenly his shoulders went back and he raised his hand, pointing toward the far end of the bay. "There she is." His voice was firm, but his finger trembled. "There, gentlemen, is the *Virginius*."

Mingo followed the direction and there was a little craft tied to a crumbling wharf; her paint peeling, her smokestacks rusty. She was a paddle-wheeler and her paddle boxes were slightly aft of midship. "Is that her?" His voice was flat.

"That is our ship."

There was a catch in Mingo's throat and his heart sank. Even he, a woodsman, perceived the utter destitution of the pitiful little craft, for the *Virginius* had been beaten by all the seas and was ready for scrap. Once a passenger ship, then a freighter, then a castoff, she told her own story.

Moored there by a neglected wharf, awaiting her new command, she was a tragic thing, cowering in the shadows of her distant cousins, the proud merchantmen of a dozen flags.

Thompson turned away. "A doughty ship, Captain Fry."

"She is my ship, Mr. Thompson. My first command in thirty years."

Captain Thompson called to his helmsman and the *Robert C. Turner* wheeled and began creeping to her berth. "Your retirement, sir, has been the sea's loss. I wish you well."

The old man bowed. "I thank you for your many courtesies." He turned to his clerk. "Come, Mr. Dabney, let us prepare to go ashore."

They went to their quarters and strapped and fastened their gear. Mingo glanced from the porthole to the *Virginius* and said slowly, "She's no great shakes as a ship, is she?"

The old mariner squared his shoulders again. "A ship, son, is as good as the men who sail her."

The pilgrim stared at the derelict for a moment more, her sagging stacks and her rusty sides, then turned abruptly and went to the deck of the barque, walking alone so none of his shipmates could see the disappointment on his face.

A crowd was swarming on Kingston's piers, waving to the *Robert C. Turner* and jabbering its excitement, a spectacle of flowing mantillas and Panama hats, of gaudy silks and white linens. Fry joined him at the rail and nodded toward the crowd. "The Jamaica *Junta*," he explained. "The Friends of Cuba."

Mingo's eyes swept the throng, eagerly, hopefully, although he doubted that she would be there to welcome a forgotten sea captain and his clerk. *La Entorcha* never went to men. Men went to her.

The crowd inched forward, careful of the lines the sailors were heaving to the wharf, and Mingo studied the host of faces, upturned and blurred in the blinding Caribbean sun.

The simple mantilla, the protecting cowl in a pageant of finery, caught his eye and he gasped, leaning over the rail and shielding his eyes against the glare. The black cotton dress among silks. The white bone buckle at her waist.

He almost raised his hand to her. He almost cried out his jubilation, but Captain Fry touched his arm and shook his head, a fatherly warning, a brave man's caution.

Only then did the pilgrim notice the towering man just behind her, his shadow shielding *La Entorcha Blanca;* a bronze giant who seemed so near to her and yet so far away.

Macéo! That would be General Antonio Macéo, creator of a symbol, guardian of thunder in the sun. His skin was the color of cocoa and milk and he was immaculate in gray Dutch linen.

The pilgrim had only a glance for The Brown One, but he stared at Rafaela Galban, unaware that he was staring. She did not return the stare, but Antonio Macéo did.

Mingo tugged at his hat and made ready to follow his captain ashore.

There was a cheer from the crowd as Fry stepped from the gangplank. The old man was proud and erect, but Mingo was grinning, the inshore breeze tousling the black hair over his ear. He put their luggage on the pier, glancing in Rafaela's direction as Fry swung forward to accept an introduction and acknowledge the tributes. The Lebanon man hung back. This was his captain's hour.

"Viva Fry!" The crowd welcomed him. *"Cuba libre!"*

Rafaela, holding her mantilla tight against the breeze, walked through the throng and the people made way for her. Her hand was extended to Fry and she was smiling. Macéo was directly behind her. He was not smiling.

There was a flurry of introductions and Captain Fry bowed pompously, grasping the hand of Antonio Macéo and accepting the plaudits of dignitaries as Rafaela presented them.

84

She did not look toward Mingo Dabney at all. He might not even have been there.

"*Viva Virginius!*" It was a roar and it echoed across the bay, against the little ship there, the waves slapping foam against her sides, peeling rust and sloughing rot.

Mingo leaned against a post, watching the ceremonial welcome; happy for his captain and proud of the old man's dignity and demeanor. There were many presentations and Rafaela made them without haste, pronouncing each name carefully.

The woodsman rested his foot on his captain's sea chest, a spectator and nothing more, his restless eyes upon Antonio Macéo while really watching Rafaela Galban.

The Brown One was a tower of reserve and grace. His thick black beard, as coarse as his hair, was trimmed precisely and his mustaches were heavy, twirling upward at the ends and exposing his full lips, firmly pressed when he was silent, scarcely moving when he spoke. His eyes were jet black, set well apart under his dark brows.

It was Joe Fry who turned first to Mingo, motioning for him to join the group and share this minute of his captain's triumph. Mingo straightened and took off his hat, then stepped jauntily across the pier, grinning his delight while trying to be serious.

Rafaela spoke to him then, turning from Fry to greet him. "Welcome, Señor Dabney."

She did not offer her hand and he bowed in his most gallant manner, politely expressing the honor of seeing her again. He wasn't embarrassed or ill at ease. They bowed to ladies back in Lebanon.

"General Macéo." She addressed her guardian formally. "It is my pleasure to present Señor Mingo Dabney. I mentioned to you that he was with Captain Fry."

Antonio Macéo nodded courteously in the Latin manner, but the woodsman put out his hand. That's the way they did it back in Lebanon, and Mingo offered his hand in the free open way of his kind. Macéo was surprised, almost startled, by this evidence of informality, but he was quick to offer his own hand. "*La Entorcha* told me of your family's kindness to her. I am in Lebanon's debt." His voice was low-pitched and soft, but his eyes were cold, expressing nothing. Then the lid of his left eye drooped slightly. "José Martí also mentioned you to me."

"I've heard a lot about you, too," Mingo said. "And I'm mighty glad to know you."

Rafaela gave all her attention to Captain Fry, and the old man beamed his delight. Mingo was in the background again and Macéo waited until the brief welcoming ceremony was over, then addressed Fry. "I know you are anxious to visit your ship. I hope we can sail in a day or so. Martí and Gómez are in the Oriente, and I should be there."

"I am sure Captain Fry is as anxious to sail as we are," Rafaela volunteered tactfully. "I am sure he knows that the *grito* has already been sounded."

"Naturally." Fry said it in measured dignity. "We kept ourselves informed in Mobile."

"Then you are aware of the emergency," Macéo persisted. "I assume we will sail without delay."

Joe Fry set his sea cap firmly on his massive head, tugging at the visor. The Cuban Navy, and he was the Cuban Navy, had no intention of taking dictation from the Cuban Army. "My ship will sail the minute she is ready. I will not commit myself until I have inspected my ship."

Mingo felt the grin coming and put his hand over his mouth to hide it. Rafaela smiled, but Macéo was brown marble, aloof and distant. "I will be at headquarters of the Jamaica *Junta* if I am needed." He bowed stiffly to Fry and, ignoring Mingo, turned to his ward. "You have had a trying day, *La Entorcha*."

"It has been a memorable day, General Macéo. And, now —" She looked at Fry, then at Mingo, and back to Macéo. "If you gentlemen will excuse me, I will return to my abode."

86

The pilgrim stepped past Antonio Macéo and stood so close to the girl that he saw the tiny beads of sweat on her lips. "With your permission, Rafaela, I will see you home." There was no brashness in his offer. It was the way they did things back in Lebanon.

She remembered the customs of Lebanon and was framing a discreet refusal when Macéo spoke: "*La Entorcha's* escort has been arranged."

Her chin rose and she looked quickly from the impetuous American to her excited guardian, bowing to her protector, then nodding to Mingo. "An escort is not necessary. My lodgings are only three blocks away." She turned swiftly and walked through the crowd, the people opening a path for her.

Mingo was very still for a second, staring after her and slowly twisting the tuft of hair. A frown, almost a scowl, crossed his face and his smoky brown eyes were somber as he turned to Macéo, studying him. Then he wheeled to Captain Fry. "I am ready when you are, sir."

The lines of worry, of premonition, were deep across the old man's brow and he put his hand on Mingo's arm, giving public witness of his friendship, his support.

The Brown One's bearing was rigid and the lid of his left eye drooped until his eye seemed to close. "Señor Dabney." His tone was studiously polite. "*La Entorcha* needs no escort among her own people."

The woodsman brushed his hand across the brim of his hat and stood with his feet well apart and firmly braced on that bit of foreign soil that was his anchor for the moment. "Back where I come from a gentleman always offers his company to a lady, if he happens to know her."

"In my country," Macéo said, "a gentleman never offers his company to a lady unless he knows her well." And so saying he bowed and took his leave, walking alone through the crowd. Again the people stepped back, making a path for Antonio Macéo, the mulatto.

Fry did not rebuke his clerk although Mingo expected some word of reproof. Instead, the old man merely said, "Let's go to our ship." He summoned a hack and a porter saw to their gear.

They rode over the rough streets and through alleys and between warehouses. Joe Fry was silent, his mouth grim and set. The pilgrim was silent, too, the black mood of the Dabneys upon him.

They came to the water front again and the hack swung toward the far end of the harbor. Salt was in Fry's nostrils, the odor of wet wood and pitch; and only just ahead, just beyond that dilapidated warehouse, his first ship in thirty years rocked with the lazy wash of the sea, awaiting the step and voice of her commander.

Mingo suddenly was excited and no longer morose. He leaned out of the buggy, looking up the ways between the warehouses, trying to spot their ship. Fry was squirming in his seat and squinting toward the dock and the buggy was slowing down, the hoofs clattering on the cobblestones.

The driver halted his team and pointed toward the harbor, using his whip. Beyond the skeleton of a rotting warehouse was the wharf and the *Virginius*. Mingo lifted the sea chest and his own bag out of the hack. "I can carry our gear." He was embarrassed because nobody was there to greet his captain.

"You take the chest." Fry adjusted his cap and squared his shoulders. "I'll take your bag." He looked around at the warehouse and sniffed the wind, the odors of decay and neglect. Then he reached for the bag, but drew back his hand and touched Mingo. "I won't preach, son —"

"Yes, sir." The pilgrim looked up at his captain, respect in his look, even homage. The rebuke must come and Mingo was ready for it, knowing he would accept it without protest or argument. Such was his affection for the old man.

"You are a Southerner, Mingo." Joseph C. Fry was erect

again, his own feet braced on the crumbling wharf of a foreign land.

"Yes, sir."

"But you are an American before you are a Southerner. Our country will be judged by your behavior, and you will live, or die, by a new code. Antonio Macéo's guiding star is his faith in *La Entorcha Blanca*. Do not crowd him, but do not cringe. Spit on no man, son, but let no man spit on you." He turned away. "Now for our ship."

They walked beside the warehouse, toward the dock and their ship. The wharf creaked under their tread, and the rusty little castoff was bobbing with the swell. Her funnels were dented, her decks buckling, and her rails secured with wire. Captain Joseph C. Fry stared straight ahead, swinging on with long strides toward his first command since he furled his Confederate flag, and put it away forever.

MINGO DABNEY

Chapter 7   The smell of rum was heavy on
the first mate of the *Virginius* when he came to the wharf to
receive them. The harassed look in his eyes and his hollow
face partly told his story, and Mingo scowled in disappointment. A derelict mate for a derelict ship.

"I'm Smith, sir." His hand shook as he offered it to Fry.
"First officer."

"John Smith?" Fry glanced at him quickly and put down
the bag.

"John Smith." He said it without mystery or admission.
"I brought her down from New York."

Joe Fry studied his first officer, the only deck officer of his
ship. He had known a hundred John Smiths; good officers
who lose their ratings for any of a dozen reasons: women,
whiskey, hard luck, women, whiskey. This flotsam was from
the Connecticut coast. Fry said, "It was a risk to bring her
through the Windward Passage."

"The shortest course, sir. I was in a hurry." His mouth
twitched and his watery gray eyes smarted in the bright sun.

"Encounter any Spanish ships?"

John Smith shrugged. "Sighted four blockaders. Ships of
the line. But we had a fog and they lost us." He looked over
his shoulder at the *Virginius*. "She's in bad shape."

"So are you," the captain said gently.

There was no salute, no pipes, as Joseph C. Fry boarded his
command, followed by a dejected Mingo and a shaky mate.

90

The old man went direct to his quarters, scarcely glancing at the nondescript crew loafing around the rail and aft near the paddle houses. Mingo was to share the captain's cabin to conserve space.

The first officer left them and they stowed their possessions, and returned to the deck. There was rust where paint should be and rot where oil should be, and the pumps were pounding slowly to keep the *Virginius* afloat. Mingo and Fry went below to the boiler room and First Officer Smith joined them. His hand was steadier and the odor of rum was heavier.

"We did the best we could." John Smith was defiant, even truculent, as he waited for judgment.

"All's well," Fry said. He had expected nothing and he had nothing.

A heavy thudding sounded in one of the boilers and the captain glanced at his first officer, then at the furnace. "It's the first engineer," John Smith explained. "Trying to patch a boiler." He raised his voice to be heard above the noise. "Mr. Caldwell?"

The thudding ceased and a greasy bald head poked out of the furnace door. Mingo almost laughed. The man's face was ruddy and his eyes were a sharp blue, warm and snapping. He was too young to be bald, but his head was as bare as a doorknob.

"What you want?" Then he saw the captain and crawled out of the furnace, wiping his hands on a knot of waste. He tossed the rags aside and pulled himself erect. He was lean and lanky, his long arms reaching almost to his knees.

"Captain Fry," the first officer said. "Mr. Caldwell. Ben Caldwell, chief engineer."

The captain offered his hand. "What shape's she in?"

"God awful." Ben Caldwell ran his fingers across his bald head, wiping off the sweat and smearing the grease. "Both furnaces about burned out. Fire bricks loose. Pressure shot to hell."

They all were silent for a moment and Mingo felt the

sweat trickling down his face. "Ships have souls, Mr. Cald-well." Fry spoke reverently. "You know that. Ships are good and evil, like men; and this is a good ship because she was bought with the pennies of poor people and is dedicated to Cuban liberty."

"Ay, sir." Ben Caldwell nodded and knuckled his forehead. "Her soul may be first-class, but her boilers are falling apart."

Captain Fry made no reply. He turned away and began inspecting the engine room, the corroded pipes, the wheezy old machinery. The steam gauges were almost useless and the steam lines were patched and rusty. "How soon, Mr. Cald-well?" Fry snapped the question.

Caldwell blinked and chuckled. Here was a master worth working for. Everything was old and rusty and out of order, but the captain was asking how soon. "It'll take three days —"

"General Macéo is impatient to be in Cuba," Fry broke in.

The engineer slid his hairy arm across his face and fingered the grime out of the corners of his eyes. "Swimming ain't crowded," he growled. "I wouldn't sail this ship on a heavy fall of dew, shape she's in. I'm saying three days."

John Smith nodded agreement and Fry accepted the obvious. "Three days. I will so notify General Macéo." The old man flipped sweat from his beard and rubbed his hand-kerchief around the inside of his cap, drying the band. "And now, gentlemen—" He smiled, happy to bring good news, "There is a ball tonight at Government House. You gentle-men are invited." He mopped his face and returned his handkerchief to his pocket.

John Smith grimaced, then quickly thanked the captain for his courtesy and left them, hurrying back to his quarters and his rum.

Mingo lowered his voice for only his captain to hear. "Will Rafaela be there?"

"No." The throbbing pumps were louder than his words. "*La Entorcha* never attends such functions."

"Think I'll stay with the ship." He grinned at Ben Caldwell and glanced around at the machinery, fascinated by it all.

The engineer leaned against the cold boiler. "Give my regards to the ladies, cap'n. Just tell 'em I'm waltzing with a steam pipe." He dabbed a greasy finger at Mingo. "Ever line a firebox?"

"Nope —"

"Mr. Dabney is a passenger." Fry broke in quickly, a bit flustered. "He volunteered to help out as my clerk, but, officially, he is a paying passenger."

"Paying to get to Cuba?" Ben Caldwell began laughing. "That's like paying your own grave digger."

Mingo liked the lanky engineer. If Ben Caldwell had lived in Lebanon they'd have cut trees together. "I don't know anything about a firebox, but I'm pretty handy with tools."

Fry started to protest. It was not proper for his clerk and passenger to work on the furnaces. However, he was anxious to be under way and every hand hastened his ship's departure. He led the way from the engine room and Mingo followed him to their cabin and helped him prepare for the reception at Government House, then slipped into his denim trousers and went below. He hung his shirt on a valve and reached for a Stillson wrench.

It was steaming hot inside the fireless furnace and the pilgrim, wiping sweat and straining, learned fast. Ben Caldwell almost praised him once or twice. They lost track of time, working by lantern light, until the heat left them limp.

Ben crawled out of the furnace and motioned for his shipmate. "I got a drink hidden in my duffle. Come on."

Mingo pressed his hands to the small of his back and stretched. "Have to hide it?"

"If you want to keep it."

"John Smith?"

The engineer nodded and headed for the ladder, ducking the pipes. "A rummy from hell to breakfast, but a sailor if I ever saw one. Canvas man."

Mingo ducked one pipe only to bump his head against a second. He cursed under his breath, then said, "Wonder what his real name is?"

Ben Caldwell had one hand on the ladder and he turned quickly to the woodsman. "Down here, Dabney, you don't pry about such things. He's John Smith and he hates Spaniards."

Mingo did not resent the tone or the words, aware that both were justified. He also reached for the ladder. "You hate Spaniards? Or is that prying?"

"Don't know much about Spaniards. But I heard a little fellow named Martí talk one night. And here I am." The engineer scampered up the ladder, his hands scarcely touching the guard rail.

There was a breeze on deck and the two men propped against the starboard wheelhouse, their drinks in their hands and the harbor breeze pleasant to their skin. The water front was lonely and lifeless, a few lanterns swaying on the anchored ships, but Government House, up a slope from the quay, blazed lights from every window. Music floated down and the two men listened, sipping their whiskey as they looked at the lights.

Mingo spoke first. "Strauss waltzes. We play 'em back where I'm from."

Ben looked down into his glass, then pushed himself up and stretched his arms above his head, relaxing. "Let's go back. We can't get to Cuba on Strauss waltzes."

The firebox was cramped and Mingo's stocky frame ached as he crawled around in the confinement, groping for footing, rubbing his skin raw against the bricks. He had ridden a white horse into a cracked and broken furnace on an aged, dilapidated little ship. The romance was out of the pilgrimage and he tasted sweat, licking his lips and wiping his mouth. His lips were puffing and his tongue was parched.

They paused often for air and the music drifted down from Government House. The engineer began humming and Mingo joined him. Tales of the Vienna Woods . . .

94

Mingo Dabney noticed it first. The music had stopped.

Perhaps the dance was over. But surely it was not that late. Besides, if the ball was ended, Fry would be back on his ship. Then Ben noticed it and frowned. "What the hell? Takes a hurricane to make a Cuban quit dancing."

"Maybe something's wrong." Mingo rested his wrench against a fire brick and listened, hearing only the waves slapping the *Virginius*.

"Don't be expecting trouble." The engineer felt for a loose connection. "We'll have trouble enough without looking for it. They're probably toasting Macéo and the fiddlers are taking a drink."

"Or Captain Fry is making a speech."

They both laughed and went back to work. Five, ten— perhaps fifteen minutes passed and the music was not resumed. Again Ben Caldwell frowned. "Even Fry wouldn't be talking that long." There was a hint of nervousness in his tone.

Mingo thought first of Rafaela, then of his captain. Maybe Macéo had crossed Fry. "I'm going up there." He was crawling toward the furnace door.

"Go ahead." Caldwell gave him room. "I can't leave the ship. Smith will be drunk by now. . . ."

A hollow, frightening blo-o-ong jarred the stillness—a rumble from the bell tower of Government House, a dismal blo-o-ong.

Mingo dashed for the ladder, snatching up his shirt as he ran. A second stroke reverberated across the King's Town and he swung himself up the ladder.

The bell tolled again before he reached the deck and he leaped for the wharf, breaking his fall with his hands and sprinting for the hill and the marble house on its crest.

His shirt was open and his denim trousers were greasy; his hair streaked with oil and brick dust. It mattered not. He was thinking only of Rafaela and his captain.

The doorman at Government House was struggling to hold back a frantic, blabbering crowd and Mingo brushed past him, running down the long corridor leading toward the ballroom. He paused at the doorway and looked around frantically. The resplendent dancers were huddled in little groups, the men whispering and the women sobbing, some wailing.

Again the bell pealed and Mingo blinked in the bright lights until his vision cleared, then he stepped into the big room, his eyes darting and his heart throbbing.

She was not there. But Joseph Fry was at the side of the room, his massive head high above all the others and his countenance marred by distress and fury.

Antonio Macéo was drooped in a chair by the captain, his bronze face a mask of abject misery. Macéo! The indomitable Macéo of twenty Spanish wounds was trembling like a ceiba leaf in his native land, a bewildered and helpless giant; Achilles with an arrow in his heel.

A scream of anguish shrilled near the empty orchestra chairs and a woman fainted. The whispers rose to a murmur, to a quivering babble. The pilgrim was awed; not frightened, yet gripped by a great fear. Fry saw him and moved quickly to him, bracing himself before his countryman. "Martí—" The name loosed the old stalwart's grief and tears welled to his eyes, spilling over, and he was not ashamed. "José Martí has been killed."

"Oh, my God!" The words rasped Mingo's dry throat and again he thought first of her. Martí dead! The prophet stilled! Isaiah with a bullet in his body. Joab cut down by a sword. For a moment he stood motionless, his shoulders sagging, and he put out his hand to his captain, seeking to comfort him and thereby comfort himself. Then he glanced over at Macéo, and the loneliness and hopelessness in The Brown One's face flooded him with horror. "Sagaldo?" Mingo whispered the question and dreaded the answer.

"No." Fry cringed and a shudder passed through his body. "God spared us that. He was betrayed. Led into ambush and shot." The captain was composing himself and standing very straight, an example for the others.

The vibrating babblings rose clearer and some of the words were distinguishable; shrill and jerky, then trailing into incoherence. . . .

The prophet was killed at a place called Dos Ríos!

His whole detachment was wiped out —

No! Two men escaped. The one who betrayed him and the one who brought the news —

There was another shriek and a woman collapsed in hysteria. Antonio Macéo stared at her, not seeing her; slumping forward in his chair, a lost and desolate man from whom the spirit had fled. Mingo Dabney yearned to go to him and take his hand, and he might have done it, but there came a swelling gasp from the huddled groups and he spun toward the doorway.

Rafaela Galban was walking down the long hall, her mantilla cowling her face and her lips bloodless. Her black cotton dress brushed the silks of the mourners, and the crowd melted a path before her, murmuring her name and finding strength and solace in the name of *La Entorcha Blanca*.

She passed so close that Mingo might have touched her had his awe been less, so close that he saw her trembling chin, her eyes blazing the fire of her dedication.

Antonio Macéo lifted his face to her and she crossed the room and stood before him, tightening her mantilla, the symbol before the creator, the miracle of thunder in the sun.

"Mambi!" She hurled the word at him, unleashing it in the fervor of the zealot, in the wrath of its meaning. Common clay! The mold of all mankind. The seal of the brotherhood. Mambi!

"*La Entorcha*." The Brown One spoke her name and rose slowly from the chair, his face blanched in desolation. "The soul of Cuba is dead."

"Mambi!" She spoke again, cold, merciless, oblivious of the misery of her guardian. "Souls do not die! As Martí was the soul of Cuba, you are her sword!"

"Mambi—" He mumbled the word.

"They betrayed him, sire." She was Cuba, the torch above the sword. "Madrid is feasting in honor of his death."

His massive shoulders went back, the huge head lifted.

"The Mambises are wailing—"

"La Entorcha!"

"Martí struck the fire that will free us." She touched his arm, flowing strength to the believer. "I am leaving for Cuba tonight—"

"The *Virginius* is not ready—"

"Tonight!" She drew back from him, her eyes flaming her indictment, burning her judgment. "You have spoken of faith, sire! Where is your faith? We came here in a fishing smack. It will take us to Cuba."

The cloud passed from his face and he was himself again; the indomitable Macéo, maker of signs and disciple of the sword. "Baire!"

He spoke only for her to hear but the crowd heard and their hearts were lifted up. Joe Fry heard and the grim lines deepened about his mouth. Mingo Dabney heard and muttered her name. *La Entorcha.* He said it like all the rest.

She clutched her mantilla and faced the people. "Baire!" She called out the challenge and moved away, the people falling back again as she swept from the room, showing the way for Macéo, opening the way for The Brown One.

Then they were gone.

The room was hushed and Mingo was entranced until his captain touched him, awakening him, and he followed the old man, stumbling behind him. His shirt still was open and the lights of the room were bright in his smoky brown eyes.

No word was spoken all the way from Government House to the *Virginius* and none was spoken as they crossed the deck. Fry climbed down the ladder to the engine room, and Ben Caldwell was standing by the boiler, staring at the floor.

"Have you heard the news, Mr. Caldwell?"

"Yes, sir."

"We sail tomorrow, Mr. Caldwell." Joe Fry removed his coat, tugging at the sleeves.

"Yes, sir." The engineer was biting his lip as he stooped and pulled himself back into the furnace.

Without orders, without delay, Mingo tossed his shirt across a steam pipe and watched Joseph Fry drop to his hands and knees and crawl into the firebox of the second furnace. The pilgrim crawled in after him and the old man handed a lantern to Mingo. "Hold the light, son —"

"I'll handle the bricks," Mingo volunteered quickly. "You take the lantern —"

"Take the light, Mr. Dabney." Fry shoved the lantern toward him and scrouged against the furnace wall, feeling for the loose bricks.

Mingo did as he was ordered, afraid to do otherwise, suddenly afraid of a righteous old man, coldly angry. "Will Spain be watching that fishing smack?" He had to ask it.

"Spain is watching every rowboat," Fry snapped. His face was pouring sweat and his hands already were rubbed raw by the bricks.

They worked in silence, too despondent for talk, too cramped and limp for the exertion of words. Mingo found a shelter for the lantern and put it there, then moved closer to his captain and they worked together until Mingo's muscles twitched their agony.

He heard the footsteps on the ladder, and Fry must have heard them although he did not look up. Then First Officer John Smith was standing by the furnace door, staring inside at his captain, bracing himself against the boiler. He wiped his mouth and chin. "I commanded a schooner that Martí sailed on once." His bleary eyes roamed about the engine room. "He loved sails as much as I do." John Smith steadied himself and went to Caldwell's furnace, bending low as he crawled through the door and into the sweltering firebox.

Mingo handed a wrench to Fry and himself lifted a crowbar, wedging against the bricks, feeling the pipes warm against his back.

He lost all idea of time and the minutes melted into hours, and the slow rhythm of the harbor pulsed the ship, the waves slapping it. Martí dead! The slap of the waves throbbed in his aching head. How could there be a revolution without its soul? Ol' Elmo. How sad he must be. And Nick González and Stockingcap and all the others of *El Delfín* . . .

"Another wrench, son. And hold the light a little closer."

The day was borning when they tightened the last brick and crawled out, Mingo too weary to hold up his head. John Smith was sodden, his bony elbows raw and bleeding, and Ben Caldwell gulped his exhaustion. Joe Fry pulled himself erect, grasping a pipe for support. "What do you think, Mr. Caldwell?"

The engineer's head drooped to his chest. "They might hold for two or three days. No longer."

"Fire her up," Fry ordered. "Bring her up to about ten pounds. Come, Mr. Smith. Mr. Dabney."

They went to the deck and the cool air nearly took their breath. Fry sent a courier to the *Junta* with word that he was ready to sail, and then ordered breakfast for his crew. Mingo ate bread and beef, but Captain Fry was too tense to eat and drank only a cup of coffee. Steam was hissing in the engine room and smoke curled from the two stacks of the little tramp. The firebox was holding heat and Ben Caldwell was increasing pressure gradually, shouting for his engine room crew to assemble from the pumps and make ready to get under way.

The sun scarcely was full up before people began thronging the wharf, staring at the ship, at those on her deck. The captain went to his bridge and shouted to his first officer, "We will receive the passengers, Mr. Smith."

The passengers came marching down the cobblestone

street. "Soldiers," the first officer mumbled. "Every damn one of 'em a soldier. Look at 'em step."

Mingo's heart leaped to his throat. One hundred and three soldiers coming aboard the *Virginius*: Cuban exiles, mercenaries, gentlemen and derelicts.

They were stacked into the cabins and jammed on deck, crowding every inch. None of the passengers were armed. Mingo noticed that. There was not a gun aboard the *Virginius* except a pistol in Fry's cabin. There was no cannon, not even a salute piece.

The passengers finally were checked and John Smith reported all accounted for. Captain Fry came down from his bridge and held up his hand to his passengers, quieting them before he spoke:

"Gentlemen. This ship flies the American flag." He nodded toward the flag, its stripes limp and its stars huddled.

It was a Cuban ship. Mingo Dabney knew it was a Cuban ship, a filibuster. He gave it not a thought, wondering only how soon they could get away, and about the whereabouts of the fishing smack.

"Our papers are in order." Captain Fry spoke flatly. "We are a passenger ship bound for Haiti to pick up a cargo for Port Limón, Costa Rica."

Of course it was subterfuge. But there were no rules in revolution. José Martí had said that.

"Our protection is the American flag." Fry locked his hands behind him and rocked on the balls of his feet. "If any man cares to leave this ship, let him leave now."

No man moved and Fry went back to his bridge. Mingo hurried below, feeling his way through the steam and heat. "How's she doing?" he asked Caldwell.

"Straining." The engineer was checking his gauges and none was accurate.

A jangle of bells on the bridge and the order from the deck came clear. "Cast off. . . ." John Smith spoke it, relaying instructions from his captain and Mingo scampered up the ladder.

The little ship puffed around, her paddles churning foam, and creaked away, a light wind touching the flag. Ben Caldwell came up for air and he and Mingo watched Kingston falling behind.

"How long would it take a fishing smack to get from Kingston to Cuba?" The pilgrim was leaning over the rail, watching the foam spray white from the paddle.

"That depends on weather and Spaniards." Caldwell rubbed his bald head and put on his cap. "Spain knows everything that goes on in these islands. They're watching us already." He looked around at the *Virginius,* her humped deck, her rusty stacks. "Only crazy men would sail on this ship. Or damn fools who want to die."

MINGO DABNEY

Chapter **8**   The engines were in trouble
before they cleared the harbor and Mingo stayed with Ben
Caldwell, helping him patch machinery, using wire and rope
and rags. Then he caught a quick nap, sprawling on deck
while the muggy heat drained sweat from him.

They raised Morant Point at the tip of Jamaica by mid-
afternoon and were in the Caribbean, sailing almost due
east for Haiti while Mingo wondered if this were the course
her little ship had taken.

A burst of thunder startled him and a spearhead of lightning blinded him, and the rain broke and he was drenched.
"The rainy season," Caldwell explained. "It'll last until fall."

Mingo wrung out his shirt and grinned. "Anyway, it's
cool. You'll never get me to volunteer for engine room duty
again."

Caldwell raised his hand quickly, a warning gesture.
"Watch that word *volunteer*. In Cuba, a Volunteer is a rich
Spaniard who serves in the militia. They just about run the
island, and the real Cubans—the Mambises—hate 'em like
snakes."

Mingo was not particularly interested and was watching
the island speck to starboard. Maybe her ship passed right
there.

Night found them huffing through the blue-green water,
the paddles plopping away and the boilers hissing. The
passengers ate their supper on deck and by black dark Mingo
was in his berth, too tired to dream.

He judged the hour at about three A.M. when he was awakened by Fry. The *Virginius* was leaking and Ben Caldwell was asking for him.

"Where are we?" Mingo shook the sleep from his head.

"Jeremie. At the western tip of Haiti." Fry was waiting for Mingo to button his shirt. "Just across the Windward Channel from Cuba."

They reached the companionway, the *Virginius* rocking on the off-shore swells. Then Mingo heard it; a hollow echo, a rhythmic pounding in the Haitian hills. He grabbed his captain's arm.

"Drums," Fry said laconically. "The talking drums of Haiti!"

The younger man listened. "What are they saying?"

"I've never known a white man who could read them." The old seaman led the way to the deck where most of the passengers were huddled, peering off into the darkness toward the island, straining to hear the pulsing of the drums. Mingo hastened to Caldwell, his spine tingling in the mystery of the low, monotonous booming.

One of the forward pumps was clogged and he and the engineer cleaned it. The brooding darkness just before dawn was heavy when he climbed back on deck, gulping the cool air.

Fry and John Smith were forward, their heads cocked toward the shore and a lantern on the anchor winch beside them. The captain's face was grim and John Smith's face twitched nervously. The drums had reached a crescendo, pounding frantically down from the mountains that dropped sheer into the sea.

"Good God! What is it?" Mingo glanced from them toward the shore, sensing a thing from another world.

John Smith grunted, but Fry shook his head slowly. "We don't know, son." He nodded toward a group of Cubans, leaning far over the rail, their ears tuned to the drums. All the passengers were tense.

"Mambi." John Smith cupped his hands and called softly. "What now, *compadre*? Can you make them out?"

The Cuban, a Negro, held up his hand and shrugged, then spat. "Sagaldo is in Santiago de Cuba."

"Blockaders?" Fry demanded. "Have they mentioned blockaders?"

The Cuban shrugged again and shook his head as the drums softened to an eerie roll. "Martí!" The Mambi's face showed his fury, a contortion of hate and sadness. "The Spaniards gave Martí a Christian funeral."

"That's strange," John Smith said, a frown passing his forehead. "It's not like the bastards to show such consideration."

Mingo gripped the anchor winch, straining toward the Cuban who understood the drums, waiting and hoping. "Anything else?" He had to ask it.

The Mambi scowled him to silence as the drums drifted from the roll, then began a furious clattering. Even John Smith leaned forward; even Fry.

"Gómez!" The Mambi threw the name at them, never turning his head from the drums. "General Máximo Gómez is marching westward —"

The clatter broke off suddenly, sharply, and there was a second, two seconds of brooding silence. It seemed forever to Mingo, and he opened his mouth to ask an explanation. A pounding signal from the hills choked off his words, a hollow boom! Boom! . . . Boooooom—

"Macéo!" The Mambi almost screamed the name.

Rrrrr—oo-oo-oo-oo-oo—tat—tat—tat—Boom! Boom!

"They have landed! Guantanamo Bay!" The Mambi shouted the tidings to his compatriots. "They are safe in the hut of a goatherd!" *La Entorcha* and Antonio Macéo were in Cuba again; the sign and the sword.

Mingo's head drooped to his chest and he breathed slowly and deeply, swallowing to melt the lump in his throat. His eyes still were closed when he heard Fry turn away. "We'll take her out now, Mr. Smith." He put his hand on Mingo's shoulder. "You'd better turn in, son."

The gray, sticky shadows of dawn were poking over the Haitian mountains and the drums softened; a quick flurry, an echo, then silence.

Mingo slouched to his cabin and sprawled on his bunk, breathing slowly in deep sleep. The little vagabond ship stole away from Jeremie, sailing in close along the southern peninsula, slipping toward Port-au-Prince. She crept into a coastal indenture and dropped anchor, waiting for darkness before entering the Haitian capital.

The lights of Port-au-Prince were showing in the hazy distance when Mingo woke, hearing the command from the bridge. "Mr. Smith, we're going in. Hold her inshore close as you can."

The full darkness of another night was upon the harbor when the *Virginius*, showing no lights, stole in. She eased to a shelter and dropped anchor.

Fry sent a small boat ashore with a message for the Haitian *Junta* and soon lighters were pulling away from land, bobbing in the bay and moving silently toward the ship. Lanterns were covered, giving only a ghastly glow. Mingo forgot his exhaustion, forgot everything except that they were trying to hide from Spain and load a cargo for Cuba.

Fry summoned him. "You will check the cargo, Mr. Dabney."

The lighters tied alongside and the passengers removed their shirts and helped haul the boxes aboard. Ben Caldwell brought his crew from the engine room and every hand helped, stacking crates in the hold and on deck, announcing their contents in hushed tones.

"Remington rifles—100."

"Remington rifles—100." Mingo repeated the muffled call, and wrote it down.

"Winchester rifles—50."

A lantern blinked over near the shore and then a launch

put out, poking among the lighters, coming on. Fry challenged.

"Harbor master," the reply came.

Three Haitian officials came aboard and called the captain aside, speaking to him softly and rapidly. Then they bowed and backed away, climbing down the ladder to their launch. The crew and the passengers, all the hands, stopped their work and looked up at Fry, awaiting orders. He put a lantern near the bow and spoke:

"Spain's consul has demanded that the Government of Haiti hold us. The Government of Haiti is embarrassed. Spain is a friendly power." He took a deep breath. "However, Haiti has granted us until dawn to load and sail. It's away by dawn—or internment."

There was no cheer, only a moment of silence; and then one of the sailors asked the time. Dawn was two hours away. Fry ripped the covering from the lanterns. No need for caution. The men must have light. Mingo and John Smith lifted a crate and hove it amidship. Quickly, silently, the men bent to their work, stopping only to glance toward the east.

Ammunition, clothing, foodstuff. It was all piled aboard and dumped wherever space was found. It could be sorted later, after the *Virginius* was at sea again, out from under the long hand of Spain.

The first red glare of dawn broke in the east and the lighters began edging away. The captain ordered it so, although one of them still was partly loaded; eight cases of *machetes*, two crates of rifles. Mingo cried his protest and the first officer called out. Captain Fry ignored them and ran to his bridge, lumbering like an old bear. Away at dawn! He had promised. Away at dawn—or internment! He spoke his engine room, demanding steam, then braced himself and roared:

"Up anchor."

John Smith pulled the lever of the anchor winch. A hiss

and a spurt of steam. The winch turned once, rattled, then grumbled to a stop. The mate yanked the lever again. Mingo joined him, tugging at the release. "She's stuck!" Smith yelled. "The anchor winch is stuck!"

The red glare of dawn was softening into gray. A Haitian government launch began moving from its dock.

"Strip her!" Fry bellowed the order, then shouted into the speaking tube, "All you've got, Mr. Caldwell." He reached for the wheel, relieving the helmsman and began rocking the wheel, whipping his ship to free her.

The *Virginius* squeaked and strained, wallowing as her paddles bit into the bay, foaming the water. John Smith grabbed a *machete* and struck the chain, denting his blade. His face worked convulsively and he chopped at the chain until he shattered the *machete*, and stood peering down at the stump of the handle, sobbing and cursing. "God damn it! Gimme a hawser! Gimme back my rope and canvas."

The little vagabond heaved to free herself, heeling and quivering. She was down at her nose as if stumbling, trying to rise and cracking and tearing herself apart. There was a pale green slit low in the east; and a thin blue haze, streaked with pink, at the top of the sky. The government launch was under way.

Old Joe Fry braced himself and his big, hairy hands locked on the rim of the wheel, and his massive shoulders heaved. The *Virginius* flung to starboard and held there, leaning and trembling. He whirled the wheel back, jamming it and locking it down, his foot heavy against a spoke. The old ship shuddered and racked and the old man held her locked. His ship must go on or go down. She raised her head once more, gulping, then buried her nose in the sea, wallowing and groaning. Fry held her steady. Go on or go down! She clawed the sea, hunching for a hold, and her anchor slipped; then slipped again, sucking free, and she dragged it out of the mud.

Go on!

Fry spun his wheel, caressing it as it slid through his fingers, and the *Virginius* lifted her head from the trough and chugged out of the harbor.

Mingo never knew if his tears were pride or a testament of love for an old man who had drunk deep from the chalice of failure, and now was refusing the cup. The *Virginius'* bow was pointing again to the sea, and the wind was streaming her flag, curling the stripes, quivering the stars. Captain Fry called from his bridge, "Mr. Dabney."

Mingo went to him and the master gave over the ship's manifest. "Check the bills of sale against this list."

"Yes, sir." Mingo wanted to say something more, but he didn't know what to say, and he went to his cabin and spread the manifest before him, sorting the bills of lading to check against his figures.

Clothing and ammunition. They balanced. Remington rifles, 500. They tallied. Revolvers, 400—tally. He repeated it under his breath, staring hard at the manifest and at the words written plainly and boldly.

It was Elmo's handwriting and Mingo ran his fingers over the words, almost trying to feel them. Then he filed the manifest and returned to the deck.

Captain Fry was watching the waves break across the bow of his command, and calling the course to his helmsman. "Two points. Starboard two points. Steady."

John Smith was standing by the rail, repeating the course to himself. "It's Cuba," the first officer said to Mingo. "It's Cuba and Guantanamo Bay."

All that day the *Virginius* steamed due west, armed only with a pistol in her captain's cabin and protected only by the flag at her mast; thirteen stripes for the colonies, forty-four stars for the states.

Mingo Dabney, moving from the bridge to the bow and among the passengers, gave no thought to the status of the creaking little paddle-wheeler, to the legality of her papers or her cargo. He simply wanted to get to Cuba and see Rafaela Galban.

The Caribbean was calm and the passengers were in cheerful humor, excited and joyous. They were going home to overthrow Spain, to drown their mother country in her own blood. They had no flag of their own and their only protection was the American flag rustling above an orphan ship; their only safeguard was Spain's fear of that striped and starred silk.

If Joseph Fry was worried, he gave no indication of it and laid his course for the Spanish blockade. Everybody ate on deck and scraped their plates into the sea. The gulls dived and called and all afternoon the *Virginius* steamed west, sighting nothing; not a stack, not a sail. The tip of Cuba was to the northwest and all was becalmed, even the sea around the island seemed dead.

Mingo spent the night on deck, watching the stars and thinking of her. Then he slept until wakened by a thunderclap, and was drenched by the quick rain.

It seemed he'd scarcely got back to sleep before the lookout called a sail to the south. It was well past daybreak and Mingo hurried to the rail, joining the first mate. "A schooner," Smith said. "I can't make out her flag."

The cry woke all passengers and they were rising from the deck and stretching. The smell of coffee came from the galley and the men dropped buckets into the sea and hauled them aboard, drawing up water to wash their faces. The sun came up and was a copper cauldron pouring its heat upon a burnished sea. The schooner disappeared toward Jamaica.

"We should have sighted a Spaniard by now," John Smith said. There were lines around his eyes and his eyes were bloodshot.

Mingo ate breakfast with the first officer and together they went to the bridge. Captain Fry took only a cup of coffee and a piece of dry bread. He kept his eye to the north, to the starboard, and sipped the coffee without looking at it; some of the liquid spilled into his heavy beard and he wiped it with his hand. To the north was Cuba and when the sun drove away the mist, the low outline of the island was visible, green, breaking the blue of the sea.

"About twelve miles away," John Smith said, then peered at the compass and the chart.

Captain Fry cut the side-wheeler's speed to three knots, barely enough to keep her under way, barely enough to make her heed her rudder. "We'll stay about twelve miles offshore until night."

"Then run for Guantanamo Bay, sir?" Smith asked.

Captain Fry nodded.

Mingo watched the compass flick. The ship's bow curled no foam, lazily rising and falling in the swells, barely moving. The morning passed and Fry veered slightly to the north, cutting in closer to shore. Cuba was only ten miles away.

Two bells—three . . . The afternoon was wearing on and the sun was heading down. Darkness meant the dash to a beleaguered land.

"Ship to starboard!"

The lookout shrieked the warning and the passengers ran to the rail.

Fry snatched his spyglass and studied the coastline. "See anything, Smith?" he demanded.

"Yes, sir. Smoke."

"So do I," said Mingo. His blood began churning and his mouth suddenly was dry. Black smoke was traced against the green of the shore.

"Can you make her out?" Fry demanded.

"Spanish man-of-war, sir," the first officer said, slowly. Then, "Good God!"

They all saw her at that instant. She lunged from the cover of the coastline and broke into the clear. Smoke was boiling from her stacks.

"The *Tornado*," Fry said, trying to hide his emotion under

his heavy calm. "She has ten guns and is ten miles away." He turned to his helmsman. "Steady as she is. We are a passenger ship cruising to Costa Rica."

John Smith was the first man on the bridge to see the puff of white smoke and he gasped. It was a gasp of surprise, not alarm. Then Mingo saw it, a rolling, spreading puff over the water. Captain Fry gripped the side of his bridge, staring at the smoke, then at the men on the wing of the bridge.

No one spoke. The passengers pointed at the *Tornado* as though they had witnessed a miracle. Perhaps they had, for they had seen a Spanish man-of-war fire on the American flag.

The dull boom of the shot echoed, sounding like thunder over the ridges of Lebanon. So that was a cannon. Mingo was fascinated.

"A warning shot." Fry's face and body were immobile. "They're warning us away from the coast."

"Your pardon, sir." The first officer was polite, but insistent. "I'm obliged to remind you that a shot across the bow is an order to come around and lay to."

A cloud passed over Joe Fry's face, the cloud, perhaps, of his failures. "I will not let the Spaniards board my ship."

Quickly, but without haste or alarm, he altered his course, swinging his ship to the south and the open sea. He raised her up to eight knots and the *Virginius* began groaning.

The Cuban passengers were milling about the deck, their faces dark and wrathful, and glancing at the Stars and Stripes as though expecting that woven symbol to cry halt. The *Tornado* was throwing foam.

"She intends to overhaul us," John Smith said.

"We can make the high seas. She won't dare molest the American flag on the high seas." Captain Fry lifted his glass and studied the oncoming Spaniard. The *Tornado* was making twelve knots. "Open her up, Mr. Smith." He lifted the speaking tube to his engine room. "More pressure, Mr. Caldwell."

"We haven't got any more," Caldwell shouted back.

"We must have more steam, Mr. Caldwell—"

"She's tearing her guts out now—"

"More steam!"

The *Virginius* quivered under the shock of full speed, whipping her paddles until spray drenched the deck. The *Tornado* was within six miles, almost within range.

Captain Fry called his engine room again, but there was no reply. Caldwell was at his boiler. "Mingo," Fry ordered. "Strip the galley of fat meat and take it below. Mr. Caldwell will understand."

Mingo shouted for men to follow him and they lugged all the meat to the engine room; hams and bacons and greasy fatback.

Ben Caldwell took one look at the meat and bellowed, "She'll blow up!" He was black and greasy and he reached for the furnace door. "This ain't the God damn Mississippi River! This ain't the Confederate Navy!" He heaved an armful of pork into the firebox and jumped back, slamming the door with his foot.

Mingo scampered back to the deck and through the clustered passengers glaring at the *Tornado* plunging in full pursuit.

The stench of burning meat rose from the engine room and the smoke thickened black, streaked red with fire. The funnels began to glow, turning yellow and orange and dull red and the *Virginius* was racking and groaning, steam spurting from cracks in her buckled decks.

Fry was pacing the wings of his bridge, glancing at the funnels of his ship, glancing back at the *Tornado*: five miles away. The *Virginius* was clawing for her ten knots, all she could make, and the agony was tearing her apart.

"Leak in the engine room!" The alarm came from Ben Caldwell.

"We are on the high seas," Fry declared.

"The Spaniard either doesn't know it, or doesn't care," John Smith said. "They are clearing for action—"

"Leak forward!" The cry came from below.

Fry touched Mingo's arm and they hastened below, making a rapid inspection. The caulking in the bow was loose and the *Virginius* was shipping water, her bottom already a'slosh. Captain Fry's heavy beard trembled and his face was taut. A specter of fear haunted his eyes, the fear of another failure, the feel of the dreaded cup in his hand again.

He went back to his bridge and held his megaphone to his mouth, shouting for attention. All passengers crowded amidship. "You gentlemen will destroy any documents that might compromise you or this ship." He sent Mingo to his cabin to destroy the manifest.

The *Tornado* was now four miles astern and Mingo glanced back at her and ran to his chore.

Fry was standing with his back to the Spaniard. "Mr. Smith. Throw all war material overboard —"

"Sir!" John Smith shouted his surprise.

"Throw all war material overboard. We must lighten ship."

"Yes, sir." John Smith called all hands, and they began pushing the crates and boxes into the sea.

Every man bent to the task and the *Virginius* trembled and churned on. The crates floated a few minutes, then one by one they sank and Mingo watched them vanish. Elmo's work, months of buying and bartering, the hoarded pennies of Cuban patriots.

The *Virginius* staggered to a crawl and began settling forward, her speed dropping to seven knots. The *Tornado* was under full pressure, thick smoke streaming back, low, almost flat from her stack.

The engine room called once more. "She's about done for." It was Caldwell. "So are we."

"Thank you, Mr. Caldwell." Fry was watching his deck, the passengers huddled there. "We are now on the high seas."

"We are in Jamaican waters," John Smith said, still panting from the exertion of jettisoning the cargo.

114

The *Tornado* was four miles astern. She swung to her starboard, then straightened, bringing the *Virginius* under her guns. The puff of smoke was seen only a few seconds before the thud was heard and Mingo Dabney saw the ball skimming and skipping over the sea. He closed his eyes and ducked, flinging his arms in front of his face. It was a low shot, a line shot, intended to hull the *Virginius* and it struck the water and came on, topping the waves, only to drop heavily into the sea about four cable lengths from the ship.

"Merciful God!" Fry little more than whispered the words. "Do they want war with the United States?"

Mingo's nerves were tingling his spine and his brain. The Cuban passengers began cursing and shaking their fists and John Smith folded his arms and stared contemptuously at the raider, a man-of-war plunging toward an unarmed paddle-wheeler.

The Spaniard was less than three miles away and her forward gun bellowed. Again Mingo ducked. The shot fell harmlessly beyond the *Virginius*.

"Cowards." Fry thundered the word. "Contemptible cowards."

"Garlic bastards," Mingo shouted. He was not conscious he shouted.

The *Virginius* was down to three knots, steam hissing, her pumps scarcely throbbing.

The *Tornado* swept in, swerved, and her port guns roared. A shot whined through the rigging and Mingo yelled, then ducked again. The *Tornado* straightened and her bow gun spoke. Mingo heard the shrill scream and he trembled. The *Virginius'* aft stack clanged and shuddered and a cable sundered, whipping across the deck and felling a seaman.

Captain Fry braced his feet wide apart and rang his engine room. "That's all, Mr. Caldwell." To his first officer he spoke clearly, "Bring her around, Mr. Smith."

The engines choked to a stop and in the sudden silence of the ship, and the great quiet of the sea, the *Virginius* labored around in a slow sweep, and lay helpless and waiting, her colors limp at the mast.

The Spaniard came on at full speed, her pennants whipping and the flag of her empire rippling over a free sea. The foam was boiling white at her bow. Her gun crews were at battle stations as she steamed past, then came about and quickly two cutters were lowered. A party of sailors and marines entered the boats: thirty men and two officers. The *Tornado* leveled her port guns at the *Virginius* and stood to.

The first cutter drew alongside and demanded a ladder. "Lower away," Fry commanded. "Obey orders to the letter."

A Spanish lieutenant threw his leg over the rail and straightened, glancing at the men, at the Cubans particularly, then at the American flag. "Who is your captain?" He demanded.

Fry stepped forward. His cap was low over his forehead. "I am captain of this ship. And I place my ship, my passengers, my crew and myself under protection of the American flag."

"You fly that flag illegally," the officer said. "These men —" He waved toward the passengers. "These men are traitors and rebels. This ship is a pirate ship and you are Joseph C. Fry, a mercenary. Take down your colors."

"Take them down yourself!" Fry clasped his hands behind his back.

"Haul down your colors." The Spanish officer raised his sword and his guards lowered their bayonets, thin blades, needle-pointed.

The passengers and crew crowded together and Ben Caldwell glanced around for a weapon. So did Mingo Dabney. Fry raised his chin and his jaw was firm. "If that flag is lowered, you will lower it."

The Spaniard turned to a subordinate. "Haul it down!"

Two sailors ran to the stern and loosened the halyard. The flag dropped, and lay on the deck.

One of the sailors spat on it. The other sailor spat on it. The officer moved as if to order the sailors away, then shrugged and turned again to Fry, demanding his papers.

Captain Fry surrendered his documents, the spurious papers that indicated his destination was Costa Rica. The Spaniard crumpled them and tossed them to a sailor. "Illegal papers," he muttered. "Fraudulent papers. Fraudulent ownership. A pirate masquerading behind the flag of the United States."

Mingo looked around at his shipmates and at the thin bayonets of the guards. A sailor picked up the flag and threw it in a heap on the deck. Three others raised the red and yellow standard of Spain.

"*Viva España!*" they cried, and the officers flourished their swords.

Fry held out his hands to his men. "Steady. A false move will endanger your shipmates." His jaw was twitching and when he lowered his hands, his fists clenched.

The crew and passengers were driven to the bow and the Spaniards circled them with bayonets. "Search the prisoners," an officer commanded.

Fry began his protest. "I demand to be taken to the captain of the *Tornado* —"

"If he speaks again," the officer said, "run him through."

Each prisoner was searched. A marine of eighteen searched Mingo, taking his purse and his watch. "You greasy little bastard," the woodsman snarled. He was no longer afraid; the slow, burning fury of the Dabneys was upon him.

A quick command and each prisoner was forced to strip to his drawers. All clothing, all possessions were taken away and they were herded to the sweltering fo'castle as twilight began shadowing the Caribbean, a few stars peeping out.

Another sharp order and a towline was thrown aboard the prize. A sailor waved, and the *Tornado* tilted her nose proudly and was under way, her pitiful little prey wallowing in her wake.

117

Dionisio Castillo, commander of the victor, checked the towline and went to his cabin to prepare his report. A Spanish man-of-war, endowed with courage, had captured a pirate on the high seas, a filibuster flying the American flag. So reported Dionisio Castillo of His Catholic Majesty's Imperial Fleet. The Spaniard mused on his triumph, then sent for his supper.

The sun was down blood-red behind the mountains of Cuba, and the stars were full out, bright and frosty white.

MINGO DABNEY

Chapter 9   Mingo Dabney's first sight of her homeland, the realm of his quest, was from the reeking forecastle of a prison ship.

At daybreak, he looked over the calm water and saw the mountains in the graying light, and they were dim and formless until suddenly tipped with fire, the sun flaming down their sides and into the sea.

There was a command from topside and guards herded the prisoners on deck. Fry breathed deeply of the fresh air and Mingo leaned against the rail, his head drooping in the clawing misery of his helplessness.

John Smith, alone and unknown, stared ahead at the *Tornado*, a little frown of resignation spreading over his face. "My luck is running out," he mumbled and turned away.

Mingo shielded his eyes against the sun and gulped his amazement at the old castle, guarding the entrance to the bay of Santiago de Cuba. The gray stone fortress towered like a medieval chateau, its guns turreted and jutting out over the sea. The *Tornado* slacked to a crawl, drawing her captive close and snaking through the narrow channel, the needle's eye through which Columbus sailed four hundred years before.

The sun swept over the Sierra Maestra, the Mountains of Our Master, searing the cloudless sky; and the *Tornado* and her prize crept on toward the city of St. James of Cuba, through the widening straits and into the bay. Terraces of brightly colored houses ascended row upon row up the side of a hill. Above the bay, above the houses, stood the spires of the cathedral, thrust up like two great arms in prayer, a monument to God, a testament to Spain.

The *Virginius* was moored about a cable's length offshore and the *Tornado* was made fast to a wharf. Her captain and two officers hastened down the gangplank.

"Sagaldo," Ben Caldwell mumbled. "They are going to report to Sagaldo."

Mingo Dabney spat, then ran his tongue along his swollen lips. They were without water to drink, without food or clothes. Fry stepped to a guard. "Put me in touch with one of your officers. At once!"

The guard flashed his bayonet toward the old man's face.

A crowd began gathering along the waterfront, gaping at the *Virginius* and the half-naked prisoners. Mingo shaded his eyes and stared at the spectators.

There was only one black man among them, a stooped little man, spry as a gamecock. He squirmed through the crowd, cocking his head from side to side, darting and peering. The Mississippi man noticed him only because he was so black, a speck of midnight in a mass of brown. "Hops around like a bantam rooster," Mingo mumbled.

A band came marching down a winding street and was followed by a throng, shouting and singing. Vendors moved among them, selling small yellow and red flags of Spain and the people waved the flags and shouted, *"Viva Tornado! Viva España!"* Some of the people were laughing and most of the women were smiling.

The pilgrim gawked at them. They were enjoying themselves, laughing at his misery. "Aren't they Cubans?" He turned to John Smith. "I thought the Cuban people were our friends."

"Sure they're Cubans." The first officer spat toward the shore. "They are toadies who lick the boots of the rich Vol-

120

unteers. They don't care anything about freedom. Just want little jobs and favors for themselves."

Ben Caldwell joined them and they watched the swelling crowd, more and more people hurrying to the water front. The throng began milling, slowly at first, and the prisoners heard the low mumblings. Mingo was awed and a bit frightened. "Where are the folks on our side?"

"In the hills with Macéo." Caldwell pointed beyond the city.

"Reckon they know we're here?" There was a catch in his voice. The crowd was shifting; growling and muttering.

"Sure." John Smith kept his eyes on the throng. "The Mambises know everything. There are Haitians in this part of Cuba, and their drums are always talking." He lifted his chin and spat again toward the shore. "But Macéo can't help us now. . . ." He turned his face toward the open sea. "We dumped his supplies, and he hasn't got a damn thing to fight with except *machetes*."

"And his faith in a sign," Ben Caldwell said.

The pilgrim changed the subject quickly, and once more he noticed the little man flicking through the multitude, jerking his head and listening to the babble. Mingo almost pointed him out, but the crowd swelled its mumblings and he looked around for his captain.

Fry was moving among the prisoners, calming them. "There is no danger. The crowd is excited, but there is no danger."

A young midshipman approached the group at the rail and ordered a guard to disperse them. Fry called out, "Convey my compliments to the commander of the *Tornado*. Request him to notify the American consul of Santiago de Cuba of our presence —"

The midshipman backed away and Fry followed him.

"Request him, further, to ask the American consul to come aboard this ship. Convey that message to your commander!"

The stilted words sounded ridiculous to Mingo.

The young Spaniard looked up, and for all his resplendent uniform he seemed trivial standing before the towering old man, naked except for his drawers. The youth hesitated, then summoned a small boat and was rowed to the *Tornado*.

Captain Fry rejoined the group. "Our consul should be aboard within an hour. The Spanish Navy will not dare ignore the official request of an American master mariner."

John Smith turned his head slightly as he studied Fry. "Captain." He drawled his words. "The Spanish army is in command in Santiago de Cuba. Sagaldo commands the army." The first officer resumed his position at the rail, staring at the throng milling, waving the red and yellow flags and shouting occasionally.

The young midshipman left the *Tornado* and was rowed back to the *Virginius*, his face scarlet as he came over the side. Fry approached him and a guard lowered his bayonet.

"Well?" Fry demanded.

The midshipman did not reply.

Captain Fry's face was livid, then white. "I remind you," he shouted, "that to deny a prisoner access to his consul can be a cause of war."

The young Spaniard wheeled and scowled. "I am ordered to inform you that any further offense on your part will cause disciplinary action against every prisoner aboard this ship."

Joe Fry reeled from the words and passed his hand over his brow. "Merciful God. It's incredible —"

"It's Sagaldo," John Smith said.

Captain Fry spread his hands over his head, trying to keep off the sun. Some of the spectators saw the gesture and laughed at him. He disdained them. "It is impossible that Spain dares treat Americans in this high-handed fashion." He glowered at his first officer as though expecting agreement.

Again John Smith drawled his words. "Everything we thought they wouldn't dare do, they have done. It's time to stop worrying about your ship and start worrying about Joseph C. Fry."

"Humbug," the old man snorted.

John Smith looked away. "I know Spaniards. I've been mixed up with them before —"

"Good heavens!" Fry lowered his voice. "Will they recognize you?"

"I doubt it. My face has changed." The first officer spoke bitterly, glancing over his shoulder at the shore.

For the first time, Mingo Dabney began thinking of Cuban prisons, of Spanish dungeons. And for what? For the rhetoric of José Martí? The burning eyes and snow-white hair of Rafaela Galban? For the meek? The stupid meek standing there on the shore jeering him?

A shout sounded up the street and the prisoners raced to the rail, peering beyond the water front. Down the way a carriage came, lunging toward the wharf, and instantly the crowd was silent, moving back to make room, then standing stiffly erect as the carriage passed; the men doffing their hats and the women lowering their heads.

"An admiral," Fry said as the passenger stepped from the carriage.

"And two butchers," snarled John Smith as two colonels rode through the throng and saluted the admiral. "Sagaldo's men. Sent along as observers. The Spanish army never trusts the navy."

"What does it mean, cap'n?" Mingo's voice was husky.

"Conference of some kind, son —"

"A palaver of buzzards." John Smith smiled the careless smile of a gambler who had lost. It was the first time Mingo ever saw him smile.

The guards brought buckets and ropes and the prisoners drew water from the bay and washed themselves. The water was foul, but Mingo plunged his face into a bucket and poured water on his chest. Buckets of drinking water were fetched and a guard tossed loaves of bread on deck.

"Throwing us food like dogs," Ben Caldwell muttered.

No man moved to pick up the bread. They were hungry,

123

but none chose to stoop for food. Finally, Joe Fry, glancing at his men as they eyed the bread, knelt and picked up a piece and began nibbling it. The others followed their captain's lead, gnawing the dry food. Fry edged to the rail and dropped his bread overboard.

The sun had passed its zenith and the crowd ashore was sweating and squirming, impatient for excitement. The band struck up a tune and the spectators rocked and swayed.

A light wind blew in from the open sea and the prisoners drank in the air. Their bellies were full and their thirst was slaked. Suddenly one of the crew stalked up to Fry. "I got a bait of this. How long before we're getting off —"

"I don't know," the captain said.

"Then, by God, somebody better know. I ain't no Cuban. I'm an American and ain't nobody going to treat me like this —"

"The same goes here," a second man called out and strode forward, drawing back his fist as he passed a guard.

Mingo moved over and joined the group.

The guards edged in closer and a sailor knocked a bayonet aside. "Keep that frog sticker out of my guts, you pasty-faced bastard."

"Steady!" Fry roared the command, then lowered his voice. "We have nothing but our bare hands —"

"Then what you aim to do, cap'n?" The sailor glared at Fry. "Let us roast out here in the sun?"

The captain returned the sailor's glare, and pointed at the guards that ringed them. "I will not allow any of you to imperil the lives of all of you. I say hold steady. But if any man can suggest a better course, then, so help me God, I will take it."

Mingo was hoping they would ignore his captain's caution and strike. A piece of plank from the buckling deck was a good club. A spike was a weapon.

"He's right," John Smith called from the rail. "All they want is an excuse to shoot us down."

"You damn right," Caldwell added. "Use your heads."

Then Joe Fry was speaking again. "I'll hear no more complaining." He glowered at his crew. "Not one word —" The old man's jaw dropped and his mouth hung open. Mingo heard his gasp and heard the quick roll of drums of the *Tornado.*

The admiral and two naval captains were coming from their cabins. They moved quickly across the deck and took their places at a table under a canopy. Sagaldo's observers stood behind them.

"What is it?" Mingo edged closer to his captain.

Joseph Fry's lips were moving but he made no sound, and John Smith replied. "Spanish court-martial. No counsel. No mercy."

A messenger boarded the *Virginius* and delivered a written order to the midshipman. He read it, then read it aloud. "All prisoners will go below. They will dress and return here immediately."

Fry started below at once and the others followed. A guard handed Mingo his clothes and he pulled on his trousers. His watch was gone and his purse was almost empty; only $14 left from the sale of Shannon. His keepsakes, including his passage receipt to Cuba, had not been disturbed, however. He wasn't angry that he had been robbed, only surprised that all his money had not been taken. He fastened his shoes and tugged on his old black hat.

Their commander led them back on deck, over the side and down a ladder to longboats. The crowd on shore gawked, then began cheering. Sweat dripped from Mingo's forehead and into his eyes and he wiped the sweat away, glaring at the spectators. The little black man was gone.

Guards on the *Tornado* flanked the rail and Fry was the first prisoner aboard the man-of-war. John Smith was second. Ben Caldwell was next, then Mingo, and all the prisoners swung over the rail and formed a line, mumbling and mouthing.

A guard approached Fry to pinion his arms, but the old man clasped his hands against his chest and locked his elbows to his side. "You will not secure me." He spoke slowly, clearly, speaking in Spanish. The admiral heard the defiance and the staff looked at the admiral. He chewed his lower lip and frowned, weighing the problem.

The guard turned to his immediate superior for instructions and some of the prisoners began laughing. "Make 'em eat them lines, cap'n."

Mingo reached out and snatched a rope from a guard, hurling it to the deck.

Captain Fry thrust his finger at the admiral. "If a rope is laid on one of my men, I will not be responsible for your lives." Deliberately, and with exaggerated insolence, he turned his back to the court and addressed his men. "If we strike, seize weapons and kill the officers first!" Impudent and scornful, Joe Fry insulted Spanish dignity, waiting for the Spaniards to give or take.

They took.

The admiral consulted one of Sagaldo's colonels and announced: "The prisoners will not be bound if they are orderly. They will line up, facing the court."

Mingo Dabney laughed, forgetting his anger and laughing his ridicule. John Smith sneered and Ben Caldwell chuckled.

Fry strode forward and stood before the admiral, waiting until all prisoners were in line and accounted for. Then he folded his arms. "I demand access to the consul of my country. The United States of America."

The admiral shifted his weight and squirmed. He, too, was sweating and the chair was hard and wet with his sweat. He looked up at the tip of the *Tornado's* smokestack. "It is my duty to inform you," he parroted, "that due to inflamed patriotism of the populace, General Leopold Sagaldo has ordered all foreign consuls detained in their quarters." He lowered his eyes.

126

Joe Fry leaned forward, his face almost in the face of the admiral. "You have imprisoned an American consul! Are you people crazy?"

The admiral drew back and nodded to an officer. Immediately sailors and marines stepped behind the prisoners, leveling bayonets. Mingo felt the steel point touch the base of his spine and drew in his stomach, squaring his shoulders.

Captain Fry ignored the bayonet at his back. "Sir," his manner indicated his contempt, "Your stupidity is exceeded only by your cowardice. Read the charge!"

There was no mention of counsel. No preliminaries. Not even oaths. The admiral, fingering the tip of his beard, looked over the heads of the prisoners, and away. "Joseph C. Fry, you accepted pay to command the *Virginius*. Pay from Cuban traitors. Our reports so show."

One hundred and fifty dollars! Paid by Martí; raised by Nick González.

Fry snorted, shaking his massive head. "The chicanery of Spanish agents is the disgust of the civilized world."

The admiral waved his hand, dismissing the truth. "Captain Joseph C. Fry. You carried arms and ammunition on the *Virginius*."

"Sir." Fry recited the ritual of the sea: "My country holds inviolate that no American vessel, regularly documented and carrying the flag of the United States, can, in time of peace, be visited and searched on the high seas." He paused for an instant only. "The *Virginius* was so documented and flew the flag of the United States. I do, therefore, protest these proceedings."

The admiral glanced back at Sagaldo's observers, then indicated the next man in line, the first officer. "Did the —" He hesitated and peered at John Smith. A frown passed over the Spaniard's face, a search of his memory. "Did the *Virginius* carry arms of war?"

John Smith slouched against the table. "Aw, for God's sake get on with this farce. Spain's queen-mother might even leave

127

her lovers and pimps long enough to cite you for your victory."

Fry frowned, but the others laughed and the guards stuck bayonets against their flesh.

"Such bluster merely is evidence of your American breeding," the admiral said. He picked up a sheaf of documents, opened them on the table, and read:

"The steamship *Virginius* was purchased by revolutionists and registered in New York to hide behind the flag of a friendly power. . . ."

Chicanery or not, Spain's agents were thorough.

The admiral cleared his throat. "The *Virginius* carried war supplies purchased by Señor Elmo Batson of Mobile, Alabama, and shipped to Haiti as machinery." He flipped a page and touched his beard again. "The *Virginius* carried 500 Remington rifles, 300 Spencer and Winchester rifles. . . ."

Mingo felt a scalding flush of anger in his stomach. Betrayed! Somebody had betrayed the manifest. He glanced down at the document, then at the crowd on the wharf. It was increasing, men and women hurrying from side streets, waving their arms and shouting their excitement.

The document was finished and the fiscal of the court, a bored henchman, laid it before Captain Fry. "Sign it," the admiral ordered.

The old man clasped his hands behind him and gazed out to sea.

The admiral shrugged and shoved the papers before John Smith. "Sign it!"

The first officer smiled sadly at the admiral, but his indictment was full of loathing. "You're still a Spaniard."

The Spaniard dropped both hands flat on the table and moved to rise. "Moran!"

"My name is Smith."

"John Smith again?"

"That's right."

The Spaniard sank back in his chair and sat for an instant

128

in silence, perhaps recalling braver days before he was a pawn under the dry, waspy eyes of Leopold Sagaldo. Then he remembered his chore and spoke to his fiscal. "Have some of the sailors document it."

Ben Caldwell spat at the paper as it was passed in front of him and Mingo snatched for it, only to have it jerked away. However, seven prisoners scrawled signatures. Two signed "John Smith." One signed "Natty Bumppo." Another, "John Smith, Jr."

The fiscal folded the document and returned it to the admiral who adjusted his plumed hat and went below.

The crowd on shore was quiet. A horse pawed. A woman moved her parasol and a child began crying. Sagaldo's observers strolled to the rail and looked out over the throng, their backs to the prisoners as they chatted casually.

A pipe sounded and there was an upstir on deck as marines and sailors moved about swiftly, bayonets fixed. The crowd pressed around the *Tornado's* gangplank, stretching and craning for a better view.

The marines formed a double line, facing inward; a passageway from the ship's hold to the gangplank. The admiral, followed by his staff, returned to the deck and took his place at the table. He drew his sword and the sun flashed from the naked blade as a drummer beat the challenge, a quick flurry.

"Take them away," the admiral commanded, and gave his back to the prisoners, seeking commendation of Sagaldo's observers. They nodded approval.

Captain Fry cautioned his men again, demanding discretion. "Obedience is next to valor," he said. "Your raised hand will mean massacre."

He and John Smith led the file from the *Tornado*. Mingo marched beside Ben Caldwell, and the company trudged between lines of soldiers who pressed back the crowd. The spectators jeered and the prisoners returned the jeers, spitting back at those who spat at them. The column dragged up the steep, narrow street and soon the bay was behind them. Only once did Fry look back, turning and looking at his ship. Spanish sailors were cleaning the deck. Mingo Dabney did not look back. The sun slipped behind the balconied buildings and the street was in shadow, and none of the men talked as they plodded up the hill.

Four blocks and the column marched right, passing the cable office. A company of Sagaldo's infantry was on guard and the office was closed. Every man in line realized the significance of the drawn blinds, the locked doors; but no man commented.

A turn, a twist, another narrow street, a filthy alley, and the file reached the jail of Santiago de Cuba, passed through the outer gate and into the inner courtyard, an enclosure about forty feet square. The prisoners stared around, then broke for a well in the center of the courtyard. They gulped the water and lifted their heads from the buckets, panting, then drinking again.

Mingo passed a bucket to his captain, and walked away, swinging quickly around the courtyard, testing the doors and measuring the walls of gray stone. There was a balcony on the second floor, jutting over the courtyard. Underneath, on the ground floor, the cells were jammed with municipal offenders who thrust their hands through the bars, shouting greetings and obscenities.

An officious little man, his mustache and goatee trimmed precisely, hurried into the courtyard. "I am the jailer," he explained, bobbing his head subserviently to Fry. "I objected to the military sending so many men to my care. But . . ." He shrugged and spread his hands. "I am only a jailer. I trust you gentlemen will give me no trouble."

"My men are hungry," Fry interrupted.

The municipal offenders set up a clamor. "Give us our slop before you feed them," one shouted.

The jailer ordered the city prisoners locked away for the night and bustled out of the courtyard. Fry stood watching his men, then walked to the side of the enclosure and stood alone, his feet braced. Mingo joined him and stood by his captain while guards distributed plates of bread and stew, a thick hash of goat's meat, beans and cabbage. The men wolfed the food, sopping their plates with their bread.

Long shadows raced across the courtyard, pacing the quick night of the tropics. In the swift darkness that closed them in, the men were restless, milling about and growling.

The first drum echoed to the north, back in the Mountains of Our Master; a slow, measured boom—boom. The flesh quivered around Mingo's spine and the drums rolled their hollow beat, rising, falling, pulsing. Fry's face was white under his heavy beard and Mingo's blood tingled to his fingertips. "Sounds like the drums we heard in Haiti." He whispered it, although there was no need to whisper.

"Haitians are with the Mambises. With Macéo." The old man whispered, too. "The Mambises know everything. . . ."

"Even before it happens." John Smith joined them, staring over the wall and to the north, toward *la tierra del Mambi,* the land of the Mambi.

Every Cuban Negro among the prisoners was still, looking from one to the other, their ears tuned to the drums, then glancing furtively toward the white men.

A throbbing heat, a quick wild clatter from the hills, then only echoes. Mingo heard his own breathing and the heavy, hollow breathing of Joe Fry.

"Mambi!" John Smith called to one of the Negroes. "Can you make them out?"

The Cuban was staring full at Captain Fry, pity and fear and horror in his face, then at all the other white men, the crew of the *Virginius,* and his eyes were wide and white in the murk. He did not answer, just stared.

"What was the message?" John Smith demanded.

"*Si,*" Mingo broke in. "What the hell did they say?"

"*Compadre.*" The Mambi said it tenderly. "There is no news from *la tierra del Mambi* except that it is raining in the mountains." He shrugged and turned away.

131

MINGO DABNEY

Chapter **10**   The terror of things not seen
was on Mingo Dabney and he moved closer to Joe Fry, seeking comfort from a well-spring of comfort and strength from
an old man who was not afraid. There was no thought of
Rafaela Galban, only fear for himself and his comrades.

The courtyard was hushed and the sole sound was the
wind in the ceiba trees beyond the gray walls, the wind whispering up from the sea and on to the Mountains of Our
Master and *la tierra del Mambi*.

The men shifted their nervousness, glancing at Fry in the
murky lantern light and mumbling soft curses. They all
jumped and craned their necks when a guard crossed the
courtyard to a heavy door and unlocked it, the bolts clanging,
and passed on down the corridor, lighting lanterns fastened
in the dank walls. The jailer came from a side entrance,
stepping rapidly across the yard and hurrying into the corridor.

"He's up to something," Mingo whispered hoarsely.

All the band was quiet, glancing into the corridor, then
turning to watch their captain until a sailor broke the spell.
"Time's running out on us —"

"They've got us spread-eagled," Caldwell broke in. "They
even had our manifest —"

"What difference does it make?" John Smith snapped at
them. "We gambled and we lost."

Caldwell grunted and might have continued the harangue,

but the little jailer came quickly back into the yard, stepped under a lantern and unfolded a paper. "The following men will please line up before me." He began reading: "Joseph C. Fry. John Smith. Ben Caldwell. Mingo Dabney —" The lantern was smoking and the jailer lifted the paper nearer the light. "Mal Hatson. Walter Searman. Hal Bostwyck. William Dolsen. Wyzee Cannon —"

Fry was the first to move. There was no confusion, no delay. Fifty-three names were read, the officers and crew of the *Virginius,* the leaders of the passengers; and fifty-three men took their places in the corridor, blinking under the lights.

The jailer checked his list. "That's all. Now follow me." He led the way along the passage and the door was slammed behind them, shutting them off from their shipmates huddled in the yard.

Double doors at the far end of the corridor were swung open, admitting the fiscal of the *Tornado* and a detachment of soldiers. They leveled their guns and advanced toward the prisoners.

Fry stood very straight, but Mingo was crouching, his lips trembling his terror.

The fiscal numbered off the prisoners and lifted his eyebrows, studying them. He opened a paper, flourishing it. "The following men —" He swallowed and raised his voice, and then read the names of the fifty-three, lowering the paper as he drew back slightly into the protection of the soldiers. "You, all of you, have this day been convicted of piracy —"

"Piracy!" Fry's hands jerked upward and he shifted his weight forward, tense and ready to spring. Two soldiers dropped their bayonets to his belly and the fiscal nodded to the guards.

Four men shouldered their way among the prisoners and fastened shackles on their wrists. One grabbed Fry's arm and

133

locked the chain, shackling him to the nearest man, to Mingo Dabney.

The prisoners were too stunned, too shaken to cry out, to fight back. Mingo and Fry raised their chain, peering at it and at each other, bewildered and incredulous.

The fiscal lifted his paper and began reading again:

"The sentence of each man is to hang at the yardarm until dead.

"However, the admiral commanding, not wishing this defilement of his ship, has altered this sentence —"

Fry leaned forward and Mingo felt the old man's arm quiver. "—each man will, therefore, be shot.

"The sentence of death before a firing squad will be executed at daybreak tomorrow."

No man moved. No man spoke. Some trembled, some stood firm; but each stared at the fiscal, at the guards, at the jailer.

The double doors at the end of the corridor clanged open again and the guards forced the prisoners forward. They moved slowly down the passageway, some stumbling, and into a chapel where priests already were intoning a Mass for their souls, a Mass for the dead.

Captain Fry was the first to kneel and Mingo, shackled to him, knelt also, gazing about the room, gazing at the priests, listening to their prayers for the dead while the dead still lived. It was his first Mass and he was awed, strangely comforted by the mystery of the living condemning a life to dust while imploring peace for a soul.

The droning of the priests ended and the murmuring of the men ceased. The Mass gave way to muskets and the prisoners were marched out of the chapel and to the second floor of the jail, none speaking, none looking about. Even John Smith was silent, even Ben Caldwell.

Captain Fry and Mingo were locked in a cell and the shackles removed. Fry began rubbing his wrists, but Mingo stepped quickly to the door, peering through the bars, his muscles taut and his ears strained. Doors all along the balcony were clanging shut and he heard his condemned comrades scraping their feet as they paced the stone floor. He twisted his neck to see them but the balcony was dim, and he stared down into the courtyard. The other prisoners, wondering about their fate, were grouped in a far corner, hushed by the nearness of death, the brush of the raven's wing.

He wet his lips, then wiped them dry with the palm of his hand. Fry walked over to a cot and sat there, stroking his beard. He was composed, calm and resigned, a man of faith in the promise of his Church. After a moment he raised his eyes and watched Mingo, then said, "Son, I know you are not a Catholic. But are you at peace with God?"

"I have never been at war with God, Captain Fry." The pilgrim glanced around the cell and went to the window that opened on to the city; a few lights showing, and the bay in the distance, shimmering darkly.

Fry said humbly, "I have failed again."

Mingo examined the two cots, the dirty straw mattresses, and felt the stones of his cell, running his hands along them. "I reckon it's every man for himself now."

"It is. Your life is your own, to spend as you will."

"And I want you to know that if they kill me, they'll kill me right here." He was breathing deeply, inhaling the odors of the jail, the moist clammy smell of the stones. A dozen ideas raced through his brain, ridiculous ideas born of desperation, but his scheming drove the terror from his mind, clearing it.

A quick rain washed the city and there was a call of the drums in the hills, a mournful throbbing. The Mambises knew everything. And if they knew it, she knew it.

Captain Fry called softly to a guard, requesting pen and paper, then spoke to the younger man. "Do you mind if I write some letters?"

"No, sir." Mingo went to the door. "What time is it?" The guard pulled out his watch. "Nine thirty."

Fry dragged the straw mattress from his cot and laid his

paper on the smooth wood. He got on his knees, leaning over, and wrote first to his children, then to friends and relatives.

Mingo was at the window, watching the mist roll in from the sea, hooding the bay and hiding it. The stars were out again and the cathedral spires rose clear.

Captain Fry rested his head on his hand and tested his pen, edging nearer the lantern:

Dear, dear Dita:

When I left you I had no idea that we should never meet again in this world; and it seems strange that tonight, and on Annie's birthday, I should be writing to take my last leave of you.

I was tried today, and at sunrise tomorrow I shall be shot. There is to be a fearful sacrifice of life from the Virginius, *and, I think a needless one. I hope God will forgive me if I am to blame for it. . . .*

The last act of my life will be a public profession of my faith and my hope in Him of whom we need not be ashamed.

Your devoted husband,
Joseph Fry.

He kissed the letter and folded it. Mingo whirled from the window and motioned a guard. "What time is it?"

The guard held his watch close to the lantern. "Twenty minutes past ten."

Fry laid his letter aside. "I thought it was later than that." He paused, then spoke his thoughts. "There's one more thing I can do. Write General Sagaldo for clemency."

Mingo did not reply, but walked back to the window and Fry picked up his pen, begging mercy from a man who knew no mercy.

He wrote deliberately. "If I, a master mariner, was ignorant of any law proclaiming death as penalty for blockade running, how then could my crew be expected to know of such a law? But beyond all this, consider the souls of these men. I know that you must fulfill your duty, but my blood should be sufficient. I implore you."

He signed the message and poked it through the bars to the guard. "Please take this to the jailer."

The guard turned away.

"I insist." The old man wilted as he added his plea, "Take it to him in the name of the Mother of Heaven."

The guard stopped and came back. Mingo saw the uncertainty in his face and ached to take the Spaniard in his hands and choke him to death. "All right," the guard said. "I'll try." He called another to take his place, and padded softly down the balcony and out of sight.

"What time is it?" Mingo asked.

"A little after eleven," the new guard replied.

High in the hills the drums throbbed and Mingo swung back to the window, clamping his hands around the bars and straining at them, jerking and tearing until the muscles in his arms knotted and the veins showed in his forehead. Fry said nothing, pretending not to see. Mingo sobbed his helplessness and leaned his head against the bars, cursing them.

The big door at the far end of the balcony clattered open and light streamed in. Mingo spun away from the window and all the condemned men pressed against their bars.

The jailer and a stranger hurried along the balcony, around the corner to Fry's cell. The jailer nodded and stepped back without unlocking the door and the stranger said, "I'm Carson. British vice-consul —"

"Thank God!" Joseph Fry believed in miracles. "Where is the American consul —"

"Locked in his residence —"

"Then how come you out?" Mingo demanded, glowering at the Englishman, a man of medium height.

The vice-consul turned to the jailer. "Unlock this door." The man hesitated, fingering his keys. "Unlock it," the Englishman commanded. The little jailer opened the door and

Carson entered the cell. "Let me talk first." He clipped his words. "Then I'll answer questions."

Carson sat on the cot, sniffing the odors of the jail. Fry sat beside him and Mingo leaned against the wall.

"I sent a message to the Spanish authorities," the captain began.

"They'll never get it," Carson snapped. "And let me do the talking." He ran a handkerchief over his face and took out a list, holding it to the light. He scowled and called to the jailer. "Move that lantern closer." The jailer complied and the consul studied his list. "Sixteen of your crew and passengers are British subjects?"

"That's correct," Fry said.

Mingo took two steps toward the cot. "You haven't told us how come you're out, and our consul locked up —"

"The guard was removed from our consulate less than an hour ago." Carson still was looking at his list, checking the names and not troubling even to glance at Mingo. "A British man-of-war is on her way from Jamaica. The *Niobe*."

Fry jumped to his feet. "Can she arrive in time?"

"No. She can't possibly arrive before noon tomorrow."

Mingo eased toward the door, measuring the distance to the jailer, to the lantern. Both were beyond his reach and he turned back to Carson. "What about an American ship? Don't our folks know what's happened?"

"Who is that fellow?" Carson glanced from Fry to Mingo, then back to his list again. "Never mind. Never mind. Yes, an American ship is coming. The *Wyoming* has sailed from Colon." He folded the list and returned it to his pocket. "I'm sorry," he said, speaking more slowly. "But I can offer you gentlemen no assistance. Sagaldo is determined to execute you at dawn."

"And the others?" Fry pointed toward the courtyard. "What of them?"

"They are all to be shot." Carson's face was white. "Half

138

tomorrow afternoon. The remainder the next morning. It's butchery."

The old man pressed his finger tips to his eyes, "There's no hope?"

The vice-consul chewed his lower lip, weighing his words. "I can offer none. You accepted pay from the Cuban revolutionists —"

"He knows that," Mingo snapped. "Why harp on it?"

Carson ignored him. "Sagaldo and the Volunteers are so arrogant they have cut themselves off from Madrid and Havana. They are acting on their own authority."

"What's that got to do with us?" Mingo demanded.

Again the Englishman ignored him and got up from the cot. "God knows I'm sorry, Captain Fry." The stiff cloak of officialdom dropped from him. "The world knows the *Virginius* was bought, paid for and dedicated to the Cuban revolution. Even your passengers took pay and passage from the *Juntas*—" The consul drew back, gaping at Fry. "What is it, man?"

"My Lord!" Fry gasped. "Merciful God!" His huge frame trembled. "That boy!" He pointed at Mingo. "That boy paid his passage to Cuba!"

Carson visibly was skeptical, and a minute, the eternity of a minute, tapped at Mingo's memory. He was back in Mobile. Twenty dollars for a passage! Twenty dollars for medicine! He felt in his pocket for his purse, blindly groping for the straw that fate drops at the feet of her favorites.

Fry clutched the consul's shoulder, whispering hoarsely in his face. "That boy was a bona fide passenger on the *Virginius*. A paying passenger —"

"Then why did he come to Cuba?"

"A girl!" Mingo took three quick strides and was beside his captain, facing the Englishman. "I came to Cuba to see a girl!"

"Your passage receipt!" Fry grabbed the boy, hoping to give him life. "I signed your passage receipt!"

Mingo opened his purse and fumbled for the receipt, then held it trembling toward the consul.

Carson unfolded the paper carefully. It was sweat-marked and brittle. He flicked away the brown dust and read it, deciphering it in the smoky light of the lantern. For an instant he was motionless and his mind, steeped in the ways of nations, measured the potentialities in this sweat-stained receipt. The revelation of its meaning surged through him and George Carson knew that he, custodian of trivia, was at that moment the most important servant in Her Majesty's Government.

"In God's name!" He crashed his fist upon the cot, and struck it again. "This man is war!" To him the American was only a cause, an immeasurable threat. "His death could mobilize a dozen nations."

Mingo snarled, "What the hell are you talking about?"

"Stay out of this!" Carson folded the receipt quickly, his brain leaping for a dozen details. "This man is protected by every international law —"

"I know! I know!" Fry's tongue raced over his words. "My country will be forced to fight —"

"My God, man!" Carson put the passage receipt safely in his own purse. "The whole world may fight. It is for Sagaldo to say." He motioned to Mingo, snapping his fingers. "Come, you." He kicked the door. "Turnkey! Open this door!"

The jailer signaled for the prisoners to go to the far end of the cell.

"That man," Carson pointed to Mingo, "is going with me —"

"No!"

"That man is going with me. To Sagaldo."

The jailer stepped back, his keys rattling in his hands. "I have no authority."

"Then take it, you idiot!" Carson shouted the words. "Open that door or you'll hang at a yardarm! A British yardarm!"

"I'll have to send guards with you." The jailer was whining and the key clattered in the lock.

"Send the Spanish army, but open that door."

The other prisoners began shouting. They didn't know what was happening; but, aroused by the urgency of the consul's tone, they began shouting and stamping their feet.

Fry stepped to the back of the cell and the jailer swung open the door. The old captain put his hand on Mingo's back, pushing him. "Go, boy! Go!"

Carson stalked out and Mingo stumbled after him, dazed as the jailer lifted his lantern and led the way.

"Hurry, Dabney." It was Ben Caldwell. "Don't forget us!"

"Remember the *Virginius*!" It was John Smith.

All the prisoners on the balcony, all the doomed, began cheering him. They knew only that a shipmate was going outside into the free air, perhaps to plead for them, perhaps to liberty. "Hurry, Dabney!—Remember the *Virginius*! . . ."

The big doors at the end of the balcony swung open, then closed; and Carson glanced back at Mingo, urging him down the winding steps and to the passageway, thence to the jailer's office. Four soldiers marched out of the office to the sidewalk, untied their horses and swung into their saddles.

The drums boomed suddenly in the hills that fringed the city of St. James, that looked down upon the Spanish capital of Cuba's Oriente; a pounding, frantic booming, spreading on to *la tierra del Mambi*.

Carson caught Mingo's arm and pushed him toward a carriage, climbing in beside him. He spoke sharply to the coachman. "To the residence of General Sagaldo."

The coachman leaned over and spat, then tapped his horses with the reins.

MINGO DABNEY

Chapter **11** Mingo Dabney slumped back
on the seat and tilted his head, gulping the air as the carriage
swayed over the cobblestones and into the night. He was too
shaken to think, or speak. Two sentries challenged near the
cathedral, waving the party through when they saw the
mounted guard.

Then the prisoner found his voice and blurted, "What are
my chances?"

The vice-consul made a quick gesture, dismissing the
question and scheming his plans. The drums were silent,
poised; and the night was broken only by the ring of the
horses' hoofs and the muffled voice of the coachman speaking
his team. A cock crowed to the west, another answered in
the east. A dog barked, the sharp yelp of a hungry cur.

"Listen, Mr. Carson." Mingo ran his fingers through his
hair and his fingers were sticky with sweat. "I'm damn near
crazy."

Carson turned to Mingo, trying to see him and able to
make out only the whiteness of his face. "I don't know what
your chances are. That depends on Sagaldo."

Mingo hitched forward, rubbing his hands along his legs.
"For God's sake, get me out of this."

Any effort to think, to bring his predicament into focus,
exhausted Mingo and his head dropped to the back of the
seat. They rode through narrow alleys, thence along boule-
vards to the residence of General Sagaldo. Carson whispered,
"Let me do the talking. All the talking."

The coachman wheeled directly in front of Sagaldo's palace, his horses almost treading the toes of the guards. The house was ablaze with light and Carson leapt from the carriage and hurried toward the door. Mingo was two paces behind him.

The captain of the outer guard, startled by the boldness of the maneuver, glanced nervously at the mounted escort, then posted himself in front of the intruder. "I have orders to admit no one." There was a trace of doubt in his tone, "I must ask your business —"

"*My* business!" Carson puffed out his cheeks until his face was red, simulating wrath. "You dare ask *my* business!"

The captain faltered. Too often he had been ordered to protect the general's house, then reprimanded for barring some important personage whose allegiance Sagaldo wished to encourage. The Englishman waved a sheaf of papers under his nose. "Here is my business. Stand aside." He reached out and brushed the Spaniard from his path, and the soldier gave way.

Carson strode to the big door and pounded, fuming noisily at a second's delay, then pounded again, fiercely rattling the brass knocker. A halberdier, resplendent in red barred with gold, opened the door and lowered his halberd across the entrance. Again Carson drew himself up, haughty, contemptuous, and flipped his paper under the sentry's nose.

Mingo heard the rustle of silk in the salon adjoining the entrance hall, then a tinkle of glasses and laughter. The Englishman heard it, too, a wry smile on his lips. Raising his voice, the vice-consul, an infinitely petty official in Her Majesty's Empire, thundered:

"Inform General Leopold Sagaldo, Don of Valencia, Knight of the Golden Fleece, Grandee of all Spain, that George Carson of Her Majesty's Britannic Government presents his immediate compliments."

It was a daring thrust, an arrogant gesture of British bluff. Mingo's heart was thudding his ribs. The merry babble of voices in the other room trailed to a whisper, then was still.

143

The halberdier opened his mouth to challenge, but Carson cut him off with an imperious wave of his hand. "Inform General Sagaldo that my visit is a matter of state." His voice carried sharp and clear. "I am instructed to wait five minutes, and no more, for admittance or an explanation."

He folded his arms and stared stolidly past the halberdier, ignoring him. Mingo moved to Carson's side and gazed over the handle of the halberd and into the brightly lighted hallway.

The guard was reciting the ritual of his post when a slender man, erect and graceful, strolled out of the salon. He wore black boots and black trousers, striped thin with scarlet at the seams. His blond hair was parted and carefully waved, and the clean-shaven face looked youthful.

The halberdier saluted and only then did Mingo Dabney realize, realizing it instinctively, that the man was Sagaldo. His jaw fell and he gawked, for this man was smiling, amused and detached, as he came into the hallway, every movement marked with a flowing, pliant strength.

"And who is it—" The voice was almost pleasant. "Who is it who limits the time of Leopold Sagaldo to five minutes?"

"George Carson of the British Consulate." The Englishman hurried into the hall, nodding for his companion to follow.

Mingo entered the palace, stepping upon the white tiles, and walked toward the general, a Mississippi woodsman face to face with a grandee of Spain.

"You are liberal with your time, Mr. Carson." The Spaniard's eyes actually were twinkling. "Leopold Sagaldo will grant you one minute to state your mission." He stood behind a chair of carved and polished teak. "But first—" He looked at Mingo, appraising the bloodshot eyes and the unshaved face. "Just who is your companion?"

Carson walked toward the general, pointing back toward the dazed woodsman. "That man, sir, is war."

Sagaldo half opened his hand, as if boredom prevented his

opening it further. "Come, come. Let us have no melodramatic nonsense." A frown darkened his face. "I was enjoying conundrums with my guests when you interrupted. I do not enjoy conundrums with you, Mr. Carson. Let's get to the point: Is this oaf one of the filibusters from the *Virginius?*" The softness was out of his voice and his eyes were expressionless.

Mingo Dabney wet his lips and slid his hands into his pockets to hide his clenched fists. Oaf! Now he was an oaf. He remembered his promise to Carson and kept silent, his eyes fixed on Leopold Sagaldo.

The Englishman moved one step nearer the blond Spaniard and pointed back again at Mingo Dabney. "That prisoner," he said slowly and distinctly, "is an American citizen who paid his passage to Cuba—"

"Preposterous!" Sagaldo's assumed ennui no longer masked his annoyance, and his fingers lightly tapped the back of the chair. His eyes were fastened upon Carson and they were cold, motionless. "The *Virginius* was a pirate—"

"Pirates do not pay passage." Carson spoke without visible excitement. "I have proof that he paid his way—"

"Show me the proof." The grandee's annoyance was approaching anger, but there was a hint of consternation in his voice.

Mingo fidgeted for Carson to show the receipt, but the Englishman rammed his hands in the side pockets of his coat. "I am prepared to submit the proof to my Government who, I assure you, will pass it to the Government of the United States of America." He was taking control of the interview. "I caution you that you have condemned a man protected by the first and last word of international law."

"Why is he in Cuba?" Color was mounting in the Spaniard's cheeks.

"A lady! He came to see a lady!"

Sagaldo struck the back of the chair and his face was contorted with rage and scarred by hate. He sat down in the chair, glaring at the Englishman, ignoring Mingo.

Carson stepped directly in front of the grandee. "The whole *Virginius* affair is a matter of grave concern to my Government and will be dealt with later. But the execution of a neutral passenger captured on the high seas by a Spanish man-of-war could cause a world conflagration —"

"Absurd!" Sagaldo spat the word. "Diplomatic nonsense!"

"Nonsense?" Carson's voice rose for the first time. "You blunder into the execution of that man and the American people will rise in such fury that the Spanish people, like their monarchy, will bleed forever —"

"Sir!" The grandee sprang to his feet.

Mingo looked around for a weapon, edging toward a spiked mace on the wall. The halberdier moved nearer his master. Carson, however, shook his finger in the Spaniard's face. "Save your threats for helpless people, General Sagaldo." He almost purred the words.

The Spaniard reached behind him, feeling for the arms of his chair, and sat down again. His lips were pinched and dry.

Carson stepped so close that he saw the flecks of red in the Spaniard's blue eyes. "If the United States mobilizes, my government probably will evidence sympathy." His voice was low, emphatic; for at that instant George Bennet Carson, custodian of trivia, spoke for Empire. "And if my government moves, Germany will move. Then France. Every major power is arming for war. I warn you!" He stepped back, slipped his hands into the side pockets of his coat and awaited a decision.

Mingo smeared his palm across his mouth, rasping it over the stubble on his chin, and swallowed. He was breathing rapidly, almost in gasps, and Sagaldo glanced at him. "Perhaps," he said slowly, "our navy should review this case."

"You will not entangle this man in a Spanish snarl." Carson pronounced each word precisely. "You will make your

146

own decision, and make it now. Another war will relegate Spain to the mausoleum of nations."

"Stop this tirade!" The grandee was standing erect and the color flowed from his face as he flung his open hands to Mingo. "Take him away." He spoke to Carson but was looking steadily at the woodsman, etching the dirty unshaved face on his memory. "I commit him to your custody."

The tightness in Mingo's chest broke, and his knees sagged and he was weak and trembling. Carson took his arm and, without another word to the Spaniard, led him through the door and out of the palace to their carriage, walking proudly between the rows of soldiers. The coachman touched his horses and the carriage whirled away.

Mingo's head rolled to the back of the seat. "You saved my life," he mumbled, and there was measureless feeling in his simple words.

"Your life?" Carson felt for his handkerchief and wiped his brow, suddenly dripping sweat. "It is possible I have helped delay a world war for five, perhaps twenty years." He, too, relaxed, staring out at the darkness of the city.

"What about the others?" Mingo asked.

"Everything that can be done is being done."

Mingo felt nauseated, and fear and relief stabbed along his nerves. His head was throbbing and his muscles were knotted into hard balls of pain. The drums called to the east. A reply from the north, then a steady frenzied pounding. Carson gave them no heed, but Mingo looked up. The coachman's head was cocked to one side and he leaned forward and flicked his horses.

They drove toward the cathedral and the plaza and the night was ebbing toward dawn. The drums throbbed to an echo and the city was quiet, panting in its restless sleep.

"I will take you to the British residence," Carson said. "As soon as possible we will arrange for you to return to the United States —"

"No, sir."

Carson snapped his head forward in surprise. "I beg your pardon —"

"I am not going back home." There was no bravado in his words, only the quiet assurance of a pilgrim who had chosen his quest and intended to follow it. "I had a reason to come down here, and I'm going to stay awhile."

Carson looked closely at his companion and was much too much a diplomat to ask her name. "You are a free man, Mr. Dabney. But for God's sake get out of Santiago de Cuba."

"I aim to." He was watching the coachman, the whip curling above the horses. "I'm going to join Antonio Macéo."

The carriage lurched and there were quick tears in the driver's eyes as he reached out and snapped his whip. Carson jerked erect and his voice was harsh, accusingly so. "Then you are a filibuster —"

"I told you the truth, Mr. Carson." The carriage was swaying and Mingo braced his feet. "I paid my way to Cuba."

The consul rubbed his chin thoughtfully, tallying his behavior. "My procedure was entirely proper. You were a bona fide passenger and my duty was to prevent an incident." He reached for the handle of the seat as the carriage rocked and creaked. "Slow down, driver!"

The coachman pulled his panting horses to a walk and guided them to the front of an austere house, shadowy in the darkness. Carson stepped from the carriage and walked toward the gate, motioning for Mingo to follow him.

Mingo moved to pull himself out of the comfort of the seat and the coachman touched his arm and whispered, "Baire!"

"Baire!" the pilgrim answered, his heart leaping to his throat.

"You come with me—the consulate will be watched." The coachman raised his whip. "I will pass you along."

Mingo Dabney sank back into the seat, glancing toward the house and Carson. Let gratitude be spoken later! The pilgrim's first thought was for himself, then for his comrades. The driver lashed his horses and the carriage surged around a corner and into a narrow alley, and there the team was reined to a walk that would attract no attention.

"Where are you taking me?" Mingo leaned forward, poised and tense.

The man shifted, holding up his hand as the drums sounded a rapid message, then eased. *"La tierra del Mambi."* He pointed to the north with his whip.

"How far?"

"Not far. And now you will be quiet."

Mingo did his bidding, scrouging down in the seat as the carriage wheeled out of the alley and up a steep hill, almost to the edge of town. Only a few houses were there and the water front was below them. The coachman halted his team under a ceiba tree. "You sleep now. I will watch while we wait here —"

"For what?"

"For daybreak. You must go part of the way alone and the hills are not kind to a stranger at night." He tapped himself on the chest. "I am Pepe Barea. A Mambi. You will trust me."

Mingo peered through the darkness at the brown face, the eyes somber and unwavering. "I will trust you." He settled into the cushions and a paralysis of weariness crept through his muscles, and through his mind.

A streak of gray showed over the mountains and cocks crowed to the east. A cart rumbled down the hill, a farmer prodding his donkey; but the pilgrim barely heard the sounds of dawn. His mind was leaping from Lebanon to a girl, a ship, a jail. He strove to bring it all into focus, particularly his condemned comrades; to plan, to scheme for them, but the world was a formless place, without motion, hovering in darkness. His mind slowed until he drifted into lethargy, collapsing into sleep. . . .

The sun touched the spires of the cathedral and the jail of Santiago de Cuba, steaming heat from the old stones; but it was cool under a ceiba tree where Mingo Dabney slept the sleep of the exhausted while a Cuban Mambi watched over him.

A clatter of horses' hoofs, and the gates of the prison swung wide, creaking as they swung. Joseph Fry and John Smith were at the head of the column, their arms pinioned as they shambled along, rattling their ankle chains. The old man's massive head was erect and he was staring straight ahead. Disdain and scorn were etched on the face of John Smith. Ben Caldwell was slumping along, his head lowered. Some of the others were weeping, some praying, others cursing.

Down the winding street, the heat waves danced in the first glare of the day. But it was cool under the ceiba tree where the pilgrim slept, where the Mambi sat trembling, berating himself for stopping there. No, he must not wake. *Madre de Dios,* let him sleep! He must not see this thing.

To the water front the column plodded, and a mob lined the street, the spectators of yesterday howling their cry for blood. A cavalry unit rode into the people, forcing them back, opening a way for the doomed.

One of the mob scooped mud at the prisoners and another snatched up horse dung and hurled it at Fry, splattering the front of his shirt. Calmly the old man walked on without deigning to notice.

There was a gray adobe building near the water front and its roof overhung a wall. In front of the wall was a gutter, a drainage for blood, for this was the slaughterhouse of Santiago de Cuba, the place to kill beeves for the City of St. James.

The prisoners were marched to the wall and forced to kneel as an officer paced the distance. Seven—eight—nine. Ten feet. The firing squad raised their rifles and the mob's scream gurgled to an end.

A blast of Spanish Mausers and some of the sailors fell and lay motionless, some sprawled, writhing and twisting. John Smith slid to the ground and lay on his side. Ben Caldwell toppled across him.

Mingo Dabney moved, his leg jerking the spasm of a man prostrated by exhaustion. The Mambi held his breath, praying and weeping. No. Mercy of the Merciful, let him sleep. Spare him this horror.

A second volley thundered, its echo rolling up from the water front, clapping against the hill. Mingo sat up quickly, blinking his eyes against the sun. Pepe Barea was frozen to the seat, slobber bubbling at the corners of his mouth.

Captain Fry was on his knees, rocking from side to side, his sightless eyes uplifted. Two more bullets tore into his breast and he pitched forward, his face to the sea.

"My God!" Mingo grabbed the hand rail and leaped, stumbling to his knees. "Cap'n Fry! Ben!" He was running down the hill, his reason suddenly drugged by madness.

Pepe Barea sprang after him, clutching for his arm and pleading. "—*compadre!* It is too late."

Mingo tore his arm from the Mambi's grasp.

"*Amigo!* They are dead. We are two against two thousand. . . ."

Mingo halted, staring down toward the slaughterhouse, then wavered and slumped against the Cuban, sobbing his helplessness, the clawing knowledge of abject futility. The Mambi drew him back to the buggy and he stared once more toward the slaughterhouse, clutching his hands until his nails cut his flesh, calling God as a witness to this minute. Then he put his hands over his face, covering it, and sobbed.

The mob began roaring and the soldiers, without orders or formation, ran to the dead men and ripped open their bellies, ripping low to the groin, slashing the mark of Sagaldo.

The people, the meek frenzied into a mob, broke through the soldiers, snatching swords from the officers and cutting their hands as they grasped the blades. Then they surged to the bodies, to the fifty-two dead, and bent low, hacking and chopping, severing the heads.

They ripped poles from the porch of the slaughterhouse and

thrust the poles through the throats and into the heads, holding the heads aloft and screaming: *"Venga Mambi!* Come on, dirt! *Viva Sagaldo!"*

The madness gripped the cavalrymen and they spurred their horses over the headless bodies, riding back and forth until the dead were mangled, sodden masses.

A bugle sounded and the cavalry swung into column, riding stiffly away, the bloody hoofs of their horses splotching the ground. A butcher drove a cart from behind the slaughterhouse, threw the bodies into the cart and clucked to his donkey.

The mob, roaring and holding their trophies aloft, came tramping back into the city, trudging toward the plaza, the cathedral, the palace of Leopold Sagaldo. And as they walked, the poles swayed and the heads of the dead men shook. The heavy beard of Joseph Fry was flecked with gray and dripping red.

MINGO DABNEY

Chapter **12**   It was at this moment that
Mingo Dabney shed the last remnant of his heritage and became a man obsessed with vengeance. An abomination rooted
in his heart and he feasted on the abundance of his hate.

It wasn't the rhapsody of José Martí, the rapture of Rafaela
Galban, that riveted him to Cuba. It was the aroused fury of
a Dabney who had seen his comrades butchered and defiled,
and there under a ceiba tree he lifted his face to the cobalt
sky and pledged his creed: death to Spaniards.

Never again would any man call Mingo Dabney an oaf.
Never again must his pride be trampled or his dignity despised, for Mingo Dabney would spit on no man, but no man
would spit on him. He sought only the right to live and love,
and be loved; for that right, he was willing to die.

He reached out and gripped the coachman's shoulder.
"Where is Macéo?"

Pepe Barea jerked free and struck his horses. They traveled
swiftly until the pavement ended, the carriage lurching on
to a rutty road at the edge of the city where the hovels of the
poor moldered in dank misery.

Flies, black and green, swarmed up from the filth, and the
people looked from their doorways and smiled at the driver,
ignoring his passenger. The shacks stood eave to eave and
Mingo stared at the blight, at the open sores of Cuba festering on the edge of the city, a squirming, steaming mass of
human beings.

The men sprawled before their *bohios*, their huts, looking out with vacant eyes. Sugar sacks were knotted about their loins. The women were pot-bellied and moved with heavy, dragging feet. The hair of their naked children was matted with filth.

The coachman was weeping, nodding toward the *bohios* as tears streamed down his face. "My country, *amigo*."

The horses bent their necks, climbing rapidly and soon they were beyond the hovels and into the clean country, out of Santiago de Cuba, away from the city of St. James. To the west and north, rising gently, were the Sierra Maestra, purple and green in the morning light, the shadows of dawn streaking their slopes.

The pilgrim looked back at the bay, clear and sparkling, the *Virginius* wallowing in the slow swell, her stack upon her deck and Spain's standard at her mast. He turned from the bay and the *Virginius*, the city and the slaughterhouse, and faced the hills, watching both sides of the trail. Around a bend and to the right was a clump of marubu trees, their thorns brown and hard, and the team was halted. "We wait here a few minutes," said Pepe Barea.

A sharp hiss sounded from the brush and Mingo jumped, then glanced around nervously.

"*Grillo*," the Mambi said. "Hissing bug. A pest."

One of the insects hopped to the seat, grinding hisses. It was only a cricket and Mingo brushed it away. "What are we waiting for?"

The Mambi held up his hand for silence and cocked his head toward the mountains, watching the sun, and when it was full upon the crest he pointed toward a path. "Follow that. About a league up the mountain, it forks. You go there."

"And then what?"

The driver shifted his weight and pulled his sweaty trousers from his flesh. "His name is Soto. He is coming. You wait at the forks."

154

The woodsman stepped from the carriage. "How will I know him?"

"You will know him." Pepe Barea braced his feet against the dash. "And may the Mother of God go with you." He slapped his reins and drove away, leaving Mingo Dabney in a clump of marubu trees, alone in a strange land with only his hands to save him.

The path was bare, weaving up the hills and around the rocks, a thin trail leading on into the land of the Mambi, the land of the talking drums, the jungles; on into Macéo's Cuba. Mingo started up the slope, walking as a woodsman walks and studying the things about him, memorizing the path, the boulders and the trees.

He didn't realize how fast he was climbing until his breath shortened and labored. He was a lowlander and this was a world he didn't know. The *grillos* endlessly grinding hisses. Small parrots whistling shrilly. Pigeons moaning in the trees, in the brush. All this was new to him and he breathed deeply until his lungs were no longer straining, then pulled himself erect and resumed his climb.

The path wove through the trees, ever mounting, until it split against a boulder, forking sharply. Mingo looked about him and knew that here he must wait.

The wind from the sea drifted through the ceiba trees, through the mahogany and the piñon, rippling the green and purple cape, and hastening on into Cuba. He heard horses coming down the mountainside and knew by the sounds of their hoofs that they were unshod. He used his foot to edge a rock within reach and leaned against the boulder, assuming casualness, concealing his expectance and fear.

The first horse came into sight and the rider was leading a second horse. Mingo studied the man in the twilight, his black face and his bearing. Suddenly the woodsman's brow wrinkled and his heart began thumping: a warning or a recollection, a signal or a memory.

Then it came to him. This was the little man he saw the

day before at the water front, the one who darted through the crowd like a bantam rooster. His first impulse was to hail, but this man had moved freely among the Volunteers. His hand slid near the rock.

The horseman gave no heed until he reached the boulder and checked his horse, sitting forward in the saddle. His *machete* was sheathed at his side. "I am Soto." His voice was soft and friendly.

Mingo didn't move.

"I am to pass you along." The man had swift eyes and his small face was piquant.

Still Mingo didn't move. "I saw you yesterday. You were at the water front. With the Volunteers."

The Cuban rested his arms on the pommel of his saddle, slouching in his saddle. "I was there, Señor." He spoke almost casually.

Mingo stepped close to the rider. He smelled of goats and sweat. "But you were with the Volunteers."

The stranger smiled, perking his head and again Mingo thought of a banty. "You are wise to challenge everything in the hills." He eased to one side of his saddle, resting his weight on that stirrup. "Pepe Barea brought you to the marubu thicket. You were told to come to this fork and wait for Soto." He bowed. "I am Soto. I am to pass you along."

"Where?" Mingo demanded.

The little black man hesitated, for an instant puzzling his answer, then he leaned down. *"La Entorcha!"*

Mingo snatched the bridle of the second horse and swung into the saddle. "Where is she?" The Cuban didn't answer quickly enough and Mingo grabbed his arm. "Where is she?" His voice was rising.

"Not far." The guide turned his horse. "She sent for you." He started riding up the slope.

"Is she all right?" The pilgrim was trembling.

The guide tightened his reins and looked at his companion. "If *La Entorcha* was not safe, Soto would not have left her in the *bohio* with the duenna."

"Then you are her friend?" He was hungry for news of Rafaela Galban, even a morsel.

Soto halted his horse and leaned out of the saddle, touching Mingo's arm. "I am a goatherd from Guantanamo, a mountain man. Sometimes Macéo honors me to be the guide for *La Entorcha*."

Mingo's horse lowered his head and smelled the *kaquaso* grass, rattling his bit as he tore the grass and fed on it. The woodsman tugged his hat tight on his forehead and lifted the reins. "Let's get going, *amigo*."

"First we eat and rest. Your eyes are red and your hand is heavy —"

"Let's get going."

"You will do as I say, *amigo*." The little guide swung from his horse and reached into his saddlebag. "This is *la tierra del Mambi*. And I am a Mambi."

Mingo did not protest. He must trust and follow, so he accepted corn cakes and yams from the Mambi and stretched on the ground in the shadow of a rock. Soto stood watch.

The shadows were reaching long down the slopes, stretching gray and black, wiping the colors from the mountain palette. The trail was so narrow the two men traveled single file, the Mambi about a length in front. They were riding in silence, climbing steadily, when night came quickly on, the final, blood-red streaks turning black in the sky and the day was gone from the Oriente.

There was no moon, but Mingo's eyes adjusted to the darkness and he watched the trail, glancing up often at Soto. The Mambi slipped his left leg around the horn of his saddle and rode easily, rocking with the movements of his horse. Mingo did likewise and Soto smiled. "That's the way. Trust your horse."

"We're making slow time." Mingo pointed impatiently up the mountain. "Is there no shorter path?"

The little black man lifted his shoulders and spread his

hands in a gesture of resignation. "The climb is steep. The way is dangerous. A man is allowed but two falls in these mountains. One for knowledge. Two for eternity. We will get there when we get there." He dropped his head and yawned.

The mountain world was silent except for the humming of the night things and the soft, sure-footed climbing of the horses. Mingo's mind darted from one thing to a hundred kindred things, and always came back to Rafaela Galban. He raised his head quickly, surprised to hear Soto singing and amused at his high squeaky voice. It was a sharp, ringing song that the little man was trying to sing:

> *Don't fear a glorious death,*
> *For to die for the Fatherland is to live!*
> *Run to arms, Valiants!*

It was *La Bayamesa,* the battle hymn of Cuba, and Mingo listened as Soto, swinging lightly in the saddle, sang the death chant and the resurrection of the Mambises.

The sudden pulsing of drums to the north, fast throbbing in the mountains above them, caused Mingo to tighten the reins; but Soto was ignoring the throbbing crescendo and continued to sing his song. The drums rolled again, a vibrating echo, and there was an answer from the south. Mingo dug his heels into his horse's flanks and the animal scampered up the incline to Soto's side. "What is it?" he asked, glancing at the goatherd's *machete,* their only weapon.

The Mambi perked up his head, cocking it from side to side. "Eh?" For a moment he peered at his companion, then the line of his teeth showed white as he smiled in the darkness. "Oh-h-h-h. The drums." He clucked his tongue. "Pay no heed to the drums, *amigo.* They are the Haitians, and Haitians talk, talk, talk. Like old women in Guantanamo." He pulled his horse's head to one side and bent forward, examining the trail.

"What are they saying?" Mingo was fascinated. This was a thing he must understand.

"Saying?" Soto's mind obviously was on other matters. *"Por Dios!* Those Haitians. They forever talk on their drums." Again he raised his shoulders and spread his hands, shrugging his placid acceptance of the inevitable. "All night and all night and every night. Little news. Big news. No news. They talk." He loosed the reins and they began climbing again.

Mingo's horse stumbled and the woodsman jerked him up, helping him hold his balance. "But what are they saying?"

Soto turned his head toward the north, listening. "The mayor of Baracoa became a grandfather today. There is yellow fever in Havana. *Recristo.* There is always yellow fever in Cuba during the rainy season."

Mingo's horse flung his head away from a firefly and dipped his ears. "Where do they get their information?"

Soto chuckled again. It was a gurgling chuckle, a happy sound. "From the Mambises. The Mambises know everything that happens in the hills. And the Haitians talk, talk, talk about it. Ah-h-h!" He broke off his own idle talk and listened. The drums were from the south, from the direction of Santiago de Cuba. "Ah-h-h. A British warship has arrived. Your other shipmates have been spared —"

"Thank the Lord!"

The Mambi motioned for silence. "So-o-o. Your country is talking of war." He sucked in his breath, deep, tilting back his head. Then slowly he nodded. "Spain is begging. *Madre de Dios!* Spain is always begging when a strong hand is raised. It will be settled." Their horses were breathing hard, but Soto gave them no rest until they reached the top of the mountain. There he halted.

"Amigo." This was the best time for the pilgrim to ask. "I have some friends in Cuba. One is named Nick González. Do you know him?"

"González?" There was a quick smile on the Mambi's face.

159

"A fat man."

The goatherd still was smiling. "I do not know him. . . ."

"I thought the Mambises knew everything."

"*Recristo!*" The Mambi extended his hands and shrugged. "I go to your country and ask for a fat man named Smith. Do you know him?"

Mingo smiled for the first time and touched his hat, slanting it a bit. "How much further?" He spoke louder than he intended.

Soto laid a quick, restraining hand upon him. "Now we do not talk. We ride and listen."

There was no trail that Mingo could see, but the guide moved in and out of the brush, weaving his way. A quarter moon was coming up behind them but it gave no helpful light in the thicket. Fireflies speckled the darkness, stabbing the black with a million golden dots. *Grillos* shrilled their endless hisses, high-pitched and piercing.

Mingo leaned back in the saddle, rocking with the uneven steps of his horse. The brush was thick and the *grillos* began hopping on him, into his hair and ears and he tried to brush them off. One slipped down his collar and he squirmed in contortions until he put his finger on the bug and crushed it against his flesh. To the north, the drums were sounding. In the south, they were rolling and throbbing.

He was beginning to tire and he estimated they had ridden five or six miles down the side of the mountain when they came to a small valley. They were in a thicket of laurel trees and beyond was a grassy clearing. In the clearing was a *bohio,* dark, and no sound came from it.

"There," Soto whispered, pointing toward the hut, then dismounting.

Mingo swung from the saddle. His throat was dry and his fingers shook as he fastened his horse in the grove. Soto put his lips to his ear. "You wait." The guide circled the *bohio* quickly and when he came back, Mingo studied his face for a sign; but there was none, only the darting eyes and the expressionless face. Soto cupped his hands toward the hut and sounded the soft cry of the pigeon. Once. Twice. A pause. Then again.

A light flickered in the *bohio*. Swiftly it was brighter, streaming from the window. The door opened and an old woman, the duenna, stood framed in the doorway, holding a lamp.

Only then did Soto smile, his smile glowing like the lamp and he gripped Mingo's arm. "Holy Mother! All is well. Macéo would cut me to bits if she was harmed." He walked toward the hut and Mingo followed, the long grass whipping about his legs, the dew wetting his feet.

The duenna drew back and Soto held up his hand, halting Mingo, and he stood there by the doorway, looking at the old woman and her lamp. Soto stepped into the hut and said, saying it proudly, "*La Entorcha,* I have brought him."

He turned and motioned, and Mingo entered, bowing to the duenna as he passed. And there, in the glow of the lamp, was Rafaela Galban, her face pale and troubled. She did not move to meet him, but stood for him to go to her; and he did, bowing his greeting and waiting for her to offer her hand.

She did not. She merely nodded and was aloofly polite, her decorum precise and rigid. "You have had a horrible experience, Señor Dabney. General Macéo will avenge the *Virginius.*"

"So will I." He, too, was stern, quickly tense and unbending. "Where is Macéo, Rafaela?"

She looked at him, almost stared at him; the cold light in his eyes where fire had been, the brittle temper of his voice. "We will discuss that later."

The duenna lit a second lamp and Soto pulled a bench to the door and sat there, resting, leaning his head against the wall. Rafaela led the way to the end of the room and Mingo followed her, hearing the rustle of her cotton dress, the garment of the poor.

161

The collar of her white blouse lay smooth on her wide shoulders, and was fastened at her throat by a brooch of beaten silver, a laurel leaf, token from a Mambi too old to fight. Her black skirt, close-fitting at her waist, fell in soft folds to her feet. The ring of Martí, the ruby, was on her finger and her lace mantilla hooded her head, covering her hair and framing her face.

She reached the end of the room and sat down, smoothing her skirt as she indicated he was to sit in a chair a few feet away. "There will be food in a few minutes." She fingered the laurel leaf at her throat.

"Maybe I can reach Macéo tonight." He folded his arms and leaned back in the chair. "Has he recovered from the shock of Martí's loss?"

At mention of Martí's name, Soto looked from one to the other. He got up and went to the duenna and spoke to her, and they began setting the table in the center of the room.

"He has recovered," Rafaela said, staring again at Mingo, at the tuft of hair he was twisting around his finger, and some of the frigidity went out of her. She asked about his family, seeking perhaps to veer his thoughts from the horror of the *Virginius*. Her feet, primly placed, showed under the hem of her skirt and the toes of her black shoes were scuffed and scarred. "I suppose you know that Elmo Batson is in Cuba."

"Where is he?" Mingo asked quickly, lowering his hand from his hair and watching her.

"He has been in Cuba a week. He was to receive the cargo of the *Virginius* and get it to Macéo." She turned her head and her hair shone silver through the black lace of her mantilla. "Soto! Where is Señor Elmo Batson?"

The guide was watching the old woman arrange the yams and the *malanga* on the table. "At sundown he was crossing the ridge of San Juan. He was riding a mule."

"Why did you not tell Señor Dabney about his friend?"

The little Mambi shrugged and leaned over the table, pinching one of the yams and drawing back his hand when

162

the duenna glared at him. "I did not know they were friends. He asked me only about a fat man named González."

"Señor Batson is on his way to Macéo." Rafaela stood, gesturing toward the table. "The food is ready. Come and share it."

They stood in their places, their heads bowed, and Soto said grace, mumbling it. They crossed themselves before and after the blessing and the duenna sat down first. The food was plentiful and well cooked, the baked yams and the squash, the roasted corn and the *malanga*.

The old woman uttered no words and Soto was busy with his eating, tearing his food with his fingers and smacking. The conversation was Rafaela's responsibility, but she was silent, picking at her food. Mingo accepted a second cup of coffee, glancing over at her, the lamplight on her mantilla. The wind was in the laurel trees and the pigeons called. The peace of this moment was on the pilgrim and he spoke to Soto: "Must we go to Macéo tonight?"

"*Sí.*" It was emphatic.

Rafaela glanced up then, and felt for the laurel brooch, fingering it. "You might prefer joining Máximo Gómez. He is commander in chief and would welcome an American on his staff."

Mingo lowered his fork and looked at her, surprised and perplexed. In Pensacola she had urged him to join Macéo and now she was suggesting Gómez. She was Macéo's ward and he remembered The Brown One's agitation on the wharf at Kingston, and remembered the admonition of Captain Fry: "—Antonio Macéo's guiding star is his faith in *La Entorcha Blanca*. Do not crowd him, but do not cringe." Her motives he did not understand, her purpose he dared not question. He was mulling a reply when Soto spoke up:

"*Por Dios!*" The guide pushed the potato peelings to one side of his plate and reached for an orange, stretching far. "*Caramba, La Entorcha!* My friend Señor Dabney is a

163

Macéo man. He seeks Spaniards, not the honor of epaulets on Gómez' staff."

Rafaela changed the subject, veering the talk to other channels, the formation of Cuba's provisional government, the dozens of chieftains whose bands were roaming the hills of the Oriente, burning and looting Spanish property.

They finished the meal and Rafaela and Mingo returned to their chairs at the end of the room. The old woman cleared away the dishes, and, reading Rafaela's glance, went outside, and Soto followed her.

The girl smoothed the cuff of her blouse, pulling it lower over her wrist and began twisting the ruby ring of Martí. There was a strained silence, and Mingo was the one who broke it. "You sent for me, Rafaela."

Her chin came up slowly and she calmly folded her hands in her lap, aloof again and as distant as frost on the rim of the world. "You must go to Máximo Gómez. Not to Macéo." It was her bidding, the dictation of *La Entorcha Blanca*.

Mingo got up, resting his hands on the back of the chair. "Don't you think that is for me to decide?"

A flush surged to her cheeks. *La Entorcha* could not plead, and her authority was only as strong as the Mambises' faith in a sign, in thunder in the sun. Protected from childhood by the fierce shadow of Antonio Macéo and dedicated as a mystic symbol to a people, she suddenly was in a world she did not understand, facing a man she did not know at all. There was no more to be said. This man was not a Mambi. She could not tell him what to do.

"I must return to the camp of my guardian." Hauteur was back in her manner and surety in her bearing. She stepped to the window and looked out. "You may go now." Then there was a flame in her eyes, austerity in her tone. "Only four persons know of this meeting. Soto. The duenna. You and I."

"Only four persons, Rafaela." His expression did not

164

change, although his blood quickened for now he shared a secret with her.

She walked to the doorway and the duenna appeared in the shadows. Soto came from the laurel grove. Mingo reached for his hat and thanked the old woman for the food. Soto took corn cakes from the table and wrapped them in a banana leaf.

Rafaela turned to the Mambi. "See that Señor Dabney reaches the camp of General Macéo."

Soto bowed, and turned to the woodsman. "I have fed and watered the horses." He waited for his companion to go through the door, then followed. "We have a long ride."

MINGO DABNEY

Chapter **13**   The trail away from the *bohio*
was wide and clear, but they traveled slowly, the Mambi setting the pace. The drums were pounding again, a question
from the west, a reply from the east. Their throb became a
monotonous overtone to the other sounds of the night, the
hisses of the *grillos,* the whistle of the parrots, the droning
buzz of the insects.

The strange sights and sounds no longer disturbed Mingo.
His horse was at an easy walk and he propped his elbows on
the pommel of his saddle, relaxed and swaying with the gait.

Soto reined to a walk so slow, so aimless, that Mingo wondered why, and kept glancing ahead. He saw no reason for
delay and again was impatient. However, these were Soto's
hills and he was no man to challenge a guide in his own
country. But he was curious, nevertheless, and gave his horse
enough rein to overtake the Mambi, riding beside him. Soto
was looking up at the trees. *"Monte*—little jungle," he explained, indicating the thin brush through which they rode.

"And where is Macéo?"

Soto chuckled. "Learn one thing now, *amigo,* and never
forget it. Tonight Macéo is here. Tomorrow he is gone. And
no man knows where except Spaniards—dead Spaniards with
their throats cut and their shoes walking away on Mambi
feet."

The trail was hard-packed and Mingo remembered the
horses were unshod. Perhaps that explained the slow gait,
but there was no reason for Soto idling along in this lazy

fashion. "The trail is plain." He pointed at the wide path, clearly marked in the moonlight. "Our horses are fresh —"

"Um-m-m-m!" It was a sound of understanding, of meditation and sly merriment. "You wonder why we do not hurry to Macéo. "Um-m-m-m." He held up his finger, and his hand swung like the slow wagging of a metronome. "No—no—no!" His head tilted with the slow tempo of his hand and his voice rose and fell. *"Recristo, amigo!* A lady cannot travel as fast as a man."

Mingo scowled at his own lack of perception. Of course, she must be back under Macéo's surveillance before he arrived at the camp.

The Mambi halted his horse, staring toward the woods at their right. The air smelled of water, heavy and cool, and they dismounted. Soto led the way down an abrupt slope and there was the creek, languid and dark. "We will rest here." He sat on the ground, resting his back against a tree and opened the banana leaf, sniffing and sucking his teeth as he looked at the corn cakes.

Mingo sat on the spongy earth and stretched out his legs, tensing them and relaxing them, easing their weariness. He bit into a corn cake and it was cold, but it was good. The earth smelled dank and musty, of rotting leaves and mold. He looked about at the underbrush close to them. "Snakes?"

"No snakes." Soto nibbled his cake.

"Do we build a fire?" He always built a fire when he slept in the woods of Lebanon.

"No fire." Soto kicked off his shoes, untanned leather held together by rawhide thongs. He wiggled his black toes and yawned, lolling back his head and enjoying the yawn.

"Why not?"

"Spaniards."

The Lebanon man felt no fear, only anticipation. "The hell you say! There are Spaniards around here?"

"Señor." Soto finished his cake and sucked the crumbs from the end of each finger, then picked up a stick and began scratching away leaves and trash, digging himself a bed.

"Spaniards are everywhere." The little Cuban raked leaves under his head for a pillow and squirmed himself into comfort.

Mingo sat pondering the night, the strangeness of the mountains. "Reckon the Spaniards know we are nigh?"

Soto cocked open one eye. "*Amigo*, aren't you sleepy?"

"No." He began scooping out his bed. The drums were talking through the hills. "What are they saying this time of night?"

"Listen, *amigo*, this time of night a man goes to sleep. But the Haitians are saying Pepe López stuck a thorn in his bare foot." Soto snorted and turned over, then yawned and smacked his lips, mumbling to himself.

The woodsman pulled the leaves together, mounding them, and stretched on the earth, expecting *grillos* and worms to crawl on his bare feet and up his trousers. He missed the warmth and the protection of a fire and couldn't get to sleep, flopping from one side to the other, restless and impatient. There were many questions he wanted to ask and he looked over at the Mambi, expecting to see him asleep; but Soto's eyes were open and his head was perked toward the northeast.

"What is it?" Mingo whispered.

"Your friend Elmo Batson has traded his mule for a horse and is making better time."

Ol' Elmo. Still swapping. A whirl of memories turned in Mingo's head, memories of Lebanon and Elmo popping his suspenders and telling spicy stories, the loafers at the Dabney store guffawing and slapping their legs. "The last time I saw Elmo he was with José Martí."

The little Cuban rose on one elbow and was wide awake. The piquancy and sly playfulness were gone from his face. "The last time I saw José Martí he was riding a white horse. Then he threw up his arm, and slid from the saddle, and he was dead."

Mingo sat up, demanding quickly, "You saw Martí killed?"

"*Si.*"

"Only two men escaped from the trap that killed him —"

"Only two." Soto tapped his chest. "I am looking for the other."

Admiration for the Mambi warmed his blood. Here was the kind of man to tie to. Light from the young moon filtered through the trees and dappled the floor of the forest. For a moment the drums were still. "I knew Martí," Mingo said.

"No, *amigo*." Soto shook his head. "You met José Martí, but you did not know him." He raised his hand. "No offense. It is only the truth."

Mingo spoke quietly. "Did you know him well?"

"Me?" Soto put his finger on his chest. "Why, *amigo* . . ." His memories showed gentle in his face. "My father was a slave in the Havana household of Martí's father. We spent our childhood together, a wild little black boy and a sad little white boy. José Martí taught me to read and write. I can even read his poetry." It was the boast of a man who has risen, the joy of all men who achieve.

Mingo was silent, hearing a goatherd talk of his idol. "I tell you something." Soto dabbed his finger toward his comrade and leaned forward. "José Martí lived long enough to strike the flint that will fire the Cuban people. Then he was led to a Spanish death by a Cuban." The little man cringed. "Holy Mother of God! He was led to his death by a Cuban!" Soto the Mambi sat up straight. "So I look for a man."

This was one of the meek, one of the lowly of Martí's dreams. "Soto." He sought to seal a friendship in a compact of hate. "I have a debt, and you have a debt. I will help you find him."

Mingo was shocked by the Mambi's ferocity, then realized the depth of his hate. "If you need me, let me know." He looked a long time at the guide, remembering the drums of Jeremie. "You are a goatherd from Guantanamo, huh?"

"*Sí*." Soto lay down again, wiggled his toes again, and was still. "Eight goats I keep. Five of them I milk." He waved his arm in a gesture of grandiloquence. "I am a rich man. Eh?"

Mingo pressed for the information he wanted. "*La Entorcha* and Macéo went to the *bohio* of a herdsman when they landed at Guantanamo —"

"You talk too much." Soto was gruff, pretending annoyance. "A Haitian, maybe. Now go to sleep." He flopped on his side, his back to his companion.

The woodsman, accustomed to sleeping on the ground, could not relax, even though the leaves were thick and soft, almost a carpet. He twisted and squirmed and held his eyes shut, only to open them again and stare up through the trees at the curved moon and the stars. Long he lay there, until the drums softened in the west, softening into a lullaby for a weary man.

Mingo woke at dawn, almost choking with the stench of death. He scrambled to his feet and saw Soto moving cautiously in the thicket. The wind had shifted and was blowing strong from the west, laden with the sickening smell. He grabbed his shoes and jerked them on and was heading into the brush when the Mambi raised his hand, reassuring him, signaling him to silence. The guide pointed toward their horses.

They mounted quickly and rode due west, following an arroyo that curved and twisted up the side of the mountain. Soto looked everywhere, seeing every tree, every bush. Frequently he stopped and listened and once he stood in his stirrups, staring over the wall of the gully. Then he eased back in the saddle, muttering and cursing. They rode up the arroyo until they came to a plateau. There the smell was stronger and Mingo's stomach squirmed and he wished he had bathed his face in the creek near where they slept.

Soto picked his way through the laurel and ceiba trees, then stopped abruptly, peering ahead into the brush. Mingo drew alongside and there was the bloated carcass of a mule, its legs sticking up, stiff as pegs. The woodsman glanced at his companion, expecting a smile. They had been stalking a dead mule.

There was no smile on Soto's face. His lips were tight and his little eyes darted, taking in every detail. He slid from his horse and hurried to the dead mule. Using his *machete*, he pried off the iron shoes and brought them back and tied them carefully to his saddle. So they saved horseshoes! Mingo turned his head from the stench and waited for the Mambi to remount.

The guide warned him to be on the alert, and began easing through the woods, his *machete* loose in his right hand. Mingo shifted in the saddle and his horse shied. Mingo steadied him, glancing again at the carcass. Suddenly he bent forward. The mule's throat was cut, slashed deep. He whistled softly to Soto and pointed at the carcass. "That mule was knifed."

"*Sí.*" The Mambi was facing west, watching through the thicket, his nostrils quivering.

"Maybe his leg was broken. Maybe they cut his throat instead of shooting him. . . ."

"No." Soto shook his head. "No Mambi would leave precious shoes on a dead mule." He flung up his hands, his *machete* flashing in the early sun. "No Mambi would leave a dead mule. He would drag it to Macéo's camp for food."

"Then who killed him? Spaniards?"

"Perhaps. Spaniards or Volunteers." He stuck his *machete* back into its rawhide scabbard and swung into the saddle. "Or *guerrilleros*. Cubans hired by Spaniards. Buzzards who pick their country's bones for sixty dollars a month." He slapped his horse with the palm of his hand.

The odor of death still was before them and Mingo peered forward, suddenly tense. The way was screened by a tangle of thorn trees but Soto hacked a path, swooping from the saddle as he swung his broad *machete*, cutting silently, swiftly.

Then the way was open and a clearing lay before them.

Mingo Dabney recoiled in stark horror, gagging under the impact of the sight and the stench. A few charred logs remained of the *bohio*, a few scorched palms. Even the *kaquaso* grass was burned and near the hut, sprawled and bloated, were five bodies. Two were the bodies of men, one of a woman and two were children.

Soto jumped from his horse and ran to the men, peering at their faces. The pilgrim dismounted and stood gazing down at the bodies. "My God!" He said it over and over.

The belly of each body was ripped open and the Mambi shrugged. "Sagaldo." He said it flatly and without feeling. "The mark of Sagaldo." He turned away, searching the clearing, poking in the debris.

Mingo could not look away from the bodies. "Then Spaniards did it. . . ."

"No. Spaniards use swords. This is *machete* work. Sagaldo's *guerrilleros* were here." The guide scratched in the ruins of the *bohio* and found a steel ramrod and a tin plate. These he tied to his saddle, alongside the horseshoes.

Mingo walked away from the dead. He stood in the shade of a laurel tree and took off his hat, mopping his brow and his face. The sun was full over the hills and he was hot and sticky. Soto joined him and Mingo said, "What can we bury them with?"

"Bury them?" The Mambi shook his head. "No, *amigo.* If you stop to bury all the dead you find in Cuba you will be nothing but a grave digger." He bowed his head, mumbling a prayer. "We can do no more. We have prayed for the family of Pablo Cortés. A cocoa farmer. A *pacifico*. He took no sides in the war, but once he gave a night's shelter to General Macéo."

Mingo caught his breath in short gasps. "That stink will stay with me forever."

"It is the smell of *la tierra del Mambi*. You will get used to it." Soto led the way back to their horses and they rode rapidly away, still going west.

The jungle fell behind them and they came to cocoa groves

and small patches of pineapples, each tended by a barefooted family. The morning shower of the rainy season caught them not far from the village of El Cobre, a copper mining community, but they plodded on in the rain until the sun came out again, drying them and reviving their spirits. At noon, they stopped at the *bohio* of a swine herdsman who shared his food with them.

The long ride began telling on the woodsman by mid-afternoon and he nodded, his head bouncing low as he rode, and frequently he dozed in the saddle. The trail widened into a wagon road and they passed a train of two-wheeled carts, larger than any Mingo ever had seen. The wheels were huge and each cart was pulled by four oxen, harnessed with head yokes instead of neck yokes.

"Sugar carts," Soto said. "Hauling supplies to Macéo."

The road was churned to mud and they hurried along, waving at the carts as they passed. "Ah-h-h, Soto!" the drivers called. The guide peered into each cart, then acknowledged the greetings.

The first picket of Macéo's army, the Army of the Oriente, challenged them as their horses waded a small creek and scampered up the west bank.

"Por Dios!" Soto leaned from his horse and slapped the picket on the shoulder. "Do you expect me to remember passwords?" He unloosed the tin plate from his saddle and handed it to the sentry. "For your beans and bread, Pepe."

"Soto!" The picket grasped the hand of his friend. "You always bring us something. What a beautiful plate. Ah-h-h . . ."

"And you can use it for a mirror," the goatherd said.

The sentry examined the plate carefully, holding it up to the sun and blinking his eyes in the reflection. He pointed his thumb at Mingo. "Friend?"

"Sí." Soto leaned over and confided. "His name is Dabney."

"So-o-o-o." The sentry nodded. "He is a strong man. He will eat a lot."

Mingo was amused and delighted, particularly when the

173

picket stepped back and bowed elaborately. Soto motioned for the guard to draw closer and lowered his voice. "*La Entorcha*. Did she pass this way an hour ago? Maybe two hours?"

The picket nodded. "Two hours."

Soto was visibly relieved and waved good-bye to the picket and they entered the lines of the Army of the Oriente, nine hundred Mambises with five hundred rifles and nine hundred *machetes*. Spain had a quarter of a million.

The road followed a bend around a mango swamp and there they came upon the baggage carts, piled high with a confusion of utensils and hammocks. The carts were in the road, beside the road, across the road, while their drivers stood or squatted near the vehicles, laughing and shouting obscenities at one another.

"Camp followers," Soto explained. "The *impedimenta* of Macéo's army."

"Army!" The wanderer's heart sank. "Are they part of the army?" He looked down at the assortment of vagabonds. Mostly they wore soiled sugar sacks twisted around their loins, and nothing else. They were dirty and indolent. Here, indeed, was a fine bunch of rag-tails.

Soto read the disappointment in his comrade's face. "*Sí.*" He lifted his shoulders and spread his hands. "They are part of the army. They follow along, stealing and robbing to help supply Macéo. Riffraff. Thieves and brigands and cutthroats." The Mambi raised his hand in greeting to the sanguinary crew. "*Saludo, amigos!*"

"Ah! Soto!"

They gawked at Mingo, looking covetously at his clothes and his horse. They all wore *machetes* at their belts and a few had guns, firelocks, musketoons, and two had blunderbusses, trophies from Spanish *haciendas* they had sacked. Proudly they waved these relics of Spain's early colonial days, brandishing them as if they were superior to Sagaldo's Mausers. The ancient weapons had not been fired in two hundred years and had hung as treasures on the walls of the rich

Spaniards. One man, a toothless, grinning Negro, his skin peeling its own filth, wore a Damascus sword at his waist, and several had Toledo blades. There was not the slightest evidence of discipline among them, or organization.

"Do not be scornful," Soto cautioned. "The *impedimenta* are worse than *grillos*, but without them Macéo's army would starve. They obey no man. They go and come as they please and they handle the carts and the baggage. But do not sneer, *amigo*. They are the stealing hands and the carrying feet of the Army of the Oriente."

Mingo was almost sick with disappointment. The *impedimenta* numbered less than one hundred men; slovenly, surly trash. They were worse than the rednecks back home.

A woman's coarse laugh came from one of the carts and several of the *impedimenta* glanced quickly at Soto. "Get her out of there," the guide commanded.

"She does no harm," an ox driver protested.

Soto reached for his *machete* and struck the man across his back with the flat of the blade. "You filth! Son of a goat and father of goats! Get her out of there! *La Entorcha* is in camp!"

The man flung up his arms. "I did not know. By the Holy Mother, I did not know. Don't tell Macéo. Please, Soto."

The Mambi struck him a second time. "Get her out of there. I will not tell."

The ox driver stepped to the side of the wagon and spoke a few words. The back flap was lifted and a woman, fat and greasy, slid out of the cart. The men laughed and Soto rapped her bare backside with his *machete*. "Slut! Bag of sores!"

The woman tugged her dress free and ambled away, rubbing her behind and shaking her fist, calling back maledictions and insults. "They are fools to crawl into a cart with her," Soto grumbled. "She will kill more Mambises than Sagaldo." He turned in his saddle and watched the woman out of sight, then heeled his horse and motioned for Mingo to follow him. "Come, *amigo*. We are there."

175

MINGO DABNEY

Chapter 14   The headquarters of Lieutenant General Antonio Macéo was a thatched *bohio* in a mango grove and, in a creek nearby, Mingo Dabney doused himself with cold water, washing off the grime of his journey.

Down along the stream rested the Army of the Oriente, nine hundred *machete*-men of every color and every shade of color. Those gaunt barefooted men skinning a *jutía* were Quintín Banderas' hill fighters, and the *jutía* was a big rat, feast meat for Macéo's ravenous warriors. Those men around the camp fires were the merciless clansmen of the Ducasse brothers, Juan and Vidal. Some wore earrings of looped silver or copper, and not much else. The swaggering gallants of Alfonso Goulet had rooster feathers in their hats, and *machetes* swung low from their sashes. All were scarred, these cock-feathered fangs of Goulet, and they numbered forty.

These were the Mambises; these the envenomed fighters that Sagaldo called mountain goats, derisively scorning them, unwisely disregarding them.

They had no uniforms and they might have been scooped from the alley of any Cuban slum, the shacks of Cuban farms. Most of them wore the *chamarreta*, a short cotton jacket, and their crude breeches were of cocoa bark, ragged and loose fitting. Their hats, hand-woven from the tough leaves of the palm, were cone-shaped and the wide brims rolled up. Less than half had rifles and only a few had cartridges, con-

176

tributions of Cuban whores who collected them from Spanish customers.

But every man had a *machete*, a farmer's tool, and Antonio Macéo schemed to cut the spine of the Spanish empire with the curved blade in the hands of peasants who had heard thunder in the sun.

This was the Army of the Oriente, this the tattered legion of The Brown One, the mulatto carpenter who had shaped his hammer into a sword. Nine hundred Mambises against two hundred and fifty thousand Spaniards; three hundred to one. *Viva Mambi!* History hardly knows you and the poets will pass you by. *Viva* you rag-tails! You stink of oil and garlic and sweat, of caked blood and scabs. *Viva Mambi! Viva eternalmente!*

Mingo Dabney scooped water in his cupped hands and poured it down his back as he stared through the grove at the slovenly mob. A hundred or more were beyond the creek, circled close about a cockfight, waving their arms and shaking their fists, banging their chests and bragging on the black cock, on the red cock, laughing and cursing and screaming their excitement.

Soto came down to the creek from the direction of headquarters, his arms filled with clothes. "Ah-h-h." He was pleased with himself. "Your friend, Elmo Batson, will be here tomorrow. And I got word to General Macéo that you had arrived."

"Did he send his brass band?" Mingo stepped to the bank and shook himself, sliding his hands down his body, slicking off the water.

Soto chuckled and glanced over toward the cock fight. "No, but he sent you some clean clothes."

Mingo shoved his fingers in his thick black hair and massaged his scalp, rubbing it hard. "Now, that was mighty nice of him." He lifted the clothes by his finger tips. The underwear was pure silk. "What the hell? I don't wear silk drawers."

The goatherd grinned, proud of his general, a man of many foibles and affectations. "Silk underwear—that is Macéo. A bath every night—that is Macéo. Oil on his hair—that is Macéo."

The woodsman held out the drawers and pulled them on as if they were hot, but they felt good, and he rubbed the silk against his legs. The trousers were gray Dutch linen, the finest cloth he had ever seen. He recalled that The Brown One wore Dutch linen in Jamaica.

Soto produced a razor and Mingo shaved, then wet his hair, combing the part carefully on the left side. He slipped into the coat and it was a bit too big, but he rubbed his hands and strutted. "Ah-h-h . . ." He said it as Soto did, the inflection rising and falling. "If I just had a cigar, I'd feel like a horse trader at a county fair."

"No. No." The Mambi wagged his finger fast. "No cigar. The smell of tobacco makes him sick." He poked out his lips, pondering the vagaries of Antonio Macéo. "He does not smoke. He does not drink—that is Macéo." He stepped in front of his charge, nodding approval. "And now, *amigo* . . ." His brow knotted and he was hesitant to speak. "There is one thing more."

"So?" For some reason, Mingo was expecting a warning about Rafaela Galban.

The little Cuban's face was grave and two lines curved deep at the corners of his mouth. "Antonio Macéo is one of eleven brothers. All are fighting for Cuba. José Macéo is a general." Soto was trying to say what he felt must be said, the caution that must be spoken. "Antonio Macéo is a proud man, proud of his brothers, proud of himself. He is sensitive, too." The Mambi touched Mingo's arm. "Antonio Macéo is a mulatto. . . ."

"I know that." Mingo was relieved that she had not been mentioned.

"But you are a Southerner. . . ."

"Wait a minute." He held up his hand. "I don't give a

hooray about Macéo's color." He picked up his old black hat and tugged it on his head. "And I didn't come down here to listen to you, or anybody else, lecture like a blue-bellied Yankee. They're always shooting off their big mouths, telling us what to think and how to get along with folks." He patted Soto. "Don't you do it, *amigo*." He began walking toward the headquarters of the Army of the Oriente. "Come on."

Mingo Dabney had to bend his neck to enter the *bohio* of General Antonio Macéo and when he raised his head he saw The Brown One standing in the center of a group of officers.

He was immaculate in Dutch linen, the coat tight-fitting, and he stepped toward Mingo, his face a calm mask of reserve and dignity, but the lid of his left eye was slightly drooping. Soto drew himself erect, standing as tall as he could between the two men, and announced pompously: "General Macéo. Señor Mingo Dabney."

The general did not offer his hand.

Neither did the Lebanon woodsman.

"God has spared us both, Señor Dabney." He nodded stiffly, a punctilious greeting.

"We've been lucky." Mingo was as reserved and dignified as his host. "I thank you for the clothes, sir." The address was deliberate, an effort to match Macéo's rigid courtesy. "I will return them as soon as mine are clean."

The Brown One dismissed the matter with a flip of his hand and a slight shrug. "They are rags. I know that in your country gentlemen wear much better."

It was on Mingo's tongue to say that never before had he worn such clothes, nor had he known any man who insisted on silk next to his skin. However, he did not speak, for suddenly it came to him that Macéo, in belittling his silks and linen, was calling attention to them.

The general turned toward the table where his staff waited. "Come, sir, and meet my officers." He led the way across the room and presented each officer in turn. First there was General José Miro Argenter, chief of staff. Then Alfonso Goulet.

Pedro Díaz and the Ducasse brothers, black and almost surly, themselves called butchers.

All the officers bowed to Mingo and, after congratulations on his escape from the *Virginius*, filed out of the *bohio*. Soto followed them, heading for the creek and the cockfights.

Antonio Macéo, arrogant and implacable, remained standing until his guest accepted a place on a plank bench, then he sat on a goods box near a larger box that served as his desk. He eased the tightness of his trousers over his knees and leaned forward, cupping his hands upon his knees, and for the first time his eyes wavered and he looked away. "You may be certain, Señor, that my army will avenge the *Virginius*."

"I aim to help." Mingo leaned back against the wall; then, remembering the coat was not his and might be soiled, he sat up straight again. "That's one reason I came to join you."

"And what is another reason?" The general asked quickly, frigidity in his voice.

Mingo Dabney would not evade the issue or resort to guile. He met Macéo's sharp stare and spoke frankly. "I've heard folks say you are a fighting man. Captain Fry said so. And Elmo Batson. So did Señorita Galban, and when I saw her back home she told me you wanted recruits."

The Brown One folded his arms, retreating into his dignity. The left lid almost closed. "I assume you know that *La Entorcha* is in this camp?"

"I'm glad to hear it." He was non-committal, betraying nothing. "I hope for the privilege of seeing her."

Macéo slid the tips of his fingers over the ball of his thumb, watching the slow movements of his fingers. "Naturally," he said, without looking up.

"Then you will send for her?" Mingo asked it hopefully, a bit too hopefully.

"No, Señor." His words were emphatic though his voice still was soft. "There is much that you do not understand," he spoke slowly. "I am a Mambi. We Mambises do not send for *La Entorcha*. We go to her."

The way he said it, the tense reverence of his tone, the wisp of rapture in his eyes, touched a chord of comprehension and a truth was born within the pilgrim. Antonio Macéo believed the legend he had created. She was thunder in the sun, a symbol to all Mambises and the star of the east to this man, the greatest Mambi of them all. Superstition he himself had created, or miracle of heaven, Antonio Macéo believed it. This bronze man built his faith in himself and in Cuba's destiny upon a sign, the roll of thunder as he held a child aloft. "I understand," said Mingo. "I, too, will go to her if she will receive me."

The Brown One got up and walked to the window and stood there, one hand resting on the sill. He looked down toward the creek, toward his troops and came back and sat on the goods box, facing Mingo once more. "Señor, I will take you to *La Entorcha*. She recruited your presence here and you have earned the honor of her blessing." The light was gone from his face and he straightened his massive shoulders, sitting more erect. "First, though, may I trouble you with a few questions?"

"I am at your service." Mingo crossed his legs and his right leg dangled.

Macéo's mood was thoughtful. "Señor Dabney, do you think your country will intervene in Cuba?"

The question surprised Mingo and threw him off guard. He had no idea what the United States was planning to do in Cuba. "I reckon you know more about that than I do. But I'll bet my country is having a fit over the *Virginius*. I bet some folks are talking war."

"The United States will not go to war over the *Virginius*." Macéo said it bluntly. "However, some of us are afraid that, sooner or later, your country will intervene —"

"Afraid?" Mingo gaped at the general, amazed that a little neighbor like Cuba should fear the United States. "What's there to be afraid of?"

His artlessness was apparent and the Cuban shrugged.

"The money lords of your country have determined a policy of aggressive imperialism. They call it manifest destiny and speak eloquently of service to the weak."

The full meaning of the remarks was lost on the woodsman, but he didn't like Macéo's tone or his manner as he spoke of the United States. "Suppose we leave my country out of this." He was twisting the tuft of hair. "But let me tell you something. The best way to keep my country from coming down here and throwing the Spaniards out, is for you Cubans to throw 'em out first."

Macéo's jaw set and he spoke from behind closed teeth, his lips scarcely moving. "You are a forthright man, Señor Dabney." He stood and walked away, going to the far side of the room and looking at a map of Cuba pinned on the wall.

Mingo Dabney rose and stepped toward the general. He intended to say more, it was in his heart to say more; but the words never came, for he glanced out of the door and there, walking alone through the grove of mango trees, was Rafaela Galban.

La Entorcha never came to men! But there she came toward the *bohio* of her guardian, to the hut where a Dabney waited.

Antonio Macéo turned from his map and saw the startled look on Mingo's face, then peered out into the grove, gasping his astonishment. Mingo shifted nearer the window and Macéo stepped to the door and was standing there, his shoulders erect but his head slightly bowed, when Rafaela entered the hut.

Her black mantilla was over her hair and hung loose down her back. Her linen dress was almost to the floor, cool flowing linen. She glanced appraisingly at her guardian, then quickly and searchingly at Mingo. "Señor Dabney." There was obvious relief in her voice and she extended her slender hand. "We welcome you to the Mambises' Cuba."

He held her hand only a moment, freeing it as he bowed. "It is a privilege to see you again, Rafaela."

The sunlight streamed through the doorway, touching her

mantilla, glowing the silver sheen beneath. Macéo looked from one to the other, and drew back into the shadows. *La Entorcha* was wearing linen; she who usually wore the cotton of the poor, the fabric of the meek. *La Entorcha* never came to men, but she had come to the *bohio* where this *gringo* was, this alien.

"—Soto says I blab more than a Haitian, but there is a lot I got to know about Cuba. . . ." He was friendly and free with her, the unbeliever chatting with thunder in the sun.

Rafaela laughed. It was a merry laugh and Macéo's black eyes clouded. The symbol was laughing. She was gay. She sat on a bench, smoothing her dress and nodding to the men. "Please sit down."

Mingo sat on a camp stool by the window. The Brown One sat at his desk, his eyes roving from his lodestar to the infidel. This was Antonio Macéo who maddened the Spaniards by his genius, this the apostle of José Martí, challenger of an empire. Now, sitting by a goods box that was his desk, his hands cupped over his knees, he was baffled and bewildered as he felt the temple shaking at its foundation. His misery gnawed at his fears and his superstitions and he was silent, moody, watching this threat to a faith he had created and that now balanced so precariously.

"—And what do you think of *la tierra del Mambi?*" She was chit-chatting and it was such a trite thing to ask that she laughed at the triteness, tossing back her head, and her mantilla hung free and wavered.

"Some mighty fine timber in these hills." Mingo scarcely was aware that he said it, for he was thinking of the lonely, distracted man in the shadows, seeing a thing that Rafaela did not see.

The Brown One's hair and lips were the only visible indications of his Negroid heritage, and yet Africa was the explanation of the pride and sensitiveness of Antonio Macéo. He never allowed himself to forget he was neither black nor white in a society where white was the color of the overlords, the saints of heaven, God Himself. Therefore, he remained stolidly behind the gap of color, dreading the snub or the equally humiliating exaggeration of hospitality.

Mingo's compassion, the affinity of one brave man for another, suddenly was pity, and that was wrong. Macéo's brown skin bore twenty wounds for his country; but it was brown in a world ruled by a white sword, a sword with a cross at the hilt. The pilgrim yearned, at that instant, to reach out and touch this man and therewith tell him things no words could explain. But Antonio Macéo, silent and aloof and stunned, was brown marble, the embodiment of all the bitterness flourishing in the spirits of those men set apart, forbidden the fruits of the arbors they till. This man, this maker of symbols, was himself a dark symbol, a page from the somber story of the disjointed brotherhood of man. . . .

Rafaela was talking and Mingo heard her mention the United States. "Many of our people wonder if your people will intervene in Cuba."

Again Mingo was puzzled, but replied politely, "If I was a little fellow fighting a big fellow, I'd be mighty glad to get a big fellow on my side." The whole thing was as simple as that to Mingo Dabney.

Rafaela lowered her head slightly toward her left shoulder, glancing at her guardian. "You see, sir, Americans speak bluntly."

The general spoke for the first time since they sat down, addressing the *gringo*. "I, too, will speak bluntly." He raised his finger to emphasize his solemn utterance. "If Cuba does not defeat Spain soon, America will intervene and if she does, she will seek to dictate our policies. That was José Martí's fear. And mine."

Mingo turned to Rafaela. "You've been to my country. Do you think we're hard to get along with?"

She stared at him in surprise and Macéo scowled. Mingo realized immediately that he had said the wrong thing, and

184

looked to her for an explanation, but she said, "I must return to my *bohio*. If you gentlemen will excuse me . . ."

"I'll see you home." He said it naturally, without thought, then, remembering Jamaica, was sorry the second he said it.

Macéo flinched as though he had been struck and Rafaela lifted her head disdainfully. "I need no escort among the Mambises, Señor." She swept out of the hut and into the late afternoon sun.

Mingo Dabney watched her until she was beyond sight and instantly was aware of the vibrating tension within the room. Quickly he looked at Macéo, and the Cuban's eyes were bright and sharp, his demeanor plainly antagonistic, even hostile.

"Señor Dabney!" Mingo had never heard a voice so cold, so bitter. "*La Entorcha's* political opinions are not asked. Never!"

"I'm sorry. I was only being polite." A hint of rebellion flared in his tone and he sat down, resentment smoldering within him. He was a stranger and how was he to know the taboos? He wanted only to love and to be loved, but his pride had taken all the slaps his pride intended to take. Mingo Dabney, too, was sensitive. He would spit on no man, but no man would spit on him.

Macéo walked to the window and looked out, judging his words before he spoke them. "*La Entorcha* is a symbol to all Mambises and is beyond politics —"

"All right," said Mingo, interrupting. "I get it, and next time I'll know better." He was no longer flustered or embarrassed. He was not being treated with the courtesy and hospitality that Lebanon gladly gave to all strangers. "Up where I live we have customs, too. And you, or anybody else, might violate 'em." He got slowly to his feet, facing the general. "I must ask your pardon for ignorance of Cuban ways. You see, sir, when Señorita Galban and Señor Martí came up to see us, they didn't tell us about your symbols and our intervention. They just wanted American men and

185

American money. I came here to join your army. May I direct our conversation to that aim?"

Macéo wheeled and stepped to the desk. "*Sí.* I think it better if we come to an understanding."

"So do I." Mingo said it quickly and with emphasis.

The Brown One tapped his fingers on his desk, looking squarely at the *gringo*, this threat to his destiny; a remote threat surely, but a threat, nevertheless. He must be rid of this restless intruder, the cloudy brown eyes and reckless confidence. "General Máximo Gómez has crossed into Camagüey. He needs men badly and will welcome you to his staff. I will give you a letter of introduction."

Mingo's resentment boiled over. "Wait a minute, mister. I came a long way to fight with you. If you don't want me in your army, just say so!"

"That is not the point." Macéo waved his hand, brushing the remark aside. "My army is an attacking force and my officers must be trained men —"

"I didn't come here to be an officer. I came to fight."

Macéo glared at him. "My officers fight! Casualties among my officers are forty per cent."

Again Mingo had blundered, but he didn't care. He was indignant and hurt. "I went to a hell of a lot of trouble to get here, and now you tell me I'm not wanted —"

The Brown One suddenly was on the defensive, floundering as he offered an explanation that really was an evasion. "Since your experience with Sagaldo you are marked by the Spaniards. I can not take the responsibility for your life —"

"Wait a minute." Mingo gripped both hands on the goods box and the veins showed in his wrists. "I thought every Cuban was a marked man —"

Macéo flushed. "I will send an escort with you to General Gómez —"

"Like hell you will.'" The woodsman's emotions were raw and his manners were raw and it mattered not to him that Antonio Macéo was a general. His pride was in turmoil and he knew, and the knowledge chilled him, that if Macéo said the wrong thing now, he would hit him. Mingo Dabney was afraid of the urge, not because Macéo was a commander, not because of any thunder in the sun or symbolism; but because he, Mingo Dabney, was a Southerner and Antonio Macéo was a mulatto. The pilgrim wanted to seal a brotherhood, not rip it further apart. He took a deep breath, controlling himself, and said, "I heard a lot of pretty words about Cuba needing strong men to help the meek. Well, I'm husky and I'm here. And I sure as hell don't like the way I'm being treated."

The brown cheeks of Antonio Macéo were red, a hot red. His pride was as strong as Dabney pride and he compressed his lips, beating back the insult that burned his tongue. He steeled himself, holding his silence, and began sorting papers on his desk. Mingo turned sharply and stepped toward the door, each step jarring his anger. "I'll send your clothes back as soon as I get my own."

Macéo looked up, the hot flush still in his cheeks. "Never mind —"

"I'll send your clothes back." He reached the door.

"Very well." The Brown One busied himself with his papers again. "I will have your quarters arranged until you are ready to go to General Gómez. Or to some of the bands roaming the hills. Or—" He looked up then. "Back to the United States."

"Don't bother yourself." Mingo was standing in the doorway. "Soto will arrange for me to eat and sleep."

"No!" The general smacked his desk with the flat of his hand. "No, I say. Soto lives with the *impedimenta* when he is not scouting. I have no military control over the *impedimenta*. . . ."

"And, by God, you have no control over me!"

Macéo banged the desk again, but smothered his anger. "We gain nothing by this talk. The *impedimenta* are civilians and camp followers. Riffraff. A man of your position cannot eat with the *impedimenta*. You cannot compromise yourself and my army."

The pilgrim put one hand against the door jamb and stared at the idol of the Mambises, himself a slave to caste. The American had come to fight for the meek, but must not eat with the lowly. A dozen angry retorts flashed in his mind, but he spoke none of them. Instead, he stood silent, his eyes speaking his mind. He stuck both hands in the pockets of the Dutch linen coat and remembered sugar sacks on men in the hovels of Santiago de Cuba. "Sir," he said in deliberate disdain. "As long as I am not a part of your army, I will eat where I please and with whom I please."

Macéo accepted the stare, and his eyes wavered and he glanced down at his papers again. "Good day, Señor Dabney."

Mingo turned his back on Antonio Macéo and walked into the sunshine of the late afternoon. It streaked through the mangoes, and in the golden shafts there shimmered dust from the feet of Quintín Banderas' hill fighters, dust from the feet of Alfonso Goulet's *machete*-men, they of the cock feathers, dust from the bare feet of the Army of the Oriente.

He walked slowly down the path toward the creek. His anger was gone, leaving only a great emptiness. He was hurt, deeply hurt, and humiliated; for he asked only the right to live, and love, and be loved.

He walked on through the mango grove until he saw Soto coming toward him. The goatherd was grinning until suddenly the grin was gone, and he peered at Mingo, shaking his head slowly. "Ah-h-h, *amigo*. Not good, eh?" He touched his arm, and the touch was warm.

"Where are my clothes?" The voice was flat and dull.

The Mambi fell in step. "Down by the creek. Nice and clean." Again he peered at Mingo. "Hear me, *compadre*! General Macéo . . ." He shrugged. "Macéo is not Martí. Martí would never send a man away unhappy. Um-m-m . . ."

"He doesn't want me in his army."

Soto stopped abruptly and his head lifted until his eyes

188

rested full on Mingo's face. "S-o-o-o. Macéo prays for soldiers, but does not want a *gringo*." He held out his open hand. "So! *La Entorcha* flames and a recruit follows, but her guardian does not want him. Ah-h-h . . ."

"That's right. He gave me a dozen reasons." Mingo swooped his hand through the air. "To hell with it." He lengthened his stride, Soto trotting beside him, until he reached the creek. His clothes were on the grass and he removed the linen, taking it off fast, stripping off the silk.

The Mambi sat on the ground, rocking to and fro and pursing his lips, mumbling to himself. Often he glanced at Mingo, darting his glances from under lowered brows. Finally, though, he seemed to find the words he sought. "*Amigo,* I know why he does not want you in his army."

The American did not reply, but pulled on his shoes, stamping his feet until his shoes fitted snugly again. He began lacing them, ignoring Soto.

"Um-m-m-m . . ." The Mambi tilted back his head, peering from under lowered lids, and there was patience and wisdom in his smile. "First we will eat. Then we will feel better."

"Where'll we eat?" Mingo demanded. He jerked his thumb over his shoulder toward the camp. "I sure as hell won't eat with Macéo's army." It was a petulant, childish thing to say.

"But no-o-o!" Soto spread his hands in surprise that anyone should ask such a question. "We eat with the *impedi- menta*. They forage for the army and help themselves first. The best portions."

"I'm not hungry," Mingo said, still petulant.

The Mambi dismissed such talk with a flip of his hand. "Sometimes a man is not hungry in his mind, but always he is hungry in his belly. You will eat. Chicken, perhaps. Ah-h-h!"

"I said I'm not hungry." Mingo jerked his hat into place, slanting it from force of habit.

Soto stepped to the pilgrim's side and touched his arm. "Antonio Macéo is Cuba's destiny, and his destiny is a child he found in the mountains." Soto, the guide of Guantánamo,

189

the herder of eight goats, was sad. "*Amigo*, a living symbol is a dangerous symbol, for all living things change. A girl-child is a dare to fate, for a girl-child grows into a woman."

Mingo did not speak. He was watching the shadows stretch through the mango grove. The Army of the Oriente was building campfires for the night. A lantern was lighted in Macéo's *bohio* and two sentries took their posts at his door.

"We will go eat," Soto said, laying his hand on his friend's shoulder. "Warm food in the belly eases the pain in the heart."

"I told you I'm not hungry."

"Then let us go to a fire." He patted Mingo's shoulder. "A fire is warm and friendly. The *impedimenta* sing songs and make jokes."

"I'm not cold."

The Mambi took his hand away. "Then it is true." He said it slowly. "Ah-h-h, *amigo!* You have ridden so far, but you are not hungry. The sun is almost down and it is cold in the hills, but you need no warmth." He was smiling as he talked, nodding and smiling a blessing upon his friend.

Mingo turned his eyes from the forest and looked into the face of the goatherd; and Soto said, "A beautiful thing has happened to my comrade. He has come into the hills where the white torch burns, and its flame is bright in his heart."

The pilgrim was ashamed that he had been abrupt with this little man, and he put his arm around Soto's shoulder. "Let's cross the creek, *amigo*. Let's get some food and warm ourselves. Me and you."

MINGO DABNEY

Chapter **15**   The foul, half-naked *impedimenta,* foragers and scavengers for the Army of the Oriente, received Mingo with curiosity and suspicion, and Soto with raucous affection. Their carts and oxen and campfires were jumbled on the slope across the creek, snarled in senseless confusion. Some of the oxen had running sores and stiff joints. So did some of the *impedimenta*.

No wonder the proud warriors of Macéo spat on these outcasts, cursing them as dogs that defiled their mother's milk. They hunted like wolves until the kill was made, then fought and snarled among themselves for the loot. A cart was their bed, a blazing log their hearth. Theft was their right, battle their amusement, death their pardon. These pickpockets and murderers were not the meek; they were the merciless.

Their hook-pointed *machetes,* carried in hard leather holders, were fastened at the back of their belts, the scabbards down the crease of their buttocks. The *machete* was the lengthening of a man's arm, an implement to take or give life; a halberd for a Spaniard, an ax for a tree, a knife for a beef. The broad side was a bludgeon for a lazy ox, the filed edge was a saber, a scimitar.

Mingo Dabney, accustomed to the camaraderie of a Lebanon lumber camp, was fascinated by the *impedimenta,* but appalled by their slovenliness. However, the things he saw took his mind off Antonio Macéo, slackening his wrath and his disappointment. He would eat and sleep with the *impedimenta*, and wait for Elmo Batson, then decide his next step.

Several of the scavengers crowded around Soto and Mingo, slapping the guide on the back, calling him goat bile and hugging him. Some of them reached boldly to feel Mingo's shirt. Others eyed his shoes. The woodsman was cautious and silent, leaving everything to Soto. There was no indication of trouble, only childish curiosity and open envy of a man who had a shirt, and pants, and shoes; a man who had everything. Soto pushed the crowd away and pointing at Mingo said over and over, "My friend, Señor Dabney. *Amigo. Compadre.*"

One of the men stepped close to Mingo. "Ah-h-h. From the *bohio* of Macéo to the wallow of the *impedimenta*. So-o-o!" He stepped back and bowed elaborately. "A muckety muck! Why does he come to us? Why should a washed lamb come to a pigsty?"

"Because he is my friend." Soto grinned at the circle that had formed about them. "He is a big man and has a big belly. So I tell him the *impedimenta* have the best food and are the best comrades."

Mingo grinned, too, and one of the *impedimenta* returned the grin and pressed close. "What does he bring us, Soto? You say he is a big man, what does he bring?"

The goatherd shrugged and glanced at the pilgrim, indicating he should give them something. Mingo Dabney had nothing. He propped against the huge wheel of one of the carts and looked at the Mambises, at their battered faces, their scarred bodies. This time he didn't grin. He locked his fingers together, holding them across his chest and tapping his thumbs together. "I bring you nothing. I have nothing." There was neither pride nor pity in his words.

The Mambises looked from one to the other, then at Soto and back at Mingo. One of them scowled. "Nothing!" He snorted and scuffed the ground with his naked heel. "A *gringo* with nothing!"

"Nothing," Mingo repeated.

"*Recristo!*" Several Mambises slapped their thighs, wagging their heads and laughing. "A poor *gringo!* All the miracles are not of the Church." They half raised their hands in the slouchy, careless salute of a careless brotherhood. "*Saludo, compadre!* Welcome, El Dabney."

"El Dabney!" Some took up the name and others repeated it, chanting it like children at play. More scavengers came running from their campfires and joined the rhythmic jubilee. One was Pepe Barea, the coachman, and he shouted, "El Dabney! I know him. I served him in Santiago de Cuba. And then I ran away." He began weeping his excitement.

The sight of the Mambi flooded Mingo's memories and his heart tightened, and he slapped Pepe Barea on the back and watched him dance away, stamping his bare feet in the dust and waving his *machete*.

The rhythm of the mumbo-jumbo, the pounding of the naked feet, pulsed into Mingo's blood and he threw back his head and laughed. The campfires and the coming twilight, the smell of smoke hanging low in the woods, the beauty of camaraderie. All this he found in the Cuban hills. And there was more. Oxen again and wheels, things they had in Lebanon, things he understood. So he laughed, a man strong again, feeling his strength among strong men.

The *impedimenta* broke off their chanting, their crazy antics, and laughed, too. Laughter, they could own because it was free.

Soto motioned for Mingo to follow and they walked among the carts. The guide peered into them until he found one he liked. It was better than most and he said, "We will sleep here tonight. This is our cart."

The vehicle was almost as large as some of the *bohios* Mingo had seen, and he judged its length at twelve feet, its width at eight. A high canvas top was fastened to bent ribs and protected the bed and sides, making the cart snug and comfortable. It was a hut on wheels, a Conestoga wagon with one axle.

Mingo braced his hand on the back and vaulted inside. He kicked a pile of hammocks out of the way and pulled an ax out of a barrel, freeing it from an assortment of pots and scrap. He ran his thumb along the ax edge and it was nicked, but the handle was straight and smooth. "Soto. Who owns this wagon?"

"Nobody." The Mambi was standing outside, amused at the *gringo* taking so much trouble to prepare a place to sleep. "It was a Spanish sugar cart and the *impedimenta* stole it. They will cut it up for wood and eat the oxen that hauled it."

"Like hell they will." The woodsman was tugging at the bent ribs, testing them. "This is a good wagon." He stamped on the boards. Two were warped and loose, but the others were sound. "A man could live in this thing. . . ."

"Men do," Soto said, then asked, "Aren't you hungry yet?"

Mingo jumped out of the cart and rubbed his hands together, "Uh huh. Sort of."

The *impedimenta*, numbering less than a hundred, had at least twenty campfires and each smoked worse than the others. They squatted around the fires in small groups, each group preparing its own food. There was no organization, for none took commands, and none dared give them. Mingo asked Soto about it and the guide shrugged. "Guttersnipes. Garbage collectors." He leaned against the cartwheel and shook his head. "They are lost in the woods, *amigo*. They hop about like *grillos* and die like flies."

"Why don't they eat together? Save food and time and work."

"Together!" Soto sneered and spat. "That bunch of bones and scabby flesh . . ." He pointed toward a group whose cook fire was so big it drove them back. "They are from Santiago de Cuba. Carriage drivers and stable cleaners." He tossed up his hands in exasperation. "And that collection of carbuncles . . ." He pointed at another group coughing and rubbing their eyes as they tried to cook over a smoke smudge of green wood. "Butchers and meat skinners from the slaughterhouses of Bayamo." He lifted his shoulders and sighed. "A man from Santiago de Cuba and a man from Bayamo might steal together, and kill together, but they could never be comrades."

Things were better back home: Yankees and Southerners at least ate together.

"They don't know much about oxen either." Mingo nodded toward a grove where several oxen, still yoked, were standing in smoke, their heads low, seeking clean air. One, a big red beast, was badly crippled. "Why don't they do something for that one?"

"Why should they?" Soto was patient with the *gringo's* ignorance. "The red ox belonged to Pepe Sánchez and Pepe Sánchez is dead. Soon they will eat the ox of Pepe Sánchez."

"Good God!" Mingo flapped his hands in disapproval. "What will they use to haul their carts?"

"Señor!" Soto poked out his lips and cocked his head to one side. "They will steal an ox." He started toward one of the fires. "We go and see if we can find a chicken. Do you like chicken?" He wrinkled his nose and sniffed. "Or roast kid, um-m-m." He sniffed again. "Or perhaps a nice fat *jutia.*"

"Chicken," said Mingo emphatically, fanning away the smoke.

Pepe Barea and three more Mambises were at the campfire, walking round and round, poking at it with long sticks and ducking to avoid the smoke. An iron pot, sunk in the midst of the roaring logs, was bubbling furiously, smelling of chicken and onions.

The woodsman circled the blaze until he was upwind. "Why do you make such a big fire?" He asked it innocently, glancing at Soto and cautioning him to silence.

The Mambises looked from one to the other and shrugged. What an ignorant man the *gringo* was. What a babe in the woods. One of them, a tolerant fellow with a big red nose, assumed the burden of explanation. "A big fire, Señor, makes more heat. And there is plenty of wood."

Mingo meditated the words as though turning the wisdom in his mind, then said politely. "Your fire is too good. It is so big and hot you cannot get close to tend your chicken."

"So!" The man spoke tersely, his chin uplifted. "I am Pepe Rosado and I made the fire. You will teach us poor Mambises how the *gringos* do it, eh?" His tone was sharp, accentuating the sarcasm.

"Ah-h-h, no!" Mingo Dabney was learning fast. "In my country we are the worst fire builders in the world. But in Mexico —"

"Um-m-m." They stuck out their lips and lifted their heads. "Mexico!" They cut their eyes around at one another. Here was something; an American admitting the *gringos* did not excel in everything. *Por Dios!* All the miracles were not of the Church.

Soto was grinning. Mingo never had been near Mexico, but he sensed a deep-rooted feeling against the big-talking way of some of his countrymen. He put his hands over his face, protecting it from the heat, and pushed one of the blazing logs aside. "In Mexico they build the best fires. In Cuba they have the fattest chickens." He shoved another log aside, rolling it until the blaze was extinguished. "Ah-h-h." He smacked his lips.

"*Sí!*" The men began yanking logs from the fire. Pepe Barea burned his hand in his excitement and Pepe Rosado berated him as a clumsy simpleton, fit only to clean stables.

Mingo scowled at Soto, warning him to hold his laughter, then looked around until he found an armful of dry branches. The wood was hard and heavy and he smelled it, wondering what wood it was. It should make good embers and he placed the sticks around the pot, gently blowing them into a

196

small blaze that caught and crackled. He stepped back and was proud. He should have been. Mingo Dabney, a tree man, was burning mahogany.

A thin chimney of smoke trickled up from the logs and the pot simmered, and the Mambises looked into the kettle and at one another. Others of the *impedimenta* joined the circle, staring at the little blaze and at the man who made it. Mingo hopped onto the bed of a cart and sat there, swinging his legs and grinning at his admirers while he waited for his supper.

The oxen were lowing, for darkness was near and the fires excited the beasts and the smoke troubled them. Mingo went to an abandoned cart and tore strips of canvas from its covering. He borrowed palm oil from another cart and bandaged the stiff leg of the red ox. The Mambises watched him, none speaking, swag-jawed as they saw the *gringo* use his beautiful time to help the ox of Pepe Sánchez when he could be sitting down and swapping tales of valor and love.

"*Mira!* Look! And Pepe Sánchez is dead." The Mambises were whispering among themselves. "El Dabney is a good man. A kind man. He eats with us instead of Macéo. Ah-h-h."

The chicken was tough and stringy and needed seasoning, but the American sat on the bed of the cart, gnawing the bones and spitting out the gristle, licking his greasy fingers. Other Mambises, jealous at being slighted, joined the group and one of them brought El Dabney a corncake dipped in sugar syrup. Another gave him the bone of a roasted kid and smackingly demonstrated how to suck the marrow.

The pilgrim feasted and was at peace with himself, almost. These men liked him, and he liked them. Someone slipped away to the carts near headquarters and came back with raw rum. They shared that with Mingo, too, and as they drank they related grandiose stories about themselves, boasting their prowess with women, their courage against Spaniards.

Pepe Rosado, his red nose bright with rum, hopped up on the cart beside Mingo and pounded his back. "Ah-h-h."

He nodded, and his looped earrings of beaten silver swung as he nodded. "Are you not happy you found us?"

"I sure am," Mingo said and meant it.

"Here . . ." The Mambi flung out his arms at his comrades. "We feast and drink and laugh. There is no rum in the *bohio* of Macéo. Ah-h-h. It is terrible to be a leader, eh, El Dabney? What hell to be a hero."

The crowd was singing *La Bayamesa*, the anthem of the revolution, and Mingo was learning the words when the courier came for Soto to report to headquarters. Mingo walked with him to their cart. "Now what? Do you reckon Macéo aims to run me off? Or try to?"

"No." The guide was emphatic. "Macéo cannot afford to notice you while you are with the *impedimenta*." His grin flashed in the light of a blazing log. "Perhaps he wants me to teach him to build a Mexican fire." Soto pointed at the cart. "You wait here."

Darkness spread down from the hills and the woodsman watched the night chase the last shadows away. The *grillos* were hissing and rain frogs called from the creek. The fires, helter-skelter up the slope, stabbed the night and the Mambises were lean, ragged figures in the reflection. The oxen lowed. The men laughed.

Two enormous Negroes, drums at their backs and scars on their faces, came out of the night and walked among the *impedimenta*, holding out their right hands for food; and their hands were piled high. Haitians. Bound to be. Their drums were hollow logs with goat skins stretched tight across each end. Mingo wanted to ask for news of Elmo, but they did not come close enough for conversation. Too, he was afraid he might say the wrong thing or ask the wrong question. Already he had run into so many taboos. He must wait until Soto returned.

The Haitians heard his name and peered at him through the smoke, then vanished as quickly as they came and Mingo stretched out on the floor of the cart, his head cradled in his hands, listening to the throb of the camp. The rum in his belly was warm and his muscles relaxed, easing into the good tired feeling of a strong man weary.

The drums were talking, Haitian hands pounding the hollow logs. A challenge sounded just outside the camp, and the slow roll began, telling the news . . . "Rrrrr-oo-oo-oo-oo-oo— tat—tat—tat—Boom! Boom! . . ." El Dabney, a big man, was in the camp of the *impedimenta*. Ah-h-h! He bound the leg of the ox of Pepe Sánchez and Pepe Sánchez is dead!

The drums joined their rumble to the sound of the night things, the hissing and screeching, and the low, soft singing that came from the banks of the creek. A feeling of exhaustion spread through Mingo's body and he stretched and sighed. Tomorrow he would decide his course. Tonight he would stretch and feel warm in his belly; and he would sleep.

Soto put his hand on Mingo's knee and the woodsman snapped open his eyes and sat up quickly. "What is it? Is it Elmo?"

The guide shook his head. "She sent for you. At her *bohio*."

Mingo sprang from the cart but the Mambi halted him. "She is going to the plains to raise recruits. It is her work —"

"I know that. Come on."

Soto gripped his arm. "I will guide her to the plains. I will remain two, perhaps three weeks. I have learned that the man who betrayed Martí was trusted by Martí." He tightened his grip. "So I look for a Cuban he trusted."

"I hope you find him." Mingo was impatient. "Now let's go."

They circled the fires of the *impedimenta*, and at the creek Soto halted. "*Amigo —*" He was irresolute, debating a decision. "You may want to go to Gómez' army. Or to a band of hill fighters perhaps. When I return, I will go with you."

Mingo was touched. "Thanks. I'll be around somewhere." He did not care to say more. "Let's hurry along."

They crossed the creek and followed the path beyond

Macéo's headquarters to a thicket of piñon saplings, their red blooms faintly silvered by the moon. An escort of six soldiers, Goulet's warriors, were resting in the shelter of the piñons, close to an opening in the trees. Mingo and the guide pushed through and came to the rear of a small *bohio*. A lamp glowed inside and lanterns hung before the door, and the thicket was dim yellow, streaked black by the trees.

Two mules with sidesaddles drowsed near the corner of the *bohio* and Soto stopped, pointing ahead. Mingo picked his way into the dull light.

Rafaela Galban and the old duenna were sitting on a bench in front of the shack. He paused for an instant, looking down at her. "You sent for me?"

"Yes. Sit down, Mingo."

The old woman went inside and Mingo remained standing. Her riding skirt and jacket were black, and a dark shawl covered her forehead. Her face was pale and her eyes were wide and black.

"Sit down." She glanced up at him and moved nearer the end of the bench. "I am going away —"

"Soto told me." He sat down then, sliding his hands around the brim of his hat.

The ruby ring glowed in the light and she touched it, twisting it. "I must raise recruits. The Army of the Oriente will strike for the plains soon, and there must be more recruits."

"Macéo is sending you away?"

"No. Macéo never gives orders to me." She folded her hands in her lap and was as calm, as cool as winter twilight. "You would not leave, so I decided it best for me to go." She hesitated as though expecting him to pick up her words, at least to comment, but he was silent, looking at her.

A second passed, then two, and an expression of annoyance, maybe vexation, was on her face. Still he said nothing, only watching her, and slowly turning his hat between his fingers.

"Mingo." She accepted the issue his silence made inevitable. "My guardian is agitated. Perhaps frightened —"

"Of what?" He, too, was constrained, expressing nothing, betraying less.

"Of you!" Her chin went up and her demeanor was haughty. "I assured him that your impetuosity affects neither him nor me, but I could not placate him—no, don't interrupt —" She lifted her hand. "We must come to an agreement. My guardian is a man of foreboding. I do not understand his fear, but I never question General Macéo. Just as he never gives commands to me —" She stopped abruptly, looking from him to the lanterns, the woods.

Mingo put his hat beside him and locked his hands around his knee. "Yes. I'm listening."

She was gazing beyond the thicket at her escort, the fangs of Goulet. "Antagonism between my guardian and the son of a family I visited in the United States could lead to disaster. So I am going away for a while."

"If Macéo doesn't want me around, he can run me off —"

"No!"

"Why not? He's the boss."

Rafaela frowned her irritation, tossing her head in impatience. "Your perception, Mingo, is no match for your persistence. Already you are El Dabney, and should Macéo order you away, the Mambises might wonder —" Again she raised her hand, halting his interruption. "Please. I must be heard. You leave me no choice, so I will say it." She stared straight ahead, almost as though he were not there at all. "If my guardian drives El Dabney from his army, the Mambises will wonder if the light in a *gringo's* eyes is hate for Spaniards or infatuation for *La Entorcha*."

"Or love for Rafaela Galban," he said and took his hands from his knee and began twisting the tuft of hair.

She sprang to her feet and glared down at him, her chin trembling her exasperation. "Señor Dabney! A nation's soul is more important than a man's heart. I am going to the plains. You will not follow me!"

"I have no intention of following you, Rafaela." He stood, too, and picked up his hat from the bench.

Her lips parted, a tiny frown wrinkling the bridge of her nose, and she looked at him, turning her head to look, to stare. Then she bit her lower lip, her teeth whitening the skin. "The *Virginius*?"

"That's right. I have a debt, and you have a duty." He put on his hat and propped one hand against the *bohio*, the other on his hip. "A woman can not forget her dedication. Well, Rafaela, a man can not forget the cries of his comrades."

She touched her shawl, drawing it tighter about her head, and moved to leave him, then hesitated. "I am going to the plains —"

"Yes. You said that."

"Macéo should reach the plains by the dry season. Will you be with his army, Mingo?"

"I don't know."

She turned away, slowly, then quickly, and stepped to the door, motioning for the duenna. The old woman blew out the lamp and came outside into the light of the lanterns. She took *La Entorcha's* arm, and they walked toward the mules, leaving the pilgrim alone by the doorway.

Soto came from the shadows and helped the women mount and they rode away, none looking back except the Mambi, and he waved his hand in a gesture of farewell.

Mingo waited until they were out of sight, watching them through the piñons until the night closed behind them. He felt for the bench and sat down, staring into the woods. The drums were pounding to the northwest, the direction she was traveling. The *grillos* were out again, hissing and hopping, and the soft call of the pigeon mourned in the thicket. Mingo Dabney got up and put out the lanterns, leaving them hanging by the door, and walked through the camp of the Army of the Oriente.

Quintín Banderas' hill fighters muttered as he passed. "*Compadre*." They were calling him comrade.

The cock-feathered fangs of Goulet smiled their greetings. "El Dabney. *Amigo*." They were calling him friend.

He crossed the creek and went to his cart. The *impedimenta's* fires were embers and the foragers were bedding down. Mingo crawled into his cart and a great weariness eased over him and he reached for one of the hammocks, folding it under his head. From the camp of the Army of the Oriente came the bugle call of *silencio,* and the camp was hushed.

Only the drums quivered the stillness of the Mountains of Our Master, echoing the news of *la tierra del Mambi*. Máximo Gómez was across the Jabobo River—out of the hills. Elmo Batson was deep in the hills, traveling fast. *La Entorcha* was riding to the plains. A *gringo* was with Macéo's *impedimenta*. They called him El Dabney. . . .

MINGO DABNEY

Chapter **16**   Elmo Batson arrived at the camp with a light touch of chills and fever, a supply of quinine and a quart of whiskey, half gone. He was singing *John Henry* and shouting for Mingo Dabney.

> *This war's gonna kill me dead, Lawd, Lawd,*
> *John Henry —*

The woodsman heard the old song from beyond the bend of the path and he sat up quickly, shaking sleep from his eyes. Daybreak was squeezing out the night and pulling the clammy mist from the mountain coves.

"Where the hell is Mingo Dabney?" Then, "Lawd, Lawd, John Henry —" The words came again and Mingo leapt from his cart and ran along the path. Elmo's horse, drooping tired, was climbing the last stretch to the camp and the Lebanon man, suddenly homesick, was laughing and crying. He waved his arms and Elmo swung down and they stood there pounding each other's back and talking at the same time. "I got a million questions," Mingo said.

"So've I." Elmo caught the reins of his horse and they walked up the path. The *impedimenta* smiled and waved at El Dabney. "Be John Brown, son," the drummer said. "You running for sheriff around here?"

Mingo was grinning, his first really broad grin since Jamaica. "Nope. Just lit yesterday and haven't paid my poll tax. Everything all right with you?"

"Uh huh." They were among the carts and Elmo glanced at the dilapidated equipment. "How 'bout you?"

"Not worth a damn."

The drummer took off his floppy Panama hat and scratched his bald pate, red and peeling within its rim of sandy hair. Some of the Mambises had built a fire near Mingo's cart and his coffee was boiling. Elmo glanced around and broke out laughing. "We're a long way from taw, ain't we, bud?"

"A long way," the pilgrim said.

Elmo climbed on the bed of the cart, grunting his exertion. "All right. Let's have it."

"Let's get some food first." Mingo walked over to a campfire and got two plates of corn cakes and pork, and Elmo wolfed his food, washing it down with coffee and whiskey. Mingo began his account as far back as Mobile, but Elmo interrupted. He knew about Mobile.

"Start with the *Virginius*," he said and frowned. "It's all got to be done over again."

"Another supply ship?"

"Uh huh." The drummer slid his thumbs under his suspenders, loosening them. "Cap'n Fry trusted to luck. His luck was bad. Yours was good. So what's eating on you?"

Mingo jerked his head toward Macéo's *bohio*. "He doesn't want me around here."

Elmo felt for a cigar, bit off the end, and spat. "Well, now. I wonder how come?"

Mingo's attempted evasion was clumsy. "Maybe it's color. Me white and him mixed. Hell, that doesn't make any difference —"

"Hogwash." The drummer lit his cigar, puffing slowly, then examining the ash. "You can say 'Negro' all you please, but you still think 'nigra.' Americans just ain't color blind yet, but color's got nothing to do with your mixup."

"All right." He had to trust somebody. "It's Rafaela Galban —"

"Course it is," Elmo snorted. "Macéo puts his luck in a

sign, and along comes a Mississippi man threatening his luck. That's why he don't want you around. And I sure as hell don't blame him."

"Well, I sure as hell ain't leaving." Mingo picked up a nail from the floor of the cart and tossed it in a box.

The drummer got up and slapped dirt from the seat of his britches. "I'm going to Macéo. You come along—"

"Not me! I've been up there once and nobody's going to treat me that way again."

"You come along, son. Maybe I can get you two together." He reached for his bottle. "Got a touch of chills and fever." He put the bottle aside and wiped his lips, and stuck his cigar back in the corner of his mouth. "I aim to sell you to General Macéo—"

"Maybe I don't want it that way."

"Maybe I do!" Elmo hurled his cigar away. "I got to get supplies to this army. Best of everything, and I'm not trusting it to the Mambises." He jabbed his finger against the woodsman's shoulder. "You're the only man in these parts who knows pea-turkey about good equipment."

Mingo still was not convinced. "If you tried to ram somebody down my throat, I'd buck."

Elmo snorted. "If you were cornered like Macéo, you'd do what he'll do. You'd trade." He wagged his finger, emphasizing the words. "I'm in a hurry, son. So you just come on along with me." The drummer was smiling but he wanted no tampering with his plans.

The younger man hesitated a moment longer, then walked across the creek with Elmo, and through the camp toward headquarters of the Army of the Oriente.

General Macéo was attending to routine duties and several hundred Mambises crowded around, watching their brown idol pass judgment and fix punishment for offenders in his army. Elmo and Mingo inched and nudged their way through the spectators until they reached the inner circle. The commander was by the door of his *bohio*, surrounded by his staff, and seeing Elmo, nodded a greeting.

"I am happy to see you again, Señor Batson," he said properly. "I will be with you as soon as I wind up these routine matters."

He ignored Mingo Dabney completely.

Most of the cases concerned simple matters of discipline and he heard the complaints quickly, smiling at one or two, frowning at others. To one Mambi, accused of knifing a comrade in the arm, he said quietly, "I am displeased, Pepe."

The other Mambises scowled at the offender, accepting their idol's displeasure as a severe reprimand, and the man hung his head. Macéo's frown was punishment enough for most misdemeanors, but rape, murder and theft of supplies were punished by death. A frown for rascals, death for criminals.

Mingo and Elmo waited and watched, impressed by the general's infinite patience with his men. His staff was restless and Miro kept glancing at Elmo, but Macéo heard each case, nodding as Pepe López wailed that Pepe Brito had dulled his *machete*. "Did he steal your *machete*?" There was sudden wrath in Macéo's eyes.

"No-o-o," said Pepe López. "He borrowed it to cut wood —"

"Brito!" Macéo scarcely raised his voice and yet his voice snapped. "Why did you not use your own *machete*?"

The accused Mambi, a gangling black man with a huge brass bracelet on his left wrist, scratched his head and pondered. He looked from the general to the other officers, then at the company. "Use MY *machete* to cut wood? Why dull my *machete* when Pepe López will lend me his?"

Elmo chuckled and the pilgrim grinned. However, Macéo was stern and shook his head slowly. "I am displeased, Pepe Brito." He turned his back and the Mambises stirred. "Ah-h-h," they said, glaring at Pepe Brito. They would attend to him later. Ten *machete* slaps across his naked rump would teach him a lesson. . . .

A mutter of deep-seated rage vibrated through the outer fringe of the crowd and Mingo wheeled quickly. Memory of the mob of Volunteers on the water front at Santiago de Cuba surged back to him. The sound was the same, the low grumble, the excited anticipation. Two enormous Negroes, naked to their waists, shoved their way through the Mambises and between them two whimpering Cubans shuffled along, shaking in terror.

"So-o-o! Ah-h-h!" The grumbling swelled. "*Guerrilleros.*" The Mambises spat and swayed. "Sagaldo's butchers."

Elmo gulped, and Mingo gawked at the prisoners. Never before had he seen men as frightened as these men. Slobber oozed from their mouths and their eyes rolled. Their knees buckled and the two guards jerked them to their feet, dragged them forward and threw them on the ground before Macéo. The Mambises crowded closer, mouthing their hate.

Macéo spoke a few words to Miro, then pointed to one of the accused. The sniveling man was yanked to his feet. "Mercy," he pleaded and dropped to his knees. "For the love of the Mother of God, mercy."

"You will have mercy if you deserve mercy." Macéo seemed almost unconcerned. "Where are the witnesses?"

Nine Mambises testified against the prisoner, a cringing animal, kneeling in the dirt and vomiting his fear. He was a *guerrillero,* one of the loathed Cubans who sold themselves to Spain. There was Spanish money in his pocket when he was captured.

"Mother of God," the man cried. "I stole the money. . . ."

He had a Spanish Mauser.

"Mercy, General Macéo." He held up his trembling hands. "On the grave of my mother, I stole the rifle from a Spaniard. On the Cross, by the Conception, I am an innocent man."

Elmo leaned close to Mingo and whispered, "He's guilty as hell."

However, all the evidence was circumstantial and Macéo said, "The evidence is not positive." He looked down at the man. "You are free."

A Mambi stepped forward and flung out his hands. "No, no." Another struck the soldier across the mouth. *"Silencio!"*

"Release the accused," Macéo ordered.

For a fleeting second, the groveling Cuban stared up at Macéo, then ducked his head and ran for the woods, screaming like a frightened jackal. He collapsed on the edge of the forest and dragged himself into the brush as the guards yanked the second prisoner to his feet. He, too, was a cowering animal, but for some reason Mingo's sympathy went out to him. He was so thin, so pitiful, so bewildered.

General Miro searched his reports, wetting the tip of his finger as he ran through them. He selected one, holding it to the sunlight. "This prisoner is accused of leading a band of *guerrilleros* against the *bohío* of Pablo Cortez—"

Pablo Cortez! The five bodies, mutilated. The dead mule, its throat cut.

A dozen or more Mambises pushed forward to testify. "He is leader of a band we ambushed near the burned hut of Pablo Cortez. We killed the others and captured this one."

He had a Mauser and plenty of cartridges. He had Spanish money and he had Pablo Cortez' *machete*.

"Does anyone know this man?" Macéo asked, turning his head slowly and searching the faces of his soldiers.

"Si. Si." There were many replies. "He is Juan Méndez. He is one of Sagaldo's *guerrilleros*."

The prisoner opened his mouth to beg for mercy. No word came, however, and he pitched forward, falling like a log, his face in the dirt. The Brown One scarcely glanced down at the man, but turned to Miro and shrugged his left shoulder slightly.

The Mambises sucked in their breath. "Ah-h-h! The shrug of death!" The two Negroes gripped the prisoner's shoulders and lifted him to his feet. They began laughing, baring their *machetes.* Juan Méndez shrieked, and the guards shoved him along, pushing him through the ranks of the soldiers who cursed him and spat on him.

Then it happened and so quickly that Mingo never was sure of every detail. Juan Méndez was hurled into a ditch about thirty yards from headquarters and the two guards leaped on him, brandishing their *machetes* and still laughing. Juan Méndez screamed once like a trapped rabbit, and a *machete* split his skull. A second strike severed his head and the guards hacked and laughed, hacking him to bits.

Mingo Dabney stared in nauseous horror at the dripping *machetes* rising and falling. "Good God," he said hoarsely. "Good God a'mighty!"

Elmo's face was white and his mouth sagged.

Antonio Macéo did not glance toward the ditch, but turned to the drummer. "Won't you please come in, Señor Batson." He ignored Mingo.

Elmo nudged his friend and shrugged. "I'll meet you back at the cart." He lowered his voice. "Don't get all steamed up because he didn't ask you in."

"It's a good thing he didn't," Mingo snarled. "The butcher!" He glared toward the hut a second, then stalked away toward the creek, his stomach squirming and his lips compressed tight to hold back the hot surge in his throat.

None of the *impedimenta* had crossed the creek merely to see a man hacked to death, and already were about their morning chores of cockfighting and squabbling.

"El Dabney!" They shouted their welcome and several hurried to his cart. Two or three brought food and Mingo's face twitched and he turned away. Pepe Rosado, he of the big nose, pointed at an ox, its leg splotched with sores. "Fix him. Like you did the ox of Pepe Sánchez."

"*Sí.*" The others nodded. "We have crippled oxen, too."

The disgust began leaving the Lebanon man and he looked around at the men standing there so expectantly, waiting for him to perform wonders. "All right. Get palm oil and canvas strips."

"*Si. Si.*" They held up their hands in salute, bragging on El Dabney as they hurried away. He reached into the cart for the ax. Might as well sharpen it; anything to keep him busy until Elmo returned.

They brought their oxen and he bound their sores. They brought their goats and he treated them. Some pointed to their own sores, and he washed them and dressed them. "Ah-a-a, El Dabney." They mumbled their gratitude and went away telling fabulous tales about the *gringo*: he could treat an ox, and treat a man, and build a Mexican fire.

Pepe Barea brought a mule to be shod and the woodsman threw up his hands in exasperation. There was no anvil or forge, but within an hour four of them were back with an anvil, laughing and snickering as they lugged it into the cart. He set it up and shod the mule, using the ax as a hammer. . . .

And Mingo Dabney forgot he was in Cuba, even forgot Rafaela Galban for the minute. He was back in Lebanon, doing the things he did well, and he broke into the words of Elmo's song.

> *This war's gonna kill me dead, Lawd, Lawd,*
> *John Henry* —

The Mambises were awed by his skill and delighted by his song. This was El Dabney. This was their friend. They slouched against the huge wheels of the carts, or squatted on their haunches, watching every move as he sweated and cursed and sang.

> *This war's gonna kill me dead, Lawd, Lawd* —

He didn't realize he was singing it. It was a work song of men cutting trees and tilling the earth, and the Mambises tapped their feet and repeated the words, with no idea of their meaning.

211

Mingo was beating a nail, but the ax was a clumsy tool for such work. "I need a hammer." He was talking to himself, never looking up. Then he chuckled and put down his ax and motioned for Pepe Rosado. "Get me a hammer, John Henry."

The Mambi looked blank, glancing from his comrades to Mingo. "John Henry?"

"*Sí*. John Henry. *Amigo*. *Compadre*. Pepe—I need a hammer."

"No-o-o-o." Pepe Rosado dolefully shook his head. "There is no hammer."

The woodsman rested against the cart, folded his arms and gazed at the sky. "No hammer, no work."

"*Sí. Sí.*" Another Mambi jerked his head up and down vigorously. "There is a hammer at Macéo's *bohio*. The best hammer in all Cuba." He pursed his lips and looked down, cutting his eyes at his fellows. They all grinned and walked off, Pepe Rosado leading the way.

Mingo was heating a shoe red hot when they returned and poked the hammer at him "Ah-h-h." He put the ax to one side. "*Muchas gracias*, John Henry." He patted the Mambi on the back.

"John Henry!" they echoed. It was a good name. *Viva* John Henry.

The woodsman laughed and began shaping the shoes and Pepe Rosado perched on the end of the cart and watched; his big nose dripping and his notched ears dangling rings. "Macéo did not need that hammer, eh, El Dabney?"

"No, no-o-o," said Mingo, and the hot iron threw sparks.

"I did not steal it, did I?"

"No-o-o. John Henry would not steal."

The Mambi cocked his head to one side and shut his left eye. "If I steal from the army, Macéo will shrug his shoulder at me. *Por Dios*! That would be bad, eh?"

The hot flush of anger came back to Mingo and he hurled the hammer to the ground. "Listen, *amigo*." He shook his finger at Pepe Rosado. "Listen all of you." He turned his head, facing them, then jerked his thumb toward Macéo's camp. "If any of those fellows over there bother you, just let me know." It was the boast of an angry and excited man, but he was foolish enough to make it and, at the minute, desperate enough to back it up.

"So-o-o." The scavengers looked about them and poked out their chests. El Dabney was not afraid of Macéo's soldiers. "So-o-o, John Henry." They slapped their thighs and laughed as they tangled the words. "This war's gonna kill me dead." They repeated it until they learned it. Lawd, Lawd!

A quick shower scattered them and drove Mingo to shelter inside his cart, and then the sun came out bright and he returned to his work. The *impedimenta* were about other duties, most of them kindling fires for the noonday meal. Mingo Dabney was alone and enjoyed being alone.

The woodsman was tempering his ax and burning out the old handle when Elmo walked back into camp. Mingo didn't see him until he stuck his foot on the spoke of a wheel. "Who do you think you are? The village blacksmith?"

Mingo jumped in surprise, turning quickly to face his friend. "What'd Macéo say about killing that poor devil?"

Elmo ran his fingers inside his shirt and scratched his chest. "Nothing. It's dog eat dog." He climbed into the cart and sat there, swinging his feet over the edge of the bed. "I'm heading for home." His eyes were bright, evidence that his fever had returned.

The metal of the ax head was flaking and Mingo brushed it with a handful of leaves. "I got a notion to go with you."

The older man grunted his dissent. "You can't go back."

"How come?"

Elmo began whistling so softly it scarcely could be heard, and when he spoke his voice, too, was soft. "You left home on a white horse, looking for a girl. And now you got a debt. Besides, boy —"

213

"Besides what?" He was homesick again.

"There's no room in the South any more for men who ride white horses." It was the truth, the sad truth and Elmo spoke it sadly. "The South is bowing down to money same as Yankees do. It ain't who you are any more. It's how much you got. The South is hanging a mail order necktie around its red neck."

Mingo wet his fingers and picked up the ax head, tossing it under the cart to cool. He leaned against a wheel, mulling Elmo's words and waiting for a report of his visit to headquarters. Almost a minute passed and Mingo's curiosity plagued him. "Did Macéo mention me?"

"Well . . ." Elmo worked a splinter out of the bed of the cart and stuck it in his mouth like a toothpick. "Wouldn't exactly say he mentioned you."

Mingo hopped into the cart and sat beside his friend. "What happened?"

Elmo broke the splinter between his teeth and spat out the bits. "He told me what he needs. I told him I'd get it. And I told him you're the man to handle it."

"What'd he say?"

The drummer's face was fever-flushed and dry. "He had to trade. I didn't budge, so he did."

"Then he'll take me in his army?"

Elmo locked his hands around his knee and leaned back. "Miro put me straight on things. As long as you stay with the *impedimenta*, Macéo won't mess with you."

"I aim to kill Spaniards. Not shoe mules." He pointed toward the Army of the Oriente. "Those are the fighting men over there."

"Those men . . ." Elmo tilted his head, pointing with his chin toward Macéo's Mambises. "They are dead men." He slid from the cart. "Now let's get some food."

They walked down the path to a campfire and got boiled mutton and a pot of coffee, and returned to their cart. The drummer picked up a piece of hot meat and blew on it. "What you aim to do when this war's over?"

"I haven't thought about it." The coffee was bitter and burned his lips.

Elmo poured whiskey in his coffee and gulped it. "This country is wide open for the right men." He pushed his cup aside. "Somebody's got to deal a new hand down here. New deck. New players. I'm going to sit in that game." He was watching Mingo intently. "You thought anything about it?"

Mingo Dabney shook his head. He wasn't interested in tomorrow in Cuba, or in a new game in an old land. "How come Macéo's soldiers are dead men?"

Elmo Batson chewed his cigar, turning it in his mouth. His loud confidence was gone and there was a cloud on his face. "I got to get to Haiti and pick up the supplies the *Virginius* left behind. Got to send 'em to a place called Baragua, just north of here." He was talking quietly. "Macéo will be in Baragua in a few weeks."

Mingo wished he'd get to the point. "Where do I come in?"

The drummer ignored him and went on talking. "From Haiti I'm heading home for some new stuff and I'll ship it to Pinar del Río." Only then did he look up, studying Mingo.

The name Pinar del Río slowly registered in Mingo's mind. *Pinar del Río?* That was at the other end of the island. Nine hundred miles away. "Who's going to handle it way down there?"

"You are, son."

"Like hell I am. I'm going to be with Macéo."

Elmo tossed his cigar away and rubbed his hand across his forehead. "That's right. And Macéo is taking his army to the other end of the island."

"He's crazy!"

"Maybe." Elmo didn't raise his voice. "Maybe he is."

Mingo blew out his breath slowly and his spine tingled. "What are his chances?"

"None, if you want to be sensible, but there's no telling what a crazy man can do." Elmo motioned across the creek. "He'll lose those fellows. He'll have to raise another army in Pinar del Río!"

Mingo rubbed his hands slowly down his legs. "How much time has he got?"

"He figures three months."

"Nine hundred miles in three months!" Mingo's mouth dropped. "Spain's got a quarter of a million soldiers on this island—"

"Then there ought to be enough to go around." A hot flush came to Elmo's brow and he went to his saddlebag for quinine, gagging at the bitter taste. "Any more of that whiskey?"

Mingo held up the bottle. "A little."

Elmo drank in noisy gulps, then slumped against the wheel, suddenly weak from fever. "I got to be leaving—"

"How come Macéo's in such a hurry?"

The drummer's eyes were running water and he reached for his handkerchief. "He figgers he's got to whip Spain before Uncle Sam does. Now, I got to be going."

There was no need to try to delay him, so Mingo led the horse alongside the cart and tossed him the reins. Elmo climbed to his saddle and fumbled in his pocket for the quinine. "You keep that. I can get some more."

Mingo accepted the medicine. "Didn't Macéo give you a pistol or a gun? Spaniards all around here."

"I had a pistol, but I traded it for that quinine." Elmo lifted the reins. "Anyhow, I can't hit the side of a barn with a shotgun." He blinked his watery eyes. "So long, bud. Don't take no wooden nickels." He kicked his horse's flank and rode down the path, and out of camp. . . .

The pilgrim turned back to his cart and went to work, shaping an ax handle for the one he had burned. The wood was ceiba and it worked easy. A bugle sounded in Macéo's camp and the *impedimenta* scattered like quail. Mingo wondered why, then forgot it.

He needed a good knife. And some files. Ol' Elmo must be a mile away. Maybe more. Lawd, Lawd. Mingo was humming again.

There was a shout from across the creek and he looked up from his ax handle. Macéo's Mambises, the cock-feathered gallants of Goulet, the clansmen of the Ducasse brothers, were pounding the dust into clouds, taking down hammocks and rolling them.

Mingo stared about him. The *impedimenta* were yoking oxen, piling baggage into their carts. "Lawd, Lawd, John Henry —"

Hurry, John Henry. Load the carts. Pile 'em high.

Hurry, Mingo Dabney. Maker of vows. Debtor to dead men.

The Army of the Oriente was moving out. Nine hundred miles in ninety days. *Saludo, compadre! Venga, Mambi!* Come on, dirt! And die!

Baire!

MINGO DABNEY

Chapter **17**   The heavy feet of the oxen dragged up little clouds of dust from the *kaquaso* grass, covering it gray. The *grillos* hissed their protests and scuttering lizards pulsed their money bags as the Mambises plodded beside their carts, their faces sweat-streaked, dust caking at the corners of their eyes.

The Army of the Oriente was moving, a crawling mile of men and animals, led by Antonio Macéo and his Toledo sword. Behind him, walking in the dust, were the warriors, and stretched out far behind, groaning under the burden of baggage, the oxcarts of the *impedimenta* slowly moved, and broke down, and were patched, and slowly moved again.

Only The Brown One knew their destination. They were creeping west, the morning sun at their backs, and there was no sound except the occasional scrape of a dry wheel on a dusty axle. The minute Mingo Dabney heard the grinding warning he called that wagon out of line and greased the wheel, then told the driver, "All right, John Henry. Keep moving."

The oxen were sleek, for after thirteen days of travel, El Dabney had sorted the animals, killing the sick and forbidding their meat to the Mambises. Only the strong steers were yoked. The weak were tied to the carts and saved for meat. Mingo took the best cuts for his own men, providing a common mess for them. Eat together or not eat at all.

He tolerated no waste and permitted no mistreatment of

equipment, and repaired carts and animals and men. Soon his foragers were down to eighty-seven men, all fit. And they had forty carts, all sturdy.

The Mambises knew not where Macéo was leading them, and it didn't matter. But the Spaniards knew and made their plans. Macéo must be held in the Oriente. The ancient *trochas*, the line of forts across the island, must be manned, blocking The Brown One from the sugar plains. He must be held in the hills while Martínez Campos, the captain-general, and Leopold Sagaldo chewed up the impudent rebels. Sagaldo would take care of The Nigra. . . .

Mingo was walking beside his oxen, pondering the problem of defending the *impedimenta* from surprise attack. All afternoon the army passed burned *bohios* and ravaged farms. The Spaniards were in the hills. Over to the west, perhaps. To the south, perhaps. No one was sure.

He waved his whip and his oxen quickened their gait. Good Lord, if only he had some of the rifles from the *Virginius*. The line toiled on through a gap in the hills and he looked back over his shoulder, motioning for Pepe Barea. "Where are we?"

The Mambi rubbed the dust from his eyes. "On the road to Manzanillo. The next village will be Maffo." The dust clung to his eyelashes. "Macéo will camp there, perhaps."

There was no village of Maffo, only a few burned huts. The army turned off the road, veering south toward the sea until the sun slanted, and then the army straggled to a halt, the woodsman waving his caravan off the trail and into the forest.

The carts were driven into circles, tongue to axle, and they became forts and corrals. Mingo sent a courier forward and requested riflemen to protect the baggage train from surprise. There were no guards and he posted his own watchmen. They had only *machetes* and he told them, "If the Spaniards jump you, warn us some way. Yell. Do something."

Yell? The Mambises shrugged and grinned. A man can't yell with a knife in his throat.

The pilgrim was moody at supper and, as darkness closed in, he sat by his fire, staring into the woods. The Haitians were talking again, their drums throbbing, and the Mambises sang and danced in the dust.

They were unconcerned that Spaniards might be all around them. That was Macéo's worry. On other nights, Mingo had joined their songs, but tonight he was sullen, in the despondency of his Mississippi heritage. What chance did they have? No guns. No way to fight back.

He tried to sleep but couldn't. The *impedimenta*, sensing battle, were excited and danced late, beating their breasts and bragging. He ordered them to their carts and they obeyed him, giggling like truants and laughing among themselves.

"Put out those fires," he called and when they did not obey quickly, he scattered the embers, stomping them.

The Mambises looked from one to the other. Ah-h-h. El Dabney was nervous. Tired, perhaps. Surely he was not afraid of Spaniards. *Por Dios!* Spaniards meant loot. Naturally a few comrades would die, but more always lived than died. And, besides, Spaniards had shoes! Who would not risk his life for a pair of shoes?

Sleep was beyond Mingo and he brooded, jerking his head at each sound in the woods. His Mambises were not sleeping and called to one another, hissing for attention. Pssst-psst! Then they scurried from one cart to the next, some hopping like crickets. The woods, the night, the smell of battle and the hope of loot aroused them.

Finally the American could stand it no longer. His nerves were frayed and his temper boiled. He jumped from his cart and stalked to the center of the circle and called the men around him. "Now, dammit, get to sleep. Quit hopping around like a bunch of *grillos*."

Some of the scavengers laughed. El Dabney was making a

joke. He was calling them *grillos*. Crickets, eh? Hissing bugs. They lowered their heads and grinned, looking at one another out of the corners of their eyes. "*Grillos*. Psst-psst." They hissed the sound. "John Henry! *Grillos!*"

It was a name for men who had no names. It was something to call themselves. The soldiers called them scum and filth. The Spaniards called them lice and leeches, but El Dabney called them *grillos*. There is unity in a name, and pride if the name is given in affection. The Lebanon woodsman had no idea that then and there he named the *impedimenta* of the Army of the Oriente. El Dabney's *Grillos!*

The men drifted away to their carts, and he watched until they were quiet, then walked back to his own place. There was muffled laughter from the cart next to his. John Henry! *Grillos!* Psst-psst. They whispered the names among themselves and Mingo shook his head in wonderment. They had nothing and wanted nothing, and were proud even to have names.

He folded a hammock under his head and stretched out on the boards of his cart, wiggling to adjust his body. There was a soft bed back home and he called himself a fool. Why risk his neck for a bunch of scabby riffraff? They didn't understand freedom. Somebody would always tell them what to do. Somebody must run things for them and the man with the purse, the pistol and a brain would always be the leader. The meek? The meek were cattle to be driven to pasture.

And yet, Mingo Dabney dared believe there was a rift in the darkness engulfing the lowly. Such was the faith of a pilgrim who rode a white horse on a quest for a girl, but now dreamed of brotherhood, and found comfort in his dream. If he lived, there was the friendship of the Mambises. If he died, there was the earth of Cuba, and the earth itself is a brotherhood. . . .

Thin, white smoke curled up from an ember bed that panted for life and Mingo lay in his cart watching the glow of the fire. His *Grillos* were sleeping and the camp was quiet. The drums to the north were louder.

Hoofs made muffled sounds in the woods and Mingo sat up straight. One of the oxen was out, perhaps. No. Those were horses' hoofs, a horse moving softly upon the thick carpet of the forest. A mule from Macéo's army. No! That was a horse and none of El Dabney's men had horses. He reached for his ax and slid out of the cart and ducked beneath it just as Soto walked into the circle, leading his horse and staring around. Mingo almost called out in relief and his heart slowed to its normal beat.

The guide dropped his reins over a cart tongue and peered in, looking at every face. One of the *Grillos* grumbled, "Go away, Soto. I am not the man you seek."

"Psst! Soto!" Mingo crawled from under his cart.

The Mambi spun around and grinned. "Ah-h-h, *amigo*." He came toward him quickly. "She is all right. I left her in Camagüey."

Mingo waited for more news but Soto had nothing more to say, and the American placed his ax on the bed of his cart, easily within reach. "You didn't find your man?"

"No. But I learned he was a lifelong friend of Martí's, and I can trace all Martí's friends." He glanced around at the orderly circle and whistled his surprise at El Dabney's miracles.

The woodsman swung into his cart and plied the guide with questions, clinging to every word about Rafaela. Finally he asked, "See any Spaniards?"

The Mambi shook his head. "No Spaniards the way I came. But there —" He pointed to the southwest. "They are swarming like bees. Campos has 6000 men —"

"That many?"

"*Sí.*" The goatherd shrugged. "Campos is near Manzanillo. The Spaniards are coming toward us, and we are going toward the Spaniards." He threw back his head and yawned, snuffling and smacking his lips in the luxury of relaxation.

"How you know Campos has so many?" Mingo's flesh was creeping up his backbone.

Soto cocked his head, listening to the drums in the north, then to the answer from the southwest. "Campos has more than 6000 now. They are swarming from the Gulf of Guacanayabo up to Peralejo. Ah-h-h." He held up his palm to delay Mingo's question, still reading the drums. "They are in Yara and Barrancas. They are in Macéo's path, between us and Manzanillo." He nodded earnestly. "There will be a fight." He glanced over his shoulder. "Do you know where we are?"

"I know we're in a hell of a mess."

"*Amigo* —" The Mambi pointed. "Tomorrow we will be just south of Baire. The *grito* was sounded there. . . ."

"Uh huh. I know it." Sweat was forming under Mingo's arms. "You know where we can get some guns?"

The guide was puzzled and frowned. "Guns? There are no guns for the *impedimenta*."

"What do we do if they jump us —"

"We run, *compadre*. Into the woods."

El Dabney glowered at the Cuban. "I'll be damned if we do. I don't aim to run away and let Spaniards take my carts and oxen."

The Mambi shrugged again. "The Spaniards will cut your throat. But it is your throat."

"I reckon Macéo expects us to fight with sticks." Mingo's disgust rankled.

Soto wagged his finger in warning. "Macéo does not expect the *impedimenta* to fight. That is why he does not take them into his army." The Mambi hated to see his friend disillusioned, but better that he be told the truth now than learn it in battle. "For nights and nights the Haitians have talked of the *impedimenta*. A *gringo* leads them and is trying to make proud those who have no pride." He shook his head, sorrowfully. "But wait until the Spaniards strike. The *impedimenta* will scatter like fleas, the drums say." His eyes popped open and he sat up quickly, listening, then leaned out of the cart, his head tilted to the northwest.

The drums rolled rapidly to the south. A call, a plea; a booming, pounding roll.

There was no answer from the north.

"What is it?" Mingo asked hoarsely. "What's wrong?"

Another call from the south. A frantic throb. A minute of stillness, and another roll, a query, a demand. But the north was silent.

The Mambi licked his lips. "Sagaldo! Only Sagaldo travels so fast. They are silencing the drums —"

"That's in the northwest!" Mingo felt his flesh creeping again. "You said there were no Spaniards there —"

"There are Spaniards there now." Soto went quickly to his horse and led him to one side of the cart, fastening him to the rim of the wheel.

El Dabney rubbed his sweaty hands down his trouser legs and, instinctively, reached for his ax. There were sudden shouts in Macéo's camp, and muffled commands were passed along. "Up. Up, Mambises." Curses greeted the commands. "No fires. No coffee. Up. Up." Down the line came the commands. "No straggling. Close in. . . ."

The army was moving again, streaking into the woods, into the black of night. Mingo watched the northwest as though expecting death to roll down from the hills. Sagaldo was in the hills and Campos was at the sea. The hills came down almost to the sea, and Macéo was between them.

Up! Up, Mambises!

El Dabney's *Grillos* began yawning and cursing. Mingo walked among them. "Up, John Henry. Let's go. We're pulling out. . . ."

Teams were spanned and carts fell into line. "No straggling. Keep your distance, John Henry." El Dabney's *Grillos* were moving again.

The south drums were rolling, calling pitifully.

The north was hushed, and slowly a glow spread in the

hills. Some Mambi's *bohio*. Sagaldo was burning again. A bayonet for the belly. A torch for the hut.

The army moved fast and the ox train plodded on behind, and the night was half away when the glow in the north spread red across the ridges.

"Baire!" Soto whispered. "Mother of God, they are burning Baire."

All that night the Army of the Oriente snaked southwest, creeping down the Mountains of Our Master toward the Gulf of Guacanayabo, wedging itself between Sagaldo in the hills and Campos near the sea.

Stray reinforcements drifted in hour after hour, little bands of Mambises flushed out of their hiding places by Sagaldo's raid. Each band was led by its own chieftain and followed by its *impedimenta* and they all mingled with Macéo's column, moving on down the mountain passes, down the road to Manzanillo. El Dabney's *Grillos* slumped along at the rear, grumbling and mouthing.

The dust hung heavy in the air and seeped into their noses and they sneezed and muttered their curses upon the dust, and the darkness, and the slow dragging on. Mingo Dabney was weary almost to collapse as he plodded beside his cart, curling his whip over his grunting team. He was aware that Macéo was squeezing his band into the gap between Campos and Sagaldo, that The Brown One was risking his army in a daring gamble, and he was scared. "Haw, Big Red." He tried not to think what would happen if the Spanish trap snapped closed. "Step along, Slow Foot."

The Army of the Oriente was creeping into battle.

They were hungry, but they did not halt. They were weary, but did not rest. The night was Macéo's cloak, the trees his allies, and he must do again those things the Spaniards thought no man could do.

A few of the Mambises staggered and fell and the other

soldiers dragged on by, leaving them for the Spaniards, for the ants, for the wild dogs. None cried out; none whimpered.

Soto crawled into a cart and slept, gaining the rest a scout must have. Mingo mumbled his exhaustion, and the drums tolled the hours, pounding in the south, silent to the north. No gossip from the Haitians, only the sobbing boom— boom—boom of awesome finality. Spaniards in Baire! Mind your *machetes*, Mambises. Spaniards in Yara! Remember Martí, Mambises. Spaniards in the hills! Remember the *Virginius*, El Dabney.

The glow in the north died down and the Mambises glanced that way, knowing Baire was gone. *Viva Baire!* They were too tired to lift their heads and look to the north; but they rolled their eyes and mumbled their troth with revenge.

There was a muffled shout up ahead, a few cries of welcome and another band joined the column. Some of the newcomers were mounted, cavalry for Macéo, and they and their frightened *impedimenta* brought fantastic rumors but no news. Sagaldo had two thousand men in the hills. Five thousand. Nobody knew. Campos had five thousand by the sea. Ten thousand. Nobody knew. Did it matter? Close up, Mambises.

Mingo Dabney tried to reason with himself and quell his fears. The Brown One, with so little, was deliberately crawling between Campos and Sagaldo, with so much. It was crazy and the pilgrim coiled his whip to lash his oxen. Damn Macéo! Silk next to his brown skin and riding a horse while a Dabney walked in the dust, heading for his first battle with no gun to shoot, no stone to hurl. Nothing but an ox whip in his hand. To hell with Macéo, riding a horse while a white man walked.

That he might be killed never occurred to him and he stumbled on, his head bobbing, his thick black hair sticky with sweat. Rafaela Galban was miles away. Soto was asleep. And Mingo Dabney was alone, breathing dust and spitting grime. He picked the dirt from the corners of his lips, and cursed. So this was war: a gnawing belly and heavy feet. So

226

this was the pilgrimage: ox dung and sweat. Keep going, Big Red. Haw there, Slow Foot.

Dawn came so quietly he was not aware of its coming until the trees turned from black to gray and he looked over his shoulder, glancing to the east.

Soto poked his head out of the cart, his little face squinting, and Mingo Dabney grinned for the first time that night. The *Grillos* saw his grin and they grinned, too, nudging one another and nodding toward El Dabney. The *gringo* was happy again and they were happy, for it was coming full dawn and the Army of the Oriente was going to fight; and a fight meant dead Spaniards and dead Spaniards meant loot. A gold earring, perhaps. A rifle, perhaps. Shoes, perhaps. Mother of God! Shoes for feet so long cut by briers and bruised by stones.

A heavy pall of smoke hung over the hills to the north. It was black and thick and lay low like a hooding fog until the sun, red and angry, sprang over the crest of the Sierra Maestra and lifted the smoke from the mountains, revealing them green again.

A courier rode back from Macéo's staff and summoned Soto forward, and the march was halted, the Mambises sprawling beside the road. The *impedimenta* prepared food and passed it to the soldiers.

The commanders were in conference under a mahogany tree and Macéo was talking quietly to General Miro. Mingo sent a bucket of coffee to the staff, and looked around for Soto, but the little Mambi was nowhere in sight. General Miro saw Mingo, and smiled. Macéo saw him and did not smile.

The morning dragged by and rumors spread among the ranks. They were going to retreat. No, they were waiting for Gómez. *Recristo!* Gómez was on the plains. Then came reports that Macéo's scouts were in the hills and that was the only report Mingo believed. It explained Soto's absence and Macéo's delay.

A quick rain left the earth soggy and the trees drooping, and the spirit of the men drooped, too. Mingo sensed their mood and put them to work.

It was mid-afternoon when he heard the report that Soto was back, his horse foaming. He had been in the hills. *Por Dios!* Miro was excited. Goulet was raging. Banderas was pleading for an attack. Only Macéo was calm.

The tension vibrated back through the line and the *impedimenta* began cutting their eyes from one to the other, spitting and wiping their mouths. A dozen times they examined their *machetes,* easing their thumbs along the blades, and they talked in low tones about casual things; weather, and food, and women.

Mingo was fidgeting on the edge of his cart when Soto rode back and slid from his horse and straightway asked for food.

"What's going on?" The American demanded. "Where you been?"

The guide wolfed his dried beef and gulped his coffee and some of it trickled out of the corners of his mouth, washing streaks in the sweat and dirt. "We have scouted as far as Baire —"

"Did you spot Sagaldo?"

Soto shook his head slowly, a fear in his look; a mystery. "They have vanished. There are no Spaniards in the hills."

"The hell you say." A tight hard knot twisted in the pit of Mingo's stomach. "Then who burned Baire?"

"Sagaldo was there last night. But he is gone."

"Where?"

"God knows."

Why should Sagaldo travel so far to destroy so little? Baire was not important except for a memory. It was too much for the woodsman. "He must have some mighty fast horses."

"*Si.*" Soto paused and awe was on his face again. "To go so far and come out so fast . . ."

Mingo was wary and baffled, and a suspicion would not be denied. "You know your hills—I reckon."

"We scouted every valley," Soto said. "We found Cuban dead. Ripped open. We found four Haitians. Their bodies were slit. But no Spaniards."

El Dabney still was puzzling the raid when General Miro rode up and the *Grillos* welcomed him with shouts. The chief of staff was more popular than Macéo. The Brown One was an idol. Miro was just another man. He was flesh. Macéo was brown marble.

"You have handled the supplies well, Señor Dabney." Miro glanced around at the carts, the oxen yoked and ready to move. "And I have come, sir, to ask a favor."

El Dabney was cautious. "What's on your mind?"

General Miro looked down at his feet and pursed his lips. "We have word that Elmo Batson has got supplies through to Baragua."

"Is that a fact?" Mingo was not committing himself. Baragua was thirty miles northeast, back in the foothills of Sierra de Nipe.

The chief of staff moved closer. "We will not mince words, Señor Dabney. This army will meet the enemy tomorrow. We will ambush him and cut him to pieces, then hasten to Baragua."

Mingo sensed a development he did not like. "General Macéo wants me to go to Baragua, huh?"

"The entire staff thinks it's best," the Cuban replied tactfully. "You can be of much service if you have the equipment ready when the army reaches Baragua."

"And miss the fight?"

"You would leave immediately." Miro spoke softly, almost pleadingly. There was something pitiful about a chief of staff asking an ox driver to help his country.

The *Grillos* wanted loot and now El Dabney must tell them to give up their chance of getting it. Maybe they wouldn't follow him. There was no way to force them, and if they refused he was discredited. For a moment he weighed the situation, then called to Soto. "I'm going to Baragua, *compadre*."

The Mambi's look darted from his friend to Miro, then back to his friend, and his little eyes were troubled.

"Tell the men to gather here." El Dabney glanced off toward the hills and ran his tongue along his lips, moistening them. He was nervous inside, but his voice was calm.

Soto walked among the men and Mingo edged back onto the cart, sitting there dangling his legs, risking his toe hold in the army on the loyalty of scavengers. Miro felt the tension of the test, the trial of one man's dignity and the loyalty of other men.

The *impedimenta* gathered slowly, eyeing their leader skeptically and Miro suspiciously. They stood around the cart, wiggling their bare toes in the dirt, and Mingo Dabney glanced at each of them. "I'm heading for Baragua. I want you *Grillos* to go with me —"

"No! No, no!" The protest came from the rear of the crowd. "There will be a fight and we want shoes." The man pointed at his feet.

"Get out!" Mingo's eyes sought the fellow and fastened on him. "Take your cart and get out."

The man looked around quickly for comrades to support him, seeking strength in numbers. But none joined him and he glanced about frantically.

"Get along!" the woodsman ordered. "Right now, John Henry!"

"He is no John Henry!" Soto yelled it from the crowd.

"*Por Dios!* He is no John Henry." The crowd took it up. "No. No. Get out."

The man might have changed his mind; he wanted to change his mind and stay with his comrades, but they pushed him away and he hung his head. Mingo felt sorry for him and almost called him back, for it was hard to send a man from the company of his kind.

"We will go with you, El Dabney." Soto called it out.

"Sí!" Pepe Rosado shouted. "We will go."

Mingo cut his eyes at Miro and the chief of staff nodded, and El Dabney faced his men again. "There are shoes in Baragua."

"Sí! Sí! And there are women in Baragua, eh?" They were strutting and bragging and waving their arms.

"There are women in Baragua," Mingo promised. "And a little rum, perhaps." He waved his *Grillos* away and slanted his old black hat on the side of his head. He was swaggering as he moved toward Miro. "You will give us an escort?"

The chief of staff flushed. "We cannot spare an escort."

El Dabney rubbed his hands along the edge of the wagon bed. "Then you will give us guns?"

"We have no guns."

The lines tightened around Mingo's mouth. "General Miro, these men must go thirty miles through the mountains. One Spanish patrol could wipe us out."

"There are no Spaniards in the hills. The way is open."

Mingo Dabney peered at the chief of staff. "We'll start first thing tomorrow." He watched Miro ride away, then called his men around him. They would rest that night and move at dawn.

The sun started down, streaking down the road to Manzanillo and the shadows were stretching long when Macéo's order was passed from headquarters to the soldiers, "Up! Up!" The Army of the Oriente was crawling forward again, churning the dust down the road to Manzanillo.

El Dabney's *Grillos,* a handful of men without a gun, were left alone in a valley between the hills and the sea, not far from the charred hamlet of Baire.

MINGO DABNEY

Chapter **18**   The moon came up mellow
and El Dabney ordered them to bed, and they went quickly
because they were tired.

He took off his shoes and rubbed his toes, then tied his
shoes to the cartwheel, high enough to avoid the dew. The
night air felt good to his feet and he stretched on the cart
floor, wiggling his toes and yawning. Soto crawled into the
cart beside him and the fires died down and the stars popped
out, tingling bright and cruising low above the forest.

Mingo Dabney did not dream that night. His muscles were
tight and cried out for rest, then slowly they relaxed and he
groaned the good, long groan of a strong body resting. Soto
was mumbling, turning restlessly, and the other Mambises
were snoring. There was no guard; no need for a guard. Sagaldo was out of the hills. Miro had said so, M-m-m.

The moon melted down behind the ceibas and waned
away. A cool wind rustled the camp and Mingo turned on his
side, his head slipping off the hammock he used as a pillow.
It jarred him from sleep and he reached for the pillow to
push it back under his head.

Then suddenly he sat up. Something urged him to sit up,
and he sat up quickly, leaning forward, poised, motionless.
His eyes blinked rapidly as he stared out toward his camp.
Mist seeped down from the mountains and drifted low and
thick about the carts, twisting and swirling white. The first-
dawn was slipping into the eastern sky, pale green and blue,
and brushed with gold.

232

Mingo felt for the cartwheel and his hand slid down the wheel, reaching for his shoes. They were gone. He cursed under his breath, for he had lost his shoes and the man who stole them. A pair of shoes was prize enough to warrant desertion.

Soto raised his head. "What is it?"

"Some son of a bitch stole my shoes."

The little Mambi grinned slyly. "There are shoes in Baragua. It is only thirty miles away. Ah-h-h, John Henry."

The woodsman grunted and rubbed his cold feet, then yawned. Now the pilgrim was barefooted. Like the Mambises. Like common clay. A Dabney was barefooted in the hills of Cuba. *Por Dios!*

An uneasy feeling began slapping at his mind, a sense of unreality stirring his sleepy thinking. The mist was clammy and he wanted coffee and, dammit, he wanted his shoes.

A cock crowed to the east and a dog barked. Then a horse neighed, high and shrill, and the sound quivered, piercing his ears, awakening a memory. The neigh of a horse. So that was what woke him. He shook his head to clear it, and yawned again. "That was a horse," he said.

"*Si.* A horse." Soto closed his eyes and stretched out his hands, spreading his fingers wide, relaxing and yawning.

Mingo grimaced his discomfort, and suddenly the expression froze on his face. "Soto!" His tongue was thick. "Where's your horse?"

"There—See him?"

Mingo grabbed his comrade's arm. "Soto!" The word was a whisper. "Macéo has horses, but he's miles away. And that was a horse—" He pointed to the north. "Over yonder."

"Mother of God!" The guide bolted upright, his eyes wide and his jaw trembling.

Mingo slid out of the cart, and the earth was damp to his bare feet. "The Spaniards have horses." He was staring at Soto and quaking with cold and fear.

The Mambi moved closer and whispered, "They came back to the hills last night —"

"They've never been out!" El Dabney was scared, and bit his words sharply. "They've been there all the time. Sagaldo tricked you scouts —"

"We beat the brush for miles and miles. . . ." The bewildered goatherd spread his hands in a gesture of resignation.

"To hell with that! They are out there now, ain't they?" Fear spread from Mingo's mind to his legs, and the muscles in his legs knotted and hurt.

"I'll wake the men," Soto whispered. "Then we'll run." He pointed to the south. "We'll run that way."

"You get to Macéo." It was his first compulsion. Warn The Brown One.

Soto drew back. "Perhaps it is not Spaniards." He was cautious and uncertain. "Macéo is riding to meet Campos —"

"Don't argue with me! Get to Macéo! Tell him Sagaldo is back here and aiming to jump him —"

"But, *amigo* —"

"God damn it, get moving! Tell him to get here quick or there won't be any more war."

Soto scampered for his horse and cut back into the woods where the sod was thick, then headed southwest, down the road to Macéo. The sun was prying a path through the murk.

A few of the *Grillos* woke up and huddled around El Dabney, and he nodded toward the hills. "Sagaldo!"

"Holy Mother!" They hurried among their comrades, laying hands over the mouths of the sleeping men and whispering close in their ears. "Up, John Henry. Sagaldo!"

Like shadows in the white mist they stole toward El Dabney, clustering around him, waiting for him to speak. Like hornets they swarmed, buzzing their excitement. He looked at them and was helpless. "There's not a gun among us." He was confused and bewildered. "Besides, somebody stole my shoes."

"Ah-h-h." Pepe Barea lifted his head, slowly nodding. "We will get shoes." He slipped his *machete* from its scabbard, and all the others bared their weapons.

234

"You will lead us, *compadre.*" They whispered the words in confidence. This was El Dabney of a hundred miracles, the tree cutter, the fire maker, the healer.

Mingo's face was clammy. He was afraid of those hills, but he felt the eyes of his men. "You will do as I tell you?"

"*Sí.*" Eagerly they nodded their agreement.

A horse neighed and Mingo jumped. Spanish patrols were slipping out of the hills, probing down the slopes, waiting for the sun to burn the mist away.

The woodsman lifted his ax from its rack, balancing it as he peered up the slope, wondering how close they were. Soto should be with Macéo by now. Thank God for the mist. "All right." He gripped his ax handle tight. "Some of us will go after shoes. The others will stay here —"

"No." The men raised their hands and shook their heads. "We will all go with you, El Dabney."

"I will take twenty men." He indicated the group he wanted. "The rest will stay here and get the carts and oxen off the road."

Most of them were sullen and silent and Mingo tried to explain. "Macéo will come back this way. He'll need room to fight. Get the carts in the woods and out of his way. . . ."

A cannon sounded to the southwest and the low blo-o-o-m rolled and mumbled. Campos was attacking. A sharp rattle of musketry pricked the echo of the cannon, and Macéo was replying. The Army of the Oriente and Campos' Spaniards were joined in battle down the road to Manzanillo.

Mingo Dabney stood still an instant, then forced himself to head up the slope, motioning for his twenty *Grillos* to follow. He had no plan. His bare feet were tender, sensitive to the broken twigs, and the sharp *kaquaso* grass lashed at his feet, cutting them until they bled. Praise the Lord for the mist. It was so thick and lay so close to the ground that the carts were shadows and the tops of the palm trees had no trunks.

The cannonading increased to the southwest and the men

whispered, "Peralejo." Mingo didn't know the place. Perhaps the Spaniards were pressing so hard that Macéo could not come back. Perhaps he must leave his rear exposed to Sagaldo.

Another horse neighed high above them, then another. Mingo held up his hand, halting his men. "Hug the ground." He whispered the words and they almost stuck in his throat. The rim of the sun poked over the ridges, but the sun was hazy in the mist.

They crawled about half a mile, slipping over logs and around trees and Mingo was dripping sweat. His feet were scratched and bruised and bleeding, yet he was not aware his feet were raw. He shifted his ax from his right hand to his left hand, then back to his right hand, balancing it, testing the feel of the handle.

The Spanish patrol was resting in a clearing, sheltered by laurel trees. Mingo saw them through the brush and fell flat on his belly, pointing to them. They numbered sixteen and their arms were stacked. He studied them, watching them move as the mist drifted, blotting them from view, then shifting to expose them again. They were young; most of them younger than he. Frightened boys, pasty-faced and scared.

They were looking toward the southwest, toward Peralejo, the rumble of cannon down there, the staccato of rifles.

The *Grillos* were restless, fingering their *machetes* and waiting for a sign from El Dabney.

One of the Spaniards moved away from the group and glanced down the slope. Mingo's heart swelled and he wiggled into the ground, trying to bury himself in the grass. The Spaniard stood motionless, staring, then yelled and leaped for his rifle.

Mingo sprang up and his hand slipped down his ax handle and he hurled it, hurling it underhanded as he had done so often in Lebanon. His men screamed at the same moment and lunged forward. The ax struck the nearest Spaniard on the chest and there was the startled look of fear, then a contortion of pain as the man dropped his head, clawing at his chest before he fell.

There was no command and no need for command. The Mambises swarmed over the Spaniards like bees crawling on a honeycomb, slashing at their necks, chopping and hacking as they fell to the ground. The pilgrim was sobbing in sudden terrible anger and in suffocating fear. He grabbed his ax from the ground and swung it and felt it sink in soft, and pulled it back and swung again. Remember the *Virginius!*

Most of the Spaniards went down in the first rush and the others were borne and beaten to the ground. They lay there pleading for mercy. The Mambises laughed and slit their necks and unlaced their shoes and slid them off.

"Get their guns!" It was El Dabney's first order. He jerked up a rifle and examined it hurriedly. One of the Spaniards was crawling away and Mingo aimed at his head and fired. It was the first shot of the fight and the man spilled forward and twisted slowly to his side. The Mambises snatched up other rifles, cackling their laughter as they shot the pitiful few who had not finished their business of dying.

It was all over, and they had sixteen rifles and sixteen pairs of shoes and Mingo stood and looked around. There were shouts at the top of the hill, and a few scattered shots came whining down the slope, cutting the grass. Sagaldo's army was forming to attack.

"Shoot back!" El Dabney pulled his gun to his shoulder and fired. It was a waste of powder and the Mambises scowled. They held their precious rifles in the crooks of their arms and scurried among the dead, ripping off clothes and tearing out earrings, scooping up handfuls of cartridges and chopping off fingers for rings. Each stuffed his pockets until there was nothing else to garner; then they all began drifting away, exhibiting their loot and excitedly jabbering their glee.

A fusillade roared down from Sagaldo's army, drowning out the sound of musketry at Peralejo. One of the Mambises gripped his stomach and sprawled forward in the grass. The others watched him, then slid to their knees and crawled toward Mingo Dabney, gathering quickly around him and waiting for him to tell them what to do.

They didn't have a chance if they tried to run across the clearing, and because they didn't have a chance Mingo took one, taking it instinctively, without reason, without design. "Shoot back!" In the sudden return of terror, his command was half a sob, half a wild scream. "All together. Shoot that way." He pointed to the right and got to his knee and fired. The others fired too and Mingo loaded and fired to the center, foolishly rising and standing upright. The *Grillos* shot to the left and swung back and shot to the right. They were blindly confused and in their desperation they confused the Spaniards as they poured volley after volley up the slope. Sagaldo hesitated and there were cries from the hilltop and hurried commands, evidence of their confusion.

"Now run!" The pilgrim gripped his rifle and started down the slope, driving his men before him.

The hilltop was quickly silent, and the *Grillos* dashed through the woods, racing madly for the road and their carts. They had rifles and they brandished them, swinging them aloft, and they had shoes.

They were halfway down the slope, screaming their triumph when a shower of rifle fire scattered them. Mingo dived for a bush and crept behind a log, melting himself into the earth while the shots sprinkled the slope, shaving the leaves and slicing bark from the ceiba trees.

For a minute he lay there, his face burrowed under the log and his hands clasped behind his neck. Then all was quiet again and he raised his head. His *Grillos* were out of sight and he heard their shod feet plopping down the road to the carts. He crawled to his knees, and slowly to his feet, crouched and tense as he peered back up the hill, and down toward the road.

A cautious man in the woods, he abandoned any idea

of quick flight and resorted to stealth. His instinct urged him to dash for the road, but his hunter's training told him to circle, and approach the road from another direction. He gripped his rifle in his left hand, glanced sharply toward the brink of the hill and headed around the ledge of the slope instead of down it.

The laurel grove directly ahead offered shelter and he hunched his back and crept toward it, keeping the brush between him and the hilltop. He reached the thicket and turned to dash for the road when a jumble of voices brought him up sharp. He straightened and wheeled; and almost cried out.

Leopold Sagaldo and two staff officers were about thirty yards away at the uphill edge of the thicket, their horses reined tight as they surveyed the slope, nodding back toward the crest and pointing toward Peralejo and the sound of battle.

Mingo Dabney was wedged to his tracks, his mouth open in stark terror as he gaped at the dreaded grandee, his young-looking, clean-shaven face and the delicate skin. Then Sagaldo saw him and spoke sharply: "Mambi!"

"The *Virginius!*" El Dabney screamed it and never knew why he screamed it. He jerked his rifle to his shoulder, and his whole body was quaking, wavering his aim.

The two staff officers fumbled for their pistols, but Sagaldo stared at him, a flicker of recognition in his startled expression. He reached for his saber and raked his spur down his horse's flank.

Mingo fired and the bullet creased Sagaldo's horse and he reared in pain, pawing the air and breaking his stride. Sagaldo reined him down.

That was all Mingo saw. A shot from one of the officers kicked up dust beside him and he crouched and plunged into the thicket. It never occurred to him to turn and fire again. El Dabney of the *Grillos,* the pilgrim of the vows, scurried like an animal flushed by the hounds. He paused only once, cocked his ear uphill, and stood poised and trembling. There was no sound of pursuit and he ducked his head and raced for the road, then down the road, crying and screaming, "Sagaldo! I saw Sagaldo!"

There was none to hear him and, now that he was safe, he suddenly was ashamed of his fear. He slowed his pace to a fast jog, hurrying down the road toward his camp.

And when he got there, the carts still were standing right where he left them. The Mambises on the raiding party were proudly showing their shoes to the others who had been ordered to move the carts. They saw him coming and waved their rifles and *machetes*. "Ah-h, El Dabney. You cannot run as fast as us. Ah-h."

"I saw Sagaldo!" Mingo was among them, pushing them aside as they crowded around. "He'll jump us in a minute —"

"Ah-h, El Dabney. We did not see Sagaldo." They looked at him and at one another, and grinned.

Mingo threw down his rifle and stamped his naked foot and winced with pain. Wildly he cursed mankind in general and specifically he cursed Cuban Mambises. "Yoke 'em!" He ran among the oxen, herding them toward the carts. There was smoke in the sky down near Peralejo and silence in the hills, but Sagaldo was forming and soon would sweep down. "Get the carts off the road."

His small band responded, hopping about like crickets and laughing, jumping up and down like children in a game, showing their new earrings, aiming their rifles, bragging of their courage.

The sun was strong and the mist was rising, exposing the slope and exposing them. Mingo was gushing sweat as he struggled with the oxen, flogging them into the woods, over logs and deep into the brush.

The road was open for Macéo if Macéo came back; if he dared divide his little army and turn on Sagaldo while Campos still was attacking. The din from Peralejo swelled.

240

"Be ready to clear out," Mingo yelled. "Be ready to run if Sagaldo jumps us —"

The pounding of hoofs down the road drowned his words and he looked to the south, hearing horses he could not see. But the Spaniards saw and the challenge stabbed down from the hills:

"*Viva España!*"

Spain was calling her defiance, crying her ancient glory. Aragon and Castile. Granada and the Alhambra. *Viva España*. . . .

"*Cuba libre!*"

The answer swept up from beyond the woods, up from the road to Manzanillo. "*Cuba libre! Viva Baire!*"

"Santiago! *Venga Mambi!*" It was the Spanish taunt, the Spanish dare and disdain. "St. James! Come on, Mambi! Come on, dirt, and die!"

Mingo Dabney tore at his collar and screamed toward the hills. "They're coming! They're coming, you greasy bastards!"

Macéo was coming back!

He had dared divide his little army and turn on Sagaldo, even while Campos was in full attack.

Soto was the first man Mingo saw; hunched over his horse's neck, beating the foaming animal with the flat of his *machete*, pounding through the woods, picking the short cuts, leaping the logs.

"Macéo!" he screamed. "Clear the road. Macéo is coming back."

"She's clear!" Mingo ran toward him, waving his rifle. "She's clear, Soto. Let him come."

"Campos is falling back!" Soto jumped from his horse and into Mingo's open arms. He was shrieking the news, "Campos is retreating!" Even the little Mambi did not know it was a ruse, Macéo's trick to pull Sagaldo out of the hills. "We are winning at Peralejo!" Soto was shouting the news that Macéo had planted.

"Good God A'mighty!" Mingo yelled. "Campos is falling back!"

El Dabney's *Grillos* took it up, racing through the woods and screaming it. "Campos is running away. Macéo is coming—"

A flash of time and a wave of dust and Antonio Macéo charged out of the woods, leading a hundred horsemen up from Peralejo, up the road from Manzanillo. Mingo Dabney swallowed his heart and almost choked on the breath that hung in his throat.

There he was; there was The Brown One, swaying slightly as he rode, rocking slightly, brown marble on a red horse. There were lines deep in his face, the marks of a man risking one against a score. Miro was back at Peralejo. So was Goulet. The Ducasse brothers. Pedro Díaz. Quintín Banderas. All except Macéo, and Macéo was leading his charge alone.

"Campos is fleeing!" The horsemen shouted the news, roaring it toward the hills. "We are coming, Sagaldo. The *machete*! On, on, you Mambises! The *machete*! We are coming!"

And come they did, pounding up the road, churning the dust into clouds that almost hid them, beating the dust into layers that seeped through the woods; their own horses choking and themselves waving their naked *machetes* and shrieking.

Mingo's breath refused to come, locking in his throat, and he stood trembling as they flashed by. Macéo saw him and Macéo, The Brown One, smiled and drew his sword, his gleaming Toledo blade, and saluted Mingo Dabney, galloping by at the full salute of El Dabney and his *Grillos*. The sword flashed for an instant and was gone and Macéo was gone, on toward the hills.

"Cuba libre! We are coming, Sagaldo! *Viva Baire!"*

The pilgrim jumped on his cart and took off his hat and screamed. "Macéo! Macéo!" He threw down his hat and leaped to the ground and shrilled: "Cre-e-e-e-o-o-o-o." The old catamount cry of the Dabneys.

The Mambises stared at him and Soto moved toward him and some of Macéo's horsemen, galloping by, turned their eyes from the road to El Dabney of the *Grillos*.

The army surged by and the dust rolled behind them and the *impedimenta* ran after the horsemen. More shoes! Maybe a shirt! It was all over in a minute, a minute of thundering horses and flashing *machetes*. Mingo and Soto were left alone with the carts, staring wild-eyed up the road as though they had seen phantoms gallop by. A volley rolled down the hill and Macéo dashed up the slope, and confusion settled over the woods, merging into cries and curses and death.

"No quarter!" The Mambises roared it.

"No quarter!" The Spaniards roared it.

"Baire!"

"Santiago!"

Macéo wheeled to the right, skirting the hilltop, then wheeled left and struck Sagaldo's flank, rolling it up. "Campos is retreating!" It sounded above all else and soon the Spaniards were saying it, repeating it among themselves, scarcely believing it, yet repeating it.

Mingo and Soto stood by their carts, staring at each other, struggling to collect their reason. There was fighting to the north and fighting to the south and El Dabney looked down at his feet and they were bleeding. "My feet are all cut up, Soto. Somebody stole my shoes. And I saw Sagaldo. I got a shot; and missed."

The little Mambi leaned against the cart and panted.

"We'd better go help 'em," Mingo said, saying it calmly, for suddenly he was strangely at ease.

"There's nothing we can do," Soto said. The cascade of musket fire from Peralejo and the deep belching of the cannon mingled with the shrill cries from the hills. "We better stay here with the carts."

"We can help the wounded."

"There will be no wounded."

The battle was raging around the crest of the hill and Sagaldo was falling back, retreating westward. The rattle of shots was dying down and only occasionally the crack of a rifle spurted out of the dust that swirled around the hilltop and drifted down the slope.

"Santiago!" The defiant cry came from west of the slope and Sagaldo was riding away, extracting his men, pulling them out of the hills and racing to the aid of Campos, to reinforce the main army at Peralejo.

Campos wasn't falling back. Campos was attacking, throwing his men against Miro, against Goulet and the others, hurling his Spaniards against the rabble.

Sagaldo was riding hard to help a man who didn't need his help, skirting the hills to reach his captain-general.

Macéo flung his men out of the hills, racing straight for Peralejo to turn Campos before Sagaldo arrived. . . .

The dust hung low over the hilltop and rolled down the slope and the Spaniards were gone. Macéo's Mambises were gone, too, except those who would never go. Mingo and Soto went among the dead, the Spaniards and the Mambises alike, taking off their clothes and their shoes.

The *impedimenta* began drifting back, laughing and giggling and pointing to their treasures; guns and cartridges and shirts and earrings. And shoes! *Por Dios*, soft Spanish shoes!

The sky over Peralejo was a pall of smoke and red flames fingered into the black, streaking it. The hills were still and silent, but around Peralejo the first great battle of Cuba's revolution still was raging, the cannon thundering along the road to Manzanillo.

Soto said, "The way is open to Baragua." He whispered it. "This time I am sure." There was no need to whisper except to appease the awe that gripped him.

"Then we'll pull out." Mingo whispered, too, glancing

down toward Peralejo, at the boiling black roof over the valley and the streaking red and yellow.

The morning was half away and El Dabney lined up his carts and ordered the loot piled beside the road to be shared. The *Grillos* muttered against giving up anything, but they grudgingly piled it up and Mingo instructed each man to take one pair of shoes, one shirt, one gun.

Then he searched among the shoes, eagerly clawing for a pair to fit him, but the largest was too small for him. "Spaniards all have small feet," he said to Soto. He said it again. "Spaniards all have small feet." There was a swing to it, like, "Shave and a haircut, bay rum."

The tune was in his mind and he hummed it over and over, stilling the excitement of the morning. "Spaniards all have small feet—shave and a haircut, bay rum."

There was nothing for him to do but walk barefooted to Baragua and trust that Elmo Batson had sent a pair of shoes big enough for his Mississippi feet.

"All *gringos* have big feet." Soto hummed it and grinned, and the *impedimenta* began humming and singing as they loaded the carts with loot.

There were cries in Peralejo. Macéo was there. So was Sagaldo.

El Dabney's feet were bleeding and his head hurt from a dull, slow throbbing, but he cracked his whip over his oxen and they headed out; the pilgrim hobbling barefooted beside his team, leaving some of his blood in the woods not far from Baire.

All morning they moved north and the sounds of Peralejo were behind them as they veered east for Baragua. Mingo's feet cracked open and he greased them with suet and wrapped them in canvas. The night came and the night brought the drums.

Macéo had won at Peralejo! Campos, the fat one, was in full retreat and Sagaldo, the haughty one, was storming his contempt of the captain-general.

245

Goulet was dead.

Macéo was wounded twice; a nick in the arm, a sear in the thigh.

Campos was never able to unite his force, to mount a concentrated attack.

"Let's get going," El Dabney told his men as the drums still rolled. "Whip 'em up and let's get going."

They traveled until the oxen stumbled from weariness and Mingo gave them six hours rest, then moved at daybreak. Throughout the hot simmering day of July 14, the day after Peralejo, the caravan lumbered on and the day ended without rain, the first dry day of months. That night the drums told them more:

Macéo was leading his horsemen east toward Santiago de Cuba.

Miro was bringing the infantry over the hills to Baragua.

The *Grillos* reached the village of Cauto Abajo at twilight the afternoon of July 15. The swelling was almost out of Mingo's feet, but they were cracked and calloused. His trousers were torn, frayed to shreds around his ankles. His hair jutted low over his neck and his shirt was matted stiff. But he had a gun, a Spanish Mauser, and he slanted the greasy brim of his hat; his step was jaunty again.

Darkness came fast and the drums talked, stirring the night with news and rumors.

The Mountains of Our Master had swallowed Macéo. There was no word from The Brown One, no hint of his destination.

Gómez' army numbered 1200 in Camagüey.

La Entorcha was on the plains rallying the Mambises.

And that day, July 15, 1895, Cuba announced her Declaration of Independence.

The drums pounded the story through *la tierra del Mambi*. The members of revolutionary government, most of them still in exile, hurled a declaration at Spain and at all the other powers. All men were equal before the law . . .

246

Life . . . Liberty . . . It sounded vaguely familiar as the drums recited the dare, the declaration of a new nation.

"What does it mean, El Dabney?" The Mambises stared their wonder. "A declaration of independence? What does it mean, *compadre*?"

The pilgrim could not tell them. He was not sure himself. Something like they had back home, he reckoned. Something like that.

MINGO DABNEY

Chapter 19 Baragua was not a town at all, only a cluster of thatched huts in a mango grove. However, Palmarito was a stone's throw away and Palmarito was a center of trade, twenty miles north of Santiago de Cuba.

There were women and rum and gambling in Palmarito and the *Grillos* scurried there to barter their loot and, after they were drunk enough, sell their shoes. Only Soto was left with Mingo at Baragua to guard Elmo Batson's supplies.

It would be days before his *Grillos* worked again, and Mingo had no intention of waiting that long. Miro was coming with the *machete*-men of the Army of the Oriente and Macéo might sweep in any day with his horsemen. El Dabney recruited labor, promising no pay for their work but Macéo's wrath if they refused, and he went to work uncrating the supplies.

First he sought a pair of shoes for himself, but there was none. There were guns packed in grease, and cartridges and dynamite, but no shoes. The need for shoes became an obsession with the pilgrim and he grumbled through the days, growling even at Soto.

His *Grillos*, poor as ever, drifted back from Palmarito, giggling and boasting their wild lies of love and merriment. El Dabney put them to work building a camp in the mango grove.

General Miro and the dog-tired veterans of Peralejo arrived July 20. But what of Macéo? Miro shrugged and even the Haitians were silent about The Brown One.

248

Recruits from as far away as the sugar plains converged on Baragua and Mingo hoped some of his friends of *El Delfín* might be among them, maybe Nick González or Stockingcap. However, he knew none of the recruits and they spoke two names: Macéo who would lead them, *La Entorcha* who had rallied them.

They did not know the whereabouts of Antonio Macéo, and the drums still were silent.

The mobilization at Baragua spoke its own story in the dust of restless feet, in the orders of impatient chieftains. The time was near for The Brown One to invade the heartland of Cuba. This was as obvious as the big, red nose of Pepe Rosado, as the big, calloused feet of El Dabney, whose feet were so big the *Grillos* made puns about them and called him The Big Feet when he drove the men too hard.

The first inkling of Macéo's whereabouts came from Spanish deserters. He was down near Santiago de Cuba, herding a force into a valley, fattening them for the kill.

Then the drums broke their silence! Macéo had crushed a force within two days of Baragua, compressing them into a knot, and cutting the knot to bits. That was all! The night swallowed him, the night and the hills.

General José Macéo, The Brown One's brother, was laid up with sciatica near Guantanamo and Spaniards were all around him, but where was The Brown One?

July of 1895 melted into August and the rains slackened. Baragua swarmed with fifteen hundred Mambises and El Dabney's carts were tight and snug. His oxen were fat and his men were fat. They prepared dynamite, wrapping the fuses, making the explosives ready, and waited for orders to pounce out of the mountains and strike for the plains. The Army of the Oriente was primed, but where was Macéo?

In Daiquiri? In Daiquiri, the drums said, and the Spaniards heeded the lie and sent an army to Daiquiri to rot in the monotony of waiting. In La Maya, the drums said and the Spaniards hurried to La Maya. In La Lima. The drums scattered the enemy through the hills and the Haitians laughed.

The strain of idleness began to tell on the Army of the Oriente and a few Mambises deserted. But Macéo knew what he was doing. A mobilized army at Baragua was a threat, and The Brown One, riding one day and hiding the next, kept the Oriente in turmoil and the Spaniards in despair.

There was criticism of Campos in Madrid, then slurs from Havana. Gómez was raiding in the sugar country and the overlords demanded protection, draining off Spanish soldiers to protect private property, splitting the cumbersome Spanish army into useless little units. *Por Dios!* Macéo knew what he was doing. And old Gómez, too.

Captain-General Campos hastened to Havana and Sagaldo commanded in the Oriente. General José Macéo, sick as he was, made a show of force and Sagaldo turned his wrath toward José Macéo, maneuvering his forces to trap the brother of The Brown One and bring Cuba to tears.

Madrid was appalled by the Cuban hornet she had aroused and the cabinet tottered. Spanish liberals begged justice for the Mambises and autonomy for Cuba. It was too late. The Volunteers were frightened and demanded an aggressive war from the crown and the removal of Campos.

Then the Church spoke, instructing the Mambises to sheathe their *machetes* and return to their fields. The queen-regent was a devout Catholic. Pope Leo was godfather to the boy king. So the bishops said, "Your allegiance, Mambises, is with your Church and your king." They didn't point out that Spain owed money to the Church and was paying in government bonds, and the bonds were no better than the prosperity of the Volunteers in Cuba.

Here and there a few priests gave aid to the Cubans, and it was whispered that the Bishop of Pinar del Río favored the revolution; but now, while the mango grove of Baragua swarmed with Mambises, every organized and orthodox force in Cuba was turned against them—God and gold and guns.

Day after day, on into August, Mingo Dabney drove his men, patching and repairing and foraging wide for food. But the silence about Macéo was unbroken. Gómez was encamped in Camagüey, the wily old chief awaiting a sign from the Oriente, the spark from the hills, the fire. But still no news of Macéo.

A silence settled, too, over *La Entorcha,* a frightening silence, and men whispered. She was on the plains, rallying recruits to Gómez. No, she was in Sancti Spiritus, reciting the words of Martí. Then even the rumors ceased and there was nothing from the plains, only silence.

El Dabney made a pair of shoes for himself. They were crude and bulky, and the *Grillos* laughed at The Big Feet with lumpy shoes. They pointed and snickered; it was very funny to all except Soto and without a word he disappeared, riding away one night.

Mingo assumed that the little Mambi was seeking Martí's betrayer and thought no more about it, until his comrade returned with a pair of shoes large enough for the *gringo's* feet. The pilgrim grinned, taking long steps in his new shoes, and the *Grillos* cheered. Miro sent his congratulations and the Ducasse brothers proclaimed the Army of the Oriente safe now that the big feet of El Dabney were shod.

"Where did you get them?" Mingo asked.

Soto pointed his chin toward the east. "Out there."

El Dabney did not press him. They were Spanish shoes and that meant another dead Spaniard. "Did you find your man? Or anything about him?"

The guide of Guantanamo, the keeper of eight goats, lifted his face to his comrade, a riddle in his eyes, a question; then turned his head quickly. "I was not seeking him. I went for shoes. I was sick of your grumbling."

The *Grillos* heard the talk and one demanded, "Who is your man, Soto?" They had asked him a hundred times and it was their favorite joke, pestering the goatherd for the name of a man he expected to kill.

"I am not sure. . . ." Always before he had said he did not know.

"Is he Pepe López?" It was like asking if he was John Smith.

Soto shook his head. Usually he enjoyed the play, but now he was moody. "I will find him."

"Is he Pepe Pozo?"

"No."

The *Grillos* rolled on the ground in laughter, beating the ground with their fists and laughing until their sides hurt. It was a big joke. Ah-h-h! A man always looking for a man.

"Pepe Roca, perhaps?"

"Aw, leave him alone." Mingo winked at Pepe Rosado. "There is no man. It is a woman —"

"A woman, El Dabney!" They feigned severe looks of astonishment. "Soto runs away to see a woman?"

"That's right."

Soto scowled. "Some day I will tire of your jokes."

"Is she a big woman, El Dabney?" The *Grillos* asked it in unison, shouting the question. It was always like that.

"*Sí.* She is a big juicy woman." Mingo cupped his hands in front of his chest, far out. "She cradles Soto. Ah-h-h." He touched his fingers to his lips and smacked, blowing a kiss to the air. "Mm-m-m. I have heard him talk about her in his sleep —"

"His sleep? What does he call her, El Dabney?" It was very funny.

"His little nanny goat!" Mingo said.

The *Grillos* beat their legs and laughed and the pilgrim laughed and Soto walked away.

It was always the same. Work and sweat all day, then a joke and a laugh, and the drums at night . . .

Sagaldo was closing in on General José Macéo, and the staff at Baragua began fidgeting. The Ducasse brothers were glum and Pedro Díaz wanted to pull out enough men to race to the aid of their ailing comrade. Miro restrained

252

them. He had served The Brown One long enough to learn patience.

Where was Macéo? Havana asked, and Camagüey pleaded, and the Mambises whispered in the mango grove.

Then the drums thundered the news, booming the tidings. The Brown One's brother was a bait, a lure. Sagaldo struck for the sick man and Antonio Macéo swept out of the hills, scattering Sagaldo's army like leaves running low and fast before the wind. The drums told it all, pounding so furiously that Soto cursed the Haitians for their frenzied stammering, the slurring and blurring of the drumbeats.

The Spaniards were immobilized in the Oriente! Now for the plains!

Havana wailed her fears. The capital was six hundred miles from the Oriente but what were six hundred miles to The Nigra who struck and was gone, and struck again.

And Gómez was moving, clearing a path through Camagüey. *La Entorcha* was with him.

Macéo was heading for Baragua.

Ah-h-h. Come back to your Mambises, Macéo. Come lead us out of the hills and down to the plains. We will march with you to Pinar del Río. We will tear the tyrant's colors from Havana's Morro Castle. Come to your Mambises, Macéo.

Germany scowled at England and Uncle Sam arched his eyebrows, peering down his long nose at the little island near his feet. Um-m-m. Well, now, I do declare. They might pull it off. Maybe we ought to help 'em. Nope. Better tend to our own knitting. But they might do it. Sure as the Lord made little apples they might pull a miracle. Like Yorktown. Humbug! Crazy talk. Like the cow jumped over the moon— like thunder in the sun.

The first Cuban constitutional assembly met at Jimaguayu on September 13, 1895 and elected Salvador Cisneros Betancourt president of the republic conceived in the soul of José Martí and now borning.

Uncle Sam ran his tongue around his cheek and pondered.

Jimaguayu? Where the hell is that? Why didn't they pick an easy name? Like Philadelphia.

Now they want guns. On credit! Uncle Sam tugged at his goatee and fretted. Business is mighty bad, but not bad enough to sell guns on credit. We'll just tend to our own knitting. . . .

The drums told none of that. The drums told that Antonio Macéo was heading for Baragua, traveling slowly because he spent much time in his hammock.

Macéo in his hammock! The Mambises looked at one another, and the drums hinted.

Macéo's head drooped as he rode. He was tired.

Macéo tired? Brown marble tired! Tell us the truth. Don't hint. What is it?

Macéo was sick.

Soto wept as he read the drums and Mingo Dabney closed his eyes to shut in the tears. Lord, have mercy. Not now.

Yellow fever? The Mambises asked it in their glances at one another, in their stares at Miro.

Malaria, the drums said. He could no longer sit his saddle. They were bringing him to his Mambises on a stretcher.

The road from Palmarito to the mangos of Baragua was lined with his warriors and even the Haitians came down from their lookouts and stood close by the cock-feathered fangs of Goulet—Goulet who was dead; close by the hill fighters of Quintín Banderas, the clansmen of the Ducasse brothers, and close by the *Grillos* of El Dabney.

The men broke into sobs and wails as he passed lying unconscious on a stretcher lashed between two mules. He did not open his eyes and the men stood on tiptoe and stared at him, and turned away. His mouth was tight around his teeth and the teeth were bare in the stupor of fever. His skin was the color of old parchment; but he wore linen, and his Toledo blade lay sheathed beside him.

They carried him to a *bohio* in the mango grove and his doctor came and looked at him and shook his head.

All that night the Mambises wailed and the Haitians muffled their drums, tolling the news through *la tierra del Mambi*. Mingo sat on the edge of his cart, staring at his fire and thinking of Rafaela, her sorrow; then searching the fates that snarled the destiny of men like Antonio Macéo. Twenty-two Spanish scars on his body, yet there he lay helpless of a disease as common as a cold.

Soto sat by Mingo, his head bowed and his lips moving, mumbling his ritual. The goatherd believed in prayer and in his Church and her saints, and over and over he prayed, his black fingers telling the beads on his rosary. Five Hail Marys he tolled on each hand, and an Our Father.

Mingo Dabney believed in prayer, too, but Macéo needed quinine to break his fever and blankets to break his chills. Quinine and heat and fresh air.

All that night rumors swept through the camp and left the Mambises trembling. Macéo was sinking. His eyes were glazed, and a priest was hurrying to his bedside. The sickness of The Brown One was a sign from heaven. The Church had put a curse on the revolution and God was angry at the Mambises, and was taking Macéo away.

"All right. All right . . ." The Lebanon woodsman broke into Soto's mumbling. "But has he got quinine? Go see if he has plenty of quinine."

"He has plenty. He has a good doctor —"

"A poultice at his back?"

"I do not know." Soto shook his head and fumbled his fingers.

"Go find out! I can make poultices. Don't sit here and watch a man die. Go find out!"

The little guide was weeping. "It is not my place. I am only a Mambi. I cannot prescribe for Antonio Macéo. Neither can you —"

"The hell I can't. I'm no Mambi."

The goatherd put his hand on the pilgrim's knee and looked up at him. "You are a Mambi, *compadre.*" It is the heart that borns one into the humble. Not the father, or the mother, but the soul that leads one up to the meek.

El Dabney tried to work the next day, but his men would not work. They huddled in little groups, staring toward the sick-hut. Macéo was delirious and tossed in his hammock, murmuring, "María, María."

The priest heard and crossed himself. Antonio Macéo was calling to Mary, calling to The Virgin.

General Miro shook his head at the doctor and did not tell the priest, but Macéo was calling for María, his wife.

Then The Brown One sat up in his hammock, breaking free from those who would hold him down, sat up straight and cried, "The *machete!* Baire!"

They forced him back and he lay limp, rolling his head, and his skin was fire to the touch; and his eyes opened in delirious wonder. "It is the sign! Thunder in the sun! *La Entorcha!*"

Miro went to the carts of the *impedimenta* and called Soto into the shadows. Then Miro walked away, and Soto came back to the camp and began saddling his horse.

Mingo Dabney watched him, but the guide did not look at him and Mingo walked over and bridled the horse while the Mambi secured the saddle, tightening the straps.

"Maybe you'll find your man."

Soto did not reply. He tossed the reins over the pommel and put his hand on the saddle and turned to the pilgrim. "He is calling for *La Entorcha.* He cries out for the sign. I, Soto, will bring her to him."

"You will bring Rafaela Galban here?"

The Mambi touched his comrade's arm. "*Amigo.* I am going to Camagüey and I will return with *La Entorcha.* With *La Entorcha, compadre.*" He swung up and gathered the reins and Mingo held the reins. Soto leaned out of his saddle and his voice was a plea and a claim. "I am a Mambi, and I am your friend. I will bring *La Entorcha* to this camp and I ask you to forget, for a while, that she is Rafaela Galban."

"Is there anything I can do for you, Soto? Any way I can help?"

"You can promise, El Dabney. You can make a vow to me, Soto, your friend and your brother."

There was an instant's stillness, and the pilgrim drew his hand from the reins. "I promise," he said, and stepped back and watched the horse spring away, running west toward Camagüey, the roofs thudding an echo to the toll of the muffled drums.

MINGO DABNEY

Chapter **20**   The September moon was at final quarter and the *kaquaso* grass was curling brown the night Soto brought Rafaela Galban back to the Oriente. They went straight to Macéo's hut and Mingo did not know they were back until the little Mambi came to his cart and woke him.

"You rode fast." Mingo blinked sleep from his eyes and rubbed them. "Is she all right?"

Soto nodded and blew the embers into flame and put a coffee pot on the ashes. "I found her just beyond the Spanish forts, the *trochas*."

"Think Macéo is any better?" Mingo was eager for talk.

The Mambi shrugged, watching the coffee. It came to a boil and Mingo handed him a cup and began his queries about the journey. Did she stand it all right? Were the fortifications hard to get through? Did Macéo recognize her?

"I am tired, *amigo*." The guide's eyelids were drooping. "*La Entorcha* is all right. Spain has manned the *trochas*. To-morrow we will talk." He poked out his arms, yawning and stretching, and climbed into the cart.

Mingo poured himself another cup of coffee and squatted by the fire, glancing frequently toward the sick-hut. She was only a few hundred yards away and yet she was the moon away because he had made a promise to Soto, his comrade.

A lantern moved in the *bohio*, dimly yellow for a moment, and General Miro and Rafaela walked out of the hut and toward his camp. Miro lifted the lantern high and called, "El Dabney."

"Here I am."

She stepped past Miro and into the light of the fire, nodding a greeting and holding her mantilla tight as she nodded. "Señor Dabney." Her black eyes were wide.

"Señorita Galban." Then he remembered and said, *"La Entorcha."*

"He is very sick. We need you."

Mingo reached for the lantern. "Let's get going." He swung away from his fire, holding the lantern high, walking fast, and she took two steps to his one, trying to keep up.

The doctor gripped his hand and thanked him for coming. They all were grateful that a well man was willing to help a sick man. Back in Lebanon, folks expected it. He stepped to Macéo's hammock, looked at the parched lips, and spoke over his shoulder to the doctor, "Got plenty of quinine?"

"Sí." The doctor was near exhaustion.

"I'll watch him at night. You watch during the day." He glanced around the room. "Now all of you get some sleep."

Miro walked toward the door, but Rafaela hesitated. "Do you need me?"

"If we do, we'll send for you. Get some rest."

The doctor snapped open his eyes, first at her, then at the *gringo* who dared give her orders. Rafaela Galban turned from them without a word and went swiftly out of the hut and into the mango grove.

"It's malaria," the physician explained to El Dabney.

The woodsman had lived with malaria all his life. The dry parched skin and the hollow eyes he recognized, but the quick, labored breathing frightened him. "Any signs of pneumonia?"

"Sí, but it's not pneumonia yet." He ran his hand across Macéo's forehead, brushing back the black coarse hair. "Pneumonia will kill him."

"He mustn't get pneumonia." Mingo pulled back the covers and put his ear to Macéo's chest and lungs.

For the first time in days, the doctor smiled. He had a nurse he could trust. "There are the medicines." He pointed to the table. "Quinine every three hours. No morphia unless you wake me." He lay on his cot and, after one heavy sigh, began breathing deeply.

Mingo turned the lantern low and moved it close to the hammock and sat on a box, applying cold towels to Macéo's forehead, wringing out each towel before he used it. He unbuttoned The Brown One's bedshirt and bathed his neck and chest, rubbing gently. He had no idea of time, of time passing, but when the sky was gray he blew out the lantern and got a basin of cold water and bathed Macéo's feet and legs, wiping them dry and covering him again, wrapping him close.

Rafaela came to the *bohio* before sunup and her eyes were red from worry and loss of sleep. She tiptoed into the room and stood by Mingo and her presence startled him. The doctor still was sleeping and Macéo's lips were drawn tight over his teeth.

"What can I do?" she whispered.

"Fill this pan with cold water."

Her hand trembled as she reached for the basin and some of the water spilled as she tilted the pitcher. But she obeyed. *La Entorcha Blanca* obeyed El Dabney of the *Grillos*; Rafaela Galban y Torres took orders from Mingo Dabney.

"We'll need some coffee." He dipped a towel in the water and laid it on Macéo's forehead, smoothing the ends close against the temples. Then he glanced at her and she was staring full at him. "You can make coffee, can't you?"

"Of course I can make coffee, Mingo."

"Make a heap of it. The doctor will want some."

Her collar was open at her throat, the laurel leaf pinned there. Her mantilla was loose to her shoulders and she did not touch it, but went outside to do as she was told. She got on her hands and knees and blew on some embers, blowing them into a blaze. She made the coffee strong and took a cup to him.

He nodded his thanks and she poured herself a cup and sat beside him. The doctor stirred in his sleep, mumbling his exhaustion. Mingo got up, stretching and easing his tiredness. "You sit here and keep cool towels on his head."

"Where are you going?" she asked quickly.

"Down to my camp. I'll be right back." He stepped into the morning air and drank deeply of it, and hurried on through the grove.

The *Grillos* were stirring and Soto was up, squatting by the fire and cooking goat meat. "I didn't go buttin' in up there," Mingo explained. "She and General Miro came for me."

The Mambi handed him a piece of meat. It was dripping hot and Mingo laid it on a slab of mahogany to cool, then gathered up an armful of sugar sacks and some rocks. Soto was eating his meat and licking his fingers, watching his friend. El Dabney reached for his own food. "Soon as the men eat, pick out a crew and meet me up there."

"*Sí*. Is *La Entorcha* with you, *compadre?*"

"*La Entorcha* is with Macéo," the pilgrim said and trudged back through the mangos.

The doctor and Rafaela were busy at the side of the hammock. Miro and the Ducasse brothers were in the room, and so was the priest. The *bohío* was hot and stuffy and Mingo put the sacks and rocks by the door and cut his eyes at the doctor, who nodded slightly.

"Gentlemen," said El Dabney of the *Grillos* to the staff of the Army of the Oriente. "There will be no more visitors until General Macéo is on the mend."

Miro started for the door, but the Ducasse brothers scowled their disapproval. Rafaela put a wet towel in a basin and her head came up haughtily. "Are you speaking to me, Señor Dabney?"

"It means all of you." He met her gaze and her eyes wavered. Thunder in the sun might perform miracles, but the Mississippi woodsman was trying to cure malaria.

Rafaela moved away without another word, without a glance at him, and the others followed, the Ducasses still scowling.

The doctor beamed his gratitude and reached for his coffee cup. "*La Entorcha* and Miro said you could do anything. I believe it."

"Don't." Mingo pointed to the rocks and sacks. "I'll heat the rocks and wrap 'em, and we'll be ready when the chills hit." Soto and his crew were coming up through the grove and he pointed toward them. "They'll build another hut and we can move him from one to the other, and fumigate the empty one."

He walked out and met his men and gave his orders quickly. No noise. The rafters must be tied in place. Thatch it with palm leaves and side it with banana leaves.

"How is Macéo, El Dabney?" Pepe Rosado asked.

"Alive."

"*La Entorcha* will cure him," said Pepe Barea.

"Ah-h-h," they all crossed themselves and nodded, all except Soto.

Mingo agreed with them and assigned their jobs. There was no waste of motion or time. Timber down. Haul away, *compadre*. Lawd, Lawd, John Henry. They worked silently lest they disturb their idol, and the *bohio* took form, a dry dirt floor and steady rafters. The soldiers gathered around, smiling encouragement and boasting that these were their *impedimenta*, a part of their army.

The *Grillos* were very proud, leaping about the rafters and tossing their tools from one to another. Pepe Barea was too proud. Never before had anyone admired anything he did, yet here were Macéo's Mambises watching him and praising him. It was too much for Pepe Barea. He began weeping and his tears made him nervous. No man must know that he wept, so he flourished his *machete* higher than anyone, and dropped it. It clattered down from the rafters and Pepe Barea blushed to the roots of his hair.

Some of the warriors smiled. They never dropped a *machete*. El Dabney braced himself and dropped the bar he was using to inch the logs into place, dropped it clumsily and laughed at himself. "Dropped my bar, John Henry," he called to Pepe Barea.

"I dropped my *machete*, El Dabney."

"You're almost as clumsy as I am." Mingo swung down and tossed the *machete* back to Pepe Barea. None dared smile at El Dabney's mistake and the shame left the face of Pepe Barea, and he grinned. Lawd, Lawd, John Henry.

They knocked off for dinner and by mid-afternoon the *bohio* was finished and Mingo winked at Soto. "These fellows did right good. How far is it to Palmarito? Five miles?"

"Four miles, El Dabney." His *Grillos* chorused the answer. "Only four miles."

"Well, now, I thought it was five miles." He turned his back and they scooted away. They had no money; but it didn't cost anything to look at the women of Palmarito, and there might be a bottle of rum with no one watching too closely.

Mingo walked into the sickroom and to the hammock and looked down at Macéo, then at the doctor. "Can we move him?"

"The sooner the better. I'll call some help."

"Never mind." The pilgrim wrapped the covers tight around the unconscious man, and lifted him into his arms, cradling him close and feeling the fever hot through the covers. He carried him into the new *bohio* and covered him over again.

He helped the doctor move his medicines, and boarded up the old hut and burned sulphur in it. It was almost suppertime before he finished, and he went to his cart and napped.

Soto waked him. It was night again and the Mambi handed him a cup of coffee. "She made it," Soto said. "She came

263

here and made it and told me to give it to you. She said I must wake you when the moon came up."

Mingo sipped the brew slowly and it tasted better than any coffee he'd ever drunk before, better even than Lebanon coffee. "Pretty good coffee," he said, and swung out of his cart and walked through the mangos to take his turn again. . . .

Antonio Macéo's fever began breaking the third night while Mingo Dabney sat by him, fanning his face and mopping his forehead. A few tiny drops of perspiration came to Macéo's forehead and to his neck and the pilgrim bent quickly and felt his lips. There was sweat on his lips and in his mustache.

Mingo started to call the doctor, but waited a minute to be sure, and Macéo opened his eyes, staring wildly around him. Mingo watched him, hoping his eyes would clear. They didn't, and he leaned over and whispered, "*La Entorcha* is here."

Macéo relaxed and a faint smile crossed his face. Then he groaned and slipped into a coma. Mingo aroused the doctor and they examined the sick man. "The fever is breaking up in a chill," the physician said. "A night without morphia would help."

"Let me try it."

The doctor rubbed the back of his neck and sat on the edge of his cot, probing the ends of his little finger into the corner of his eye. "All right. Call me if you need me."

The woodsman heated the rocks and put them at Macéo's feet, and loosened the covers, letting the air circulate to his body. The Brown One shivered and Mingo tightened the covers again. The doctor nodded and closed his eyes.

A hundred little fires were banked in the camp and the Mambises slept fitfully, waking often and glancing toward the *bohio*. El Dabney turned down the lantern until it flickered, and pulled his chair close to the hammock. The Brown One groaned again and he touched the hammock, swaying it gently.

There was no way for him to know how long he sat there, rocking the hammock of Antonio Macéo. There was no clock in the room and the moon was hidden. His eyes got heavy and he rubbed them, closing them tight and blinking back the sleep; and he began singing to keep himself awake, softly, almost humming.

> *Is it not fine to dance and sing*
> *When the bells of death do ring?*
> *When the winds blow and the seas flow?*

He crossed his legs and rested one arm on his lap, swaying the hammock and almost dozing in the quietness of the night and the softness of his own singing. The past parted and he was back home, the people toiling and chanting their lament:

> *Was you there when they crucified my Lord?*
> *Was you there when they nailed Him to the tree?*
> *Sometimes it causes me to tremble, brother—tremble. . . .*

The Brown One opened his eyes and Mingo hushed his song. "El Dabney?"

"Yes, sir."

"You were singing. . . ." Macéo's head rolled to one side and his look wandered around the *bohío*, to the rafters, the dim lantern.

Mingo drew the covers gently into place. "You go back to sleep now." He whispered it.

The sick man glanced around again. "I thought *La Entorcha* was here."

"She is at her *bohío*. I will send for her."

A flick of light was in Macéo's eyes and he looked sternly at Mingo. "We Mambises do not send for *La Entorcha*. We go to her." He sighed deeply and closed his eyes again.

The pilgrim adjusted the covers and rocked the hammock, swaying it until Antonio Macéo lapsed into natural sleep.

Mingo Dabney gave credit for the general's improvement to the doctor, and the doctor gave credit to his medicines and the *gringo* nurse. So did Rafaela Galban. The Mambises, however, called it a miracle and looked to the sign.

A few priests gave prayers of thanksgiving and Martínez Campos, commander of all Spain's armies, publicly announced his gratitude that heaven had spared such a brave adversary. Havana was infuriated by the statement. Antonio Macéo was a nigra bandit and Campos was a sniveling fool. Send us a strong man, the Volunteers instructed Madrid and tightened their purse strings. The crown instantly took notice, looking around for another captain-general. But who was a strong man? Sagaldo? Spain dared not flaunt him to the world.

Then there was Lieutenant General Weyler, idle in Spain because the crown did not trust him. He was a quiet little man, always wearing alpaca. But he was a soldier, brave enough to cry justice, daring enough to advocate a Spanish republic. Weyler was too strong and Campos was retained in Cuba. Besides, His Majesty's ministers were not unduly worried. Macéo was still bedridden and Gómez was only growling; too old to bite. There was no hurry, the ministers said, no hurry in October of 1895. . . .

The Haitians' drums, muffled so long, pealed the tidings that The Brown One was recovering and *la tierra del Mambi* quickened, raising its eyes and looking toward the west, toward the *trochas*, and beyond the forts to the heartland of Cuba. The rainy season eased off, dying in a patter of showers, and the clouds soared high.

The Mambises gathered in the mango grove, squatting in little huddles, and watched the door of Macéo's *bohío*, waiting for him to arise and lead them away. The invalid, however, was too weak to sit up and scarcely strong enough to feed himself. So Mingo fed him, and the doctor fed him, and sometimes Miro came and spooned soup for his chief.

He was winning back his strength and growled for peppery soups, but the doctor shook his head and Mingo cooked rich, creamy broths. The color began returning to his cheeks and he was aloof again, withdrawing within himself. The pilgrim felt the barrier between them rising once more and made no effort to breach it. The doctor sensed the tension and was troubled, aware that the barrier rested on the soft shoulders of *La Entorcha*; a barrier as high as Macéo's superstitions, broad as his emotions.

Rafaela came to the *bohio* late each afternoon, about twilight, bringing fruits and sometimes flowers. Always it was the same: she came through the door smiling, wearing linen, and walked to the hammock. "You are looking better, sire."

He always replied, "I thank you, *La Entorcha*."

Then she turned and spoke to the doctor and to Mingo, and always Mingo answered impersonally. A promise was a promise and she must remain *La Entorcha* until her guardian was strong again.

Each day when her visit ended, the doctor, or Miro, or some other visitor walked with her to the door and bowed to her. Each day, until there came that twilight when Mingo was alone with Macéo and she came earlier than usual.

The Brown One was propped in his hammock and she talked with him until it was time for her to go, and Mingo escorted her to the door. There he bowed and turned back into the hut, and she motioned to the bench outside the doorway, indicating he was to sit by her. They were in full view of General Macéo, but beyond his hearing, and he did not look their way, closing his eyes to blot out the sight of *La Entorcha Blanca* by an unbeliever.

Mingo was nervous, even embarrassed, but Rafaela calmly smoothed her skirt, her eyes darting at him, and away. "The dry season has come," she said.

"Uh huh." He shifted slightly on the bench, looking out into the mango grove. "Nice and pleasant out here. Think I'll put up a shelter and move the general into the fresh air."

She folded her hands in her lap and the breeze rustled her mantilla and she did not tighten it. "Where did you learn to do so many things, Mingo?"

He grinned his pleasure at the flattery. "Around the lumber camps back home. You remember how it was."

She remembered little about Lebanon. "Why, yes, I recall. There were so many trees."

"Pine trees. And some hardwood . . ."

"I remember. . . ."

"There was a big tree up in front of our house." He wanted to talk about home, to talk about anything to detain her there in the pleasant twilight; and again the past opened and he took her with him back to Lebanon. The Dabney store. The days when Elmo Batson came, peddling his wares and popping his suspenders. Mingo grinned and twisted the tuft of hair as he talked. "Elmo was a scamp, all right."

"Scamp?" Rafaela was puzzled. "What's a scamp?"

"Oh, I don't know. Just a saying."

"Are you a scamp?"

"Me?" He began laughing and shoved his hands deep in his pockets. "I suppose so."

"Am I a scamp?"

The laughter went out of his throat and he faced her, looking first at her mantilla, the silver sheen under the silk, and at her eyes, and into her eyes. "You are the most beautiful woman who ever lived."

She caught her breath and lowered her eyes, then raised them slowly, saying nothing, only looking at him. She got up from the bench and he stood, too, and she looked up at him, watching his eyes. *"Minguillo,"* she whispered and touched his arm.

He felt for her hand, but she turned quickly and walked alone through the mangos, and he watched her until she was out of sight, knowing he must not follow her. He stood there until darkness awakened the hissing bugs and the pigeons, and he stepped back into the *bohio* and lighted the lantern.

The hot flush on Antonio Macéo's face was not fever. It was fear. She had asked this man to sit beside her and she had laughed like a little girl. Macéo had heard her laughter, ringing and carefree, and there should be no gaiety in thunder in the sun, no merriment in a symbol.

"Señor Dabney." His voice was strong again. "I am grateful, but I will not trouble you further. The *impedimenta* need you more than I."

Mingo Dabney put the lantern on a table and turned the wick until the light flooded the room. He gathered his sugar sacks and the rocks, and tossed the rocks out of the door. "You are right," he said. "I'll be with the *Grillos* if you need me again." He started for the door.

"El Dabney!"

Mingo turned abruptly, in no mood for further discussion. He hoped the general would not mention Rafaela to him. That would be a mistake.

"I have not had an opportunity to thank you for Peralejo." The Brown One was staring at his emaciated hand, the skin in folds. "They might have trapped us."

"I saw Sagaldo." He rested against the door, affecting a careless slouch although his nerves were coiled. "I got a shot, and missed."

Macéo looked up, his black eyes holding the American, piercing his mood. "So I heard. Sagaldo recognized you."

"That makes us even, sir. I recognized him, too."

They parted without another word and Mingo walked back to his cart and ate his supper with the *Grillos*, and one of them went to the camp of the *machete*-men and stole rum. Another came back with cigars and they sat around the campfires and feasted and drank and celebrated El Dabney's return. They told him a hundred lies about all they had done, the women they'd possessed, the things they'd stolen. They brought their rifles to him and showed that they were shiny. They held up their feet, pointing to their shoes.

General Miro and the doctor came to the camp of the *impedimenta* that night, and when the *Grillos* saw the doctor they quickly hid their cigars and fanned the smell from the air. General Pedro Díaz came down and so did Banderas and the Ducasse brothers. The staff of the Army of the Oriente stood by the campfire of the *impedimenta* and thanked El Dabney and thanked his men. Pepe Barea began weeping again, this time in joy and rum. A man's pride can take just so much.

Soto was very dignified, sitting on Mingo's cart and shifting his head from side to side, not deigning to betray the emotions that welled inside.

The generals went away and the cigars reappeared and El Dabney eyed his band. "They are good cigars. And it was good rum."

"Um-m-m." The *Grillos* poked out their lips. "But he did not need the cigars," they explained. "They were going to waste, El Dabney. The doctor could not smoke around Macéo—"

"And General Miro did not need the rum," the others declared. "A general should not drink rum. *Por Dios!* Macéo does not drink rum and he is the greatest general who ever lived, eh, El Dabney?"

"I reckon so," Mingo swung to his cart and sat beside Soto.

The little Mambi's cigar was in the side of his mouth, perked upward and he took it out and puffed a cloud of smoke. Then he put it back and rolled it between his teeth. "Well?" he asked.

The pilgrim looked at him for a second, and said, "The promise is ended, *amigo*."

"*Si*." Soto nodded. "It is ended, *compadre*."

MINGO DABNEY

Chapter **21** Mingo walked to **Palmarito** and spent the last of his Shannon money for a cotton shirt and denim trousers. He tried to buy shoe blacking, but there was none in town, so he bought a cigar instead, tilting it in the corner of his mouth as he tugged his hat to a jaunty angle and swaggered across the plaza: El Dabney of the *Grillos*.

The poster caught his attention because it proclaimed *peso duro*—hard money—and he jerked his head to see it, suddenly conscious of the stares of some loiterers. He grinned at them and began reading the proclamation, and gaped, alarmed and incredulous.

The poster challenged:

PESOS DUROS!
For the Heads Of:

Máximo Gómez	100,000
Antonio Macéo	100,000
José Miro Argenter	50,000
Quintín Banderas	30,000
Vidal Ducasse	30,000
Juan Ducasse	30,000
Pedro Díaz	30,000
Elmo Batson	15,000
Soto of Guantanamo	15,000
El Dabney of the *Grillos*	10,000

271

Eighteen names in all were on the list and it was signed: "Sagaldo!"

Mingo took the cigar from his mouth and glanced around, the suspicions of a hunted man tensing his muscles. The poor craved hard money, and his head was worth 10,000 pesos. *Recristo!* His first impulse was to walk away quickly, but not too quickly, and slip back to camp where he was safe. But the sign held him, vanity overcoming his trepidation.

An old man, a beggar in rags, sidled up to him. "El Dabney?"

"That's right."

The beggar nodded toward the poster. "You are in the company of the mighty, *amigo.*" He put his hand on Mingo's arm. "My nephew is a *Grillo.* Pepe Rosado. The one with the big red nose."

El Dabney was no longer afraid and grinned at the beggar and at the others who shuffled up, eight or nine old men, for no young men remained in Palmarito. They touched him, proud to touch him and he wished he had enough cigars to pass around. One of them spat at the sign and the pilgrim borrowed a pencil stub and ran a black line through the names on the poster, and added:

For the Heads Of:

The King of Spain	Two pigs
Leopold Sagaldo	Chitterlings

He signed it: "The *Grillos!*"

The spectators laughed, bobbing their heads in approval. It was very funny and El Dabney was a brave man. Pigs for the King of Spain. Ah-h-h.

Mingo slanted his hat a bit more and puffed on his cigar. He flipped a salute to the group and sauntered away, blowing smoke into the sultry air of the autumn afternoon.

All the way back to camp he thought about it. In the company of the mighty! Ten thousand pesos for a *gringo's* neck. By God, he was somebody.

He greeted Soto with the news and the Mambi grunted. "Sagaldo is a spendthrift." It took some of the starch out of Mingo, but not all of it. He was one of the select, and that night he was going to see Rafaela.

A song came to his lips and he mixed suet and soot and daubed his shoes and, his shoes safely placed in front of him, he stripped and bathed by his cart. There was no soap, but two of his *Grillos* sauntered away toward headquarters and there was soap in the wash basin of El Dabney the *gringo*.

Soto sat on the end of the cart, swinging his legs and commenting on the ablutions, and offering suggestions about the virtues of cleanliness. He thought they were silly virtues.

The *Grillos* nudged each other when Mingo washed his head. Ah-h-h. El Dabney was going to feast with Macéo and the muckety-mucks at headquarters. Um-m-m.

Soto knew better and got a razor and fastened a mirror to the side of the cart for his friend to use for shaving.

And then, in the cool of the evening just before daydown, Mingo Dabney walked through the trees to call on Rafaela Galban. That's the way they did it in Lebanon.

The duenna met him at the door, a gaunt, stern woman of Palmarito, ordered to the camp by Macéo to chaperon *La Entorcha* and fill out the pattern of Cuban traditions and customs. The woman wore a rumpled shawl and stray black hairs stood stiff on her bony chin. She glowered at him in disapproval because there was no place for young men in this *bohio*. Miro would upbraid her and she shuddered to think what Señorita Galban's guardian might say.

Rafaela heard his voice and came promptly. She stepped around the duenna and in front of her and welcomed him. "Won't you come in, Mingo?"

It sounded like Lebanon and Mingo grinned shyly, entering the *bohio* of Rafaela Galban y Torres. He took a chair at the far end of the hut and the duenna lit a lamp and turned it high as she put it on a table by him, and paraded to a corner nearby and plopped down, watching and sulking.

"Sure has been a nice day." Mingo started to cross his legs, then sat erect, aware of the duenna's stare. He wanted to tell Rafaela about the poster in Palmarito, but that might be boasting.

"The rainy season has gone." She sat in a chair facing him. Her blouse was embroidered.

"It has not gone yet," the duenna blurted, and added the comment of those who grow old. "We don't have rainy seasons like we used to."

Rafaela smiled and Mingo was afraid to. The duenna marched to the hearth and blew on the embers. "I'll make coffee." Her tone was gruff, implying that she might as well refresh this man and let him be on his way.

"No, Señora." Rafaela said it quietly but firmly, and stepped to the hearth. "I will make it."

The old woman stared at her, and arched her brows, peering at Mingo until slowly the sternness went out of her face and it was almost soft; a memory perhaps, a recollection. Without a word, she crossed the room and sat in the shadows.

Insects swarmed through the door and buzzed around the lamp and Mingo and Rafaela drank coffee and talked about the dry season and the wet season and the clear October weather. He said, "This is the busk season back home. Harvest time."

She said, "We will have no harvest in Cuba. There are not enough men to cut the cane. Do you grow cane in Lebanon? I don't remember any?"

"A little. Enough for syrup." He put his coffee cup on the table and crossed his legs.

The hearth fire was embers again and the duenna was nodding.

"It seems so long ago that I was in Lebanon." Her hand was at her throat, touching the laurel leaf. "The trees were so big. Like the trees in the valley where I was born."

"You never told me where you were born, Rafaela."

"I'd rather talk about Lebanon," she said quickly.

"I'd rather hear about you."

Her hand moved from the laurel leaf to the ruby of Martí and she looked down at the ring, turning it. "I was born near a village north of here. My father was a cocoa farmer." There was hesitancy and reservation in her words and they were stilted, like a person talking of another person and never about herself. "I was reared in a convent. Perhaps you knew that."

"Yes. But come to think of it, I never saw a convent."

Rafaela smiled and then her smile was a laugh. This man had never seen a convent. "They taught me many things."

"How to make coffee?"

"In the Cuban way, *sí*. But I remembered how they made coffee in Lebanon and I made yours that way." She lifted her eyes from the ruby and at him, and glanced at the duenna.

Mingo cut his eyes toward the old woman, too, and uncrossed his legs and began twisting the tuft of hair.

She looked up at his hair, staring at it, the black, free abundance of his hair, then turned her face from him. "They made me study music at the convent and I couldn't carry a tune to save me." She said it hurriedly, running the words together.

"I like singing," he said.

Her favorite color was blue. She told him that. She liked sweet things to eat and pastries.

Mingo said, "I like pies, too. Can you make pies?"

"What kind?"

"Mince. Apple. I like mince best."

She tried to hide her smile and her pleasure but they would not be denied. "They didn't teach me that at the convent." Some of the blacking from his shoes rubbed off on his new trousers and she saw that he was embarrassed and pretended not to see. "Will you have some more coffee?"

"No thank you." The night had given its legacy to the land, sharing it with the moon, and it was time to go back to his carts. The duenna was rustling her dress and squirming in her chair. So he got up and walked toward the door and they stood together, looking out at the land and the moon soft on the land. "May I come back tomorrow?" That's the way they said it in Lebanon.

"Yes, Mingo."

The oxen were lowing in their corrals and lamps were burning in Macéo's hut. Mingo passed close by the hut on his walk back to camp, and scarcely glanced that way.

He was back at Rafaela's *bohio* a bit earlier the next night and the duenna was almost cordial and coffee simmered on the hearth. There was a pie beside the coffee pot, and a tiny red burn on the girl's hand.

"There is no mincemeat in Cuba." The duenna saw him looking at the pie. "I told her that —"

"It's lemon," Rafaela said. "You like lemon pie, don't you?"

"I sure do."

She poured coffee and served the pie, sharing it with the old woman who insisted the crust needed more shortening.

It was more pleasant outdoors. They agreed on that. It was nice to watch twilight linger for the short life the tropics allotted it. The pigeons always called at twilight and sometimes the parrots whistled, but never loud at twilight. He pulled up a bench and they put it by the door and sat there.

Darkness came and she went inside and got a shawl and tossed it around her shoulders. The night was so quiet, so still; a little cool, but so peaceful. He veered their talk to her and she talked freely. Martí once took her to a great restaurant in New York, and there were many lights, and she wore blue. Sometimes Martí called her Rafaela, but her guardian never called her by that name. The ruby Martí gave her—she held it out and it was dull and heavy in the moonlight—belonged to his mother.

They talked of many things that night, and he was close to saying what he wanted to say, almost opened the floodgates of his heart. But a pigeon called, or a parrot whistled, or the

276

duenna moved. Or a leaf rustled, or the moon shadowed. And he didn't say what he ached to say.

This was the courtship of Mingo Dabney.

Miro knew about it and did nothing. Antonio Macéo knew and his despair was deeper, the terror that his lodestar was only a woman. He sat up for an hour or so each day, but still was weak and spent most of his time in his hammock staring at the sky, hearing again the roll of thunder. . . .

Each night Mingo called on Rafaela Galban, and their words were whispers, a man and a girl whispering under the busk moon of late October.

He took her flowers, the free blooms of the hills, and she arranged them on the table by the lamp and fastened a red one to her mantilla.

"It is very pretty there," he said. "But I wish you'd put it in your hair. A red flower in silver hair —"

"My hair is white, Mingo." She touched her mantilla then, drawing it tighter.

"Your hair is silver, Rafaela —"

"It is white!" Her mouth was trembling and her eyes were brimming. "Do you think I do not know it is white? Or that I wanted it white?" The tears spilled over and she bowed her head, and he dared not break the moment or seek to comfort her.

Her hands were against her cheeks. "I wept when it happened, Mingo. I was ashamed and I covered it as a child covers her nakedness." Her head came up slowly and she looked past him toward the camp, the Mambises squatting by their fires. "Even my hair became a symbol and its cover became a sign. The Mambises say that as long as my hair is hidden, I belong only to Cuba—to them."

Mingo nodded, nodding slowly, and she sensed his melancholy and eased it; a smile, a toss of her head, and she asked him to sing to her.

They were sitting on the bench in front of the *bohio* and he leaned back and closed his eyes, and sang. The duenna

277

came to the door and looked down at them, at his face in the moonlight, and at Rafaela whose eyes were closed, too. The old woman tiptoed back into the shadows.

The autumn was fading, blending into the early winter and the leaves of the ceibas dropped and the marabu bushes were twisted and brown. The wind blew steadily from the east, from the Windward Channel, sometimes lulling soft through the Oriente, then shrieking down from the mountains and on to the plains. The Mambises were restless, watching Macéo's hut and his horse, and whetting their *machetes,* endlessly whetting them.

The Brown One was walking again. He leaned on his doctor and on Miro, but he walked every day, drenching himself in the sun and staring endlessly toward the plains, the *trochas,* and beyond the *trochas* where Máximo Gómez waited.

Then, one day, he got up suddenly from his hammock, motioning the doctor aside, and dressed himself, fastening on his Toledo sword. The belt hung loose and the gray Dutch linen hung loose; but he stood erect and Miro smiled. Pedro Díaz rubbed his hands together nodding to the Ducasse brothers.

The Mambises glanced at one another and whispered. Ah-h-h. We will be moving. *Por Dios!* Macéo has his sword and now we will shake the dust of this place from our feet.

El Dabney looked to his equipment, stacking dynamite in the carts and lashing it tight. He worked every day, and all day, and felt the wind strong against his cheeks, twisting the leaves of the mangos and rustling on toward the plains, the *trochas* and Máximo Gómez. He was nervous when he shaved late that afternoon, and anxious as he walked from his cart through the mango grove.

The duenna had been weeping and her eyes were red when she met him at the door, and spoke into the shadows, "He is here, Señorita."

Rafaela accepted his hand. She always did that, but this

time she did not take her hand away, and they walked into the grove until the twilight and the shadows almost hid them. "You are late today," she said.

He was a few minutes early, but she thought he was late and he, too, wondered why he had delayed so long. There was no place to sit among the trees and the ground was cool, so he went back for the bench and placed it against a mango. They sat down and she folded her hands in her lap, staring at them. "I am leaving tonight, Mingo."

Mingo was not surprised. The plains were stirring and she should be there. "We'll all be leaving soon." He was looking at the ground, at the splotched moon-shadows.

The girl nodded, slowly nodding. "I am going to Mantua. A village in Pinar del Río."

"So far, Rafaela?"

Nine hundred miles. Nine hundred miles to Pinar del Río.

She leaned against a mango at her back and looked up at the trees, the sky, the busk moon waning. "A new army must be waiting there for General Macéo. I must help raise it." The wind whined in the trees and she shuddered, although it was not cold, and drew her shawl around her shoulders. "Soto will not guide me this time."

"Then who will?" A hint of alarm was in his tone.

"There are other good guides. I will be safe." Her assurance comforted him.

"I wish I dared ask Macéo to let me guide you —"

"No!" Her hands were at her cheeks, pressing hard. "That would be most unwise."

Mingo locked his fingers behind his neck and he, too, stared at the sky, the wind in his hair, the west-bound wind. "He knows I've been coming over here. He may not let me go with him to Pinar del Río. He may try to run me off —"

"He won't do that." She let her hand rest beside her and he put his hand over hers, and she did not move it. "He will not order you away." Her eyes were closed and she bowed her head, biting her lip until it whitened, and speaking softly. "My guardian knows that if he sends you away, I will call you back." She grasped his hand, clinging to it.

"Rafaela . . ."

She touched each finger, bending each finger, and rubbed the back of his hand, caressing it. *"Minguillo."*

"My sweet." He whispered it and touched his lips to her hand, the palm, the fingers.

"You have come into my heart, my love, and now my heart is full." She whispered, too, lest the ceiba hear and tell the piñon, lest the piñon gossip, lest the wind hear and pass it from the Oriente to the palms of the plains, and on down to Pinar del Río, the pines by the river. "When I was a child, my life was put into the keeping of Antonio Macéo. Now that I am a woman, I put my heart into your keeping."

He moved his hands on her arms, high on her arms, and she took his hands away. "You must not call to me, *Minguillo,* for I will hear you, and I must not hear you now. You must wait until Mantua. Until my life is mine to give with my heart."

"I will wait." He drew back, accepting her decree. "I have come so far and have found so much, and I can wait until Mantua."

The wind fingered her mantilla and brushed it from her forehead, revealing the line of her white hair. She made no move to hide it and he gazed at its beauty, and searched her face. Her eyes were closed and he kissed her cheek and felt her quiver. He kissed her forehead, touching his lips to her hair.

Rafaela gasped and her hands flew to her hair. Her cheeks burned red and she pulled her mantilla tight over her forehead. "I must go." She got up quickly, the flush draining from her cheeks until they were pale.

Mingo felt for her hand and her hand was trembling, and they walked in silence through the grove, her hand growing warm inside his, trembling no more.

280

He bade her good-bye at the doorway, saying simply, "I will be in Mantua."

"I will be waiting." She turned into the darkness of her *bohio*, leaving him by the doorway, his hands empty, his heart so full, and the wind rustling his hair, the west-bound wind. He put on his hat and tugged at the brim, but did not slant it.

Campfires danced around Maceó's hut and wavered in the mango grove and Mingo sensed the tension in the Army of the Oriente. The Mambises seethed with expectancy, the certainty of things to come, and El Dabney, hurrying to his *Grillos,* looked back at her *bohio* and it was dark. Already she was gone.

MINGO DABNEY

Chapter 22   The night wind, blowing low, held the smoke to the ground and spread it through the mango grove. The campfires of the Army of the Oriente pulsed red in the smoke, and the faces of the Mambises glistened. Their eyes were wide, and they whispered and jabbered in the rising tension.

Mingo was panting when he reached his carts, and he licked his lips and counted his *Grillos*—eighty-two, eighty-three, eighty-four! An undertow of excitement, perhaps of destiny, tugged at the scavengers, the guttersnipes, and their nostrils quivered as they walked around their fires, glancing frequently toward Macéo's hut.

Soto moved light-footed, darting his glances, and handed his comrade a cup of coffee and a piece of corn cake. Mingo drank the coffee and did not feel its heat. He laid the bread aside. He was not hungry.

"Carts all ready?" he asked.

Soto tipped his chin, pointing at the carts. They were in line, tongue to bed.

"Dynamite safe?" His voice was low. "Tools?"

"*Sí.*" Soto glanced over his shoulder. "We are ready when Macéo is ready."

Mingo propped against the cart and watched the fire cast off sparks. His *Grillos* huddled around the blaze, and some were silent, gazing at the fire; and some leaned forward and chattered, their hands in swift and endless motion.

"She has gone, Soto. To Pinar del Río."

"*Sí.*" The Mambi looked away and Mingo turned and climbed into his cart. He examined his tools, fingering his ax and his gun.

A courier came from the west, over beyond the *trochas*, and reined at Macéo's headquarters, and a hundred whispers spread through the camp. From Goulet's handful, to the *machete*-men, to the *impedimenta*.

"Gómez!" the whispers ran. "He came from Gómez. He rode from the west. Through the *trochas*."

The Haitians were silent, strangely silent, and there was no sound from the hills except the wind in the ceibas. The moon scurried behind the clouds and hid there and the drums began, slowly at first, then faster and faster, rolling thunder down from the hills.

"Baire! Baire!" That was all they said, over and over. The camp quivered and the Mambises shuffled around the fires, their faces sweat-wet and glowing.

General Miro walked out of headquarters and among the men, and Pedro Díaz came out. His pistol hung low at his hip. The Ducasse brothers came from the *bohio* and walked among the men, showing themselves, nodding to the groups, lifting their hands. The Mambises held up their rifles and raised their *machetes*, raising them high and shaking them.

"*Compadres,*" Miro said.

"Baire!" the men replied, and the drums flung it back from the hills. "Baire!"

Somebody called, "Macéo." Another took it up, a low sweeping murmur. "Macéo. Macéo." They chanted until it swelled and burst, and they screamed and leaped from their fires and ran to the *bohio* of The Brown One, brandishing their *machetes*: "Macéo! Macéo!"

The drums pounded it back, thundering it: "Macéo!"

Mingo Dabney ran with his men, jumping out of his cart and running blindly to the clearing and moving among the fires, his blood throbbing to his brain and his feet thudding the ground in rhythm with their feet. Smoke was in his eyes and his eyes ran red and his cheeks were burning in the firelight that flooded through the trees, darting red tongues against the *bohio* of Antonio Macéo.

Miro looked at Pedro Díaz, and Díaz nodded. They withdrew into the *bohio* and a shout, a wild shout, went up from the men. They surged around the hut, circling it and waving their *machetes,* shuffling dust, drifting it up to mingle with the smoke.

"Macéo! Macéo!"

The pounding drums flung it back, booming their thunder, rolling it down from the hills, crashing it into the mango grove.

Brush was thrown on the fire and the yellow flames leaped high, withering the leaves, charring the trees. The Mambises surged forward, and back again, dancing in waves.

The wild chant was a blood beat and Mingo felt it pounding in his veins, and he screamed with the others.

Miro appeared at the door and stood there, then stepped aside. A silence, quick, brooding, fell upon the men and upon the woods. The firelight flicked into the *bohio*, lighting it, and the Mambises were hushed, peering and craning their necks.

In that moment of stillness the world hung poised, and then Antonio Macéo stood in the doorway. The lines of his sickness were deep in his face and his clothes hung loose. His sword was sheathed, but one hand grasped the hilt and his men saw the sword, and they shrieked his name, leaping and shrieking. Some screamed until slobber foamed at their mouths and others flung up their hands, swirling their *machetes*; and an acre of steel swayed under the mangos.

Macéo walked out and they drew back before him, pushing back until a wall of men formed in front of him. Again he looked at them and they were silent. And the drums were silent.

He stood erect and one hand grasped the hilt of his sword, and the other hand he raised, palm toward them. "Mambises!" This was his salutation, and this his highest praise. His voice was weak and dust and smoke eddied about him.

284

He stiffened his shoulders and called to them again, in pride and affection. "Mambises!"

And they answered him. "Macéo!"

"This army will march at dawn."

"Dawn," they shouted.

"To the *trochas!*" He raised his head higher, slowly turning his head. "To the *trochas,* and through the *trochas* to the plains."

"The plains!" The answer shook the mangos and the swirling *machetes* gleamed yellow and scarlet.

Macéo's eyes swept the grove. "I have a message from General Máximo Gómez." He unrolled the paper and raised it to the firelight. "Mambises, hear it!" Then he read:

" 'Animated by unchangeable resolution in defense of the rights of this country, humiliated and despised by Spain, I have ordered the following—' " The Brown One raised his eyes again, looking about him, steadying his men. " '*One:* All plantations shall be totally destroyed, their cane and outbuildings burned, and railroad connections destroyed.' " He waited, and the Mambises flashed their eyes toward their comrades.

Burn Cuba? A war of the torch?

Ay, burn Cuba? Burn everything!

Macéo rattled the paper and the men watched him. "*Two.*"

The men repeated it. "*Two.*"

" 'All laborers who aid the sugar factories shall be considered traitors to their country.' "

Even the Mambises gasped. The sugar workers were Cubans. They bore no arms against the Revolution. They worked for their pittance and harmed no one. Traitors? Those sweating drudges, traitors!

" '*Three*—' " Macéo folded the paper and handed it to Miro. No need to read the third article. It was as simple and direct as a *machete* thrust, as final as death. " 'All traitors shall be shot!' "

The bald horror of the orders sickened Mingo and he swallowed and closed his eyes, shaking his head. This could not be. Sagaldo was offering hard money for the heads of a handful. Gómez was condemning half the people. The torch and the *machete!* Holy Mother. This rabble turned loose on the plains. A hundred sugar mills. A thousand plantations. A million workers. Burn and kill! This rabble surging into Havana.

The Ducasse brothers and Miro exchanged glances, feeling the mood of the Mambises. Macéo felt it, too, and looked at his men, waiting for someone to speak, someone to move.

But no one spoke. No one moved.

And then, suddenly, the drums screamed it. "Burn! Kill! Burn! Kill!"

The Mambises shifted and swayed, swaying again to the drums. Soto, little Soto the goatherd, 15,000 pesos on his head, fingered his *machete*. The drums stepped up their tempo and Soto, glancing around quickly, flung back his head and screamed, "Kill! Burn!" He whirled his *machete*. "Burn! Burn!"

The spark struck the dry leaves, the flame touched the powder, and the Mambises roared in unison. Macéo unsheathed his sword and held it aloft, rigid before him, and it flashed white in the firelight.

"Kill! Burn!"

The Brown One nodded to Miro, and El Dabney heard him sigh as he turned and walked back to his *bohio*, a sad and lonely man, passing on the order of flames for Cuba and death for the poor.

Mingo stumbled away and went to his cart and drank water and washed the dust from his face. The Mambises still swarmed in the mango grove, screaming and slashing with their *machetes*, and Soto came down and joined him.

"I hope you're proud," Mingo said. "You set them on fire."

"I am not proud, *amigo*."

They went to the oxen and separated them into teams, Big Red with Slow Foot. The shouting died down and the Mambises surged to their chieftains. The *Grillos* came to El

Dabney and they yoked the oxen. The moon was wasting and the night was running away.

"Get some sleep," Mingo ordered.

It was a foolish order. There was no sleep that night. The men built up their fires and lolled around them, endlessly talking and making quick, restless gestures. The woodsman stretched on the bed of his cart and tried to sleep, but his *Grillos* were shifting about and the drums were pounding.

There was no measurement of time; and suddenly, a few minutes before the night died, a roar shook the mango grove.

Macéo's big red horse was led through the grove, and the shouting swelled, the men leaping and screaming and running after the horse.

It was still dark when The Brown One walked out of his *bohío* and the army cried his name. He took the reins in his hand and steadied himself, and mounted. The *Grillos* scurried away to see, but Mingo and Soto called them back, holding them in their own camp to put out the fires. Scatter the ashes. Tighten the yokes.

Macéo wore clean garments of soft Dutch linen and silk was next to his skin and he sat his horse rigidly, leaning against the pommel. Miro ordered the line of march.

First, the cavalry.

The horsemen dashed out of the night and to the edge of the grove. There they reined in and waited, their horses champing at their bits and flinging their heads and pawing the ground.

Next, Goulet's warriors.

Twelve ragged men, their cock feathers gleaming, ran to the edge of the mangos and formed behind the horsemen. That was all. Only twelve. Goulet was dead and his cock-feathered fangs accepted no other leader.

Banderas' hill fighters.

They were next. Then Pedro Díaz' infantrymen, and the clansmen of the Ducasse brothers. Then bands from every district, each with its chieftain. Fifteen hundred men formed into line.

They were facing west! Nine hundred miles! Ninety days! Two hundred and fifty thousand Spaniards!

Macéo touched his horse and leaned back from the pommel, bracing himself as he rode up the line to the head. There he waited, standing in his stirrups, watching the east.

It came in a low, sullen streak of red, the dawn borning, and a curtain of pink rolled up beyond the Sierra de Nipe.

The Mambises were still and hushed.

Suddenly Macéo flashed his sword, lifting it to the rising sun, and wheeled and pointed with his sword to the west.

His Mambises answered: "To the plains!"

He tightened his reins and the column moved, following a bronze man on a red horse and a naked sword pointing west.

Slowly at first, confused and cluttered, the column straggled out of the mango grove.

Close up!

The order came back from Macéo and the last groups of *machete*-men quickened their pace, taking the slack out of the line.

Mingo Dabney waited until the warriors were beyond the mangos, and turned to his *Grillos*. The sun was climbing over the mountains, widening the dawn, breaking it up and scattering it. "Let's get moving, John Henry."

He cracked his whip over his oxen, over Big Red and Slow Foot, and the *impedimenta* moved out, grinding along, eating the dust of the Army of the Oriente. The mangos were behind them; the dust and smoke settling back into the grove, and it was empty.

The pilgrim glanced over his shoulder only once, glancing toward the spot where Rafaela Galban had spoken her love. Then he set his face west, closing the door of the Oriente behind him, shutting off the mountains, shutting away Santiago de Cuba where the *Virginius* lay rotting.

And so they moved out. It was October 22. Mingo remembered because it was his mother's birthday.

MINGO DABNEY

Chapter **23**   They made twenty-one miles that day, and on the second day saw signs of Sagaldo, the bloated dead in a village where nothing lived. Even the dogs were dead, their throats ripped and their bodies still chained to the *bohios*, dead dogs guarding dead men.

"Anyway," said Mingo, turning away. "Sagaldo is running."

Soto shook his head. "Sagaldo never runs without reason."

The guide was right. The bulk of Spain's army had been sent to the plains, leaving Sagaldo only a few men and orders to delay Macéo.

Delay lightning? The Mambises laughed and their spirits soared. Ten—twenty miles. They were going to Mantua! Nine hundred miles! Close up, *compadres*.

The Brown One sat his horse straighter and bathed every night and changed his silks. El Dabney bathed in the streams they crossed and washed his jeans and put them on wet. The *Grillos* never bathed.

Posters were on the trees along the road. Spanish money for Mambi heads. Mingo still was tenth on the list, his neck worth 10,000 pesos, but Elmo Batson's value had jumped to 35,000 pesos.

"It means he's getting supplies into Mantua," El Dabney bragged to his *Grillos*.

"And *La Entorcha* is raising recruits in Mantua," the *Grillos* bragged to El Dabney.

Out of the mountains, down the hills of the Oriente. Always westward. Day after plodding day, Sagaldo turning often to flick Macéo, and running again. A skirmish at dawn. An ambush at night. Baire! The *machete*! Then silence. Push on, Mambises.

Macéo used only his cavalry and whittled Sagaldo's force to impotency, and the grandee fled the hills. The Oriente belonged to the Mambises, the mountains to common clay, and Sagaldo raced for the *trochas*, the blockhouses, Spain's barrier against the east.

The way to the line of forts was cleared and the Mambises crawled down into Camagüey, the gate to the sugar country. The flat land, the plains stretching level to the horizon, was strange and awesome to the hillmen and they began whispering among themselves; nervously glancing back toward *la tierra del Mambi*, nervously peering ahead toward the *trochas*.

Trochas. The word rang in Mingo's ears, beating a rhythm. *Trochas. Trochas.*

But on they plodded, moving out at daybreak, halting at night, avoiding the cities, crawling along the spine of Cuba. The carts soon were shaken down and the oxen were lean, and the men were lean, calluses on their feet and calluses on their gun shoulders.

A cart broke down and Mingo ordered it abandoned. Keep moving. Two of his men fell ill of dysentery and they left them and pushed on. A *Grillo* deserted, stealing two rifles and a bag of salt. Soto wanted to track him and kill him, but El Dabney forbade the waste of time.

Keep rolling.

The hills dropped behind, but the men stole nervous glances back toward their East as they plodded on toward Spain's West, and Spain's *trochas*. And then the drums were silent. "We are rid of the Haitians," Soto said. "We have left the chattering old women in the hills."

Mingo was sorry, for he missed the drums; but the Haitians never ventured into the plains and the Army of the Oriente had marched away from them.

There were no Spaniards, only dust, and the pilgrim was gay, waving his whip over his oxen, his hat slanted and his step restless and confident. Sometimes he sang as he walked, thinking of the little town of Mantua. I will be there, *Minguillo*. I will be waiting for you.

He tried to get his *Grillos* to join his songs, but they were silent, glancing back and whispering, glancing ahead and cringing, terrified of something they had never seen.

Trochas. Trochas. Trochas.

"For God's sake," Mingo grumbled to Soto. "You folks act like the *trochas* are the walls of hell."

"You will see, *compadre*. The *trochas* are not far."

Six more men deserted. They didn't steal anything. They just ran away. They ran from the *trochas*.

Soto tried to explain. The *trochas* were the legend of Spain's might, the remembrance of Spanish whips. For four hundred years Spain had owned Cuba and for four hundred years the line of forts held back the fighting men of the Oriente, guarding the sugar plains.

You must not cross the *trochas*, you dirt. Don't you dare.

There was a whip for those who tried it and death for those who succeeded.

Trochas! Trochas!

The oxen's feet beat the rhythm and the Mambises' feet echoed it. Fear began seeping into Mingo's mind and he tried to shake it off, but it fastened itself like a fungus and spread.

The Mambises talked of the *trochas* by day and mumbled by night. The *Grillos* crossed themselves as they spat out the word and Mingo's nerves were frayed by the sound. "Shut up," he told them finally. "Stop your damned blubbering. I'm sick of hearing it."

The march was one month and six days old when they came to the village of Artemisa and camped by a creek. They built little fires and huddled around them and the frogs cried beside the stream and the crickets rasped. Even the sounds were different from the Oriente, the frogs bellowing their deep call.

Mingo went to his cart early and took off his shoes and

put them under his head. His shirt was stiff with dried sweat, and dust was caked in his scraggly, black whiskers. He ought to shave. He was too tired to shave.

The *Grillos* crept to their beds and Soto came to Mingo's cart, looking down at his sleeping comrade, then bending to wake him. *"Amigo,"* he whispered.

"Huh? What is it?" Mingo felt first for his shoes and his gun.

The guide motioned him to follow and they slipped out of the cart and around the oxen. A reflection rose in the west, soaring yellow and red in the sky. There was a smell in the air and Mingo tasted its heavy, cloying sweetness, the smell of cane juice burning, of syrup-making back home. "It's sugar cane," he said, pointing toward the fire.

"It's Gómez," said Soto. "Gómez is burning a mill."

The pilgrim stared at the reflection, at the fierce red glow and the sparks spurting high above the flames. "How far?"

"Four miles, perhaps." Soto paused, then added. "Just beyond the *trochas.*"

It was too dark to see the land clearly, but on the crest of a slope were thinly scattered trees, black and forlorn in the light of the sugar mill burning, Spain oozing the thick, sweet blood of her Cuban colony, drained by old Gómez the fox.

A rocket streaked high to the northwest and Mingo jumped. He gripped Soto's arm, and Soto's arm shook. The trees were clear in the sudden light of the rocket, their branches jagged against the yellow sky.

Beyond the trees, not far beyond the trees, the *trochas* waited.

Don't you dare, you dirt.

Baire!

It was daybreak and the Army of the Oriente huddled along the stream, awaiting orders to move on the forts and pry open the door between Cuba's hills of revolt and Cuba's flatlands of submission.

El Dabney left Soto to hold the *Grillos* steady while he scouted the land alone, seeking a route for his equipment. The reflection to the west died down and the sugar mill was ashes, and Mingo crouched and waded the stream, crawling on his hands and knees through the tall grass and pulling on his elbows across the open spots. Sometimes he lay flat, wiggling and sliding like a snake.

At the crest of the slope, shadowed by the trees, he rested a moment, panting, and slowly lifted his head and peered over.

There were the *trochas*!

He frowned, pulling his brows together, and shook his head to clear it, and rubbed dust from his eyes. For a long minute he could not believe the thing he looked at, and then, believing it, could not take it in.

The *trochas* were Spain's magnificent arrogance. That, and nothing more.

A few wooden blockhouses loomed in the gray dawn. They were built on a mud bank just beyond a gully, and rusty barbed wire stretched from one blockhouse to the next. That, and nothing more.

El Dabney got off his knees quickly, defiantly; for it came to him that he, too, had been on his knees to the *trochas* and they were nothing but a tradition, shrewdly nurtured by one group of men to blind another group of men.

The fortifications stretched north and south across the island's neck and a railroad ran behind the blockhouses, paralleling them. Mingo counted four blockhouses within vision and nothing was awesome about them, no waving banners, no bristling steel.

"I'll be damned." He propped himself against one of the trees, staring down.

A dusty road stretched on across the plains and barbed wire was across the road and more barbed wire was tangled in front of the forts. A rusty little engine huffed along the railroad, hauling a flatcar on which a few Spanish soldiers huddled in the fast-breaking dawn. A few more soldiers were in the wire, patching it. They were a shabby lot.

So these were the *trochas*! There stood Spain, a haughty fraud. There was the ever-recurring line drawn by the mighty to hold back the meek. Towers of arrogance and empty monuments of insolence; modern shams and ancient myths. And they infuriated Mingo Dabney.

He took one more look, and walked back down the slope, walking erect so his *Grillos* could see him. Their eyes opened wide and he turned his head toward the *trochas*. "Build your fires," he called out. "We'll eat."

"Fires, El Dabney?" They gaped at him. "The Spaniards will see us."

"To hell with the Spaniards." With a flip of his hand he brushed the Spaniards aside. "We'll walk right through their mud bank —"

"El Dabney! Mother of Heaven . . ."

Mingo balanced his rifle in his hand, squinting along the barrel. "I'll take you through." He was hiding the shame of his old fear, wiping it clean with big talk. Big American brag.

The *Grillos* lit their fires, lying low and watching the smoke drift over the crest. There was no challenge from the *trochas*, and all along the creek, fires were lighted. Still there was no challenge, and the *Grillos* sauntered among the soldiers, carrying food and holding their heads high, their noses sharply uplifted.

The soldiers asked, "What of El Dabney? What does he think of the *trochas*?"

The *Grillos* spat and Pepe Barea even spat toward the *trochas*, though he ducked the instant he did it. "We'll walk right through their mud bank," they told the warriors. Big talk. Big *Grillo* brag.

Mingo was drinking coffee when General Miro rode up and he poured another cup for the chief of staff. The haze was lifting and the sun was full up. Miro's horse was frothing: the general had ridden the length of the army, passing on Macéo's orders for the day.

"I took a look at those two-bit forts." Mingo sneered and jerked his thumb toward the blockhouses. "Nothing to 'em."

Miro's eyes were heavy for sleep and his smile creased his cheeks. "Perhaps not, Señor Dabney. Only four hundred years of tyranny." He shook his head. "It is not what the *trochas* are; it is what they represent." He sipped his coffee and watched Mingo over the edge of his cup. "General Macéo sends his compliments."

"That's mighty nice of him." The pilgrim reared back against the wheel of his cart and folded his arms. He was free of his fear and felt expansive. "There won't be any trouble getting through. Just let the cavalry hit 'em once, and the *trochas* will fall apart." He curled his lip in scorn. "No trouble at all."

"Perhaps not. About a third of the army slipped through last night."

El Dabney was deflated and his pride was hurt because he did not know what was going on. "Who took them through?" He asked it brusquely, almost demanding it.

"The Ducasse brothers," Miro replied. "General Máximo Gómez is just beyond the *trochas* at the village of Lázaro López —"

"The hell you say." Mingo began grinning. His pride still was piqued because he, El Dabney of the *Grillos*, tenth on Sagaldo's list, was kept in ignorance of operations, but he grinned.

Miro smiled again. Perhaps he was trying to grin. "General Gómez reached Lázaro López only yesterday," he explained tactfully. "It is three miles southeast of here and he fired a sugar mill and drew the Spaniards off. The Ducasse brothers took five hundred men through the *trochas* during the confusion." He shrugged, and put his cup aside. "There was no opposition to the crossing. Spaniards will always leave their post to protect a sugar mill." He traced a pattern in the ground with a heel of his boot, then patted it out with his toe and looked up at El Dabney. "General Macéo will take the remainder of his army through today."

"In broad open daylight?"

"*Sí*. The army will cut its way through."

"So we follow the army?"

"No." Miro flipped his reins, slapping them against his palm and his horse was skittish. "The army is going through at a little place called Gil Herrera. There is no road there for the *impedimenta*. . . ."

Mingo was red-faced and angry. "How does Macéo expect us to get through? Jump over 'em?"

"General Macéo doesn't worry about the *impedimenta* —"

"You damn right he doesn't. And I'm getting pretty tired of it —"

"General Macéo hasn't worried about the *impedimenta* since El Dabney organized his *Grillos*." José Miro Argenter was a suave man and wise; he knew the taste of wormwood and how to sweeten it. "You will find a way through, *compadre*."

Mingo bit his lip, choking off his angry retort. The high command was scorning his men and Miro's tact was not enough. However, he held his temper and said slowly, "Tell General Macéo the *Grillos* will get through."

"I have already told him." Miro swung into his saddle. "I told him last night when he was trying to figure a way to escort you through." The chief of staff looked steadily at El Dabney as he said it, and the pilgrim wondered at the truth. Miro stroked his horse and glanced up the slope. "We have received word that *La Entorcha* is in safe hands in Pinar del Río. I am sure the news will cheer your men."

"It will cheer them very much, sir." Mingo bowed slightly. "It was kind of you to think of them."

Miro tightened the reins and wheeled his horse. "The

village of Reforma is about six miles due west of here, Señor Dabney. You will please take your men there. Damage what you can, except the railroad. Do not dynamite the railroad. You wait at Reforma. The Army of the Oriente and the Army of General Máximo Gómez will come there."

"We'll be waiting," Mingo said and watched Miro ride away.

The chief of staff hurried down the stream and among the *machete*-men. Already they were moving on to Gil Herrera where Macéo waited to rip aside the veil of four hundred years.

A score of *Grillos*, led by Soto, walked resolutely up the slope and opened fire on the nearest blockhouse, darting among the trees to load and fire and hide. A token answer came from the blockhouse, and then silence. The *Grillos* began grinning. They had fired on the *trochas* and the heavens did not fall.

El Dabney lined his carts behind the brink of the hill and waited until a salvo from down at Gil Herrera told him Macéo was going through. Soto's riflemen covered Mingo while he and a crew of thirty raced down the road for the barbed wire and cut gaping holes, opening a way for the oxen.

The blockhouse to the left spat a few shots and he sent back for dynamite, then crawled so near he saw the terror in the faces of the Spanish soldiers at the rifle slits. Without haste and without feeling, he lighted the fuses and hurled the dynamite. The faces disappeared and the *Grillos* hopped up and down.

"Keep still, John Henry," Mingo ordered.

"Let me throw one," Pepe Barea begged. "Let me throw a dynamite, El Dabney."

Mingo handed a charge to the Mambi and he ran almost to the blockhouse and hurled it. The explosion slapped

297

him sprawling, but he got up and raced back to El Dabney, grinning and weeping and rubbing the dirt from his hair.

Pepe Rosado threw one, crawling closer than Pepe Barea and stalking back contemptuously for all his comrades to see.

A handful of Spaniards jumped from behind the railroad embankment and tried to run. Soto's riflemen killed three and the *Grillos* began laughing, mocking the Spaniards and tormenting them. They made obscene gestures and spat at the *trochas*.

There was heavy fire down near Gil Herrera, but the *Grillos* met no resistance. Most of the Spaniards cowered in their forts, cringing from the *machetes*, and let the Cubans drive their carts through the barricades.

By noon the road was clear and four hundred years were breached. The *Grillos* were puffed up, strutting like game-cocks, thumping their chests as they danced around their carts, waiting for El Dabney to tell them what to do next, waiting as always for somebody to tell them what and when and how. Pepe Barea was weeping his pride and holding out his hands, showing the hands that threw dynamite at the *trochas*.

Soto led the way to Reforma, to a burned plantation in a thicket, and the cane still in the fields. The *Grillos* ran to the cane and cut it and sucked it. Mingo made them destroy all they could not eat. "Burn it," he directed. "Burn the cane."

"But it is good cane, El Dabney. Sweet and good —"

"Burn it!"

They shrugged and did as they were told, and brewed coffee and listened to the musketry rattling down at Gil Herrera. Mingo called Soto to him. "Go find out what's going on. And then —" he grinned at the guide. "I suppose you'll be leaving us again, eh?"

"Why do you say that, *amigo*?" Soto looked full into Mingo's eyes.

"I can tell the way you act —"

"So-o-o?"

"Uh huh." El Dabney blew on his coffee and took a big swallow. "You've been mighty quiet about him lately. Any more news?"

"No." He said it abruptly, and went for his horse and rode toward Macéo's army. Mingo unwrapped dried beef and smelled it for taint. The firing was subsiding at Gil Herrera.

"Ah-h-h." Pepe Rosado rubbed his big red nose. "We got through ahead of the army, eh, El Dabney? We fought our way through. I myself killed six Spaniards. Ten, perhaps —"

"Ten!" Pepe Barea scoffed and held out his hands that had thrown dynamite at the *trochas*. "*Por Dios*! I myself killed twelve. How many did you kill, El Dabney?"

"Oh, couple a'hundred. More or less."

"Um-m-m." The *Grillos* rolled their eyes in mockery. "Then perhaps El Dabney will be worth more than 10,000 pesos to Sagaldo. Perhaps 11,000. Spain is rich."

The Army of the Oriente began pouring through the *trochas* and into the village of Lázaro López before dusk and the *Grillos* looked in that direction, knowing that Máximo Gómez and Antonio Macéo were together, Cuba's two armies merged at last.

Lázaro López was only four miles from Reforma and the armies were spreading out, extending almost the distance between the villages. There were wild shouts and many shots and Mingo sat in his cart, staring into the distance. He wanted to be down there, but Miro had requested him to remain at Reforma and he would not ignore the request. To hell with Macéo, but he liked Miro. There was history at Lázaro López, but Mingo Dabney was missing it while he wet-nursed a bunch of scavengers. He was chagrined and bitter and once more the black mood of his Mississippi heritage was on him.

Darkness came and a thousand campfires burned along the road, and Gómez' *impedimenta* went among the soldiers, feeding them. Rum was passed out. The shouting told him they were passing rum. He had half a mind to saunter down that way, wondering again why Miro had asked him to wait at Reforma. Macéo was in it somewhere. Macéo didn't want him around when he met Gómez. That was it. Bound to be. Macéo wanted to talk to the commander in chief about the *gringo*.

Several *Grillos* edged away, watching him out of the corners of their eyes. They eased into the shadows, slipping beyond the fires and running down the road to Lázaro López. Macéo and Gómez were together. They must see it. They owed it to their grandchildren. It was their duty. *Por Dios!* They were not slipping away from El Dabney. Oh, no! They were just doing their duty to their grandchildren. El Dabney was a *gringo* and it was all right for him to wait in his cart, but they must see this glorious thing.

Mingo made no effort to stop them and was sitting on the edge of his cart, glaring at the fire, when Soto returned. "Took you a hell of a time."

The Mambi squatted by the blaze and poured himself a cup of coffee. "There was much to see, *compadre*."

"How many men has Gómez got?" Mingo swung from his cart and approached the fire.

"Two thousand, perhaps." The guide sat on a log and drank his coffee, making a loud noise as he sucked it up.

A log burned through in the fire and Mingo pushed it back with his foot. "All right. Tell me about it."

Soto put his cup aside. "It was glorious, *amigo*. Macéo was on his red horse." The goatherd's eyes were tearful. "The Mambises screamed his name. It made my heart grow big until it hurt. If José Martí could only have seen this thing." Some of the tears spilled out. "Many of the Mambises wept." He paused and bent over the fire, poking it. "Miro was there and Banderas and all the others. Gómez rode out with his staff to meet them. Gómez has a flag—"

"The hell you say." El Dabney's eyes suddenly were shining.

"*Sí*. And do you know who made it?"

"Rafaela Galban —"

"No. María Macéo made it. She sent it to Gómez."

The armies of Cuba united. A common flag. The pilgrim poured himself a cup of coffee and sat down by his friend. He was a part of all this; an ox driver, a cook, a handyman. But he was a part of it all and he was proud. "Go on," he said. "Tell me the rest of it."

A few Mambises were left in the *trochas*. They fell at Gil Herrera. Two were Goulet's warriors. Ten of his men still lived.

Gómez was riding sidesaddle: an old leg wound had ulcered and he could not sit his saddle straight. Soto told it all. Máximo Gómez looked like a shriveled Chinaman, hunched over his sidesaddle, his frail little body lost in his rumpled uniform, his heavy mustaches drooping and his white goatee jutting down stiff.

"And, *compadre,* Macéo bragged to Gómez about El Dabney —"

"How come?" Mingo was suspicious.

The goatherd shrugged and spread his hands. "He told him that El Dabney is a big man. His head worth 10,000 pesos." He looked up quickly. "Macéo suggested that such an important man as El Dabney should be with the commander in chief."

The woodsman stood and stretched. "I'm staying where I am, and they can go to hell."

Soto's mouth spread into a broad grin, almost the grin of Lebanon, and his eyes were bright in the fire's reflection. "That is what Miro said." He felt in his shirt and under his belt and pulled out a bottle of rum.

Mingo Dabney laughed. "Steal it?"

"No. Miro."

The *Grillos* slipped back into camp, smelling of rum and

boasting in whispers. They scurried to their carts, sorry that El Dabney had missed all the excitement; but then he was a *gringo* and his grandchildren would not understand. Ah-h-h.

Soto waited until the camp was quiet, and went for his horse. Mingo walked with him out beyond the circle of carts. The moon was up and they looked across the prairies, the land flat and unbroken. Only a thin scattering of trees, a few palms on the horizon, and plains again. Good Lord! It might have been Texas.

"Not many trees," the woodsman said.

"Not many."

They stood for a minute longer, looking at the land. "Sure you don't want me to help you find that fellow?"

"No! You stay out of it." The Mambi turned away, feeling for his stirrup.

"Needn't be so touchy." Mingo slid the reins through his hands, smoothing them. "I just asked."

He tossed the reins to his friend and stepped back, watching the guide gallop away, and he was alone again. Six hundred miles to Pinar del Río. Six hundred miles to Rafaela Galban. But what in the world had come over Soto?

MINGO DABNEY

Chapter **24**   The *Grillos* were full of rum
and big talk and the moon was high before they bedded
down. Mingo posted four pickets and went to work by firelight, sharpening tools; any work to dull his loneliness.

It was nigh midnight before he stretched out, his shoes
under his head and his body twitching its tension, then soothing into relaxation. A few shots from over near the *trochas*
and he sat up, squinting into the darkness. A dog barked.
Two more shots. Foragers and looters, perhaps. He called to
the nearest cart. "John Henry."

"*Sí.*" Pepe Rosado popped his head out.

"All here?"

"*Sí*, El Dabney."

He lay down again, feeling the tremor of the night, the
land shadowy and ephemeral, and nothing certain or sure,
or safe. Soto was gone. Rafaela was six hundred miles away.
He dreamed that night of frost on the sedge back home.

All the next day the two armies moved into Reforma and
El Dabney saw Máximo Gómez for the first time, riding sidesaddle, a hunched little man, wan and drawn. A tent fly was
stretched and in its shade the captains and generals crowded
around the commander in chief who lay in his hammock, a
bottle of brandy on a keg nearby to deaden the pain in his
ulcered leg.

Macéo was close to Gómez' hammock, presenting his officers to The Old Fox. There came a smooth-faced youth,

scarcely out of his teens or perhaps still in them. He stepped up to Máximo Gómez, then bowed to Macéo and the *Grillos* sucked in their breath.

"Bacardi," one said. "That's Captain Emilio Bacardi. Rich people."

Another *Grillo* rubbed his naked belly. "Maybe we'll get some rum. They make rum, the Bacardis."

The young captain walked over to Miro, his face glowing his pride as he reported as aide-de-camp to General Macéo. Old Máximo Gómez knew what he was doing, assigning a Bacardi to serve a mulatto. Color and caste were for Spaniards.

It was just as well the *Grillos* did not know all that was taking place around the hammock. They might have protested and made nuisances of themselves, for Macéo's Army of the Oriente was passing into history, merging into the Army of Liberation, Máximo Gómez commanding.

By noon of December 1st, the merger was completed and the army settled into camp, 3500 soldiers and 400 *impedimenta*. There were two cannon, Hotchkiss guns, and no shells. There were only 2000 rifles and some of Gómez' staff urged that the *Grillos'* rifles be distributed among the warriors. Miro stormed his protest and Macéo forbade it.

Mingo's chief concern was with the dust that settled on his equipment, churned up thick by Gómez' *impedimenta* padding through the burned fields to gape at the *gringo* and his *Grillos*. He was restless to roll on.

What was holding them at Reforma?

Gómez was holding them. The Old Fox had no sign, no symbol, but he knew Spaniards and he sipped his brandy, watching the railroad at his back.

That night General Martínez Campos, planning in Havana, sent five battalions over the railroad to garrison the *trochas,* to shut the door behind Macéo. The Brown One was out of *la tierra del Mambi* and the combined armies of Cuba were exposed, so the Spaniard moved his pawns into the *trochas* and planned his checkmate on the plains.

Gómez was pleased and Macéo was poised. They wanted those five battalions out of the way.

Baire!

Sagaldo struck before dawn, riding out of the north with two thousand horsemen. *Viva España!* Santiago!

El Dabney recoiled from the cry and his *Grillos* blanched their fears.

Spain was moving for her checkmate, moving Sagaldo into action to bleed the Army of Liberation and weaken it for the kill. He stormed Gómez' left wing, folding it up like a jack-knife, and wheeled to storm the center. Macéo was in the center.

The opening thrust was a mile from the thicket where the *Grillos* camped, but Mingo pulled his *impedimenta* together and pointed west. He must give Macéo room to maneuver. Give him the fields. Give him the thicket. "Pull out!" he shouted, his head cocked toward the north where Sagaldo was striking in circles.

The carts rumbled along the road for two miles and he formed them in a ring and posted his men, ready if the Spaniards broke through that far.

Macéo lay back until Sagaldo was winded, and struck from the center with four hundred horsemen and Banderas' hill fighters. They carried the flag that María Macéo had stitched. *Cuba libre!* Sweat flooded from Mingo's armpits and down his side and he chewed his lips, shielding his eyes against the sun, peering toward the clouds of dust, the cries.

Bedlam swirled in the burned fields and the battle ebbed, a mile of boiling dust and screaming men. El Dabney walked among his carts, holding his men steady.

A captain and a squad of *machete*-men rode up, leading a string of captured horses. Mingo went out to meet them. "How's it going?"

"Not too good." The officer glanced over his shoulder and

nodded at the horses. "General Miro said they'd be safe with you."

"We'll watch 'em." Now he was a horse wrangler and his band drove the mounts into the center of their circle, gazing covetously at them.

The captain turned back toward the battle. "There is a sugar mill at Trilladeritas. About four miles south of here. General Miro said tell you we'll retreat there if things go bad for us." He touched his horse and was away, the *machete*-men following him.

A sugar mill at Trilladeritas! Mingo folded his arms and slouched against the cart wheel, glancing to the north where the battle surged, then staring toward the south.

The idea was born then. In years to come, there would be myths to explain it, but the idea came to El Dabney of the *Grillos* as he tended horses at the battle of Reforma. The myths would call him a soldier. He wasn't a soldier at all. He was a woodsman and a hunter who had seen a rabbit lure foxhounds from the trail, a chipmunk confuse bear dogs. He twisted the tuft of hair and bit his lip, thinking of all he had heard about Spaniards and sugar mills, and conjecturing many things he had not heard. And he stared to the south.

The screams at Reforma, the gunfire and the tumult, slackened. Sagaldo was containing Macéo's charge and Spanish infantry was marching east to trap the Army of Liberation. This was the place, and this the time, to bleed the revolution dry. It might have happened, but there was a sugar mill at Trilladeritas and Mingo Dabney was a woodsman.

He had no orders. He needed none. "Pepe Rosado! Pepe Barea!" He called twenty-seven *Grillos* around him and sent them for their rifles. Dynamite. Torches. The others would mind the carts.

The men looked from one to the other, at El Dabney and over toward Reforma. Pepe Rosado spoke for them. "We will loot?"

306

"Maybe." Mingo reached in his own cart for his rifle, and stuffed dynamite in his shirt. "Now pick out your horses."

Horses! They were to have horses. They had shoes and rifles and now they were to have horses. *Por Dios!* It was glorious. They dashed for their mounts and swung into their saddles, beaming their pride and giggling like children. All except Pepe Barea. This was too much. He was weeping.

Mingo took the horse nearest him and again addressed his men. "We got to be where they think we won't be. Get there before they do, and get away before they catch us."

The *Grillos* nodded their understanding, and El Dabney raised his gun, pointing toward the east. "That way," he shouted. "Kick up dust and whoop and yell —"

"But Trilladeritas is south." One of his men corrected him.

"That way!" Mingo bellowed the command.

He lunged away and his twenty-seven *Grillos,* clinging to their saddles like crickets, rode after him, churning the dust toward the east, racing away from Reforma; screaming like demons. This was the sweep. A man in a black hat leading a handful of scavengers, sweeping toward the east, the rabbit confusing the hounds.

For a mile they rode, beating their horses into a froth, swirling dust that hid them and yet traced their dash across the fields. Then Mingo held up his gun and pointed south, wheeling his horse toward Trilladeritas. This was the thrust. The sweep, the thrust; a *gringo* hunter riding a horse across cane fields while the Cuban Army of Liberation fought for its existence at Reforma.

They came to a creek that furnished water for Trilladeritas, which was nothing but a sugar mill, a long low building with smoke wisping from the stacks; and a *hacienda,* the home of the Volunteer overlord.

Mingo reined down his horse at the creek and signaled for silence, and ordered his men to dismount. "Tie your horses here."

"But El Dabney?" It was Pepe Barea who protested, the one who so seldom protested.

"Leave 'em here!" Mingo checked his rifle and glanced up and down the creek, the thicket, the thorny marabu and brush. "If we get back, they'll be here. If we don't get back, we won't need 'em. Now come on with me. . . ."

The battle sounds from Reforma were a rumbling echo and they crept away from the creek and to the edge of the cane fields, all the cane ripe and much of it dry. He hid his men and he and Pepe Rosado scouted the mill, crawling through the cane. There were guards at the plant and about two hundred workmen.

Back to the rendezvous they scooted, crawling where the cane was sparse and running upright where it was thick. Mingo lit the first torch, a pitch torch dipped in tar, and held it until it burned bright, and heaved it into the dry cane. The *Grillos* scattered, throwing torches until the cane burst into flame, the fire spurting red and the smoke boiling black. They worked silently, spreading the fire until the wind caught it, whipping it across the field.

A few guards ran from the mill and one of the *Grillos* raised his gun. Mingo knocked it down. "Wait until they all come out."

The workmen streamed from the plant, jabbering as the guards rounded them up. The Volunteer overlord dashed out of his *hacienda,* conferred quickly with the guards, and *machetes* were passed out to the men. "Hack fire-breaks! Beat it out!" The orders sounded above the crackling flames and Mingo looked at his men and grinned. The owner thought the fire was an act of God, never dreaming it was the work of devils.

A nod to Pepe Rosado and he and twelve more *Grillos* ran for the *hacienda*. The others followed El Dabney, circling the field and the fire until they were within a hundred yards of the mill. Mingo felt for his dynamite and his men for their torches. "On your bellies," he ordered.

They wiggled across the field, down the rows of cane, and Mingo lit his dynamite. The first stick landed near the base of the wall and he reached for another, biting the end where the cap was set, lighting the fuse and hurling it.

The explosions shattered the wall and the stack trembled. Mingo sprinted for the mill, his *Grillos* scurrying behind him. "Torches!" he yelled.

The guards were benumbed and looked to the master for instructions. "Mambises! Mother of God. Mambises!" The overlord screamed it and the guards fired wildly. Pepe Barea ran to the mill and heaved a torch inside. Others duplicated his daring, and Mingo crouched on one knee, firing at the guards.

A rumbling explosion from the *hacienda* and the guards and workmen were frozen by indecision. A rattle of rifle fire from over near the house blasted them into panic. Pepe Rosado was over there. Mingo's group leveled a volley and the guards were trapped in a cross fire, the mill burning and the workmen running for safety, to the fields, to the woods.

The overlord went down with a bullet in his chest and was hacked to pieces. The guards staggered and some tried to crawl away. "Baire!" the *Grillos* screamed and swung their *machetes*. It was all over in a few minutes, the mill burning furiously, the *hacienda* crumbling and the *Grillos* picking off the workmen, shrieking as they cleaved with their *machetes*.

Mingo Dabney wiped the sweat and dust from his eyes and brushed his hat to the back of his head. The black smoke rose in a greasy pall and the wind spread it, a cloud from Trilladeritas to Reforma.

"Let's get out of here!" He led the way across the field, back to the creek and the horses. Pepe Barea was weeping, and all the *Grillos* beat their chests and strutted. "We did it, eh, El Dabney? We are somebody, eh, *compadre?*"

"La Cuchillada!"

It was never known who shouted it first, but it was one of the *Grillos*. Not Pepe Rosado. Not Pepe Barea. One of the others. He brandished his rifle and his *machete* and danced around Mingo Dabney the *gringo*, and shouted: *"La Cuchillada!"*

The sweep! The thrust!

The cane fields glowed all the way from the creek to the mill, the smoke lacing a black cloud over the plains. Four miles away at Reforma old Máximo Gómez saw it and plucked his goatee. Antonio Macéo saw it and ran the back of his hand across his forehead and reeled from exhaustion. His sign was a living torch. Well, there was a torch, a cloud by day; a flaming torch of a sugar mill burning, the smoke writing a dare in the sky.

La Cuchillada!

Leopold Sagaldo saw it and raised his face to the simmering skies and cursed the Spanish overlords who demanded protection, those who placed profits above victory. The Nigra was falling back, his Mambises floundering at Reforma, and this was the hour for Sagaldo to quarry his prey.

But the grandee was a soldier; and the grandee had his orders. Save the sugar mills! Protect the property of the rich! Safeguard the profits of Crown and Church! Fight a war in the name of God and under the decree of gold.

Leopold Sagaldo turned his horses and sabers from the Army of Liberation and rode for Trilladeritas. He had to pull away from a battle he was winning to save a mill already lost.

The *Grillos* watched the dust rising between them and Reforma, and Mingo led the way due east again, sweeping to the east, his men strung behind him and low in their saddles. Mingo tilted his hat over his forehead to keep dust from his eyes. He tried not to show his pride, rocking in his saddle and grinning his triumph. *La Cuchillada!*

He gave no thought to what Macéo might say. Or Gómez. He had pulled Sagaldo off balance. Remember the *Virginius!* Don't forget us, Dabney!

General Miro was waiting for him at the carts.

The *Grillos* held back, but Mingo dismounted, glancing at the chief of staff and over toward Reforma where Macéo's Mambises were looting the dead and counting their losses.

"It was a bold maneuver, Señor Dabney." They were Miro's first words and there was no reproof in his tone.

"We caught 'em flatfooted." Mingo tied his horse to a cart wheel. "We didn't lose a man."

"My congratulations, sir." Miro watched the *Grillos* slip from behind the carts, grinning their pride and deviltry.

Mingo beat his hat against his leg, flaying out the dust. "We didn't hurt your horses. They'll cool off in an hour or so."

The *Grillos* crowded closer, daring now to stand near Macéo's chief of staff. General José Miro Argenter looked at them, the sores on their bodies, the light in their eyes, and at Mingo Dabney, standing by his cart, twisting the tuft of hair, his eyes daring and restless. "The horses are yours, *amigo*. You have earned them."

"But what about General Macéo?" El Dabney was hesitant. "Will he let us keep them?"

"*Si*. He told me to decide about the horses. I have decided."

"Did he say anything else?" Perhaps there was a crumb of praise, a word of commendation; if not for him, maybe for the *Grillos*.

"He said nothing else. But Máximo Gómez asked many questions about you." Miro drew back his shoulders and looked evenly at the *gringo*. "I took the liberty of explaining to the commander in chief that I am your friend." He wheeled and walked away, leaving the pilgrim to puzzle the words, leaving the *Grillos* to expound them and spread them. General Miro was the friend of El Dabney. *La Cuchillada!* Ah-h-h.

Pedro Díaz came to the camp and shook hands with El Dabney. The Ducasse brothers came, the moody Juan Ducasse and the brooding Vidal Ducasse. They wrung his hand and smiled at him for the first time, bowing their compliments and flashing their praise to the *Grillos*. Many of the Mambises brought tribute, little gifts, homage of the meek. But Macéo did not come. He remained aloof and alone, riding the fields, reckoning his dead.

The fire down at Trilladeritas was dying to embers, and Leopold Sagaldo counted the toll: twenty dead workmen, one sugar mill, one *hacienda*. He cursed the day and offered fifteen thousand pesos for the head of Mingo Dabney.

Then the Spaniard turned from the smoldering mill and galloped toward the *hacienda* where lay the bodies of the Spanish guards and the overlord, a hole in his chest, a slash in his throat. Leopold Sagaldo rose in his stirrups, color splotching red in his fair skin:

"Twenty thousand pesos for the head of Mingo Dabney! *Pesos duros!*"

The Cubans lost eighty-seven dead that day and as many more were dying from wounds. Old Máximo Gómez ordered them abandoned. He had plans and he was in a hurry, and a wounded man was a burden.

It was Antonio Macéo who moved the wounded to the thicket, and Mambi women slipped from the farms nearby to care for them.

El Dabney saw to his oxen and his horses, but only half of the *Grillos* were with their carts. The others were over in Macéo's camp, boasting and accepting rum from the *machete*-men and lying. Big *Grillo* brag. Ah-h. El Dabney swept east and fooled them, then thrust south. *Recristo! La Cuchillada!* The sweep. The thrust. Mother of God! It was glorious.

The camp took up the name. The hill fighters of Banderas repeated it and passed it on. *La Cuchillada!* The *machete*-men of the Ducasse brothers, of Pedro Díaz. It swelled to an echo of praise, and Mingo Dabney slanted his hat on the side of his head and wished for the Haitian drummers to tell the story.

But maybe she would hear it anyhow.

MINGO DABNEY

Chapter **25** The army marched again at daybreak, trudging west all that day of December 2, 1895 and that night Miro sent word to El Dabney: there was a sugar mill at La Campana.

Mingo selected the same twenty-seven and they were away in the darkness, a sweep around the army to confuse, a thrust straight for the quarry. The guards were strangled or knifed at their posts. The fires were set while the workmen slept, then the *Grillos* butchered the workmen and rode swiftly away.

Sagaldo charged through the night to save La Campana, leaving his rear guard at Trilladeritas. Macéo raced back and wiped out the guard.

"Baire!" the *machete*-men shouted, returning from Trilladeritas.

"La Cuchillada!" the *Grillos* replied, pointing toward the glow at La Campana.

Move on. Close up. . . .

That was the pattern of things and Mingo Dabney gradually lost his horror of the slaughter; the sweep, the thrust, the knifed guards, the butchered workmen.

They entered the province of Santa Clara and a poster hung in a village plaza. Twenty-five thousand pesos for the head of El Dabney! He was worth almost as much as Pedro Díaz, as the Ducasse brothers. The *Grillos* ripped down the sign and stuck it on the side of his cart and cheered him.

La Cuchillada! Mingo grinned his pride and slanted his hat until it touched his ear.

Gómez issued orders direct to his troops. Burn everything that stands. Kill everything that crawls. The *machete* for those who toil for Spain.

El Dabney's *Grillos* made torches of dried sticks, tying them together with vines and dipping them in tar. The pattern never varied as they plodded west. Word forever coming back from Miro. A mill to the south. A plantation to the north. *La Cuchillada!* El Dabney sweeping out and thrusting, drawing Sagaldo in futile pursuit.

Macéo followed, striking from the rear, on the flank, and darting away when the Spaniard turned to give battle. El Dabney laid a trail of burning plantations and swirling dust, and Sagaldo charged after him, Macéo nipping at his heels. Sixty Mambises dead. Two hundred dead Spaniards. *Venga Mambi!* Baire!

Day after day. Mile after mile. Burn! Kill!

The Army of Liberation numbered four thousand, swelled by recruits creeping in from the plantations. Better to fight for Gómez than die like squatting rabbits in the field, die under Macéo's *machetes* or under the thrust of a swaggering *gringo* they called El Dabney.

Sagaldo finally dug in, making a stand with less than a thousand men, hoping Campos would come to his aid so that they could lure Gómez into open battle. The Old Fox dashed up, but never quite closed with the Spaniard and Macéo raced north for a cluster of *haciendas*. El Dabney swept south for a string of sugar mills. Then Gómez skipped away, and Sagaldo was left to rage his fury as the black palls boiled into the sky.

Captain Emilio Bacardi sent rum and greetings to the *Grillos*. The Ducasse brothers drank a toast with El Dabney, and even Gómez sent congratulations. Only Macéo was silent.

Leopold Sagaldo proclaimed a new price through the province of Santa Clara, and on to Havana, on to Pinar del Río.

Thirty thousand pesos for the head of Mingo Dabney! *Pesos duros* for the head of the *gringo*. El Dabney's head was worth nearly as much as the head of Elmo Batson.

Mingo picked up a cockatoo feather, a dashing red feather, and stuck it in his hat. His trousers were ripped and fastened with marabu thorns and his shirt was in shreds. But he had a feather in his hat.

Campos, under orders from Madrid, broke his army into fragments and sent forces to protect the sugar mills and the *haciendas* of the Volunteers. The fat one wept his disgust and Sagaldo retreated west, cursing the orders that rendered the army impotent.

Macéo kept slashing, eating up the Spanish rearguard, marking the roadside with Spanish dead. Old Máximo Gómez calmly sat his sidesaddle, plucking his little white goatee and watching Cuba change into a furnace, a slaughterhouse.

They came to the village of Guama the afternoon of December 14 and Mingo found a stream to refresh his men. They cooked beef for the army, building their first big fires since Reforma. Mingo took stock that night. His supplies were low and his medicines were gone. Soon they must forage. "Ah-h-h." The *Grillos* wagged their heads and grinned. Stealing was more fun than killing.

They had come four hundred and fifty miles from the mango grove of Baragua, covering the distance in less than two months.

That was the night Soto came back, riding hard for headquarters. Mingo sauntered up to meet him, waiting at the edge of a thicket until the guide came out of Macéo's *bohio* and dragged himself into the saddle, his head lolling as he rode toward the camp of the *Grillos*.

Mingo waited until he was only a few yards away, and stepped from behind a tree. "Is she all right?"

Soto's head jerked up. *"Amigo!"* Then he shook his head. "I did not see her, but she is safe." He noticed the feather and grinned.

"Did you find your man?" the American asked.

The grin gave way to a scowl. "No!"

"Maybe you need a good man to help you." He was making a joke to welcome his friend back to camp.

"La Cuchillada!" The goatherd clucked his tongue. "A red feather on a *gringo. Por Dios!"* He swung off his horse, still scowling. "If you knew what I know you would not make bad jokes." He looked back toward the Army of Liberation, couriers moving swiftly from headquarters and the warriors already spreading out across the plains. "A Spanish army has come out of Havana to greet us."

Mingo Dabney scoffed. He had seen only the backs of Spaniards for days. "To hell with a Spanish army. All they do is run."

"Big brag," the Mambi said.

They reached the carts and the men greeted Soto affectionately, carving meat for him from a beef rib. Mingo motioned him into the shadows. "What's all this talk about Spaniards?"

"Sagaldo has rallied." Soto blew on the meat, cooling it. "He has a new army from Havana and is waiting for us."

"We'll burn some sugar mills and watch him run." El Dabney waved his hand, brushing Sagaldo and his army aside.

The goatherd ate the last of the meat and licked his fingers. "Hm-m-m. A red feather and a big brag." He stuck his arms above his head, stretching. "Every sugar mill for fifty miles is garrisoned. You won't draw off Sagaldo this time."

"Then we'll fight him." He walked with Soto toward his cart.

The Mambi nodded. "That's what Macéo says. And Gómez." He closed his eyes and rubbed them. "Time has caught up with us. Time and luck and the Spaniards." He crawled far back into the cart and curled up. Let the generals worry. Soto was going to sleep.

There was no *silencio* that night and around ten o'clock word came down to put out the fires and start rolling again. No singing. Close up. Pedro Díaz to the right. The army fanned out, moving under hushed orders, moving like shad-

316

ows. Mingo worked his carts in behind Díaz and trudged out to the far tip of the fan.

Midnight passed them as they were climbing a slope, the oxen pulling hard, and then the beasts raised their heads to breathe deep and Mingo knew they were at the crest. It was pitch dark and he drove his carts to the right, but never out of sight of Díaz. He put rocks under the wheels and unyoked his oxen and the *Grillos* prodded them to the rear.

The *parana* grass was waist-high and Mingo walked through the grass and came close to Díaz' men. A few of them looked up and recognized his restless stride, the red feather. "El Dabney." They whispered it.

"*Compadres,*" he answered.

"We are going to fight, El Dabney. No longer will we hide like moles and run like rabbits."

"*Bueno.*" He spoke it like a Mambi.

"May the Queen of Heaven protect you, El Dabney."

The Army of Liberation was drawn into position, facing west. The east was closed and they must either fight and move on west again, or stay still and die. There was no other choice.

It was near three o'clock and daylight soon must come. Nevertheless, he sent out four pickets and told his *Grillos* to get some sleep. They clambered into their carts and peered to the west, wondering and waiting, and no sleep was in them. But Soto slept. He snored so loud that the *Grillos* giggled.

There was a rustle to his left and Mingo walked around his cart, staring into the dark. Díaz' men were restless. They were on their feet and he heard their chieftain order them back to ease, but they were mumbling in a wave of excitement.

Mingo was of a mind to step over there and see what was going on, when out of the darkness came Antonio Macéo, walking alone through Díaz' *machete*-men and into the camp of the *impedimenta*.

The woodsman gripped the tongue of his cart and stared at

the general. Macéo stopped and peered into the darkness. "El Dabney?"

"General Macéo." He waited and let The Brown One come to him.

And Macéo came, glancing at the red feather, the torn trousers and ragged shirt. "General Miro is sleeping," he said, offering it as an explanation, perhaps.

"Soto is sleeping, too." Mingo was flustered and it was the first thing that came to his mind.

Macéo put one hand on the tongue of the cart and looked closely at the *gringo,* and away toward the west. "We have come a long way since Baragua."

"*Sí.* How do you feel?"

"Very well." His voice was low, almost liquid. "But I am worried, Señor."

"I'm scared, too. Maybe a cup of coffee would help."

"We cannot make coffee," Macéo replied. "A fire might give us away." He walked around the cart and heard the goatherd snoring. "Soto?"

Mingo nodded.

"He snores like Miro," the general said.

One of the *Grillos* poked his head out of his cart and saw The Brown One and they all poured out, pressing close to touch his clothes, his hand. The demigod had come down to earth. It was a thing to remember and to tell their grandchildren.

General Macéo glanced into Mingo's cart, at Soto snoring, the tools, the ax, the forge. He picked up the ax and felt it, and lifted the hammer, balancing it. The *Grillos* held their breath, fearing he would recognize it. Perhaps he did, but he laid it back in place. "I used to be a carpenter."

The *Grillos* beamed and Mingo said, "The men are mighty proud you came down. Maybe there's something we can do for you."

"Yes," Macéo said without hesitation. "I want to anchor my line on the *impedimenta* —"

318

"Sir!" Mingo's jaw dropped and his men blinked in amazement. Macéo asking a favor of the *Grillos?* Macéo using them in his plan of battle? *Por Dios!* They were important.

The Brown One faced the men, glancing first at El Dabney and then at Pepe Barea. "There are people who say —" He cut his eyes at the *gringo.* "There are governments who say we Cubans are not ready for responsibility. You are the people of Cuba. You are the *impedimenta,* the fingers of the army."

"We are the *Grillos,*" Pepe Rosado declared, and the tip of his nose was twitching.

"*Sí.*" Macéo bowed to them, bending his neck slightly. "The *Grillos.*"

"El Dabney's *Grillos,*" Pepe Barea said, his face contorted with joy and weeping.

Again Macéo bowed. The commotion woke up Soto and he rubbed his eyes and his eyes popped open wide. Mingo sent for the pickets that all might see General Antonio Macéo in the camp of the *Grillos,* so that all might share the honor. He must not deny any grandchild a tale in the years to come, a tale so laden with glory.

"All the *Grillos* are here, sir," Mingo stepped back.

Macéo rested his hand on the hilt of his sword. "We will fight tomorrow —"

"Baire!" It was a murmur, a quick hot murmur.

"We will anchor our line on these carts. Will you hold?"

The *Grillos* puffed out their chests and nodded vigorously. Mingo said, "We'll hold."

Macéo bowed his thanks. "Mambises!" It was his highest praise and, without another word, he walked away.

Mingo followed him around the cart and there the Brown One paused and jerked his head around, staring over his shoulder at Mingo. A flush was on his cheeks and his eyes wavered before Mingo's gaze. He bent slightly and tugged at the *parana* grass, pulling a tuft by the roots and tossing it away. "Señor Dabney," he said it softly, "General Máximo Gómez is impressed by you and your men."

Mingo stiffened and his eyes never moved from Macéo's face. *"Es verdad?"* Like a Mambi he asked if it were true.

"Señor Dabney." Macéo was feeling his way. "General Gómez is not going to Pinar del Río."

"I am." Mingo pulled a stalk on the *parana* grass and chewed it. "I'm going to Mantua."

The Brown One rubbed his mustaches, smoothing them with the tips of his fingers. "It was not I who suggested you to General Gómez. Your own courage commended you to him. I just want you to know that."

Mingo took the piece of grass from his lips and dropped it. "I am going to Pinar del Río on a promise. I just want you to know that."

"Your promise was to Señor Elmo Batson?"

"No, sir." Mingo spoke slowly, saying each word distinctly. "My promise was to Rafaela Galban."

"La Entorcha!" It was a harsh command.

"No." Again Mingo spoke slowly. "I speak of Rafaela Galban."

The Brown One breathed deeply, almost a gasp, and a strange look came into his eyes, a wild look of fear and pleading. Then the moment passed and he wheeled and walked into the darkness; the believer whose lodestar was passing into the care of another.

Mingo returned to his band and passed out ammunition, distributing every cartridge he had hoarded. His *Grillos* were like crickets again, scurrying through the grass and preparing for battle. Only Soto was not excited. His dignity did not permit demonstration.

"Ah-h-h, El Dabney." The *Grillos* said it over and over, banging their chests. "Soldiers, eh? We will get medals, eh?"

Pepe Rosado stroked his long nose. "Will they be gold?"

El Dabney dispersed them along the crest and in front of the carts, hiding them in the grass. They could fall back to the carts, but no farther. It took him only a few minutes to get set, and he moved into the grass near the tongue of his cart and sat down, waiting for the dawn.

It came in a dreary streak of gray: the dawn of December 15.

Pepe Penalver, a scout, rode in from the northwest, and Macéo was on his horse and waiting. So was Gómez. He was riding astride. Ulcer be damned. The Spaniards had flushed The Old Fox, had treed him, and now let the Spaniards beware.

"They are at Mal Tiempo," the scout reported. "Beyond the west slope on a plain at Mal Tiempo."

The word spread through the army, traveling the crest from the Ducasse brothers on the left flank to the *Grillos* on the right. Mal Tiempo. Bad time. The Mambises whispered the name.

El Dabney looked to the northwest, to the valley and the sugar mill there, the chimneys smoking and soldiers patrolling the cane fields. He was coldly angry, though his flesh burned hot at the back of his neck. Cuban workmen were toiling for Spain and every stalk they cut delayed the revolution. His fingers itched to throw a dynamite stick into the mill. The *Grillos* saw and grumbled.

"We'll get them, El Dabney." They passed the word along. "*Sí.*"

Two more scouts came in, pointing excitedly toward Mal Tiempo. Macéo stood in his stirrups and gazed northwest. "If the Spaniards are there, we must ride over them."

Gómez reined his horse alongside Macéo and they looked down the slope at the sugar mill and at Mal Tiempo. The Old Fox stroked his white goatee, plucking it, and slowly drew out his sword, a short stubby sword without grace or beauty. He pulled it out clumsily and passed it from his right hand to his left. Macéo unsheathed his Toledo blade and the army fidgeted, some of the men raising their heads above the grass to stare down the slope.

Máximo Gómez held his sword in his right hand. "We attack," he said to Macéo. "One shot. Then the *machete*." The order ran among the men and old Máximo Gómez checked his line, then raked his spurs across the flanks of his horse.

He was the first man away, down the slope and galloping northwest, his sword held high and his frail little body bouncing in his saddle. Macéo sat straight, rocking slightly, and his head and his sword were above Máximo Gómez and yet he, the brown idol, willingly followed the little white man. *Cuba libre!*

Miro was at Macéo's left, whipping his horse into a froth and charging down from the crest, racing wide to the left and signaling for the Ducasse brothers to move.

The whole line lunged, swinging forward like the spoke of a wheel, swinging from the tip on the far left to the hub anchored on the crest, and El Dabney's *Grillos* were the hub. There were no shouts, no dares or taunts. The tall grass hid Máximo Gómez, then it thinned and he galloped into the open beside Macéo.

The Spaniards fired first. They fired from behind a low ridge and ran out onto the plain, out into the open, and formed a square.

"*Venga, Mambi!*" It was their first cry and their only cry.

The *Grillos* fingered their triggers and Mingo ran among them, shoving their guns off aim. "Don't shoot!"

A second volley from the Spaniards and Pedro Díaz' men began tumbling, and the clansmen of the Ducasses. No shots from the Cubans. No shouts. They kept moving down the slope, trotting until they broke out of the tall grass, and dropped to one knee, aimed carefully, and fired. One shot was all they had.

The Spaniards in the forward wall pitched to their faces, or slithered down, or sprawled; and the Mambises reached for their *machetes*.

Again the *Grillos* fingered their triggers and again Mingo forbade a shot. "Hold it, John Henry! Save those bullets!"

The Army of Liberation plunged into the Spanish line, slashing it. They surged through and wheeled and surged back, and dust and smoke covered Mal Tiempo and Mingo Dabney glanced at Soto and Soto nodded knowingly.

The Spaniards were running through the cane fields and toward the sugar mill. They threw down their guns and fled wildly and the Mambises sprinted after them, hacking and chopping, leaping on their backs and tearing at their throats.

The Ducasse brothers circled the field, driving the enemy back into the center, into the open arms of the Mambises. It was a mob of men, belly to belly, biting and clawing. Gómez put his sword away and took a *machete* from a dead man. Macéo sheathed his sword and swung a *machete*. It wasn't a battle at all; it was a slaughter of Spaniards. Mambi cane cutters swinging *machetes!* Mambi tree cutters swishing steel! The dust and smoke rose thick and the fighting surged northwest and Mingo Dabney looked down into the valley at the writhing wounded and the stilled dead: a Mambi here and there, and piles of Spaniards.

A rabble, half of them with rifles, was crushing the Spanish army in open fight. The haughty Spanish grenadiers had advanced without support of cavalry, scorning the need of horsemen. *Venga, Mambi!*

"*Recristo!*" The *Grillos* waved their arms. "Look at the loot, El Dabney."

Mingo glared at them. "Don't you budge."

The fight was raging beyond the sugar mill and Mal Tiempo was strewn with guns and dead men and carts burning. "All those guns," the *Grillos* wailed. "Look at them, El Dabney. They are wasting and it is a sin to waste."

"And those shoes," Pepe Barea moaned.

"We will need shoes, El Dabney. It is a long way to Pinar del Río. A rocky way. You want to be barefooted again, El Dabney?"

"Don't you budge." Mingo leaned against the tongue of his cart, his rifle loose in his hand. Pepe Barea was weeping, the tears trickling free down his cheeks, and Pepe Rosado's big red nose was running. "Wipe your nose, John Henry," El Dabney ordered. "And stay where you are."

Soto stood behind Mingo, watching the *Grillos,* loosely swinging his *machete* in his right hand and watching.

They didn't try to break. They looked down at the loot and at El Dabney, and shrugged their shoulders.

MINGO DABNEY

Chapter **26**   The first cry for *La Cuchillada*
came from beyond a ridge and the *Grillos* scampered for
their horses, awaiting no orders. "Hold it!" Mingo commanded. "Not yet!"

A courier broke from the swirling confusion of the battle
and raced up the slope, beating his horse with the flat of his
machete and screaming:

"*La Cuchillada!* The sugar mill!"

They all heard. Well, let them remember. Macéo needed
him; her guardian was sending for El Dabney the *gringo*.
Quickly he tested his gun and reached for his horse's bridle.
No word was spoken, no order sounded. He pointed his gun
toward the sugar mill and dug his heels into his horse's
flanks.

There was no sweep, no ruse. Only the thrust, the wild
dash for the mill. El Dabney was proud, arrogant, and the
sun touched his red feather and his horse foamed lather,
leaping the dead and pounding on. He was triumphant at
last. Macéo had sent for him!

The stench of battle, the bitter smoke and the clawing
dust, filled his nostrils and sweat trickled down his face, into
his eyes and mouth. The *Grillos* were bunched around and
behind him. On. On, you gutter imps! *La Cuchillada.* The
sugar mill.

"Men are fools that wish to die —"

The *Grillos* peered at him, at El Dabney singing a song

new to them, and they twisted their necks and stared at him. He lifted his rifle and shook it.

> *Is it not fine to dance and sing,*
> *When the bells of death do ring. . . .*

The first line of Spaniards, a few cowering recruits, threw down their arms and fled. Pepe Rosado leaned out and slashed one with his *machete*. Soto slashed another. And they rode on, leaving two writhing bodies in their path.

The sugar mill was before them and Mingo scanned the field, the battle raging half a mile away and to the right, a thin line of guards around the plant, and the workmen behind the barricade.

There was a gap in the line, a wide ragged gap and he laughed his joy. Stupid Spaniards! Pigs, and blood brothers of pigs! Leaving a gap for El Dabney the *gringo,* daring an opening for El Dabney of the red feather. *La Cuchillada!*

With a flourish of his rifle he rallied his band, pointed to the opening, and dashed for it. The opening spread, the Spaniards melting back. Soto looked over his shoulder and frowned. Pepe Barea blinked the sweat from his eyes and scowled. But Mingo Dabney rode on, hard for the barricades and the mill they protected, feeling his dynamite against his side and his heart thumping his ribs.

The workers began running, ducking their heads and racing for the field. The *Grillos* leveled one blast, laughing as they shot, and Mingo reached for his dynamite and picked his targets. The first stick through a window, the second by the wall. Then the torch. This one was easy —

Pepe Rosado screamed first. *"Recristo!"*

Pepe Barea shrieked. "Mother of Mercy!"

"Hold up!" Soto's face blanched and he jerked his horse to a halt, sawing the bit.

Mingo glanced back, a stick of dynamite in his hand and his red feather gleaming.

The gap in the line was closed.

326

The *Grillos* surged about him, pointing frantically. The Spaniards were crowding into the opening, locking the gap. El Dabney the *gringo* was trapped by the open door that was not open at all. He had thrust in and it had snapped shut behind him.

His fear turned to panic and he stared at the Spanish line constricting slowly, hemming him in, their Mausers dully reflecting the morning sun. His men looked from the Spaniards to him, to his red feather. They uttered no word, not a sound, just looked at him. He had brought them in, and he would take them out. El Dabney knew what he was doing.

But he didn't. He was trapped like a rat in a corn crib, the mill suddenly swarming with soldiers; and a line arced about him, waiting for him to move.

He picked the weakest spot, over to the left and pointed. "There—we'll break through there." Break through about two hundred Spaniards!

"*Sí!*" They echoed his command.

El Dabney fired first. He raised his gun, aimed at the line and fired, hoping, praying the Spaniards would divide. Then Soto fired, and they all fired, blazing a volley toward the weakest link. "Now ride!" Mingo struck his horse and lunged.

The Spanish fire seared the ground, a tight volley that tore into the *Grillos* and four of them pitched from their horses, screeching their agony. Mingo felt blood warm against his leg, and saw the gaping hole in his horse's side. He jumped to the ground, lying prone to load and fire at the line slowly advancing. "Keep shooting!" He shrieked the order. "Cut through if they give an inch —"

"Our horses! Our beautiful horses are dead." The *Grillos* wailed it and again Mingo looked around, the horses squirming in the dust and the men on foot again, crouching, looking to him and expecting a miracle.

A sudden rage gripped Mingo and he cursed blindly. The panic was gone and fear was gone, and there was only fury. Fury at the Spaniards who had trapped him. Fury at himself for his brashness and pride. "Keep shooting!" His rifle was burning hot.

Two more *Grillos* went down. "El Dabney . . ."

The cries died in the crackle of Spanish fire, dying to a whimper; and they were still.

Soto crawled to his side, hugging the ground. "The *machete, amigo?* We must cut our way out."

"It's my fault." Mingo began sobbing and his rifle burned his fingers. "How can we get out, Soto? Good Lord! How can we get out —"

"The *machete*." The little Mambi reached for the hooked knife. "Some of us can escape."

Mingo Dabney leaped to his feet, waving his men toward the line. "Cut your way out! The *machete!*"

The Mambises unsheathed their blades and wiggled forward. But Mingo had no *machete* and he balanced his rifle as a club. The first blow would shatter it, and what then, El Dabney of the red feather?

The body of a *Grillo* was at his side, and he turned him over, snatching the *machete*, the tool of the peasant, the weapon of the Mambi.

It fitted naturally into his hand.

He glanced at Soto and the little black man nodded and they raced forward together, swishing their *machetes* and screaming their taunts. Baire!

Venga, Mambi! Come on, dirt!

A blistering fire pinned them down and when Mingo Dabney looked up there was Leopold Sagaldo, calmly sitting his horse, waiting in the line, waiting for his quarry.

Thirty thousand pesos for the head of Mingo Dabney!

Leopold Sagaldo smiled his assurance and raised his sword, pointing directly at the man who had tricked him twice —

The explosion in the mill rocked the earth.

"Macéo!" Pepe Rosado screamed it and Mingo looked

back, his tongue cleaving to the roof of his mouth and his eyes bulging.

"Baire!" It came from the sugar mill, and the mill was crumbling, smoke billowing up and the scorching blast rumbling through the plant. Macéo was there! The Brown One was at the mill, lancing through the *Grillos'* rear and on toward Sagaldo. The Nigra was facing the grandee!

The Spaniards hung back, massing around Leopold Sagaldo, and he snarled his helplessness. Save the mill. He shouted the order with which Madrid had dulled his sword. "Advance to the mill!"

The Spanish line thinned like leaves before a hurricane and the way out was open. Macéo! Macéo! They were calling his name back at the mill, the Mambises in triumph, the Spaniards in dread. A red horse circled the mill, a Toledo blade flashed, and Antonio Macéo raced through the smoke and the flame, hard by the *Grillos* and into the Spanish line.

A minute, two minutes, and Soto lay panting on the ground, staring at the sky where the saints were. Macéo charged and Sagaldo fell back, and the battle of Mal Tiempo dwindled into blood and cries and prayers, the sticky smoke from the mill hanging low over the ground and the bitter smoke of gun powder curling the grass.

"We are safe now," Soto said.

El Dabney said nothing. He got to his feet and began walking back up the slope, the *machete* still in his hand, loose in his hand.

His *Grillos* filed after him, their heads bobbing their exhaustion, and all on foot; all except nine who lay in the dust back by the mill.

Up the slope, trudging slowly, dejected and silent. The carts were waiting, the oxen munching the grass. Soto went for a pail of water and the *Grillos* sprawled on the ground, their eyes closed and their tongues lolling.

Mingo went to his cart and took off his hat, resting his face in his hands, hiding his face. Soto brought him a gourd of water, but Mingo did not look up. The little Mambi put the dipper back in the pail and, saying nothing, reached over and took the red feather from the old black hat and dropped it to the ground.

The *Grillos* were sad. El Dabney had lost his red feather and his head was bowed. "May we loot now?" They asked it almost timidly.

He nodded his approval and went to his oxen and watered them. He was an ox driver, not a soldier. She would hear about it, but that didn't matter. Macéo had sent for him and he had failed, and that didn't matter. The *Grillos* had trusted him and there were nine to trust him no more, and that did matter.

The sun passed its peak and glared down on five hundred Spanish dead, and forty of Macéo's Mambises, and nine *Grillos*. A breeze stirred the ashes of the sugar mill and lifted the bloody grass of Mal Tiempo, and the fighting was beyond the ridge and beyond sound.

The battle was over by four o'clock and word came back for Mingo to bring up his *impedimenta*, and the carts bumped down the slope and over the bodies. The *Grillos* wandered out of line, picking up rifles and shoes, tearing out earrings and corralling horses.

El Dabney found a new rifle and a fresh horse. His black hat rested squarely upon his head, no longer slanted, and he rode without speaking, staring straight before him.

Miro met them on the road beyond Mal Tiempo and looked long at the *gringo*, at the hat where the feather had been, and there was no rebuke within him. "The Spaniards are routed," he said.

"I lost nine men, General Miro."

José Miro Argenter put his hand on El Dabney's shoulder, knowing that failure had humbled him. He glanced at the *machete*, at the dust streaked where the tears had fallen, saying nothing, for the salt of the *gringo's* defeat still was raw in the wound.

"Did we lose many?" Mingo wiped his arm across his face.

Not many. Gómez' ulcer was broken and bleeding and he was riding sidesaddle again, raging his pain. Macéo was untouched. Juan Ducasse had lost blood. The last of Goulet's men were dead.

"Shall we feed?" Mingo asked.

"No," Miro replied. "There is a railroad up ahead."

"Want us to blow it up?" He asked it quickly, doubt in his tone.

Miro nodded. "General Macéo said tell you to destroy it."

So they still trusted him, and some of the bitterness passed from El Dabney. He cracked his whip and his carts rumbled on, and his spirits rose. It was dark when they reached the railroad, and they blew it up and blew up a bridge.

His *Grillos* laughed as the crossties sailed into the air and the rails buckled. Mingo Dabney did not laugh because there was no laughter within him. The broad grin of Lebanon was gone, but there was a slight smile as his work was done. Like a Mambi, perhaps . . .

Havana held its breath in the shock of Mal Tiempo and Madrid trembled from the cardinal to the crown, for the meek had turned to bite the jeweled hand of Church and State. It couldn't be! But the dead at Mal Tiempo were not a lie. The wounded streaming into Havana, and the terrified unwounded, were not a lie. The Army of Liberation had crushed Campos' army and the Volunteers closed their purses and shook their fists at Madrid. Send us a strong man.

Spain had a quarter of a million soldiers in Cuba and yet a rabble, armed with peasant *machetes*, was advancing on Havana. The Spanish army was tied down in garrisons as far back as the *trochas*. Tied down in cities that the Mambises by-passed.

England rubbed her chin and pondered newspaper accounts of Mal Tiempo. Incredible! The foolish journalists insisted the Cubans might win their independence. Germany watched England. The United States watched the stock market, fretting over the rise of sugar, and wondering when the panic would end. Mal Tiempo? It meant bad times. Well, there were bad times in the United States, too. Money was tight, but those little fellows down in Cuba won 'em a good battle. Maybe we ought to help 'em. Might be a good investment. Neighbors, ain't they? . . .

The Army of Liberation pushed on west; ten, fifteen, seventeen miles a day. The memory of Mal Tiempo began to leave El Dabney and some of his old ways came back, but there was no swagger in his walk. The *Grillos* were happy that he was himself again. *"Bueno?"* They smiled the question.

"Bueno." He smiled the answer.

There was a skirmish every day, Macéo slashing, the *Grillos* burning and Gómez pushing on. Mingo watched his oxen wither under the strain, two of them staggering and dropping in their tracks. No oxen could stand such a pace, and few men. Ten—twelve—twenty miles a day.

Dysentery hit the *Grillos* and three of them went down before Mingo knew what it was. He left them and pushed on. It was Christmas Day.

Pepe Barea came down with fever and they left him in a farmer's hut; left him weeping for them to take him along and give him the right to die in his cart. "Take me, El Dabney," Pepe Barea pleaded. "I'll never get back to the Oriente. Don't leave me here, *compadre* —"

El Dabney cracked his whip over his oxen. "Push on. Keep going." He did not look back at his comrade. He must not let his men see that he could weep.

Pepe Barea raged all night and, crazed and delirious, slipped into the woods before dawn, staggering after the *Grillos*. Sagaldo found him and left him in the woods, his belly slashed.

Push on. Keep moving.

Big Red, the off ox, stumbled and never got up. Mingo

butchered him where he lay and fed the wounded, the few still able to travel.

Sagaldo tried to stop them at Calimete. He had twelve hundred men and Macéo brushed him aside. Captain Emilio Bacardi was wounded and Máximo Gómez assigned his own son, young Francisco Gómez, to Macéo's staff as aide-de-camp, and they pushed on.

It was January 1, 1896, and they crossed into Havana province and watered their horses in the Almendares River. Gómez had promised they would reach the river by January 1, and they were there.

The *Grillos*—the forty-one who survived—rested by the stream and a few of them bathed, but most of them scorned the water. El Dabney was as lean as a sapling and hard as a brier, and there were wrinkles at the corners of his eyes; and he never laughed. Soto kept hoping for gaiety again now that they were so near Mantua, but there was no merriment in El Dabney and he wished only to move on.

The men patched their clothes and polished their weapons and lolled by the river, and at headquarters lanterns burned all night and Máximo Gómez and Antonio Macéo and the combined staffs pored over plans. The Army of Liberation was to be split and Gómez was to remain on the plains. The army of the west, the Army of the Occidente, was formed and given into the hands of The Brown One. It numbered less than seven hundred men, and Macéo was to march on down to Mantua and the end of the island.

That was the plan.

Máximo Gómez folded his maps and reached for his brandy bottle. His leg ached and he was surly with pain, and The Old Fox was worried.

The Ducasse brothers were brooding and Pedro Díaz was despondent. Miro was alarmed.

There were furrows across the troubled brow of Antonio Macéo. He was almost at Pinar del Río, but there were whispered reports from the far end of the island, vague, dismal reports from Mantua.

The people were not rallying to *La Entorcha*.

Gómez heard it and watched Macéo. Macéo heard it and paled. The people were listening to *La Entorcha*, but turning away. The fire was gone from the torch, for her eyes were misty and she was a woman waiting in Mantua, watching the east.

The Mambises themselves must not know that something was wrong in Pinar del Río. The staff agreed on that: the men must not be told. Above all, El Dabney of the *Grillos* must not learn that *La Entorcha* looked to the east, the way he would come.

The plans for the two armies were drawn. Pedro Díaz and the Ducasse brothers were to go with Macéo. Old Máximo Gómez ordered it so, and hobbled to his hammock. He wanted brandy and he wanted sleep. He slept in his boots and his rumpled clothes; but Antonio Macéo put on silken underwear and a clean linen suit and went out into the night.

The camp was sleeping and the fires were dead or dying, and he walked among his men, the new Army of the Occidente, and along the river bank to the camp of the *Grillos*. He stood in the shadows, alone and proud, near the *gringo's* cart until Mingo saw him and went out to meet him. This time Mingo Dabney went to Antonio Macéo.

The Brown One rested his hand against a tree and fastened his gaze on Mingo. "General Gómez is moving east tomorrow. I will move west. General Gómez has asked for your services."

El Dabney shook his head. "I am heading west. To Mantua."

Antonio Macéo struggled with himself to contain his wrath. "It was I who made the suggestion to General Gómez. I want you to know that."

Mingo spoke quietly. "It doesn't make any difference. I want you to know that."

334

"I cannot order you away for many reasons." He smoothed his beard and his hand shook. "I made an agreement with Señor Elmo Batson not to order you away."

"That's right," Mingo said. "You can't order me away for many reasons —"

"But I can remind you of your duty, Señor Dabney. The commander in chief needs you and I do not want you. You will interfere with my plans and I am trying to win a war."

Mingo stepped closer to the tree and closer to The Brown One. "I have a stake in this war, too. And I am trying to win a woman." He measured each word, weighed it, then spoke it. "I expect to stay in Cuba. I will build my home here, and up where I come from we build a home around a woman." There was no boast in his words or in his demeanor.

Macéo was motionless. His cheeks were ashy and his eyes burned. He opened his mouth to speak, perhaps to plead, the believer to the infidel, but no words came and he turned and stalked away.

MINGO DABNEY

Chapter **27**   The new Army of the Occidente bade farewell to their comrades at the River Almendares and Macéo and old Máximo Gómez embraced before all their men and some of the men wept, but mostly they cheered.

The *Grillos* lined along the stream as the commander in chief led his warriors away, their feet kicking the dust into little clouds. Young Francisco Gómez rode a few miles with his father, kissed him good-bye and returned to the river, his sire's injunction ringing in his ears: Your duty is to protect Antonio Macéo with your life.

Mutton and beans for dinner that day, and a little rum, and the Western army—seven hundred Mambises—pulled out late in the afternoon; Macéo up front with Miro, the *machete*-men in close ranks and the *Grillos* straggling despite El Dabney's admonitions to keep up. They were in new country and the *Grillos* stretched their necks to see everything, scurrying into the woods, seeking *bohios* to loot and willing women.

Pepe Rosado found a woman and boasted of her youth and beauty, snapping his fingers to indicate the ease of his conquest. Mingo sought out the woman and she was forty and toothless, but he made sure there was no rape. Rape meant certain death in the Army of the Occidente and El Dabney

336

couldn't afford to lose Pepe Rosado now that Pepe Barea was dead.

Soto left them on the third day, left them at dusk and rode northwest toward Havana. There was a skirmish the night of January 8 and Macéo lost five men; and passed into the province of Pinar del Río.

The woodsman looked around for pines and there were no pines, only a few scattered blockhouses and muddy *trochas* —the forts of the west. This line of blockhouses, dividing Havana province from Pinar del Río, was even more flimsy than the *trochas* of the Oriente, and Macéo passed boldly through, his men singing *La Bayamesa*.

The march quickened, eighteen, twenty miles a day and no Spaniards, only dust and mosquitoes and Negro workmen in the fields, gaping at the wild Mambises from the hills.

The great sugar plantations were behind them and tobacco fields flanked the route, stretching in even rows from the ornate *haciendas* to the dirty *bohios* of the workmen.

Pinar del Río was a province of easy-living landowners loyal to Spain and passionately loyal to things exactly as they were, Cuban Tories stubbornly opposed to any change.

The hillmen of the Oriente were fierce and independent, but the workmen of Pinar del Río were servile, dragging out their weary lives in bondage to the land and to usurious Spanish merchants. These Negro field hands, many imported from the Canary Islands, had no heart for the Revolution and thought the Mambises were savages; they stared at them, and sometimes ran away. Macéo did not molest the workers and Mingo wondered why, not aware that the high command had agreed on a policy of the open hand for the Occidente.

Some of the *Grillos* wanted to chase the frightened field hands, for they all had shoes and the women were young and dumpy and jiggled when they walked. Pepe Rosado, on El Dabney's orders, swore a beating for any *Grillo* who left the line of march. However, two of Pedro Díaz' Mambises slipped away and there was a charge of rape. Macéo shrugged: the men were shot and the army moved on.

The woodsman saw his first pine tree at Paso Viejo, the Old Pass, and he stared at it a second, and ran up there. The *Grillos* thought he was crazy and glanced at one another, and some of the Ducasse clansmen peered at him as he ran toward the tree.

Mingo was disappointed. It was a scrubby tree, fit only for kindling back home or maybe a fence rail; but the clean, sharp smell tingled his nose and he stripped off some of the needles and crushed them. Um-m-m. Smelled mighty good. Anyhow, they smelled like Lebanon pines.

He looked around at the rolling land and it looked familiar. Could be Mississippi, almost. The Oriente, with its mountains, was like North Alabama. Santa Clara and the central plains were Texas. Pinar del Río could be Mississippi. Change the tobacco to cotton and raise the stubby pines into tall pines, and it might be like Lebanon. The houses were high off the ground and the Negro children in Pinar del Río were no different from the Negro children back home, just as naked and just as shy, hiding and peeping big-eyed around their mothers' skirts.

"Is it like back home, El Dabney?" his *Grillos* asked.

"Sort of." Mingo smeared his hands together and smelled the pine needles again. "Now let's get going." Mantua was only sixty miles away and January was half gone.

The Spaniards and Volunteers attacked at the Old Pass, rising up from the tobacco fields and striking hard to turn back the invasion in its final hours. Macéo slapped them aside and they marched to Sabalo and Mingo thought Sabalo was a pretty name. Even the country thereabouts was pretty, the streams deep and cool and fast-running. It was all beautiful to the pilgrim because Mantua was less than twenty miles away.

He wanted to push on that night, but Macéo ordered a

338

camp and directed his men to clean themselves and polish their *machetes*. The *Grillos* poked out their lips and sulked. They cleaned their *machetes* all right, using sand and ferns; but they refused to go into the water and when El Dabney stripped and waded in, they squatted on the bank and laughed at him. Some tossed rocks at him and he caught the rocks and threw them back and they all laughed. Mantua was nigh, and it was a pleasant land of tobacco and good coffee and dumpy women.

That night a priest came into camp, astride a donkey, and Mingo wondered about it. He hadn't seen a priest since the Oriente and wondered about a man daring to defy his Church and come to the Mambises. The priest went to headquarters, but was there only a minute or so before he walked out of Macéo's hut, and young Francisco Gómez pointed the way to the camp of the *Grillos*.

"El Dabney?" the priest called. He had a lean face and black eyebrows, thick and tangled. Mingo stepped forward, still wondering, and the padre spoke in a quiet voice. "I am Father Tomás. I am from Mantua." He looked directly at Mingo as he spoke.

Mingo held his breath. "Yes, Father?" If there was a priest in Mantua to be trusted, she would know him.

"I have news for you. Señor Elmo Batson was in Mantua last month. He said you would be along —"

"Is he still there?"

The priest shook his head. "He was there only a few days. He said tell you your family was all right —"

"What else?" Mingo asked quickly and a dozen other questions followed.

Father Tomás held up his hand and stopped him, and reached under his cassock for a square of frayed paper. "I've been carrying it a long time. He said give it to you."

Mingo took the letter and stepped over to a fire and unfolded it. It was written on heavy brown wrapping paper.

Mantua, December 23, 1895

Dear Mingo:

Take care of these supplies. It took all I could rake and scrape to buy them.

You can trust this priest. His bishop, too, but don't make too much noise about it.

Everything is about the same back in Lebanon.

The United States is getting stewed up about Cuba and it won't take much shoving to push us in.

Save me a corner down here for a store. I'm getting old and this is a good place to settle down. I want my store next to the post office.

Don't do anything I wouldn't do.

Your friend,

Elmo Batson

P. S. Merry Christmas

No mention of Rafaela Galban. Ol' Elmo was too smart for that. The priest might get caught. "*Servidor de usted.* Your servant, Father. And I am grateful."

"I am indebted to you, El Dabney." The priest put his hand on the pilgrim's shoulder and looked around at the *Grillos,* lazying in their carts and sipping coffee and cutting their eyes at the padre suspiciously. "I am a Mambi, too."

"Are you going back to Mantua tonight?"

The priest nodded. "*Sí.* And I am going alone. I asked General Macéo your whereabouts and he told me. He told me to return to Mantua alone. I promised."

A flush of temper spread across Mingo's face and he accompanied the priest out of camp, walking slowly at his side. "I will be in Mantua tomorrow."

"*Bueno.*" Father Tomás paused and again put his hand on Mingo's shoulder. "The supplies are hidden near the village —"

"Hidden!" The implications of the word alarmed him.

340

Why were the supplies hidden? There should be enough Mambises in Mantua to protect them, recruits rallied by *La Entorcha*, recruits for Macéo's withered Army of the Occidente. El Dabney was cautious. "You will show me where they're hidden?" He tried to stifle the premonition that tapped at his brain, demanding acknowledgement.

Father Tomás lowered his voice. "She will show you, my son."

"Is she all right, Father?" It was a hurried nervous whisper.

"*Sí*. She lives in a convent near the church." The priest was agitated. "Now do not ask me more. I promised."

Macéo again. Always Macéo. The Brown One had pledged the priest to silence about Rafaela Galban and Mingo's anger rose—only to be swept aside by sudden fear. Something was wrong in Mantua. Was that the reason Macéo hushed the priest? Rafaela in a convent! The supplies hidden! Where were the Mambises she had rallied? Troublesome thoughts surged through his mind as he trudged back to his camp.

Pepe Rosado poured him a cup of coffee and the cup trembled in Mingo's hand, the coffee spilling. The *Grillos* could steal him a horse from under Macéo's nose and Mantua was only a few hours away. He could trust Pepe Rosado to handle his crickets until he got back. Or could he? The women of Pinar del Río were plump and rape meant death.

The thought of Macéo shrugging his death shrug at one of the *Grillos* chilled his blood and he pushed the thought out of his mind and scowled into his coffee. A man does not live so long with comrades and then desert them even for a few hours, even for his love of a woman.

General Miro sauntered casually into camp, too casually perhaps, and greeted Mingo with obvious distaste for his mission. "Everything is well, El Dabney?"

"*Sí*." Mingo sensed the meaning of the visit and resented it, and asked testily, "Is there something I can do for you?"

Miro looked at the ground and scratched a pattern in the dust with his boot. "You must not hold the performance of my duty against me. A soldier takes orders, *compadre*. I came down for a little visit."

El Dabney poured a cup of coffee for Miro and refilled his own cup. "You may tell General Macéo it is not necessary to send his chief of staff to watch me. I am not going to Mantua, until I march with this army. Or, if I decide otherwise, I shall ride by headquarters and so inform General Macéo."

Miro bowed. "Your word is your bond, El Dabney. *Servidor de usted*. I am always the servant of an honorable man."

They drank their coffee in silence and Miro rose to go. "We are almost there. It has been a long journey and we will move again before daybreak. So I bid you good night."

Mingo touched Miro's sleeve, halting him. "I have never asked anything of the staff of this army. Now there's something I've got to know. Why is she in a convent? What about the army she came to raise —"

"There is no army in Mantua, Señor Dabney!"

"No—!" It was a stunned cry of uncertainty. "*La Entorcha* failed!"

"Rafaela Galban failed!" Miro's face was stern and his words were ringing. "There are no recruits in Mantua because the people will not rally to Rafaela Galban y Torres. . . ."

El Dabney's mouth opened and his chin quivered. "Did she recite the words of Martí? The story of thunder in the sun?"

"She tried. But there was mist in her eyes where fire should be." Miro's mouth was a hard line. "There was no thunder in the sun. Only a lonely woman watching the east, and the people scoffed and turned away." His words were his testimony and his demeanor was his indictment. "General Macéo will never tell you because he cannot admit it to himself. But I will tell you. You have torn down a symbol. You have done to Antonio Macéo what Spain could never do. You have weakened his faith in himself —"

342

"*Hombre!* Wait a minute. . . ." Mingo gripped his arm, pleading.

"No!" Then the sternness went out of Miro's face and sadness was there. "I hold no blame, *amigo*. The heart has reasons of which the mind is not aware." He stepped into the shadows and walked away, erect and proud and going into the darkness.

Mingo Dabney stood there alone, his hands open before him, and empty. He turned his face slowly toward his carts, the *Grillos* waiting, they who had shared their bread with him and spilled their blood for him. Then his eyes wandered over all the camp, the Mambises sleeping—the common clay who called him comrade, the believers; and he the infidel.

The little Army of the Occidente limped into Mantua early the morning of January 22, 1896.

Nine hundred and sixty miles in three months, and there was nothing in Mantua except a handful of vagrants and adventurers, a cluster of dusty buildings, a church, a convent and the frightened people of the village.

The Mambises felt the emptiness of the hour, the dream unfounded, and they looked ahead to the source of their strength. There was Macéo and the Mambises were untroubled. Their idol would pilot them, and his sign would pilot him; there was thunder in the sun among the pines by the river.

But there was silence in the pines. *Silencio!* A brooding silence in Mantua and silence in the hearts of the faithful.

The staggering column came to a dead stop, the end of the journey; six hundred dead men still breathing. No flags to furl, no drums to hush. They did not sing or cheer, merely looked ahead to Macéo and, at the signal of his raised hand, they grunted their exhaustion and slumped in the dust beside the road, staring around at the westerners gathering in sullen little groups.

343

Mingo waited a minute, glancing at the strange faces. Then he pushed his *machete* scabbard back of his hip and tossed his whip to Pepe Rosado. "Unyoke 'em, John Henry."

He did not delay to comb his hair or wash his face, but slid his fingers through his hair and it was dry and dusty. He walked away from his carts, up the street of Mantua and among the Mambises, swinging along toward the church, its spire rising above the people, and the town, and all the countryside.

The convent was next to the church and Macéo's horse was at the gate, almost blocking it. El Dabney slapped the horse on the flank, turning him out of the way, and walked up the path and to the front door. He knocked firmly and did not step back, but stood by the door waiting for it to open.

No answer, and he knocked again, harder than before. A sister opened the door, sliding back the big bolt. She stared at him, at his sheathed *machete*. "Yes?"

"I am here to see Señorita Rafaela Galban."

The nun hesitated, avoiding his gaze. "Won't you come in, Señor Dabney."

He stepped inside and the hallway was shadowy and musty, and, suddenly ill at ease, he fumbled with his big hands, resting one on the hilt of his weapon. Father Tomás came into the hall, his long face grieved, and motioned for him to enter the reception room.

She was not there, but Antonio Macéo was there, slumped on a bench by the window; again Achilles with an arrow in his heel. He did not raise his head, just staring at the floor, his eyes vacant and his face tortured in misery and desolation.

A nun watched Father Tomás and he nodded and she tiptoed to the foot of the stairs and called softly. "Señorita. Señorita Galban."

Rafaela brushed by the sister, hurrying along the hallway, her eyes streaming tears and her mantilla loose around her forehead. *"Minguillo!"* She called to him and ran into the

344

room, scarcely glancing at her guardian, her arms out to Mingo Dabney.

He did not speak, and she dropped her arms, and he could not speak, only looking at her and remembering those things the vengeful and the valiant must remember.

"Mingo—" She whispered it in the stillness of the room.

—Comrades at a slaughter wall, and Soto searching for a man.

"Mingo?" The white hair was free on her forehead, the forbidden silver revealed.

—The hillside at Peralejo and his comrades in the mist . . . *La Cuchillada* and the red feather at Mal Tiempo . . . The dust and Pepe Barea.

"Minguillo." She touched him, her hand warm on his arm.

And he drew back; the pilgrim drew away from her, denying the quest, and his eyes were wrathful. *"La Entorcha!"*

She stiffened, a shudder racking her body and her chin trembling; and she closed her eyes and lowered her head, hiding her face from his judgment. He put his hand tight under her chin and lifted her face, then jerked the mantilla low on her forehead, hiding her hair, imprisoning it again.

There was no blood in her cheeks and no life in her eyes, only a wonderment, and obedience. Father Tomás murmured a benediction and the sisters began sobbing. Antonio Macéo raised his eyes, his stare fixed on El Dabney the *gringo*.

Rafaela Galban cringed into the shadows and Mingo stepped to the light of the window, towering above the crumbled idol, the brown marble broken.

"Mambi!" He hurled the dare, the gauntlet to the cheek of Antonio Macéo. The *gringo*'s black hair hung wild to his shoulders and his eyes smoldered, then blazed. *"Recristo,* sire! By the blood of your dead! Baire!"

The priest flung up his hands to halt the blasphemy. The nuns pressed their fingers to their cheeks and swayed closer to Rafaela, their protection against this fierce transgressor.

Mingo bent low, a merciless antagonist, and his face was

345

close to The Brown One. "Nine hundred miles your Mambises followed you. Their faith was the promise of God to the meek. But you, their idol, sought a sign of your own creation—your own vanity." His voice was taut and cold with fury. "A sign for Macéo! *Madre de Dios!* I will give you a sign! From the scavengers of your army, sire!" He unsheathed his *machete* and swung it free; the farmer's tool, the workmen's blade. "Here is your sign! Death to Spaniards!"

A stifled cry from Rafaela Galban and she moved from the shadows and was close to Mingo. A sobbing whimper from the sisters. A blessing from the priest.

Macéo's eyes swept them, lingering on her, resting on El Dabney of the *Grillos*. Then he rose from the bench and stood tall in the room. "Keep your *machete*! You will need it!" The light flooded through the window, gleaming the coarse hair of the greatest Mambi of them all. "I will raise an army! An army of dead men, perhaps. But I will raise an army." He coiled the words on his tongue, and loosed them. "Captain Dabney! Your *impedimenta* is dissolved. . . ."

A tremor ran through Mingo's spine to his finger tips and his muscles jerked, and he felt her close beside him but saw only his chieftain, meeting The Brown One's gaze and accepting the command.

"Burn your carts! Butcher your oxen, Captain Dabney! We will use pack mules!"

"*Sí.*" Mingo brushed the black hair from his temples.

Macéo's gaze darted to Rafaela, his face reflecting the remembrance of things past: the child, the thunder, and his fate. "Señorita Galban!"

The name rang out as he spoke it for the first time. It echoed in the room and then the room was hushed. The sisters turned away, some weeping, and the others cupping their cheeks with their palms. Tears surged to Mingo's eyes and his heart hurt, a tender hurt for the lonely man standing there, his symbol shattered, the thunder stilled.

Rafaela Galban moved still closer to Mingo and tightened

her mantilla, holding it low. "General Macéo." She bowed her head, accepting his salutation.

"My Mambises are trapped and their faith must not be weakened."

"*Sí.*" Her voice was as clear as his. "None of us must lose faith. You in yourself, and us in you." Her chin came up and she spoke directly to him. "Or you in us."

The Brown One stepped close to them, so close that Mingo saw the deep pools of Africa in his eyes. "Señorita Galban." Macéo repeated the name and there was no mysticism in it. It was a name and nothing more. "As long as we are in Pinar del Río you are *La Entorcha* to my Mambises."

"It is a covenant, sire," she said softly, and the sisters lowered their hands from their faces. Macéo was watching her, and Mingo turned his face toward her, his pride deep and his confidence strengthened. "However . . ." she said it slowly. "I cannot keep my heart from beating, and each beat is for the day when I will be free of this covenant of Mantua."

The pilgrim's impulse was to take her hand and pull her to him, and shelter her, but he restrained the desire. Her confession was sufficient, and her troth was the promise of tomorrow.

"You will lead us to the supplies." It was the first order Antonio Macéo ever gave Rafaela Galban y Torres. "Then you will go to Los Arroyos. You will speak there tonight."

"I have spoken there. The words of Martí and they turned away —"

"You will speak the vow of Macéo!" He put his hand to the hilt of his sword; a mystic severed from his symbol, cold and aloof. "They will join us, or I will turn every hill of Pinar del Río into a bastion, every valley into a burial place. Tell them that! It is the vow of Macéo!"

All the blood drained from her face, but faith and hope gushed to Mingo's heart, filling it. Father Tomás mumbled a quick benediction and the sisters looked at one another, and were sorely afraid.

347

Rafaela moved away from Mingo and, standing alone, she held her head high. "I will be ready in a few minutes." She swept out of the room and all eyes followed her; all except Macéo's, and Macéo was watching the *gringo*.

MINGO DABNEY

Chapter **28**   The supplies were in a cave
and Rafaela led them there, and continued down the road
toward the sea. Father Tomás was beside her, his cassock
pinned to his waist and his long legs dangling about his
donkey.

The *Grillos* unpacked the equipment and burned their
carts, wailing their dole at the announcement that they were
soldiers of the Army of the Occidente. "Soldiers! Poof!" Pepe
Rosado sat on the ground, his legs extended, and sulked.
"Soldiers get killed."

"Heroes get praise. *Sí!*" They nodded their heads and
shook their fists. "*Por Dios!* But they are dead."

Mingo ordered the oxen slaughtered, and turned his back
on the *Grillos* and walked toward Macéo's headquarters.
They cried their lamentations, keening until he was out of
sight, then looked at one another and shrugged. Pepe Rosado
loosed his *machete* and they all went to the oxen and asked
their forgiveness, and cut their throats, saving the best meat
for themselves and slipping delicacies to the plump young
women of Mantua.

Headquarters was bare except for a box and a hammock
and Miro greeted Captain Dabney warmly and the others
greeted him casually. He was not proud that the door to headquarters was open to him at last. He was not particularly

349

pleased about it; there was no place for pride in his heart.

Macéo accepted his report on the slaughter of the oxen. "Now we need mules. Send the *Grillos* to the plantations."

By nightfall, sixty mules were in the corrals and a throng of farmers were calling down heaven's wrath on the Mambises. "Thieves!" they stormed. "Wait until the Spaniards come. You mountain goats."

Macéo eventually wearied of the insults and the farmers were driven off, the Mambises flaying them with their *machetes*. The army feasted on hot beef and loaded the mules, and pulled out about midnight for Los Arroyos, down by the sea.

There were no recruits and Rafaela was gone, she and Father Tomás moving on to the next village. The army camped on the outskirts of Los Arroyos and three spokesmen for the village came to headquarters and reviled Macéo for his impudence.

"We do not want war," they said. "Go away and leave us alone. We are loyal to Spain."

Their Negro servants held their horses while the masters were inside talking to The Brown One. The *Grillos* crowded around the horses and eyed the servants, looking from their good heavy shoes to their fat jowls. The servants were frightened and ran away and the *Grillos* led the horses back to their own camp.

The masters were furiously indignant and spluttered their abuse. "Robbers!" They wagged their fingers in Macéo's face. "The Spaniards are right. You are a gang of bandits."

The Brown One looked from one to the other and turned his back and walked away. He did not shrug. He just walked away and Miro walked with him.

It was Juan Ducasse who raised his eyebrows slightly and his men grabbed the three Tories and dragged them to a tree. The jeers of the Mambises, assembling fast, drowned out the cries and they hanged the three on one limb, using pack ropes. Captain Dabney did not protest. If this was to be the new pattern, so be it.

He and Macéo rode the next day to a plantation of six *bohios* and a *hacienda* and were welcomed by its master, an unctuous white man with a mulatto wife. He gave them cocoa and sweet cake and was very polite. News of the hangings had traveled fast.

"I need soldiers," Macéo said.

The master rolled his eyes toward the ceiling. "I am no soldier, *compadre*. And I have only enough men to tend my tobacco."

Macéo and Mingo took their leave and rode back to the army. "I need a Mambi who is shrewd," The Brown One said. "A soldier from the ranks."

"Pepe Rosado," El Dabney said.

"He must look like a lout, but he must be cunning."

"Pepe Rosado," Mingo repeated.

So Pepe Rosado was dressed like a tobacco worker and his gold earrings were removed and he was sent to the village to spread rumors that Antonio Macéo was fed at the *hacienda*. The Tories hastened to the plantation and burned it and hanged the master.

That night five workmen slipped into camp. "We will fight against the Tories. They burned us out and killed our master."

Macéo moved from one plantation to the next. If a master declared for Spain, the Mambises burned his home. If an overlord declared for the Revolution, the Tories burned his home.

Eighty workers, caught between Mambi and Tory, joined Macéo, but twice that many hid in the hills, and Spain sent them rifles and officers, goading the Cuban West against the Cuban East, the rich Occidente against the ragged Oriente.

Two gaping yokels came from Río Hondo bringing word of a Spanish pack train. "*La Cuchillada*," Macéo ordered.

The *Grillos* swept around the town, and Pedro Díaz thrust

in, but there were no supplies in Río Hondo, only a poster, the first since Havana province. Thirty-five thousand pesos for Mingo Dabney! The men cheered the rise in the price of their captain's head, and spat at the sign and loosed their *machetes*.

A blast of rifle fire from the catacombs of the church, and the trap was sprung. A wave of Díaz' men were cut down and six *Grillos* sprawled in the street.

"The hills," Mingo yelled. "Get out!"

He threw a stick of dynamite toward the church and ran, looking back only when he reached a roadside shrine and crouched behind it. The church was burning and Spanish soldiers ran out to the *Grillos* lying in the road. They jabbed their bayonets in, and ripped low.

Sagaldo! El Dabney shouted the name to Macéo and The Brown One glanced around for the two spies, but they had slipped back to the Spaniards.

Macéo pulled out fast. The Army of the Occidente had less than seven hundred men. Sagaldo had two thousand.

And there was no news from the plains—no news from Máximo Gómez.

Macéo hid his Mambises in the hills and licked his wounds and sent out scouts. *La Entorcha* was at Taco Taco. Father Tomás was with her and she was hiding by day and speaking by night: a handful in a *bohio*, a crowd in the woods.

The army waited for word from Máximo Gómez, but no word came and The Brown One assembled his staff. "This army is returning to the plains. I must have recruits. We leave tonight." He spoke rapidly. "Only Captain Dabney and his *Grillos* will remain here and hold Sagaldo while the army slips into Havana province."

"*La Entorcha*—" El Dabney stepped close to the general.

"She will remain in Pinar del Río."

Mingo looked from one to the other, feeling the gaze of the staff. There were thirty *Grillos* left and two thousand Spaniards to stamp them into the earth. He wished he had Soto,

352

but Soto was somewhere on the plains. "We will raid west tonight, and draw Sagaldo while the army moves east."

Macéo nodded curtly and all the staff nodded at El Dabney. Juan Ducasse, the somber Ducasse, spoke out. "Cuba will sing your praises."

"*Amigo!*" Mingo lifted his hand, jaunty again. Thirty against two thousand, but he was jaunty. Cuba would sing his praises. And Rafaela Galban was to remain in Pinar del Río.

But swiftly the truth came to him. The simple, blinding truth. He must not see her. The rabbit must not lead the hounds to *La Entorcha*. Macéo's assignment had put her farther from him than ever, for any approach to her was a threat to her. Thirty-five thousand pesos for El Dabney, but a saint's ransom for *La Entorcha*.

The Brown One offered his hand and mumbled, "*Compadre.*"

Macéo was calling him comrade.

Mingo bowed, his long black hair falling over his eyes, and he brushed it back. He bade farewell to Miro and the others, shaking hands with each of them, and started away.

"El Dabney!" The command was soft.

"*Sí?*"

The Brown One ran the tip of his finger to the ends of his mustaches, and felt in his Dutch linen coat, drawing a feather from the pocket. A red feather. He held it up for all to see, twirling it in the light. Mingo swallowed, choking back the lump in his throat.

"My brother, General José Macéo, sent this feather." Antonio Macéo touched it almost lovingly. "I asked for a feather from the finest red cock of the Oriente. He sent this one." The Brown One stepped to Mingo and, without a word, stuck the feather in the band of the old black hat, slanting the feather. "I will be back before the next dry season," Macéo promised. "God willing."

All other men in the room were blurred in the mist of Mingo's eyes, but Macéo, standing alone, was distinct. "I will be here when you return," El Dabney promised. "God willing." He wheeled and was gone.

The *Grillos* rolled their eyes and blinked at the red feather. Quickly, he gave his orders. Quickly, they obeyed, packing meat and salt, stuffing cartridges inside their shirts and hissing their excitement. *"Por Dios!* It is hell to be a soldier. Soldiers get killed —"

Mingo tied dynamite to his saddle and slanted his hat, touching the feather. "Baire," he called to his men, and they mounted, following him out of camp. He didn't see the Army of the Occidente pull out, but by dawn it was gone.

They raided first at the village of Diana, a tobacco warehouse. Sagaldo followed, and El Dabney wheeled and thrust, and dashed away. *La Cuchillada!* Sagaldo was off balance, and Macéo broke out on the plains.

Forty thousand pesos for the head of Mingo Dabney!

It was posted in Loma China, on the walls of a cigar factory. Mingo blasted the wall with dynamite, and skipped for the hills. Pepe Balderas straggled that night, hanging back for loot; and then Pepe Balderas was dead, his belly ripped open while Sagaldo looked on. . . .

The winter passed, and the days were tolled by black arcs in the sky of Pinar del Río, smoke from the ruins of a dozen towns, a hundred plantations. The sweep. The thrust. In, then out, and the hills. A dead *Grillo*, quickly dead. A wounded *Grillo*, soon dead.

He saw Rafaela in the village of Neptuno, but only long enough for her eyes to fill at sight of him. Father Tomás was with her, and the Mambises swarmed around her and the pilgrim made no effort to see her alone, and she encouraged no effort. She was pale and her face was drawn and her shoes worn. *La Entorcha* was almost barefooted. So was Mingo Dabney.

She spoke to the *Grillos* and they whirled their *machetes*,

354

daring Sagaldo and his two thousand to cross their path. Mingo did not cheer. He just watched her, a great pride in his heart and a longing. She was not safe in Neptuno, so he ordered her deep into the hills.

"Stay there until General Macéo comes back," he told her. "If he is not here by the dry season, I will take you to Máximo Gómez."

"Yes, *Minguillo*," she whispered and did not look up. The Mambises must not see the light in her eyes.

She rode for the hills and Father Tomás went with her. His donkey was dead and he walked beside her mule. The priest was wholly barefooted, his feet puffing sores and bleeding.

The *Grillos* burned Neptuno, covering the trail of *La Entorcha*, and slipped away to rest and patch their arms. The rainy season was full upon them, the quick showers, the long sun. Soon Macéo must return, and El Dabney was holding Sagaldo in Pinar del Río, the red feather never drooping, even in the summer rains. . . .

Soto rejoined them in the hills, riding in from Havana province, and Mingo hugged him. No! He hadn't found his man and he would not discuss it. Macéo? The Brown One was on the plains. Recruits? Only a few. The little Mambi grimaced and cursed:

Captain-General Valeriano Weyler had arrived in Havana!

Campos was gone and the Volunteers had their strong man!

Mingo handed a cup of coffee to the goatherd and called Pepe Rosado. "Get to *La Entorcha*. Tell her and Father Tomás that Weyler has arrived. Warn them to stay hidden."

They gave raw corn meal to Soto, the only food they had, and he washed it down with coffee. "Weyler brought his own staff." The guide mumbled the words, his mouth full. "Havana dropped roses in his path."

"So-o-o." The *Grillos* rolled their eyes. "Will they drop roses for us in Havana? Eh, El Dabney?"

"They'll throw rocks at you. What else, Soto?"

Captain-General Valeriano Weyler had ordered the Volunteers out of his path and tossed the deadwood from his army, heeding only a man's ability and not his patrons. He had 176,000 first line soldiers, 191 cannon and 76,000,000 rounds of ammunition. Weyler, too, was in a hurry. He, too, feared the United States might step in and settle things.

"It will be different now," Soto warned.

"Maybe," Mingo replied, and wasn't thinking of what he said. It was apparent that Gómez and Macéo had planned to win before Spain aroused herself. The plan had failed; perhaps because there was no army to meet Macéo in Pinar del Río, perhaps because his lodestar had waned. El Dabney flinched at the thought. He didn't want to think about that too much. "Is your man still around Havana?"

"He is with Sagaldo." The little Mambi looked down quickly, scooping the meal in his hands.

"Then you know his name?" Mingo persisted.

"I know his name." That was all Soto said; nothing more.

El Dabney cocked his head and smiled, a quick warm smile. Like a Mambi. "Sagaldo will be after us tomorrow night."

The guide glanced at his comrade, at the red feather, and grinned.

They rode hard for a hamlet just over the hill, and Sagaldo was after them again; the hound on the rabbit's trail, the rabbit running. *La Cuchillada!*

A village burned, a *hacienda* razed. El Dabney had been that way.

Forty-five thousand pesos for the head of Mingo Dabney! It was a sign in every plaza.

Weyler needed Sagaldo in Havana, but El Dabney held him in the Occidente. The grandee dared not leave the province exposed, and El Dabney taunted him, a torch to a plantation, a sweep, a thrust. A rope for Tories, a *machete* for Spaniards. El Dabney had passed that way.

Fifty thousand pesos for Mingo Dabney!

Tumbra de Estorino. It was a pretty village with a pretty name, and then it was ashes.

Pepe Rosado rejoined them, reporting *La Entorcha* was safe in the hills. But Father Tomás was dead. Pepe Rosado wept as he told it, his watery red eyes pouring their tears, his voice a wail.

The *Grillos* crowded around, all silent, Mingo biting his lip and Soto staring into the distance.

"He slipped out of the hills for food." Pepe Rosado rubbed his hand across his eyes. "They caught him down at Isabel María and they stripped off his cassock. Mother of God! They stripped him naked and hanged him, and ripped him open. Slaughtered him like a pig, El Dabney. And he was such a good man —"

"Wipe your nose, *amigo*." Mingo said it gently, and went that afternoon into the woods and hunted and found a red cockatoo, and plucked him.

The town of Isabel María was ashes by nightfall. The torch, and five Tories on a limb. Sagaldo's camp was raided, a colonel hanged; a red feather stuck over his ear.

Then they were away again, wild dashes by night and hide-outs by day. Raw corn meal and coffee and a little stolen rum. And the fagot.

A red feather pinned to Sagaldo's tent, and Havana snickered. A red feather on Sagaldo's couch, and Madrid laughed.

La Cuchillada! They tormented Sagaldo to madness and left their own dead where they fell. Vultures followed them, circling low by day and perching near at night. And they rode on.

Ceja del Negro. The red fire, and the red feather . . .

Soroa . . .

The villages rolled by in the beauty of their names, then only their names remained to mourn that El Dabney the Mambi had passed that way.

A storm; and the rainy season was gone and Antonio Macéo returned to Pinar del Río. He had only his veterans, the fanged ones of Peralejo, of Baragua and Mal Tiempo. The people of the plains had not joined him. There was no torch to fire them. And Gómez had no men to spare.

Captain Mingo Dabney and his eighteen *Grillos*—the eighteen and Soto—hurried down from the hills to meet the army. Miro embraced El Dabney, and the Ducasse brothers embraced him, saluting the red feather. But Macéo was aloof. What of *La Entorcha*?

"She is safe," Mingo reported.

"She will remain in hiding." Macéo ventured no explanation of the command.

"Perhaps she should go to the plains. . . ." El Dabney presumed to suggest. "Maybe she can rally the people." The minute he said it, he was sorry.

Macéo's left lid drooped, almost closing. "She failed to raise an army here. There is no reason to suppose the plains will heed her." He changed the subject abruptly. "Havana has offered a fabulous price for her arrest."

"It proves Weyler is desperate." Mingo wanted to get the subject entirely away from Rafaela.

"*Sí*. Weyler must win quickly. The United States won't wait forever." He leveled his gaze at El Dabney. "And we must win quickly. Or not at all. There is an election in the United States this year. . . ."

Mingo was thoughtful. It was all so far away, so vague. "*Sí*," he said slowly. "This is election year. They elect in November." He smiled then. "*Por Dios!* I do not even know who's running."

"Señor McKinley and Señor Bryan. They talk of gold and silver while the press screams of Cuba." Antonio Macéo looked out at his army, shrunken to five hundred. "November is three months away. We must be back with Gómez in three months." His eyes swept the fields and lifted to the hills. "Pinar del Río will feed the Revolution, or Pinar del Río will feed the vultures. We move tonight."

MINGO DABNEY

Chapter **29**   A red feather became the lance tip for an army of phantoms, the *Grillos* scouting the way and heeding only their chieftain, a Mambi with black hair long to his shoulders and restless brown eyes without mercy.

They fought to the last western mile of Cuban earth and wheeled, fighting east once more, seeking support and finding none. A few recruits straggled in, but not enough to replace the Mambises lost to Spanish steel, to fever and dysentery.

The Army of the Occidente was down to less than five hundred warriors and ranged from the Hills of Purgatory to the Valley of Despair, and the people scorned the sword of Macéo as they had scorned the pleas of *La Entorcha Blanca*.

She sent word from her mountain hiding place that she was coming out to try again. Macéo firmly forbade it. Spanish units were at every crossroad, on every trail.

The Brown One admitted in a message to Gómez that his campaign was failing and requested help. The commander in chief could send no help, and Weyler held him in a pocket on the plains; The Old Fox was dodging and hiding, skulking for his life.

That was the hour García came back to Cuba, Calixto García with a bullet scar in his forehead and a diseased heart. He slipped into the Oriente, calling recruits from the cradles, from the couches of *la tierra del Mambi*. His return was the only good news of '96, the best news since Mal Tiempo.

360

Macéo received the information without comment and went into camp at Lomas de Tapia to replace horses and patch equipment. The Mambises were there when the storm struck: thunder from Weyler, lightning from Sagaldo.

Spain's captain-general ordered five thousand troops into the west—power enough to squeeze Macéo to death.

Send us the head of Antonio Macéo! The red feather of Mingo Dabney! One hundred and fifty thousand pesos for the head of The Nigra. One hundred thousand pesos for the head of the *gringo*. A *machete* was his ax and the grin of Lebanon was gone, but Spain still called him a *gringo*.

Then Weyler sent his engineers to build *trochas* across the gateway from Pinar del Río, raising a wall from Mariel on the north to impassable swamps on the south.

Macéo raced to get out before the wall was sealed. Barbed wire and steel stopped him and cannon drove him back. The Army of the Occidente was locked in Pinar del Río with Sagaldo; and Sagaldo had five thousand.

All his blood seemed to drain into Mingo's legs when he saw the *trochas*. Miles of stone and guns! The Mambises crossed themselves and even the *Grillos* blanched.

The warriors of the Ducasse asked it first: "Where is *La Entorcha?* Where is the lodestar of Macéo, the luck charm of the Mambises?"

"There is a price on her head," The Brown One said.

"There is a price on your head," they protested. "Gold for your neck, sire. A rope for ours. Send for *La Entorcha.*"

Antonio Macéo turned to Mingo, a pitiful sadness in his eyes and loneliness graven on his face.

Mingo did not hesitate. "You will send for her?"

"You send for her, El Dabney." Macéo turned away.

Miro watched Mingo, and all the staff looked at him. He called Soto. "Go for *La Entorcha, compadre.*"

The Brown One said, "We are going back to Lomas de Tapia."

"Then lead her there, Soto," Mingo directed. "Tell her to wait there for the army."

So they turned from the *trochas* and moved west again, plodding over the ashes of fields they had burned, dragging across plantations with no food for men or animals. Only charred trees, their limbs blackened, and the patient buzzards tilting in the sky.

Sagaldo circled them and Pedro Díaz hurled his men at the line and broke it, and broke his band of warriors. Macéo led the way through, his sword sheathed and a *machete* in his fist. El Dabney was at his side, swinging his blade.

They clawed their way over the trail to Lomas de Tapia. Vidal Ducasse was weak from three wounds and his men carried him, except when he staggered in to fight. Pepe Rosado had a bayonet thrust in his thigh. It festered, and Mingo burned it clean. There was a bullet hole through Miro's arm and a saber slash on El Dabney's shoulder. They all were barefooted; all except Macéo, and his boots were cracked and broken, and he was threatened with fever again.

Their rifles were rusty, their cartridge belts empty, and their pack mules were dead and eaten. Blood caked their *machetes* and they jabbed them in the earth to clean them. Even the sun gave no mercy, the Spaniards even less; the burning sun day after day, the Spaniards night after night, and the Mambises stumbling and dying.

La Entorcha was at Lomas de Tapia with nine recruits and she led them out of the village to meet the Army of the Occidente—four hundred and sixteen Mambises, their bones bare under open wounds.

She ran first to Mingo and he ordered her to Macéo, the Mambises watching as she turned from El Dabney to her guardian. She showed them the trail into the hills, to her camp, and the men wept at sight of the protecting boulders, the trees, the cool stream and a cluster of thatched *bohios*.

"We can hold this place forever," Macéo said and ordered the wounded and sick under shelter.

The *Grillos* built more *bohios*, using pine rafters, and El Dabney swung his *machete* with one hand; the saber cut was on his left shoulder and pained him. He made no effort to see Rafaela alone and they both went about their work, he building and she tending the sick. He was just another Mambi, and she was the lodestar of them all.

The shelters were finished in a week and Soto saddled his bony horse and led him past the shade where Mingo was cleaning rifles. Mingo glanced up, and rose and followed his comrade to the edge of camp.

"I am going to Mantua," Soto said.

"Is he there?"

"I have heard mention of a man." He reached for the pommel of his saddle.

El Dabney raised his eyes but not his head. "We need you here, *compadre*."

The Mambi's hand slid from his pommel and he stared at the long black hair, the cloudy brown eyes. "I must go to Mantua."

"We need you here." Mingo repeated it.

"*Amigo!*" The goatherd lifted his palms. "It has been a year and a thousand miles. And he may be in Mantua."

Mingo Dabney turned his back and walked away. Soto watched him, and then, without a word, unfastened the belly-band and pulled off the saddle.

That night he raided with El Dabney and they came back with cartridges and eighteen pairs of shoes. The Mambises cast dice for the shoes. Pepe Rosado won a pair, but they were too small and he traded them to Soto for his saddle.

For a month the army rested, looking toward the valleys where Sagaldo plugged every hole and blocked every trail. Vidal Ducasse's wounds mended and El Dabney was sound again. Macéo's threat of fever left him and he withdrew into himself, eating his corn meal and yams alone in his hut. But he bathed every night and washed his own clothes in the stream by his *bohio*.

They broke out of the hills in November and cut Sagaldo's supply line and raided for two weeks. Máximo Gómez was moving on the plains; The Old Fox stealing out of his burrow and snapping Weyler, biting and sometimes tearing the flesh. Calixto García was moving in the Oriente, stinging and jerking back to sting again.

And Macéo was driving Sagaldo to fury, El Dabney tormenting him to frenzy. A red feather upon the breast of Sagaldo's chief of staff. A red feather woven into the mane of Sagaldo's horse while the Spaniard attended mass. There was talk of recalling the grandee. *La Cuchillada!*

Spain was bleeding slowly from myriad wounds, and England mused, looking to her empire, patching the weak spots, thinking twenty years ahead. Germany sent her armies to maneuvers and France watched the Rhine. The busk season was passing, the harvest moon wasting, and Spain was bleeding.

Uncle Sam took his eyes off the stock market and blinked slowly. A new shuffle was coming. The same old deck, but a new shuffle, and Uncle Sam stroked his goatee and blinked. Wait a minute! Who's dealing what? Maybe he'd better pull up a chair and draw a hand. He was big enough to play with the men. Some folks said he wasn't old enough, and maybe he wasn't smart enough, but Lord knew he was stout enough. . . .

A courier arrived from Gómez on November 16.

William McKinley was president of the United States.

General José Macéo was dead in the Oriente, killed in battle.

A shudder passed through the gaunt frame of Antonio Macéo. All the brothers were dead, all except The Brown One.

"What else?" he asked the courier, the words heavy-laden. "How did you get through the *trochas?*"

He didn't. He came around the northern end, by rowboat

at night. Spain was watching every pass, the sea, the land, but he slipped through.

Weyler was sending more cavalry to Pinar del Río.

And Gómez wanted Macéo on the plains by Christmas!

Three Mambises volunteered to get to the commander in chief and tell him the Army of the Occidente would be there. *La Entorcha* baked bread for the messengers and El Dabney dug yams for them. The *Grillos* honed their *machetes* and the three men wished aloud for a priest to give them communion.

Macéo ordered the camp abandoned and burned, and sent *La Entorcha* deeper into the hills. She did not look back at Mingo as she rode away.

Captain Francisco Gómez applied the torch and the smoke billowed black, and Macéo led his Mambises to the valleys. The campaign had failed and Pinar del Río remained loyal to Spain; the fat land bled to ashes and graves, but it was loyal to State and Church.

So they went down from the hills to stab for the plains and Gómez, and The Brown One was brooding. Soto, scouting a *hacienda*, brought news of Weyler's thrust:

"I, Don Valeriano Weyler y Nicolau, Marquis of Tenerife, Governor-General, Captain-General of this island, and Commander in Chief of the Army, hereby order and command —"

Every Cuban civilian outside the cities must come into the cities.

No food to be moved without permission of the Spanish army.

All herds to be brought to Spanish commanders.

Each refugee to move only the possessions he could carry on his back.

The penalty for disobedience was death.

Reconcentrado!

Concentration camps. Imprisonment of a population. Weyler could not protect Spanish sympathizers in the hinterlands, or tolerate Cuban spies, so he herded them all into the cities.

Mingo Dabney's fury rose hot, but Antonio Macéo smiled. Spain had blundered again.

Every wheel in Cuba ground to a stop.

The world held up its hands in horror.

The old people trudged into the cities, lugging their pots and pans, their crucifixes, their starving children.

But the young men defied the order and honed their *machetes* and hid in the woods, sending their families to the cities to eat Spanish food while they stayed on the plains and cut Spanish throats. Gómez' army began swelling.

Reconcentrado!

The smile of Antonio Macéo, the first in months, was a shrewd smile of calculation and resolve. A million people caged, wrapped in by barbed wire! Fever and starvation. Pellagra and green flies. Imbeciles! Spain was bled to madness. Up, Mambises. The plains by Christmas . . .

They found one of the messengers to Gómez in a *bohio* near the *trochas*. He was dying of dysentery. The others were dead, their bellies slit. Only he had come so far.

Soto, the guide of Guantanamo, heard the sick man talk and went to Macéo. "I will go to Máximo Gómez."

The Brown One stroked his mustache and looked a long time at the keeper of eight goats. He could get through if anyone could.

"Tell Gómez I will be on the plains by Christmas." His face was flushed, the only indication of the turmoil within him.

El Dabney heard the message and went for Soto's horse, saddling him carefully, tightening every strap. The guide mounted and Miro handed him the reins and turned away. "Baire," the little Mambi said, sitting erect in the saddle.

"Baire," said Antonio Macéo and he, too, turned away.

Mingo walked beside the horse until they reached the trail to the *trochas*. "I will be back in two weeks," Soto said. He, too, wished for a priest, but there was no comfort for the goatherd of Guantanamo, the avenger of Martí. "Look for me in two weeks. *Si Dios quiere.*"

"*Bueno, compadre,*" El Dabney said. "Two weeks."

Soto looked east toward the Spanish forts, and his eyes fired bright, then were sad. He hitched the reins in his right hand and leaned down and put his hand on Mingo's shoulder. "I must pass this thing to you, *amigo.* You know him— you have shared his bread. His name is González. Nicolas González —"

A cold tingle at the base of Mingo's spine, a flood of memories and a spasm of doubt. "No. *No!* A fat man? Two silver teeth?"

"A fat man. Two silver teeth. *Saludo, compadre.*" He lifted his foot to his horse's flank and was away.

Nick González! The keeper of *El Delfín.* The fat man of a thousand questions. Nick González the betrayer of José Martí.

Mingo stared after Soto, his mind dazed by the revelation, and he began piecing the parts together, and they fitted. Soto's recent behavior, knowing he must kill a man who had shared bread with his comrade. *Saludo,* Mambi—keeper of eight goats.

And poor old Fry. The bartender had known every move he made. Nick González toasting Baire and leaving so soon after Martí landed in Cuba. Mother of All Men!

Mingo Dabney was not angry, but deeply hurt in his heart for Soto. For Joe Fry and John Smith. And for Elmo Batson.

If Soto did not come back, then he who had shared the salt of *El Delfín* must find Nick González, and kill Nick González.

The dust was churning on the trail to the *trochas* and the rumble of horses' hoofs echoed to the east. He looked that way and lifted his face, listening until the hoofs were silent, until there was no sound toward the *trochas.*

The army moved down, a few miles each night, hiding by day. It took them a week and November was passing, and then they were near enough to probe the *trochas*, pawing for a gap. They found none, and two weeks passed.

Soto did not return.

Mingo Dabney was barefooted and his muscles ached. Soto was dead, and his heart ached. . . .

It was November 22 and Macéo called his Mambises around him. Miro was weeping openly and El Dabney was staring at his hand, the calluses there. "I must leave you," The Brown One said.

"Leave us?" The Mambises looked from one to the other, and at him. "Leave us in Pinar del Río?"

"I must leave you. No army can get through the *trochas*."

"But how will you get through?" They gave no thought to themselves, believing they could hide in the western hills and fight forever.

"By sea," he said. "North to Mariel, across the Bay of Mariel, and around the end of the *trochas*."

A rowboat or a raft. Spaniards waiting on the beach. This was what it meant, but it was the only way to get out. The swamps at the south end were impassable.

He gave command of the Army of the Occidente—three hundred skeletons—into the keeping of the Ducasse brothers, and announced the group to go out:

Miro. Of course, Miro. Colonel Nodarse, wounded six times. General Pedro Díaz, wounded four times. General Martel Piedra, seven times. Captain Francisco Gómez, once. Lieutenant Justiz, nine times; one eye. General Antonio Macéo, twenty-five times.

There were sixteen in all, and Mingo Dabney was not among them.

Neither was Rafaela Galban y Torres.

"What of *La Entorcha*?" the Mambises queried.

Macéo smoothed his beard and glanced down at the ragged cuff of his linen coat. Then he raised his head, and his eyes rested on them all. "Mambises! I am giving *La Entorcha* into

368

the care of Captain Mingo Dabney, my friend and my brother."

Mingo rubbed his thumb across the calluses of his palm and did not look up, just staring at his hand, and down at his feet, unshod and dirty. The red feather was frayed but staunch in the old black hat. His long hair was tangled and his eyes were misty and he closed them, shutting off the mist and the sight of the man who called him brother, the idol whose symbol he had changed into a woman.

"El Dabney! *La Cuchillada!*" The Mambises cheered him and he looked up at them, first at them and then at Macéo.

"Captain Dabney will take *La Entorcha* out of Pinar del Río." The Brown One paused and looked to the east, and turned his back and walked away. Miro went with him.

The *Grillos*, the fourteen who lived, crowded around Mingo, jostling to get close to him. "How will you get through?" Pepe Rosado asked.

"Somehow. *Si Dios quiere.*" He was not going by sea; not daring to take Rafaela into Spanish rifles on the beach. That much he knew. And that was all he knew.

"Will you come back to us? Or do we go to you?"

"I don't know. But I will find you."

He walked over to Macéo's hammock. There was fever in the eyes of The Brown One and he sat up in his hammock and held out his hand. "Her life is yours, *amigo.*"

El Dabney said, "Give me three days to find a way."

"Three days," Macéo said. "Miro will go for her. She will be here when you return."

MINGO DABNEY

Chapter **30**   He selected one of the five mules that were left and rode openly until the *trochas* were in view, then swung south, keeping shelter between him and the forts. It was almost twilight when he reached the morass of Majana, the southern anchor of the *trochas*, and the swamps were murky and foreboding, but they were swamps and Mingo Dabney came from swamps.

The mule sloshed into the bog and when his hoofs pawed for dry ground, Mingo dismounted and felt the earth. It was spongy and dank, but there was no ooze.

He scooped a hole in the ground and it filled slowly, and the mule sniffed the water, then drank it. The woodsman smiled and poked a reed to the bottom of the hole, drinking his own needs. The water was sweet. The sea was near, but the water was sweet. It seeped down from the hills instead of in from the sea.

The night came, the night things calling and crawling, and Mingo listened; the frogs rumbling, the owls pitching from low limbs. It was the swamps of Lebanon again, and he put his saddle on the ground for a pillow, and slept.

The mule woke him, straining to reach a grass hammock, and Mingo loosed the tether and let him eat. Mist rolled low over the swamp, shrouding it. It was false dawn, day stillborn.

He saddled at daybreak and moved due south into the morass, glancing back occasionally to the northeast at the last fort on the edge of the marshes. Water began forming where the mule trod and his hoofs sucked ooze. Mingo watched the hoofs sink, and turned him quickly and went back to dry ground.

Por Dios! He rested both hands on the pommel and stared at the swamp, wondering what its secret was. There were a few cypresses and cypresses meant water, and there were twisting mangoes and twining vines and orchids. The morass was impassable from that approach. The Spaniards had known it all along, and now he knew it. He headed his mule straight west, away from the *trochas*, skirting the bog.

For three hours he rode, feeling for an opening and finding none. He was veering south again. The sun told him that. The salt air told him he was near the sea, the salt air and the birds and the reeds, a savanna of reeds crisping in the wind. Cranes flew up from the savanna and circled, spearing on to the south.

If there was a way through it wasn't apparent to Mingo Dabney, but, because he was a desperate man, he heeled his mule directly into the marsh, heading in from the west.

The mule bogged deep and he kicked him forward, then dropped the reins and let the animal pick his way, climbing the hummocks and stepping slowly and surely across the black morass. The savanna was at his back and the waving reeds hid him. He watched the hoofs sink less and less with each step, and then they were dry, and he looked up.

Mingo Dabney caught his breath and stared at the sky and the land around him, an awe suddenly upon him in the infinite silence, in a revelation.

There lay the valley, stretching from the savanna at his back to the swamp ahead. A stream flowed out of the swamp and down the valley, vanishing in the muck of the savanna.

It could have been the valley of Lebanon.

It could have been because he wanted it to be, and man's imagination is an architect, and his hope is a builder. There were the slopes down to the stream and there were the pines trooping down, teetering to the pranks of the wind.

371

He rode up the bank of the stream and already was calling it the East Fork, like back home. It came out of the swamp about two miles from the savanna, cutting through the marsh, offering a passage through the barrier.

There, on the slope of the creek, he would build his house, first of logs; then a small sawmill to cut timber for his big house and lumber for people to buy. Drain the savanna and build a road.

A site there for Elmo's store. A bench on the porch and a rocking chair for the cool of evening and Ol' Elmo rocking and talking.

El Dabney pulled his mule into the stream, watching his footing, and rode on. The last fort, the anchor blockhouse, was to his left and behind him. Ahead was Havana province and the plains.

This was the way through for one, two, maybe three persons if they were cautious and lucky.

He turned and went back down the stream, heading out again, marking his way well. He rode back across the savanna to dry land, then circled away from the *trochas* and once more turned north. . . .

Rafaela was with Macéo and Miro when he got back and she hurried to him, holding out her hands, and he took her hands, holding them fast. Her black cotton dress was spotted brown, the skirt ragged and the rents unmended. Her shoes were patched with undressed leather and sewed with rawhide, but her mantilla was tight over her forehead and her eyes were lustrous bright.

"Can you get through?" Macéo glanced at their hands joined.

"I think so."

Miro stepped up to him and offered his hand, then embraced him and turned sharply away.

Macéo stood erect, aloof and impassive. "Meet me at Punta Brava." His voice almost betrayed him, coming deep from within his emotions.

"Punta Brava." El Dabney repeated the name.

"It is a town just south of Havana." Macéo fingered the ragged cuff of his coat, and his face was calm; a lie to his heart, a mask to his loneliness.

He looked a long time at Rafaela, and bowed. "God's mercy on both of you." He said it clearly and turned from them and followed Miro.

Mingo selected a mule for her and the Mambises gathered around, touching the hem of her skirt. He pointed down the path and said to her, "Meet me there."

She rode away and El Dabney called the *Grillos* around him. "Pepe Rosado will take my place."

"I?" Pepe Rosado touched himself. "I was but a scavenger in Santiago de Cuba —"

"You, John Henry. And wipe your nose. Your eyes, too. Come close, all of you."

They were so close he smelled the brine of their sweat. "His name is Nicolas González." He said it without feeling, calmly pronouncing doom for a man he had trusted.

"Nicolas González." They said it for themselves, their lips scarcely moving.

"He has two silver teeth. He is a fat man." El Dabney completed the sentence, the judgment of vengeance.

"He is a dead man," said Pepe Rosado, and they nodded slowly.

Mingo swung into his saddle and looked at their upturned faces, black and brown and white, all dusty with the powder of the earth. He motioned for Pepe Rosado, and felt for the red feather, holding it a second and twirling it. Then he leaned over and stuck it in the band of the *Grillo*'s floppy palm hat, hand-woven and cone-shaped. Pepe Rosado slanted the brim of his hat, tilting the feather, and El Dabney lifted the reins. *"Saludo, compadres."* And he was away, his *Grillos* wailing.

Rafaela was waiting and he urged his mule into a trot and motioned for her to keep up and ride at his right side, the off side from the *trochas*. It was almost noon and they had to be through the Spanish wall that night. . . .

The shadows were on the savanna and the reeds streaked a web of shadows, and Mingo reached out and touched her hand. "There is a way through. Follow me and let your mule pick his own footing."

She wasn't afraid. She followed him into the marsh and there was no sound except the cranes sweeping up, and the mules' hoofs sucking mud.

The sun drowned golden into the sea and they crossed the savanna and were in the valley. Twilight brushed the pines, deepening their green. "It's Lebanon," Mingo said.

Rafaela was surprised. "This is El Paso del Pinos. The Pass of the Pines." She dropped her reins to the pommel. "It is very old. People lived here once and then the marsh filled. It blocked the pass, and the people moved away."

He swung down and lifted his hands and helped her from the saddle. "People will live here again. I'll drain the marsh."

"Drain the marsh?"

"*Sí.*" He took her hand and led her up the stream and the mules followed, pausing to nip the sweet grass. "We'll wait here until it's black dark."

She walked up the side of the slope and under a pine and sat there, and he brought corn cakes from her saddlebag and a yam. She broke the yam in half and handed him his portion. Darkness was quick upon the land and they sat there, neither speaking, both watching the fireflies come out of the swamp.

"I'll build a house right there." He pointed to the spot. "Up yonder . . ." He raised his hand toward the opening where the stream came through. "That's the north cut." They called it the north cut to the valley back home.

"That's east," Rafaela said, factually and womanlike.

"I know it's east." A trace of annoyance was in his voice. "But it's the north cut."

"How can it be north if it is east?" She asked, insistent on her point.

"Never mind." The moon spun over the swamp, scattering the low clouds and fringing the high ones. "I'll build a mill up on the slope." He pointed the way. "And a store right over yonder."

She sensed his mood and that, too, was womanlike. So she slipped her hand over his, covering his hand. "Will Elmo Batson be here?"

"*Sí.* At the store."

"Farms for the *Grillos?*"

"If they want farms." He nodded toward the savanna. "Down there. That's the south cut." There was a south cut in Lebanon, but this one was due west.

"The south cut." Rafaela laughed as she said it. There, almost under the *trochas*, she laughed the gay laugh of a woman who knew the mood of a man, and dared his mood because she was a woman.

He lifted her hand to his mouth and kissed it, first the tips of her fingers, and the palm.

"*Minguillo.*" She let her head rest against the pine, looking at his eyes burning bright and his lean cheeks and his mouth. Then she closed her eyes and put her hand to her forehead, pushing back her mantilla until the silver showed.

Mingo gasped at the radiant beauty of her hair and touched it, stroking it. She slipped back the mantilla until the moonlight was full on her hair, and it was soft silver, falling to her shoulders.

He kissed her high on her forehead, then brushed his lips against her ear and found her mouth, and it was warm and without shame or regret. She held to him, whispering his name over and over, her eyes still closed and the moon silver on her hair.

All the doors behind him were closed, sealed tight at that moment. He might remember them in years to come, perhaps even reach for them in the memory of things past, but remembering this minute, he never again must touch the latch that held the doors immovable between this minute, in this

375

place, and all other minutes in all other places. The quest was fulfilled. The pilgrimage ended . . .

The moon was clouded and Mingo Dabney looked up at the sky and it was dark. The valley was dark and he held out his hand to her and lifted her up.

"*Sí,*" she murmured. "It is time."

He went for the mules and they rode down into the stream and into the swamp. The frogs bellowed their protest and the owls drifted deeper into the marsh.

They listened, and moved on, slowly up the stream, out of Pinar del Río and through the swamp to dry land.

The Spaniards were in Punta Brava!

Mingo and Rafaela learned it in time to avoid the town and veer for the hamlet of San Pedro. There a band of Mambises from the plains rested in a clump of aroma trees.

Antonio Macéo was half a mile away at Molina Farm and El Dabney thanked the Mambises for the information and gave them six cartridges and a hatful of corn meal.

They crossed Conception Farm and through a palm grove and down a dusty lane to a stone wall, an old Spanish rock wall that fenced the fields.

Captain Francisco Gómez saw them and then Miro, and they both waved and Miro walked out to meet them. "Thank God," he said. He looked at Mingo's face and into the merry eyes of Rafaela. "Macéo is resting. Did you have trouble?"

"Not a bit." He swung down and helped Rafaela dismount. "Did you?"

"Not much." Miro motioned for an orderly to take the mules. Mingo handed his rifle to the man. There was no danger now. "The Bay of Mariel was stormy and we had only one rowboat." Miro shook his head. "Macéo was ill, but the storm kept the Spaniards from the beach. Macéo called it a sign."

A sign again. Always a sign.

The Brown One lay in a hammock under a laurel tree and he sat up quickly, staring at Rafaela, at the mantilla high on her forehead, the sun touching her hair. "Señorita Galban." He removed his hat and bowed.

"Sire." She nodded with dignity.

"Sit here in the hammock and tell me about the journey. Sit beside her, Captain Dabney."

An orderly fetched a box and Macéo placed it against the laurel tree and sat down, resting his back against the trunk. Mingo traced their route and Macéo turned to Rafaela, "El Paso del Pinos?"

"*Sí.*"

"People lived there once," The Brown One said.

"People will live there again," Mingo said.

"He is going to drain the marsh," Rafaela explained.

"So-o-o." Macéo looked down at his boots, then put his hands on his knees and stood. "I will leave tomorrow for Gómez. This is December 7th and I will be there December 10th—*Si Dios quiere.*"

El Dabney said, "We will go with you."

The Brown One did not reply immediately. His look was far away. Then he spoke only to Rafaela, saying, "The covenant of Mantua is ended."

She reached for Mingo's hand. "*Sí.* It is ended."

Mingo felt the sadness of the moment and wished for it to be over. Antonio Macéo turned his face from them and stared toward the east, the Oriente and the Mountains of Our Master where he found her that day the thunder shook the sun. He looked up at the sky once more and his black eyes filled. "Heaven will send us another sign," he whispered. "Heaven will not forsake my Mambises."

Rafaela trembled slightly and Mingo stared at The Brown One, seeing the mysticism and faith of an unfathomable man.

A wind from the east, a hot wind from the plains, rustled the laurel leaves and then they were still and the earth was hushed. The spell passed quickly, Mingo shaking it off, nervously drawing away from it, and he got up from the hammock. Rafaela stood too.

"We will be ready this afternoon," El Dabney said.

They walked away, past Miro and Francisco Gómez and along a hedge of piñon trees. Rafaela's eyes were dancing again. . . .

The first shot came from beyond the stone fence of Conception Farm and Captain Francisco Gómez sprang for his horse. A cry sounded in the aroma thicket and the Mambises pointed toward the wall, screaming the alarm. Mingo pushed Rafaela into the shelter of the piñons and raced for his rifle, running close by Macéo's hammock. The Brown One's face was white and he cried out, "My horse!"

Three more shots crackled over the stone wall and Macéo stabbed his spurs into his horse, drawing blood. The horse leaped toward the fence, overtaking Captain Gómez. Macéo reached for his sword and cried out, "Rally to me, Mambises! Baire!"

He and his aide were over the barrier at the same second. A crash of rifle fire met them.

Young Gómez fell backward and Macéo stood high in his stirrups, blood spouting from his throat. He pointed his sword at the ambush and wilted in his saddle, crumpling to the ground.

Miro was to him first and then Mingo Dabney. Mingo glanced only once at the body and leaped to the wall and strode along it, cursing as he walked, firing until his rifle burned his hands and the powder burned his eyes.

A second Spanish company burst out of the woods and charged across Conception Farm. Miro and Pedro Díaz rallied the Cubans in the aroma thicket. Lieutenant Justiz raised his *machete* and fell with two holes in his chest. Colonel Nodarse was down with a wound in his leg and General Martel Piedra was writhing in the palm grove.

378

El Dabney stalked the top of the wall, firing into every bush, and several Mambises joined him. They had no rifles, but they swung their *machetes*, hacking the wounded and the living, the half dead and the dead. Mingo sobbed his fury, but the Mambises were silent, hacking as if they were cutting cane.

A hundred yards, two hundred, they walked the stone fence flushing Spaniards from both sides. There was a piñon thicket ahead, and more Spaniards. Mingo slipped behind the wall, motioning for the Mambises, and they crawled along, their movement hidden in the tall grass.

There were six, maybe seven Spaniards in the thicket, all mounted, gazing south toward the skirmish around the farm. The man on the white horse was Leopold Sagaldo.

Mingo pressed his rifle to his shoulder and the Mambises gasped and crossed themselves. The idea came to him then, the justice of the minute. Let the meek pull down the mighty. Let the poor humble the proud.

He lowered his rifle slowly and handed it to the nearest Mambi. Pepe Sánchez, perhaps.

"I?" The Cuban's hand trembled as he accepted the gun, the judgment. "I, El Dabney?"

Mingo nodded and the Mambi rested the rifle on the stone wall, taking slow aim. Mingo raised his voice toward a man doomed. "The *Virginius*!"

Leopold Sagaldo jerked his head that way. A searing flame, spurting red, the lazy coil of smoke, and the shot tore into his chest just above the ribbon of the Golden Fleece. The Mambi dropped the rifle for Mingo to pick up, and scampered over the wall, his *machete* gleaming and his comrades close behind him.

Mingo watched an instant, the judgment done, and turned slowly, walking back along the wall. The Spaniards were fleeing toward Punta Brava. . . .

The bodies of Antonio Macéo and Francisco Gómez lay alone for a few minutes, and a Spaniard sneaked out of a

379

ditch and looked around. The fighting had passed him and he slipped to Macéo's body and rifled the pockets.

There was no money. Only some papers and four letters; one from José Macéo, written years before, two from María Macéo, and one from a child—a tattered letter, scarcely legible.

The Spaniard could not read and stuffed the letters in his shirt, and turned to the body of Francisco Gómez. Again he found no money and, in his anger, reached for the young man's *machete* and split open the skull of the son of old Máximo Gómez, cursing both bodies for Mambi paupers. Macéo's head was worth one hundred and fifty thousand pesos, but the Spaniard did not know who he was, and could not read, and ran away. . . .

Miro was with Macéo's body when El Dabney returned. "Sagaldo is dead." He said it dully and, without another word, hurried to Rafaela. She was crouched in the hedge, her hands covering her eyes and her chin quivering.

"I saw him leap the wall. Macéo! I saw him fall —"

Mingo touched her. "We must get away from here."

"I saw it. He rose and pointed his sword —"

"We must get away, Rafaela." He stroked her face, quieting her. "They'll be back. We must hide his body."

She looked at him, her eyes wide. "The sign! He asked a sign for his Mambises. Blessed Mother!" She murmured it reverently. "He himself is the sign —"

"Rafaela!" Mingo tilted her chin and shook her, breaking the spell. Enough of signs! A Mauser rifle was the Spanish sign and by its token the Spaniards soon must know they had killed The Nigra. "We must go." He shook her again. "And we must take his body."

She shuddered, and then her eyes flared open and she was calm. "Go to Miro. I will get the mules."

They buried Justiz under the aroma trees and Francisco Gómez under the rock wall, and the Mambises took the wounded deep into the woods.

Pedro Díaz found Macéo's horse and Mingo lifted the body, cradling The Brown One, and laid him across the saddle.

"Where shall we take him?" Miro asked, glancing toward Rafaela for instructions.

"South of here," she said. "I will show the way." She was trembling again as she led the group away from Conception Farm and down the path beside the stone wall. Miro was at her side, and Pedro Díaz led Macéo's horse, sitting his own saddle almost sideways. Mingo Dabney walked behind the body to guard it. He blew into the barrel of his rifle. It was dirty and he must clean it soon. Macéo's big red horse kicked up little patches of dust and it hovered in the air, some of it falling on the pilgrim.

They moved due south, crossing field after field of burned cane, little farms where nothing lived. All night they traveled, Rafaela staring straight ahead, Mingo frequently glancing over his shoulder in the direction of Punta Brava, and the Spaniards.

After dawn, they came to Babadilla Farm and the *bohio* was burned and the cane was ashes. Rafaela looked back at Mingo and then at Miro. "This is the place."

"Why this place?" Miro asked.

She waited until Mingo came to them. "The Spaniards will never come here again. It is burned so badly they will never come back." She held out her arms and Mingo lifted her down. "There is another reason. Martí came here as a boy and played in these fields."

"Maybe Soto was with him," Mingo said.

"Perhaps." She pointed at the base of a laurel tree, blackened and charred. "There . . ."

They had only the *machete* of Pedro Díaz and they dug into the earth that was hard and dry. The *machete* blistered Miro's hands, and Pedro Díaz could not dig fast. He had only one arm.

The tool fitted the hands of Mingo Dabney and he dug most of the grave, and his sweat dripped onto the ground where Macéo would rest.

Rafaela said, "General Miro, you take his sword —"

"We must bury his sword with him."

"Take his sword, General Miro. It must go back to the Oriente, to María Macéo." She had the right to speak thus, she who was his thunder in the sun, child he found and symbol he dedicated.

Miro bowed, then stooped and unclasped the heavy belt and lifted the Toledo blade. Mingo and Pedro Díaz laid the body in the earth. They turned to Rafaela and she bowed her head and they all bowed. Miro mumbled, "Baire."

A pillar of black smoke swirled up in the west. His Mambises were burning the cane, and that, too, was a sign. A cloud by day.

They covered the body and Mingo said, "We should raise a headstone." They always put up stones for the dead in Lebanon.

"No. The Spaniards might find it. Only we know where he is buried." She stooped and smoothed the earth over the grave, the old earth newly turned. She reached for ashes of the burned cane and sprinkled them on the spot, and the spot was gray like all dirt.

Venga, Mambi. . . .

Mingo took her arm and they walked to the mules nuzzling in the ashes for grass and finding none. "We must go to Gómez," he said.

"Sí." She put her hands on his shoulders and he lifted her to the saddle. "I will go where you say."

Miro and Pedro Díaz heard the words and they rode on ahead, neither looking back.

She held Mingo's rifle while he tightened the girth of her saddle. Then she handed the rifle back to him and touched his hand and touched his face. He tightened the girth of his

382

own saddle and swung up, lifting the reins. The girths must hold fast. It was a long way to Gómez, and to a free Cuba.

It was a long way back to Pinar del Río, but the Pass of the Pines was very old. It had been there a long time. It would be there when they got home.